Lecture Notes in Computer Science   14045

Founding Editors

The series Lecture Notes in Computer Science (LNCS), including its subseries Lecture Notes in Artificial Intelligence (LNAI) and Lecture Notes in Bioinformatics (LNBI), has established itself as a medium for the publication of new developments in computer science and information technology research, teaching, and education.

LNCS enjoys close cooperation with the computer science R & D community, the series counts many renowned academics among its volume editors and paper authors, and collaborates with prestigious societies. Its mission is to serve this international community by providing an invaluable service, mainly focused on the publication of conference and workshop proceedings and postproceedings. LNCS commenced publication in 1973.

Abbas Moallem
Editor

HCI for Cybersecurity, Privacy and Trust

5th International Conference, HCI-CPT 2023
Held as Part of the 25th HCI International Conference, HCII 2023
Copenhagen, Denmark, July 23–28, 2023
Proceedings

 Springer

Editor
Abbas Moallem
San Jose State University
San Jose, CA, USA

ISSN 0302-9743   ISSN 1611-3349 (electronic)
Lecture Notes in Computer Science
ISBN 978-3-031-35821-0   ISBN 978-3-031-35822-7 (eBook)
https://doi.org/10.1007/978-3-031-35822-7

This Springer imprint is published by the registered company Springer Nature Switzerland AG
The registered company address is: Gewerbestrasse 11, 6330 Cham, Switzerland

Foreword

Human-computer interaction (HCI) is acquiring an ever-increasing scientific and industrial importance, as well as having more impact on people's everyday lives, as an ever-growing number of human activities are progressively moving from the physical to the digital world. This process, which has been ongoing for some time now, was further accelerated during the acute period of the COVID-19 pandemic. The HCI International (HCII) conference series, held annually, aims to respond to the compelling need to advance the exchange of knowledge and research and development efforts on the human aspects of design and use of computing systems.

The 25th International Conference on Human-Computer Interaction, HCI International 2023 (HCII 2023), was held in the emerging post-pandemic era as a 'hybrid' event at the AC Bella Sky Hotel and Bella Center, Copenhagen, Denmark, during July 23–28, 2023. It incorporated the 21 thematic areas and affiliated conferences listed below.

A total of 7472 individuals from academia, research institutes, industry, and government agencies from 85 countries submitted contributions, and 1578 papers and 396 posters were included in the volumes of the proceedings that were published just before the start of the conference, these are listed below. The contributions thoroughly cover the entire field of human-computer interaction, addressing major advances in knowledge and effective use of computers in a variety of application areas. These papers provide academics, researchers, engineers, scientists, practitioners and students with state-of-the-art information on the most recent advances in HCI.

The HCI International (HCII) conference also offers the option of presenting 'Late Breaking Work', and this applies both for papers and posters, with corresponding volumes of proceedings that will be published after the conference. Full papers will be included in the 'HCII 2023 - Late Breaking Work - Papers' volumes of the proceedings to be published in the Springer LNCS series, while 'Poster Extended Abstracts' will be included as short research papers in the 'HCII 2023 - Late Breaking Work - Posters' volumes to be published in the Springer CCIS series.

I would like to thank the Program Board Chairs and the members of the Program Boards of all thematic areas and affiliated conferences for their contribution towards the high scientific quality and overall success of the HCI International 2023 conference. Their manifold support in terms of paper reviewing (single-blind review process, with a minimum of two reviews per submission), session organization and their willingness to act as goodwill ambassadors for the conference is most highly appreciated.

This conference would not have been possible without the continuous and unwavering support and advice of Gavriel Salvendy, founder, General Chair Emeritus, and Scientific Advisor. For his outstanding efforts, I would like to express my sincere appreciation to Abbas Moallem, Communications Chair and Editor of HCI International News.

July 2023   Constantine Stephanidis

HCI International 2023 Thematic Areas and Affiliated Conferences

Thematic Areas

- HCI: Human-Computer Interaction
- HIMI: Human Interface and the Management of Information

Affiliated Conferences

- EPCE: 20th International Conference on Engineering Psychology and Cognitive Ergonomics
- AC: 17th International Conference on Augmented Cognition
- UAHCI: 17th International Conference on Universal Access in Human-Computer Interaction
- CCD: 15th International Conference on Cross-Cultural Design
- SCSM: 15th International Conference on Social Computing and Social Media
- VAMR: 15th International Conference on Virtual, Augmented and Mixed Reality
- DHM: 14th International Conference on Digital Human Modeling and Applications in Health, Safety, Ergonomics and Risk Management
- DUXU: 12th International Conference on Design, User Experience and Usability
- C&C: 11th International Conference on Culture and Computing
- DAPI: 11th International Conference on Distributed, Ambient and Pervasive Interactions
- HCIBGO: 10th International Conference on HCI in Business, Government and Organizations
- LCT: 10th International Conference on Learning and Collaboration Technologies
- ITAP: 9th International Conference on Human Aspects of IT for the Aged Population
- AIS: 5th International Conference on Adaptive Instructional Systems
- HCI-CPT: 5th International Conference on HCI for Cybersecurity, Privacy and Trust
- HCI-Games: 5th International Conference on HCI in Games
- MobiTAS: 5th International Conference on HCI in Mobility, Transport and Automotive Systems
- AI-HCI: 4th International Conference on Artificial Intelligence in HCI
- MOBILE: 4th International Conference on Design, Operation and Evaluation of Mobile Communications

List of Conference Proceedings Volumes Appearing Before the Conference

1. LNCS 14011, Human-Computer Interaction: Part I, edited by Masaaki Kurosu and Ayako Hashizume
2. LNCS 14012, Human-Computer Interaction: Part II, edited by Masaaki Kurosu and Ayako Hashizume
3. LNCS 14013, Human-Computer Interaction: Part III, edited by Masaaki Kurosu and Ayako Hashizume
4. LNCS 14014, Human-Computer Interaction: Part IV, edited by Masaaki Kurosu and Ayako Hashizume
5. LNCS 14015, Human Interface and the Management of Information: Part I, edited by Hirohiko Mori and Yumi Asahi
6. LNCS 14016, Human Interface and the Management of Information: Part II, edited by Hirohiko Mori and Yumi Asahi
7. LNAI 14017, Engineering Psychology and Cognitive Ergonomics: Part I, edited by Don Harris and Wen-Chin Li
8. LNAI 14018, Engineering Psychology and Cognitive Ergonomics: Part II, edited by Don Harris and Wen-Chin Li
9. LNAI 14019, Augmented Cognition, edited by Dylan D. Schmorrow and Cali M. Fidopiastis
10. LNCS 14020, Universal Access in Human-Computer Interaction: Part I, edited by Margherita Antona and Constantine Stephanidis
11. LNCS 14021, Universal Access in Human-Computer Interaction: Part II, edited by Margherita Antona and Constantine Stephanidis
12. LNCS 14022, Cross-Cultural Design: Part I, edited by Pei-Luen Patrick Rau
13. LNCS 14023, Cross-Cultural Design: Part II, edited by Pei-Luen Patrick Rau
14. LNCS 14024, Cross-Cultural Design: Part III, edited by Pei-Luen Patrick Rau
15. LNCS 14025, Social Computing and Social Media: Part I, edited by Adela Coman and Simona Vasilache
16. LNCS 14026, Social Computing and Social Media: Part II, edited by Adela Coman and Simona Vasilache
17. LNCS 14027, Virtual, Augmented and Mixed Reality, edited by Jessie Y. C. Chen and Gino Fragomeni
18. LNCS 14028, Digital Human Modeling and Applications in Health, Safety, Ergonomics and Risk Management: Part I, edited by Vincent G. Duffy
19. LNCS 14029, Digital Human Modeling and Applications in Health, Safety, Ergonomics and Risk Management: Part II, edited by Vincent G. Duffy
20. LNCS 14030, Design, User Experience, and Usability: Part I, edited by Aaron Marcus, Elizabeth Rosenzweig and Marcelo Soares
21. LNCS 14031, Design, User Experience, and Usability: Part II, edited by Aaron Marcus, Elizabeth Rosenzweig and Marcelo Soares

47. CCIS 1836, HCI International 2023 Posters - Part V, edited by Constantine Stephanidis, Margherita Antona, Stavroula Ntoa and Gavriel Salvendy

https://2023.hci.international/proceedings

Preface

The cybersecurity field, in all its dimensions, is exponentially growing, evolving and expanding. New security risks emerge continuously with the steady increase of internet interconnections and the development of the Internet of Things. Cyberattacks endanger individuals and companies, as well as vital public services and infrastructures. Confronted with spreading and evolving cyber threats, the system and network defenses of organizations and individuals are falling behind, as they often fail to implement and effectively use basic cybersecurity and privacy practices and technologies.

The 5th International Conference on HCI for Cybersecurity, Privacy and Trust (HCI-CPT 2023), an affiliated conference of the HCI International Conference, intended to help, promote and encourage research in this field by providing a forum for interaction and exchanges among researchers, academics and practitioners in the fields of HCI and cyber security. The conference focused on HCI principles, methods and tools in order to address the numerous and complex threats which put at risk computer-mediated human activities in today's society, which is progressively becoming more intertwined with and dependent on interactive technologies.

In this regard, and motivated by recent worldwide developments driven by the ongoing pandemic, such as increased usage of internet and IoT services for remote working, education, shopping and health management, papers accepted in this year's proceedings emphasize issues related to user privacy and data protection. Furthermore, they focus on the usability of solutions in the field, as well as on user-centred perspectives on security and privacy.

One volume of the HCII 2023 proceedings is dedicated to this year's edition of the HCI-CPT Conference and focuses on topics related to usable security and privacy, data privacy, sovereignty and governance, cybersecurity challenges and approaches for critical infrastructure and emerging technologies, user-centered perspectives on privacy and security in digital environments, as well as human-centric cybersecurity: from intrabody signals to incident management.

Papers of this volume are included for publication after a minimum of two single–blind reviews from the members of the HCI-CPT Program Board or, in some cases, from members of the Program Boards of other affiliated conferences. I would like to thank all of them for their invaluable contribution, support and efforts.

July 2023   Abbas Moallem

5th International Conference on HCI for Cybersecurity, Privacy and Trust (HCI-CPT 2023)

Program Board Chair: **Abbas Moallem**, *San José State University, USA*

Program Board:

The full list with the Program Board Chairs and the members of the Program Boards of all thematic areas and affiliated conferences of HCII2023 is available online at:

http://www.hci.international/board-members-2023.php

HCI International 2024 Conference

The 26th International Conference on Human-Computer Interaction, HCI International 2024, will be held jointly with the affiliated conferences at the Washington Hilton Hotel, Washington, DC, USA, June 29 – July 4, 2024. It will cover a broad spectrum of themes related to Human-Computer Interaction, including theoretical issues, methods, tools, processes, and case studies in HCI design, as well as novel interaction techniques, interfaces, and applications. The proceedings will be published by Springer. More information will be made available on the conference website: http://2024.hci.international/.

General Chair
Prof. Constantine Stephanidis
University of Crete and ICS-FORTH
Heraklion, Crete, Greece
Email: general_chair@hcii2024.org

https://2024.hci.international/

Contents

Cybersecurity Challenges and Approaches for Critical Infrastructure and Emerging Technologies

User-Centered Perspectives on Privacy and Security in Digital Environments

**Human-Centric Cybersecurity: From Intrabody Signals to Incident
Management**

Usable Security and Privacy

Transparency of Privacy Risks Using PIA Visualizations

Ala Sarah Alaqra[1]([envelope]) [iD], Simone Fischer-Hübner[1,2] [iD], and Farzaneh Karegar[1] [iD]

[1] Karlstad University, Karlstad, Sweden
as.alaqra@kau.se
[2] Chalmers University of Technology, Gothenburg, Sweden
http://www.springer.com/gp/computer-science/lncs

Abstract. Privacy enhancing technologies allow the minimization of risks to online data. However, the transparency of the minimization process is not so clear to all types of end users. Privacy Impact Assessments (PIAs) is a standardized tool that identifies and assesses privacy risks associated with the use of a system. In this work, we used the results of the PIA conducted in our use case to visualize privacy risks to end users in the form of User Interface (UI) mock ups. We tested and evaluated the UI mock-ups via walkthroughs to investigate users' interests by observing their clicking behavior, followed by four focus group workshops. There were 13 participants (two expert groups and two lay user groups) in total. Results reveal general interests in the transparency provided by showing the risks reductions. Generally, although participants appreciate the concept of having detailed information provided about risk reductions and the type of risks, the visualization and usability of the PIA UIs require future development. Specifically, it should be tailored to the target group's mental models and background knowledge.

Keywords: Privacy Impact Assessment · User Interface · Usability · Transparency · Privacy-Enhancing Technologies

1 Introduction

Personal data analysis based on Machine Learning is increasingly used, e.g. for enabling new eHealth services or for commercial applications, but may result in privacy risks for the individuals concerned (specifically data subjects). Consequently, there is a need to develop and use Privacy-Enhancing Technologies (PETs) to mitigate privacy risks. PETs can support users' privacy and data protection by enforcing the legal privacy principles of, for example, data minimization through anonymization or pseudonymization of personal data [15]. There are several data minimization PETs, including homomorphic encryption (HE) and Functional Encryption (FE) schemes for data analyses as well as differential privacy for federated learning [5,6]. The above-mentioned PETs were developed

A. Moallem (Ed.): HCII 2023, LNCS 14045, pp. 3–17, 2023.
https://doi.org/10.1007/978-3-031-35822-7_1

and demonstrated in the PAPAYA Horizon 2020 EU project[1]. PAPAYA stands for PlAtform for PrivAcY preserving data Analytics.

Given the approaches of different PETs for minimizing risks to one's online data, the use of PETs, however, cannot guarantee absolute risk abolition in practice. This study investigates the transparency and communication of Functional Encryption (FE) risk reductions. Through user interface (UI) visualizations of the conducted Privacy Impact Assessment (PIA) for FE, we investigate users' perspectives of the PIA elements. We take into consideration users' technical knowledge (lay and expert users) and further report on recommendations for future PIA visualizations and designs.

1.1 Objective and Research Questions

The purpose of this study is to evaluate user interface mock-ups explaining how privacy-preserving data analysis is working with the PAPAYA platforms developed in the project. Therefore, the following are the research questions of this study:

RQ1: What are the users' (experts and lay) perceptions of the visualizations of PIA risks in a user interface?
RQ2: What are the recommendations for future UI visualization implementations of usable PIAs?

1.2 Outline

In the following section (Sect. 2), we present the background and related work to this study as well as the UI mock-ups of the PIA of the use case used in this study. In Sect. 3 we describe the methodology and study design. Results are presented in Sect. 4. Derived recommendations for the UI visualizations are discussed in Sect. 5. Finally, our conclusions are found in Sect. 6.

2   Background and Related Work

We present the background and related work to our study in the following subsections. That includes the use case scenario used as well as work on the PIA user interfaces.

2.1 Privacy Impact Assessment

For assessing the extent and type of privacy risks of data processing practices a Privacy Impact Assessment can be conducted [11].

A PIA is used to evaluate the potential privacy risks associated with a system and could be defined as "a process whereby the potential impacts and implications of proposals that involve potential privacy-invasiveness are surfaced and

---

[1] https://www.papaya-project.eu/.

examined" [10]. According to [11], a PIA's definition has evolved throughout time and the specification varies depending on the jurisdiction.

The EU General Data Protection Regulation (GDPR) requires data controllers to conduct a PIA for applications which are likely to result in high privacy risk [13]. A PIA can help communicate how the PETs in place reduce privacy risks, which contributes to improving users' trust and their willingness to share their data. Furthermore, previous research has shown users' existing interest in knowing about the underlying PETs in place (i.e., how PETs protect their data and the potentially remaining risks despite PETs used), which can help them in making informed privacy decisions [2,16]. Consequently, for enhancing transparency for different stakeholders, including end users, our objective is to explore how and to what extent we should explain to stakeholders how the PETs in place can reduce their privacy risks with a focus on communicating the results of PIA.

While a PIA is needed for complying with regulations, especially in the case of data analyses of medical data, we see an opportunity of using PIAs also as a means to inform different stakeholders of how PETs can reduce privacy risks. Promising results of a previous study show that the stakeholders appreciated and had more trust in the PET– a privacy-enhancing data analytics platform enabling medical data analyses on homomorphically encrypted patient data– by the mere fact that the service provider has conducted and displayed results of the PIA [3].

However, details and visualization of specific elements of the PIA were requested by participants of the study conducted in [3]. Furthermore, participants requested information about the PET method (incl. information on how Homomorphic Encryption (HE) works), the PIA method and how it was conducted, and the qualification of the individuals that conducted the PIA [2].

2.2 PETs and Transparency

Functional encryption is an encryption mechanism enabling an authorized party, which has the functional decryption key (a.k.a. evaluation key), to compute and learn an authorized function of the encrypted data (see also [4]). In contrast to homomorphic encryption, the result of the computed function is not encrypted meaning that the authorized party gets the result of the computation in an unencrypted form.

Transparency is a legal privacy principle (pursuant to Art.5 (1), 12 GDPR) and usable transparency concerning privacy-enhancing technologies can be a means for enhancing trust in those technologies (see e.g. [7,18]).

However, providing transparency of PETs in a usable manner poses several challenges. For instance, our previous studies on metaphors for illustrating PETs and making their privacy functionality transparent revealed misconceptions that users have, also for the reason that users may assume that a PET would be functioning in a similar way as security technologies that they are familiar with and would thus have comparable security properties [2,3,16]. Commonly used metaphors (such as the metaphors often used for explaining differential privacy i.e., the pixelation of photos) may also rather provide a structural explanation for a PET, while recent research has shown that functional explanations of privacy and security technologies are better understandable for end users [12].

Therefore, higher emphasis should be put on functional explanations, and explaining how PETs can reduce privacy risks via PIA illustrations can be one usable form of such a functional explanation. Such PIA illustrations should also provide guidance on adequate (residual) risks per context and what this implies (as suggested in [16,19]).

2.3   Use Case Scenario and Visualizations for Users

We utilized a specific commercial use case for the PAPAYA project involving data analyses for functionally encrypted data. The PIA results were produced with an extended version of the PIA tool by the French Data Protection Agency CNIL [1]). While the CNIL PIA focuses on assessing and displaying risks in terms of the classical security goals of Confidentiality, Integrity and Availability, an extended PIA tool version was developed in the PAPAYA project [14] (and is in the rest of this paper referred to as the "PAPAYA tool"). The PAPAYA tool, in addition, assesses and displays privacy risks in terms of the privacy goals of data minimization, intervenability and transparency and shows how they can be reduced by the use of a PET.

Moreover, the enhanced tool produced graphical output of the assessed risks and risk reductions for mobile devices, i.e., with limited screen sizes. The graphical output of the assessed risks by the enhanced tool was used in the design of the UI mock-ups of the study reported in this paper. We displayed the results of the PIA as a part of multi-layered structured consent forms of the use case in which we provided more details about the PET. Table 1 displays the list of the risks, the corresponding name of the risk in the UI, and descriptions.

In the use case, a Telecom provider called TelecomAB offers a service in their application. In their service, app users are prompted with a consent form asking if they would participate and contribute their personal usage data for a statistical survey study. The UI shows a declaration that the data should be protected by PAPAYA's Privacy by Design approach and offers details in the UI mock-ups.

Figure 1 gives an overview of the UI mock-up figures presented in this paper. The UI mock-ups present the consent form for participating data for a study by TelecomAB (Fig. 2a), information about PIA and Privacy by design (Fig. 2b and 2c), and the risk reductions and illustrations (Figs. 2d, 3a, and 3b).

2.4   PIA User Interfaces

In Fig. 2a, the UI illustrates the screen where the consent, for contributing one's data to a study, is presented to end users. In this UI, we show the consent prompt for users to contribute their specified data with MediaSurvey Corporation on behalf of TeleComAB (the data controller). In return, users would receive a monetary incentive of a five-euro voucher in this case. Further, we show that

Table 1. List of Privacy/Security aspects at risk and the corresponding name and description of the risk in the UI

Aspect at risk	Name of risk in UI	Description of remaining risks
Confidentiality	Illegitimate Data Access	The risk seriousness and likelihood that TeleComAB could access your data (age and social network usage) are reduced from 'Important' to 'Negligible'
Integrity	Unwanted Modification of Data	The risk seriousness that data could be falsified is reduced from 'Important' to 'Limited' while the risk likelihood is reduced from 'Important' to 'Negligible'
Availability	Data Disappearance	The risk seriousness that data could be lost is reduced from 'Important' to 'Limited' while the risk likelihood is reduced from 'Important' to 'Negligible'
Transparency	Intransparent Data Processing	The risk seriousness and likelihood that the data processing is not made transparent to the users is reduced from 'Important' to 'Limited'
Unlinkability	Linkable Data Processing potentially identifying users	The risk seriousness that TeleComAB could identify users and their social network usage profile based on the provided data is from 'Maximum' to 'Negligible', while the risk likelihood is reduced to reduced from 'Important' to 'Negligible'. There are small (negligible) risks remaining that personal data could be inferred from the calculated statistics
Intervenability	Lack of User Control	Not impacted. As TeleComAB cannot identify the users (data subjects), TeleComAB is not obliged to allow users to exercise their data subject rights according to Art 11 GDPR

data would be aggregated and securely encoded as well as the purpose for using the specified data (age, ad social network usage in this use case scenario). Here we provide a link to TeleComAB's PIA and Privacy by Design (PbD) approach presented in Fig. 2b.

We present information about the PIA and PbD approach in the UI of Fig. 2b. Regarding the PbD, TeleComAB state that "Our **Privacy by Design** approach ensures that your data will only be sent to us and statistically analysed by us in aggregated and securely encoded form. We will not be able to decode your data and can only derive statistics from your and other user's data". Reasons for conducting the PIA are illustrated under "Why did we conduct a PIA" UI

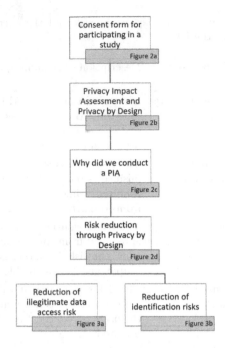

Fig. 1. Overview of mock-up UI figures

(Fig. 2c. We show that there are privacy risks for sharing the data in this scenario and how these risks are reduced by the PbD approach. An overview of the PIA results showing the list of risks reduced by the PbD approach is illustrated in Fig. 3a. Details and visual illustrations of specific risk reductions are shown in Figs. 3a and 3b.

In Fig. 3a, the user interface shows a risk heat map with an overview of reductions of risks based on the PIA, in addition to the details about the specific risks (clicking the 'more' link). For instance, in Fig. 3a, the visualization of the illegitimate data access risk is shown. It shows that both risk seriousness and risk likelihood are reduced from serious to negligible. Further details relating to specific data (age and social network usage) as well as actors (TeleComAB) accompanied the visualization of risks relating to the use case. Similarly, in Fig. 3a, the UI illustrates the reduction of identification risks associated with participating/sharing their data in the scenario. We further present remaining negligible risks entailing possible inference of personal data from the calculated statistics results.

**Consent Form
for participating in a study**

Do you consent to first collect and later send data for participating in a study?

Renumeration: 5 Euro Amazon Voucher

Data: Aggregated and securely encoded data about:
• Your age
• Your social network usage

Purpose: Statistical Analysis of the average time users use social network apps per day, depending on their age.

Data Controller: TeleComAB, Sweden,...dpo@telecomab.com

On behalf of MediaSurvey Cooperation

More on TeleComAB's Privacy Impact Assessment and Privacy by Design approach

Full Privacy Policy

Cancel   **Consent**

(a) First UI: consent form

**Privacy Impact Assessment
& Privacy by Design**
by TelecomAB

Consent / PIA & PbD

Why did we conduct a Privacy Impact Assessment (PIA)?

Our **Privacy by Design** approach ensures that your data will only be sent to us and statistically analysed by us in aggregated and securely encoded form.
We will **not** be able to decode your data and can only derive statistics from your and other users' data.

How does it work?

How are Privacy Risks reduced by our Privacy by Design approach?

Back

(b) PIA and Privacy by Design

Why did we conduct a PIA?

Consent / PIA & PbD / **Why PIA?**

We conducted a Privcay Impact Assessment (PIA) to assess

• The privacy risks that may arise by the our application through the statistical analysis of usage profiles and data at a large scale;

• How these risks are reduced by our Privacy by Design approach (more).

Back

(c) PIA: Why

**Risk Reduction through
Privacy by Design**

Consent / PIA & PbD / Why PIA? / **Risk Reduction**

Our PIA shows that our Privacy by Design approach leads to **Reductions of Risks** of

• Illegitimate data access (more)
• Unwanted modification of data (more)
• Data disappearance (more)
• Intransparent data processing (more)
• Linkable data processing potentially identifying users (more)
• Lack of user control (more)

More on the Privacy Impact Assessment Process and Results

Back

(d) Overview of risk reductions

Fig. 2. Overview of the use case UIs

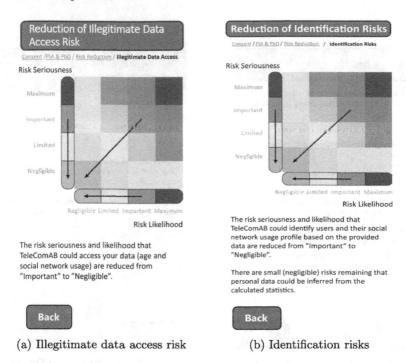

(a) Illegitimate data access risk   (b) Identification risks

Fig. 3. Risks reduction UIs

3   Methodology

The PAPAYA project followed a PbD approach [8,9], where we focus and take privacy considerations in the early stages of the development process of the project's PETs. As our objective is to investigate how to communicate/make transparent the PIA results to users, we, therefore, designed UI mock-ups to display PIAs risks and visualize each risk mitigation for our use case (found in Sect. 2.4). Based on the UI mock-ups we conducted the user studies as described below.

3.1   Study Design

The method used in this study is two-fold. First, we had individual walkthroughs of the UI mock-ups. Second, we had four focus group workshops with 3–4 participants in each. All studies were conducted online due to COVID19 restrictions at the time. We used Zoom (a video conferencing service) and Mentimeter (an interactive presentation software) to remotely facilitate the interactions and discussions of the studies. Participants were asked to share their screens for the UI walkthroughs as they clicked around the interactive UI mock-up. After consenting to participate in the study, participants were also asked to consent to the screen recording and the voice recording of the sessions.

In total, there were 13 participants with varied technical backgrounds. Our focus group participants were divided into lay (FG0, FG2) and expert groups (FG1, FG3). Table 2 shows participants numbered in each group and their expertise. During the recruitment process, we sampled lay participants who had no knowledge of cryptography. As for the experts, we sampled participants who had knowledge of cryptography but no knowledge of functional encryption specifically.

Table 2. Participants in each focus group and their expertise.

Focus group number	Expertise	Participants
G0	Lay	P1, P2, P3
G1	Expert	P4, P5, P6
G2	Lay	P7, P8, P9, P10
G3	Expert	P11, P12, P13

The individual walkthroughs of the mock-ups had a focus on the UIs for the PIA and privacy by design descriptions as well as the risk reduction illustration (as seen in Figs. 2 and 3.

The focus groups included a group discussion of participants' inputs of the walkthroughs as well as investigating participants' perspectives and thoughts about (1) the presentation of the risks (2) understanding of the illustration and (3) thoughts on what is missing. The moderator facilitated the discussion by allowing each participant to first respond and then go around for comments.

Data from the focus groups were collected via the recordings, transcribed, and then coded via Nvivo (a qualitative data analysis software). The analysis of the data followed an inductive approach and we present our findings in Sect. 4.

3.2   Ethical Considerations

We submitted the proposal and study materials (including information letters, consent forms, and study guides) to the local ethical committee at Karlstad University and have received approval from the ethical advisor. Participation in the studies, the recording of the sessions, screen sharing, as well as the demographic questions were optional and based on the users' consent that we obtained before the studies. We provided an information letter about the studies, and consent forms with details about our data collection and processing.

4   Results: Walkthroughs and Focus Groups

Most participants clicked either on consent (6) or back (2) without going through the links in the first UI (Fig. 2a). The remaining five participants clicked through the UIs and reached the risk reduction visualization such as the ones found in

Fig. 3. The following results are based on the discussions of the focus groups mainly, as they indicate their input on the visualization of the risks as well as the PIA information provided.

Overall, all the non-experts except one in FG3 found the graph confusing and difficult to comprehend to some extent. Similarly, half of the experts (P4, P12, P6) specifically indicated that the graph was confusing and not understandable. Despite not directly mentioning confusion, the other half expressed several concerns about missing information and what they needed to know. In general, the confusion and difficulty in understanding the graph and our participants' concerns stem from different factors. There are issues with visual-related aspects, a diversion from what users expect of a typical graph, and more importantly insufficient information and clarification regarding the terminology used, the context, and the purpose. In the following subsections, we provide details about the sources of confusion, concerns, and difficulties participants experienced in understanding the PIA representation, along with what they appreciated.

4.1 UI Design Aspects

The use of different colors in the risk heat map (as seen in Fig. 3) to convey different levels of seriousness and likelihood was not appreciated equally and did not appear as intuitive for all of the participants. P11 found the'colorfulness' good because the colors "point to like negligible on the risk seriousness and likelihood". P8 made a connection with traffic lights and stated: "I think it is clear because of traffic lights, red is like no don't do that it's just dangerous, danger color, and green is like good, go, and yellow is in between". On the other hand, P9 found the colors confusing stating: "Why are there different colors ...? I don't know, and what does the mixture between different color, what does that mean? No idea". P9 requested clarification about what the colors and the arrows represent. Although no participants from non-experts voiced a comment regarding their appreciation of the graph, a few experts (3) commented on the validity of the graph and the fact that it was 'nice' in their opinion. P11 stated that "this depiction is like the standard like risk analysis results that you just put on this, like, graphical shape with different colors [..] But as a general graphical, like, a depiction it is valid". P5, similar to P13 who found the visualization 'nice' and 'ok', stated that "it could have been nice to keep the image". Despite positive opinions about the existence of such graphical representations among experts, P4 indicated uncertainty regarding the need for the visualization as they did not appreciate it: "I don't know to be honest. I don't want to say that I don't think there should be a like visualization, but yeah, I just don't know to be honest. But I did not like what I saw here anyway in front of me, yeah". P4 added that understanding such a graph requires a previous background in reading graphs: "If you're not used to looking at graphs this graph is probably confusing as well".

4.2   Deviation from Users' Expectations of a Typical Graph

Both P3 and P1 requested a graph that reads from left to right, contrary to the UI mock-up, as that is the way they are used to seeing and reading graphs. P3 stated that: "If I write a graph I have to start- yeah. From the left side to the right... I think the graph looks like it's upside down for me. Because the graph that I normally read starts from the left to the right. So, what I see here is a bit confusing. It's like...somehow the linear has to start from the left side and finish". P1 states: "It's not in the way I'm used- that I am used to when it comes to reading graphs and such...[] well... flip the graph. Somehow you need to move the axis to the right position as well, but just... the graph needs to start from the left and then go to the right. Yeah, that would help me at least". Despite the confusion, P1 believed that the context and the accompanying text helped clarify the graph better.

Experts as well as non-experts had specific expectations regarding the graph based on what they had previously seen. P6 expected to have scatter points and stated: "If it were like linear instead of just a grid. Because I understand that there are two variables, the seriousness and likelihood, but I... I don't know I would expect maybe scatter points".

4.3   Need for More Information and Clarifications

Non-expert participants' feedback generally included that they perceived the graph and text below it as reducing the risk. They believed the accompanying information made it clearer what the graph related to. For example, P1 conveyed that: "[..] seeing the graph confused me from the start, but when I read the text under, I can understand what you mean". Nevertheless, due to the lack of information about how the risk reduction would be accomplished and the similarity between the graphs showing two different types of risks, non-expert participants were confused about the purpose of the graph and what it really depicted, as P10 stated: "I don't see the purpose of this graph. Because it can be applicable for all kinds of risk and we don't see how it is reduced, so. It's just a graph saying you can have some big risks and you- We are trying to reduce them. But how do you try to reduce them? You have no idea". P7 also referred to the similarity of the graphs for different risks and said: "It is extra confusing that the same figure shows up here. I think it's the same. Risk likelihood, risk seriousness, yeah. Okay yeah, so that's confusing. [..] There is a missing description here. And I think a lot of this is incomplete". Despite understanding what the graph represents, P8 thought the purpose and credibility of the graph are unclear, as the graph and accompanying text do not convey how risk is reduced: "So, you know, it shows that they are simply making in such a way that the risk is neg- You can neglect it and also the likelihood is also decreased. So, I can understand what it says, but I can draw it myself. So, why is it there? I would like to know how are you doing this?".

In addition to the lack of information about risk reduction, non-expert participants also felt that the content provided was lacking in other aspects. Among these were the meanings of the two axes on the graph, risk seriousness and likelihood, the scales associated with them, and how risk seriousness and likelihood would correlate. For example, P7 stated: "I am uncertain what it shows. It does not show how they correlate. It says that the likelihood is reduced and the risks are reduced". P9 also voiced their desire for more information about the labels included by adding: "I feel like there is too little information about what it means. This 'Maximum', 'Important'".

In a similar fashion to non-experts, experts wanted to know how risks were reduced, not just that they had been reduced. P11 stated that: "the only thing that is missing is that like why was that at that level and what controls were used to reduce it. Yeah, like so why was there before and what was done to move it there". In addition, P5 wanted to know how the risks are mitigated with examples of risk evaluation: "but I'd need some risk that you really evaluated. [..] but just taking one or two examples and then on the image [..] showing that there, I don't know from red color, for example, and then going into details to explain why you can take them to the green case". Interestingly, experts disagreed regarding the usefulness of a graph lacking information about how risks are reduced. While P11 appreciated the graph by stating: "nice to see that this was the initial state, and this is the end state after the controls are applied", P11 highlights: "it does not say how it has been done". P4 and P5 did not like the graph/explanation and believed that it was not conveying much information as P5 said: "I don't really like this explanation because it feels like you want to say something, but you don't say enough to actually say something". While familiarity with PIA and related backgrounds may have contributed to a positive opinion about the graph despite its lack of information (as mentioned by P11), it may not necessarily be a factor influencing users' desire to know 'how' and not 'what'.

In addition to how risks were reduced, experts wanted a deeper explanation of the exact meaning of the risks (e.g., illegitimate data access). Moreover, similar to non-experts, they wanted more clarity about the meaning of the risk seriousness and likelihood, and the meaning of the scales presented, as P13 stated: "Example of risk seriousness, what is high? [..] Some scale to- so that we can... more understand more easily... What risks means, and the likelihood what it means also". The scales also appeared confusing for participants, as P6 mentioned: "the two-dimensional stuff doesn't really give something better than just- probably just one dimensional... like very risky- like, what is it... like 'Important' to 'Negligible' or the other way around and just doing it one way. it's too confusing."

Participants in both groups, during the walkthrough, had the chance to see some information regarding the remaining risks which was conveyed below the PA graph as accompanying text (see Fig. 3b). Although very few (one expert and one non-expert) commented on the information regarding the remaining risks, it appeared that communication of such risks was appreciated as it could give users more information on what could happen to them and "that zone zero does not exist", as P5 stated it. Still, P5 wanted to know more details about how personal data could be inferred or recovered from statistics.

5   Discussions

Based on our results, participants (lay and experts) have indicated their appreciation for the transparency of having information about privacy risk reductions. Therefore we believe providing information about risk reductions from the PIA tool to users is necessary. However, further clarifications and development of the visual aspects of PIA risk representations should take place. We present our recommendations for future work on usable PIA visualization in the following subsections.

5.1   UI Design Conventions and Clarifications

Participants showed varied opinions about the visualizations of the risks in terms of colors. The use of colors to illustrate the severity of risks could be considered useful in illustrating the seriousness of risks. In general, expert participants that were already more familiar with risk heat maps were more appreciative of the color scheme. However, due to the other information illustrated in the graph (arrows and simplified information), the perception of the color could have been affected accordingly. We, therefore, recommend design considerations when following conventions for the choice of color that must suit the target users, whether it is the familiarity with severity ratings (as used commonly in risk heat maps) or the accessibility for perceiving the colors presented correctly. Furthermore, a clarification for all UI elements must be available to users in a user-friendly manner.

5.2   Mental Models Considerations

As some participants were familiar with risk analysis and graphs in general, that created some confusion due to the mismatch in the mental models of some participants. Specifically, the arrow in the UI represents the transition of the risk from a higher risk seriousness/likelihood (up/right-hand side indicated by red) to a lower risk seriousness/likelihood (down/left-hand side indicated by green. This form of illustration (graph) has left participants, who are familiar with other types of graphs, confused. Their reasoning was that points should move from left to right and not the other way around. This format, which we used in the UI design, is taken directly from the PAPAYA tool, and participants who are familiar with risk heat maps seem to appreciate this format.

Furthermore, representing similar risk reductions for different risks seems to confuse participants. For example, the illegitimate data access and identification risks look the same in the UI as shown in Fig. 3. This could have had an impact on how users perceived the graph, as an image rather than a specific illustration of the risk at hand. Only those familiar with different risk types were able to notice the distinction. We, therefore, advise a consideration for the mental models and design conventions based on the target users, i.e., use risk heat maps with caution and possibly offer alternative illustrations for different users.

5.3   Need for More Information and Clarification Regarding the Terminology Used, the Context, and the Purpose

Participants indicated on many levels the need for more information and clarification regarding the terminology used, the context, and the purpose of the UI mock-ups. We, therefore, recommend improving the information provided on the following:

– Informing on the 'how', relating to how are the risks being reduced using the PETs. Providing information on 'how' the PET is done contributes to users' trust in the system. A graph like the one depicted in Fig. 3 was perceived by participants as a broad claim about risk reduction that anyone can make because it lacks the reasoning about 'why' the reduction is claimed in the figure. It should be made clear that the graph is based on a professional PIA tool, such as the one we used in PAPAYA.
– Clarifying the terminology used. Not all users, even experts, are familiar with the concepts of seriousness and likelihood in the context of risk management and it is better to exemplify them. Even the risks themselves (e.g. the meaning of illegitimate data access) should be clarified. Not knowing what the risk is makes it useless to know if and how it is being reduced.
– Taking precautions regarding remaining risks. To prevent PIA visualization from functioning as a privacy theatre (Privacy theatre dictates that PETs may provide the "feeling of improved privacy while doing little or nothing to actually improve privacy" [17]), we should always refer to remaining risks. By just emphasizing a lot on risk reduction, the remaining consequences of sharing data with a particular service and what it means for users to share their data are thwarted which can affect their decisions and may lead to regrets about sharing. The information about the remaining risks provided was also appreciated by the participants who got exposed to it. Therefore we recommend development of descriptions of remaining risks as seen in Table 1.

6   Conclusions

In our work, we show how PIA visualization in the user interface faces some challenges as well as opportunities for making the privacy-enhancing functionality and value of PETs transparent. Based on experts' and lay users' feedback, we present recommendations for future work and the development of usable PIAs for the transparency of privacy risks that should target different types of users.

Acknowledgment. We would like to acknowledge the PAPAYA (H2020 the European Commission, Grant Agreement No. 786767) and the TRUEdig (Swedish Knowledge Foundation) projects for funding this work. We extend our thanks to the project members for contributing with their valuable inputs throughout the projects. We further thank Tobias Pulls and Jonathan Magnusson for their technical input of the PAPAYA tool, John Sören Pettersson for his input to the user studies, and Elin Nilsson for her help in implementing the mock ups in adobe and transcribing results.

References

1. Privacy impact assessment (pia)—cnil. https://www.cnil.fr/en/privacy-impact-assessment-pia. Accessed 23 Jan 2023
2. Alaqra, A.S., Fischer-Hübner, S., Framner, E.: Enhancing privacy controls for patients via a selective authentic electronic health record exchange service: qualitative study of perspectives by medical professionals and patients. J. Med. Internet Res. **20**(12), e10954 (2018).
3. Alaqra, A.S., Kane, B., Fischer-Hübner, S.: Machine learning-based analysis of encrypted medical data in the cloud: qualitative study of expert stakeholders' perspectives. JMIR Hum. Factors **8**(3), e21810 (2021).
4. Boneh, D., Sahai, A., Waters, B.: Functional encryption: definitions and challenges. In: Ishai, Y. (ed.) TCC 2011. LNCS, vol. 6597, pp. 253–273. Springer, Heidelberg (2011). https://doi.org/10.1007/978-3-642-19571-6_16
5. Bozdemir, B., et al.: D3.3 complete specification and implementation of privacy preserving data analytics—Papaya (2020). https://www.papaya-project.eu/node/157
6. Bozdemir, B., et al.: D4.3 final report on platform implementation and PETs integration—Papaya (2021). https://www.papaya-project.eu/node/161
7. Camenisch, J., et al.: Trust in prime. In: Proceedings of the Fifth IEEE International Symposium on Signal Processing and Information Technology, 2005, pp. 552–559. IEEE (2005)
8. Cavoukian, A.: Privacy by design, take the challenge (2009)
9. Cavoukian, A.: Privacy by design in law, policy and practice (2011)
10. Clarke, R.: Privacy impact assessments. Xamax Consultancy Pty Ltd. (1998)
11. Clarke, R.: Privacy impact assessment: its origins and development. Comput. Law Secur. Rev. **25**(2), 123–135 (2009).
12. Demjaha, A., Spring, J.M., Becker, I., Parkin, S., Sasse, M.A.: Metaphors considered harmful? an exploratory study of the effectiveness of functional metaphors for end-to-end encryption. In: Proceedings of the USEC, vol. 2018. Internet Society (2018)
13. EU-GDPR: Article 35 EU general data protection regulation. Data protection impact assessment. (2022). https://gdpr-info.eu/art-35-gdpr/
14. Simone, F.-H., et al.: D3.4 transparent privacy preserving data analytics (2021). https://www.papaya-project.eu
15. Heurix, J., Zimmermann, P., Neubauer, T., Fenz, S.: A taxonomy for privacy enhancing technologies. Comput. Secur. **53**, 1–17 (2015).
16. Karegar, F., Alaqra, A.S., Fischer-Hübner, S.: Exploring {User-Suitable} metaphors for differentially private data analyses. In: Eighteenth Symposium on Usable Privacy and Security (SOUPS 2022), pp. 175–193 (2022)
17. Khare, R.: Privacy theater: why social networks only pretend to protect you (2022). https://techcrunch.com/2009/12/27/privacy-theater/
18. Murmann, P., Fischer-Hübner, S.: Tools for achieving usable ex post transparency: a survey. IEEE Access **5**, 22965–22991 (2017).
19. Nanayakkara, P., Bater, J., He, X., Hullman, J., Rogers, J.: Visualizing privacy-utility trade-offs in differentially private data releases. Proc. Priv. Enhancing Technol. **2022**(2), 601–618 (2022).

Overcoming Privacy-Related Challenges
for Game Developers

Marissa Berk[1]([✉]), Tamara Marantika[1], Daan Oldenhof[1], Marcel Stalenhoef[1],
Erik Hekman[1], Levien Nordeman[1], Simone van der Hof[2], Linda Louis[3],
Aletta Smits[1], and Koen van Turnhout[1]

[1] Utrecht University of Applied Sciences, 3584 CS Utrecht, The Netherlands
marissa.berk@hu.nl
[2] University of Leiden Law School, 2311 EZ Leiden, The Netherlands
[3] The Hague University of Applied Sciences, 2521 EN The Hague, The Netherlands

Abstract. Design and development practitioners such as those in game development often have difficulty comprehending and adhering to the European General Data Protection Regulation (GDPR), especially when designing in a private sensitive way. Inadequate understanding of how to apply the GDPR in the game development process can lead to one of two consequences: 1. inadvertently violating the GDPR with sizeable fines as potential penalties; or 2. avoiding the use of user data entirely. In this paper, we present our work on designing and evaluating the "GDPR Pitstop tool", a gamified questionnaire developed to empower game developers and designers to increase legal awareness of GDPR laws in a relatable and accessible manner. The GDPR Pitstop tool was developed with a user-centered approach and in close contact with stakeholders, including practitioners from game development, legal experts and communication and design experts. Three design choices worked for this target group: 1. Careful crafting of the language of the questions; 2. a flexible structure; and 3. a playful design. By combining these three elements into the GDPR Pitstop tool, GDPR awareness within the gaming industry can be improved upon and game developers and designers can be empowered to use user data in a GDPR compliant manner. Additionally, this approach can be scaled to confront other tricky issues faced by design professionals such as privacy by design.

Keywords: Privacy · GDPR · Game development · Game design · Gamification

1 Introduction

The European General Data Protection Regulation (GDPR) was implemented by the European Parliament in 2018 to give individual users more rights in how their data is processed [1]. The GDPR has strict rules that are complex and hard to understand [2]. The punishment for noncompliance consists of hefty fines that can reach upwards of 20 million Euros [1]. At the same time, the GDPR contains legal jargon that is difficult for non-legal experts, such as game developers, to understand and implement. Therefore, game developers struggle with designing in a privacy-sensitive way [3].

A. Moallem (Ed.): HCII 2023, LNCS 14045, pp. 18–28, 2023.
https://doi.org/10.1007/978-3-031-35822-7_2

The use of data and analytics is common in the online gaming industry as it improves game design and user testing procedures [4]. Video game developers and/or designers often collect data from users in order to improve or add new features [5] or to create adaptive games [6]. Lack of GDPR understanding among game developers, combined with their fear of receiving large non-compliance fines, can deter them from using this valuable data to optimize games. Consequently, the games that are developed either inadvertently violate privacy [7] or underutilise user data - as a defensive maneuver to avoid noncompliance fines [8]. Therefore, we must identify what is preventing game developers from understanding and complying with the GDPR and devise solutions to address those issues so that game developers can confidently utilise user data without violating user privacy under the GDPR. This research explores these obstacles through a user-centered design case and introduces a potential solution in the form of a gamified questionnaire; The GDPR Pitstop tool. With the design of the GDPR Pitstop tool we explored how game practitioners could be empowered to better apply the GDPR in the game development process.

2   Related Work

2.1   Understanding and Implementing GDPR for Game Developers

The changes brought about by GDPR legislation have had severe impacts on businesses and organizations in the EU territory [9]. Organisations are having difficulties understanding what compliance is and how to properly implement it [10]. The complex nature of the GDPR causes uncertainty about its content and scope [11]. According to Sirur, Nurse and Webb [2], deciphering the semantics behind the words of GDPR is a burden for organisations. In this study [2], respondents expressed that without a legal background or assistance from a legal professional, implementing the regulations would prove challenging.

This is also true for developers, Alhamazi & Arachchilage [12] cite developers' lack of familiarity with GDPR principles as a cause for their inability to create applications that comply with GDPR principles. Research shows that most game developers do not know enough about the GDPR and the risks that occur when it is not properly adhered to [3, 13]. These studies also show that even developers with a bit of knowledge of the law still struggle to properly implement it.

User data collection is a common practice in the gaming industry. The online gaming industry deals with a lot of transmission of information between networks, making the proper handling of user data paramount to user privacy [7]. According to Kröger et. al [14] the amount and richness of personal data collected by (video) games is often underestimated. Examples of personal data collected through games include specifics of a user's device including type of device and browsing history and personally identifiable information such as name, email address, and geolocation [15]. Even if users do not provide personal data, personal information can be inferred based on data collected from in-game behaviour [14]. Therefore, the GDPR's legislature encapsulates gaming as well, and game developers may not even be aware of how much personally identifiable data their game designs are collecting. Game development practitioners' understanding of the GDPR law is often limited, leading to illegal or alternatively overly self-regulated data collection practices [7, 8].

3 Design Case

To come up with a solution to help game developers combat their uncertainty, we employed a user-centered design process [16]. As an initial attempt to solve this problem, we created a GDPR decision tree, in collaboration with legal scientists and gaming practitioners. The decision tree became overly complex and had 21 levels, the first four are depicted below in Fig. 1.

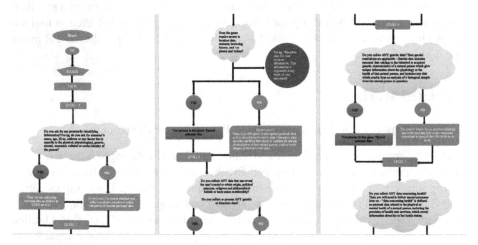

Fig. 1. Decision Tree levels 1–4

The decision tree framed compliance as a linear problem; however, walkthroughs with game developers showed this type of solution had fundamental flaws. Seeing as non-compliance with one GDPR principle does not necessarily imply non-compliance with the other principles, a more versatile solution was needed. Since game development is multifaceted [17] there is not a 'one size fits all' solution. Even the legislators for the GDPR deliberately avoided recommending specific technical frameworks or methods for implementing the GDPR legal requirements, since technical innovations are always evolving [9]. It became clear that a more flexible and user friendly solution was needed to solve this problem, so we developed the GDPR Pitstop tool [18]. The GDPR Pitstop tool is a gamified questionnaire that simplifies the complex legal jargon of the GDPR and delivers it in easily implementable bits of information.

3.1 Stakeholder Workshops and Interviews

To gain a better understanding of the game development process, we organised workshops with a group of six game developers to determine when GDPR knowledge is required during the game development process. These sessions provided insights into how game developers are currently working with the GDPR, how information is gathered and what sources are used, and when key decisions regarding privacy, data collection and data processing are made. In these sessions it was discovered that the game development process is not linear, that client desires, or design choices evolve during the development process and therefore there are multiple moments throughout this process in which GDPR compliance should be checked. It was also discovered that many, specifically smaller game development organisations, attempt to avoid data collection due to lack of legal understanding and fear of violating the GDPR. Therefore it is vital that the tool is flexible and employs language and design choices that game developers are familiar with.

We followed up with individual interviews conducted with nine game developers and four legal experts to gain a comprehensive understanding of the game development process and GDPR challenges from industry professionals. These further revealed that game developers need an adaptable, legally substantiated decision aid that presents a risk analysis in regard to GDPR compliance. These expert interviews led us to discover four GDPR themes that are highly relevant to the game development process. These themes are; necessity, consent, data subject rights, and security & storage. The GDPR Pitstop tool focuses on these themes and addresses them in the seven quick scan questions and quick scan result. Each question in the quick scan relates to one of the four themes. For example; Question 2: *How do you decide whether to collect / process the data or not?* Relates to the theme of necessity.

3.2 Flexible Design Structure

Having a sense of the most important areas of privacy concern in the game development process opened the possibility for a layered solution. We could provide a quick scan enabling the designer to check the areas of concern and a deep scan to enable a more thorough diagnosis of this area. We quickly check all four relevant GDPR themes (necessity, consent, data subject rights, and security & storage) in a quick scan by asking users seven questions. Users are then provided with a quick scan result with specific control points indicated (Fig. 2). Any of those areas that may be problematic, based on the answers of the quick scan, can then be further investigated with more detailed questions in the deep scan.

The combination of a quick scan and a deep scan was implemented to limit the number of initial questions and give users a quick sense of overview and detail. The user is shown the major themes that need to be re-evaluated. Then, within each area, the user is provided with the details that require attention in order to comply with GDPR. They can select a theme (highlighted in the quick scan) and will be presented with more questions on the topic (in the deep scan). The user is then presented with tips and tricks on how to solve the non-compliant parts of the different themes. They are then guided through the different possibilities and given examples for the questions and solutions from other games. This setup allows game developers and designers to focus on the areas or themes that need the most attention for their game. Instead of addressing the entirety of the GDPR, the flexible design of the tool draws attention to the themes that the user needs to address.

3.3 Careful Language Crafting

Much effort went into crafting the questions. The goal of the tool is to make the complex GDPR law comprehensible for game developers who have little to no legal expertise, thus, the questionnaire's questions must bridge the gap between legal jargon and game developers' understanding. It has long been known that legal jargon is difficult to understand [19]. However, successful questionnaire design requires that questions use clear and unambiguous language [20, 21]. Cognitive interviews are an effective method for pre testing questionnaire understanding, specifically for complex questions [22], therefore this is the method we used to carefully craft the language in the GDPR Tool questionnaire.

The questions were drafted in close collaboration with legal experts to ensure that they maintained legal relevance. To determine whether the questions in the quick scan and deep scan were comprehensible, we conducted cognitive interviews with 10 communication and design experts who had no prior legal experience. In these interviews, the questions and answers were tested for legibility and clarity amongst lecturers of the Communication and Multimedia Design programme at the Utrecht University of Applied Sciences recruited via convenience sample. Since the main goal of the tool is clarity for the user, it is vital that the questions and related advice are understandable and unambiguous for non-legal experts. These lecturers were used as a proxy for game developers since they have no legal knowledge of the GDPR but have knowledge of communication and design. The results of the cognitive interviews showed that the simplified legal text was still too complex for non-legal experts to understand and apply. Therefore, the questions were rewritten to increase comprehension levels amongst game developers. The quick scan and deep scan questions went through three rounds of such language revision. For each round of revision, two legal experts assisted in the rewriting of the questions to ensure that rephrasing did not compromise the legal validity of the content.

An example of question rephrasing can be shown using quickscan question number 5. This question pertains to the 4th GDPR theme addressed in the tool; security and storage. The legal text of the GDPR states:

"Taking into account the state of the art, the costs of implementation and the nature, scope, context and purposes of processing as well as the risk of varying likelihood and severity for the rights and freedoms of natural persons, the controller and the processor shall implement appropriate technical and organisational measures to ensure a level of security appropriate to the risk, including inter alia as appropriate..." [1]. The law goes on to list conditions and requirements. For the GDPR Pitstop Tool the section of this law was simplified to pertain to gaming practitioners which resulted in the following question: "Do you have knowledge about the requirements and standards that apply to the storage of data, as described in the GDPR?". In the first round of cognitive interviews, participants suggested a simplification to this question and in collaboration with legal experts it was updated to "What do you need to know about proper data storage under the law?" In the second round of cognitive interviews it was still experienced as unclear and was therefore updated as follows: "Where is the collected data stored? Is that within the EU?". The final version of the question asks only what is relevant to game developers and further details can be elaborated upon in the deepscan.

3.4 Gamification

We opted for a gamified questionnaire because gamification and game elements such as challenge, theme, reward, and progress can be used to make non-game products more enjoyable and increase user retention [23, 24]. Game elements have successfully been used to teach software developers about privacy and how to embed it into designs [12, 13]. Therefore, we found it was an appropriate method to teach game developers and designers about privacy.

The metaphor of a pitstop was chosen because regular user privacy maintenance is required and there is an association of danger if it is not done correctly, much like a pitstop in automobile racing. In the pitstop tool, the users first go through a quick scan which checks for compliance in the four GDPR areas by asking users questions about how their game collects and handles user data. These four areas coincide with the four GDPR themes relevant to game developers; necessity, consent, data subject rights, and security & storage. The areas include data purpose limitation (necessity), procedure of permission for using data (consent), data integrity and confidentiality (data subject rights), and location of data storage (security & storage). After a quick scan, the game developer is shown a dashboard with the four broader GDPR themes colour coded according to the GDPR compliance of the developers quick scan answers, as shown in Fig. 2.

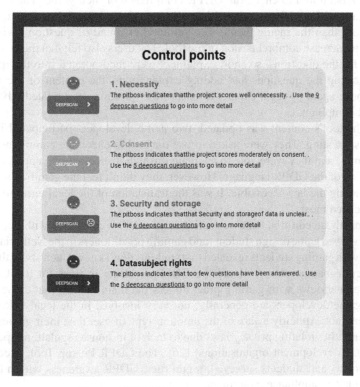

Fig. 2. GDPR Pitstop tool quick scan result

Some of the themes are green, which signals to the user that they do not require immediate attention. Some themes are greyed out, meaning more questions need to be answered to provide a result. Some themes are orange, which indicates that there are some problems in this theme. And some of the themes may be red, which indicates that there are issues with noncompliance in this theme. There are also corresponding smiley icons to indicate whether the theme needs more attention. The user should then conduct a deep scan on the themes that are red, orange, or grey to better understand how he or she can improve these areas in the games' data collection and processing methods. The quick and deep scan results should not be taken as legal advice, rather they can be used as a guide to help developers become more aware of where in their game designs they are at risk of violating user privacy. Game elements, specifically challenge (completing all the quick scan questions with a green result) and theme (the racing theme and pit boss character) are used in the GDPR Pitstop tool to increase motivation and questionnaire stamina.

3.5 User Testing

The look and feel of the GDPR Pitstop tool was tested with five game developers recruited via convenience sampling from game development firms in the Netherlands. The game developers were asked to use one of their games as an example and to run through the GDPR Pitstop tool to check the GDPR compliance of their game. The developers reported that they found the content of the tool (the quick scan and deep scan questions) more relevant than the racing theme. So, yet another round of question revision was conducted to increase comprehension of the tool. The users also felt that there was a lack of context for the questions, so short explainers were incorporated into the questions. After rephrasing the questions and adding explanations, the content of the tool was reviewed once again by legal experts to ensure the questions and related advice were still GDPR compliant.

After the tool's content was updated, two game developers participated in a final round of user testing. They were asked to use the tool to check the compliance of one of their games, and they were able to navigate through it successfully, appreciating the simplification of the GDPR language. However, they didn't feel the gamification helped much in making the law accessible. It was the translation of the legal terminology that they appreciated most.

Additionally an editorial team consisting of journalists connected with our research group interviewed game design students and gaming practitioners in the Netherlands. The interviews with gaming students revealed that students don't know much about the GDPR and have even inadvertently violated the GDPR resulting in fines for the University [25]. In the interviews with gaming practitioners the main themes that came forward were that game developers are generally; not very involved in the legal side of game development, not explicitly aware of the amount/ type of user data their games collect, and inadvertently violating privacy laws due to lack of in-house regulation (specifically smaller game development organisations) [26]. The GDPR Pitstop Tool, according to the practitioners and students surveyed, might raise GDPR awareness within the game sector and make compliance more manageable.

4 Discussion and Conclusion

The complex jargon combined with the non-linear nature of the GDPR makes developing GDPR compliant games challenging for those without legal expertise. Game developers are in need of tools that help them adhere to complex legal regulations within their game designs. The GDPR Pitstop tool offers a low-threshold, hands-on way of accessing this information space. Professional gaming practitioners have been involved in the design throughout the whole design process to ensure that the tool is useful and relevant for game developers. Although there are areas that can be improved upon, overall, the tool was well received by the community. There are three design choices that worked for this target group: 1. Careful crafting of the language of the questions; 2. a flexible structure; and 3. a playful design.

4.1 Careful Crafting of the Language of the Questions

Frequent collaboration with the game development field revealed that the most important aspect of the tool was the content (the questions). Therefore, this was the focus of the GDPR Pitstop tool - to speak the language of the game developers, while remaining valid in terms of the GDPR. The process of breaking down the GDPR law for game developers began by identifying four main GDPR themes (necessity, consent, data subject rights, security & storage) that are especially relevant to the game development process. The questions in the GDPR tool all relate to one of these four themes. The questions and answers for the quick scan and deep scans were crafted through workshop sessions, cognitive interviews, user testing, and collaboration with legal experts to be understandable for game developers while remaining legally valid. From this process we learned that questions should be drafted with an iterative process that incorporates feedback from users. This allows for the recontextualization of legal terms into language and context that game practitioners are familiar with. By doing this, we were able to take general legal text and craft it to refer to specific background knowledge and goals. The benefit is that gaming practitioners can actually understand the questions and how they apply to their game designs; the disadvantage is that the topics are oversimplified. While the GDPR Pitstop tool can raise GDPR awareness in the gaming industry by drawing attention to it, the simplification of complex legal texts may cause gaming practitioners to undervalue the topics.

4.2 Flexible Design Structure

The structure of the tool allows the users to adapt their journey based on the needs of the specific case study the game developers use. By guiding users through the quick scan first, they can identify the areas of the GDPR they need to improve on and dive deeper into the deep scan. This flexible design allows users to focus on problem areas specific to their game rather than addressing the GDPR in its entirety, which has proven to be overwhelming and difficult for non-legal experts. During the user tests, game developers mentioned that since game development is an iterative process, the tool can be useful as a 'check-up' to be used occasionally throughout the development process. The flexible design structure facilitates an easy checkup process, allowing game developers to quickly identify areas that require improvement via a quick scan and then zoom in on only the areas that require attention as needed.

4.3 Playful Design

Gamification can be an effective method for increasing user retention and enjoyment, specifically when it comes to complex topics such as privacy. Therefore, we decided to incorporate gamification elements into the tool. Gamification has been used in surveys and questionnaires to increase user enjoyment and attention [27]. While users were successfully able to complete the questionnaire within the GDPR Pitstop tool, the user testing resulted in mixed reviews about the playfulness of the design. Some professionals were not interested in the theme at all, and others appreciated the gamification elements. Therefore, there was less focus on the gamification and game elements of the tool, and more focus on testing and improving the content - the questions. The gamification elements in the tool are simple and only aim to increase user attention and enjoyment. Additionally, the game itself was not user tested as thoroughly as the quick scan and deep scan questions. Therefore, as a next step, user tests with more game developers should be conducted.

4.4 Discussion

Overall, gaming practitioners appreciated the GDPR Pitstop tool and felt it could be useful to raise awareness of GDPR requirements for game developers. The tool's simplified GDPR language, flexible structure, and playfulness have the potential to raise GDPR compliance awareness within the gaming industry and empower game developers and designers to use user data in a GDPR compliant manner without fear of facing substantial fines. Additionally, this approach can be scaled to confront other tricky issues faced by design professionals such as privacy awareness outside the scope of gaming. Privacy by Design (PbD) refers to a proactive integration of technical privacy principles in a system's design in order to prevent privacy risks before they happen [28]. According to Spiekermann [29], even if organisations are committed to PbD, there are many challenges that make implementation difficult including an unclear methodology for its implementation and insufficient knowledge of the pros and cons related to privacy and privacy breaches. The same is true for privacy in game development. Therefore, a similar flexible solution could be implemented to increase awareness of privacy and PbD outside the scope of gaming.

References

1. Regulation (EU) 2016/679 of the European Parliament and of the Council of 27 April 2016 on the protection of natural persons with regard to the processing of personal data and on the free movement of such data, and repealing Directive 95/46/EC (General Da.) Official Journal of the European Union (2016). http://data.europa.eu/eli/reg/2016/679/oj
2. Sirur, S., Nurse, J.R., Webb, H.: Are we there yet? Understanding the challenges faced in complying with the General Data Protection Regulation (GDPR). In: Proceedings of the 2nd International Workshop on Multimedia Privacy and Security (MPS 2018), pp. 88–95 (2018). https://doi.org/10.1145/3267357.3267368

3. Alhazmi, A., Arachchilage, N.A.G.: I'm all ears! Listening to software developers on putting GDPR principles into software development practice. Pers. Ubiquit. Comput. **25**(5), 879–892 (2021). https://doi.org/10.1007/s00779-021-01544-1

4. Bauckhage, C., Kersting, K., Sifa, R., Thurau, C., Drachen, A., Canossa, A.: How players lose interest in playing a game: an empirical study based on distributions of total playing times. In: 2012 IEEE Conference on Computational Intelligence and Games (CIG), pp. 139–146 (2012). https://doi.org/10.1109/CIG.2012.6374148

5. Drachen, A., Thurau, C., Togelius, J., Yannakakis, G.N., Bauckhage, C.: Game data mining. In: Seif El-Nasr, M., Drachen, A., Canossa, A. (eds.) Game Analytics, pp. 205–253. Springer, London (2013). https://doi.org/10.1007/978-1-4471-4769-5_12

6. Charles, D.K., Black, M., Moore, A., Stringer, K.: Player-centred game design: player modelling and adaptive digital games. In: Proceedings of DiGRA 2005 Conference: Changing Views – Worlds in Play. Digital Games Research Association: DiGRA, pp. 285–298 (2005)

7. Zhao, C.: Cyber security issues in online games. In: AIP Conference Proceedings, vol. 1955, p. 040015, 1–5 (2018). https://doi.org/10.1063/1.5033679

8. Holl, A., Theuns, M., Pieterman, N.: Schiet uit de privacykramp! Hoe technologie privacy eenvoudiger kan maken. Retrieved from Trends in Veiligheid 2021 (2021). https://www.trendsinveiligheid.nl/wp-content/uploads/2020/08/TiV-2020_Schiet-uit-de-privacykramp.pdf

9. Politou, E., Alepi, E., Patsakis, C.: Forgetting personal data and revoking consent under the GDPR: challenges and proposed solutions. J. Cybersecur. **4**(1), 1–20 (2018). https://doi.org/10.1093/cybsec/tyy001

10. Tankard, C.: What the GDPR means for business. Network Security, 8. The Centre for Information Policy Leadership. 2017. 2nd GDPR Organisational Readiness Survey Report (2016). https://www.informationpolicycentre.com/global-readiness-benchmarks-for-gdpr.html

11. Bygrave, L.A., Yeung, K.: Demystifying the modernized European data protection regime: cross-disciplinary insights from legal and regulatory governance scholarship. Regul. Gov. **16**, 137–155 (2022)

12. Alhazmi, A.H., Arachchilage, N.A.: A serious game design framework for software developers to put GDPR into practice. In: ARES 2021: The 16th International Conference on Availability, Reliability and Security, Article no. 64, pp. 1–6 (2021). https://doi.org/10.1145/3465481.3470031

13. Arachchilage, N.A., Hameed, M.A.: Designing a serious game: teaching developers to embed privacy into software systems. In: Proceedings of the 35th IEEE/ACM International Conference on Automated Software Engineering Workshops, pp. 7–12. Association for Computing Machinery, New York (2020). https://doi.org/10.1145/3417113.3422149

14. Kröger, J.L., Raschke, P., Campbell, J.P., Ullrich, S.: Surveilling the gamers: privacy impacts of the video game industry. Entertainment Comput. **44**, 100537 (2023). https://doi.org/10.1016/j.entcom.2022.100537

15. Moon, S., Reidenberg, J.R., Russell, N.C.: Privacy in Gaming and Virtual Reality Technologies: Review of Academic Literature (2017)

16. Abras, C., Maloney-Krichmar, D., Preece, J.: User-centered design. In: Bainbridge, W. (ed.) Encyclopedia of Human-Computer Interaction, vol. 37, no. 4, pp. 445–456. Sage Publications, Thousand Oaks (2004)

17. Petrillo, F., Pimenta, M., Trindade, F., Dietrich, C.: What went wrong? A survey of problems in game development. Comput. Entertain. **7**(1), 22, Article no. 13 (2009). https://doi.org/10.1145/1486508.1486521

18. Human Experience and Media Design (2018). GDPR Pitstop Tool. https://www.avgtool.org/index.html

19. Miner, R.J.: Confronting the communication crisis in the legal profession. NYL Sch. L. Rev. **34**, 1 (1989)

20. Conrad, F., Blair, J., Tracy, E.: Verbal reports are data! A theoretical approach to cognitive interviews. In: Proceedings of the Federal Committee on Statistical Methodology Research Conference, Tuesday B Sessions, Arlington, VA, pp. 11–20 (1999)
21. Dillman, D.: Mail and Internet Surveys: The Tailored Design Method, 2nd edn. Wiley, New York (2000)
22. Drennan, J.: Cognitive interviewing: verbal data in the design and pretesting of questionnaires. J. Adv. Nurs. **42**(1), 57–63 (2003)
23. Deterding, S., Dixon, D., Khaled, R., Nacke, L.. From game design elements to gamefulness: defining "gamification". In: Proceedings of the 15th International Academic MindTrek Conference: Envisioning Future Media Environments (MindTrek 2011), pp. 9–15. Association for Computing Machinery, New York (2011). https://doi.org/10.1145/2181037.2181040
24. Flatla, D., Gutwin, C., Nacke, L., Bateman, S., Mandryk, R.: Calibration games: making calibration tasks enjoyable by adding motivating game elements. In: Proceedings of the 24th Annual ACM Symposium on User Interface Software and Technology (UIST 2011), pp. 403–412. Association for Computing Machinery, New York (2011). https://doi.org/10.1145/204 7196.2047248
25. Human Experience and Media Design (2022). https://hemdmissies.nl/hanze-university-gro ningen-avg-wetgeving-voorlichting/
26. Human Experience and Media Design (2022). https://hemdmissies.nl/gdpr-pitstop-op-dutch-media-week/
27. Triantoro, T., Gopal, R., Benbunan-Fich, R., Lang, G.: Would you like to play? A comparison of a gamified survey with a traditional online survey method. Int. J. Inf. Manag. **49**, 242–252 (2019)
28. Cavoukian, A.: Privacy by design (2009)
29. Spiekermann, S.: The challenges of privacy by design. Commun. ACM **55**(7), 38–40 (2012)

Parents, Passwords, and Parenting: How Parents Think about Passwords and are Involved in Their Children's Password Practices

Yee-Yin Choong[1]([✉]) [iD], Kerrianne Buchanan[1] [iD], and Olivia Williams[2] [iD]

[1] National Institute of Standards and Technology, Gaithersburg, MD, USA
{yee-yin.choong,kerrianne.buchanan}@nist.gov
[2] University of Maryland, College Park, MD, USA

Abstract. Though much is known about how adults understand and use passwords, little research attention has been paid specifically to parents or, more importantly, to how parents are involved in their children's password practices. To better understand both the password practices of parents, as well as how parents are involved in their children's password practices, we conducted a survey study of 265 parents in the United States (US) with school-aged children (kindergarten through 12th grade, 5 to 18 years old). We asked parents about their general technology use, the kinds of technologies and password-protected accounts they have; how they make and maintain their passwords; and about how, if at all, they help their children create and maintain passwords. We found that parent password practices align with research surrounding adult password practices, and that parents, especially those of younger children, are very involved in the creation and maintenance of their children's passwords. With these findings, we conclude with both recommendations for future research, as well as a call for the cybersecurity community to better support parents' password understandings and practices so that parents can better support their children.

Keywords: Privacy and Online Security · User Survey · Usable security · Passwords · Parenting

1 Introduction

Passwords continue to be the de facto authentication method for most devices and accounts that a typical digital user accesses online. Over time, these "typical digital users" have increasingly come to include youth at younger ages. These youth use a variety of technologies every day, sometimes for more than eight hours a day [20]. In doing so, they access dozens of security measures, applications, and accounts that all require the creation, use, and maintenance of passwords [20]. As youth age, the number of passwords they require—and the sensitivity of the data that those passwords

---

This material is based on work supported by the UMD and NIST Professional Research Experience Program (PREP) under Award Number 70NANB18H165.

A. Moallem (Ed.): HCII 2023, LNCS 14045, pp. 29–48, 2023.
https://doi.org/10.1007/978-3-031-35822-7_3

protect—increases, and the password practices they learn at a young age can turn into habits over time. The ubiquity and importance of passwords in youth's online lives demands an understanding of how children are using passwords. An important facet of this understanding is knowing more about from where youth password knowledge comes.

Parents and guardians[1] are often the first external point of contact in a child's password learning journey. Most youth's earliest exposure to technology and passwords happens under the supervision of their parents or guardians. Examining what parents know and how they are involved in their children's passwords is an important starting point for understanding how and from where children develop password understandings and behaviors. While we have an idea of what children do online [20, 23], and we know that parents are actively involved in children's online lives [13], there is still much to learn about the development of children's knowledge and behavior regarding the use of passwords, and the role parents play in this learning process. We designed this study to provide insights on how parents can best support their children's password practices by answering two research questions: RQ1–What are parents' password practices? and, RQ2–How, if at all, are parents involved in their children's password creation and maintenance? If so, does parental involvement differ across children's grade bands?

When conceptualizing this study, we found it important to ask parents not only about their involvement with their children's passwords, but also about their own password practices. This choice was made for two reasons: one, we wanted to know if there was something about the experience of being a parent that influenced their own password behavior, for example, being responsible for a young person's information online in addition to their own. Two, we wanted to see if and how parents were involved with their children's password creation and maintenance in order to understand more about parents' conceptualizations of youth's password needs. We also explored whether parent's involvement depended on the age of their child.

2 Related Research

The existing body of literature concerning password behaviors, password understandings, and password policies is enormous. To situate our current study of parents and their involvement in their children's password behavior in this vast landscape, we first synthesize recent literature regarding adult password knowledge and behavior, as most parents are also adults. Then we explore studies that address the same understandings in youth. Finally, we examine the few studies that investigate the role that parents play in youth password knowledge to lay the groundwork for our exploration of parents' password behavior and their involvement in their children's password practices.

2.1 Adults' Password Habits

Although most adults are generally aware of basic password hygiene [1], studies find that many adults still enact undesirable password behaviors [10, 16, 26]. Some research

---

[1] Both parents and legal guardians are referred to as "parents" hereafter throughout the paper.

suggests these undesirable behaviors stem from flawed password creation beliefs [28], such as believing that the inclusion of a symbol like an "!" automatically increases security [28], or that reusing passwords is acceptable if those passwords are strong [15]. Multiple studies have found that re-use of passwords is especially common [5, 17, 31], indicating that adults struggle to balance security, usability, and convenience in having many passwords for a variety of devices and accounts [6, 24, 25].

Indeed, many studies have shown that this cognitive dissonance between usability and security in password priorities results in users who know good password and security behavior but do not enact them [30]. For example, Ur et al. found that participants perceived a tradeoff between security and memorability, rating more secure practices as more difficult to remember [29]. In such cases, if users valued the usability of a password—i.e., the ease of remembering and entering it into a website or device—more than security, they were likely to sacrifice some level of security even if they knew what secure behaviors were [18, 32]. A study of 902 participants' adoption and/or abandonment of 30 common security practices found similar results, such that participants ignored or deserted good practices due to inconvenience, low perceived value, or because they just thought they knew better [34]. These findings collectively suggest that understanding good password behavior, alone, is a far cry from ensuring good password practice.

Because most parents are also adults, these findings about adult password behavior both inform an understanding of parent password behavior, while also raising further questions. It is unclear whether parental responsibilities—such as having to help teach children about passwords or being generally responsible for the online privacy and security of others—are related to one's own password knowledge and practice development. It is also unclear whether and how parents' complex and sometimes disjointed password understandings and practices are related to their conceptualization of appropriate password practices for themselves and for their children. Our study aims to contribute to these understandings.

2.2 Youth Password Knowledge and Behavior

Like their adult counterparts, there seems to be a gap between what children understand in theory and what they practice in real life [4, 11, 19]. For example, Zhang-Kennedy et al. found that study participants (7 to 11-year-olds) had good foundational password knowledge, such as knowing that they should not share their passwords with strangers and that passwords are secrets [33]. However, these participants had conflicting behavior, like one participant who stated the importance of not sharing passwords with anyone including family members, but who also reported that their mother had made their password for them, and later shared one of their passwords with the researchers [33].

Other studies have noted developmental trends in youth password habits; while youth may know that complex passwords are important, from a developmental standpoint, they may not be ready to create and reliably use them [12]. Moreover, some studies have found that password understandings and behavior change over time. For example, a study of 1,505 3rd to 12th grade students revealed that while middle and high school students were more likely to report that they keep their passwords private, they were also significantly more likely to report sharing their passwords with friends and using the same password across multiple accounts than their elementary school counterparts

[27]. Other studies suggest that the older children get and the more passwords they have to make and maintain, the more some of their habits tend to reflect those of adults [21].

Fortunately, children's password knowledge and behavior are in constant development, and thus can be changed with support, good information, and encouragement. For instance, in a password simulation activity, Maqsood et al. found that their 20 preteen participants believed that their simple passwords containing personal information were secure. But when participants were introduced to the rule and value of including special characters in password creation, the participants quickly understood [14]. As a result of their study, Maqsood et al. leveraged a call for "further studies with parents [to] explore their knowledge of secure passwords and what they teach their children about the topic" (p.543) [14]. As social learning theory supports that children's learning is a direct result of their environment and the people in it [3], and parents are the first and often most prominent figures in children's environments, we agree with Maqsood et al. that exploring what parents teach children about passwords is important. Our current study of parents' password knowledge and their involvement in their children's password behavior is a direct answer to this call.

2.3 The Involvement of Parents in Youth Password Behavior

There is little research dedicated to understanding the involvement of parents in their children's password behavior, but those studies that do exist lay important groundwork for this study. They find, first and foremost, that parents actively choose to involve themselves in their children's password creation [19]. From the children's perspective, Choong et al. found that many elementary school children reported having parental help with password creation and tracking [4]. From the parent perspective, in Zhang-Kennedy and colleagues' 2016 dyadic study of parent/child perception of cyber threats, all 14 of the study's parent participants reported controlling their young (7–11 years old) children's passwords and accounts and talking with their children about how to create passwords [33]. Unfortunately, parents reportedly felt torn between wanting to teach their kids good behavior with the reasoning behind that behavior and wanting to shield their children from the harsh realities of the world. For example, some of the advice these parents provided to their children included choosing a weaker but easier to remember passwords [33].

Our study builds onto this limited body of work by focusing on a larger sample of parents and extending the grade range of children to include kindergarten through 12th graders. As described earlier, children's learning can be influenced directly from their parents [3]. If parents are involved in passing down their password knowledge to their children, understanding more about how this involvement happens is an important precursor of understanding children's password knowledge and behavior. Our study examines the password understandings and practices of a larger group of parents, looks for trends in parent involvement in children's password creation and maintenance across several developmental stages, and explores how, if at all, parents' own practices are impacted by working with their children.

3 Methods

To answer our two research questions, we conducted an online survey study with US parents of children from kindergarten to 12th (K-12) grades (typically 5 to 18 years old).

3.1 Survey Development

Guided by our two research questions, the objective of the survey was to gather information on household technology use, parents' password practices, and parents' involvement in their children's password practices.

We developed a list of survey items based on findings from literature and past studies. Three types of reviews were conducted iteratively. Content experts in usable security evaluated and provided feedback on the alignment of survey items with the scope of the survey goals. Survey experts reviewed each item for clarity for the intended audience, appropriate format, and alignment of response options. Then, cognitive interviews with parents were conducted using a talk-aloud protocol to determine if questions were being appropriately interpreted. The survey instrument was refined iteratively based on the feedback from each type of review. The final survey was implemented by a contracting research firm to collect responses online. The survey was divided into two major sections, corresponding to the two research questions.

Parents' Password Practices. There were seven sets of questions to address RQ1.

1. Family devices (*desktop computers, laptops, tablets, cell phones, game consoles, smart TVs*), number of devices owned and number of password-protected devices
2. Number of personal accounts across eight account types (*email, social media, banking, shopping, bill payment, entertainment, games, accounts related to children*) and number of accounts requiring passwords
3. Number of personal passwords
4. Password creation:
   a. Importance of considerations (*easy to remember, easy to type, strong–hard to crack, same as other passwords*)
   b. Whether password generators are used (*Always, Sometimes, Never but know about it, Never and don't know about it*)
   c. Create a password for a hypothetical account on family doctor's website
5. Password tracking and maintenance:
   a. Methods used to keep track of personal passwords (*memorize, browser/device saved and auto-filled, use mnemonics, someone else remembers, write on paper, save in files, save in emails, password manager, do not track*)
   b. Frequency of changing personal passwords (*30, 31–60, 61–90, 91–120, 121–180 days, change only when necessary, change depending on accounts*)
6. Sources for password help and perceived effectiveness of those sources (*family members, friends, internet provider, account websites, internet search, media, paid technical support, public library, children's school, government agencies*)
7. Technology landscape: usage, technology savviness, technology adoption
   a. Daily hours spent on computers/devices (*< 1, 1–3, 3–5, 5–7, 5–9, > 9*)
   b. Technology savviness (response options in Table 1)

c. Technology adoption (response options in Table 1)

Technology savviness and adoption responses were labeled to aid in statistical data analysis and discussion. The response options and their labels are shown in Table 1.

Table 1. Labels for Technology Savviness and Adoption.

Technology Savviness	
Labels	Response Options
Novice	*I have limited experience using technology and I don't know much about how technology works*
Average	*I have some knowledge about how technology works, but often need to ask for help to perform more advanced activities – such as to configure the privacy settings on my cell phone*
Advanced	*I can do most things that I want to do with technology and only need help occasionally*
Expert	*I can do all things that I want to do with technology without help from others*
Technology Adoption	
Labels	Response Options
Laggard	*I only adopt new technologies when it's required*
Late majority	*I wait until my old technology dies*
Early majority	*I let others work out the kinks first*
Early adopter	*I follow technology trends*
Innovator	*I try the latest technologies as soon as they come out*

Parents' Involvement with Children's Passwords. There were three sets of questions. to address RQ2. This section was repeated for each child within the grade range of K-12 as reported by a parent participant. For parents with more than one child, they had the option to select if their answers were the same (if "*same*", then the question block was skipped for that child) or different from a previously entered child.

1. Do you help this child create passwords? (*Always, Sometimes, Never*)
   a. If *Always* or *Sometimes*, how (check all apply)?

   - *I create passwords for this child.*
   - *This child and I work together to create his/her passwords.*
   - *I only give this child guidance, but he/she creates the passwords.*

b. If *Always* or *Sometimes*, rate the importance of considerations when helping this child with password creation (*easy to remember, easy to type, strong–hard to crack, same as other passwords*)

2. Do you help this child keep track of passwords? (*Always, Sometimes, Never*)

  a. If *Always* or *Sometimes*, how (check all apply)?

- *I have a list (paper or electronic) of this child's passwords.*
- *I memorize this child's passwords.*
- *I have this child create a list of passwords and he/she is responsible for keeping the list.*
- *I give this child guidelines on how he/she should keep track of the passwords.*

3. Has helping your children with their passwords changed your own password practices? (*Yes–why, No–why not?*)

3.2 Participant Sampling and Demographics

The study was approved by our institution's Research Protections Office and the Institutional Review Board (IRB). All responses were collected anonymously.

We used a research firm for participant sampling utilizing double opt-in research panels. Panelists were notified about the survey through online advertisements. Interested panelists were qualified if they met these criteria at the time of taking the survey: (1) be at least 18 years old; (2) reside in the US; (3) be parents or legal guardians; (4) have at least one child within the K-12 grade range. Participants received proprietary internal currency that, while not equating to an exact dollar-for-dollar value, holds monetary value of approximately $1 US dollar.

A total of 265 panelists self-selected to complete the survey; 82.64% were female and 17.36% male. A majority of the parents were under 45 years old (18–34: 30.42%; 35–39: 20.91%; 40–44: 16.73%; 45–49: 15.97%; 50 or older: 15.97%). Nearly a third (32.95%) of parents had a Bachelor's degree, 29.50% had less than high school or a high school degree, 19.92% had an Associate's degree or some other degree, and 15.71% had an advanced or professional degree.

A majority of the parents had one (n = 136, 51.32%), two (n = 87, 32.83%), or three (n = 32, 12.08%) children within the target grade range of K-12. Only 10 parents (3.77%) had four or more children. Parents were asked to indicate each of their children's grade and sex. Grades were categorized into three grade bands: Elementary school (ES)–kindergarten through 5th grade; Middle school (MS)–6th through 8th grade; High school (HS)–9th through 12th grade.

This paper focused on data and results of the first child parents entered the survey, as the majority of parents only had one child, and parents with more than one child tended to report that their answers for subsequent children in their family were the same as their answers for the first child. For parents with two children, answers only differed from the first child for 23 parents (26.44%). For parents with 3 or more children, only 15 (34.88%) differed from a previously entered child. Future efforts will examine patterns between and across parents with multiple children. Table 2 shows percentages of the grade bands and sex of the parent participants' first child reported.

Table 2. Demographics of First Child Reported (n = 265)

Grade Band (%)			Sex (%)	
ES	MS	HS	Boy	Girl
47.55	21.89	30.56	52.34	47.66

Each participant was assigned a unique alphanumerical identifier, for example, p123456789. In this paper, any quotes provided as exemplars are verbatim from survey responses and presented in italics with its unique participant identifier.

3.3 Data Analysis

Primary Analysis. We used descriptive statistics to examine participants' responses to survey questions. For categorical questions, we computed frequencies and percentages for parents' responses to each question. For variables with continuous data, we computed averages (i.e., accounts requiring passwords, personal passwords, password tracking strategies). We also examined the relationship between continuous variables with a correlation. The strengths of hypothetical passwords created were scored using the zxcvbn.js[2] script, an open-source tool which uses pattern matching and searches for the minimum entropy of a given password. Password strength was measured by assigning passwords with scores ranging from 1 to 5, with 1 as the lowest strength.

We used inferential statistics to find significant differences between demographic subgroups in the data. We examined if parent password behaviors depended on parents' demographic characteristics (i.e., sex, age range, education, technology savviness, and technology adoption). We also examined if parents' involvement with their child depended on the child's grade band. We report Chi-square tests (the statistic, degrees of freedom, and p-value), which evaluated significant differences between groups on categorical outcome variables.[3] Significant Chi-Square tests were followed up by examining adjusted standardized residuals [2, 22]. Wilcox and Kruskal-Wallis non-parametric tests were conducted for responses measured on an interval scale (e.g., password strength) and/or were not normally distributed (e.g., number of password tracking strategies). Significance for all inferential tests was determined using an adjusted alpha level of α = 0.01 and all effect size estimates were calculated using Cramer's V. All significant effects had effect sizes ranging from small to moderate. In this paper, only statistically significant test results are presented.

Because all survey questions were optional, only valid responses were used in analyses. Thus, the total number of responses differed for each question. Additionally, as stated previously, analysis was conducted on the first child parents entered the survey.

Post Hoc Tests. We also examined the association between parents' password priorities and parents' priorities for their child's passwords. We conducted a Chi-Square test to

---

[2] https://www.bennish.net/password-strength-checker/.

[3] In cases in which the Chi Square test could not be run due to small cell sizes, Fisher's exact tests were conducted. In some cases, p-values were simulated to ascertain statistical significance.

examine this association for the four password priority items. Significant tests were followed up by examining the adjusted standardized residuals.

4   Results

4.1   Technology Savviness and Adoption

Parents in the study tended to report as savvy with technology (Fig. 1), with over 86% reporting having advanced or expert experience. Figure 1 also shows that most parents reported as *"early majority adopters"* or *"early adopters"* of technology.

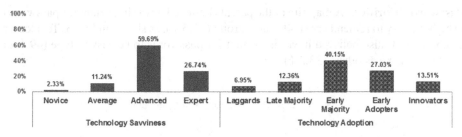

Fig. 1. Parents' self-reported technology savviness and adoption

4.2   Parents' Personal Devices, Accounts, and Passwords

We examined parents' ownership and password protection of six different device types: cell phones, tablets, laptops, game consoles, smart TVs, and desktop computers. For each, we calculated the percentage of parents who owned at least one of the device types and the percentage of parents who password protected at least one of the device types. A majority of parents owned each of the six devices asked in the survey with high ownership (over 85%) of having cell phones, tablets, and laptops (Fig. 2).

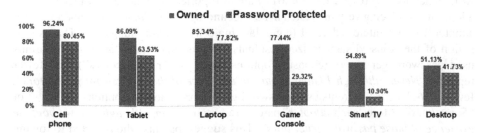

Fig. 2. Parents' ownership and password protection of devices

However, fewer parents reported password protecting their devices than owning devices (Fig. 2). For example, while 96.2% of parents owned a cell phone, only 80.5%

reported password protecting a cell phone. This suggests some parents do not always password protect their devices.

The survey asked parents for their total number of personal passwords and the number of online accounts they had that require passwords. Parents reported an average of 10.5 personal passwords (SD = 13.5, range: 0–99), and 15.9 accounts (SD = 14.7, range 0–128) requiring passwords. Parents' personal passwords were significantly correlated with the number of accounts requiring passwords ($r = 0.63, p < .01$). Further, the number of personal passwords is smaller than the number of accounts requiring passwords. This indicates personal passwords may be reused for some accounts.

4.3   Parents' Password Behaviors

Password Priorities. A majority of the parents believed it was important for passwords to be both easy to remember (80.4%) and strong (75.5%), as shown in Fig. 3. To a lesser extent, parents also believed it was important for passwords to be easy to type (49.1%) and be the same as others (33.2%).

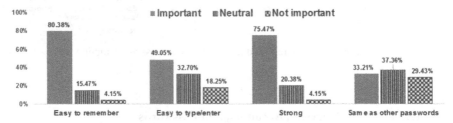

Fig. 3. Parents' priorities for own passwords

Password Generators. Fewer than 20% of parents used password generators when creating their personal passwords. While some (41.7%) had heard of password generators, nearly as many (39.1%) were not aware password generators existed.

We found a significant effect of parents' reported technology adoption on use of password generators ($\chi^2(6) = 21.5, p < .01$). Parents reported different levels of technology-adoption: from being very interested in new technology (e.g., "*innovator*" and/or "*early adopter*") to not interested at all (e.g., "*late majority*" and/or "*laggard*"). The examination of the adjusted standardized residuals revealed that more "*innovator*" parents used password generators (choosing options "*Always*" or "*Sometimes*"), and fewer reported "*Never, although I know about the existence of those password generators*"; fewer "*late/laggard*" parents used password generators (choosing options "*Always*" or "*Sometimes*"). More "*early adopter*" parents reported "*Never, although I know about the existence of those password generators*". This suggest parents who reported following and trying the latest technology were, if not using, at least more aware of password generators.

Password Tracking Strategies. Parents on average chose two of the 13 listed methods as how they track their passwords (SD = 1.1, range = 0–6). A majority of parents used memorization techniques (mnemonics or memorized passwords; 78.5%). To a lesser extent, parents used technology (browser/device autofill or password management software; 43.0%), physically wrote down passwords (37.7%), or saved their passwords electronically (e.g., email, file; 17.4%). Nearly 1 in 10 parents (9.1%) also reported using the "forgot password" feature instead of tracking passwords.

We found significant effects of parents' reported technology adoption ($\chi^2(3) = 11.5$, $p < .01$) and age ($\chi^2(4) = 20.8$, $p < .01$) on use of memorization techniques to track passwords. Analysis shows fewer "*late/laggard*" parents used memorization techniques to track their passwords. Additionally, across age ranges, more parents between 18 and 34 years old and fewer parents over 50 years old used memorization techniques to track their passwords. This suggests older parents and those who reported being less interested in adopting new technology do not tend to use memorization techniques.

Frequency of Password Change. A majority of parents (53.4%) changed their passwords only when necessary. Over a third of parents (34.2%) changed their passwords between 30 and 180 days and 12.4% changed their passwords depending on the account type.

Passwords Generated for Hypothetical Accounts. Passwords generated for a hypothetical account were on average 10.71 characters in length. Most parents used lowercase letters (59.5%) and numbers (23.0%), and fewer used uppercase letters (10.8%), symbols (6.1%), and white space (0.5%). Very few parents (4.7%) had lowest strength passwords (score = 1), and only 22.8% had a password scored at the highest level (score = 5). Thus, most parents (72.5%) created password with strength scores ranging from 2 to 4 (out of 5).

How/Where to Seek Password Guidance. Parents sought a variety of sources for information or guidance of passwords including family members (41.7%), internet searches (29.9%), and websites where accounts are created (23.9%). A majority of parents felt that each source was effective, with family members being rated as most effective (70.9%) followed by websites (60.3%) and internet searches (50.6%). However, for internet searchers, nearly as many parents were neutral (48.1%).

4.4   Parents' Involvement with Children's Password Creation

Helping Children Create Passwords. Parents tended to help their children with password creation. About 74% of parents ("*Always*": 33.0%; "*Sometimes*": 41.0%) helped their children with password creation, and 26.0% "*Never*" helped. However, parents' help significantly depended on their child's grade band ($\chi2(4) = 35.2$, p < .01), with more parents helping younger children and fewer helping older children (Fig. 4).

More parents "*Always*" helped their ES child and fewer "*Sometimes*" helped. More parents helped with their MS child "*Sometimes*" and fewer "*Never*" helped. More parents "*Never*" helped their HS child and fewer "*Always*" helped.

Parent Strategies for Involvement with Child's Password Creation. Parents who "*Always*" or "*Sometimes*" (n = 189) helped their children with password creation did so in various forms. Most parents helped their child by creating passwords together (46.6%),

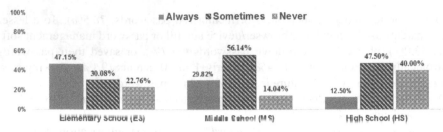

Fig. 4. Responses to "Do you help this child create his/her passwords" by child grade band.

but some created passwords for their child (29.6%) or gave their child guidance (25.4%). Few parents (1.1%) reported they helped their child in some "*other*" way.

The number of parents creating passwords for their child ($\chi^2(2) = 23.8, p < .01$) and giving guidance ($\chi^2(2) = 18.1, p < .01$) significantly differed depending on the child's grade band, but working together with the child did not. More parents created passwords for their ES child, and fewer parents did so for their MS or HS child. More parents gave their MS child guidance for password creation and fewer gave guidance to their ES child. Figure 5 displays parents' strategies for their involvement with their child's password creation by child grade band.

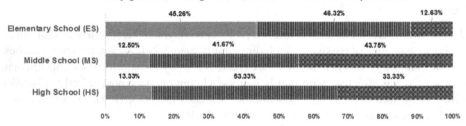

Fig. 5. Parent strategies for involvement with child's password creation by child grade band.

Password Priorities for Children. A majority of parents believed it was important for their children's passwords to be easy to remember (73.7%), strong (64.5%), and easy to type/enter (53.5%). About 30% of parents believed it was important for their children's passwords to be the same as other passwords (29.0%). When helping their children with password creation, parents' priorities significantly differed depending on the child's grade band for being easy to type ($\chi2(4) = 27.5, p < .01$), strong (Fisher's exact test p < .01), and the same as the child's other passwords ($\chi2(4) = 19.0, p < .01$). These differences are described below.

- **Easy to type.** More parents of ES children indicated it was important for their child's password to be easy to type and fewer were neutral. More parents of MS children were neutral for their child's password being easy to type and fewer indicated this was important. More parents of HS children indicated this was not important for their child's password and fewer indicated it was important.

- **Strong.**[4] More parents of HS children indicated it was important for their child's password to be strong. More parents of ES children indicated this was not important or were neutral about this for their child's password.
- **Be the same.** More parents of ES children thought it was important for their child's passwords to be the same and fewer thought this was not important. More parents of MS children were neutral on this priority for their child. More parents of HS children thought this was not important and fewer thought it was important.

Post Hoc Test of Association of Password Priorities. Parents' own password priorities and parents' priorities for their child's passwords were significantly related for being easy to remember ($\chi 2(1) = 57.1$, p $< .01$), easy to type ($\chi 2(1) = 49.8$, p $< .01$), strong ($\chi 2(1) = 71.2$, p $< .01$), and the same ($\chi 2(1) = 56.1$, p $< .01$). For all priorities, more parents thought that if the priority was important for their own passwords, it was also important for their child's passwords. Likewise, priorities not important to parents or if parents were neutral, they believed the priority was also not important or neutral for their child's passwords.

4.5 Parents' Involvement with Children's Password Tracking

Helping Children Track Passwords. Almost 80% of parents (*"Always"*: 40.4%; *"Sometimes"*: 38.9%) reported helping their children keep track of passwords and 20.8% reported that they *"Never"* helped with password tracking.

Parents' help significantly differed depending on their child's grade band ($\chi^2(4) = 38.2$, $p < .01$). More parents of ES children *"Always"* helped their child, and fewer *"Sometimes"* or *"Never"* helped. More parents of MS children *"Sometimes"* helped their child and fewer *"Always"* helped. Fewer parents of HS children *"Always"* helped their child and more *"Never"* helped. Figure 6 displays frequencies of help by child grade band.

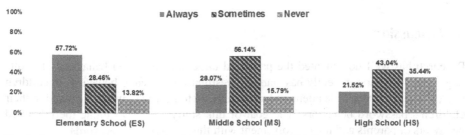

Fig. 6. Responses to "Do you help this child keep track of his/her passwords" by child grade band.

---

[4] Due to small cell sizes, "not important" and "neutral" items were combined for follow-up analysis. This yielded a significant Chi-Square $\chi^2(2)=12.9$, p$<.01$.

Parent Strategies for Involvement with Password Tracking. Parents who *"Always"* or *"Sometimes"* (n = 205) helped their children with password tracking did this in various ways. Most memorized their child's passwords (47.8%) or made a list of the child's passwords (43.4%). Few gave the child guidance for tracking (14.6%) or had their child create their own list they were responsible for (14.2%).

4.6 Has Helping Children with Passwords Changed Parents' Password Practices?

A majority of parents (80.38%) reported that they had not changed their password practices as a result of helping their children with passwords. However, changing password practices depended on parents' technology adoption ($\chi^2(3) = 17.736$, $p < .01$). More *"innovator"* technology adoption parents reported their password practices changed after helping their children with passwords, and fewer *"early majority"* technology adoption parents did.

Of those parents who reported that helping their children had not changed their own password behavior, 140 parents offered reasoning for why. For most, they believed they already had good password practices that they did not want to change, or they did not think it was important to change their current behaviors. For example, one parent commented that they were *"set in my ways with no need to really change"* (p558784107) while another explained that they *"already had enough ways to formulate various types of strong passwords"* (p55901423). Other common reasons were age-specific, as in the case of p100000982 who indicated that they were *"more capable of memorizing more complex passwords than my 5-year-old. Her passwords are much too simple for me to use and still feel like I am somewhat secure when I log in."*

Only 19.62% of parents reported that helping their child has changed their own password habits, and 36 of them offered their reasoning. Some of these parents said working with their child served as a reminder of good habits, while the rest learned something new in the process. These new, learned behaviors included knowledge about how to make a strong password, information about how often passwords should be changed, insights into how to manage multiple passwords, and new memorization strategies.

5 Discussion

Research has well documented the password understandings and behaviors of adults (e.g., [32]) and more recently has started investigating the same behaviors in children (e.g., [27]). However, little attention has been given to how parents are involved in their children's password behaviors. The goal of this study was to examine the password behaviors of parents and their involvement with their children's passwords.

5.1 RQ1: Parents' Own Password Behaviors

Our first research question was to examine parents' password practices in order to gain insight into parents' password perceptions and practices. Although parents in this study prioritized both high usability (easy to type, easy to remember) and high security (strong) for their passwords, our results indicate parents' practices may favor usability over security. For example, despite valuing strong passwords, a majority of parents created hypothetical passwords of moderate strength and containing mostly lowercase numbers and letters. Further, a large majority of parents in this study relied on memory and mnemonic strategies. Very few reported using password generators, which often produce passwords that are secure but may be difficult to type and remember. Additionally, parents in this study reported having more active accounts than personal passwords, suggesting a habit of reusing passwords. Wash and Rader suggests this behavior may be due to the challenge and cognitive difficulty of having many passwords [32]. Therefore, while parents desire passwords that are both strong and usable, practically they may be unsure how to achieve both goals simultaneously, especially given the large number of passwords they have and the current state of password requirements and guidance from technology providers [9]. This may result in parents placing more weight on practical usability than on high-level security when creating and maintaining passwords. Taken together, this suggests that parents (as well as users generally) can benefit from having more support and guidance for how to have both strong and usable passwords.

Indeed, our findings suggest parents may have few reliable sources of password guidance. Parents most often cited other family members as a key source of password guidance, which raises some practical questions. If parents struggle with balancing priorities and practices, but are themselves an important source of other family members' password guidance, how, when, and where are good resources for parent behaviors introduced and circulated? Additionally, our findings revealed few relationships between parent demographic characteristics (e.g., self-reported technology adoption) and password behaviors. Thus, it is unclear what qualities and experiences are related to alignment of priorities and practices.

Understanding parents' password perceptions and behaviors are important for examining if, how, and when these information are translated to their children. Given parents themselves have discrepancies between their priorities and practices, the study's next major goal was to examine parents' password approaches for their children.

5.2   RQ2: Parents' Involvement in Children's Password Behaviors

Parents in this study were involved in helping their children make and maintain passwords. Our study also shows that parents demonstrated developmental awareness when it came to helping their child with password creation strategies, tailoring help to their child depending on their age. For example, parents of ES children emphasized making passwords easy to type, while parents of HS children valued password strength. Further, differences in parents' reported involvement in password creation and maintenance with ES, MS, and HS children suggests that a gradual release of parental participation as children age. For example, parents reported often helping their ES child with passwords, but only helping MS and HS aged children sometimes or not at all. Involvement was also more direct (i.e., helping create and track the passwords) with ES children versus indirect (i.e., providing guidance or advice). Although this study was not longitudinal, the differences between parents' reported involvement depending on their child's age makes the gradual release theory worthy of further study. Developmental awareness and the possible gradual release of password control to children over time are both encouraging parent practices. However, this raises the question of when, how, and why parents may replace the developmentally appropriate password behaviors targeted at younger children with strategies for strong, adult-appropriate password behaviors for older children? Future work examining parenting behaviors over time is encouraged to answer these questions.

Although the child's grade band was an important factor for parental involvement in password practices, our results also suggest that parent's own perceptions are related to how they approach their child's passwords. Parents' priorities for their own passwords aligned with their priorities for their child's passwords. For example, parents who believed it was important for their passwords to be easy to remember, easy to type, strong, and/or the same as other passwords found these same priorities important for their child's passwords. Similarly, when parents found these priorities to be neutral or unimportant for themselves, they also believed the priorities were neutral or not important for their child. This raises the question of how parents' perceptions are related to the child's own password practices and perceptions. If parents do not believe strong and/or usable passwords are important for neither themselves nor their child, are these beliefs transferred to their child? From this study alone, it is unclear if and to what extent, children learn and practice: a) their parent's own priorities, b) their parent's priorities for the child, or c) their parent's actual password behavior. Understanding how children's learning takes place may be important for understanding how parents can instill their children with effective password practices.

While the impact of parents on their child's practices needs further investigation, our study did find some evidence suggesting that helping children with passwords can change parents' own password practices. Although most parents did not change their password practices as a result of being involved with their child's passwords, nearly one in five did report changing their practices, with many reporting positive changes. This suggests it is worth exploring if there are important bidirectional effects between parents and their children on their password practices. Research examining both parents and their children together is needed to understand the impacts of parents' and children's' perceptions and behavior on one another.

5.3 Practical Implications

Our findings show that there is a strong need to help parents with their own password behaviors and with teaching password behaviors to their children. Because parents are a primary influence on children's perceptions, understandings, and behaviors [8], it is important that parents are well equipped to teach password practices to their children and model good practices themselves. Results from this study suggest there are several areas where cybersecurity researchers and practitioners can support parents.

First, there is a need for guidance on effective password creation and maintenance strategies for parents. Guidance should be both practical and usable given the large number of devices, accounts, and personal passwords parents have and given parents' prioritization and practice of creating and maintaining usable passwords. For example, new password guidelines published by the National Institute of Standards and Technology (NIST) state that password complexity requirements do not ensure strong passwords;

instead, longer passphrase-like passwords are encouraged [7]. It will be helpful to provide guidance to parents and youth on how to evaluate what they want to protect, how strong a password is needed, and how to create an appropriate password. Relatedly, researchers and practitioners should promote effective tools to help parents create and track their passwords. Tools such as password generators and password managers may help parents to achieve their goals of creating strong passwords that are easy to remember and use. However, our results suggest few parents use these tools and are aware they exist. Therefore, increased awareness and communication on benefits of such tools are needed.

Second, parents need guidance on effectively teaching password creation and maintenance to their children. Guidance must consider age-appropriate strategies for teaching password practices, as well as assist parents in modifying teaching password practices as children age. Finally, researchers and practitioners should increase outreach to provide resources and best practices to parents.

6 Limitations

Our study has few limitations that are common to many usable security studies. First, results of this study are specific to the parent sample from a panel who self-selected to participate. Thus, our results may not generalize to the broader parent population. Second, the survey gathered parents' self-reported password practices. Parents' actual password behaviors were not measured and may differ from the behaviors reported. Although measuring parents' actual behaviors is an important area for future study, the value of self-reported data should not be minimized, as it can be vital for obtaining insight into the mental models that drive human behavior. Third, like many other studies of password behavior, to prevent privacy concerns of asking for passwords with an authentic scenario, we asked parents to generate hypothetical passwords. Using a hypothetical password scenario constrains our ability to understand genuine password behavior and to gain a nuanced understanding about parents' contextually specific password behavior.

7 Conclusion

This study focused specifically on parents in order to understand their password behaviors and involvement with their children's password practices. Not surprisingly, we found that parents' password practices do not differ much from password practices of typical adults which include parents and non-parents; parents in our study understand the importance of creating strong and usable passwords, but may struggle to practically implement these priorities, as parents also tend to have many personal passwords. We gain important insight on that parents are actively involved in their children's password behaviors, especially helping elementary school children create and maintain their passwords. Cybersecurity researchers and practitioners can help parents by providing guidance, tools, and outreach to successfully support both parents' own password practices as well as with teaching their children to establish good password practices.

There are several areas for future work. First, research should explore parents' involvement over time as children age. Longitudinal research may be able to identify how and when gradual release of parental involvement in children's password practices occurs. Second, research is also needed to understand dynamic and bidirectional influences between parents and children within the same family. While the current study focused on parents' experiences with the first child they reported in the survey, future work should examine the experiences of parents and children together, as well as understand the influence and role of family members, such as siblings. Third, additional research is also encouraged to examine the role of influences outside the family such as schools, educators, and peers on children's password understanding and practices.

References

1. Abraham, M., Crabb, M., Radomirović, S.: "I'm doing the best I Can": understanding technology literate older adults' account management strategies. In: Parkin, S., Viganò, L. (eds.) STAST 2021. LNCS, vol. 13176, pp. 86–107. Springer, Cham (2022). https://doi.org/10.1007/978-3-031-10183-0_5
2. Agresti, A.: An Introduction to Categorical Data Analysis, 3rd edn. Wiley, Hoboken (2018)
3. Bandura, A., Walters, R.H.: Social Learning Theory, vol. 1. Prentice Hall, Englewood Cliffs (1977)
4. Choong, Y.-Y., Theofanos, M.F., Renaud, K., Prior, S.: Passwords protect my stuff"—a study of children's password practices. J. Cybersecur. 5(1), 19, Article no. tyz015 (2019). https://doi.org/10.1093/cybsec/tyz015
5. Das, A., Bonneau, J., Caesar, M., Borisov, N., Wang, X.F.: The tangled web of password reuse. In: NDSS 2014, vol. 2014, pp. 23–26 (2014). 15 pages
6. Florencio, D., Herley, C.: A large-scale study of web password habits. In: Proceedings of the 16th International Conference on World Wide Web, pp. 657–666 (2007)
7. Grassi, P.A., et al.: Digital identity guidelines: authentication and lifecycle management. Technical Report 800-63B, NIST Special Publication (2017). https://doi.org/10.6028/NIST.SP.800-63b
8. Hernández-Alava, M., Popli, G.: Children's development and parental input: evidence from the UK millennium cohort study. Demography 54(2), 485–511 (2017). https://doi.org/10.1007/s13524-017-0554-6
9. Inglesant, P.G., Angela Sasse, M.: The true cost of unusable password policies: password use in the wild. In: Proceedings of the SIGCHI Conference on Human Factors in Computing Systems, pp. 383–392 (2010). https://doi.org/10.1145/1753326.1753384
10. Kawu, A.A., Orji, R., Awal, A., Gana, U.: Personality, culture and password behavior: a relationship study. In: Proceedings of the Second African Conference for Human Computer Interaction: Thriving Communities, pp. 1–4, Article no. 36 (2018). https://doi.org/10.1145/3283458.3283530
11. Kumar, P., Naik, S.M., Devkar, U.R., Chetty, M., Clegg, T.L., Vitak, J.: "No telling passcodes out because they're private" understanding children's mental models of privacy and security online. Proc. ACM Hum.-Comput. Interact. 1, CSCW, 1–21, Article no. 64 (2017). https://doi.org/10.1145/3134699
12. Lamichhane, D.R., Read, J.C.: Investigating children's passwords using a game-based survey. In: Proceedings of the 2017 Conference on Interaction Design and Children, pp. 617–622 (2017). https://doi.org/10.1145/3078072.3084333
13. Livingstone, S., Helsper, E.J.: Parental mediation of children's internet use. J. Broadcast. Electron. Media 52(2), 581–599 (2008). https://doi.org/10.1080/08838150802437396

14. Maqsood, S., Biddle, R., Maqsood, S., Chiasson, S.: An exploratory study of children's online password behaviours. In: Proceedings of the 17th ACM Conference on Interaction Design and Children, pp. 539–544 (2018). https://doi.org/10.1145/3202185.3210772

15. Mayer, P., Volkamer, M.: Addressing misconceptions about password security effectively. In: Proceedings of the 7th Workshop on Socio-Technical Aspects in Security and Trust, pp. 16–27 (2018). https://doi.org/10.1145/3167996.3167998

16. Morris, R., Thompson, K.: Password security: a case history. Commun. ACM 22(11), 594–597 (1979). https://doi.org/10.1145/359168.359172

17. Pearman, S., et al.: Let's go in for a closer look: observing passwords in their natural habitat. In: Proceedings of the 2017 ACM SIGSAC Conference on Computer and Communications Security, pp. 295–310 (2017). https://doi.org/10.1145/3133956.3133973

18. Pearman, S., Zhang, S.A., Bauer, L., Christin, N., Cranor, L.F.: Why people (don't) use password managers effectively. In: 15th Symposium on Usable Privacy and Security (SOUPS 2019), pp. 319–338 (2019)

19. Ratakonda, D.K., French, T., Fails, J.A.: My name is my password: understanding children's authentication practices. In: Proceedings of the 18th ACM International Conference on Interaction Design and Children, pp. 501–507 (2019). https://doi.org/10.1145/3311927.3325327

20. Rideout, V., Robb, M.B.: The Common Sense Census: Media use by tweens and teens. Common Sense Media 2019 census full report. Common Sense Media. San Francisco (2019). https://www.commonsensemedia.org/sites/default/files/research/report/2019-census-8-to-18-full-report-updated.pdf

21. Rim, K., Choi, S.: Analysis of password generation types in teenagers–focusing on the students of Jeollanam-do. Int. J. u-and e-Serv. Sci. Technol. 8(9), 371–380 (2015)

22. Sharpe, D.: Chi-square test is statistically significant: now what? Pract. Assess. Res. Eval. 20(1), Article no. 8 (2015). https://doi.org/10.7275/tbfa-x148

23. Smahel, D., et al.: EU Kids Online 2020: Survey results from 19 countries. EU Kids Online, London (2020). http://hdl.handle.net/20.500.12162/5299

24. Tobert, E.S., Biddle, R.: The password life cycle: user behaviour in managing passwords. In: 10th Symposium on Usable Privacy and Security (SOUPS 2014), pp. 243–255 (2014)

25. Tam, L., Glassman, M., Vandenwauver, M.: The psychology of password management: a tradeoff between security and convenience. Behav. Inf. Technol. 29(3), 233–244 (2010). https://doi.org/10.1080/01449290903121386

26. Taneski, V., Heričko, M., Brumen, B.: Password security—no change in 35 years? In: 37th International Convention on Information and Communication Technology, Electronics and Microelectronics (MIPRO), pp. 1360–1365. IEEE (2014). https://doi.org/10.1109/MIPRO.2014.6859779

27. Theofanos, M., Choong, Y.-Y., Murphy, O.: "Passwords keep me safe"–understanding what children think about passwords. In: 30th USENIX Security Symposium (USENIX Security 2021), pp. 19–35 (2021)

28. Ur, B., et al.: "I added '!' at the end to make it secure": observing password creation in the lab. In: Eleventh Symposium on Usable Privacy and Security (SOUPS 2015), pp. 123–140 (2015)

29. Ur, B., Bees, J., Segreti, S.M., Bauer, L., Christin, N., Cranor, L.F.: Do users' perceptions of password security match reality? In: Proceedings of the 2016 CHI Conference on Human Factors in Computing Systems, pp. 3748–3760 (2016). https://doi.org/10.1145/2858036.2858546

30. Walia, K.S., Shenoy, S., Cheng, Y.: An empirical analysis on the usability and security of passwords. In: 2020 IEEE 21st International Conference on Information Reuse and Integration for Data Science (IRI), vol. 1, no. 7, pp. 1–8. IEEE (2020). https://doi.org/10.1109/IRI49571.2020.00009

31. Wang, C., Jan, S.T.K., Hu, H., Bossart, D., Wang, G.: The next domino to fall: empirical analysis of user passwords across online services. In: Proceedings of the Eighth ACM Conference on Data and Application Security and Privacy, pp. 196–203 (2018). https://doi.org/10.1145/3176258.3176332

32. Wash, R., Rader, E., Berman, R., Wellmer, Z.: Understanding password choices: how frequently entered passwords are re-used across websites. In: Twelfth Symposium on Usable Privacy and Security (SOUPS 2016), pp. 175–188 (2016)

33. Zhang-Kennedy, L., Mekhail, C., Abdelaziz, Y., Chiasson, S.: From nosy little brothers to stranger-danger: children and parents' perception of mobile threats. In: Proceedings of the 15th International Conference on Interaction Design and Children, pp. 388–399 (2016). https://doi.org/10.1145/2930674.2930716

34. Zou, Y., Roundy, K., Tamersoy, A., Shintre, S., Roturier, J., Schaub, F.: Examining the adoption and abandonment of security, privacy, and identity theft protection practices. In: Proceedings of the 2020 CHI Conference on Human Factors in Computing Systems, pp. 1–15 (2020). https://doi.org/10.1145/3313831.3376570

Refining the Understanding of Usable Security

Wesam Fallatah$^{(\boxtimes)}$, Steven Furnell, and Ying He

School of Computer Science, University of Nottingham, Nottingham, UK
{Wesam.Fallatah,Steven.Furnell,Ying.He}@nottingham.ac.uk

Abstract. Cybersecurity technologies and processes must be usable if users are to make effective use of protection. Many security practitioners accept the value of usable security, but few can precisely define it in practice and in terms of how it influences users' security behaviour and the wider security culture in organisations. This paper investigates how different sources characterise usability and usable security to identify the key aspects that affect usability and determine the degree to which usability aspects are relevant in cybersecurity. This has resulted in a definition of usable security and a framework that supports the cybersecurity community's efforts to make security more usable. The motivation for examining the definitions of usable security in detail is to characterise the potential linkage between usable security and the wider security culture within an organization (with the usability of the technology being a factor that could clearly help or impede the acceptance and operation of security, and therefore impact the related culture). The study suggests that, to some degree, the cybersecurity community is catching up with notions that the HCI field has understood for longer. The lack of consistency in defining usable security motivates the proposal of a working definition. Furthermore, a primary outcome of assessing the usability and usable security studies is establishing a framework of usable security, integrating the key aspects identified in the literature. The proposed framework offers a mechanism for operationalising usable security by incorporating principles from both IT/HCI and cybersecurity perspectives.

Keywords: Usability · Usable Security · Security Culture

1 Introduction

There have been significant advancements in developing technical security solutions that would support safeguarding information in organisations. These solutions, however, cannot solely protect organisations and stop cyber threats on their own. Human perceptions and behaviour while interacting with security solutions and other security controls are essential to the overall security systems. According to Verizon [1], the human element is a factor in 82% of data breaches. As a result, organisations started to realise the importance of strengthening security culture as establishing a strong security culture and engaging it can play a crucial role in protecting organisations against breaches. Moreover, security solutions need to be integrated into people's habits, behaviours, and daily actions, i.e., security culture. In order to achieve that, we have to examine the

© The Author(s), under exclusive license to Springer Nature Switzerland AG 2023
A. Moallem (Ed.): HCII 2023, LNCS 14045, pp. 49–67, 2023.
https://doi.org/10.1007/978-3-031-35822-7_4

factors that could potentially enable the promotion of good security behaviour and its transition into a security culture. One of the factors to consider is whether making security usable would eventually improve the overall security culture. This study reviews usability definitions from an IT/Human-Computer Interaction (HCI) and cybersecurity perspective by looking into usability definitions and key aspects. In doing so, the study first looks at how usability is defined from both IT/HCI and security perspectives, which led to building a usable security framework that aims to support the efforts of the cybersecurity community to capture the key elements detailed in the HCI studies. The prime outcome of this study conceptualises usable security and offers organisations a practical contribution that they can rely on to strengthen the general security culture.

The remainder of this paper is organised as follows. Section 2 provides an overview of usability and usable security definitions in previous work. A working definition and a framework for usable security are proposed in Sects. 3 and 4, respectively. Section 5 discusses the future work, and Sect. 6 concludes the paper.

2 Defining Usability

The usability of products is essential for functioning, and it affects how users achieve a desired task. In addition, users leave products that are difficult to use and choose alternatives [2]. Thus, creating usable products attracts users and help organisation benefit from users' engagement. To create usable measures, it is vital to understand what characteristics usability entails. This section investigates the various ways in which different sources characterise usability, as a foundation for later discussion of usable security. The goal is to identify what key aspects affect usability and determine the degree to which these aspects are then relevant in cybersecurity.

A comprehensive definition of usability can guide the creation of effective systems and services. Many definitions of usability and its related attributes have been introduced in the literature. It is imperative to note that usability is not a single-dimensional issue, but its attributes connect it to qualities covering many disciplines [3]. Although various usability definitions are discussed in the literature, they nonetheless have attributes in common. Therefore, it is helpful to investigate what characteristics of usability have been identified and what characteristics have the more significant impact on systems' usability in order to consider these while designing usable systems and services. Moreover, Quesenbery [4] believes that it is important to utilise our understanding of each usability dimension to better generate usable products. The International Organisation for Standardisation (ISO) defines usability as the "extent to which a system, product or service can be used by specified users to achieve specified goals with effectiveness, efficiency and satisfaction in a specified context of use" [5]. Still, ISO's definition is not 'universal', and other studies have proposed various usability definitions.

Table 1 demonstrates an illustrative set of usability definitions in an IT/HCI context. The search string: usability AND (definition OR meaning) was formalised to query relevant online indexes and publisher repositories: Springer, Scopus, IEEE Xplore, Web of Science, and Google Scholar. In the search, we considered widely cited data sources that are related to IT/HC and with free access. The list includes sources that suggest a usability definition. However, definitions that are derived from other sources are not taken into account. Finally, definitions from authoritative sources were also included in the list. For each identified source, the table directly quotes its main definition of usability and then abstracts what are considered to be the key aspects from it. These are then able to be used to show how frequently each aspect was recognised in prior definitions. Most importantly, the resulting data from Table 1 will be crucial in determining how the usability key aspects are relevant in a cybersecurity context and the extent to which these aspects are recognised in usable security studies.

Table 1. Usability definitions and key aspects

Source	Definition	Key aspects
Abran et al. [6]	"a set of multiple concepts, such as execution time, performance, user satisfaction and ease of learning ("learnability"), taken together"	• Execution time/efficiency • Performance • User satisfaction • Ease of learning (learnability)
Bevan and Macleod [7]	"a) the product-centred view of usability: that the usability of a product is the attributes of the product which contribute towards the quality of use; b) the context of use view of usability: that usability depends on the nature of the user, product, task and environment; c) the quality of use view of usability: that usability is the outcome of interaction and can be measured by the effectiveness, efficiency, and satisfaction with which specified users achieve specified goals in particular environments."	• Product • Quality of use • Environment/context • User • Task • Interaction outcome • Effectiveness • Efficiency • User satisfaction • Goals
Bevan et al. [8]	"the ease of use and acceptability of a product for a particular class of users carrying out specific tasks in a specific environment."	• Ease of use • Acceptability • Product • Users • Tasks • Environment/context

(*continued*)

Table 1. (*continued*)

Source	Definition	Key aspects
Constantine and Lockwood [9]	"Usability is influenced by many factors. Highly usable systems are easy for people to learn how to use and easy for people to use productively. They make it easy to remember from one use to another how they are used. Highly usable systems help people to work efficiently while making fewer mistakes. We can think of these characteristics as five facets of usability[…]: - Learnability - Rememberability - Efficiency in use - Reliability in use - User satisfaction"	• Systems • People (users) • Ease of learning (learnability) • Productivity • Fewer mistakes/Error tolerance • Ease of remembering (memorability/rememberability) • Efficiency of use • Reliability of use • User satisfaction
Eason [10]	"the degree to which users are able to use the system with the skills, knowledge, stereotypes and experience they can bring to bear"	• Users • System • Users' skills, knowledge, stereotypes, and experience (user literacy)
EC [11]	"Usability refers to how easy it is to navigate through your website. This is determined by aspects including the way your site arranges and displays information, as well as how comfortable it is for users to interact with it."	• Website • Ease of use • Information display/ user interface • Comfort of use • Interaction
Edwards [12] for Hewlett Packard (hp)	"When using HCI to develop new tech, it was agreed that four main components factor into the equation: the user, the task, the interface, and the context."	• User • Task • User interface • Environment/context

(*continued*)

Table 1. (*continued*)

Source	Definition	Key aspects
Gould and Lewis [13]	"Any system designed for people to use should be easy to learn (and remember), useful, that is, contain functions people really need in their work, and be easy and pleasant to use."	• System • People (users) • Ease of learning (Learnability) • Ease of remembering (memorability) • Useful functions • Use satisfaction
HHS and GSA [14]	"the quality of a user's experience when interacting with products or systems, including websites, software, devices, or applications. Usability is about effectiveness, efficiency and the overall satisfaction of the user"	• User experience (user literacy) • Interaction • Product/system/websites/software/devices/applications • Effectiveness • Efficiency • User satisfaction
Holzinger [15]	"usability is most often defined as the ease of use and acceptability of a system for a particular class of users carrying out specific tasks in a specific environment"	• Ease of use • Acceptability • System • Users • Tasks • Environment/context
IBM [16]	"Usability is the discipline of applying scientific principles to ensure that the application or website being designed is easy to learn, easy to use, easy to remember, error tolerant, and subjectively pleasing"	• Application/website • Ease of learning (learnability) • Ease of remembering (memorability) • Error tolerance • User satisfaction
IEEE [17]	"The ease with which a user can learn to operate, prepare inputs for, and interpret outputs of a system or component."	• Ease of learning (learnability) • User • Input preparation/Output interpretation/ task performance • System/component
IEEE [18]	"the extent to which a product can be used by intended users to achieve specified goals with effectiveness, efficiency, and satisfaction"	• Product • Users • Goal achievement • Effectiveness of use • Efficiency of use • User satisfaction

(*continued*)

Table 1. (*continued*)

Source	Definition	Key aspects
Interaction Design Foundation [19]	"Usability is a measure of how well a specific user in a specific context can use a product/design to achieve a defined goal effectively, efficiently and satisfactorily"	• User • Environment/context • Product/design • Goal achievement • Effectiveness of use • Efficiency of use • User satisfaction
ISO [5] Also adapted by most HCI experts and organisations including [20–24]	"extent to which a system, product or service can be used by specified users to achieve specified goals with effectiveness, efficiency and satisfaction in a specified context of use"	• System/product/service • Users • Goals achievement • Environment/context • Effectiveness of use • Efficiency of use • User satisfaction
Krug [25]	"making sure that something works well: that a person of average (or even below average) ability and experience can use the thing—whether it's a Web site, a fighter jet, or a revolving door—for its intended purpose without getting hopelessly frustrated"	• Person (users) • Experience (user literacy) • User satisfaction
Microsoft [26]	"Usability is a measure of how easy it is to use a product to perform prescribed tasks."	• Ease of use • Product • Performance • Tasks performance
Nielsen [3]	"usability is not a single, one-dimensional property of a user interface. Usability has multiple components and is traditionally associated with these five usability attributes: - Learnability - Efficacy - Memorability - Errors - Satisfaction."	• User interface • Ease of learning (learnability) • Efficacy • Memorability • Errors tolerance • User satisfaction

(*continued*)

Table 1. (*continued*)

Source	Definition	Key aspects
Preece [27]	"a measure of the ease with which a system can be learned or used, its safety, effectiveness and efficiency, and the attitude of its users towards it"	• Ease of use • Ease of learning (learnability) • System safety • System effectiveness • System efficiency • User attitude/user satisfaction
Quesenbery [4]	"For each of the five dimensions of usability (the 5Es), we think about how it is reflected in requirements for each of the user groups. The 5Es are: - Effective: How completely and accurately the work or experience is completed or goals reached - Efficient: How quickly this work can be completed - Engaging: How well the interface draws the user into the interaction and how pleasant and satisfying it is to use - Error Tolerant: How well the product prevents errors and can help the user recover from mistakes that do occur - Easy to Learn: How well the product supports both the initial orientation and continued learning throughout the complete lifetime of use."	• Effectiveness • Efficiency • Interaction • Users • Goals achievement • User interface • Interaction • User satisfaction • Product • Error tolerance • Ease of learning (learnability)
Schumacher, Lowry [28] for the National Institute of Standards and Technology (NIST)	"the effectiveness, efficiency, and satisfaction with which the intended users can achieve their tasks in the intended context of product use"	• Effectiveness • Efficiency • User satisfaction • Task • Environment/context • Product • User

(*continued*)

Table 1. (*continued*)

Source	Definition	Key aspects
Shackel [29]	"the capability in human functional terms to be used easily and effectively by the specified range of users, given specified training and user support, to fulfil the specified range of tasks, within the specified range of environmental scenarios A convenient shortened form for the definition of usability might be 'the capability to be used by humans easily and effectively', where Easily = to a specified level of subjective assessment Effectively = to a specified level of (human) performance."	• Users • User literacy • Ease of use • Effectiveness of use • User support • Tasks • Performance • Environment/context
Sharp et al. [30]	"usability is generally regarded as ensuring that interactive products are easy to learn, effective to use, and enjoyable from the user's perspective. It involves optimising the interactions people have with interactive products to enable them to carry out their activities at work, school, and in their everyday life. More specifically, usability is broken down into the following goals: - effective to use (effectiveness) - efficient to use (efficiency) - safe to use (safety) - have good utility (utility) - easy to learn (learnability) - easy to remember how to use (memorability)."	• Products • People (users) • Interaction • Activities/tasks • Environment/context • Effectiveness of use • Efficiency of use • Safety • Utility • Ease of learning (learnability) • Ease of remembering (memorability) • User satisfaction

(*continued*)

Table 1. (*continued*)

Source	Definition	Key aspects
Shneiderman and Plaisant [31]	"1. Time to learn: How long does it take for typical members of the community to learn relevant task? 2. Speed of performance: How long does it take to perform relevant benchmarks? 3. Rate of errors by users: How many and what kinds of errors are made during benchmark tasks? 4. Retention over time: Frequency of use and ease of learning help make for better user retention 5. Subjective satisfaction: Allow for user feedback via interviews, free-form comments and satisfaction scales"	• Time of learning/ Ease of learning (learnability) • Speed of performance/ Efficiency • Rate of errors/ Error tolerance • User satisfaction • Task • Users
Usability Professionals Association [32]	"the degree to which something - software, hardware or anything else - is easy to use and a good fit for the people who use it."	• Software/hardware • Ease of use • User satisfaction
Usability.gov [33]	"How effectively, efficiently and satisfactorily a user can interact with a user interface."	• User interface • Effectiveness • Efficiency • User satisfaction • Interaction

Table 1 presents an overview of usability representations from usability studies and authoritative resources. The list has, nonetheless, captured the most significant sources of relevance. The output shown in Fig. 2 supports the conclusion drawn from usability studies, including a systematic review of usability, which covers 790 papers from 2001 to 2018 [34]. The study confirms that the HCI community has primarily adopted ISO's definition of usability and standardised it in an unchanged form. The study also asserts that the most frequently identified usability aspects are "efficiency (70%), satisfaction (66%) and effectiveness (58%)", which are derived directly from the ISO definition. Figure 1 shows the total percentage of the most identified usability key aspects highlighted in our study. Hence, we opt to have consistent vocabularies for the key aspects across all of the sources we are examining, as some of the different terminologies can/may end up being combined together. For instant, systems, products, websites, software, devices, apps, service, etc. can be characterised as touchpoints. Also, cognitive load, consciousness, and mental image are all defined as 'mental model'. Figure 2 provides a visual insight concerning the most common terms associated with usability generated using an online Word Cloud tool [35] by pasting all the definition text into it to illustrate the most common terms from the definitions presented in the list. A total of 165 occurrences were fed in the key aspects entries. Based upon this grouping, the findings suggest that recognition of the 'touchpoint' is the most considered aspect in usability studies. Also, facets such as 'user satisfaction', 'user', 'efficiency', and 'effectiveness' have been mentioned more repetitively than the other usability aspects.

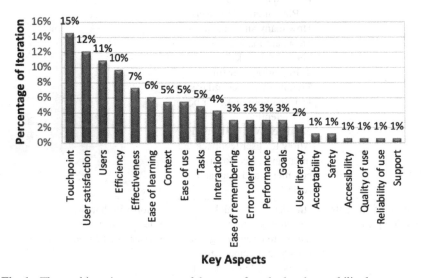

Fig. 1. The total iteration percentage of the terms found related to usability key aspects

Generated using Davies [37]'s Word Cloud Generator.

Fig. 2. Word Cloud denoting prominence of words relating to usability

3 Defining Usable Security

Having determined the key aspects in usability definitions, next we examine how different sources also address usable security to see how the usability aspects are relevant in cybersecurity context. To identify sources that define usable security, the paper took the same approach presented in Sect. 2 above but by using the search string: ("Usable security" OR "Cybersecurity usability" OR "security usability") AND (definition OR meaning). Unlike 'usability' definitions, there do not seem to be many definitions that specifically focus on what it means for a system or service to be both 'usable' and 'secure'. Table 2 presents illustrative examples of existing usable security definitions and the associated key aspects.

Table 2. Illustrative examples of existing usable security definition

Source	Definition	Key aspects
Caputo et al. [36]	"delivering the required levels of security and also user effectiveness, efficiency, and satisfaction"	• Security • User effectiveness • Efficiency • Satisfaction
Zurko and Simon [37]	"security models, mechanisms, systems, and software that have usability as a primary motivation or goal."	• Security models • Mechanisms/system/software • Goal

The definitions in Table 2 are provided as illustrative examples of existing definitions that can be found in usable security related studies. The key aspects associated with these definitions are also highlighted. Table 3 below summarises the key aspects from the definitions suggested by multiple authors, including the two examples in Table 2.

As shown in Table 3, there exists a considerable body of research that aim to represent usable security. There are different perspectives when addressing usable security, and there is no widely accepted formal definition has been observed so far. In addition, few studies clearly outline the different dimensions that may contribute to understanding usable security despite some efforts. Figure 3 shows the total percentage of the most identified usable security key aspects highlighted in our study. Figure 4 provides a visual representation of the most common terms associated with usable security, generated by pasting all of the definition text from the sources shown in Table 3 into an online Word Cloud tool [35].

Compared to usable security, the representation of usability is more consistent in the literature and to some degree, the cybersecurity community is catching up with notions that the HCI field has understood for longer. Figure 3 shows the total percentage of the most identified usable security key aspects highlighted in our study, where a total of 73 occurrences were fed in the key aspects entries. Figure 4 provides a visual insight concerning the most common terms associated with usable security. Notably, 'touchpoints', 'user', 'user satisfaction' are some areas of commonality between usability and usable

Table 3. Summary of usable security key aspects presented in studies

Caputo et al. [37]	Theofanos [38]	Zurko and Simon [36]
• Security • User effectiveness • Efficiency • Satisfaction	• Cybersecurity • Usability • Interaction	• Security models • Mechanisms/system/software • Goal
Johnston, Eloff [39]	Saltzer and Schroeder [40]	Whitten and Tygar [41]
• User interface / Aesthetic/minimalist design • Visibility • Users • Learnability • Error • User satisfaction • Trust • Environment	• User interface • Users • Ease of use • Protection • Mental image • Mechanisms • Goals • Rate of errors/mistakes	• People (users) • Reliability • Tasks • Performance • Errors • User satisfaction • User interface
Hof [42]	Nurse et al. [43]	Yee [44]

• Consciousness
•
  Availability/understandability
• Empowerment
• Activities/Tasks
• Interaction
• Efficiency
• Ease of remembering
  (memorability)
• Interaction
• System/application
• Support
• User satisfaction
• Error tolerance
• Consistency
• Users
	• Accessibility
	• Users
	• Support
	• Error prevention
	• Visibility
	• Cognitive load
	• System/application
	• Tasks
	• Performance
	• User satisfaction
	• Aesthetic/minimalistic
	  design/user interface
	• Technical terms
	• Mental model
	• Tools
		• System/ Software
		• Explicit Authority (safety
		  related)
		• Visibility (safety related)
		• Revocability (safety related)
		• Path of Least Resistance
		  (safety related)
		• Expected Ability
		• Boundaries Appropriation
		  (safety related)
		• Expressiveness
		• Clarity
		• Identifiability, Trusted Path
		  (safety/protection related)

security, whereas important usability aspects such as efficiency and learnability are still considered as outliers in cybersecurity studies. In addition, the 'context of use', which has a degree of importance in usability studies also is not given the required attention from the cybersecurity community. The lack of consistency and clarity in defining and presenting usable security motivates this work to create an initial definition, which will be discussed in the next section.

As a result, this study establishes a working definition of usable security that aims to support the efforts of the cybersecurity community to capture the key elements discussed in the HCI community. The definition is:

'Usable security is utilising usability concepts to enable cybersecurity concepts'

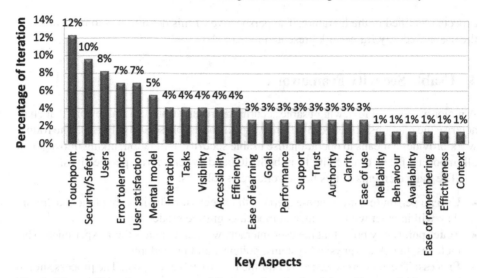

Fig. 3. The total iteration percentage of the terms found related to usable security key aspects

Generated using Davies [37]'s Word Cloud Generator.

Fig. 4. Word Cloud denoting prominence of words relating to usable security

where:

'Usability concepts' = all usability key aspects and requirements,

and

'Cybersecurity concepts' = all cybersecurity aspects and requirements

Furthermore, a primary result arising from our assessment of usability and usable security studies is establishing a framework of usable security, looking at the different aspects identified in the literature. The perspective of this definition is to be detailed in the usable security framework presented in Sect. 4.

4   Usable Security Framework

A major outcome of reviewing usable security representations is a framework that characterise the relationship between different aspects of usable security (Fig. 5). The frame work provides a means to operationalise usable security definiation, taking into account all important facets of usability from both HCI and cybersecurity perspectives.

The main elements of this framework are as follows:

- **User:** a person (expert or non-expert) with expectations/beliefs about the touchpoint they will interact with (i.e., mental model, cognitive model, etc.).
- **Touchpoint:** any point that the user interacts with and creates their experience. This includes digital and physical systems, policies, and procedures.
- **Process:** The action(s) constructed for the user to achieve a goal. The process should be centred on users' needs and meet the usability key aspects based on the context of use.
- **Goal:** a specific aim that users/organisations ought to achieve by considering cybersecurity best practices, each in their context.
- **Context:** the set of conditions that accommodate the process to achieve the goal.

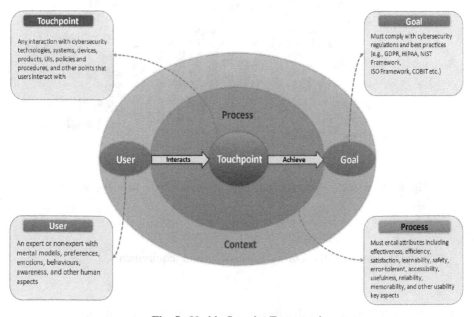

Fig. 5. Usable Security Framework

The framework provides a mechanism to define usable security, taking into consideration all the usability key aspects from both HCI and cybersecurity perspectives. The mechanism implies that a user with a level of experience/awareness/emotions/certain behaviour interacts with a touchpoint (technology, device, product, U.I., etc.) to achieve a goal which should comply with the cybersecurity best practices/requirements in a specified context of use. The process of interaction to achieve the goal should fulfil a set of multiple attributes (i.e. effective, efficient, satisfactory, safe, simple, accessible, reliable, error tolerance, trustworthy, aesthetic, etc.). Organisations can use the existing evaluation methods to assess if the process meets these attributes or if they should value one quality over another based on the context of use and threat modelling process. Also, designers and policy/procedure makers should keep in mind that the touchpoint they create for the user to interact with should make the process cybersecurity compliant.

One example to clarify the operation in the proposed framework is that a user interacts with a banking application using a biometric signature to log into the system to make a bank transfer. In this context, the biometric authentication facilitates a simple, secure, and efficient interaction with the application (touchpoint) to achieve a certain goal in accordance with the best cybersecurity practices. The journey of the user experience once they log in to the system until they make the transfer holds a number of attributes that would leave the user with a positive experience while complying with cybersecurity requirements. Another example is an organisation with a clean desk and clear screen policy, which requires all users to clear their desks at the end of the day and lock their devices' screens as they leave their offices. In this case, the policy is the touchpoint. If a user has to deal with this policy, the organisation is responsible for making the process effective, efficient, and satisfactory. For example, while implementing such a policy, the organisation should provide the employees with clean desk equipment (lockable drawers, storage boxes, etc.) as an alternative to keeping documents lying on the desk.

If it is not usable for users to interact with the touchpoint once they start the process, it will not be guaranteed that the goal they are trying to achieve will comply with best cybersecurity practices because users are always going to find ways to make the touchpoint usable for themselves, which can sometimes damage the whole security system. In many cases, the user cannot be blamed for not abiding by the cybersecurity policies and rules set by organisations if these are not usable while there is a less secure and more usable way to complete a task. Further, some users would be encouraged to bypass the unusable security rules to achieve more important goals (e.g. a doctor bypass/ignore the security system to access a patinate record to save their life.

5 From Usable Security to Security Culture

Examining the concept of usability from both IT/HCI and cybersecurity perspectives contributes into refining our understanding of usable security. It is also a vital step towards characterising the linkage between usable security and security culture. This work further investigates security culture by reviewing the different definitions of security culture presented in studies and the most discussed factors influencing organisations' security culture for the past ten years. There are various definitions of security culture, yet there is no commonly accepted definition. Therefore, most papers suggest a definition to show how their working definition fits into the overall study. In addition, the research addresses a variety of shared characteristics when investigating factors that impact establishing and maintaining strong security culture. Many studies emphasise the importance of top management and leadership support. This support is arguably critical in enforcing and fostering other factors such as increasing awareness and knowledge, applying policies and procedures, and complying with corporate governance [45–47]. Cybersecurity activities may not seem important without the support from top management; therefore, management must guide employees' security culture efforts and manage resources effectively [48]. Despite the importance of top management's support for cybersecurity awareness and training programs, a recent study suggests that compliance is the primary driving factor while conducting awareness and training programs because regulations require businesses to provide regular cybersecurity awareness and training programs [49].

Policies and procedures also appear in many papers as a vital factor. It is worth noting that policies and procedures are frequently associated with users' awareness and knowledge, and the training programs organisations offer to their employees. For example, Chen, Ramamurthy [50] assert that security education, training, and awareness programs are key components that influence employees' understanding of organisational security policy and that the awareness will ultimately positively impact the overall security culture. By contrast, the lack of awareness and knowledge to implement the necessary policies and procedures might negatively impact the organisation's security culture. Other factors, such as change management, communication, trust, technological aspects, and national culture, also appear in multiple studies. However, a further important implication is to consider all internal (e.g., management and awareness) and external (e.g., national culture and technological) factors while establishing and maintaining robust security culture, besides determining the degree to which the organisation's security culture is dependent on each of them [47].

Notably, no study has directly stated the usability of security as a factor influencing security culture, although few studies identify usability as an embedded/integrated quality in other factors. For example, Furnell and Rajendran [51] emphasise that usability is an aspect that can enhance user behaviour, Padayachee [52] asserts that usability increases the likelihood of compliance, and Hassan and Ismail [53] discuss how change management improves security through multiple elements including usability. Although previous studies consider some aspects of usable security, no explicit connection is identified between usable security and security culture. Further, a practical implication is to assess the security culture in organisations and determine the extent to which a particular factor impacts cultivating a strong security culture. We plan to continue this work by designing a means to assess the influence of usable security on security culture. This can be achieved by creating a security culture framework focusing on the usability aspect as an enabler. Also, to further examine security culture representation in studies in terms of definitions, influential factors (e.g., significant factors, contributing factors, and marginal factors), and measurement approaches then to identify whether taking a usable security approach can help them maintain good security culture.

6   Conclusions

Significant progress has been made in creating technical security solutions that would help organisations mitigate serious security risks. However, on their own, these solutions are unable to fully safeguard organisations against threats. The effectiveness of the overall security systems depends on how people perceive and behave while dealing with security solutions and other security measures. As a result, security studies and security professionals began to realise the need to investigate factors that can strength security culture in organisation. One way to establish and maintain a strong security culture is to consider a usable security approach. As a method of achieving this, we proposed a definition of usable security. Without a clear definition of usable security, it becomes difficult to identify how to implement security measures that are both secure and usable. A usable security framework then accompanied the definition to provide a structured approach that supports previous studies' efforts and helps ensure that all relevant usability aspects are considered while implementing security measures. Further, Organisations can take cybersecurity safeguards without falling into usability mistakes that often accompany their implementation. Consequently, users will be able to make informed decisions about the measures they are asked to follow and comply with, which can presumably be a major factor in fostering a robust security culture. Additionally, there does not seem to be a specific single definition of security culture that is widely acknowledged. However, most publications include definitions to demonstrate how their working definitions fit into the larger research. Moreover, the characteristics of security culture appeared to be a topic of considerable interest in the literature. Although many studies highlighted the significance of usable security, previous research did not specifically investigate the linkage between usable security and security culture.

References

1. Verizon: 2022 Data Breach Investigations Report. https://www.verizon.com/business/resour ces/reports/dbir/. Accessed 10 July 2022
2. Nielsen, J.: Usability 101: Introduction to Usability (2012). https://www.nngroup.com/art icles/usability-101-introduction-to-usability/
3. Nielsen, J.: Usability Engineering. Morgan Kaufmann (1993)
4. Quesenbery, W.: Using the 5Es to Understand Users - Whitney Interactive Design. WQusability - Whitney Quesenbery (n.d.). https://www.wqusability.com/articles/getting-started.html. Accessed 15 Feb 2022
5. ISO. Ergonomics of human-system interaction—Part 11: Usability: Definitions and concepts (2018). https://www.iso.org/obp/ui/#iso:std:iso:9241:-11:ed-2:v1:en
6. Abran, A., Khelifi, A., Suryn, W., Seffah, A.: Usability meanings and interpretations in ISO standards. Softw. Qual. J. 11(4), 325–338 (2003)
7. Bevan, N., Macleod, M.: Usability measurement in context. Behav. Inf. Technol. 13(1–2), 132–145 (1994)
8. Bevan, N., Kirakowskib, J., Maissela, J.: What is usability. In: Proceedings of the 4th International Conference on HCI. Citeseer (1991)
9. Constantine, L.L., Lockwood, L.A.: Software for Use: A Practical Guide to the Models and Methods of Usage-Centered Design. Pearson Education (1999)
10. Eason, K.D.: Information Technology and Organizational Change. CRC Press (1989)

11. European Commission. Usability. Internal Market, Industry, Entrepreneurship and SMEs. https://ec.europa.eu/growth/sectors/tourism/business-portal/usability_en. Accessed 17 Feb 2022
12. Edwards, M.: Exploring Human-Computer Interaction. HP (2018). https://www.hp.com/us-en/shop/tech-takes/exploring-human-computer-interaction. Accessed 15 Feb 2022
13. Gould, J.D., Lewis, C.: Designing for usability: key principles and what designers think. Commun. ACM **28**(3), 300–311 (1985)
14. HHS and GSA: The Research-Based Web Design & Usability Guidelines, Enlarged/Expanded edition. U.S. Government Printing Office. https://www.usability.gov/what-and-why/usability-evaluation.html. Accessed 31 Jan 2022
15. Holzinger, A.: Usability engineering methods for software developers. Commun. ACM **48**(1), 71–74 (2005)
16. IBM. User Experience. Usability (2008). https://www-03.ibm.com/services/ca/en/mobility/offerings_userexperience_usability.html#:~:text=Usability%20is%20the%20discipline%20of,error%20tolerant%2C%20and%20subjectively%20pleasing. Accessed 15 Feb 2022
17. IEEE. IEEE Standard Glossary of Software Engineering Terminology (1990). https://ieeexplore.ieee.org/document/159342/definitions#definitions. Accessed 27 Feb 2022
18. IEEE. Usability and Accessibility (2022). https://brand-experience.ieee.org/guidelines/digital/style-guide/usability-and-accessibility/. Accessed 27 Feb 2022
19. Interaction Design Foundation. Usability (2022). https://www.interaction-design.org/literature/topics/usability#:~:text=Usability%20is%20a%20measure%20of,deliverable%E2%80%94to%20ensure%20maximum%20usability. Accessed 27 Feb 2022
20. HFES. Human Readiness Level Scale in the System Development Process (2021)
21. ANSI. Ergonomics of Human-System Interaction - Part 11: Usability: Definitions and Concepts (2022). https://webstore.ansi.org/standards/iso/iso9241112018?_ga=2.3299568.111955288.1644355252-1926938011.1644355252. Accessed 20 Feb 2022
22. BSI, Ergonomics of human-system interaction - Usability: Definitions and concepts. https://shop.bsigroup.com/products/ergonomics-of-human-system-interaction-usability-definitions-and-concepts/tracked-changes. Accessed 20 Feb 2022
23. Jordan, P.W., Thomas, B., McClelland, I.L., Weerdmeester, B.: Usability Evaluation in Industry. CRC Press (1996)
24. IEC. Usability (2018). https://www.electropedia.org/iev/iev.nsf/display?openform&ievref=871-01-08. Accessed 15 Feb 2022
25. Krug, S.: Don't Make Me Think!: A Common Sense Approach to Web Usability. Pearson Education India (2000)
26. Microsoft, Usability in Software Design (2019). https://docs.microsoft.com/en-us/windows/win32/appuistart/usability-in-software-design#defining-usability. Accessed 11 Feb 2022
27. Preece, J.: A Guide to Usability: Human Factors in Computing. Addison-Wesley Longman Publishing Co., Inc. (1993)
28. Schumacher, R.M., Lowry, S.Z., Schumacher, R.M.: NIST guide to the processes approach for improving the usability of electronic health records. US Department of Commerce, National Institute of Standards and Technology (2010)
29. Shackel, B.: Usability-context, framework, definition, design and evaluation. Interact. Comput. **21**, 339–346 (2009)
30. Sharp, H., Rogers, Y., Preece, J.: Interaction design: beyond human-computer interaction (2019)
31. Shneiderman, B., Plaisant, C.: Designing the User Interface: Strategies for Effective Human-Computer Interaction. Pearson Education India (2010)
32. Usability Professionals Association (2010). What is Usability? https://www.usabilitybok.org/what-is-usability. Accessed 15 Feb 2022

33. Usability.gov. Glossary: Usability. https://www.usability.gov/what-and-why/glossary/u/index.html. Accessed 15 Feb 2022
34. Weichbroth, P.: Usability of mobile applications: a systematic literature study. IEEE Access **8**, 55563–55577 (2020)
35. Davies, J.: Word Cloud Generator. https://www.jasondavies.com/wordcloud/. Accessed 25 May 2022
36. Caputo, D., Pfleeger, S., Sasse, M., Ammann, P., Offutt, J., Deng, L.: Barriers to usable security? Three organizational case studies. IEEE Secur. Priv. **14**, 22–32 (2016)
37. Zurko, M., Simon, R.: User-centered security. In: Proceedings of the 1996 Workshop on New Security Paradigms (1996)
38. Theofanos, M.: Is usable security an oxymoron? IEEE Comput. **53**(2), 71–74 (2020)
39. Johnston, J., Eloff, J.H., Labuschagne, L.: Security and human computer interfaces. Comput. Secur. **22**(8), 675–684 (2003)
40. Saltzer, J., Schroeder, M.: A proteção de informação em sistemas de computador. Proc. IEEE **63**(9), 1278–1308 (1975)
41. Whitten, A., Tygar, J.: Why Johnny can't encrypt: a usability evaluation of PGP 5.0. In: USENIX Security Symposium (1999)
42. Hof, H.-J.: User-centric IT security-how to design usable security mechanisms. arXiv preprint arXiv:1506.07167 (2015)
43. Nurse, J., Creese, S., Goldsmith, M., Lamberts, K.: Guidelines for usable cybersecurity: past and present. In: Third International Workshop on Cyberspace Safety and Security (CSS) (2011)
44. Yee, K.-P.: User interaction design for secure systems. In: Deng, R., Bao, F., Zhou, J., Qing, S. (eds.) ICICS 2002. LNCS, vol. 2513, pp. 278–290. Springer, Heidelberg (2002). https://doi.org/10.1007/3-540-36159-6_24
45. Mahfuth, A., Yussof, S., Baker, A., Ali, N.: A systematic literature review: Information security culture. In: 2017 International Conference on Research and Innovation in Information Systems (ICRIIS). IEEE (2017)
46. AlHogail, A., Mirza, A.: Information security culture: a definition and a literature review. In: 2014 World Congress on Computer Applications and Information Systems (WCCAIS). IEEE (2014)
47. Da Veiga, A., Astakhova, L., Botha, A., Herselman, M.: Defining organisational information security culture—perspectives from academia and industry. Comput. Secur. (2020)
48. Uchendu, B., Nurse, J., Bada, M., Furnell, S.: Developing a cyber security culture: current practices and future needs. Comput. Secur. **109**, 102387 (2021)
49. Bada, M.: Stakeholder Analysis: Motives, Needs, and Drivers for Cybersecurity Awareness Training in Modern Work Environments, in AwareGO (2022)
50. Chen, Y., Ramamurthy, K., Wen, K.-W.: Impacts of comprehensive information security programs on information security culture. J. Comput. Inf. Syst. **55**(3), 11–19 (2015)
51. Furnell, S., Rajendran, A.: Understanding the influences on information security behaviour. Comput. Fraud Secur. 12–15 (2012)
52. Padayachee, K.: Taxonomy of compliant information security behavior. Comput. Secur. 673–680 (2012)
53. Hassan, N., Ismail, Z.: A conceptual model for investigating factors influencing information security culture in healthcare environment. Procedia-Soc. Behav. Sci. 1007–1012 (2012)

Survey of Services that Store Passwords in a Recoverable Manner

Kazutoshi Itoh and Akira Kanaoka[✉]

Toho University, Miyama 2 2 1, Funabashi, Chiba 274–8510, Japan
akira.kanaoka@is.sci.toho-u.ac.jp

Abstract. Passwords entered by users in web services and applications are essential and confidential information. Therefore, it is ideal for difficulty storing them to decipher in case of unauthorized intrusion from the outside. As a typical example, passwords are converted into hash values using the SHA2 algorithm and stored. However, not all web services and applications implement the ideal storage method. There have been many incidents in which personal information has been leaked. In some cases, the passwords were not stored correctly on the server-side but in plain text or encrypted in a reversible form. The passwords were leaked when there was an unauthorized intrusion or other damage. This research aims to clarify the actual situation of how services and applications store users' passwords in plaintext or reversible form on the server-side through external observation surveys. The method is to list the survey targets for each service or application and conduct the survey for each service or application. As a result of the survey, there were no services or apps that were confirmed to have implemented inappropriate storage methods in both the top sites in the Alexa ranking and the top apps in the Google Play ranking, and the survey revealed that there were not many services that returned plain text in general.

Keywords: Password · Plaintext · Web Technologies

1 Introduction

Passwords entered by users in web services and applications are essential confidential information, and therefore, it is ideal for keeping them in a complex state to decipher in case of unauthorized intrusion from outside. As a typical example, there is a method of storing passwords by converting them into hash values using a cryptographic hash function such as SHA-256. However, not all web services and applications implement the ideal storage method.

There have been several incidents where personal information has been leaked from web services and applications. Although there are various causes, there are cases where passwords themselves are leaked in the event of an unauthorized intrusion because the server did not store the passwords properly and encrypted them in plain text or reversible form.

Ideally, users should have different passwords for different services and applications, but in reality, it is known that users often tend to use the same password

A. Moallem (Ed.): HCII 2023, LNCS 14045, pp. 68–77, 2023.
https://doi.org/10.1007/978-3-031-35822-7_5

for multiple services and applications [1]. Given that it is difficult to change such users' behavioral characteristics, storing passwords in plaintext or reversible encryption should be avoided.

In this research, the current state of what services and applications store passwords in plaintext or reversible form on the server side is investigated, and the commonalities specific to these services are examined. In order to investigate whether or not services and applications store passwords on the server side in plain text or reversible form, observations are conducted on typical web services and applications.

A survey was conducted on services that store passwords in plaintext or reversible form. The results of a survey of Alexa's Top Japan Domains (#1 to 103) and Google Play's Top Free Android Apps (#1 to 28) did not reveal any web services or apps that can be determined to be storing passwords in plain text or reversible form. No web services or apps were found that could be determined to store passwords in plaintext or reversible form.

Forty services were surveyed, and seven services were found to store passwords in either plain text or reversible form. Based on these investigations, we analyzed the similarities among the services that store passwords in plain text or reversible form from two perspectives: the appearance of the web service or application and the HTML data provided by the server. When the HTML data were compared, no common points were found, and no common points that could be considered the cause were discovered.

The structure of this paper is as follows. First, in Sect. 2, several cases of password leaks are listed, and related studies are explained in Sect. 3. Section 4 presents the methodology, target of the survey, and results of the external observation survey of password storage methods conducted in this study. Section 5 discusses future issues, and Sect. 6 summarizes.

2 Examples of Plaintext Password Leaks

2.1 Largest Breach Cases

An investigation by UpGuard [2] reported that in October 2015, information from the Chinese service NetEase was leaked, and that the leaked information included hundreds of millions of plaintext passwords.

In the case of the Evite breach, 101 million records containing plaintext passwords were compromised in 2013, but it was not discovered until 2019.

In the case of Russia's VK in 2012, 93 million records were compromised, including plaintext passwords and email addresses.

The cases described here are the largest plaintext password leaks in history, but it is not hard to imagine that a massive number of plaintext password leaks, including small ones, occur frequently.

2.2 Facebook Password Breach

On March 21, 2019, Facebook announced its stance and efforts in response to the security incident in "Keeping Passwords Secure—Facebook," [3] which revealed that some passwords for Facebook and other applications were recorded in log files in plaintext format. On April 18 of the same year, Facebook announced its stance and efforts in response to the security incident. It was followed by an update to the release on April 18 of the same year. Facebook explained that it would notify the affected users.

2.3 Google's Plaintext Storage of Some G Suite Passwords

In a blog post on May 21, 2019, US time, Google informed customers of its G Suite service that some passwords were being stored on internal servers without encryption [4]. In the post, Suzanne Frey, vice president of engineering at Google Cloud Trust, said that the bug only affects enterprise users.

3 Related Works

3.1 Behavioral Tendencies of Developers

Naiakshina et al. have been conducting ongoing research on how software developers implement password storage. They surveyed students, freelancers, and corporate developers, and the results showed that a large percentage of the participants implemented password storage inappropriately [5–8].

These results suggest that it is generally difficult to implement proper storage, as participants in experiments who have not received proper lectures tend to store without encryption or hashing in the first place, and even when hashing, salt and stretching are not used.

3.2 Password Reuse

In today's world, where it is not uncommon to use multiple services, it is desirable to set different passwords for each service, but in reality, users tend to reuse passwords and share passwords across multiple services. While these were empirically known, In 2016, the first academic study was conducted by Wash et al. [1]. They studied the behavior of 134 people over six weeks and found that among the participants in the experiment, each person reused their password on 1.7–3.4 sites.

Based on the assumption that users are likely to reuse passwords, secure password storage becomes even more critical.

4 Observation Survey of Password Storage Methods

4.1 Methodology

The purpose of this research is to clarify the actual situation of what services and applications store users' passwords in plaintext or reversible form on the server-side. There are two approaches to this: external observation and internal observation. Internal observation is not realistic because it cannot be realized unless the confidential information on the server-side can be viewed. Therefore, in this research, we use external observation.

In this research, a survey is conducted on typical services and applications, and after discovering the services that store passwords in plain text or reversible form on the server-side, the method is to classify them and find common and similar points. First, typical services and applications try to reset their passwords and check if the service or application sends back the set password in its response. It is then checked whether the password is stored in plain text or reversible form.

Next, services and applications that store passwords in the reversible form are categorized, and similarities or commonalities are examined and analyzed. By taking these steps of investigation and consideration, we thought we could discover the root cause of implementing problematic storage methods. In this section, we describe these investigation targets, methods, and environments and the results of our investigation.

4.2 Website Survey of Alexa's Top Services

In order to investigate the status of password storage for typical services, a survey is conducted on the top Alexa sites.

The first step is to register as a user for each of the services on the top Alexa sites, log off, and then take action as "forgot password" when logging back in, and then check the response. There are two possible responses: one is to disclose the original password, and the other is not to disclose the original password. In this survey, the ones with the original password disclosure are searched.

Survey Target. Although there are many web services, including those operated by individuals and companies, this study decided to investigate the status of password storage for typical web services, and referring to "Japan Top Domains[1]" provided by Alexa, web services ranked from 1st to 103rd were targeted.

If the web services are used frequently by users and have a relatively high level of attention, storing passwords in plain text or reversible form suggests that the social impact of security threats is high.

Research Methods and Environment. In order to search for commonalities and similarities in what services store passwords in plain text or reversible form, items that can be used as indicators are listed. In order to list the survey targets, Alexa's Top Japan domain is accessed using a web browser, and the service name, URL of the registration page, and the existence and type of ID linking are listed. The listing was performed in one day. The Alexa rankings may change after a while, so the list should be compiled in a day. Although some services allow ID integration, each service should create its account without using ID integration.

---

[1] https://www.alexa.com/topsites/countries/JP.

After the list is completed, the survey is conducted one by one, starting from the first place. The survey method is described below.

- Access the registration page URL and actually register as a user.
- Save screenshots of the registration screen and any emails received during registration.
- After the user registration is completed, the user can take an action to the same service saying "I forgot my password" and record the pattern of the reaction, such as whether the service sends back the original password, and if not, what procedures are taken, using screenshots and memos.
  - If there are features specific to that service, such as how to register or reset passwords, record those as well, using screenshots or notes.

When registering for an account, some services read the past login information and log in automatically. Therefore, in order to avoid saving the login information and to proceed with the registration process smoothly, everything was performed in Google Chrome's incognito mode.

Result. The survey was conducted for the services ranked from 1st to 103rd. The detailed information of each service should not be presented from an ethical point of view.

A screenshot was used to save each transition through the registration screen of each service during the registration process. After the 51st place, the policy was to take screenshots only for those with the original password disclosure.

After listing and investigating Alexa's "Japan Top Domains" from No. 1 to No. 103, none were found to have the original password disclosure. Of the 103 cases, there were 9 cases where there was no user registration, 26 cases where registration was impossible during the survey experiment due to overseas services and the need to register a phone number, and 1 case where the service had been terminated.

There were 67 sites that had completed membership registration, of which 48 were duplicates, excluding sites that had duplicate registration accounts, such as those dependent on Google.

The duplicates were Google account, Livedoor account, DMM account, Microsoft account, and Amazon account.

Figure 1 shows the registration screen of Google with Alexa rankings of 1, 2, 5, and 31, as well as the corresponding screen when you forget your password. Google has a unified authentication mechanism for its various services, and all logins are redirected to a page on the same domain.

4.3 Google Play Top Ranking Apps Survey

A "forgot password" action is taken on the top apps in Google Play to see how they respond. There are two possible responses: one is to disclose the original password, and the other is not to disclose the original password. This study will search for those with the original password disclosure.

Fig. 1. Google (Alexa Rank: 1, 2, 5, 31) registration screen and the response screen when you say "forgot password"

Survey Target. Although there are many applications distributed on Google Play, both paid and free, we decided to investigate the password storage status of representative applications in this study. We referred to Google Play's popular overall ranking "Free Top Android Apps[2]," and targeted applications ranked 1st to 28th. If the apps that are used frequently by users and have a relatively high profile store passwords in plain text or reversible form is considered to have a high social impact on security threats.

---

[2] https://play.google.com/store/apps/top?hl=ja.

Research Methods and Environment. In order to search for commonalities and similarities in what apps are storing passwords in plain text or reversible form, index items are listed. As a list of targets for the investigation, the free Top Android apps in Google Play's overall popularity ranking are installed from the top, and user registration is checked. Since the Google Play ranking may fluctuate over time, the listing is conducted in a single day. An Android device is used for the survey to install the apps.

The survey is conducted one by one, starting from the first place after the list-up. The survey method is described below.

– Register users for the installed application.
– Save screenshots of the registration screen and any emails received during registration.
– After the user registration is completed, the application is erased to return to the state before the user registration. After that, take action "I forgot my password," and record the pattern of the reaction, such as whether the app sends back the original password, and if not, what procedures are taken, using screenshots and notes. Use screenshots and notes to record the reaction.
  • If there are features specific to that app, such as how to register or reset passwords, record those as well, using screenshots or notes.

Result. The survey was conducted for the apps ranked from 1st to 28th. The detailed information of each app should not be presented from an ethical point of view.

A screenshot was used to save each transition of the registration screen of each application during the registration process. After 11th place, the policy was to take screenshots only for those with the original password disclosure.

After listing and investigating Google Play's popular overall ranking of "Free Top Android Apps" from No. 1 to No. 28, I could not find any with the original password disclosure. As a breakdown, out of 28, 6 apps were not registered, and 5 apps could not be registered. 16 apps completed registration, of which 3 were automatically linked to the device's Google account, and 12 were duplicates, excluding apps that depended on Google for the registered account. The duplicated ones were Google account and d-account.

4.4   Survey of Services Where Information on Inappropriate Password Storage Was Obtained Through Web or SNS Searches

Alexa's survey of the top 103 Japanese Top Domains and the top 28 Free Top Android Apps in Google Play's overall popularity ranking did not reveal any services that store passwords in plain text or reversible form. Therefore, as an additional survey, a survey was conducted not only on typical sites and apps, but also on web and SNS services that reportedly store passwords in reversible form.

Survey Target. In order to discover services that store passwords in plain text or reversible form, this survey will be conducted on services that have been informed that their original passwords are returned through web searches and SNS searches.

Research Methods and Environment. Since this survey will be conducted on the services that were informed when the original password was sent back, the survey method and environment is the same as the method and environment for Alexa top sites.

The list of survey targets was made based on web search results and Twitter search results. The search was conducted using the following free words, and then the listed targets were further scrutinized.

- "password" "plain text" (in Japanese)
- "password" "e-mail" (in Japanese)

Result. The number of cases actually investigated after listing was 40. As a result of our survey, a total of seven services that had disclosed the original password was found. In addition, we found three services that did not disclose the original password but sent a new or temporary password to the email after the user said, "I forgot my password.

The survey was limited to services informed that the original passwords would be sent back, but the survey results showed that few services sent back the original passwords. Among the services that were informed that the original passwords were sent back, it can be inferred that there were several cases where the passwords were stored in plain text when the information was provided but was later modified.

4.5 Analyze the Common Elements Between Services that Store Passwords in Plaintext or Reversible Form

The survey discovered services that store passwords in either plain text or reversible form. An analysis of the commonalities among services that store passwords in either plaintext or reversible form are conducted. The purpose is to understand how this situation is driven by a specific implementation or a specific operator.

Analysis Method. The method used is to analyze the similarities between services that store passwords in plain text or reversible form in terms of appearance and HTML data provided by the server. We have found several services that store passwords in either plain text or reversible form, and the unique characteristics of these services are recorded. These features are compared from two perspectives, the appearance and the HTML data provided by the server, and the common parts are searched for.

Result. The results of the analysis show a similar format in appearance between the two services. We avoid presenting detailed information about each service for ethical reasons.

We then compared the HTML data provided by the servers of the two services (let us call them Service A and Service B). The HTML for Service A had "action="index.aspx"" and the HTML for Service B had "action="/7cn-webapp/mobile/WMShinkiTorokuNyuryoku.do?&timestamp=20200129170029". There was a description. It is a description related to the location where the data entered by the user is sent, but there were no similarities because the architectures of the services were different, with Service A being .aspx and Service B being .do. The other services were also compared from the two perspectives, but no common points could be found that could be considered the cause.

5   Future Works

In this study, the password management status of famous websites and applications was investigated, the similarities between services that store passwords in plain text or reversible form were searched for, and the causes were analyzed. In this study, an approach based on external observation was adopted. However, since there is a limit to the information that can be obtained in an experiment based on external observation, we believe that the accuracy and efficiency of the investigation can be improved by using internal observation or a similar method. It is also necessary to increase the number of services compared and analyze the common parts of services that store passwords in plaintext or reversible form. One of the future tasks is to identify the root cause of the services that store passwords in plaintext or reversible form based on the analysis results.

6   Conclusion

Passwords entered by users in web services and applications are considered to be important confidential information, so it is ideal to store them in a manner that is difficult to decipher in case of unauthorized intrusion from the outside, but there have been incidents of personal information leaks in web services and applications. However, there have been incidents of personal information leaks in web services and applications, partly due to storing passwords in plain text or reversible form.

The purpose of this study is to find out what kind of services and applications store passwords in plain text or reversible form on the server side. As an approach to this, a survey was conducted from typical web services and applications. as a result of surveying web services ranked from No. 1 to No. 103 in Alexa's "Japan Top Domains" and from No. 1 to No. 28 in Google Play's "Free Top Android Apps" ranking of overall popularity, it was found that passwords were stored in plain text or reversible form. As a result, no web service or app was found that could be determined to be storing passwords in plaintext or reversible form. Therefore, a separate survey was conducted on services that were reported to store passwords in plain text or reversible form. 40 services were surveyed, and 7 services were found to store passwords in plain text or reversible form. Based on these investigations, we analyzed the similarities among the services that store passwords in plaintext or reversible form from two perspectives: the appearance of the web service or application and the HTML data provided by the server. When the HTML data was compared, no common points were found, and we were not able to discover any common points that could be considered the cause. Future tasks include increasing the number of services to be compared, analyzing the common parts of services that store passwords in plaintext or reversible form, and improving the accuracy and efficiency of the survey by using internal observation or similar methods if possible. The results can then be used to identify the root cause of the service storing passwords in plaintext or reversible form.

The fact that we did not find any services storing passwords in plaintext or reversible form on Alexa's top sites or Google Play's top-ranked apps indicates that the risk is not urgent. However, the services that have been reported still store passwords in plain text or reversible form, and some of these services have a large number of users. This study shows that the risk itself continues to exist, and the reality of the risk has been clarified.

Acknowledgements. This work was supported by JSPS KAKENHI Grant Number JP22K12035.

References

1. Wash, R., et al.: Understanding password choices: how frequently entered passwords are re-used across websites. In: Twelfth Symposium on Usable Privacy and Security (SOUPS 2016) (2016)
2. Tunggal, A.T.: The 62 Biggest Data Breaches (Updated for January 2022). UpGuard Blog (2022) https://www.upguard.com/blog/biggest-data-breaches. Accessed 11 Feb 2022
3. Keeping password secure—Facebook. https://about.fb.com/news/2019/03/keeping-passwords-secure/. Accessed 08 Oct 2019
4. Notifying administrators about unhashed password storage. https://cloud.google.com/blog/products/g-suite/notifying-administrators-about-unhashed-password-storage. Accessed 08 Oct 2019
5. Alena, N., et al.: Why do developers get password storage wrong? a qualitative usability study. In: Proceedings of the 2017 ACM SIGSAC Conference on Computer and Communications Security (2017)
6. Alena, N., et al.: Deception task design in developer password studies: exploring a student sample. In: Fourteenth Symposium on Usable Privacy and Security (SOUPS 2018) (2018)
7. Alena, N., et al.: If you want, I can store the encrypted password a password-storage field study with freelance developers. In: Proceedings of the 2019 CHI Conference on Human Factors in Computing Systems (2019)
8. Alena, N., et al.: On conducting security developer studies with CS students: examining a password-storage study with CS students, freelancers, and company developers. In: Proceedings of the 2020 CHI Conference on Human Factors in Computing Systems (2020)

(I Can't Get No) Satisfaction: On the Existence of Satisfaction as a Component of Usable Security and Privacy

Akira Kanaoka[✉]

Toho University, Miyama 2-2-1, Funabashi, Chiba 274–8510, Japan
akira.kanaoka@is.sci.toho-u.ac.jp

Abstract. In the ISO definitions of usability, user satisfaction is specified as an element and effectiveness and efficiency. Jakob Nielsen, who is well known for his work on usability in web and UI design, defines satisfaction as one of the five qualitative elements in usability. Whitten and Tygar's paper, one of the earliest usability studies on usable security, also includes "sufficiently comfortable" as one of the usability definitions for security, which relates to user satisfaction. Although many usable security researches have been conducted and usability evaluations of the proposed methods have been done, most of them have mainly evaluated the effectiveness and efficiency of the proposed methods, and there is a possibility that satisfaction or comfort has not been sufficiently evaluated. Therefore, this paper investigates how satisfaction or comfort is evaluated in usable security research and discusses the results.

Keywords: User acceptance of security and privacy technologies ·
Usable Security and Privacy

1 Introduction

As cybersecurity, privacy, and trust (CPT) technologies continue to develop, one of the most critical research issues is users' appropriate use of these technologies. Human Computer Interaction (HCI) is the technology that can contribute most to solving this problem. The relationship between HCI and CPT has been the subject of much academic discussion in the usability of CPT technologies, i.e., usable security and privacy (USP). The USP field, which Whitten and Tygar pioneered in 1999 [1], has expanded over the past 20 years into the academic field of CPT. Many sessions at USENIX Security, one of the most challenging international conferences in CPT, have been devoted to discussing the human aspect.

ISO defines the usability of software and systems [2]. Jacobsen's ten principles are well known for web and UI usability [3]. However, there is no common definition of USP meant to the best of our knowledge. However, if security and privacy are one of the non-functional requirements of software and systems, and if the USP is an attempt to improve the usability of security and privacy, then the elements listed in those usability definitions may be familiar to the USP. If we look at the ISO definition, three elements make up usability: effectiveness, efficiency, and satisfaction. Of these three elements, "effectiveness" and "efficiency" have been the main focus of evaluation in USP research. But what about the remaining factor, "satisfaction"? It is difficult to say that this has been the focus of the discussion.

For example, a study by Felt et al. on the display of icons indicating the status of certificates in browsers evaluated usability by questionnaires asking whether participants felt safe or not and the difference in their behavior due to the difference in icons and wording [4]. However, the level of satisfaction with using the icons and wording has not been investigated. In the same way, in the study on the display of certificate errors in browsers [5], effective display using colors and wording was discussed and evaluated, and the results were shared widely, and technology was proposed that has become the mainstream of modern browsers, but again, there was no survey on the level of satisfaction with the use of colors and wording.

Let us focus on one of the most successful studies in USP research, the study of password management. Tan et al.'s study [6], the most recent and comprehensive work in the field, surveyed items such as fun and annoyance but did not discuss satisfaction in terms of these items in the paper.

Therefore, the following two research questions were raised in this paper.

RQ1: Has satisfaction been sufficiently discussed in the past USP studies?
RQ2: Can satisfaction be a component of USP?

To answer RQ1, we first surveyed past USP papers to determine whether satisfaction with the proposed methodologies was surveyed in those papers or whether satisfaction was on the agenda when discussing the surveyed content. As a result of surveying 53 papers in SOUPS 2019 and 2020, 47 papers had usability evaluations, and 6 of them were surveyed and discussed under the title of satisfaction.

Next, we also surveyed the evaluation criteria for USPs that have been proposed and used to date to see if any of them had criteria for satisfaction. After surveying the seven evaluation criteria, we found that none directly incorporated satisfaction into the evaluation criteria. At the same time, a few incorporated factors that can be said to be similar to satisfaction into the criteria.

Based on these results, we discussed RQ2. It is interesting to note that the results of RQ1 did not directly cite "satisfaction" as a criterion for survey and evaluation, but at the same time, the USP technologies were surveyed using keywords such as annoying, difficulty, and frustration. This result is fascinating. CPT technology is not the original purpose of the system or software but the technology that supports the execution of that purpose. It has been pointed out that CPT technologies sometimes have a negative impact on user interaction with the original purpose of the technology, so in evaluating the USP technologies, the USP researchers wanted to show that the negativity had been reduced or eliminated.

According to the above results, "No" was obtained for RQ1, and no clear answer was obtained for RQ2. Then, a new research question was clarified, "Is the impact of CPT technology on users as HCI only negative? Is there any positive impact?" This new RQ could be central to HCI-CPT. These possibilities will be discussed further in the paper.

2 Components of Usability

The definition of usability in ISO 9241-11 [2] is "extent to which a system, product or service can be used by specified users to achieve specified goals with effectiveness, satisfaction" is an element of usability. It indicates that "Satisfaction" is an element of usability. The same document states that Satisfaction is the "extent to which the user's physical, cognitive and emotional responses that result from the use of a system, product or service meet the user's needs and expectations."

Jakob Nielsen, an authority on the usability of websites and information systems, stated in his book that usability comprises the following five attributes [3].

- Learnablity
- Efficiency
- Memorability
- Errors
- Satisfaction

One of which is Satisfaction. He described it as "The system should be pleasant to use, so that users are subjectively satisfied when using it; they like it.".

In the context of usable security, Whitten and Tygar identified the following four usability requirements for security software in 1999 [1].

- are reliably made aware of the security tasks they need to perform
- are able to figure out how to successfully perform those tasks
- don't make dangerous errors
- are sufficiently comfortable with the interface to continue using it

The last of the four listed above is "are sufficiently comfortable with the interface to continue using it", and the keyword 'comfortable' is mentioned.

They further stated that.

> If an average user of email feels the need for privacy and authentication, and acquires PGP with that purpose in mind, will PGP's current design allow that person to realize what needs to be done, figure out how to do it, and avoid dangerous errors, without becoming so frustrated that he or she decides to give up on using PGP after all?
>
> – Whitten, Tygar [1]

They, therefore, noted the existence of frustration, which is a subjective factor as opposed to time performance or accuracy. Their research is arguably the paper pioneered in the USP field and still contains several important research factors. The same applies to 'satisfaction,' the factor we focus on in this paper. Unfortunately, their user experiments did not evaluate subjective factors such as satisfaction.

3   Usability Evaluation Item Survey

The System Usability Scale (SUS) is often used in questionnaire surveys in usable security research. SUS is a 10-item questionnaire in which each question is answered on a 5-point Likert chart. The results are scored on a 0–100 scale [7]. The survey items include whether the user wants to use the system frequently, whether it is easy to use, and whether it is not unnecessarily complicated, but there are no items that directly ask about satisfaction.

There are several other common questionnaire items in the HCI field to evaluate usability, validity, and reliability. QUIS (Questionnaire for User Interface Satisfaction) by Chin et al. is a UI-focused questionnaire that includes satisfaction in its title [8]. In the QUIS, frustrating and satisfying were listed as opposing factors in one of the 10-point scales of the overall reaction to the software. The questionnaire asked the respondents which of the two they felt more satisfied with.

In the Computer System Usability Questionnaire (CSUQ) by Lewis [9] , two of the 19 items are related to satisfaction. The first and last questions are unique in that they each ask about the overall satisfaction of the system. On the other hand, the 100-item Purdue Usability Testing Questionnaire (PUTQ) did not include satisfaction or items related to it, probably because many of the questions were about the specific operation of the system rather than about general feelings [10]. The PHUE (Practical Heuristics for Usability Evaluation) by Perlman also asked questions about specific behaviors, etc., and did not include items on satisfaction or related topics [11].

A questionnaire designed explicitly for usable security research is the SeBIS (Security Behavior Intentions Scale) by Egelman et al. [12]. This is not a usability questionnaire but a questionnaire to measure the security behavior of end-users. Therefore, the questionnaire did not ask about the usability of specific technologies, and there was no item asking about the level of satisfaction. The SA-6 by Faklaris et al. was also a questionnaire to measure users' security awareness, but not usability or satisfaction [13]. The UPSP (Users' Perceived systems' Privacy) by Ayalon et al. measures users' perceptions of system privacy and does not ask about usability or satisfaction [14].

4   Satisfaction Survey in Usable Security Research

Have any satisfaction surveys been conducted in the previous usable security and privacy research? In this section, previous papers are surveyed to show whether and what satisfaction surveys have been conducted.

Table 1. User experimental method classification in SOUPS 2019 and SOUPS 2020

User Study Type	Num. of Papers	Papers
Interview	27	[16,17,20,23–25,28,31–35,38,41,42,45,53,56–61,63,65–67]
Survey	24	[15,21,22,29,34–37,40,43,44,46–64]
(no user study)	6	[18,19,39,52,54,62]
SUS	2	[17,51]
Observation	2	[26,30]
Focus Group	1	[23]
Heuristic Walkthrough/ Cognitive Walkthroughj	1	[27]

4.1 Survey Method

The survey covers the international conference SOUPS 2019 and 2020, and 53 papers were surveyed.

The evaluation part of each paper was focused on. First, it was checked whether surveys such as interviews or questionnaires were conducted. If a survey was conducted, the content of the survey was checked to see if it included items or references to satisfaction. In the research on usable security and privacy, in addition to the research that proposes technologies to make it usable, there are many researches on the survey method itself, such as SeBIS and SA-6 mentioned above, and researches on the principles of user behavior that are the background of technological proposals.

4.2 Result

As a result of the survey, among the papers surveyed, there were 47 papers in which evaluation was conducted by user experiments [15–17,20–38,40–51,53,55–61,63–67]. Among them, six papers were identified as having a satisfaction survey [17,21,37,59,60,65]. The questionnaire using SUS was not counted as a satisfaction survey.

Although not directly in line with the objectives of this study, Table 1 shows how users were evaluated in each study, as it is valuable as a trend in USP research.

Among the papers that evaluated satisfaction, Kitkowska et al. analyzed the survey results to find that the proposed method contributed to user satisfaction in evaluating the visual design of privacy notices [37].

In Pearman et al.'s survey on password managers, they interviewed participants about their satisfaction/dissatisfaction with current methods of password management, and several responses were discussed [59].

As for the others, one of the three questionnaires only included a brief satisfaction-related question, and any mention of the results was limited to simply stating the results and not discussing them in-depth [21]. The other two were indicated in the questionnaire but were not mentioned in the text [17,65].

In many of the papers, there was no satisfaction survey. On the other hand, there were many papers where the purpose of the research was not to evaluate the usability of technology or software but to investigate user behavior and awareness of various security/privacy-related events. In such papers, the evaluation of satisfaction may be out of scope.

5   Discussion

In Whitten and Tygar's paper, comfort is listed as one of the definitions, but in the section that corresponds to the Research Question, they state "*If an average user of email feels the need for privacy and authentication, and acquires PGP with that purpose in mind, will PGP's current design allow that person to realize what needs to be done, figure out how to do it, and avoid dangerous errors, without becoming so frustrated that he or she decides to give up on using PGP after all?.*" Moreover, use the word "frustrated" rather than referring to comfort, suggesting that they believe that satisfaction and comfort with security technology are "no/low." If an average email user feels the same as the average user of email, it is because they are dissatisfied.

Even in papers that do not have a direct questionnaire on satisfaction, many items ask about Difficulty and Annoying, indicating that researchers in usable security and privacy tend to do so, although there is no unified opinion.

It cannot be denied that even in studies where satisfaction can be investigated, some have not been investigated. And may decrease in terms of satisfaction while increasing effectiveness and efficiency. In some studies, there were questionnaire items regarding satisfaction, but the results did not mention it [6,17]. In these studies, it is possible that there was no statistically significant difference or that there was a significant difference in the lower satisfaction level that was not mentioned.

6   Conclusion

In addition to the fact that there is room for re-evaluation of existing research with satisfaction evaluation as part of Replication Work, the question "Is satisfaction evaluation vital in usable security research?

To clarify the question, "**If there are a group of elements that constitute usable security, are satisfaction and comfort included in the elements?**" and "**Can we consider satisfaction and comfort to be synonymous with dissatisfaction and annoyance?**" These are new questions in this field. These questions may be considered new research questions in this field for further study.

References

1. Whitten, A., Tygar, J.D.: Why Johnny can't encrypt: a usability evaluation of PGP 5.0. In: Proceedings of the 8th Conference on USENIX Security Symposium - vol. 8 (SSYM 1999). USENIX Association, USA, 14 (1999)
2. ISO, "Ergonomics of human-system interaction - Part 11: Usability: Definitions and concepts," Iso/Np 9241–11 (2018). https://www.iso.org/obp/ui/#iso:std:iso: 9241.-11.cd-2.v1:en. Accessed 22 Oct 2021
3. Nielsen, J.: Usability Engineering. Morgan Kaufmann, Burlington (1994)
4. Felt, A.P., et al.: Rethinking connection security indicators. In: Twelfth Symposium on Usable Privacy and Security (SOUPS 2016) (2016)
5. Felt, A.P., et al.: Improving SSL warnings: comprehension and adherence. In: Proceedings of the 33rd Annual ACM Conference on Human Factors in Computing Systems (2015)
6. Tan, J., et al.: Practical recommendations for stronger, more usable passwords combining minimum-strength, minimum-length, and blocklist requirements. In: Proceedings of the 2020 ACM SIGSAC Conference on Computer and Communications Security (2020)
7. Brooke, J.: SUS: a quick and dirty' usability. Usability Eval. Ind. **189**, 4–7 (1996)
8. Chin, J.P., Diehl, V.A., Norman, K.L.: Development of an instrument measuring user satisfaction of the human-computer interface. In: Proceedings of the SIGCHI Conference on Human Factors in Computing Systems (1988)
9. Lewis, J.R.: IBM computer usability satisfaction questionnaires: psychometric evaluation and instructions for use. Int. J. Hum. Comput. Interact. **7**(1), 57–78 (1995)
10. Lin, H.X., Choong, Y.-Y., Salvendy, G.: A proposed index of usability: a method for comparing the relative usability of different software systems. Behav. Inf. Technol. **16**(4–5), 267–277 (1997)
11. Perlman, G.: Practical usability evaluation. In: Conference Companion on Human Factors in Computing Systems (1996)
12. Egelman, S., Peer, E.: Scaling the security wall: developing a security behavior intentions scale (seBIS). In: Proceedings of the 33rd Annual ACM Conference on Human Factors in Computing Systems (2015)
13. Faklaris, C., Dabbish, L.A., Hong, J.I.: A self-report measure of end-user security attitudes (SA-6). In: Fifteenth Symposium on Usable Privacy and Security (SOUPS 2019) (2019)
14. Ayalon, O., Toch, E.: Evaluating users' perceptions about a system's privacy: differentiating social and institutional aspects. In: Fifteenth Symposium on Usable Privacy and Security (SOUPS 2019) (2019)
15. Jayakrishnan, G.C., Sirigireddy, G.R., Vaddepalli, S., Banahatti, V., Lodha, S.P., Pandit, S.S.: Passworld: a serious game to promote password awareness and diversity in an enterprise. In: Proceedings of the Sixteenth USENIX Conference on Usable Privacy and Security (SOUPS 2020). USENIX Association, pp. 1–18. USA (2020). Article 1
16. Farke, F. M., Lorenz, L., Schnitzler, T., Markert, P., Dürmuth, M.: You still use the password after all - exploring FIDO2 security keys in a small company. In: Proceedings of the Sixteenth USENIX Conference on Usable Privacy and Security (SOUPS 2020). USENIX Association, pp. 19–35. USA (2020). Article 2
17. Samuel, R., Markert, P., Aviv, A.J., Neamtiu, I.: Knock, knock. who's there? on the security of LG's knock codes. In: Proceedings of the Sixteenth USENIX Conference on Usable Privacy and Security (SOUPS 2020). USENIX Association, pp. 37–59. USA (2020). Article 3

18. Lee, K., Kaiser, B., Mayer, J., Narayanan, A.: An empirical study of wireless carrier authentication for SIM swaps. In: Proceedings of the Sixteenth USENIX Conference on Usable Privacy and Security (SOUPS 2020). USENIX Association, pp. 61–79. USA (2020). Article 4

19. Dev, J., Moriano Salazar, P., Camp, J.: Lessons learnt from comparing WhatsApp privacy concerns across Saudi and Indian populations. In: Proceedings of the Sixteenth USENIX Conference on Usable Privacy and Security (SOUPS 2020). USENIX Association, pp. 81–97. USA (2020). Article 5

20. McDonald, N., Larsen, A., Battisti, A., Madjaroff, G., Massey, A., Mentis, H.: Realizing choice: online safeguards for couples adapting to cognitive challenges. In: Proceedings of the Sixteenth USENIX Conference on Usable Privacy and Security (SOUPS 2020). USENIX Association, pp. 99–110. USA (2020). Article 6

21. Fanelle, V., Karimi, S., Shah, A., Subramanian, B., Das, S.: Blind and human: exploring more usable audio CAPTCHA designs. In: Proceedings of the Sixteenth USENIX Conference on Usable Privacy and Security (SOUPS 2020). USENIX Association, pp. 111–125. USA (2020). Article 7

22. Geeng, C., Hutson, J., Roesner, F.: Usable sexurity: studying people's concerns and strategies when sexting. In: Proceedings of the Sixteenth USENIX Conference on Usable Privacy and Security (SOUPS 2020). USENIX Association, pp. 127–144. USA (2020). Article 8

23. Obada-Obieh, B., Spagnolo, L., Beznosov, K.: Towards understanding privacy and trust in online reporting of sexual assault. In: Proceedings of the Sixteenth USENIX Conference on Usable Privacy and Security (SOUPS 2020). USENIX Association, pp. 145–16. USA (2020). Article 9

24. Danilova, A., Naiakshina, A., Deuter, J., Smith, M.: Replication: on the ecological validity of online security developer studies: exploring deception in a password-storage study with freelancers. In: Proceedings of the Sixteenth USENIX Conference on Usable Privacy and Security (SOUPS 2020). USENIX Association, , pp. 165–183. USA (2020). Article 10

25. Chalhoub, G., Flechais, I., Nthala, N., Abu-Salma, R.: Innovation inaction or in action? the role of user experience in the security and privacy design of smart home cameras. In: Proceedings of the Sixteenth USENIX Conference on Usable Privacy and Security (SOUPS 2020). USENIX Association, pp. 185–204. USA (2020). Article 11

26. Palombo, H., Ziaie Tabari, A., Lende, D., Ligatti, J., Ou, X.: An ethnographic understanding of software (in) security and a co-creation model to improve secure software development. In: Proceedings of the Sixteenth USENIX Conference on Usable Privacy and Security (SOUPS 2020). USENIX Association, pp. 205–220. USA (2020). Article 12

27. Smith, J., Do, L. N., Murphy-Hill, E.: Why can't Johnny fix vulnerabilities: a usability evaluation of static analysis tools for security. In: Proceedings of the Sixteenth USENIX Conference on Usable Privacy and Security (SOUPS 2020). USENIX Association, USA, pp. 221–238 (2020). Article 13

28. Tiefenau, C., Häring, M., Krombholz, K., Von Zezschwitz, E.: Security, availability, and multiple information sources: exploring update behavior of system administrators. In: Proceedings of the Sixteenth USENIX Conference on Usable Privacy and Security (SOUPS 2020). USENIX Association, pp. 239–258. USA (2020). Article 14

29. Reinheimer, B., et al.: An investigation of phishing awareness and education over time: when and how to best remind users. In: Proceedings of the Sixteenth USENIX

Conference on Usable Privacy and Security (SOUPS 2020). USENIX Association, pp. 259–284. USA (2020) Article 15

30. Becker, S., Wiesen, C., Albartus, N., Rummel, N., Paar, C.: An exploratory study of hardware reverse engineering technical and cognitive processes. In: Proceedings of the Sixteenth USENIX Conference on Usable Privacy and Security (SOUPS 2020). USENIX Association, pp. 285–300. USA (2020). Article 16

31. Michalec, O., Van Der Linden, D., Milyaeva, S., Rashid, A.: Industry responses to the european directive on security of network and information systems (NIS): understanding policy implementation practices across critical infrastructures. In: Proceedings of the Sixteenth USENIX Conference on Usable Privacy and Security (SOUPS 2020). USENIX Association, pp. 301-317. USA (2020). Article 17

32. Alomar, N., Wijesekera, P., Qiu, E., Egelman, S.: You've got your nice list of bugs, now what? vulnerability discovery and management processes in the wild. In: Proceedings of the Sixteenth USENIX Conference on Usable Privacy and Security (SOUPS 2020). USENIX Association, pp. 319–339. USA (2020). Article 18

33. Mai, A., Pfeffer, K., Gusenbauer, M., Weippl, E., Krombholz, K.: User mental models of cryptocurrency systems - a grounded theory approach. In: Proceedings of the Sixteenth USENIX Conference on Usable Privacy and Security (SOUPS 2020). USENIX Association, pp. 341–358. USA (2020). Article 19

34. Wermke, D., Huaman, N., Stransky, C., Busch, N., Acar, Y., Fahl, S.: Cloudy with a chance of misconceptions: exploring users' perceptions and expectations of security and privacy in cloud office suites. In: Proceedings of the Sixteenth USENIX Conference on Usable Privacy and Security (SOUPS 2020). USENIX Association, pp. 359–377. USA (2020). Article 20

35. Story, P., Smullen, D., Acquisti, A., Cranor, L.F., Sadeh, N., Schaub, F.: From intent to action: nudging users towards secure mobile payments. In: Proceedings of the Sixteenth USENIX Conference on Usable Privacy and Security (SOUPS 2020). USENIX Association, pp. 379–415. USA (2020). Article 21

36. Barbosa, N.M., Zhang, Z., Wang, Y.: Do privacy and security matter to everyone? quantifying and clustering user-centric considerations about smart home device adoption. In: Proceedings of the Sixteenth USENIX Conference on Usable Privacy and Security (SOUPS 2020). USENIX Association, pp. 417–435. USA (2020). Article 22

37. Kitkowska, A., Warner, M., Shulman, Y., Wästlund, E., Martucci, L.A.: Enhancing privacy through the visual design of privacy notices: exploring the interplay of curiosity, control and affect. In: Proceedings of the Sixteenth USENIX Conference on Usable Privacy and Security (SOUPS 2020). USENIX Association, pp. 437–456. USA (2020). Article 23

38. Rader, E., Hautea, S., Munasinghe, A.: I have a narrow thought process: constraints on explanations connecting inferences and self-perceptions. In: Proceedings of the Sixteenth USENIX Conference on Usable Privacy and Security (SOUPS 2020). USENIX Association, pp. 457–488. USA, Article 24 (2020)

39. Bird, S., Segall, I., Lopatka, M.: Replication: why we still can't browse in peace: on the uniqueness and reidentifiability of web browsing histories. In: Proceedings of the Sixteenth USENIX Conference on Usable Privacy and Security (SOUPS 2020). USENIX Association, pp. 489–503. USA (2020). Article 25

40. Cobb, C., et al.: How risky are real users' IFTTT applets? In Proceedings of the Sixteenth USENIX Conference on Usable Privacy and Security (SOUPS 2020). USENIX Association, pp. 505–529. USA (2020). Article 26

41. Hayes, J., Kaushik, S., Price, C.E., Wang, Y.: Cooperative privacy and security: learning from people with visual impairments and their allies. In: Proceedings of the Fifteenth USENIX Conference on Usable Privacy and Security (SOUPS 2019). USENIX Association, pp. 1–20. USA (2019)

42. Frik, A., Nurgalieva, L., Bernd, J., Lee, J., Schaub, F., Egelman, S.: Privacy and security threat models and mitigation strategies of older adults. In: Proceedings of the Fifteenth USENIX Conference on Usable Privacy and Security (SOUPS 2019). USENIX Association, pp. 21–40. USA (2019)

43. Ayalon, O., Toch, E.: Evaluating users' perceptions about a system's privacy: differentiating social and institutional aspects. In: Proceedings of the Fifteenth USENIX Conference on Usable Privacy and Security (SOUPS 2019). USENIX Association, pp, 41–59 USA (2019)

44. Faklaris, C., Dabbish, L., Hong, J.I.: A self-report measure of end-user security attitudes (SA-6). In: Proceedings of the Fifteenth USENIX Conference on Usable Privacy and Security (SOUPS 2019). USENIX Association, pp. 61–77. USA (2019)

45. Fulton, K. R., Gelles, R., McKay, A., Abdi, Y., Roberts, R., Mazurek, M.L.: The effect of entertainment media on mental models of computer security. In: Proceedings of the Fifteenth USENIX Conference on Usable Privacy and Security (SOUPS 2019). USENIX Association, pp. 79–95. USA (2019)

46. Das, S., Dabbish, L., Hong, J.: A typology of perceived triggers for end-user security and privacy behaviors. In: Proceedings of the Fifteenth USENIX Conference on Usable Privacy and Security (SOUPS 2019). USENIX Association, pp. 97–115. USA (2019)

47. Busse, K., Schäfer, J., Smith, M.: Replication: no one can hack my mind revisiting a study on expert and non-expert security practices and advice. In: Proceedings of the Fifteenth USENIX Conference on Usable Privacy and Security (SOUPS 2019). USENIX Association, pp. 117–136. USA (2019)

48. Wu, J., et al.: Something isn't secure, but i'm not sure how that translates into a problem: promoting autonomy by designing for understanding in signal. In: Proceedings of the Fifteenth USENIX Conference on Usable Privacy and Security (SOUPS 2019). USENIX Association, pp. 137–153. USA 2019

49. Simoiu, C., Gates, C., Bonneau, J., Goel, S.: I was told to buy a software or lose my computer. i ignored it: a study of ransomware. In: Proceedings of the Fifteenth USENIX Conference on Usable Privacy and Security (SOUPS 2019). USENIX Association, pp. 155–174. USA (2019)

50. Kum, H.C., Ragan, E.D., Ilangovan, G., Ramezani, M., Li, Q., Schmit, C.: Enhancing privacy through an interactive on-demand incremental information disclosure interface: applying privacy-by-design to record linkage. In: Proceedings of the Fifteenth USENIX Conference on Usable Privacy and Security (SOUPS 2019). USENIX Association, pp. 175–189. USA (2019)

51. Qin, L., et al.: From usability to secure computing and back again. In: Proceedings of the Fifteenth USENIX Conference on Usable Privacy and Security (SOUPS 2019). USENIX Association, pp. 191–210. USA (2019)

52. Drury, V., Meyer, U.: Certified phishing: taking a look at public key certificates of phishing websites. In: Proceedings of the Fifteenth USENIX Conference on Usable Privacy and Security (SOUPS 2019). USENIX Association, pp. 211–223. USA (2019)

53. Mhaidli, A.H., Zou, Y., Schaub, F.: We can't live without them! app developers' adoption of ad networks and their considerations of consumer risks. In: Proceedings of the Fifteenth USENIX Conference on Usable Privacy and Security (SOUPS 2019). USENIX Association, pp. 225–244. USA (2019)

54. Patnaik, N., Hallett, J., Rashid, A.: Usability smells: an analysis of developers' struggle with crypto libraries. In: Proceedings of the Fifteenth USENIX Conference on Usable Privacy and Security (SOUPS 2019). USENIX Association, pp. 245–257. USA (2019)
55. Voronkov, A., Martucci, L., Lindskog, S.: System administrators prefer command line interfaces, don't they? an exploratory study of firewall interfaces. In: Proceedings of the Fifteenth USENIX Conference on Usable Privacy and Security (SOUPS 2019). USENIX Association, pp. 259 271. USA (2019)
56. Li, F., Rogers, L., Mathur, A., Malkin, N., Chetty, M.: Keepers of the machines: examining how system administrators manage software updates. In: Proceedings of the Fifteenth USENIX Conference on Usable Privacy and Security (SOUPS 2019). USENIX Association, pp. 273–288. USA (2019)
57. Mecke, L., Rodriguez, S.D., Buschek, D., Prange, S., Alt, F.: Communicating device confidence level and upcoming re-authentications in continuous authentication systems on mobile devices. In Proceedings of the Fifteenth USENIX Conference on Usable Privacy and Security (SOUPS 2019). USENIX Association, pp. 289–301. USA (2019)
58. Mecke, L., Buschek, D., Kiermeier, M., Prange, S., Alt, F.: Exploring intentional behaviour modifications for password typing on mobile touchscreen devices. In: Proceedings of the Fifteenth USENIX Conference on Usable Privacy and Security (SOUPS 2019). USENIX Association, pp. 303–318. USA (2019)
59. Pearman, S., Zhang, S.A., Bauer, L., Christin, N., Cranor, L.F.: Why people (don't) use password managers effectively. In: Proceedings of the Fifteenth USENIX Conference on Usable Privacy and Security (SOUPS 2019). USENIX Association, pp. 319–338. USA (2019)
60. Ciolino, S., Parkin, S., Dunphy, P.: Of two minds about two-factor: understanding everyday FIDO U2F usability through device comparison and experience sampling. In: Proceedings of the Fifteenth USENIX Conference on Usable Privacy and Security (SOUPS 2019). USENIX Association, pp. 339–356. USA (2019)
61. Reese, K., Smith, T., Dutson, J., Armknecht, J., Cameron, J., Seamons, K.: A usability study of five two-factor authentication methods. In: Proceedings of the Fifteenth USENIX Conference on Usable Privacy and Security (SOUPS 2019). USENIX Association, pp. 357–370. USA (2019)
62. Di Martino, M., Robyns, P., Weyts, W., Quax, P., Lamotte, W., Andries, K.: Personal information leakage by abusing the GDPR "Right of access". In: Proceedings of the Fifteenth USENIX Conference on Usable Privacy and Security (SOUPS 2019). USENIX Association, pp. 371–386. USA (2019)
63. Habib, H., et al.: An empirical analysis of data deletion and opt-out choices on 150 websites. In: Proceedings of the Fifteenth USENIX Conference on Usable Privacy and Security (SOUPS 2019). USENIX Association, pp. 387–406. USA (2019)
64. Vance, A., Eargle, D., Jenkins, J.L., Kirwan, C.B., Anderson, B.B.: The fog of warnings: how non-essential notifications blur with security warnings. In: Proceedings of the Fifteenth USENIX Conference on Usable Privacy and Security (SOUPS 2019). USENIX Association, pp. 407–420. USA (2019)
65. Alqhatani, A., Lipford, H.R.: There is nothing that i need to keep secret: sharing practices and concerns of wearable fitness data. In: Proceedings of the Fifteenth USENIX Conference on Usable Privacy and Security (SOUPS 2019). USENIX Association, pp. 421–434. USA (2019)
66. Tabassum, M., Kosinski, T., Lipford, H.R.: I don't own the data: end user perceptions of smart home device data practices and risks. In: Proceedings of the

Fifteenth USENIX Conference on Usable Privacy and Security (SOUPS 2019). USENIX Association, pp. 435–450. USA (2019)

67. Abdi, N., Ramokapane, K.M., Such, J.M.: More than smart speakers: security and privacy perceptions of smart home personal assistants. In: Proceedings of the Fifteenth USENIX Conference on Usable Privacy and Security (SOUPS 2019). USENIX Association, pp. 451–466. USA (2019)

Analysis of Information Quality and Data Security in the KPU (General Elections Commission) SIDALIH (Voter Data Information System) Application

Jaka Raharja[1][✉], Achmad Nurmandi[2], Misran[1], and Dimas Subekti[1]

[1] Department of Government Affairs and Administration, Yogyakarta Muhammadiyah University, Yogyakarta, Indonesia
{jaka.raharja.psc22,misran.psc20}@mail.umy.ac.id
[2] Department of Government Affairs and Administration, Jusuf Kalla School of Government, Muhammadiyah University, Yogyakarta, Indonesia
nurmandi_achmad@umy.ac.id

Abstract. The purpose of this study was to determine the quality of services provided and data security in the use of the KPU's SIDALIH (Voter Data Information System) application. This research uses qualitative methods by analyzing online news media. The news is collected using the NCapture feature and then the Nvivo 12 plus software is used to manage and analyze the data. The results show that the accurate indicator in the SIDALIH application service has the highest percentage of 33.33%, then the relevant indicator with a percentage of 29.17%, the completeness indicator with a percentage of 22.92%, and the timeliness indicator with a percentage of 14.58%. Infrastructure indicators have a percentage of 53.33% and management indicators have a percentage of 46.67%. The SIDALIH application can provide accurate information, but the delivery of information on the SIDALIH application takes time to be accessed. Security infrastructure needs to be improved so that it is not easy to be hacked and it is necessary to establish guidelines, rules, and task forces that play a role in tackling information technology disasters or data leaks. The limitation of this research is that the data obtained is only from online news media, so it still needs to be explored further regarding its truth and legitimacy. The findings in this study can be used as a reference for improving the quality of information and guaranteeing the security of user data in the future.

Keywords: Information Quality · Data Security · SIDALIH (Voter Data Information System)

1 Introduction

Along with the rapid development of the times, technology has become the main player in this fast-paced changing era. Technology continues to develop relentlessly, and every time it always gives birth to new things. Technology spreads to the fields of economics, politics, society, and government. Of course, the presence of this technology has both good and bad impacts. Jobs that used to be done manually are now being done by machines or computers [1]. The government has adapted to changing times by using technology in running its government. The use of Information Technology in government has evolved over the last few years to make interactions between government and citizens (G2C), government and business (G2B), and inter-agency relations (G2G) more effective, democratic and transparent [2].

Personal computers, cell phones, e-mail, and the internet have permeated all walks of life. Industrial productivity has increased and service efficiency has increased [3]. When people understand how to use the internet properly and can operate other electronic media, the government seeks to provide public services that are more efficient, transparent, and easy to access [4]. Digital-based services are the answer to this rapid technological development. The transition from manual to digital means that it has covered various activities in government, be it administration, data management, information, and management, which have worked electronically [5].

Information technology has now been used by the KPU. A mandatory condition must be met in the implementation of electoral democracy, namely updating voter data. The accuracy of voter data enhances the quality of electoral democracy and provides the widest possible platform for the public to cast their right to vote [6]. Technology plays a major role in supporting performance and convenience in processing public data as well as ease in holding elections conducted by the KPU [7]. As proof that technology has been present in general elections, namely the presence of several applications issued by the KPU, some of these applications, namely nominations with the Candidacy Information System (Silon), Political Party Information Systems (Sipol), Calculation Information System Information Systems (Situng), Information Systems Electoral District Information (Sidapil), Recapitulation Information System (SiRekap) and Voter List Information System (Sidalih) [8].

In anticipating the occurrence of things that might eliminate someone's right to vote which will lead to disputes on election day, it is necessary to register voters earlier before voting takes place. Inaccuracies and errors in voter data will have an impact on the legitimacy of general elections and the completeness of general election administration [9]. Before the determination of the DPT (Fixed Voters List), the accuracy of voter data would be accommodated in advance on the DPS (Temporary Voters List) but reflecting on the experience of previous elections this could not accommodate all voters [10]. So that this becomes a problem that triggers disputes over election results, and the majority of requests filed with the Constitutional Court are related to disputes over more requests about inaccurate voter lists [11].

Based on these problems in updating data, the use of information technology implemented by the KPU caught a lot of people's attention at the beginning of its appearance, namely SIDALIH. SIDALIH is a product of Information Technology that has efforts as a double e-government that implements the principles of e-governance and e-government so that people are allowed to be directly involved in general elections [12]. According to Wulan Suri & Yuneva (2021) SIDALIH is an online-based voter data information system centered on the KPU server. SIDALIH was created to serve voters regarding voter data, and support the work of election administration employees in compiling, coordinating, announcing, and maintaining voter data. SIDALIH performs CRUDE (create, read, update, and delete) functions. SIDALIH has advantages over previous methods from election to election, SIDALIH can overcome most of the problems at the stage of updating voter data, and SIDALIH can provide data regarding the number of voter lists accurately [14].

In research Akbar et al., (2021) This study describes artificial intelligence that is applied to the KPU's voter data updating application or SIDALIH. The results show that in terms of the effectiveness of siding, it has benefits that can assist organizers in recapitulating voter lists effectively, being able to produce accurate and precise reclaimer data, and being able to detect the presence of multiple voters. Constraints and obstacles that occur in the application of SIDALIH namely regarding the quality of human resources, the occurrence of natural disasters, the existence of population database incompatibilities, lack of community participation, there are network and system disturbances, and there are multiple voters with many voters on the previous voter list.

Research conducted by Makuta et al., (2021) The results of this study explain that the recommended model for updating data for the 2024 election is a continuous data updating model and an improved model, with voter data in SIDALIH being able to connect with regency/city KPU, Disdukcapil (Civil Registry Service Office), sub-districts, and hamlets. Data updating must be ongoing based on data generated by Disdukcapil by cooperating with SIDALIH and SIAK (Population Administration Information System) and utilizing IT, so that data that has changed in the relevant h5amlets will be known by the district/city KPU directly, Disdukcapil, sub-district, and hamlet governments. Because so far, the SIDALIH application is only available at Disdukcapil, while the KPU, sub-district government, and hamlets obtain data only from hamlets.

This research is different from previous studies because at present the implementation of SIDALIH in Indonesia faces various serious challenges for the Indonesian government with the large demands of the public for the government to get maximum service, as well as the rapid development of science and technology [17]. So the government is required to be able to provide the best quality and useful information and be able to provide a sense of security for people's data. Data security and the quality of services provided to the government will have a major impact on people's interest in adopting digital services provided by the government [18]. Research with the title Analysis of Information Quality and Data Security in Using the SIDALIH KPU Application is interesting to discuss to find out how SIDALIH plays a role in providing quality information services and how can the technology used maintain the security of user data. And is SIDALIH still relevant for future use?

2 Literature Review

2.1 Information Quality

Information is a form of data that is formed in such a way that it can be understood and has meaning for its users or recipients so that it has a real impact on users who will influence their decisions [19]. The higher the quality of the information provided about the products produced by a system, the more decisions will be made by users [20]. Reliable quality information can describe according to client needs through information services and empower them to be able to carry out their work successfully [21]. The quality of the information on SIDALIH is complete, non-misleading, and more transparent [15].

SIDALIH information quality refers to the validity, value, and usefulness of information that is the result of an information system and the quality of these results. SIDALIH information quality describes the extent to which the system can provide users with useful and significant information accurately and quickly [22]. The quality of information becomes the main determinant of the quality of the website. Good quality information can produce enjoyment and positive behavior in its use. Customers will form a positive view when information can meet their wishes during the decision-making process and is available in an adequate manner [23].

The quality of the information produced depends on several things, namely, completeness, the information disseminated or published must be complete or not partial, if the information provided is incomplete it will affect decision-making so that will affect problem-solving. Relevance, the information provided must have benefits for its use, this will influence the user in making decisions. Accurate, the information conveyed must not be negatively misleading, the information must be following the actual situation. And the timeliness of information should not be delivered late, because the information that is not on time is no longer valuable [24].

2.2 Data Security

According to Benuf et al. (2019) Personal data is individual data that is confidential which is guarded and protected. In an electronic system, personal data is protected and monitored, including data acquisition, data collection, and data dissemination. Protection of personal data in electronic systems refers to the principle of respect for personal data as privacy. Public privacy and data security are matters of serious consideration and concern in digital-based services that utilize internet media. Because the security of public data is a benchmark for the quality and ability of the government to provide digital services [26].

Protecting personal data is an obligation for users of electronic systems. The confidentiality of personal data collected, obtained, processed, and analyzed must be used according to user needs. Documents that contain personal data need to be protected to avoid data misuse. Organizations and individuals are responsible for personal data that becomes their control if personal data is misused [25].

According to Iswandari (2021) The government as the provider of information needs to guarantee its security and confidentiality so that acts of abuse do not occur. Several things become paralyzing or damaging in e-government services. These problems can be classified into 4 categories, namely: 1) Infrastructure security, government networks are built to interact between institutions and various elements on time. Building data network security is the key to infrastructure development and forms the basis of all information services. 2) Application security. The government certainly has strict regulations regarding applications in terms of security and usability. However, public access that is so broad in e-government services is vulnerable to potential security breaches so mitigation is needed in terms of security. 3) Identification of management, the management of access to information and services is the hand of the government as the spread of electronic transactions increases. The government needs to help users, so they don't have difficulty accessing it and don't jeopardize user security. 4) Information Guarantee, Information owned by the government whether it contains personal information must be accounted for by them. All Applications and Web sites must provide sufficient access to data security so that it is not misused. Information owned by the government whether it contains personal information must be accounted for by them.

Of the four categories then the indicators in data security are adequate infrastructure and Management.

3   Research Methods

The study uses a qualitative method by analyzing online news media that focuses on reporting on service quality and data security in the KPU's SIDALIH application. Data were obtained from national online news media, namely Kompas.com, Merdeka.com, Tribunnews.com, and Suara.com which are related to the SIDALIH application (Table 1).

Table 1. Data source

Online news platform	Number of news
Kompas.com	9
Merdeka.com	5
Tribunnews.com	7
Suara.com	5

Data collection begins with searching for keywords that are appropriate to the focus of this research found in reputable online media in Indonesia, then using the Extensions Ncapture feature to retrieve news from online news in the form of PDFs so that it can then be processed. The data analysis technique in this study used manual coding through the features of the Nvivo 12 Plus software. Data were analyzed by processing manually coding online news results. Manual coding was done by manually classifying data that was relevant to the topic discussed in this study. The data is presented in the form of diagrams and pictures by utilizing the Crosstab query and Word Cloud features from the coding results.

4   Results and Discussion

4.1   Information Quality SIDALIH KPU

The SIDALIH (Voter Data Information System) application presented by the KPU is to provide voter data information to the public and to make it easier for officers to update voter data. SIDALIH (Voter Data Information System) is a creative product from the KPU which has a positive value that can update and convey information about voter data so that voters can exercise their right to vote. Of course, the election will not take place if there are no participants and voters, it is the KPU's job to facilitate voters as in a democratic government system [27].

The 2014 legislative election was the first time the SIDALIH application was used, being the first step in organizing online-based voter list updates. In updating voter data, SIDALIH is expected to be able to improve the performance of the KPU. The activity of updating voter data on an ongoing basis is an activity carried out by the KPU to obtain voter data that is more accurate, up-to-date, comprehensive, continuous, and not only dependent on the election process because voter data has the following elements, namely: 1). Voter data is a guarantee so that the owner can exercise his right to vote; 2). As the main component in determining the quality of the holding of elections; 3). As supporting data in activities or processes in the administration of elections such as distribution of logistics, nominations, verification of political parties, and others; And 4) the data is used as a reference in the recruitment of TPS (Polling Station) supervisors and TPS officers [28].

The function of SIDALIH in updating and maintaining voter data was developed to assist the KPU in updating and maintaining voter data. In carrying out its function, SIDALIH is used to carry out the data input process in the form of adding new voters, improving data, and deletion of data, it can be said that SIDALIH helps to identify problems that exist on the voter list, such as duplicate data, data that does not meet the requirements, under 17 years of age, invalid KK (Family Card) and NIK (National Identity Number), voters who have died and several problems regarding other voter lists. Then the function of SIDALIH in terms of dissemination or publication of data, SIDALIH KPU opens access to the public to information regarding voter lists, both providing information about voter lists online and a copy of the voter list given to supervisors in the form of a print out that has been pasted in village office and other strategic places [27].

The quality of information generated by the KPU in the SIDALIH applications as DPT (Fixed Voters List) information is always a polemic in every election event. This is a challenge for the KPU in conveying voter data information, of course, it will affect the quality of information delivery in the SIDALIH application. The results of the analysis through Word Cloud Analysis display a few words regarding the Quality of Information in the SIDALIH application. The word SIDALIH is a word that often appears in online news that has been collected because SIDALIH is closely related to research on the variable quality of information (Fig. 1).

Then through the Nvivo Crosstab Query from the four online news Kompas.com, Merdeka.com, tribunnews, and suara.com which have been collected provide information that the Accurate indicator has the highest score of 33.33% and Timeliness has the lowest score of 14.58% (Fig. 2).

Based on the picture above it can be explained that:

First, Completeness. In the results of online news collection, it is known that the completeness of the information described in the news sources Kompas.com, Merdeka.com, Suara.com, and Tribunnews.com shows a score of 22.92% through manual coding results on completeness items, using NVivo 12 plus. Completeness is indicated by the contents of the information contained in the SIDALIH application. Completeness has a score that is below the accurate and relevant indicators. One of the provisions of quality information is the completeness of the information content available. Completeness of information

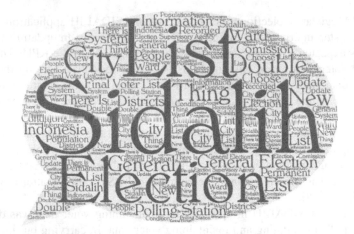

Fig. 1. Word Cloud Analysis Information Quality

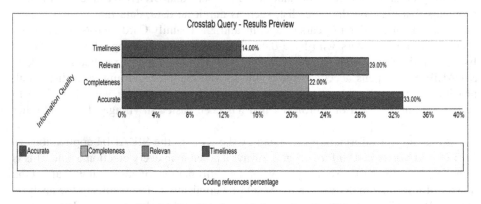

Fig. 2. Crosstab Query Information Quality

is one of the most important indicators in conveying information because incomplete information will result in future user decisions.

Second, Relevant, in the results of news collection through online news such as Kompas.com, Merdeka.com, Suara.com, and Tribunnews.com the indicator relevant has a score of 29.17% Results from coding per indicator relevant using Vivo 12 Plus. The relevance indicator has a higher score than the completeness indicator but is still below the accurate indicator. Appropriateness in the delivery of information is a component needed for the community to obtain information according to their needs and uses. The usefulness and relevance of the SIDALIH application are related to election information or information about the DPT (Fixed Voters List) of the user community so that the information conveyed is under the needs of the community.

Third, Accurate, information provided in the SIDALIH application is the most important component of this application, the accuracy of voter data in the SIDALIH application influences the running of general elections. As explained by Habibah & Safuan (2022) that the use of information technology to produce accurate data is important for optimization. Using this technology is very important in the data processing. In the picture above it can be seen that the accurate indicator has the highest score based on coding through the results of data collected from online news media with a score of 33.33%, this score is the highest compared to other indicators.

Fourth, Timeliness. The timeliness indicator has the lowest score compared to other indicators with a score of 14.58%. The results are based on data collection through online media and then coded using the Nvivo 12 Plus application. Timeliness is the indicator with the lowest score because the data available in the SIDALIH application requires time to update and re-data collection in the field related to DPT so it takes more time to input data into the SIDALIH application.

4.2 SIDALIH Data Security

Public data security is an important matter that requires serious attention and consideration in the administration of a digital-based bureaucracy that utilizes the internet network. Because one of the main things in improving service quality is the ability to provide reliable service. The development and construction of a system that supports the implementation of E-government need planning and needs to pay attention to aspects based on facts and possibilities that will occur later. Information owned by the government regarding people's data needs security and confidentiality guarantees so that it does not fall into the hands of irresponsible parties who will misuse the data and will have very serious consequences. The government needs to guarantee that public data will remain safe and will not be leaked to parties who should not know the data. Of course, a data leak will have quite a big loss for both the community as the owner of the data and the government itself. Buying and selling personal data and information without the consent of the data owner is a very dangerous crime within the scope of buying and selling which has entered the international sphere [26].

Data leaks are things that have a serious impact, leaked data will cause financial losses. Most recently, the data leak disseminated by Bjorka has become a concern for the Indonesian people because the data allegedly came from the KPU's SIDALIH application. The results of online news coding from Kompas.com, Tribunnews.com, Merdeka.com, and Suara.com use NVivo's Computer Assigned Qualitative Data Analysis (CAQDS) by coding based on indicators on Data Security, namely Infrastructure and Management. Following are the results of the Crosstab Query (Fig. 3).

First, infrastructure is needed to support information system management so that data centralization forms a definite data collection procedure to improve data security. The government needs to cooperate with non-government institutions and work optimally to fulfill the provision of good security infrastructure. Need to ensure that the data security infrastructure has been guaranteed and tested, for example by implementing a central security system on network infrastructure and a Security Operation Center (SOC) that can increase security on all devices.

Infrastructure has an influence on data leakage in the SIDALIH application. Because the infrastructure in terms of system and network security in the security SIDALIH application is inadequate, data leaks occur. Based on the results of coding from online news media namely Kompas.com, Merdeka.com, Suara.com, and Tribunnews.com the

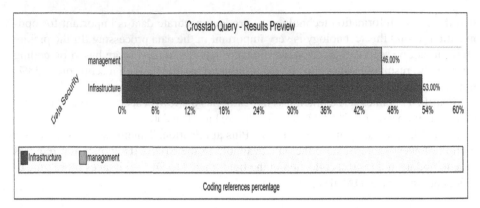

Fig. 3. Crosstab Query Data Security

security indicator has the highest score of 53.33%. The news media presents relevant news regarding weak data security infrastructure against data leaks.

The application of e-government must of course be accompanied by the construction and development of supporting elements for the security of the system. e-government development must look at several aspects that are likely to occur. Information about individuals in the community needs security guarantees so that it is not misused which results in serious impacts.

Second, Management, the management indicator has a Crosstab Querry score of 46.67%, the result is based on manual coding using NVivo 12 plus. Based on the news that has been collected and manually coded relevant news regarding security management, in general, it can be explained that agencies in the management of personal data do not yet have definite rules regarding guidelines for dealing with data leaks. The work unit that will play a role and be responsible for the prevention of leaks has not yet been formed. Data leakage is a challenge for the SIDALIH data manager they manage.

5   Conclusion

Shows that the indicator Accurate in the SIDALIH application service has the highest percentage, namely 33.33%, then in second place followed by the indicator of relevance with a percentage of 29.17%, the completeness indicator is in third place with a percentage of 22.92% and the timeliness indicator is last with a percentage of 14.58%. Then in data security, there are 2 indicators, namely Infrastructure and Management. In the results of data processing from online news media Kompas.com, Merdeka.com, Suara.com, and Tribunnews.com using the NVivo 12 Plus software as a qualitative data analysis tool with the Crosstab Query feature, it was found that the infrastructure indicator had the highest percentage, namely 53.33% while the management indicator has a percentage of 46.67%.

Based on these results, it can be concluded that the SIDALIH application can provide accurate information, but the delivery of information on the SIDALIH application takes time to be accessed because in updating data and updating data it is not impossible to experience problems in the field. In terms of data security, security infrastructure needs to be improved so that it is not easy to be hacked and it is necessary to establish guidelines, rules, and task forces that play a role in tackling information technology disasters or data leaks. Seeing this, SIDALIH is still relevant for future use but needs to strengthen system defense and change the voter list re-data collection system. The limitation of this research is that the data obtained is only from online news media, so it still needs to be explored further regarding its truth and legitimacy. SIDALIH is a useful application in elections but every year it always has problems or has problems updating data. The findings in this study can be used as a reference for improving the quality of information and guaranteeing the security of user data in the future.

References

1. Almuraqab, N.A.S., Jasimuddin, S.M., Mansoor, W.: An empirical study of perception of the end-user on the acceptance of smart government service in the UAE. J. Glob. Inf. Manag. **29**(6), 1–29 (2021). https://doi.org/10.4018/jgim.20211101.oa11
2. Yunita, N.P., Aprianto, R.D.: Kondisi Terkini Perkembangan Pelaksanaan E-Government Di Indonesia: Analisis Website. In: Seminar Nasional Teknologi Informasi dan Komunikasi, vol. 2018, no. Sentika, pp. 329–336 (2018)
3. Alshamsi, O., Ameen, A., Isaac, O., Khalifa, G.S.A., Bhumic, A.: Examining the impact of Dubai smart government characteristics on user satisfaction. Int. J. Recent Technol. Eng. **8**(2), Special Issue 10, 319–327 (2019). https://doi.org/10.35940/ijrte.B1053.0982S1019
4. Auditia, G.G.: E-government accessibility for disability persons. Indonesian J. Disabil. Stud. **5**(2), 185–189 (2018)
5. Patrisia, N.E., Anwar, F.: Penerapan Transformasi Digital Pada Pelayanan Publik di Badan Pengelola Keuangan Provinsi Bengkulu. J. Penelit. Sos. dan Polit. **10**(1), 24–33 (2021). https://journals.unihaz.ac.id/index.php/mimbar/article/view/963
6. Izzaty, R., Nugraha, X.: Perwujudan Pemilu yang Luberjurdil melalui Validitas Daftar Pemilih Tetap. J. Suara Huk. **1**(2), 155 (2019). https://doi.org/10.26740/jsh.v1n2.p155-171
7. Lestari, P.B., Zulfikar, D.H., Gunawan, C.E.: Analisis Kualitas Sistem Informasi Data Pemilih (SIDALIH) Menggunakan Model McCall. Jusifo **6**(1), 1–14 (2020). https://doi.org/10.19109/jusifo.v6i1.5526
8. Ginting, A.E., Nasution, M.A., Kusmanto, H.: Pola Rekrutmen Penyelenggara Pemilihan Umum Tingkat Kelompok Penyelenggara Pemungutan Suara Di Kecamatan Medan Selayang Pada Pemilihan Umum Serentak Tahun 2019. Perspektif **10**(2), 692–709 (2021). https://doi.org/10.31289/perspektif.v10i2.5101
9. Yandra, A., Faridhi, A., Andrizal, A., Setiawan, H., Nurchotimah, A.S.I.: The urgency of classification of the voter list as a fulfillment of political rights. Polit. Indones. Indones. Polit. Sci. Rev. **7**(1), 36–50 (2022). https://doi.org/10.15294/ipsr.v7i1.38484
10. Putra, R.N.: Implementation of Update Voter Data on Election of Riau in Bengkalis Regency, vol. 8, pp. 1–15 (2022)
11. Rahmiz, F., Yasin, H.M.: Tugas dan Wewenang Badan Pengawas Pemilihan Umum dalam Mengatasi Sengketa Pemilu Presiden dan Wakil Presiden. Al-Ishlah J. Ilm. Huk. **24**(1), 163–187 (2021). https://doi.org/10.56087/aijih.v24i1.55
12. Akbar, P., Pribadi, U., Purnomo, E.P.: Faktor-Faktor yang Mempengaruhi Kinerja Pegawai dalam Penerapan Sidalih di Komisi Pemilihan Umum Daerah Istimewa Yogyakarta. Analitika **12**(1), 1–9 (2020). https://doi.org/10.31289/analitika.v12i1.3350
13. Wulan Suri, E., Yuneva: Akselerasi Transformasi Digital Pada Tata Kelola Pemilu di Kota Bengkulu. Mimb. J. Penelit. Sos. dan Polit. **10**(2), 1–10 (2021)

14. Habibah, I.N., Safuan: Penggunaan Aplikasi Sistem Informasi Data Pemilih (SIDALIH) Berkelanjutan untuk Mewujudkan Daftar Pemilih yang Akurat dan Mutakhir, vol. 7, no. 2 (2022)
15. Akbar, P., Loilatu, M.J., Pribadi, U., Sudiar, S.: Implementation of artificial intelligence by the general elections commission in creating a credible voter list. In: IOP Conference Series: Earth and Environmental Science, vol. 717, no. 1 (2021). https://doi.org/10.1088/1755-1315/717/1/012017
16. Makuta, M., Kasim, N.M., Iljuw, L.M.: A voter list update model for the indonesian regional election. 06(1), 82–89 (2021)
17. Manoharan, A.P., Ingrams, A., Kang, D., Zhao, H.: Globalization and worldwide best practices in e-government. Int. J. Public Adm. 44(6), 465–476 (2021). https://doi.org/10.1080/01900692.2020.1729182
18. Pratama, M.S., Miftach, F., Ali, Y.: The cyber security strategy of general elections commission in facing the general election 2019. J. Prodi Perang Asimetris 4(3), 77–94 (2018)
19. Rachmawati, I.K., Handoko, Y., Nuryanti, F., Wulan, M., Hidayatullah, S.: Pengaruh Kemudahan, Kepercayaan Pelanggan dan Kualitas Informasi Terhadap Keputusan Pembelian Online. Semin. Nas. Sist. Inf. 3, 1617–1625 (2019)
20. Tulodo, B.A.R., Solichin, A.: Analisis Pengaruh Kualitas Sistem, Kualitas Informasi dan Perceived Usefulness terhadap Kepuasan Pengguna Aplikasi Care dalam Upaya Peningkatan Kinerja Karyawan (Studi Kasus PT. Malacca Trust Wuwungan Insurance, Tbk.). J. Ris. Manaj. Sains Indones. 10(1), 25–43 (2019)
21. Dewi, N.F., Ferdous Azam, S.M., Yusoff, S.K.M.: Factors influencing the information quality of local government financial statement and financial accountability. Manag. Sci. Lett. 9(9), 1373–1384 (2019). https://doi.org/10.5267/j.msl.2019.5.013
22. Rodríguez-Hidalgo, C., Rivera-Rogel, D., Romero-Rodríguez, L.M.: Information quality in Latin American digital native media: analysis based on structured dimensions and indicators. Media Commun. 8(2), 135–145 (2020). https://doi.org/10.17645/mac.v8i2.2657
23. Lee, S.W., Sung, H.J., Jeon, H.M.: Determinants of continuous intention on food delivery apps: extending UTAUT2 with information quality. Sustainability 11(11) (2019). https://doi.org/10.3390/su11113141
24. Mulyadi, A., Eka, D., Nailis, W.: Pengaruh Kepercayaan, Kemudahan, Dan Kualitas Informasi Terhadap Keputusan Pembelian Di Toko Online Lazada. Jembatan 15(2), 87–94 (2018). https://doi.org/10.29259/jmbt.v15i2.6656
25. Benuf, K., Mahmudah, S., Priyono, E.A.: Perlindungan Hukum Terhadap Keamanan Data Konsumen Financial Technology Di Indonesia. Refleks. Huk. J. Ilmu Huk. 3(2), 145–160 (2019). https://doi.org/10.24246/jrh.2019.v3.i2.p145-160
26. Iswandari, B.A.: Jaminan Atas Pemenuhan Hak Keamanan Data Pribadi Dalam Penyelenggaraan E-Government Guna Mewujudkan Good Governance. J. Huk. Ius Quia Iustum 28(1), 115–138 (2021). https://doi.org/10.20885/iustum.vol28.iss1.art6
27. Fauzi, A.M.: Pengembangan Integrasi Sidalih Antara Pilwali Surabaya dan Pilgub Jawa Timur: Optimalisasi Pelayanan Publik KPU Kota Surabaya. JPSI J. Public Sect. Innov. 3(1), 1–5 (2018)
28. Abdul Kadir, A.F.A., Yuliati, E., Effendi, R.: Implementation of digital transformation of voter data updating management using the Cianjur regency KPU's voter data information system application (SIDALIH). divers. J. Ilm. Pascasarj. 2(2) (2022). https://doi.org/10.32832/djip-uika.v2i2.5920

Towards Improving the Efficacy of Windows Security Notifier for Apps from Unknown Publishers: The Role of Rhetoric

Ankit Shrestha[✉], Rizu Paudel, Prakriti Dumaru,
and Mahdi Nasrullah Al-Ameen

Department of Computer Science, Utah State University, Logan, USA
{ankit.shrestha,rizu.paudel,prakriti.dumaru,mahdi.al-ameen}@usu.edu

Abstract. With over 1.4 billion users of Windows 10, it is the most widely used operating system in the world. In Windows, applications from unknown publishers are popular due to mass availability and ease of access. Installing such applications can lead to malware infection, including viruses and ransomware. Therefore, we explored the design of interventions to prevent the users from installing applications from unknown publishers. To this end, we conducted a lab study with nine participants to understand the perceptions and behavior of users toward the designed interventions. Then, we conducted an online study with 256 participants to evaluate the impact of reflection, contextualization, and persuasion used in the finalized interventions. In summary, our findings provide valuable insights into understanding the needs and expectations of the users for usable and effective interventions against applications from unknown publishers. Based on our findings, we provide guidelines for future research.

Keywords: Reflective Design · Contextualization · Persuasion · Security Warnings · Windows

1 Introduction

The prior study [68] on security warning points to the lack of comprehension, where technical jargons [4,68], and habituation [3,5,50,61] lead users to ignore a security notifier. In these contexts, little study, to date, focused on the Windows notifier presented to users while installing an application from an unknown publisher. However, installing such applications can lead to malware infection [25,26,68]. The Windows operating system accounts for over 76% of global desktop operating systems [54][1] with over 1.4 billion devices of Windows 10 alone[2]; we believe that it is high time to focus on improving the design of Windows security notifiers to help users with better comprehension and informed decision making.

---

[1] https://www.statista.com/statistics/218089/global-market-share-of-windows-7.
[2] https://news.microsoft.com/bythenumbers/en/windowsdevices.

A. Moallem (Ed.): HCII 2023, LNCS 14045, pp. 101–121, 2023.
https://doi.org/10.1007/978-3-031-35822-7_8

To address this challenge, we designed a security notifier where we leveraged reflective design [42] with multiple persuasion techniques, including ethos, pathos, and logos [12,15]. We then investigated the following research questions, where we evaluated the designed security notifier (treatment) and compared that with the existing one (control): (**RQ1**): *What are the user perceptions about the existing security notifier presented to them while installing an application from an unknown publisher?* (**RQ2**): *How can we help users better understand the security risks of ignoring such notifiers and making an informed decision in the process?*

To answer these questions, we conducted a lab and an online study in North America (USA and Canada). In the lab study, we conducted semi-structured interviews with nine participants. The findings from our lab study reveal the participants' perceptions towards the existing and the designed notifier. We further improved our designs based on the feedback from the lab study and evaluated the updated designs through an online study with 256 participants on Amazon Mechanical Turk (Mturk).

Our findings from the online study show that reflection with persuasion in security warnings can be helpful while supporting the users to understand and combat the risks associated with applications from unknown publishers. Overall, our study contributes to advancing the HCI and Security community's understanding of end users' needs and expectations in helping them make an informed decision while installing the application from an unknown publisher in the Windows operating system. We provide recommendations based on our findings, including moving towards more reflective and contextualized interventions in future designs.

2   Related Work

Prior research [3–5,48,50,68] showed that users often ignore security warnings due to lack of comprehension, past experiences without consequences, optimism bias and the habituation to the warning. However, a little study focused on the Windows notifier presented to users while installing an application from an unknown publisher. Installing such applications can lead to malware infection [25,26,68]. Moreover, with over 76% of the global market share, the Windows operating system is by large the most widely used desktop operating system. The mass availability of applications from unknown publishers in Windows situates its users in a vulnerable position where they may face malware infections from installing such applications. Our study focuses on improving this existing security notifier to address the users' behavior and motivations behind ignoring security warnings.

2.1   Lack of Comprehension

Prior literature showed that users need help understanding the security warnings [4]. The study of Sharek et al. [55] reported that users needed to learn to differentiate between fake and real internet popup warnings. The study of Sunshine et al.

[57] further reported that users struggled to understand the SSL warnings in the browsers as they lacked knowledge about the situation and the harm related to man-in-the-middle attacks. Prior works [21,70] have further reported that users struggle to understand the context of the warning, which leads to poor comprehension and risky behavior. Further, a set of literature [14,68,70] reported the use of technical jargon as one of the major factors leading to difficulty for users in understanding the security warnings. The study of Bravo-Lillo et al. [14] also reported that novice users need help understanding technical wordings even when they have heard about it. Therefore, our study avoids technical terms, like ransomware and malware, to create user-friendly notifiers.

2.2 Past Experience

Prior works point towards the non-consequential experience of ignoring warnings as a significant factor for ignoring the same or similar security warnings [50,61]. In cases of informing, warning, or notifying users about consequences through security notifiers, most of the users tend to disregard those security warnings passing on the same message when they do not face any negative consequences, which inevitably leads to habituation [3,5,48,61]. The study of Amran et al. [3] reported that the habituation mechanism becomes universal if there is no adverse effect when a user ignores security dialog. Moreover, habituation to frequent non-security related notifications does carry over to a one-time security warning [61]. Windows provides similar notifications for installing applications from both verified and unknown publishers, which may magnify habituation to the latter.

According to Brustoloni and Villamarin-Salomon [16], habituation occurs as users learn to avoid context-sensitive guidance (CSG). As a consequence, CSG's purpose is to prompt the user to provide them with appropriate background information in order to help them make better security decisions. Based on the latest investigation and assessments, polymorphic alerts and iterative design are a few methods used to enhance security warnings to overcome habituation [5,16]. Therefore, our study uses multiple variations of the warning, created in an iterative design process through user feedback (see Sect. 5).

2.3 Optimism Bias

Prior literature from psychology [63] showed that individuals routinely overestimate their abilities and underestimate the risk they face compared to others, termed optimism bias. The study of Cho et al. [18] reported that individuals display a strong optimistic bias about online privacy risks, judging themselves to be significantly less vulnerable than others to these risks. Further, people tend to believe that specific security software like antivirus would protect them from any security threats [50]. There is also a common misconception among the participants regarding malware having an instantly visible effect [50]. Users want to believe that they cannot be the target, assuming that they have nothing valuable on their computer [50]. The study of Wu et al. [65] also reported that users ignored the warnings when they believed the web content seemed legitimate. Therefore, our study considers optimism bias as one of the primary reasons why users ignore security warnings.

3   Design Principles

Prior works [21,34,48,65] found that users routinely ignore contextual warnings – such as banners or pop-ups. However, they notice interstitial interventions that interrupt their primary task. Therefore, we design and study multiple variations of interstitial interventions. These interventions start by shifting the primary task of the users from installing an application to self-reflection, where they are urged to reflect and understand why they want to ignore the warning (see Sect. 3.1). We then contextualize the information presented by the notifier where we focus on challenging the user's particular reason for ignoring the notifier (see Sect. 3.2). Finally, we leverage persuasion methods to present the contextualized information to motivate the users to avoid installing applications from unknown publishers (see Sect. 3.3).

3.1   Reflection on Rationales

Reflection refers to people's self examination of their own actions, understanding, and monitoring of progress [42]. Reflective designs have shown to promote conscious thought and decision making and help the users take a moment to realize their actions [23,40–42]. Moreover, prior literature [6,29,38,47] from psychology, marketing and human computer interaction showed that reflective designs are useful in increasing engagement and thoughtful decision making. Therefore, we translate and deploy reflective design in this study where users are urged to reflect on their own potential actions and understand their rationales behind it. To achieve that, we use the reasons behind ignoring security warnings (see Sect. 2) to create the reflective design (see the central interface in Fig. 2). In the reflective design, we intervene the task of installing the application from an unknown publisher and ask them to identify their reason for ignoring the notifier.

3.2   Contextualization

Contextualization in design is the process of understanding the underlying context, rationale or intention (e.g., why do users ignore security warnings?) and designing the required artifact based on the identified context [28,66]. Works [7,8,24,45] from education and human computer interaction used contextualization in designing education content and web warnings respectively. The findings from these studies points towards the importance of contextualizing the information provided to the users. Further, prior literature [31,37,50] showed that users ignore warnings that provide generic information which they perceive as distant harm. Studies from psychology [49,60] suggest conveying negative impacts as it is more effective than citing advantages. Studies from Xu et al. [67], and Kaiser et al. [34] also showed that the conveyance of specific harm to the users is an effective deterrent in convincing them to avoid risky activities. Therefore, we use the rationale selected by the users in our reflective intervention to contextualize the information in our warnings.

3.3 Persuasion Modes

We contextualized the harm based on their rationale for ignoring the warning. However, prior works pointed to the benefits of persuasion in order to motivate users to comply with the warnings [33,52]. The objective of the warning is not only to inform but also to persuade users to avoid risky activities without hindering their freedom of choice [33]. Hence, we use Aristotle's Rhetoric [15] (ethos, pathos, logos) to illustrate the contextualized harm to persuade users to avoid installing applications from unknown publishers. Ethos is persuasion using authority or credibility of character [15]. Pathos is an appeal to emotion of the user [15]. Logos is an appeal to logic by using statistics, facts, and figures [15]. Prior works [12,19,30,39] from psychology and political science used Aristotle's Rhetoric to understand persuasive communication. In our study, we use these rhetorics to persuade the users by appealing to authority, emotion or logic.

4 Lab Study Methodology

We used the existing Windows notifier as the control condition (see Fig. 1). We then created warning designs (see Fig. 2) adapting design recommendations from prior literature [12,39,42,46,48,49,60] which we call treatment condition. Using these designs, we conducted the lab study.

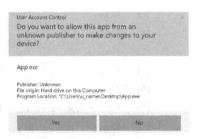

In the lab study, we conducted semi-structured interviews (see Sect. 4.1) with nine participants online through Zoom/Skype between March and April 2021. The participants for the study were recruited using snowball sampling via email. A participant had to be at least 18 years old to participate in this study. Details of the participants are available in Table 1. The Institutional Review Board approved the study at our university.

Fig. 1. Control condition for both lab and online study

4.1 Study Procedure

When a participant showed interest in participating in our study, we emailed them the informed consent document (ICD). Once they agreed to the ICD, we scheduled an online interview through Zoom or Skype. In the interview, the participants were presented with the same scenario for the control and treatment conditions in which the notifier occurred. Then, the participant interacted with the notifier and answered interview questions focused on understanding their perceptions and behavior. At the end of the interview, the participants were asked to complete a demographics survey. After completing the interview, each participant was sent an email thanking them for participating in this study.

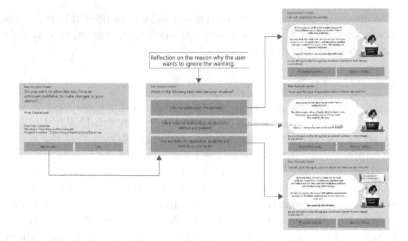

Fig. 2. Treatment condition and the flow of interaction in the lab study. (The flow is the same in online study.)

Table 1. Demographic Information of the Lab Study Participants

PID	Gender	Age Range	Education
P1	Male	18–24 years old	Graduate Degree
P2	Male	30–34 years old	Graduate Degree
P3	Female	25–29 years old	Graduate Degree
P4	Female	25–29 years old	Four-year College Degree
P5	Male	25–29 years old	Four-year College Degree
P6	Prefer not to answer	18–24 years old	Four-year College Degree
P7	Male	25–29 years old	Graduate Degree
P8	Female	25–29 years old	Four-year College Degree
P9	Female	18–24 years old	Two-year College Degree

4.2 Analysis

The audio recordings from the interview were transcribed. Then, we performed thematic analysis on our transcriptions [9,11,13,56]. Two independent researchers coded each transcript, where they read through the transcripts of the first few interviews, developed codes, compared them, and then iterated again until we had developed a consistent codebook. After the codebook was finalized, two researchers independently coded the remaining interviews. Both researchers spot-checked the other's coded transcripts and found no inconsistencies. Finally, we organized and taxonomized our codes into higher-level categories.

5   Design Evolution

In this section, we will present the qualitative feedback from the participants on our designs and the changes we have made to address the issues raised by

Fig. 3. Logos treatment condition in the online study

them. For consistency, we use these terms throughout the manuscript based on the frequency of comments in participants' responses: *a few* (0–10%), *several* (10–25%), *some* (25–40%), *about half* (40–60%), *most* (60–80%), and *almost all* (80–100%).

In the lab study, most participants reported that the control condition (see Fig. 1) needed to be more specific and clear as the notifier was unable to provide sufficient context for them to make an informed decision. In contrast, they found the treatment condition (see Fig. 2) to be informative; one of them stated, *"This [treatment] version of notifier was really like something that I was looking forward to that really solved my problem that I was facing in the previous notifier with clearly identifying what might be the issue that you are facing or what might be the consequences of you trying to access this [application from unknown publisher]."* *(P7)*.

Our participants also reported satisfaction with the presentation of options that account for the reasons behind a user's intention to ignore a warning. One of them mentioned, *"It also showed options that I don't understand this warning, or that I have already used this application before ... so that I know beforehand that, these are certain things that I will have to keep in mind when I try to access this application, ... so I can use this application fully prepared."* *(P4)*. The effectiveness of the thought-provoking questions can be attributed to the reflective design that we discussed in Sect. 3. This motivated us to retain the reflective design in our interventions for the online study.

However, the persuasion-based designs also needed improvements as presented below which we addressed through focus group discussions between the authors.

5.1 Inducing Focus

For the designs used in our lab study, we combined the three rhetorics for the treatment condition, which resulted in increased information (see Fig. 2). Some participants in the lab study found the amount of text and information in the treatment condition overwhelming. One of them reported, *"... it [treatment condition] was more clustered than I wanted to. There are certain points that are highlighted, but I would also suggest that it be more visual than more textual. So just by looking at it, we can understand that there are certain issues there that we might come across."* *(P1)*. Therefore, to reduce the cognitive burden

Fig. 4. Pathos treatment condition in the online study

Fig. 5. Ethos treatment condition in the online study

[36,58,59], we focused on creating multiple variations of the designs focused on a particular rhetoric (see Fig. 3, 4, and 5). Moreover, as the amount of information was reduced with increased focus, we could replace texts in the design with graphical components. These changes were also motivated by prior works [25,27,43,44], which use graphics to increase perception speed and memorability of the information.

5.2   Design Identity

In the lab study, some participants found it challenging to differentiate the designs for the three reflective options (scenarios). One of them reported, *"... the three instructions were on a similar fashion. Only on the bubble of the computer representative in the instruction was changed. So, what I could suggest is you have three instructions on like different graphical format or different visual format, so that they can be separated distinctly." (P1).* To help participants avoid mistaking the different designs as the same, we imbued each design with different graphics to create their identity. Since graphics are more memorable and perceived faster [43,44], we believed the changes would help the participants identify the designs for the different options.

5.3   Overcoming Experience Bias

A few of our participants reported on their experiences installing applications from unknown publishers where they faced no problems and argued against the warning we had presented. They mentioned that there are many applications from unknown publishers that are from unverified publishers. In such cases, the notification occurs, but it is not always an infected software. To overcome this

Table 2. Demographic Information of the Participants in the Online Study (N = Number of Participants)

Demographic	Demographic Group	N			
			Race	White	183
Gender	Male	146		Asian	50
	Female	109		Black/African American	6
	Prefer not to answer	1		Hispanic or Latino	5
Age range	18-24 years old	4		Native American	4
	25–29 years old	64		Mixed Race	6
	30–34 years old	36		Prefer not to answer	2
	35–39 years old	58	Education	High School Graduate	35
	40–44 years old	40		Two-year College Degree	17
	45–49 years old	15		Four-year College Degree	157
	50–54 years old	18		Graduate degree	44
	55–59 years old	7		Prefer not to answer	2
	60–64 years old	8		Other	1
	Above 65 years old	4	Major	Computer-Related Major	101
	Prefer not to answer	2		Non-Computed Related Major	146
				Prefer not to answer	9

bias based on the user's experience, we changed the sentiment of the design to convey that not having problems before does not mean there will be no problems this time. We also provided scenarios depicting the severe consequences when one might face problems to dissuade the users from avoiding the warning. Prior works [34,67] have also shown that conveying relevant adverse harm can effectively deter users from risky activities.

6   Online Study Methodology

We changed the treatment conditions' design based on the lab study findings (see Sect. 5). Then, we used them in an online study conducted through Amazon Mechanical Turk (MTurk) with 256 participants. We created our system for data collection, as we had multiple variations of interactive designs, which were not feasible for existing survey systems. We selected the widely used User Experience Questionnaire plus (UEQ+) scale[3] [51] to understand the user experience and the effectiveness of the warnings. We presented the questions in random order in the survey, with some reversed to avoid bias [20,64]. Additionally, we used nine attention-check questions in random order, following procedures suggested by prior works [32,35].

6.1   Participant Recruitment

We recruited participants using Amazon Mechanical Turk (Mturk). While imperfect, MTurk can provide data of at least the same quality as methods tradition-

---

[3] https://www.ueq-online.org/.

ally used in research, as long as the experiment is designed carefully [10,17]. Participants had to be 18 or older and live in the United States or Canada to participate in our study. We compensated the participants with USD 2.5 for the study, which took approximately 15 min, even if they failed the attention check questions. In our analysis, we only used responses from the participants who correctly answered all nine of our attention check questions. The summary of the participants' demographics is available in Table 2.

6.2 Procedure

Participants interested in our study would first accept the task in Mturk and review the ICD provided in the survey. Clicking the link to our online study system meant that the participants agreed to the ICD. The participants were greeted with information about the survey in our system. Then, the participants interacted with one of the four conditions (Control, Ethos, Pathos, and Logos). Moreover, the three treatment conditions had designs for the reflective rationales that the users could select. A survey including open-ended questions followed each design. Finally, the participants answered questions about their demographics and prior knowledge about applications from unknown publishers. At the end of the study, we provided the participants with a seven-digit code, which they entered into the Mturk Survey to complete the study.

6.3 Analysis

We use statistical tests to analyze our quantitative results. We consider results to be significant when we find $p < .05$, but further highlight results with lower p values. When comparing two conditions, we use a Wilcoxon signed rank test for the matched pairs of subjects and a Wilcoxon Mann-Whitney test for unpaired results. Wilcoxon tests are similar to t-tests but do not assume the distributions of the compared samples, which is appropriate for our collected data.

For the qualitative results from the open-ended questions, we performed thematic analysis, where two independent researchers coded the responses and later discussed and resolved the discrepancies in the codes.

7   Online Study

After making changes based on the suggestions from the lab study, we created a survey system to conduct an online study in Amazon Mechanical Turk (see Sect. 4). Each user was either provided with the control condition (see Fig. 1) or one of the three treatment conditions (see Fig. 3, 4, and 5). The three scenarios (see Sect. 4) in treatment conditions were presented randomly to mitigate order effects. We observed that the randomization was successful, as there is a lack of significant order effects between the three conditions (see Table 3).

Table 3. Order effects between the different scenarios of treatment condition

Scenarios		Wilcoxon-Signed Rank Test	
First	Second	W	p
Understanding	Experience	1430829.0	0.137
Understanding	Optimism	444029.0	0.404
Experience	Optimism	446506.5	0.959

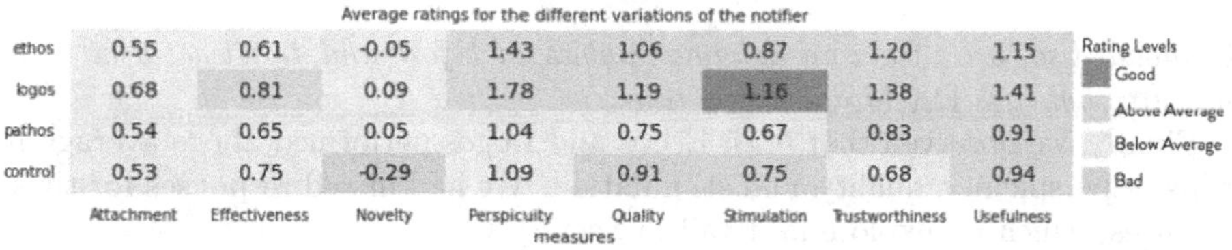

Average ratings for the different variations of the notifier

	Attachment	Effectiveness	Novelty	Perspicuity	Quality	Stimulation	Trustworthiness	Usefulness
ethos	0.55	0.61	-0.05	1.43	1.06	0.87	1.20	1.15
logos	0.68	0.81	0.09	1.78	1.19	1.16	1.38	1.41
pathos	0.54	0.65	0.05	1.04	0.75	0.67	0.83	0.91
control	0.53	0.75	-0.29	1.09	0.91	0.75	0.68	0.94

Rating Levels: Good, Above Average, Below Average, Bad

measures

Fig. 6. Average ratings for different notifier variations

7.1   User Ratings: Sensemaking in the Context of Warning Design

Figure 6 provides the average scores along with UEQ recommended category (color-coded) for all the 24 variations of the warnings we have used in the online study.

In light of the UEQ benchmark[4], we observed that all the warnings had above-average scores for usefulness. That implies most users consider it important to be notified about applications from unknown publishers. One of the participants reported, *"This alert is useful when you want to ensure the security of your PC and avoid accidental changes to important settings."* However, only Logos was rated above average in terms of effectiveness. The high scores in the effectiveness measure may be due to the factual information presented in Logos, which some participants reported as their primary reason for liking the warning. One of them said, *"I like that it provides information about the number of attacks that have happened, and it makes me really think if it is worth it to download the app."*

We also observed that all treatment condition warnings were considered above average in trustworthiness whereas the control condition was not. Most participants preferred the contextualized information about the application (see Sect. 3), which increased their trust in the warning. Further, the reflective nature of the treatment condition (see Sect. 3) helped increase the users' trust in the warning. Most participants liked the specific scenarios addressed by the warning to persuade them to avoid installing the application. One of them mentioned, *"I like the fact that the notifier will tell you exactly some of the issues you will experience if the unknown publisher has a virus that will infect your system later."* Similarly, the participants reported on particular scenarios and how the treatment condition works, convincing them to avoid the application installation. One of them said, *"It addresses a common misconception that if you have*

---

[4] https://www.ueq-online.org/Material/Handbook.pdf.

P-values of significance test between rhetoric-based treatment conditions and control condition

	Attachment	Effectiveness	Novelty	Perspicuity	Quality	Stimulation	Trustworthiness	Usefulness
ethos	.718 (E)	.284 (C)	.125 (E)	.053 (E)	.423 (E)	.739 (E)	.007 (E)	.533 (E)
logos	.346 (L)	.576 (L)	.030 (L)	<.001 (L)	.072 (L)	.025 (L)	<.001 (L)	.018 (L)
pathos	.990 (P)	.419 (C)	.032 (P)	.755 (C)	.111 (C)	.451 (C)	.550 (P)	.451 (C)

Significance level: Not Significant, $p < 0.05$, $p < 0.01$, $p < 0.001$

Larger rating for: (C) Control, (L) Logos, (P) Pathos, (E) Ethos

Fig. 7. P-values from the significance tests between the control condition and variations of treatment condition

downloaded software from an unknown publisher before and didn't get a virus or malware that it is OK to do so this time."

Finally, we observed that both Ethos and Logos performed above average in terms of perspicuity, quality, and stimulation. We had mixed responses for these measures, which we explore in detail in Sect. 7.3.

7.2 Control vs. Treatment Conditions

As we discussed the average ratings of the warnings, next, we compared the three variations of our treatment condition with the control condition (see Fig. 7). We observed that Logos and Ethos performed significantly better than the Control in terms of trustworthiness. That could be due to the factual nature of Logos and the portrayal of a credible source in Ethos, which are both lacking in the control condition [12,19,30,39]. Some of our participants also mentioned these traits of the designs; where one of the participants talking about Ethos reported, "I like how it seems credible based on the name tag next to the man."

The added useful information and the thought-provoking nature of the warnings mentioned by some of our participants could have resulted in significantly higher scores in perspicuity, stimulation, and usefulness for Logos. One participant, when mentioning Logos, said, "It's relevant and timely: The user's behavior, location, or preference triggers the notification. It's personal: The content of the push appeals to the user as an individual. It's actionable: The push makes it clear what the user should do next."

7.3 Comparison Between the Treatment Conditions

We compared the three variations of the treatment conditions with each other (see Fig. 8). We observed that Logos performed significantly better than Pathos

P-values of significance test between the different rhetoric-based treatment conditions

	Attachment	Effectiveness	Novelty	Perspicuity	Quality	Stimulation	Trustworthiness	Usefulness
Logos vs Ethos	.317 (L)	.040 (L)	.285 (L)	.003 (L)	.207 (L)	.002 (L)	.082 (L)	.005 (L)
Logos vs Pathos	.145 (L)	.073 (L)	.780 (L)	<.001 (L)	<.001 (L)	<.001 (L)	<.001 (L)	<.001 (L)
Pathos vs Ethos	.571 (E)	.583 (P)	.388 (P)	.001 (E)	.002 (E)	.090 (E)	.001 (E)	.038 (E)

Significance level: Not Significant, $p < 0.05$, $p < 0.01$, $p < 0.001$

Larger rating for: (L) Logos, (P) Pathos, (E) Ethos

Fig. 8. P-values from the significance tests between different variations of treatment condition

		P values of significance test for scenario 1: lack of understanding							
Logos vs. Ethos	.513 (L)	.195 (L)	.859 (L)	.298 (L)	.921 (L)	.254 (L)	.260 (L)	.270 (L)	Significance level
Logos vs. Pathos	.620 (L)	.112 (L)	.950 (P)	<.001 (L)	.014 (L)	.008 (L)	<.001 (L)	.004 (L)	Not Significant / p < 0.05
Pathos vs. Ethos	.846 (P)	.992 (E)	.893 (P)	.019 (E)	.013 (E)	.094 (E)	.025 (E)	.058 (E)	p < 0.01
	Attachment	Effectiveness	Novelty	Perspicuity	Quality	Stimulation	Trustworthiness	Usefulness	p < 0.001
				measure					

Fig. 9. P-values from the significance tests between different rhetoric used in scenario 1 of treatment condition

and Ethos in terms of perspicuity, stimulation, and usefulness. Qualitative responses from about half of the participants indicate that they liked the factual information presented in Logos, which immediately motivated them to avoid the warning. One of them said, *"This notice is very clear that there is a serious issue with this app. If these stats are true then I would never download something like this."*

Further, Logos was rated significantly higher than Pathos for information quality and trustworthiness. As we discussed above, participants found the factual information in Logos helpful which could have also increased their perceptions of trustworthiness and quality of information. Similarly, Ethos was also rated significantly higher than Pathos for information quality and trustworthiness. Ethos uses credible and authoritative sources to provide relevant information to the users. Some users reported that such a delivery helped them make an informed decision. One of them reported. *"That [security expert] gives me specific information 'unknown publisher' so if I know the publisher and feel comfortable I can feel safe to install it."*

7.4 Scenario-Based Evaluation: Rhetoric Behind the Interventions

In this section, we focus on each of the three scenarios we addressed as part of our reflective design and understand the rhetoric that can be useful for these scenarios.

Scenario I: Lack of Comprehension. Figure 9 summarizes the significance tests performed between the persuasion principles for scenario 1.

In this scenario where users did not understand the warning, we observed that both Logos and Ethos performed significantly better than Pathos regarding perspicuity, information quality, and trustworthiness. Comments from some of our participants revealed that they liked the easy-to-comprehend Logos and Ethos warnings. One of them said, *"It warns you in a clear and concise way what could happen by installing unknown apps and programs. It is also easy to read, and the colors are easy on the eyes."* Moreover, participants found the idea of helping the users by first understanding their level of knowledge preferable which could have resulted in higher scores for information quality and trustworthiness. One of them said, *"I like that it goes in-depth about what it means only after you said you don't understand. Good for people who aren't familiar with technology that much."*

P values of significance test for scenario 2: past experience

	Attachment	Effectiveness	Novelty	Perspicuity	Quality	Stimulation	Trustworthiness	Usefulness	
Logos vs. Ethos	.469 (L)	.723 (L)	.467 (L)	.038 (L)	.367 (L)	.101 (L)	.341 (L)	.120 (L)	Significance level
Logos vs. Pathos	.233 (L)	.761 (L)	.942 (P)	<.001 (L)	.068 (L)	.008 (L)	.007 (L)	.028 (L)	Not Significant / p < 0.05
Pathos vs. Ethos	.620 (E)	.944 (P)	.370 (P)	.041 (E)	.377 (E)	.221 (E)	.068 (E)	.500 (E)	p < 0.01 / p < 0.001

Fig. 10. P-values from the significance tests between different rhetoric used in scenario 2 of treatment condition

On the other hand, some participants found the storytelling in Pathos challenging to understand. One of them said, *"I like that it is trying to be fun and interesting, it just isn't very understandable because of it. I also like the colors and pictures used."* However, some participants thought Pathos was playful and exciting. One of them said, *"I like the way the images look, I also like it shows the hacker guy, and then you having your files locked so kind of hits harder and just like the look. Also, it tells you what could happen, like one of the worst cases of what could happen but does it in a way that's more playful"*

In conclusion, for the scenario, both Logos and Ethos performed significantly better than Pathos and should be considered in future designs to increase the understanding of the users.

Scenario II: Past Experience. In the second scenario of the user's past experience, we observed that Logos performed significantly better than Pathos in terms of stimulation, trustworthiness, and usefulness (see Fig. 10). Some participants found Logos to be thought-provoking considering how it challenges our primary task to understand and decide in an informed manner. One of them said, *"I feel like sometimes we get too busy to care about things and just accept whatever notifications when we are for instance trying to install a video game and our friends are waiting on us to complete the install. This actually happened just last night."* Some participants found the facts and statistics helpful, whereas a few found the graphics in Logos, particularly representative. One of them reported, *"I like the detailed pictorial representation in the notifier. I like it because it clearly indicates the possibility of an app not being safe even if it has been previously tested to be safe due to a past user experience."*

Moreover, Logos performed significantly better than both Pathos and Ethos in terms of perspicuity, where some participants mentioned the ease of understanding the logical reasoning provided in the Logos. In conclusion, for scenario II, Logos performed the best, but there was a significant difference between Logos and Ethos in only one measure.

Scenario III: Optimism Bias. In the final scenario of optimism bias, we observed that Logos performed significantly better than both Pathos and Ethos in terms of Perspicuity, Stimulation and Usefulness (see Fig. 11). Qualitative responses revealed that some participants found the image used in the Logos design interesting, which could have resulted in higher scores for stimulation.

P values of significance test for scenario 3: optimism bias

	Attachment	Effectiveness	Novelty	Perspicuity	Quality	Stimulation	Trustworthiness	Usefulness	Significance level
Logos vs. Ethos	.710 (L)	.062 (L)	.374 (L)	.042 (L)	.268 (L)	.011 (L)	.420 (L)	.040 (L)	Not Significant
Logos vs. Pathos	.395 (L)	.234 (L)	.679 (L)	.001 (L)	.002 (L)	.006 (L)	.023 (L)	.005 (L)	$p < 0.05$
Pathos vs. Ethos	.547 (E)	.263 (P)	.613 (P)	.192 (E)	.049 (E)	.950 (E)	.102 (E)	.299 (E)	$p < 0.01$
				measure					$p < 0.001$

Fig. 11. P-values from the significance tests between different rhetoric used in scenario 3 of treatment condition

P value for significant difference in ratings based on various factors

	Attachment	Effectiveness	Novelty	Perspicuity	Quality	Stimulation	Trustworthiness	Usefulness	Significance level
understanding	.007 (+)	.001 (+)	.394 (+)	<.001 (+)	<.001 (+)	.010 (+)	<.001 (+)	<.001 (+)	Not Significant
consequences	.002 (+)	<.001 (+)	.485 (-)	<.001 (+)	<.001 (+)	.001 (+)	<.001 (+)	<.001 (+)	$p < 0.05$ / $p < 0.01$
knowledge	<.001 (+)	<.001 (+)	.671 (+)	<.001 (+)	<.001 (+)	.025 (+)	<.001 (+)	<.001 (+)	$p < 0.001$
Seen Notifier	.123 (X)	.864 (X)	.237 (X)	.094 (Y)	.790 (X)	.941 (X)	.763 (X)	.962 (X)	Larger rating for: (+) >= mean (-) < mean
Gender	.514 (W)	.815 (M)	.114 (W)	.233 (M)	.871 (W)	.007 (W)	.526 (W)	.090 (W)	(S) Seen (X) Not Seen
Age	.025 (Y)	.220 (Y)	.106 (O)	.100 (Y)	.018 (Y)	.003 (Y)	.034 (Y)	.009 (Y)	(M) Man (W) Woman
Education	.996 (H)	.002 (L)	.030 (L)	<.001 (L)	.045 (L)	.090 (H)	.090 (L)	.676 (H)	(Y) Young (O) Old
Major	.910 (C)	.806 (C)	.078 (N)	.171 (C)	.230 (C)	<.001 (C)	.448 (C)	.031 (C)	(H) Highly ed. (L) Low ed.
				measure					(C) Computer (N) Non-computer

Fig. 12. P-values of significance tests showing the impact of various factors on the ratings of the warnings

One of them reported, *"Best thing is the image of the screen peeling back to reveal a possible ransomware warning. I like how you still have the choice to proceed or not though."* While about half of the participants found the logical reasoning easy to understand, some participants also expressed that the warning addressed the optimism bias appropriately making it useful. One of them said, *"I think the good thing is that it makes you think, it makes you question whether it is worth it to download the app. It gives you facts, and then states you could be one of them, because I think people believe things happen to other people, not to themselves."*

7.5 Impact of User Demographics on Warning Perceptions

We observed that the user demographics had varying impacts on the warning ratings (see Fig. 12). The ratings for the warnings are significantly higher for all measures except novelty for participants with a higher understanding and knowledge about the applications from unknown publishers. We further observed that there is no significant difference in ratings between the users who have seen the existing Windows notifier and the users who have not.

Moreover, female participants rated the warnings significantly higher than their male counterparts in terms of stimulation. Younger participants (18–39) rated the warnings significantly higher than older participants (older than 39) regarding attachment, information quality, stimulation, trustworthiness, and usefulness. In addition, less-educated participants (high school or less) rated the warnings significantly higher than highly-educated participants (2-year college degree or more) in effectiveness, novelty, perspicuity, and information quality.

Similarly, participants with computing backgrounds rated the warnings significantly higher regarding stimulation and usefulness. These findings imply that certain groups of participants may benefit more from the use of persuasion-based interventions.

8 Discussion

Our findings report on the perceptions of the users towards applications from unknown publishers and the effectiveness of the reflective rhetoric-based notifiers against them. In this section, we discuss the possible implications of our findings and provide suggestions to consider in future designs.

8.1 Moving Towards Reflective Design

Prior literature [22,69] reported the behavior and perceptions of users towards security warnings where they consider it the secondary task. In our study, the user is also primarily motivated to install the application from an unknown publisher. However, dealing with security warnings becomes a secondary task. Therefore, reflection is an essential step in the design of security warnings that intervenes the users to take a moment to identify their rationale in doing a risky activity. Our findings show that the use of reflective designs can be a practical approach in convincing users to avoid installing applications from unknown publishers (see Sect. 7.1 and 5). However, few works in computer science have used reflective designs that first aim to understand the context of the users and then present information based on the identified context. Our work provides the direction for future works to adopt and evaluate the reflective designs in various security warnings and beyond the scope of such interventions.

8.2 Addressing Habituation

Our findings highlight the importance of contextualizing the warning where participants appreciated addressing their selected rationale for installing applications from unknown publishers (see Sect. 7.4). In our designs, the contextualization of information and persuasion modes (see Sect. 3) have further resulted in polymorphic warnings. The study of Vance et al. [62] reported habituation as a significant inhibitor to the effectiveness of security warnings. However, prior works [5,16] showed that the use of polymorphic warnings could prevent habituation in the long term. Moreover, our findings show a significant impact of users' understanding of the applications from unknown publishers on the performance of the interventions (see Sect. 7.5). Therefore, understanding the reason behind the user's tendency to do a risky activity should be considered an important context in designing future security warnings. By doing that, we can address specific issues that the users face while simultaneously avoiding habituation.

8.3   Limitations and Future Work

Our study was limited to participants from the U.S. and Canada. However, recent HCI studies [1,2,53] highlight the importance of looking beyond Western contexts. Hence, future works should include participants from diverse regions to understand their perceptions and create effective interventions.

In our lab study, we interviewed nine participants by following widely-used methods for qualitative research [9,11,13,56]. We acknowledge the limitations of these studies, that a different set of samples might yield varying results. Thus, we do not draw any quantitative, generalizable conclusion from the lab study. Instead, we conduct an online study with sufficient statistical power, leveraging the findings from the lab study to reach generalizable results.

Our study focuses on a single security intervention, whereas further work is needed to understand the validity of the results for different warnings and designs. As we continuously improve designs in future iterations, we should move from just informing the user to promoting reflection where we can motivate and help them in context.

References

1. Al-Ameen, M.N., Kocabas, H.: "i cannot do anything": user's behavior and protection strategy upon losing, or identifying unauthorized access to online account. In: Symposium on Usable Privacy and Security (Poster Session) (2020)
2. Al-Ameen, M.N., Kocabas, H., Nandy, S., Tamanna, T.: We, three brothers have always known everything of each other: a cross-cultural study of sharing digital devices and online accounts. Proc. Priv. Enhancing Technol. **2021**(4), 203–224 (2021)
3. Amran, A., Zaaba, Z.F., Mahinderjit Singh, M.K.: Habituation effects in computer security warning. Inf. Secur. J. Glob. Perspect. **27**(4), 192–204 (2018)
4. Amran, A., Zaaba, Z.F., Singh, M.M., Marashdih, A.W.: Usable security: revealing end-users comprehensions on security warnings. Procedia Comput. Sci. **124**, 624–631 (2017)
5. Anderson, B.B., Kirwan, C.B., Jenkins, J.L., Eargle, D., Howard, S., Vance, A.: How polymorphic warnings reduce habituation in the brain: insights from an FMRI study. In: Proceedings of the 33rd Annual ACM Conference on Human Factors in Computing Systems, pp. 2883–2892 (2015)
6. Baek, E., Choo, H.J., Wei, X., Yoon, S.Y.: Understanding the virtual tours of retail stores: how can store brand experience promote visit intentions? Int. J. Retail Distrib. Manage. (2020)
7. Bartsch, S., Volkamer, M.: Towards the systematic development of contextualized security interventions1. In: The 26th BCS Conference on Human Computer Interaction, vol. 26, pp. 1–4 (2012)
8. Bartsch, S., Volkamer, M., Theuerling, H., Karayumak, F.: Contextualized web warnings, and how they cause distrust. In: Huth, M., Asokan, N., Čapkun, S., Flechais, I., Coles-Kemp, L. (eds.) Trust 2013. LNCS, vol. 7904, pp. 205–222. Springer, Heidelberg (2013). https://doi.org/10.1007/978-3-642-38908-5_16
9. Baxter, K., Courage, C., Caine, K.: Understanding Your Users: A Practical Guide to User Research Methods, 2nd edn. Morgan Kaufmann Publishers Inc., San Francisco (2015)

10. Berinsky, A.J., Huber, G.A., Lenz, G.S.: Evaluating online labor markets for experimental research: Amazon. com's mechanical Turk. Polit. Anal. **20**(3), 351–368 (2012)
11. Boyatzis, R.E.: Transforming Qualitative Information: Thematic Analysis and Code Development. Sage Publications, Thousand Oaks (1998)
12. Braet, A.C.: Ethos, pathos and logos in Aristotle's rhetoric: a re-examination. Argumentation **6**(3), 307–320 (1992)
13. Braun, V., Clarke, V.. Using thematic analysis in psychology. Qual. Res. Psychol. **3**(2), 77–101 (2006)
14. Bravo-Lillo, C., Cranor, L.F., Downs, J., Komanduri, S.: Bridging the gap in computer security warnings: a mental model approach. IEEE Secur. Priv. **9**(2), 18–26 (2010)
15. Brinks, M.: Ethos, pathos, logos, Kairos: the modes of persuasion and how to use them. Prep Scholar (2019). Accessed 20 Aug 2021
16. Brustoloni, J.C., Villamarín-Salomón, R.: Improving security decisions with polymorphic and audited dialogs. In: Proceedings of the 3rd Symposium on Usable Privacy and Security, pp. 76–85 (2007)
17. Buhrmester, M., Kwang, T., Gosling, S.D.: Amazon's mechanical Turk: a new source of inexpensive, yet high-quality data? (2016)
18. Cho, H., Lee, J.S., Chung, S.: Optimistic bias about online privacy risks: testing the moderating effects of perceived controllability and prior experience. Comput. Hum. Behav. **26**(5), 987–995 (2010)
19. Demirdöğen, Ü.D.: The roots of research in (political) persuasion: ethos, pathos, logos and the Yale studies of persuasive communications. Int. J. Soc. Inquiry **3**(1), 189–201 (2010)
20. DeSimone, J.A., Harms, P.D., DeSimone, A.J.: Best practice recommendations for data screening. J. Organ. Behav. **36**(2), 171–181 (2015)
21. Egelman, S., Cranor, L.F., Hong, J.: You've been warned: an empirical study of the effectiveness of web browser phishing warnings. In: Proceedings of the SIGCHI Conference on Human Factors in Computing Systems, pp. 1065–1074 (2008)
22. Egelman, S., Schechter, S.: The importance of being earnest [in security warnings]. In: Sadeghi, A.-R. (ed.) FC 2013. LNCS, vol. 7859, pp. 52–59. Springer, Heidelberg (2013). https://doi.org/10.1007/978-3-642-39884-1_5
23. Fang, Y.M., Chen, K.M., Huang, Y.J.: Emotional reactions of different interface formats: comparing digital and traditional board games. Adv. Mech. Eng. **8**(3), 1687814016641902 (2016)
24. Fernandes, P., Leite, C., Mouraz, A., Figueiredo, C.: Curricular contextualization: tracking the meanings of a concept. Asia Pac. Educ. Res. **22**, 417–425 (2013)
25. Good, N., et al.: Stopping spyware at the gate: a user study of privacy, notice and spyware. In: Proceedings of the 2005 Symposium on Usable Privacy and Security, pp. 43–52 (2005)
26. Good, N., Grossklags, J., Thaw, D., Perzanowski, A., Mulligan, D.K., Konstan, J.: User choices and regret: understanding users' decision process about consensually acquired spyware. I/S J. Law Policy Inf. Soc. **2**(2), 283–344 (2006)
27. Good, N.S., Grossklags, J., Mulligan, D.K., Konstan, J.A.: Noticing notice: a large-scale experiment on the timing of software license agreements. In: Proceedings of the SIGCHI Conference on Human Factors in Computing Systems, pp. 607–616 (2007)
28. Haleblian, K.: The problem of contextualization. Missiology **11**(1), 95–111 (1983)

29. Heidig, S., Müller, J., Reichelt, M.: Emotional design in multimedia learning: differentiation on relevant design features and their effects on emotions and learning. Comput. Hum. Behav. **44**, 81–95 (2015)
30. Higgins, C., Walker, R.: Ethos, logos, pathos: strategies of persuasion in social/environmental reports. In: Accounting Forum, vol. 36, pp. 194–208. Elsevier (2012)
31. Hora, A., Anquetil, N., Ducasse, S., Allier, S.: Domain specific warnings: are they any better? In: 2012 28th IEEE International Conference on Software Maintenance (ICSM), pp. 441–450. IEEE (2012)
32. Ipeirotis, P.G., Provost, F., Wang, J.: Quality management on amazon mechanical Turk. In: Proceedings of the ACM SIGKDD Workshop on Human Computation, pp. 64–67 (2010)
33. Jones, C.P., Robinson, S.J., Sabadosh, N., Bishop, D., Koyani, S.: How can rhetoric and argumentation help us make the case for UCD? In: CHI 2006 Extended Abstracts on Human Factors in Computing Systems, pp. 415–418 (2006)
34. Kaiser, B., Wei, J., Lucherini, E., Lee, K., Matias, J.N., Mayer, J.: Adapting security warnings to counter online disinformation. In: 30th USENIX Security Symposium (USENIX Security 2021), pp. 1163–1180 (2021)
35. Kung, F.Y., Kwok, N., Brown, D.J.: Are attention check questions a threat to scale validity? Appl. Psychol. **67**(2), 264–283 (2018)
36. Lenzner, T., Kaczmirek, L., Lenzner, A.: Cognitive burden of survey questions and response times: a psycholinguistic experiment. Appl. Cogn. Psychol. **24**(7), 1003–1020 (2010)
37. Lesch, M.F., Powell, W.R., Horrey, W.J., Wogalter, M.S.: The use of contextual cues to improve warning symbol comprehension: making the connection for older adults. Ergonomics **56**(8), 1264–1279 (2013)
38. Lindgaard, G., Dudek, C., Sen, D., Sumegi, L., Noonan, P.: An exploration of relations between visual appeal, trustworthiness and perceived usability of homepages. ACM Trans. Comput. Hum. Interact. (TOCHI) **18**(1), 1–30 (2011)
39. Mshvenieradze, T.: Logos ethos and pathos in political discourse. Theor. Pract. Lang. Stud. **3**(11) (2013)
40. Norman, D.: The Design of Everyday Things: Revised and expanded edition. Basic books (2013)
41. Norman, D.A.: Introduction to this special section on beauty, goodness, and usability. Hum. Comput. Interact. **19**(4), 311–318 (2004)
42. Norman, D.A., Ortony, A.: Designers and users: two perspectives on emotion and design. In: Symposium on Foundations of Interaction Design, pp. 1–13 (2003)
43. Paivio, A.: Mind and Its Evolution: A Dual Coding Theoretical Approach. Psychology Press, London (2014)
44. Parkinson, M.: The power of visual communication. Billion Dollar Graphics (2012)
45. Perin, D.: Facilitating student learning through contextualization: a review of evidence. Commun. Coll. Rev. **39**(3), 268–295 (2011)
46. Petelka, J., Zou, Y., Schaub, F.: Put your warning where your link is: improving and evaluating email phishing warnings. In: Proceedings of the 2019 CHI Conference on Human Factors in Computing Systems, pp. 1–15 (2019)
47. Peters, D., Calvo, R.A., Ryan, R.M.: Designing for motivation, engagement and wellbeing in digital experience. Front. Psychol. **9**, 797 (2018)
48. Reeder, R.W., Felt, A.P., Consolvo, S., Malkin, N., Thompson, C., Egelman, S.: An experience sampling study of user reactions to browser warnings in the field. In: Proceedings of the 2018 CHI Conference on Human Factors in Computing Systems, pp. 1–13 (2018)

49. Rozin, P., Royzman, E.B.: Negativity bias, negativity dominance, and contagion. Pers. Soc. Psychol. Rev. **5**(4), 296–320 (2001)
50. Sasse, M.A., Krol, K., Moroz, M.: Don't work. can't work? why it's time to rethink security warnings. In: 2012 7th International Conference on Risks and Security of Internet and Systems (CRiSIS), pp. 1–8. IEEE Computer Society (2012)
51. Schrepp, M., Hinderks, A., Thomaschewski, J.: Applying the user experience questionnaire (UEQ) in different evaluation scenarios. In: Marcus, A. (ed.) DUXU 2014. LNCS, vol. 8517, pp. 383–392. Springer, Cham (2014). https://doi.org/10.1007/978-3-319-07668-3_37
52. Seo, H., Xiong, A., Lee, D.: Trust it or not: effects of machine-learning warnings in helping individuals mitigate misinformation. In: Proceedings of the 10th ACM Conference on Web Science, pp. 265–274 (2019)
53. Shahid, F., Kamath, S., Sidotam, A., Jiang, V., Batino, A., Vashistha, A.: It matches my worldview: examining perceptions and attitudes around fake videos. In: CHI Conference on Human Factors in Computing Systems, pp. 1–15 (2022)
54. Share, N.M.: Operating system market share (2009). https://marketshare.hitslink.com/operating-system-market-share.aspx
55. Sharek, D., Swofford, C., Wogalter, M.: Failure to recognize fake internet popup warning messages. In: Proceedings of the Human Factors and Ergonomics Society Annual Meeting, vol. 52, pp. 557–560. SAGE Publications Sage CA: Los Angeles, CA (2008)
56. Shrestha, A., Graham, D.M., Dumaru, P., Paudel, R., Searle, K.A., Al-Ameen, M.N.: Understanding the behavior, challenges, and privacy risks in digital technology use by nursing professionals. Proc. ACM Hum. Comput. Interact. **6**(CSCW2), 1–22 (2022)
57. Sunshine, J., Egelman, S., Almuhimedi, H., Atri, N., Cranor, L.F.: Crying wolf: an empirical study of SSL warning effectiveness. In: USENIX Security Symposium, pp. 399–416. Montreal (2009)
58. Sweller, J.: Cognitive load theory: recent theoretical advances (2010)
59. Sweller, J.: Cognitive load theory. In: Psychology of Learning and Motivation, vol. 55, pp. 37–76. Elsevier (2011)
60. Vaish, A., Grossmann, T., Woodward, A.: Not all emotions are created equal: the negativity bias in social-emotional development. Psychol. Bull. **134**(3), 383 (2008)
61. Vance, A.: The fog of warnings: how non-essential notifications blur with security warnings. In: Symposium on Usable Privacy and Security (SOUPS) (2019)
62. Vance, A., Kirwan, B., Bjornn, D., Jenkins, J., Anderson, B.B.: What do we really know about how habituation to warnings occurs over time? a longitudinal FMRI study of habituation and polymorphic warnings. In: Proceedings of the 2017 CHI Conference on Human Factors in Computing Systems, pp. 2215–2227 (2017)
63. Warkentin, M., Xu, Z., Mutchler, L.A.: I'm safer than you: the role of optimism bias in personal it risk assessments. In: Proceedings of, pp. 1–32 (2013)
64. Weijters, B., Baumgartner, H.: Misresponse to reversed and negated items in surveys: a review. J. Mark. Res. **49**(5), 737–747 (2012)
65. Wu, M., Miller, R.C., Garfinkel, S.L.: Do security toolbars actually prevent phishing attacks? In: Proceedings of the SIGCHI Conference on Human Factors in Computing Systems, pp. 601–610 (2006)
66. Wyatt, T.: Understanding the process of contextualization. Multicultural Learn. Teach. **10**(1), 111–132 (2015)
67. Xu, H., Rosson, M.B., Carroll, J.M.: Increasing the persuasiveness of it security communication: effects of fear appeals and self-view. In: Workshop on Usable

IT Security Management, Symposium on Usable Privacy and Security (SOUPS), Pittsburgh, PA (2007)

68. Zaaba, Z.F., Boon, T.K.: Examination on usability issues of security warning dialogs. Age **18**(25), 26–35 (2015)

69. Zaaba, Z.F., Lim Xin Yi, C., Amran, A., Omar, M.A.: Harnessing the challenges and solutions to improve security warnings: a review. Sensors **21**(21), 7313 (2021)

70. Zaaba, Z., Furnell, S., Dowland, P., Stengel, I.: Assessing the usability of application-level security warnings. In: Proceedings of the 11th Security Conference (Security Assurance & Privacy) (2012)

Data Privacy, Sovereignty and Governance

A Trustworthy Decentralized System for Health Data Integration and Sharing: Design and Experimental Validation

Ruichen Cong[1] , Yaping Ye[2] , Jianlun Wu[2] , Yuxi Li[1] , Yuerong Chen[2] ,
Yishan Bian[2] , Kiichi Tago[3] , Shoji Nishimura[4] , Atsushi Ogihara[4] ,
and Qun Jin[4(✉)]

[1] Graduate School of Human Sciences, Waseda University, Tokorozawa, Japan
carriecong@moegi.waseda.jp
[2] Zhejiang Chinese Medical University, Hangzhou, China
[3] Department of Information and Network Science, Chiba Institute of Technology, Narashino, Japan
[4] Faculty of Human Sciences, Waseda University, Tokorozawa, Japan
jin@waseda.jp

Abstract. Personal health data collected via wearable devices can be used for sharing and utilization to provide smart healthcare services. Since personal health data involves sensitive information, it is necessary to require a secure way to manage and use data with the consent of each individual. To integrate and share health data securely, many frameworks using federated learning and blockchain-based system have been proposed. However, the issues of ensuring data ownership and enhancing privacy protection remain to be solved. In this paper, we propose a trustworthy system for health data integration and sharing enabled by decentralized federated learning. We describe the major functions and features, including health data integration, doubling data ownership, data analysis via decentralized federated learning, and incentive mechanisms. We further introduce the experiment and assume two application scenarios for sharing and utilization of personal health data and visualization feedback to users. Various types of health data are collected and integrated into the system with decentralized data analysis while sharing results and models and reducing data transmission for privacy-preserving. The proposed system can be expected to provide an effective way to integrate and analyze personal health data for personalized smart healthcare.

Keywords: Personal health data · Healthcare · Blockchain · Privacy protection · Decentralized Federated Learning · Data integration

1 Introduction

In recent years, the growth of IoT services and other data collection and utilization practices has greatly enhanced our daily lives and brought many benefits in fields such as healthcare and medical services. The continuous production of personal health data

(PHD) from wearable devices and sensors has led to its widespread use for personalized healthcare analysis and the promotion of health and well-being [1]. However, there are growing concerns about privacy-preserving and how to make the proper protection and management of collected and stored data. Therefore, individuals who utilize such information face the challenge of securing and maximizing the benefits of their data while also addressing privacy concerns.

To address these challenges, various privacy regulations have been established globally, including the European Union General Data Protection Regulation (GDPR) [2], the California Consumer Privacy Act (CCPA) [3], and Singapore's Personal Data Protection Commission (PDPC) [4], among others. These regulations highlight the increasing importance of privacy protection in data management. The GDPR, in particular, imposes significant legal penalties. Therefore, for sensitive data sharing such as PHD, it is necessary to require a secure way to manage and use data with the consent of each individual. However, there are still challenges to be overcome, including concerns with ensuring data ownership and enhancing privacy protection.

To solve these problems, many solutions using blockchain and privacy computing have been proposed [5, 6]. In our previous work [7–9], we proposed a novel model of Individual-Initiated Auditable Access Control (IIAAC) for privacy-preserved data sharing based on blockchain, Ciphertext-Policy Attribute-Based Encryption (CP-ABE) and InterPlanetary File System (IPFS). We further implemented the secure interoperation of blockchain and IPFS through a client application.

In this paper, we propose a trustworthy system enabled by decentralized federated learning in IIAAC. Federated learning is a method for collaborative machine learning, which only shares training models while maintaining all the target data on the decentralized nodes without centralized data collection [10]. By coordinating multiple nodes to execute machine learning, federated learning is suitable for health data sharing and utilization while enhancing privacy protection [11].

The remainder of this paper is organized as follows. In Sect. 2, related work on blockchain and federated learning are overviewed, and privacy protection issues on data sharing are identified. In Sect. 3, we introduce the functions and features of our proposed system and present the basic system architecture using decentralized federated learning. In Sect. 4, our simulated experiment is described, and two scenarios for health-related data sharing and utilization are assumed. Thereafter, a set of individualized visualization results are shown. Finally, this paper is summarized, and future directions are highlighted in Sect. 5.

2 Related Work

In this section, we briefly introduce the issues of health data sharing and utilization. Then, we present federated learning, blockchain, and previous related works conducted in data integration and sharing based on federated learning and blockchain platforms.

With the rapid growth of the Internet of Health Things (IoHT) in health infrastructures, large amounts of health-related data are being collected and processed in storage data centers [12]. However, securing a vast amount of health data presents a significant challenge, and it is necessary to implement innovation with privacy-preserving health data solutions.

In recent years, privacy computing has emerged as a promising privacy-preserving technology. Gartner has recognized privacy-enhancing computation as a top strategic technology trend for consecutive years 2021 and 2022 [13]. Privacy computing encompasses techniques, such as multi-party computation, differential privacy, and federated learning. Especially federated learning enables machine learning analysis without data aggregation and public transmission. In a federated learning platform, data remains stored locally while models are trained and shared in multiple nodes, preserving the privacy of the data owner [10]. Therefore, federated learning enables data processing and analysis locally while reducing the transmission of original data, allowing for secure and privacy-protected sharing of models.

However, federated learning may also bring privacy risks, such as malicious users can obtain sensitive information through the inference of data during the training process [14], and data leakage could occur when the central server or client is compromised [15].

To solve these problems, blockchain technology has been used as a complement to federated learning, which allows for trustworthy identity authentication, tamper-proof data storage, and decentralization. To counter global aggregation attacks and distributed poisoning attacks in federated learning, many frameworks and approaches using blockchain have been proposed. Heiss et al. [16] proposed a blockchain-based federated learning, which uses zero-knowledge proofs to verify off-chain computations and prove the correctness of parameters. It remains the federated learning framework with a central server. To address these several key issues, such as ensuring the reliability and quality of distributed data and considering how to motivate data owners to share data with others by using an incentive mechanism. In our previous work [8, 9], we proposed a novel model of Individual-Initiated Auditable Access Control (IIAAC) in a consortium blockchain-based system incorporating CP-ABE and IPFS. We further implemented secure interoperation of blockchain and IPFS through a client application. Based on our previous work, this paper focuses on data integration and sharing in a trustworthy way enabled by decentralized federated learning in IIAAC.

3   A Trustworthy Decentralized System for Health Data Integration and Sharing

In this section, we first introduce the functions and features of our proposed system. Then, we describe the prototype system using decentralized federated learning in IIAAC.

3.1   System Requirements

To integrate and share health data effectively and securely, a trustworthy decentralized system enabled by blockchain and decentralized federated learning is designed. The major functions and features of our proposed system are summarized as follows.

1) **Health data integration**

   Various types of health-related data are collected and integrated into the system, including health features collected via a wearable device related to bio indicators (e.g., heart rate and blood oxygen), sleep indicators (e.g., sleep score, deep sleep continuity, wake-up counts, and breathing quality) and activity indicators (e.g., step number, step distance, activity calories consumption, and moderate to high-intensity activity duration). In addition, health data in terms of Traditional Chinese Medicine (TCM) are obtained and used, which is important for predictive health risk analysis [17, 18]. These data are collected and integrated into the system for sharing and utilization in a trustworthy and secure way.

2) **Doubling data ownership**

Users in the system are classified into two types: the data owner, who generates the data, and the data requester, who uses the data. In certain situations, health data can be owned by plural users. For instance, an electronic medical record (e.g., TCM health data) is usually created by a medical staff or a medical device as the data owner. However, such a kind of health data is important for a person to manage his/her health through health data analysis. In our previous work, we allowed the system to set double ownership for the person, which is implemented by smart contracts in blockchain [19].

3) **Data analysis via decentralized federated learning**

By using the decentralized federated learning mechanism, machine learning algorithms are applied to data analysis while maintaining data decentralization. The local model and the global model are used for further personalized analysis.

4) **Incentive mechanism**

To motivate data owners to participate in data integration and sharing positively, we incorporate an incentive mechanism that provides individualized feedback to a data owner who shares the data. The individualized feedback includes comparative analysis results with a peer user or a group of users.

3.2 System Architecture

In this section, we describe the basic system architecture in IIAAC by using Hyperledger Fabric, a consortium blockchain, an IPFS distributed file system, a CP-ABE encryption mechanism, and a decentralized federated learning platform to interoperate with each other.

In a decentralized federated learning mechanism, we use the local model and the global model for personal health data analysis and feedback on the analysis results to data owners. The system architecture designed in our proposed model mainly consists of two categories of users, which are data owner and data requester. In our proposed architecture, personal health data is kept on local devices (decentralized nodes) instead of being centralized on a server or transferred data to otherwhere. In addition, important information related to the training process and model parameters in the federated learning process can be securely stored on on-chain storage and off-chain storage via blockchain. The basic architecture of the prototype system is shown in Fig. 1.

4   Experiment and Application Scenarios

In this section, we first describe the simulated experiment. Then, we assume two application scenarios for sharing and utilization of personal health data and visualization feedback to users.

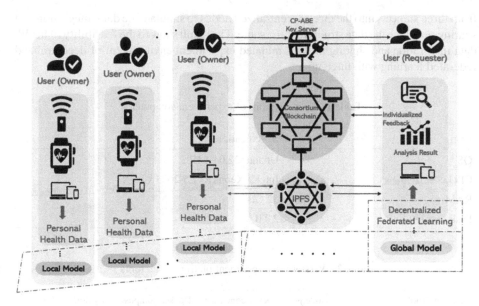

Fig. 1. Basic System Architecture

4.1 Experiment Overview

Wearable devices were used to monitor and record the daily health data of 22 recruited participants for 50 days and collecting data every day. Each participant was requested to record Self-assessed Subjective Health Score (SSHS) every day [20]. This study was conducted under the approval of the Ethics Review Committee on Research with Human Subjects of Waseda University, Japan (No. 2018-092), and all subjects for this experiment signed the informed consent.

In this paper, we design and conduct a simulated experiment based on the proposed system for health data integration and sharing using a part of the collected data, as mentioned above. The simulated experiment environment was built using a Blockchain-powered Verifiable PPC (Privacy-Preserving Computation) network, namely Delta Framework[1], which integrates blockchain and ZPK (Zero Knowledge Proof) to ensure it is verifiable that the computation is actually performed as designed on the required data in a privacy-preserving manner. Delta transforms the tasks into horizontal/vertical federated learning, or federated analytics task and executes it on the network.

For the experiment environment, we also implemented a dashboard interface on the Delta Framework for usability and use Jupyter Lab to construct these tasks, which are written in Python. In the experiment, we simulated three nodes on a computer with the Ubuntu OS. The specifications of the experiment computer are given in Table 1, and the versions of experiment platforms and tools are shown in Table 2.

In the experiment, we took three nodes as three users to simulate the integration and sharing of data in privacy-preserving computation. We put three datasets collected

---

[1] https://deltampc.com/en.

from three subjects into the three decentralized nodes to simulate the data integration and sharing, in which the data structure is the same. The result showed the feasibility of health data integration and sharing in the simulated experiment environment of decentralized federated learning with three nodes.

Table 1. Specifications of experiment computer

Item	Specification
OS	Ubuntu 22.04.1 LTS
CPU	Intel® Xeon (R) E5-2603 v4
RAM	32 GB
Disk capacity	2 TB

Table 2. Versions of experiment platforms and tools

Platforms/Tools	Delta Framework	Node.js	Docker-container	Docker-compose	Python	Jupyter Lab
Version	v 0.8.0	v 8.15.0	v 20.10.11	v 1.29.2	v 3.8.10	v 3.1.6

4.2　Application Scenarios

In our previous work [21], we proposed two types of comparisons for visualized feedback of personal health data analysis results, namely temporal comparison, and horizontal comparison. Temporal comparison is designed to show the current health indicators versus the features obtained from the data of the past. On the other hand, the horizontal comparison provides a measure to let users know where they stand in relation with others, e.g., a peer of the same gender, or a group of the same age, which is also considered to be a good way for us to know ourselves. We describe two application scenarios by showing the visualization feedback which our proposed system aims to provide as follows.

Scenario for Temporal Comparison. A female student wants to know her health indicators for the past week from January 2 (Monday) to 8 (Sunday), 2023, comparing with the averages in the last two weeks up to the day before. She selected five health indicators, i.e., resting heart rate, total sleep duration, activity calorie consumption, stress score, and SSHS (the last two as one pair). The results of these temporal comparisons are shown in Fig. 2, in which the reference range is highlighted in light green color. The user can observe from the graphs how her health features changed, to what extent they are different from the averages, and whether the selected resting heart rate, total sleep duration, and stress score are within the reference range or not.

In Fig. 2, we can see that the daily indicators in the last one week have significant fluctuations compared to the averages in the last two weeks up to the day before. Moreover, the resting heart rate and the total sleep duration on Tuesday are greatly out of the reference range and the other one is less than the reference range, which resulting a higher stress score. And the SSHS is also very low, which is kept low for continuous four days. By continuously observing the bio indicators, such as the resting heart rate, or the sleep indicators, such as the total sleep duration, the user can understand their physical strength improvement, accumulated fatigue, or stress, and their relation to her health status.

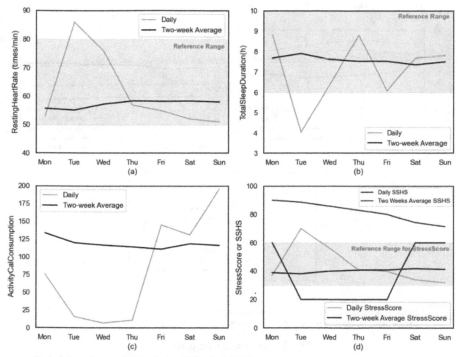

Period: from January 2 (Monday) to 8 (Sunday), 2023
Average based on the data in the last two weeks up to the day before.

Fig. 2. Temporal Comparison

Scenario for Horizontal Comparison. The female student wants to know her selected five health indicators during the period of January 2 (Monday) to 8 (Sunday), 2023, compared in terms of the averages in the last two weeks up to the day before with one of her good friends as well as a female group whose members all agree to share their data. The results of these horizontal comparisons of five selected health indicators are shown in Fig. 3, in which the reference range is highlighted in light green color. From the figures, she can observe the trends and the changes to find similarities or differences between herself and her friend or a group of chosen female users.

In Fig. 3, we can see that the trends of the average of the user, the average of a peer, and the average of a group are similar and stable. Among them, her resting heart rate and activity calorie consumption (represented in black lines) are lower than the peer and

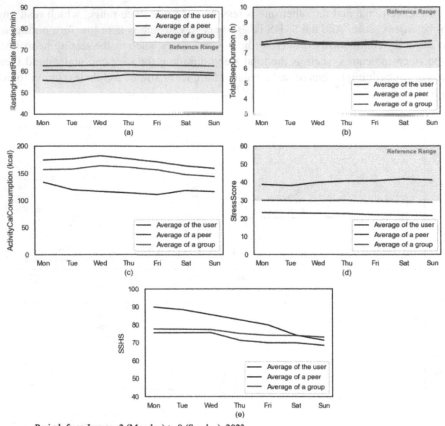

Period: from January 2 (Monday) to 8 (Sunday), 2023
Average based on the data in the last two weeks up to the day before.

Fig. 3. Horizontal Comparison

the group, while their total sleep duration is almost the same, about 7.5 h. Less activity calorie consumption of the user may imply that she spent less time doing exercises, which may result in her higher stress scores than the peer and the group, although it is still within the reference range. From Fig. 3(d), we can also see that the average SSHS of the user has a declining trend from weekdays to weekends.

5   Conclusion

In this study, we proposed a trustworthy decentralized system with the blockchain and federated learning for privacy-preserving data integration and sharing. The system introduced in this paper can be expected to realize the processes of data life cycle management and utilization with trustworthiness.

In this paper, we described the functions and features of our proposed system in terms of health data integration, doubling data ownership, data analysis via decentralized federated learning, and incentive mechanism. Then, we explained the system architecture in IIAAC. We further described the simulated experiment and assumed two scenarios for sharing and utilization of personal health data. The individualized feedback was given to a user in a visualized way, in comparison with the averages calculated from the data of a peer or a group, which can also be used as an incentive for positive data sharing.

For our future work, we will implement the proposed trustworthy decentralized system. We will conduct the validation and performance evaluation experiment on the proposed system using decentralized federated learning models to analyze the tasks in [20]. We further plan to compare the proposed system with other related works for benchmark analysis.

Acknowledgement. The work was supported in part by 2022–2024 Masaru Ibuka Foundation Research Project on Oriental Medicine, 2020–2025 JSPS A3 Foresight Program (Grant No. JPJSA3F20200001), 2022 Waseda University Grants for Special Research Projects (Nos. 2022C-225 and 2022R-036), 2020–2021 Waseda University-NICT Matching Funds Program, 2022 JST SPRING (Grant No. JPMJSP2128), and 2022 Waseda University Advanced Research Center for Human Sciences Project (Grant No. BA080Z000300).

References

1. Wang, Z., et al.: From personalized medicine to population health: a survey of mHealth sensing techniques. IEEE Internet Things J. **9**(17), 15413–15434 (2022)
2. General Data Protection Regulation (GDPR). https://gdpr-info.eu/. Accessed 9 Feb 2023
3. California Consumer Privacy Act (CCPA). https://oag.ca.gov/privacy/ccpa. Accessed 9 Feb 2023
4. Personal Data Protection Commission Singapore (PDPC). https://www.pdpc.gov.sg/. Accessed 9 Feb 2023
5. Liang, W.: PDPChain: a consortium blockchain-based privacy protection scheme for personal data. IEEE Trans. Reliab. **72**(2), 586–598 (2022). https://doi.org/10.1109/TR.2022.3190932
6. Ali, M., Tariq, M., Naeem, F., Kaddoum, G.: Federated learning for privacy preservation in smart healthcare systems: a comprehensive survey. IEEE J. Biomed. Health Inform. **27**(2), 778–789 (2022)
7. Ito, K., Tago, K., Jin, Q.: i-Blockchain: a blockchain-empowered individual-centric framework for privacy-preserved use of personal health data. In: Proceedings of the 2018 9th International Conference on Information Technology in Medicine and Education (ITME), pp. 829–833 (2018)
8. Cong, R., Liu, Y., Tago, K., Li, R., Asaeda, H., Jin, Q.: Individual-initiated auditable access control for privacy-preserved IoT data sharing with blockchain. In: Proceedings of the 2021 IEEE International Conference on Communications Workshops (ICC Workshops), pp. 1–6 (2021)
9. Cong, R., et al.: Secure interoperation of blockchain and IPFS through client application enabled by CP-ABE. In: Moallem, A. (ed.) HCII 2022. LNCS, vol. 13333, pp. 30–41. Springer, Cham (2022). https://doi.org/10.1007/978-3-031-05563-8_3
10. Elayan, H., Aloqaily, M., Guizani, M.: Sustainability of healthcare data analysis IoT-based systems using deep federated learning. IEEE Internet Things J. **9**(10), 7338–7346 (2021)
11. Nguyen, D.C., et al.: Federated Learning for Smart Healthcare: A Survey. ACM Comput. Surv. (CSUR) **55**, 1–37 (2021)

12. Sarosh, P., Parah, S., Bhat, G., Heidari, A.A., Muhammad, K.: Secret sharing-based personal health records management for the internet of health things. Sustain. Cities Soc. **74**, 103129 (2021)
13. Gartner Identifies Top Security and Risk Management Trends for 2022. https://www.gartner.com/en/newsroom/press-releases/2022-03-07-gartner-identifies-top-security-and-risk-management-trends-for-2022. Accessed 9 Feb 2023
14. Salim, S., Turnbull, B., Moustafa, N.: A blockchain-enabled explainable federated learning for securing internet-of-things-based social media 3.0 networks. IEEE Trans. Comput. Soc. Syst. (2021). https://doi.org/10.1109/TCSS.2021.3134463
15. Peng, Z., et al.: VFChain: enabling verifiable and auditable federated learning via blockchain systems. IEEE Trans. Netw. Sci. Eng. **9**(1), 173–186 (2022)
16. Heiss, J., Grünewald, E., Tai, S., Haimerl, N., Schulte, S.: Advancing blockchain-based federated learning through verifiable off-chain computations. In: Proceedings of 2022 IEEE International Conference on Blockchain (Blockchain), pp. 194–201 (2022)
17. Tago, K., Wang, H. Jin, Q.: Classification of TCM pulse diagnoses based on pulse and periodic features from personal health data. In: Proceedings of 2019 IEEE Global Communications Conference (GLOBECOM), Waikoloa, HI, USA, pp. 1–6 (2019)
18. Tago, K., Nishimura, S., Ogihara, A., Jin, Q.: Improving diagnosis estimation by considering the periodic span of the life cycle based on personal health data. Big Data Res. **23**, 100176 (2021)
19. Wang, Y., et al.: Multi-ledger coordinating mechanism by smart contract for individual-initiated trustworthy data sharing. In: Moallem, A. (ed.) HCII 2023, LNCS, vol. 14045, pp. xx–yy. Springer, Cham (2023)
20. Wu, J., et al.: Multidimensional data integration and analysis for youth health care during the Covid-19 pandemic. In: Moallem, A. (ed.) HCII 2023, LNCS, vol. 14045, pp. xx–yy. Springer, Cham (2023)
21. Li, Z., Jin, Q.: Visualization design based on personal health data and persona analysis. In: Proceedings of 2019 IEEE International Conference on Dependable, Autonomic and Secure Computing, International Conference on Pervasive Intelligence and Computing, International Conference on Cloud and Big Data Computing, International Conference on Cyber Science and Technology Congress (DASC/PiCom/CBDCom/CyberSciTech), Fukuoka, Japan, pp. 201–206 (2019)

Usable Implementation of Data Sovereignty in Digital Ecosystems

Denis Feth$^{(\boxtimes)}$ (iD)

Fraunhofer IESE, Fraunhofer-Platz 1, 67663 Kaiserslautern, Germany
denis.feth@iese.fraunhofer.de
https://www.iese.fraunhofer.de

Abstract. Products and services are increasingly being offered in so-called "digital ecosystems", where the processing of sensitive data plays a major role. In such ecosystems, the aim should always be to offer "data providers" (e.g., companies or consumers of goods and services) transparency and control over the processing of their data. This concept is called "data sovereignty." However, it is extremely challenging to present complex processes, data flows and protective measures to users in an understandable and comprehensible way. Furthermore, it is important to make users aware of the consequences of their choices when it comes to settings and consent—without influencing them inappropriately. However, users of digital ecosystems are very heterogeneous in their needs and abilities. For appropriate transparency (e.g., user-friendly privacy statements, uniform icons, traceable data flows) and self-determination measures (e.g., end-to-end consent management), these needs, abilities and some fundamental limitations must be considered. With this paper, we discuss how ecosystem providers and participants can implement data sovereignty in a user-friendly way. We extend the human-centred design process to include data sovereignty aspects and show how data usage control can help to technically implement user needs.

Keywords: Usable Security and Privacy · Data Sovereignty · Digital Ecosystems

1 Digital Ecosystems and Data Sovereignty

Products and services (so-called assets) are increasingly being exchanged and traded digitally. Providers and consumers are finding each other in so-called *digital ecosystems*. For example, consumers can book accommodation via Airbnb, commission craftsmen's services via MyHammer or buy products via the Amazon marketplace. Digital Ecosystems are defined as follows:

Definition 1 (Digital Ecosystem). *"A **digital ecosystem** is a socio-technical system connecting multiple, typically independent providers and consumers of assets for their mutual benefit. A digital ecosystem is based on the*

This work is funded by the German Federal Ministry of Education and Research (BMBF), grant number 16KIS1507.

*provision of digital ecosystem services via digital platforms that enable scaling and the exploitation of positive network effects. A **digital ecosystem service** is characterized by a brokering activity that enables the exchange of assets between their providers and consumers. Typically, asset providers offer assets over a digital platform that brokers these assets to asset consumers. An **asset broker** aims to increase the transaction rate over the marketplace and thus facilitates the harmonized exchange of assets, carrying the responsibility of onboarding the participants, matching assets between them, and enabling physical or digital fulfillment. A **digital platform** is a software system that forms the technical core of a digital ecosystem, is directly used by providers and consumers via APIs or UIs—such as a digital marketplace—and facilitates the matching of a provider and a consumer in relation to an asset within a digital ecosystem service." [18]*

Digital ecosystems offer a wide range of opportunities for their participants. These include the development of new business areas, the acquisition of new customers, and the initiation of innovations in their own industry. Economies of scale and network effects are a central component of digital ecosystems and the platform economy.

In all of this, data plays a major role. For example, the asset providers and the platform provider generally process personal data in order to provide the asset. There are even various examples where the traded asset itself is data, e.g. Caruso[1], Advaneo[2], or GovData[3]. In this context, there is an increasing demand both by legislation (in the context of the GDPR) and by the users (i.e., primarily providers and consumers) themselves that users be granted certain information and co-determination rights regarding the use of "their" data. This kind of informed self-determination is also referred to as *data sovereignty*:

Definition 2 (Data Sovereignty). *"Data sovereignty means the greatest possible control, influence and transparency over the use of data by the data provider. The data provider should be entitled and empowered to exercise informational self-determination and be given transparency about the use of their data." [16] (translated from German)*

Data sovereignty is all the more important in view of the fact that digital ecosystems consist of a highly dynamic and hard to understand network of participants that have a commercial interest in the data.

1. Users must be able to *understand, interpret and verify* with reasonable effort how their data is used and shared.
2. Users must be given the opportunity to *influence the processing* of their data.
3. Users must understand the *impact* of certain decisions on them (e.g., giving consent).
4. Users must be *free and uninfluenced* in their decision.

---

[1] https://www.caruso-dataplace.com/.
[2] https://www.advaneo.de/.
[3] https://www.govdata.de/.

These requirements relate directly to the user experience (UX) and in particular the usability of the data sovereignty measures. In very general terms, the interaction between data sovereignty and UX can be summarized as follows: On the one hand, lack of data sovereignty can have a negative impact on important UX aspects such as satisfaction or trust. Therefore, data sovereignty can be a prerequisite for good UX. On the other hand, data sovereignty can only be achieved if the measures are also implemented in a usable way. Otherwise, users will not use them (at least not correctly) and thus indirectly be deprived of their sovereignty. For example, incorrectly made settings can even have the exact opposite effect of what the user actually wants.

In this paper, we convey the importance of a usable implementation of data sovereignty measures, address the specific challenges in digital ecosystems and present solution approaches. To this end, we take a closer look at our target groups in Sect. 2 and their main goals and challenges in Sect. 3. We then elaborate on design practices and propose an approach based on human-centred design and introduce the concept of "data usage control," which is an essential building block for technically enforcing data sovereignty in Sect. 4. We conclude in Sect. 5 by summarizing our key take-aways.

2   Target Groups

Before we can think about how to implement data sovereignty in a user-friendly way, we must clarify who is responsible in the first place and who the addressed users are.

In order to understand responsibilities, we have to be aware that digital ecosystems consist of a large number of interdependent systems and components that build on one another. By their very nature, these are not designed, developed and distributed by a single provider, but by a provider chain, as Fig. 1 illustrates.

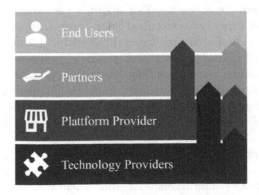

Fig. 1. Chain of providers and consumers

At the lowest level, technology providers provide generic software components, including data sovereignty components, for data flow tracking, access control or usage control. These solutions are used by the platform provider as well as by the ecosystem partners to develop their systems. These systems can ultimately be used by end users, directly or indirectly, to define and enforce their data sovereignty needs. Thus, each level is both a user of measures for the level(s) below and a provider of measures for the level(s) above. This makes the developers themselves to users when they integrate existing software libraries or system components—just on a different, more technical level than the end users. In contrast to the end-user level, however, poor usability or UX of the components to be integrated has a systemic impact on all ecosystem participants (e.g., through security vulnerabilities). A similar argument applies to system administrators, who must reliably configure and maintain security measures. Here, too, small errors can have serious consequences. In such cases, usability problems affect not only individual users, but all participants equally. Thus, one has to consider different characteristics of developers, as for example described by Clarke [5].

A general recommendation in the area of security is to develop as little functionality as possible yourself and instead to use established, possibly even certified components. At the same time, unfortunately, it must be noted that there are only a few established standard solutions, both for digital ecosystems and for data sovereignty. Looking at the research and development landscape, however, projects like GAIA-X[4], International Data Spaces[5] and solutions like MYDATA[6] illustrate a positive trend. In this respect, the background to this recommendation—namely, that security and data protection are highly complex areas and therefore errors or security gaps can easily creep in during in-house development—is of course nevertheless valid and relevant in our context.

End users are, of course, the primary stakeholder group when it comes to data sovereignty. When we talk about "the end user," we should first be aware of whether we are talking about a user whose sensitive data is being processed (i.e., the "data subject" in the area of data protection or in general the "data provider" when it comes to non-personal data) or about a user who, in turn, processes the sensitive data of others (the so-called "data user"). In addition, users differ greatly in their individual needs and capabilities with regard to data sovereignty. It is therefore worth taking a closer look at the classification of "Deutschland sicher im Netz" [Germany secure online] [6], which currently distinguishes five user types: fatalistic users (16.5 percent), outsiders (4.3 percent), gullible users (42.9 percent), thoughtful users (17 percent), and driving users (19.3 percent). DsiN also provides suggestions on how to counter the security deficits of the various user groups. Ultimately, however, general categorizations are only helpful up to a certain point, because digital ecosystems differ greatly. And even within a digital ecosystem, there can be strong cultural differences. For example, in a study by the European Union Agency for Fundamental Rights [8], 65 percent of

---

[4] https://www.gaia-x.eu/.

[5] https://www.internationaldataspaces.org/.

[6] https://www.mydata-control.de/.

participants from Cyprus said they would be willing to share their facial images with the government, compared to only nine percent of the German participants. Therefore, platform or service providers should always carefully examine their user base, classify it, and describe it using personas, for example. Corresponding methods and templates can be found in the relevant literature from the field of requirements engineering. This makes it possible to keep an eye on the specific characteristics of one's target groups during the (further) development of the digital ecosystem.

3   Goals and Challenges

From Definition 1 (see page 2), we can directly derive two main goals of data sovereignty: transparency and self-determination. In this chapter, we take a closer look on what that means and what typical challenges are in the digital ecosystem context. Furthermore, we discuss fundamental limitations of data sovereignty.

3.1   Transparency

First, let's take a look at the definition of transparency:

Definition 3 (Transparency). *Transparency means that the collection and processing of data in procedures and their use can be planned, traced, reviewed and evaluated with reasonable effort. (based on [24])*

Transparency in the processing of sensitive data is increasingly demanded by data providers (e.g., companies or consumers of goods and services) and, in the case of personal data, also by legislators. It is also a precondition for self-determination, because data subjects cannot decide about something they do not understand. In practice, complex facts have to be presented in such a way that users can understand and interpret them. Since sensitive data is processed on a large scale in digital ecosystems and a large number of companies are involved, this is no easy task. At this point, we will look at three transparency measures for digital ecosystems: user-friendly privacy policies, uniform icons and data flow tracking.

User-Friendly Privacy Policies. In practice, privacy policies are currently the only means of providing users with information about the processing of their data. However, it is well documented that the acceptance of privacy statements is already very low on "traditional" websites. Surveys (e.g., [21,29,30]) show that about three quarters of users do not read privacy statements at all, and the remaining users at most skim them. Approaches to improve the readability [7,20], comprehensibility [23], design [31], or basic structure [9,10,22] of privacy notices have so far borne little fruit in practice. In the case of digital ecosystems, this problem is exacerbated by the fact that this is a network that is difficult for users to survey and is not transparent, with each participating company having its own data protection declaration. Users are thus inundated with information, and inconsistent interaction patterns, designs, and wording make it extremely difficult for users to understand and compare.

But with all these challenges, the centrality of digital ecosystems plays into our hands. Although the individual participants are independent in the ecosystem, their role often falls into one of a few categories (e.g., service providers, service consumer). The platform provider has the power to address the aforementioned issues by imposing binding requirements on all participants regarding the structure, expected information, and design of privacy policies. In addition, the platform itself can serve as a central entry point for users, making sense of the information provided by various privacy statements.

Uniform Icons. According to Art. 12 GDPR, information must be provided "in a precise, transparent, comprehensible and easily accessible form, using clear and simple language". As already described, in practice this usually results in textual data protection statements. The possibility of using uniform icons for the communication of data protection information is explicitly provided for (cf. GDPR Article 12, paragraphs 7 and 8). These icons could, for example, help to make the privacy notices, which are so vehemently ignored by users, more user-friendly in the future. Various initiatives have tried to develop good icons, e.g. the "Privacy Icons Forum"[7], Bitkom[8] or the State Commissioner for Data Protection and Freedom of Information of Baden-Württemberg[9]. Unfortunately, none of these proposals has yet gained widespread acceptance in practice. Until this is the case, individual solutions will continue to be in demand. As with the topic of privacy policies, the platform provider has the power to establish a uniform language and icons that support the user and increases transparency.

Data Flow Tracking. Another problem with data privacy policies is that they are static and rather abstract. For example, they merely explain that certain categories of data (e.g., address data) may be passed on to certain partners (e.g., shipping service providers) under certain circumstances (e.g., when an order is placed). However, it is seldom possible to trace which specific data was actually passed on to which partner for which order. In digital ecosystems in particular, where a high degree of dynamics and a large number of participants are a core characteristic, this is precisely where added value for users would arise. Again, the centrality of digital ecosystems plays into our hands here, since it is often comparatively easy from a technical point of view to log data flows on the platform. The greater challenge here is to make the available data comprehensible and user-friendly, for example as presented by Bier et al. [1].

---

[7] https://privacyiconsforum.eu/.

[8] https://www.bitkom.org/Themen/Datenschutz-Sicherheit/Privacy-Icons.

[9] https://www.baden-wuerttemberg.datenschutz.de/datenschutz-icons/.

3.2 Self-determination

The goal of high transparency was not only to inform those affected, but also to lay the groundwork for them to take control of their own data while understanding the consequences. To make this possible, two additional steps are required:

1. the data subject must be given the opportunity to define his needs and requirements with regard to processing.
2. the defined rules must be implemented by all ecosystem participants.

Both aspects are very challenging. We will deal with the first aspect directly below by looking at the challenges of consent management and setting options in general. We will return to the second aspect in Sect. 4.2.

Consent Management. In the area of data protection, the GDPR stipulates that companies may only process personal data if at least one of six prerequisites is met. One of these prerequisites is that the data subject has given consent. In principle, there are no such restrictions for non-personal data, even though they are quite plausibly transferable and benefit the self-determination of data providers. In the case of data protection, however, the downsides also come to light at this point: due to the uncertainties created by the GDPR, users are often confronted with consent forms, even though it is not necessary. Furthermore, consent is only legally valid if it is given voluntarily and uninfluenced. "Nudging", as often occurs with cookie consent, is therefore not permissible. Even small design decisions (so-called "dark patterns") can tempt a person to select an option that does not correspond to his or her actual wishes [3]. In this case, consent is not legal.

In a study by Kettner et al. [17], consumers were presented with various designs for consent management. Based on this study, a best practice model for innovative consent management was developed using various practical examples. In the case of digital ecosystems, the question should also be asked as to whether it makes sense and is feasible to offer centralized consent management via the platform. Ultimately, this would save work and provide security for all ecosystem participants.

User-Friendly Privacy Settings. Many large platforms already offer users data protection settings. Many of these settings require the user to make tradeoffs between privacy and other features or resources. For example, restrictive privacy settings (i.e., a higher level of privacy) in Google search are accompanied by less personalized suggestions (i.e., a lower level of effectiveness). Nevertheless, the default settings should be privacy-friendly in any case, in line with the principle of "privacy by default". Regardless of this general challenge, settings options differ according to the degrees of freedom and support they provide to the user, as well as their general interaction paradigm [25]. Here, there is a wide spectrum - starting with very coarse security levels, over templates and wizards, up to special "policy languages" (e.g. XACML, ODRL or proprietary languages) to express needs and constraints. Which paradigm is most appropriate depends on a variety of factors and the target group (cf. Sect. 2). Policy languages, for example, are reserved for experts on the intermediate layers because they require detailed knowledge of the language and the system being controlled. At the same time, coarse security levels do not provide experts with the desired flexibility. At most, they can serve them to make basic settings. The choice and implementation of the interaction paradigm must therefore always be precisely tailored to the respective characteristics and needs of the user groups.

3.3 Limitations of Data Sovereignty in Digital Ecosystems

The centrality of the platform plays into our hands in many places, as we have just seen. However, there are also a number of characteristics of digital ecosystems and some fundamental trade-offs that complicate the situation:

- *Temptations:* Digital ecosystems offer great advantages to providers and consumers, especially when services can be customized based on the user's data. At the same time, the barrier to entry and the perceived risks are fairly low. This makes it tempting for users to give consent and disclose data.
- *Achieving overall trust:* Trust is essential for data being shared and used. However, it is challenging to establish trust in an entire ecosystem that potentially comprises thousands of (legally independent) participants. Since all participants are legally independent entities, it often is unclear for the user who is the data controller for a concrete use case or transaction. It is therefore important that the platform operator does everything to ensure that customers have an extremely high level of trust in him and support the user in the best possible way.
- *Volatility:* Digital ecosystems, like all ecosystems, are subject to constant change: providers come and go; services are revised; terms and conditions or privacy statements are updated; the ecosystem adapts to changing laws, etc. This means that the user would continuously need to be concerned with the protection of their data-which is, of course, completely illusory.
- *Transparency vs. monitoring:* The more data flows and data processing are made transparent, the higher the risk that sensitive information about the persons processing the data will be disclosed. For example, if the exact time and person of a data use is disclosed, the data subject can draw conclusions about the work behavior of the data user. Anonymization can at least partially resolve this trade-off.
- *Trust vs. distrust:* With a high level of transparency, there is a risk that users will not be able to correctly classify the information shown and will draw erroneous conclusions. In addition, they may become aware of facts that seem surprising to them. The reasons and objectives for new measures (such as increasing transparency) should also be made clear. Data subjects might otherwise wonder, for example, whether there was a data protection incident that led to this introduction.

– *Data sovereignty vs. social pressure:* If data providers and data users know each other, e.g., if they have a direct business relationship, data providers may face social pressure to provide their data. This, of course, then directly threatens their sovereignty.

These described examples illustrate that there is not or cannot be a "perfect" solution. Even if the implementation of data sovereignty initially appears to be ideally implemented from the user's perspective, many factors must be taken into account and weighed against each other. With regard to the data protection paradox, the question arises as to whether it is even possible to solve the described problems in a meaningful way. After all, regardless of whether users exercise their data sovereignty or not, someone else's privacy may be at risk. The maxim of granting users as much transparency and participation as possible is therefore untenable. Instead, a case-by-case approach and the balancing of interests are essential.

Finally, it should be clear to all involved that data sovereignty does not, of course, mean that users have unrestricted freedom with regard to the processing of their data. There are, of course, various situations (e.g., law enforcement) or laws (e.g., retention obligations) that have a higher priority than the self-determination of the individual. This is also regulated accordingly in the GDPR (e.g., in Article 2, paragraph 2d or Article 6, paragraph 1e). Ultimately, the following principle applies to data protection as well as data sovereignty: "The freedom of the individual ends where the freedom of others begins."

4   Methods and Tools

Having gained an overview of the different stakeholders, their goals and challenges, as well as some solution approaches for digital ecosystems, the question naturally arises how to methodically approach the user-friendly implementation of data sovereignty. In this chapter, we approach this question from an organisational and a technical side.

4.1   Organisational Implementation

In the past decades, a number of product development models and methods have been proposed to support the development of secure products (e.g., Microsoft's Security Development Lifecycle (SDL) [14]). Unfortunately, all these methods hardly consider the usability and UX of security measures. Conversely, for many application domains there are still no best practices on how to adequately consider security and privacy in a user-centric design.

Therefore, in this chapter we would like to present our approach to integrating "Usable Security & Privacy" (USP) concepts into the human-centred design (HCD) process (cf. ISO 9241). HCD is understood as an interactive and iterative design process with users, where designers use prototyping and feedback loops to understand users and their requirements. To each step of HCD, we added aspects related to the user-friendly implementation of data sovereignty.

Understand the Context of Use. The first step of HCD is to understand the context of use. According to ISO 9241, context of use includes users, tasks, equipment (hardware, software, and materials), and the physical and social environment in which a product is used. We propose to consider three more aspects:

1. *Understanding Data in the Digital Ecosystem.* First, one has to be clear about data categories processed in the digital ecosystem and who can access them under which circumstances. This can be done by analyzing the ecosystem service, the business processes, the platform architecture and interfaces.
2. *Understand Privacy Regulations.* Second, one has to know and consider data protection regulations, company policies and the Terms and Conditions and contracts in the digital ecosystem to be able to narrow down the solution space. Particular attention should also be paid to the issues of commissioned data processing and cross-border data transfer. If data leaves the GDPR's scope of jurisdiction, for example, this must of course first be clarified in legal terms.
3. *Understand User Characteristics.* Users have different needs and characteristics related to data sovereignty. For example, regardless of the legal assessment one should also check how users feel about cross-border data transfer. Are they okay with it or will they reject it because they feel their privacy is at risk? End users can be distinguished based on the characteristics shown in Fig. 2, among others. All these characteristics can have an impact on the design. For example, if a person has a strong need for privacy, appropriate privacy features could be placed prominently so that the user understands that the system cares about privacy. If a user knows little about data sovereignty, the system could educate the user about the threats and opportunities. If the user's skills are low, a tutorial could help them apply the measures. If the user is not used to being able to act sovereignly, reminders could help to establish such habits.

Fig. 2. Characteristics of end users in terms of Data Sovereignty

Elicit User Needs. The second step in HCD is to identify user needs, based on the identified user types. In our case, there are two important types of users—data providers and data users. It is important to distinguish them because they have different needs that may conflict with each other.

Data providers (data subjects in the sense of data protection) have the following types of needs:

- *Data protection needs:* the desire to protect certain types of data or certain data elements.
- *Transparency needs:* the need or desire for information about how their data is used.
- *Self-determination needs:* the need or desire for control over how their data is used.

Data users (the people who process someone else's data) have the following types of needs:

- *Data processing needs:* the need to process a data category or data item to accomplish a task.
- *Information needs for processing:* a person's need for information about the rules governing the processing of data, e.g., information about the purposes for which the specific data may be used.

Of course, it must be specifically determined which particular needs they have in the respective categories.

It is also to be noted that, data processing needs and data protection needs can be conflicting. The conflict can be resolved or mitigated by providing information about the need for and benefits of the data processing as well as the measures to protect the data.

Develop Solutions. The third HCD step is the development of solutions. Best practices from the area of USP should be known and observed here. The USecureD project[10] has collected such best practices and distinguished between three levels: principles, guidelines and patterns.

Principles: Principles are general rules for designing systems. They are based on experience, are relatively short, and are well suited for gaining a basic understanding of USP. USecureD provides a collection of 23 principles online, such as the following:

- Good security now [12]: Don't wait for the perfect.
- Path of least resistance [32]: The easiest path should be the safest.
- Conditioning [4]: Use positive reinforcement to encourage a desired behavior.

---

[10] https://www.usecured.de/.

Guidelines: Guidelines describe how to implement the principles. They are important to eliminate as many potential problems as possible early in the process [2]. They also help to ensure a high quality standard and reduce the complexity of development projects. USecureD provides a collection of guidelines online, such as guidelines for usable crypto APIs [13], for error prevention [27], and for standardized procedures [26,28].

Patterns: Patterns are proven solutions to recurring problems encountered during system development. Today, following patterns is an integral strategy in the software industry. This is reflected in a large number of collections, which contain patterns for many phases of the software engineering, e.g. architecture, documentation, organization of user interfaces or even security. In the last years also increasingly patterns for USP developed. They deal with aspects such as authentication, authorization, key management, digital signatures, encryption, secure data deletion, creation of backups, user-friendly APIs, and the design of hints, warnings, and system states [19]. USecureD provides an extensive collection online here as well.

Evaluate Against the Requirements. In the final HCD step, the developed solution is evaluated against the requirements. User tests are usually very time-consuming and cost-intensive, since users usually receive at least an expense allowance for their participation. It is therefore advisable to have a heuristic evaluation performed by experts before starting user tests. This method is less expensive, faster, and can already uncover many design flaws before getting to the users with it. To this end, we provided a list of 45 heuristics for evaluating the usability of security and privacy measures and described their application in HCD (cf. Fig. 3) in an earlier publication [11].

These heuristics cover usable transparency (e.g., it is clearly stated for which purposes data is used), authentication (e.g., password policies are directly displayed when passwords are issued), user control and freedom (e.g., users can update or delete incorrect data on their own), error detection, diagnosis and correction (e.g. error messages inform about the severity of the problem), user support and documentation (e.g., help and documentation follow process steps), and accessibility (e.g., the system supports the use of text passwords for visually impaired users).

4.2   Technical Enforcement

In the previous chapters, we have seen the challenges that need to be addressed in order to implement data sovereignty in a user-friendly way. The problem is that the complexity of many requirements and privacy settings goes beyond what can be directly implemented with standard Identity and Access Management solutions. In particular, data filtering (e.g., "Only records from the last 30 days"), data masking (e.g., "Blacken fields with purchased items"), data anonymization, and data usage requirements (e.g., "Delete data after 14 days") are gaining

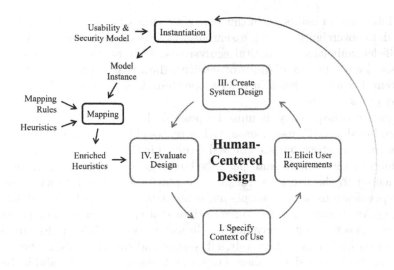

Fig. 3. Heuristic evaluation in the human-centred design [11]

importance. Especially data usage requirements, which regulate usage of data, not the access to it, are challenging. However, platform and service providers need to find ways to technically enforce such requirements in a digital ecosystem.

To this end, the following features must be implemented:

1. data usage and data flows must be controlled at relevant points in the ecosystem, e.g., in the platform.
2. desired data uses must be balanced against a variety of complex rules, which may include propositional, cardinal, and temporal aspects. Contextual factors may also need to be considered.
3. Preventive (e.g., blocking or filtering the data flow) or reactive (e.g., notifying the user or administrator) actions must be able to be performed according to the evaluation of the constraints.
4. if data is passed on, usage obligations ("delete data after 14 days") must be passed on to the target system and implemented there accordingly.

While it is still possible to implement the first three requirements oneself in traditional systems with reasonable effort, this is no longer practicable in the case of cross-company data exchange in an inherently volatile, digital ecosystem with regard to the fourth requirement. Special usage control frameworks and solutions that combine the specification, management and enforcement of data usage rules, have to be used here [15].

5 Summary and Conclusion

For digital ecosystems, the processing of sensitive data is fundamental. In particular, incentives to share sensitive data in a digital ecosystem quickly outweigh actual intentions or concerns. In this paper, we thus addressed how to implement usable data sovereignty—which essentially consists of the areas of transparency and self-determination—in digital ecosystems. Data sovereignty is not limited to personal data, but to all kinds of sensitive data that is processed in a digital ecosystem. It therefore has a broader scope than data protection, but makes use of many of its aspects.

To create transparency, it must be possible for the data provider to trace, check and evaluate the use of data with a reasonable amount of effort. Privacy policies are mandatory, but are not well received in their current form. Therefore, use different levels of detail and speak the language of the user—briefly, precisely, and oriented to the use case. Ideally, the platform provider provides binding design specifications here. Concepts like contextual privacy policies and data flow tracking allow becoming more concrete than static, abstract privacy policies.

With respect to self-determination, it has to be considered that users can only express their needs effectively, efficiently and satisfactorily if the consent and setting tools offered are tailored to them. Consents are only valid if they are given voluntarily and without manipulation of the user.

When planning and implementing data sovereignty measures, it needs to be considered that users are not homogeneous, and that there is certainly no "one-size-fits-all" solution when it comes to data sovereignty and digital ecosystems. User classification and personas help to keep track of the specific characteristics of target groups. However, one needs to be aware that data sovereignty can also have negative effects. Ultimately, the interests of all ecosystem participants must be weighed against each other.

Usability and UX are often neglected in security processes and vice versa. A user-centric approach along the HCD process we have presented can help to better understand user needs and implement data sovereignty in a user-friendly way. This process should be seen more as an inspiration, but not as something to which one must always adhere. Also, the area of "Usable Security & Privacy" covers a broad spectrum of cross-cutting and interdisciplinary topics between the areas of security, privacy, and UX. We recommend that these topics should always be considered holistically and from the outset, taking into account their mutual interactions.

Finally, with all the discussions about the user's needs, one must of course not lose sight of the technical feasibility. Usage obligations in particular are often difficult to technically implement in practice, because traditional security solutions often end at the "access gate". Data usage control [15] offers a suitable extension here.

References

1. Bier, C., Kühne, K., Beyerer, J.: PrivacyInsight: the next generation privacy dashboard. In: Schiffner, S., Serna, J., Ikonomou, D., Rannenberg, K. (eds.) APF 2016. LNCS, vol. 9857, pp. 135–152. Springer, Cham (2016). https://doi.org/10.1007/978-3-319-44760-5_9

2. Birolini, A.: Zuverlässigkeit von Geräten und Systemen. Springer, Heidelberg (2013)
3. Caraban, A., Karapanos, E., Gonçalves, D., Campos, P.: 23 ways to nudge: a review of technology-mediated nudging in human-computer interaction. In: Proceedings of the 2019 CHI Conference on Human Factors in Computing Systems, CHI 2019, pp. 1–15. Association for Computing Machinery, New York (2019). https://doi.org/10.1145/3290605.3300733
4. Chiasson, S., van Oorschot, P., Biddle, R.: Even experts deserve usable security: design guidelines for security management systems. In: SOUPS Workshop on Usable IT Security Management (USM), pp. 1–4 (2007)
5. Clarke, S.: What is an end user software engineer? In: Burnett, M.H., Engels, G., Myers, B.A., Rothermel, G. (eds.) End-User Software Engineering. Dagstuhl Seminar Proceedings (DagSemProc), vol. 7081, p. 1. Schloss Dagstuhl - Leibniz-Zentrum für Informatik, Dagstuhl, Germany (2007). https://doi.org/10.4230/DagSemProc.07081.26. https://drops.dagstuhl.de/opus/volltexte/2007/1080
6. Deutschland sicher im Netz e.V.: DsiN-Sicherheitsindex 2021 (2021). https://www.sicher-im-netz.de/dsin-sicherheitsindex-2021
7. Ermakova, T., Fabian, B., Babina, E.: Readability of privacy policies of healthcare websites (2015)
8. European Union Agency for Fundamental Rights: Your rights matter: data protection and privacy: fundamental rights survey. Publications Office (2020). https://doi.org/10.2811/292617
9. Feth, D.: Transparency through contextual privacy statements. In: Burghardt, M., Wimmer, R., Wolff, C., Womser-Hacker, C. (eds.) Mensch und Computer 2017 - Workshopband. Gesellschaft für Informatik e.V., Regensburg (2017). https://doi.org/10.18420/muc2017-ws05-0406
10. Feth, D.: Modelling and presentation of privacy-relevant information for internet users. In: Moallem, A. (ed.) HCII 2020. LNCS, vol. 12210, pp. 354–366. Springer, Cham (2020). https://doi.org/10.1007/978-3-030-50309-3_23
11. Feth, D., Polst, S.: Heuristics and models for evaluating the usability of security measures. In: Proceedings of Mensch Und Computer 2019, MuC 2019, pp. 275–285. Association for Computing Machinery, New York (2019). https://doi.org/10.1145/3340764.3340789
12. Garfinkel, S.: Design principles and patterns for computer systems that are simultaneously secure and usable. Ph.D. thesis, Massachusetts Institute of Technology (2005)
13. Green, M., Smith, M.: Developers are not the enemy!: the need for usable security APIs. IEEE Secur. Priv. 14(5), 40–46 (2016)
14. Howard, M., Lipner, S.: The Security Development Lifecycle, vol. 8. Microsoft Press, Redmond (2006)
15. Jung, C., Dörr, J.: Data usage control. In: Otto, B., ten Hompel, M., Wrobel, S. (eds.) Designing Data Spaces, pp. 129–146. Springer, Cham (2022). https://doi.org/10.1007/978-3-030-93975-5_8
16. Jung, C., Eitel, A., Feth, D.: Datensouveränität in Digitalen Ökosystemen: Daten nutzbar machen, Kontrolle behalten. In: Rohde, M., Bürger, M., Peneva, K., Mock, J. (eds.) Datenwirtschaft und Datentechnologie, pp. 203–220. Springer, Heidelberg (2022). https://doi.org/10.1007/978-3-662-65232-9_15
17. Kettner, S., Thorun, C., Spindler, G.: Innovatives datenschutzeinwilligungsmanagement. Forschungsvorhaben gefördert durch das BMJV, Berlin (2020)

18. Koch, M., Krohmer, D., Naab, M., Rost, D., Trapp, M.: A matter of definition: criteria for digital ecosystems. Digit. Bus. **2**(2), 100027 (2022). https://doi.org/ 10.1016/j.digbus.2022.100027. https://www.sciencedirect.com/science/article/pii/ S2666954422000072
19. Lo Iacono, L., Schmitt, H., Feth, D., et al.: Arbeitskreis usable security & privacy: nutzerzentrierter schutz sensibler daten (2018)
20. Milne, G.R., Culnan, M.J., Greene, H.: A longitudinal assessment of online privacy notice readability. J. Public Policy Mark. **25**(2), 238–249 (2006)
21. Obar, J.A., Oeldorf-Hirsch, A.: The biggest lie on the internet: ignoring the privacy policies and terms of service policies of social networking services. Inf. Commun. Soc. **23**(1), 128–147 (2020)
22. Ortloff, A.M., Güntner, L., Windl, M., Feth, D., Polst, S.: Evaluation kontextueller datenschutzerklärungen. In: Dachselt, R., Weber, G. (eds.) Mensch und Computer 2018 - Workshopband. Gesellschaft für Informatik e.V., Bonn (2018). https://doi. org/10.18420/muc2018-ws08-0541
23. Reidenberg, J.R., et al.: Disagreeable privacy policies: Mismatches between meaning and users' understanding. Berkeley Tech. LJ **30**, 39 (2015)
24. Rost, M., Bock, K.: Privacy by design und die neuen schutzziele. Datenschutz und Datensicherheit-DuD **35**(1), 30–35 (2011)
25. Rudolph, M., Polst, S., Doerr, J.: Enabling users to specify correct privacy requirements. In: Knauss, E., Goedicke, M. (eds.) REFSQ 2019. LNCS, vol. 11412, pp. 39–54. Springer, Cham (2019). https://doi.org/10.1007/978-3-030-15538-4_3
26. Shneiderman, B., Leavitt, M., et al.: Research-Based Web Design & Usability Guidelines. Department of Health and Human Services, Washington DC (2006)
27. Shneiderman, B., Plaisant, C., Cohen, M.S., Jacobs, S., Elmqvist, N., Diakopoulos, N.: Designing the User Interface: Strategies for Effective Human-Computer Interaction. Pearson (2016)
28. Smith, S.L., Mosier, J.N.: Guidelines for Designing User Interface Software. Citeseer (1986)
29. Symantec: State of Privacy Report 2015 (2015)
30. Tsai, J.Y., Egelman, S., Cranor, L., Acquisti, A.: The effect of online privacy information on purchasing behavior: an experimental study. Inf. Syst. Res. **22**(2), 254–268 (2011)
31. Waldman, A.E.: Privacy, notice, and design. Stan. Tech. L. Rev. **21**, 74 (2018)
32. Yee, K.-P.: User interaction design for secure systems. In: Deng, R., Bao, F., Zhou, J., Qing, S. (eds.) ICICS 2002. LNCS, vol. 2513, pp. 278–290. Springer, Heidelberg (2002). https://doi.org/10.1007/3-540-36159-6_24

Research on the Capability Maturity Model of Data Security in the Era of Digital Transformation

Zimeng Gao[1], Fei Xing[1](✉), and Guochao Peng[2]

[1] Suzhou Institute of Trade & Commerce, Suzhou 215009, China
921820868@qq.com
[2] Sun Yat-sen University, Guangzhou 510000, China

Abstract. Digital transformation has become the trend of enterprise operation in the digital economy era. In this context, data security has become the focus of academic research and industrial circles. This paper aims to develop an enterprise data security capability maturity model in the era of digital transformation. Firstly, systematic literature review (SLR) was used to build up the hierarchical model of enterprise data security, which consists of three first level indicators and twelve second level indicators. Secondly, expert interview was used to develop the capability maturity model of data security with five different maturity levels. In the end, a series of suggestions was put forward to improve enterprise data security, namely: 1) Daily maintenance is required for computer and network security; 2) Physical safety protection to avoid safety accidents caused by environmental factors; 3) Establish a complete monitoring and automatic response mechanism; 4) Enterprise data disaster tolerance measures can systematically ensure security.

Keywords: Data security · Capability maturity model · Digital transformation · Recommendation

1 Introduction

With the rapid development of digital economy, enterprises comply with the development trend of digital economy and use emerging technologies to carry out digital transformation. Enterprise digital transformation is essentially the integration of unified digital technologies across a business. From startups to multinationals, these technologies change and optimize the way a company deploys and manages its everyday operations [1]. As a result of digital transformation, the operation mode of enterprise is changing stupendously. One of the most obvious changes is to enhance the data collection in the process of enterprise digital transformation [2]. Specifically, many enterprises have accumulated a lot of data about consumers, but the real advantage comes from analyzing these data to promote enterprise business development. Therefore, digital transformation provides a mechanism to capture the right data and fully integrate it to achieve a higher level of business insight.

© The Author(s), under exclusive license to Springer Nature Switzerland AG 2023
A. Moallem (Ed.): HCII 2023, LNCS 14045, pp. 151–162, 2023.
https://doi.org/10.1007/978-3-031-35822-7_11

In the wave of digital transformation, data security has become a hot topic of concern in academia and industry due to the rapidly growing amount of data. Manita et al. (2020) considered that 'He who gets the data gets the world' [3]. Mergel et al. (2019) assumed that data is the 'gold' or 'oil' in the development of digital transformation, which is becoming the core asset of enterprise [4]. Since the significance of data security in enterprise digital transformation, there are many research results exploring it. On one hand, one of the most popular research fields are about the advantages brought by digital transformation from a macro perspective [3, 5]. Academic researchers have demonstrated the huge benefits that digital transformation brings to enterprise through theoretical and empirical studies. Besides, case analysis of digital transformation in different fields has also been investigated by academic scholars [6, 7]. On the other, researchers have made a lot of investigations in data security, mainly from the view of technology, such as tools [8], platforms [9].

However, it is worth noting that the research of studying the data security of enterprise digital transformation is scarce. Particularly, current literature and studies showed that most studies in this field focus on the advantages of digital transformation and technical angles of data security [9]. There is little research studying the combination of data security in era of digital transformation, especially in terms of data security capability maturity. Enterprise can effectively understand their data security protection capabilities in their process of digital transformation through the development of data security capability maturity model. Therefore, this paper aims to identify the indicators that affect the data security and maturity levels.

The rest of the papers is structured as follows. First, systematic literature on digital transformation and capability maturity model are presented. Subsequently, research methods namely systematic literature review and expert interview are introduced. Then, we will discuss the hierarchical model enterprise data security and capability maturity model. In the final, several suggestions on how to improve enterprise data security are put forward.

2 Literature Review

2.1 Related Studies on Digital Transformation

The digital transformation, otherwise called 'digitalization' is defined today rarely in the literature. Our literature review showed that the digital transformation is defined as a social phenomenon or cultural evolution [2], and for enterprise as an evolution of their business or operation model. In fact, it is perceived as a fundamental transition of society, driven by digital technologies such as big data, machine learning, deep learning, and even artificial intelligence. These so-called digital technologies are deeply rooted in their culture and daily practices. In this context, enterprise need to adapt themselves by changing their business pattern.

However, it is biased that regard digital transformation simply as a business mode of the enterprise, because it affects other elements of an organization like culture, organizational structure, etc. In academic research, although there is no unified concept of enterprise digital transformation, important consensus has been reached on some key elements [10]. On one hand, enterprise digital transformation is the reshaping of enterprise business activities through using advanced information technologies. Enterprise fully utilizes the new generation of digitalization and intelligence technologies to optimize the business process and management system and realizes the transformation of the organizational structure and the innovation of the business model by formulating a comprehensive enterprise digitalization strategy [11]. On the other hand, the core of enterprise digital transformation is to realize value co-creation. Enterprises can ensure their ability to obtain competitive advantages and sustainable growth in the fierce market competition by changing the operation mode [12].

2.2 Related Studies on Capability Maturity Model

The Capability Maturity Model (CMM) was first formally put forward by the Software Engineering Research Institute (SEI) of Carnegie Mellon University in 1991. It is used for the evaluation and improvement of software development process and software development capability [13]. It is an integrated model of system engineering and software engineering with organization. Academic researchers have applied the ideas and methods of CMM to the field of project management, such as enterprise information security maturity [13], enterprise intelligent manufacturing maturity [14] and enterprise intellectual property management maturity [15]. In addition to software management and project management, the basic ideas and methods of CMM can also be widely applied to the process management of other organizations like university, hospital, and governments, etc. As a result of this, the existing literature showed that CMM has been adopted and applied in a large number of organizations.

2.3 Related Studies on Data Security Capability Maturity Model

In the wave of enterprise digital transformation, data is becoming the core asset or even the 'lifeline' of enterprises. The importance of data security is self-evident. The data security capability maturity model standard, which focuses on the security of the six data life cycle processes of collection, transmission, storage, processing, exchange and destruction, providing a basic model framework for the maturity of the organization's data security capability [15]. The existing literature showed that the enterprise data security maturity model is mainly embodied in three aspects: security capability, capability maturity level and data security process [16]. In the dimension of security capability, the existing research mainly uses organizational construction, institutional processes, technical tools, as well as the safety awareness and related capabilities of data security personnel as the measurement indicators [16]. In terms of capability maturity level of enterprise data security, its maturity model is mainly divided into five levels. In the final, the data security process mainly focuses on the data life cycle process and the data security process dimension evaluation index composed of 11 general security process areas such as data security policy planning, authentication, and access control.

Existing researchers have conducted extensive and in-depth research on the maturity of enterprise data security and have achieved many research results. However, digital transformation enterprise has not taken into account, considering the unique features of the digital transformation enterprises, their maturity model construction is different from other enterprises. At the same time, digital transformation enterprises are the development direction of enterprises in the digital economy era. Therefore, there is of great theoretical and practical significance to study the data security maturity model of digital transformation enterprises.

3   Research Methods

In this study, systematic literature review (SLR) and expert interview (EI) were adopted to develop the evaluation indicators and enterprise data security capability maturity model respectively.

3.1   Systematic Literature Review

Systematic Literature Review (SLR) is a research method based on the analysis of existing literature. Unlike traditional literature analysis, systematic literature analysis method follows a rigorous and systematic literature research route [17]. It uses clear definitions to identify evidence related to research issues (i.e., past research results), and screens the literature through quality evaluation criteria. The systematic literature analysis method mainly includes four research steps: defining the scope of literature inspection, querying the initial literature, selecting relevant literature, and analyzing the selected literature data [18].

Firstly, this paper mainly selects research documents in the field of data security and capability maturity model from Scopus, ScienceDirect, SpringerLink, Web of Science, Wiley Online Library, Google Scholar and two Chinese databases namely CNKI and Wan fang. Secondly, Boolean operators were used to link the search terms in the selected database through three fields of title, summary, and keywords, which produced the initial relevant literature. Thirdly, according to the principle of literature selection and exclusion, 317 articles were excluded from the original 809 articles through the repeatability of the title and the content of the abstract. In this case, a total of 492 papers were selected as the research samples of this paper. Finally, the selected literature was coded and analyzed to develop the evaluation indicators of capability maturity model of data security.

3.2   Expert Interview

The expert interview is one of the most frequently used methods in empirical social research. It provides exclusive insights into expert knowledge and into structural contexts as well as change processes of action systems [19]. The aim of the expert interview is to discover the unknown, a person's 'insider knowledge'. Basically, expert interview will involve two or more people [20]. Mostly between the interviewer and the interviewee and the interviewer asks questions while the interviewee replies to them. Therefore, conducting expert interview helps the researcher get specific information about a specific study area.

In this study, a total of 12 experts were interviewed in the meeting room. Twelve experts come from different field such as computer, data science, enterprise management, information system, etc. Each interview lasted 40–60 min and all experts were booked in advance. Moreover, the expert interview data were analyzed through content analysis.

4 The Proposed Capability Maturity Model of Data Security

4.1 Hierarchical Model of Enterprise Data Security

After conducting the systematic literature review, hierarchical model of enterprise data security was built up, which consists of three first level indicators and twelve second level indicators. In general, data security capability of enterprise in the era of digital transformation was affected by three dimensions, namely platform risk, enterprise behavior and external risks. To be specific, platform risk mainly refers to information system defects, network protocol defects, physical environment defects, privacy security settings and hacker stealing. The risk of enterprise data storage platform will affect data security. Once there is a certain risk in the system, external hackers are easy to attack, resulting in data leakage. The existing literature showed 28% of enterprise data security problems are caused by system failures, including IT and business process failures.

Secondly, enterprise behavior refers to data security awareness, data security management system and data protection negligence. Data security awareness is one of the reasons that leads to the data leakage in the enterprise. Therefore, in order to improve enterprise data security capability, enterprises need to require internal personnel to abide by professional ethics, establish a prevention mechanism, and conduct regular safety training for employees. Lack of data privacy management system is also a major problem for the enterprise data security. Therefore, data privacy management system is also considered as the evaluating indicators to measure the capability maturity of data security in enterprise.

In the final, if platform risk and enterprise behavior are the internal evaluation index, external threat is the external dimension. In this paper, external threats primarily refer to destruction of intellectual property, policy impact, backward data security protection technology and data cross-border transmission protection. In details, data cross-border transmission protection refers to the enterprise is lack of security assessment and process control in the cross-border data transmission process, and the operation adopted is inconsistent with the internationally recognized transmission mechanism, that is, the enterprise does not have adequate security assurance in the data transmission process. The specific explanation of these indicators was demonstrated in Table 1 (Fig. 1).

Table 1. Enterprise data security evaluation indicators

First level indicator	Second level indicator	Description
Platform risk	Information system defects	Data security risk was caused by the incomplete software and hardware facilities of the computer, intentional destruction, and untimely updating, etc., leading to the difficulty in ensuring the database security

(continued)

Table 1. (*continued*)

First level indicator	Second level indicator	Description
	Network protocol defects	Defects of application, transport, network, data link and physical
	Physical environment defects	Defects of site selection, storage and surrounding environment
	Privacy security settings	Defects of various privacy security functions provided by the system for users in enterprise
	Hacker stealing	The enterprise is attacked by hackers due to the low security level of its cloud configuration, which leads to the theft of enterprise secret
Enterprise behavior	Data security awareness	The overall data security awareness of the enterprise, including the understanding of domestic and foreign data security regulations
	Data security management system	Relevant systems set by the enterprise for data security, including relevant training, confidentiality agreement, etc.
	Data protection negligence	Data loss or leakage due to negligence of enterprises in data security protection
External threats	Destruction of intellectual property	Threat and destruction of enterprise intellectual property rights caused by external behaviors
	Policy impact	Constraints and obstacles posed by domestic or foreign data security policies to enterprise data security behavior
	Backward data security protection technology	The data security technology used by enterprises is backward and it is difficult to resist external technical interference

(*continued*)

Table 1. (*continued*)

First level indicator	Second level indicator	Description
	Data cross-border transmission protection	The enterprise lacks security assessment and process control in the cross-border data transmission process, and the operation adopted is inconsistent with the internationally recognized transmission mechanism, that is, the enterprise does not have adequate security assurance in the data transmission process

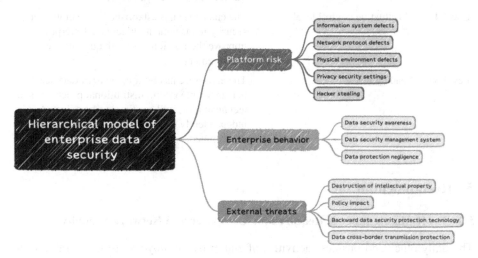

Fig. 1. Hierarchical model of enterprise data security

4.2 Capability Maturity Model of Data Security

The data was collected by expert interview, which contains of three categories of experts, namely computer science, enterprise management and information systems. Besides this, the collected interview data was analyzed through a thematic analysis. Consequently, the capability maturity model of data was developed, and it involves of five different maturity levels, namely planning level, informal implementation level, specification level, quantitative control level and leading level, the detailed explanation of capability maturity model of data security seen Table 2.

Table 2. Capability maturity model of data security

Name of level		Concept of level
Level 1	Planning level	The enterprise has realized the importance of data security and made a preliminary plan concentrate on data security, but no effective related work has been carried out
Level 2	Informal implementation level	Data security activities are being implemented, but these implementation activities are informal, and most of them are dependent on personal efforts and knowledge
Level 3	Specification level	The enterprise has invested on data security and some implementation activities are planned and tracked at the enterprise level
Level 4	Quantitative control level	The enterprise has established measurable data security management objectives. Enterprise can improve their actions through quantitative measurement
Level 5	Leading level	The enterprise has built up a smart data security management system, institutional processes and technical tools will continue to be adjusted independently to better adapt to business development

5 Recommendation

5.1 Daily Maintenance is Required for Computer and Network Security

The daily office and business activities of enterprise employees are inseparable from computers and networks, while Trojan viruses, harmful programs, security vulnerabilities, hacker attacks, etc. are all kinds of internal and external network threats. Therefore, it is difficult to guarantee the data security of enterprise in the era of digital transformation. Daily maintenance can be done from two dimensions.

Firstly, enterprise can improve the computer security protection capabilities. Nowadays, enterprise employees have recognized various risks from the network, but based on their past habits, they often ignore the impact on themselves, and even conflict with various security software and security measures [21]. The most simple and effective measures to protect computer security are to install enterprise antivirus software, update passwords regularly, update system patches regularly and other routine operations.

Secondly, enterprises can improve their network security protection capabilities. Common network security protection tools include firewall, network situational awareness, vulnerability scanning and intrusion detection system [22]. Firewall is the first barrier to prevent network sabotage. Network situational awareness equipment can help enterprises actively identify threats and risks in the company's network, and can cooperate with firewalls, intrusion detection systems, vulnerability scanning tools, etc. to form a more three-dimensional network defense system to ensure the safe operation of enterprise networks and information equipment.

5.2 Physical Safety Protection to Avoid Safety Accidents Caused by Environmental Factors

Physical security protection is one of measures to protect data equipment and data system from earthquake, fire, flood and other environmental disasters and human error operation and destruction. In this paper, physical security protection contains of environmental safety protection and equipment safety protection.

Equipment security mainly refers to protecting the information equipment and facilities of enterprises from being damaged and stolen, especially every piece of equipment in the data center is valuable. If equipment is stolen or damaged by people, the losses caused by them will even far exceed the purchase value of the equipment itself. Traditional defensive measures can play an effective role in prevention, such as controlling personnel access through fingerprint identification, swiping card access control and other technologies.

In addition to the factors mentioned above, the safety of the equipment is also affected by itself. Safety accidents caused by defects in the design and manufacture of electronic equipment or normal aging are not uncommon in enterprises [23]. Although the availability of its functions can be guaranteed through regular maintenance and clustered deployment, the equipment that is far beyond the normal service life or has problems should be resolutely eliminated to ensure that the equipment is always in good working condition.

5.3 Establish a Complete Monitoring and Automatic Response Mechanism

According to the research conducted by Xing et al., about 65% of all data security incidents are caused by human factors, so the biggest risk of enterprise information security management is the security of internal personnel [11]. Safety accidents will be caused by personnel's operation mistakes, weak sense of responsibility, lack of professional ability or failure to strictly comply with relevant safety systems and operation procedures [24]. There are even internal personnel who maliciously destroy and tamper with enterprise information systems, data, and equipment due to dissatisfaction, or steal confidential information to obtain illegal profits. In this context, enterprise must do a good preparation work in personnel security management.

First, it is necessary to formulate and improve various safety rules and regulations, including disciplinary mechanisms, according to the current situation and requirements of different companies, and strictly implement and implement safety responsibilities. Secondly, data security publicity and education and training are often carried out to eliminate the resistance of security management among employees and make security awareness deeply rooted in the hearts of the people in their daily work. Moreover, it is necessary to clearly divide the responsibilities of personnel, allocate the authority according to the principle of minimization, and follow the principle of multiple people present for key operations.

5.4 Enterprise Data Disaster Tolerance Measures can Systematically Ensure Security

Data disaster recovery refers to a systematic project to protect the data from natural disasters and man-made damage and reduce the impact of disaster events on information systems and business processes. In the practice of enterprise data protection, two important safeguards are needed, namely data backup and disaster recovery center.

Data backup refers to the process of copying all or part of data to other storage media through backup software and corresponding backup strategies to prevent data loss. Backup is the basis of disaster recovery [25]. Enterprises backup data such as databases, documents, and system applications. In this way, data can be recovered quickly when the information system is damaged or lost.

As soon as completing the backup of the important data of the enterprise, it is also indispensable to check the integrity and validity of the backup data regularly, because it can detect whether the backup strategy is successfully implemented and whether the data can be truly restored. The disaster recovery center is a redundant node that establishes one or more data centers outside the production environment for disaster recovery. When a disaster occurs, the disaster-tolerant node can take over the system and business without being damaged, so as to achieve the goal of uninterrupted business. It can be said that the substantive purpose of the disaster recovery center is to ensure business continuity.

6 Conclusions

Data security is related to the sustainable development of enterprises in the network era. Data security management is conducive to improving the competitiveness of enterprises and is also an effective integration in the process of enterprise digital transformation. To ensure the data security of enterprises, it is to achieve the organic combination of internal management and external prevention and control. This paper aims to develop the hierarchical model of enterprise data security and the capability maturity model of data security in the era of digital transformation through the combination of systematic literature review and expert interview. Subsequently, capability maturity model of data security with five different maturity levels is built up. In the end, in order to improve the data security capability of enterprises in digital transformation, a series of suggestions was put forward to improve enterprise data security, namely 1) Daily maintenance is required for computer and network security; 2) Physical safety protection to avoid safety accidents caused by environmental factors; 3) Establish a complete monitoring and automatic response mechanism; 4) Enterprise data disaster tolerance measures can systematically ensure security.

References

1. Litvinenko, V.S.: Digital economy as a factor in the technological development of the mineral sector. Nat. Resour. Res. **29**(3), 1521–1541 (2020)
2. Verhoef, P.C., et al.: Digital transformation: a multidisciplinary reflection and research agenda. J. Bus. Res. **122**, 889–901 (2021)

3. Manita, R., Elommal, N., Baudier, P., Hikkerova, L.: The digital transformation of external audit and its impact on corporate governance. Technol. Forecast. Soc. Chang. **150**, 119751 (2020)
4. Mergel, I., Edelmann, N., Haug, N.: Defining digital transformation: results from expert interviews. Gov. Inf. Q. **36**(4), 101385 (2019)
5. Fenech, R., Baguant, P., Ivanov, D.: The changing role of human resource management in an era of digital transformation. J. Manage. Inf. Decis. Sci. **22**(2) (2019)
6. Piepponen, A., Ritala, P., Keränen, J., Maijanen, P.: Digital transformation of the value proposition: a single case study in the media industry. J. Bus. Res. **150**, 311–325 (2022)
7. Datta, P.: Digital transformation of the Italian public administration: a case study. Commun. Assoc. Inf. Syst. **46**(1), 11 (2020)
8. Thapa, C., Camtepe, S.: Precision health data: requirements, challenges and existing techniques for data security and privacy. Comput. Biol. Med. **129**, 104130 (2021)
9. Yang, P., Xiong, N., Ren, J.: Data security and privacy protection for cloud storage: a survey. IEEE Access **8**, 131723–131740 (2020)
10. Xue, L., Zhang, Q., Zhang, X., Li, C.: Can digital transformation promote green technology innovation? Sustainability **14**(12), 7497 (2022)
11. Xing, F., Peng, G., Wang, J., Li, D.: Critical obstacles affecting adoption of industrial big data solutions in smart factories: an empirical study in China. J. Glob. Inf. Manage. (JGIM) **30**(1), 1–21 (2022)
12. Gao, J., Zhang, W., Guan, T., Feng, Q.: Evolutionary game study on multi-agent collaboration of digital transformation in service-oriented manufacturing value chain. Electron. Commer. Res. 1–22 (2022)
13. Chapman, R.J.: Exploring the value of risk management for projects: improving capability through the deployment of a maturity model. IEEE Eng. Manage. Rev. **47**(1), 126–143 (2019)
14. Ge, J., Wang, F., Sun, H., Fu, L., Sun, M.: Research on the maturity of big data management capability of intelligent manufacturing enterprise. Syst. Res. Behav. Sci. **37**(4), 646–662 (2020)
15. Wu, J., Ma, Z., Liu, Z., Lei, C.K.: A contingent view of institutional environment, firm capability, and innovation performance of emerging multinational enterprises. Ind. Mark. Manage. **82**, 148–157 (2019)
16. Kim, S., Pérez-Castillo, R., Caballero, I., Lee, D.: Organizational process maturity model for IoT data quality management. J. Ind. Inf. Integr. **26**, 100256 (2022)
17. Xiao, Y., Watson, M.: Guidance on conducting a systematic literature review. J. Plan. Educ. Res. **39**(1), 93–112 (2019)
18. Brereton, P., Kitchenham, B.A., Budgen, D., Turner, M., Khalil, M.: Lessons from applying the systematic literature review process within the software engineering domain. J. Syst. Softw. **80**(4), 571–583 (2007)
19. Bogner, A., Menz, W.: The theory-generating expert interview: epistemological interest, forms of knowledge, interaction. In: Interviewing Experts, pp. 43–80. Palgrave Macmillan, London (2009)
20. Xing, F., Peng, G., Zhang, B., Li, S., Liang, X.: Socio-technical barriers affecting large-scale deployment of AI-enabled wearable medical devices among the ageing population in China. Technol. Forecast. Soc. Chang. **166**, 120609 (2021)
21. Kaufman, L.M.: Data security in the world of cloud computing. IEEE Secur. Priv. **7**(4), 61–64 (2009)
22. Kong, D., Dong, H., Li, H., Wang, Z., Li, J.: Research on situation analysis technology of network security incidents. In: Proceedings of the 2020 International Conference on Cyberspace Innovation of Advanced Technologies, pp. 213–218 (2020)

23. Xing, F., Peng, G., Liang, Z.: Research on the Application of Blockchain Technology in the Cross-border E-Commerce Supply Chain Domain. In: Streitz, N.A., Konomi, S. (eds.) HCII 2022. LNCS, vol. 13326, pp. 99–109. Springer, Cham (2022). https://doi.org/10.1007/978-3-031-05431-0_7

24. Fraga-Lamas, P., Fernández-Caramés, T.M.: A review on blockchain technologies for an advanced and cyber-resilient automotive industry. IEEE Access 7, 17578–17598 (2019)

25. Nabbosa, V., Kaar, C.: Societal and ethical issues of digitalization. In: Proceedings of the 2020 International Conference on Big Data in Management, pp. 118–124 (2020)

Data Guardians' Behaviors and Challenges While Caring for Others' Personal Data

Julie M. Haney[1][(✉)] , Sandra Spickard Prettyman[2], Mary F. Theofanos[1] ,
and Susanne M. Furman[1]

[1] National Institute of Standards and Technology, Gaithersburg, MD 20899, USA
{julie.haney,marytheo,susanne.furman}@nist.gov
[2] Culture Catalyst, Chicago, IL, USA
sspretty@icloud.com

Abstract. Many professional domains require the collection and use of personal data. Protecting systems and data is a major concern in these settings, making it necessary that workers who interact with personal data understand and practice good security and privacy habits. However, to date, there has been little examination of perceptions, behaviors, and challenges among these professionals. To address this gap, we conducted an interview study of 19 individuals working in the education, finance, and health fields. We discovered an overarching theme centered on caring in relation to how these professionals feel responsible for protecting other people's personal data and take on a "data guardian" role. The identification of the experiences and challenges of data guardians can aid organizations in recognizing and supporting this critical role. Study insights can also help designers of systems that process personal data to better align with the needs and constraints of data guardians.

Keywords: cybersecurity · privacy · personal data

1 Introduction

Many professional domains – such as health, finance, and education – require the collection and use of sensitive personal data[1], which, if compromised, could result in significant harm to patients, clients, or organizations. Protecting systems and data is a major concern in these settings, making it imperative that workers who interact with personal data understand and practice good security and privacy habits.

---

[1] The terminology used to describe sensitive, personal data varies within different laws, e.g., personally identifiable information (PII) in the Privacy Act [2], personal health information (PHI) in the Health Insurance Portability and Accountability Act [11], personal data in the General Data Protection Regulation [12], and personal information in the California Consumer Privacy Act [30]. For simplicity, within this document, we standardize on the term personal data.

A. Moallem (Ed.): HCII 2023, LNCS 14045, pp. 163–183, 2023.
https://doi.org/10.1007/978-3-031-35822-7_12

There are often rules and policies that govern workers' use of personal data. For example, in the United States (U.S.), the Health Insurance Portability and Accountability Act (HIPAA) Privacy Rule [11] establishes standards for protecting personal health data. The Financial Privacy and Safeguards Rules under the Gramm-Leach-Bliley Act (Financial Services Modernization Act of 1999) [1] govern how financial institutions collect, disclose, and protect personal financial data. Organizations may also enact their own policies or communicate expectations of how data and systems should be protected.

Despite its importance, the protection of personal data can be complicated, especially given the range of people and devices that may have access to this data. Organizational security and privacy rules and policies may not be attuned to occupational workflows or the ramifications on the workers and their primary duties. A common result is the development of circumventions and workarounds to security and privacy practices [18,28]. It may also be that the cost of adhering to security and privacy advice for an individual is greater than the benefit they receive, so they rationally choose to reject it [6,15]. Ultimately, the lack of compliance with organizational security and privacy policies in professional environments can put stakeholders, including clients, at risk.

While prior research investigated security and privacy practices and perceptions of experts and the general public (e.g., [7,34]), there has been little focused examination of professionals in work contexts that require them to regularly interact with and safeguard the personal data of others. To address this gap, our exploratory study examines a group of workers who are responsible for protecting the confidentiality of other people's personal data as part of their work responsibilities.

With a goal of developing a deeper understanding of the security and privacy beliefs, behaviors, and challenges of these professionals, we conducted an interview study of 19 individuals working in the U.S. who have responsibilities for protecting the confidentiality of personal data in their daily jobs. Specifically, we interviewed professionals in three sectors that involve significant collection and use of personal data: education, finance, and health. We sought to answer the following research questions about these professionals:

RQ1: What are the professionals' beliefs about and experiences with security and privacy in relation to their work?
RQ2: What motivating constructs guide the professionals' security and privacy understandings, beliefs, and behaviors in their daily work?
RQ3: What barriers or facilitators exist for these professionals in their protection of personal data?

We identified an overarching theme centered on "caring" in relation to interactions with personal data in the context of work. This caring was exemplified by a deep sense of personal responsibility for safeguarding others' personal data, motivated by ethical, legal, and organizational expectations. However, the security and privacy-protecting actions they take vary in sophistication and are undertaken with differing levels of diligence as these workers encounter multiple challenges.

Our research makes several contributions. Based on our analysis, we coined the term *data guardians*[2] in recognition of how our participants spoke about their roles and responsibilities. Beginning to uncover the definitional boundaries of the role and associated work practices allows organizations to recognize the importance of this group of professionals and consider how to best support them. Our findings, though focused on professionals in only three domains, may also be transferable and adapted to other populations of workers responsible for personal data. Study insights can also help designers of systems that store, process, and protect personal data to better understand the perspectives of prospective system users (the data guardians) so that interfaces, applications, and tools can be adapted to user needs and constraints. Furthermore, findings can help security and privacy champions and advocates (those who promote good security and privacy practices in professional settings) better address the needs of their target audiences.

2 Related Work

To provide a basis of comparison for our findings, we summarize prior work on security and privacy perceptions and behaviors of both experts and non-expert (general public) users of online technologies.

2.1 Experts

Multiple researchers examined the practices and perceptions of security and privacy experts (those who work in and are knowledgeable about security and privacy fields). Compared to non-experts, experts generally exhibit more sophisticated and accurate mental models of security and privacy [7,16,26,34]. They are able to comprehensively identify security and privacy risks and are less trusting of the online environment. However, because of their own expertise, they feel confident that they can avoid or recover from risks since they proactively implement protections [34]. Experts display a command of and familiarity with security and privacy tools and employ mitigations considered to be more robust, such as using a password manager, using two-factor authentication, encrypting sensitive communications, and using anonymization tools [7,16,26,34].

Some experts serve in educational and advocacy roles to impart security and privacy best practices and values to employees and build security and privacy culture within organizations. Examples include security champions [13], cybersecurity advocates [14], and privacy champions [33]. These experts employ a variety of persuasive techniques and communication channels to reach their target audiences. *Privacy champions* [33] are of special interest to our area of

---

[2] The term "data guardian" does not describe a formalized cybersecurity or privacy work role (e.g., like those described in the National Initiative for Cybersecurity Education Workforce Framework for Cybersecurity [22]), but rather encompasses a range of professionals using large amounts of personal data as part of their jobs.

investigation since our targeted study population is on the receiving end of champions' privacy awareness and advocacy efforts. Champions view privacy as being a multi-faceted concept that involves aspects of data protection and control, transparency, trust, legal compliance, and ethics. Despite good intentions, privacy champions encounter numerous challenges that threaten the success of their work, including negative attitudes or misunderstandings about privacy among their stakeholders and difficulty communicating the importance of privacy to audiences with diverse backgrounds and roles. To combat these challenges, privacy champions employ a variety of strategies to promote privacy, frequently emphasizing the need to take a "collaborative tone." They regularly engage in efforts to improve their organizations' privacy culture, develop guidance, policies, and tools to help stakeholders build privacy into their processes and products, and take on training and mentoring roles.

While the privacy champions study was focused on individuals in software teams, many of the findings may be applicable to those working in other privacy contexts within organizations, including our target population within the education, health, and finance domains. We envision that insights into challenges faced by our participants can aid privacy champions in adjusting their tactics to be more effective and responsive to these workers' needs.

2.2   Non-expert General Public Users

Non-expert general public users (individuals who do not have specialized security or privacy knowledge or responsibilities) operate with a different set of assumptions and mental models than experts. Prior research findings demonstrate that these users rely on multiple mental models about security and privacy that are often incomplete or incorrect and tend to not be proactive in their approach to online security and privacy [16,17,25,36].

Non-expert users can experience a form of security fatigue: feelings of resignation, complacency, and a loss of control [29]. Fatigue and frustration can then result in a decrease in desired security behaviors [10]. In the privacy context, people often are resigned to disclosing data and rationalize their use of privacy-invasive technologies despite their own discomfort [27]. The tendency to satisfice, cognitive biases, time pressures, lack of knowledge, and desensitization contribute to users often making poor security and privacy decisions [23,37]. In organizations, non-expert employees may view stringent security measures as counterproductive and stressful since these measures impede their ability to be flexible in their day-to-day operations [19,24]. Therefore, in what is known as "shadow security," users may circumvent or devise their own security measures to counter practices perceived as overly-burdensome [3,18,28]. Furthermore, employees may view organizational security awareness training as boring, with little relevance to their day-to-day work [4].

Our target population of data guardians (those are responsible for interacting with personal data on a regular basis) is different from both the security/privacy expert and non-expert populations. However, little is known about their practices and challenges. Our study begins to address this gap.

3 Methodology

We conducted an exploratory, semi-structured interview study to investigate the security and privacy perceptions and practices of professionals who regularly interact with personal data. The NIST Research Protections Office reviewed the protocol for this research project (ITL-0010) and determined it meets the criteria for "exempt human subjects research" as defined in 15 CFR 27, the Common Rule for the Protection of Human Subjects.

3.1 Sample and Recruitment

We purposefully recruited professionals in education, finance, and healthcare domains whose jobs necessitated frequent interactions with other people's personal data but who were not privacy and security experts. Working with three domains allowed us to focus the data collection and analysis on a bounded case and permitted more thorough exploration of potential domain-related differences in worker beliefs, behaviors, and experiences.

Initially, we used both personal and professional contacts to generate names of potential participants from each of the three domains. This purposeful sampling [21] was combined with convenience sampling, in which access, availability, and willingness to participate played a role in recruitment. Twelve participants came from this initial outreach to contacts. Subsequently, seven additional participants were recruited through snowball sampling in which participants suggested others who might be willing to participate. Participants were from two regions in the U.S.: 14 from four different states in the Midwest, and five from Mid-Atlantic states and Washington, D.C.

3.2 Data Collection

We developed a semi-structured interview protocol that included questions designed to elicit information about participants' beliefs, behaviors, and challenges related to online security and privacy in their work. The protocol was largely based on a prior study that investigated expert and general public perspectives [34], with adjustments for our specific population. Several professional colleagues who work in positions similar to those of our sample reviewed the protocol for language, content, and flow. We used their feedback to revise the protocol, then conducted two pilot interviews with representative participants to gain additional feedback that resulted in minor adjustments to clarify language.

After finalizing the protocol, we conducted 19 interviews. The in-person interviews averaged about 30 min and took place in a location convenient for the participant. Participants were compensated with a $50.00 gift card.

Prior to beginning each interview, the research team provided participants with an information sheet and talked to them about the purpose of the study and how their data would be collected, used, and protected. Participants then completed a short demographics questionnaire. All but one session were audio-recorded and transcribed. Participant H05 requested not to be recorded, but agreed that the interviewer could take notes. To protect confidentiality, we assigned reference codes to participants: a letter indicating the participant's work domain (E = education; F = finance; and H = healthcare) is followed by the interview number (e.g., H04).

3.3 Data Analysis

The research team iteratively coded and analyzed the data for this study. Data analysis began with the development of an *a priori* code list based on research questions and related literature. Initially, the researchers independently read and coded the same three transcripts to determine how they were using and applying codes. Subsequently, each of the researchers read two additional transcripts and met again to identify any ongoing issues with the code list, including the need for more specific operationalization (definition) of a code or the creation of emergent codes. Subsequently, the two researchers split the remainder of the transcripts to complete the coding.

We continued to meet regularly during this process to discuss our coding. We focused not just on agreement but also on where and why there were differences in our coding and the insights afforded by subsequent discussions [5,20]. Once coding was completed, subsequent analysis included organizing the data into higher-level codes (axial coding) and discussing relationships in the codes and the data (selective coding) [21]. This process allowed us to discuss our emergent ideas and refine our interpretations as we moved from concrete codes to more abstract constructs and themes. What emerged was an overarching sense of care on the part of data guardians in relation to their access to and protection of other people's personal data.

4 Participants

Of the 19 participants, there were eight participants who worked in education, six in finance, and five in healthcare. All participants directly supported others, whether that be students and their families in the education domain, clients in the finance domain, or patients in the healthcare domain. They also all held positions requiring professional licenses or certifications within their domains (e.g., teacher, realtor, nurse).

Table 1 provides an overview of participant demographics, including self-reported security knowledge. There were similar numbers of male (9) and female (10) participants, ranging in age from 20–29 years old to 60+. Only three participants indicated a high level of security knowledge, over half (n = 10) rated themselves as having a moderate amount of knowledge, and just under a third (n = 6) said they had little or very little knowledge.

In their daily work, these professionals often interacted with a wide range of personal data. A school social worker regularly encountered student data consisting of: "date of birth, residence, grades, parent names... When I have

Table 1. Participant Demographics

Domain	ID	Occupation	Gender	Age Range	Security Knowledge
Education	E01	School administrator and teacher	F	30–39	moderate
	E02	Special education teacher	F	40–49	little
	E03	High school teacher	F	50–59	very little
	E04	School social worker	F	20–29	little
	E05	High school counselor	F	30–39	moderate
	E06	Elementary school teacher	F	30–39	moderate
	E07	High school counselor and data analyst	F	30–39	moderate
	E08	University administrator and faculty	M	40–49	high
Finance	F01	Finance banker	M	50–59	high
	F02	Accountant	M	20–29	little
	F03	Realtor	M	30–39	little
	F04	Accountant	F	40–49	moderate
	F05	Investment banking intern	M	20–29	high
	F06	Realtor	F	60+	moderate
Health	H01	Mental health professional	M	60+	moderate
	H02	Physical therapist	M	30–39	moderate
	H03	Nurse	F	50–59	moderate
	H04	Doctor	M	30–39	moderate
	H05	Nurse	M	30–39	little

access to IEPs [individualized education program] that often includes some medical,... social-emotional level of mental health" (E04). An accountant enumerated the type of client data he interacts with: "date of birth, social security number, age, address,... children, children's social security numbers,... bank information" (F02). A doctor discussed the personal data he has access to: "medical records... name, address, phone number,... insurance information,... financial information" (H04).

5 Results

Today, the work of many professionals necessitates a high degree of dependence on computers and working online. The individuals we interviewed further depended on having access to personal data necessary for them to provide support and services to their students, patients, and clients. Overall, we found that these professionals recognized and exhibited care when interacting with other people's data, essentially operating as data guardians. In the following sections, we discuss this emerging theme of *care* in the context of participants' perceptions, behaviors, and challenges related to the protection of personal data.

5.1 Privacy and Security Conceptualizations

To first understand perceptions of privacy, we asked participants what they thought privacy means in the context of their work. Privacy was frequently expressed as the protection of personal data, most commonly by limiting who has access. For example, a high school counselor said, "privacy would be having that [student and parent] information, making sure that it's protected, if we have it on our computers, that we're not sharing it outside of just the small circle that needs to know that information" (E05).

Privacy was also described in general terms of what might happen if sensitive data got into the wrong hands. A participant remarked, "It's about information that's personal that, if released, could do damage of a multitude of types" (F04).

Other participants characterized privacy as following a set of procedures dictated either by the organization or regulation. For example, a school administrator stated, "Privacy to me is a lot of there being rules and then there being people who are aware of what the rules are because I think having the rules isn't really enough" (E01).

Participants were also asked about the relationship between privacy and security. Overall, they understood that the two concepts, though not the same, were strongly related. For example, both deal with protection and controlling access. Beyond that, security was perceived as being an enabler of privacy in an *active* sense: "Privacy is kind of the goal and security's the way to get there" (F05). One participant viewed privacy as protecting data in a physical format and security as protecting digital data:

> "Privacy is more making sure that somebody's not watching what you're doing when you're on the computer so that they're not able to view something they shouldn't view when they're standing there. Whereas security is a little bit more in-depth than that, making sure somebody else can't hack into that system and access that without your being there" (H03).

5.2 What It Means to Care

Across the three domains, participants spoke about a sense of personal responsibility related to protecting others' personal data. In part, this was because their work today necessitates a different type of interaction with client data. Taking care of others (students, clients, or patients) now also means taking care of their data online. A doctor spoke specifically about this responsibility: "It's my responsibility to make sure I follow the rules, make sure I do everything in my power to keep people's information safe and make sure that I don't do anything that could lead to somebody's information getting out there" (H04).

However, participants drew a distinction between protecting their own versus others' data, often being more attentive to security in their work context as compared to their personal context. An educator said:

> "If it's my information, I can make a decision about what to send and when to send it and how to send it and if I care. But when I have other people's information,...I think I have to be a little bit more careful because, well, it's not mine. So, it shouldn't be up to me about whether or not that's put in danger" (E01).

5.3   How Participants Care

We asked participants what actions they took to safeguard personal data. Specific actions included having strong passwords, encrypting sensitive emails, and using secure wireless connections or virtual private networks (VPNs). However, some participants were vague in their articulation of actions they take. For example, an educator noted that "I'm just really super cautious" (E03), and a healthcare worker said it was about "being mindful" (E06).

Beyond their own actions, participants also relied heavily on others – service providers or Information Technology (IT) professionals within their organizations – to provide oversight and keep the data they work with safe. A high school counselor said, "I just am trusting that the makers of the software that we use...know that this information has to be protected or that there's some sort of regulation about it that keeps that information safe. But I don't know that for a fact" (E05). This reliance was often based on blind trust since data guardians did not see themselves as experts in this area, as expressed by one participant: "I'm not a cyber tech guy at all, so I just kind of take what we're given and roll with it" (F02).

5.4   Motivations for Caring

The caring that participants articulated was connected to ethical, legal, and organizational expectations. Not meeting those expectations could result in negative consequences.

Ethical Obligations. Almost all participants spoke about having an ethical obligation to protect personal data. A financial and wealth advisor said, "It's a trust factor and one that's an ethical issue too. When somebody submits their personal information, you're saying, 'Yeah. Okay. I've got it, and I'll protect it to make sure it doesn't leak out' " (F01). Participants often related ethics to what would happen if trust was lost due to a privacy/security breach. An owner of an accounting firm talked about potential loss of company reputation:

> "As a small company, it's often word of mouth. We need our clients to trust us. We need them to trust that we will keep their data and information safe, that nothing will happen to it, that others will not be able to access it, and that we are doing everything in our power to ensure that. Without that trust and without that relationship, we do not have the potential to grow as a firm. We, I believe, would suffer financially tremendously if we had a breach in that trust relationship" (F04).

Beyond reputation, other participants articulated potential consequences to those they supported. An accountant discussed financial consequences for clients should their data be breached: "Their information could be out there, and their investment portfolio could be accessed" (F02). An educator described potential dangers for students and their families:

"Many students' families and sometimes students are undocumented. And in this particular political moment, that could be really dangerous. We have really sensitive information that matters, I think, for our students' lives, for their families' lives, for their siblings' lives" (E02)

Legal Obligations. Some participants were familiar with applicable laws governing the use and protection of personal data in their domain, while others were not. Healthcare workers all mentioned HIPAA; however, their comments did not always specifically address legal obligations related to *online* privacy and security. Educators rarely noted legal obligations, with only two participants providing vague references to mandated reporting laws that do not mention online privacy and security specifically. Of the three domains, those who worked in finance articulated legal responsibilities and consequences the most clearly. An accountant identified legal consequences should a breach occur by citing a U.S. Internal Revenue Service code: "Section 7216 imposes criminal and financial penalties on tax preparers when they have knowingly or recklessly disclosed return-related information, so we take that very seriously" (F04).

Organizational Expectations. Participants were often motivated by organizational security and privacy expectations. Oftentimes, these expectations were customized to the domain and organizational needs, as noted by a small business owner: "We're a very small firm. What works for us may not work for a large, multinational corporation, but certainly, what works for a large, multinational corporation is not going to work for us" (F04).

Participants generally recognized the importance of following organizational rules and policies, even if doing so required extra effort. For example, a doctor commented on his view of the importance of following organizational rules:

"Sometimes there are things we don't want to have to do and it would be faster to do it a different way, but less secure. And so I'm always going to opt on the side of being more secure. But that might mean it takes me longer. That might mean the next patient has to wait an extra five minutes, but those are things I think we've got to do if we want things to be safe" (H04).

Most participants received some type of training or written guidance about organizational expectations. For some, training took place when they first joined the organization. A few participants said they receive training constantly throughout the year. However, more often, training was a once-a-year activity.

Even though training was common, the *importance* placed on training and communicating expectations varied. Some organizations viewed ongoing training as essential, as expressed by a small business owner: "In our field, even today, folks receive very little training on cybersecurity, on how to keep information safe, on what to do, and how to do it. And so I think the first thing is educate yourself" (F04). She continued, "We have clear policies around that, and we do try to ensure that everyone follows those. I would say that I think, for the most part, folks do" (F04). However, other organizations, especially in the education domain, were less clear about their expectations or did not communicate those in terms understandable to their employees, leaving workers unsure about how to keep data safe. E04, a teacher, said that she had received "no training" about security and privacy. In some cases, data guardians received a handbook with a long list of guidelines. This large volume of information could be overwhelming, so workers may not retain the information, as expressed by a teacher:

> "There's a whole list of things that we're supposed to do. Do I know this list? No. So it must not be that important. And we have to sign a contract or some sort of legal document that says that we read those and that we will follow those rules, but I don't know if anyone really knows what they are" (E03).

Further contributing to confusion, some organizations' actions were inconsistent with their own rules. For example, one participant discussed the contradictory ways in which his university dealt with a security issue:

> "They say we're always supposed to be using not the public, unsecure network, but the secure network. But... when tech support can't figure out how to get you onto the secure WiFi when you're actually on the premises, then they're like, 'Oh well, just use unsecure. It's not that big of a deal' " (E08).

Not following organizational policies could have consequences for employees. One educator said she is "nervous... that I could maybe... get disciplined for being careless" (E03). A financial participant commented, "some of these are fireable offenses" (F01). Another said, "Our employees know what the consequences will be by not following those policies and procedures, and it would be termination. We take this seriously" (F04).

5.5   Challenges to Caring

While participants acknowledged that they have a responsibility to protect the personal data of their students, clients, and patients, they often encountered a number of challenges that impeded their ability and willingness to do so.

Attitudes and Biases. A majority of participants – including all education participants – expressed personal attitudes that may interfere with their willingness to take protective actions. These attitudes were often rooted in the availability heuristic, in which people assess the probability of a security or privacy breach occurring based on recent events, and the optimism bias, in which people believe they are less likely to experience a negative event. For example, showing an optimism bias, a high school art teacher opined, "the chances of anybody really targeting me are so low that as long as I don't make silly mistakes and just give out my passwords, I'll probably be fine, statistics show" (E01).

While they may be diligent about protecting others' data, some participants expressed attitudes that impacted their personal practices, suggesting that their good security and privacy habits may not persist outside of the work context. A physical therapist was not as worried about his own online privacy because "I don't feel like I'm doing anything that the police would be coming to me for" (H02). Others expressed resignation that there was not much they could do to protect themselves online because giving up some privacy is "just a way of life today" (E02).

Lack of Knowledge. Participants cited their lack of security and privacy knowledge as an impediment to their behaviors. Although our participants regularly accessed and interacted with personal data, security and privacy were not their areas of expertise nor their primary focus while on the job. A health care provider remarked that security can be a burden because "it's another thing to learn... That was not something that I went to nursing school to figure out" (H03). While more than half of participants rated their level of security knowledge as moderate or high, their responses and behaviors did not always reflect this. F06, a realtor, rated her security knowledge as moderate, but made comments demonstrating that she did not understand technology or security. For example, she recounted how she had fallen prey to an online scam, expressed confusion about how her computer works, and said "I don't know that I'm qualified or smart enough to figure it out" when asked what might help her stay safe online.

Not Understanding Risks. Participants knew that bad things can happen but could not always articulate specific risks. An educator commented, "Whatever it is it could hurt people... I'm not even sure what the risks are. I just know they're out there" (E03). Since they did not fully understand the risks, they did not know if their actions were appropriate or effective, leaving them feeling uncertain, frustrated, and anxious. For example, when talking about how to protect private data, a school social worker commented, "I have no idea how people hack into that... And so when I don't understand something, I don't think that I'm able to feel confident that I'm accurately protecting myself" (E04). When asked what emotions online security and privacy invoke, she said, "I would say frustration. I would say helplessness,... Feeling like it's something that I could never get on top of given that it's not my job. I'm not in internet security" (E04).

Difficulty in Keeping Knowledge Current. The pace of change in technology and security/privacy threats, mitigations, and regulations further contributed to participants' lack of understanding and feelings of powerlessness. A realtor said:

> "I don't know all the ways things could happen, so how could I take precautions to protect myself and my clients from those things? I've taken

classes on computer security...But that can only do so much, and these hackers are coming up with...more and more clever ways to get around all sorts of firewalls" (F03).

Adapting to and educating employees about security and privacy changes was a particular challenge to organizations. H04 mentioned that his healthcare employer has to continually update training to keep up. The owner of a small accounting firm recognized the importance and complexity of keeping pace: "We need to continually update our skills, update our tools and resources, update the way we do things, update our policies and procedures. Without that, I don't think we can have real privacy" (F04).

Need for Improved Training. To address the perceived lack of security and privacy knowledge, several participants thought that they should be provided more or better training or resources at work. A nurse expressed a desire for more guidance on how to protect patient data, saying, "It'd be nice, though, if there is...some easily accessible resource out there that talks about what needs to be done and the easiest way to do it" (H03). To address the unknowns of how to best protect counseling notes, a school social worker thought that standard, secure procedures should be communicated throughout the organization: "I think it would be something good for all social workers in the network or something to have a training on security or to be told... 'This is how we're all going to track our confidential meeting notes' " (E04).

Complexity. Even though participants recognized that protecting personal data is part of their job, they often found it to be complex, difficult, and taking time away from their primary tasks. A finance banker, F01, summed up the complexity he encounters: "Lots of procedures, lots of security issues, a lot of bank regulation issues." Several mentioned that there are multiple systems and software applications they need for their jobs, which adds time and difficulty in keeping track of sometimes conflicting system security requirements. Passwords were repeatedly mentioned as an example of a burdensome security mechanism, especially when having to maintain different passwords on multiple systems.

Even though participants often articulated the importance of following organizational rules, they did not always follow prescribed practices due to complexity. To cope, they sometimes found workarounds. However, these workarounds often negated the intent of the rule. One participant thought that workarounds were inevitable: "Human nature often defaults to the easiest possible scenario and the fastest possible scenario and maybe not necessarily the safest possible scenario" (H04). Because of the desire to do what is easiest, H05 said that he rarely sees people following security and privacy procedures at work. A university educator recognized the value of security and privacy, yet "I haphazardly practice good behavior. My first emotion is just being annoyed. One more thing to deal with" (E08). In the case of passwords, participants admitted to less-secure practices, including choosing a simple password, using the same password for multiple systems, or writing their passwords down.

To address complexity, participants expressed a need for usable security and privacy solutions that could seamlessly integrate into the work environment. A participant commented, "What really is needed are tools and mechanisms that are not cumbersome and that allow us to get on with our work while at the same time protecting privacy and providing security" (F04). Another said that, although he has a duty to make good choices, the onus is not just on him:

"I think that the people who develop these tools, I think the people who come up with these programs, I think they have a responsibility, too, and their responsibility is to make sure that it's not too cumbersome on me... If you want me to be safe and secure, you need to find ways to help me do that" (H04).

Inevitability of Security Problems. Participants were often realistic in their expectations of security and their own limitations. For example, a participant said, "We know that nothing is ever 100% safe. That's true whether we're talking about handwritten records and physical files, or we're talking about things that are kept online" (H04). Even when they followed best practices and organizational procedures, they thought it may never be enough to adequately protect the personal data with which they are entrusted. A financial sector participant commented, "Our responsibility is to make sure that we're following best practice and that we do everything we can, knowing that maybe we can't do everything and that something might still happen" (F04). A realtor said, "I don't feel confident that anything is safe enough" (F06).

Because of their deep sense of responsibility for protecting others' data, the concern that, no matter what they do, personal data could still be compromised resulted in participants experiencing emotions such as frustration, anxiety, stress, and fear. F04 acknowledged that anyone can make an error that puts personal data in jeopardy: "One mistake, one click – and sometimes it's very easy to click by mistake – and who knows where you'll be, who knows what will happen, and who knows what then happens in terms of clients' data and information." As a result, F04 said:

"I feel fear and that bothers me. I don't think I should have to feel fear in my work,... but I think that it's the fact that it seems at least to be out of my control. I can put mechanisms in place and policies in place and tools in place and still we get phishing emails and still we can be hacked and sometimes we might not even know it."

Similarly, when asked what emotions he feels when thinking about online privacy and security, a doctor said:

"I'd say I'm worried, always worried. There's that level of stress I think anytime you're in charge of or have other people's information and other people's lives, if you will, in your hand... While I'd like to save that stress for saving people's lives, I think sometimes this might, in fact, be just as serious to them in some cases" (H04).

6   Discussion

In this section, based on our bounded case of the education, finance, and health domains, we compare data guardians to previously identified user populations, finding them to be a group with special needs. We then suggest ways in which organizations can better support their own data guardians.

6.1   Between Two Worlds

In their critical role in the protection of personal data, data guardians are a unique population of workers who, at times, are between two worlds: those of security/privacy experts and general public users. Like experts, data guardians are expected to know online security and privacy best practices and consistently make good choices to protect personal data. However, these workers often think and behave more like non-expert, general public users.

We observed a marked tension between data guardians *wanting* to protect personal data and *being able* to protect. Like the experts represented in prior studies [7,34], data guardians exhibit a sense of responsibility about keeping personal data secure and private, and they generally understand that negative consequences could result if they fail in those duties. However, in contrast to experts, their primary education and training are focused on roles that support people rather than systems. Their lack of security expertise may result in them not feeling empowered to protect personal data, whereas experts have confidence in their own abilities [34].

Unlike general public non-experts who often are resigned about their inability to protect their own data [27,34], data guardians have a greater sense of duty since they are stewards of others' personal data. Moreover, they may have strict organizational procedures they must follow or may be subject to significant consequences for violating national or state laws. However, despite this extra burden of responsibility, similar to general public users (e.g., as identified in [16,17,25]), data guardians may have limited understanding of security and privacy risks, technologies, and mitigation strategies and have inconsistent security/privacy experiences as they navigate different applications. Complexity and conflict with their primary tasks result in the security workarounds and justifications that exemplify the shadow security phenomenon found in prior studies [3,18]. Some participants are further unsure of organizational or legal expectations about desired security and privacy practices beyond general platitudes. These uncertainties result in data guardians often taking limited actions on their own and largely depending on others, as also reflected in prior work [16,25]. In addition, our participants clearly exhibit the "security fatigue" previously noted among the general population [29] in their expression of biases that lead to less vigilance, frustration with complex and unusable security mechanisms, and a sense of powerlessness that no matter what they do, something bad may still happen [23,37].

6.2   Domain Differences

Although our sample size was not large enough to definitively identify contrasts among data guardians in the education, finance, and healthcare domains, we offer preliminary thoughts about observed differences.

Overall, participants in the education domain had the least amount of formal security training, often saying that they did not remember much of the guidance provided by their institutions, if provided at all. These participants often did not know about applicable laws governing the protection of data in educational institutions and seemed to be more naive about the likelihood of a privacy or security breach. Education participants also were more likely to see security as complex and admit their lack of understanding. These findings suggest potential reasons behind susceptibility of education organizations to attack and the poor evaluations states received regarding their ability to protect student records [31, 35].

In contrast, finance and healthcare participants received more focused security and privacy training, often on a continuous basis. These participants also exhibited a deeper understanding of the harmful repercussions of security or privacy compromises. In particular, healthcare participants worked in a high-stakes environment in which their patients' health and lives may depend on the security of personal and medical data. In general, finance and healthcare participants, although recognizing that safeguarding data could be time-intensive, often placed its importance above convenience. They were also more knowledgeable about applicable regulations and organizational policies, likely because of clearer regulations and harsher consequences for not following those [9,11]. Finance participants working in banking or accounting were most able to articulate how they could safeguard personal data in their care.

6.3   Practical Implications for Supporting Data Guardians

Our study identifies a class of employees who work with and are expected to protect online personal data but may not be adequately equipped to do so. The following are actions organizations can take to better support data guardians.

Identify the Data Guardians in the Organization. The conceptualization of data guardians and their work practices allows organizations to recognize the importance of the role in the protection of data, their level of responsibility, and how best to support them. In some domains, it is clear which employees operate as data guardians (e.g., health professionals), but it is less clear in others (e.g., realtors). As initial steps in supporting guardians, organizations can: 1) create clear criteria for classifying data guardians (those who use personal data on a regular basis), 2) identify who the data guardians are in the organization; 3) recognize ways in which data guardians interact with other people's personal data; and 4) determine how these interactions support (or interfere with) guardians' primary tasks towards solutions that mitigate interference with primary tasks.

Work to Create a Strong Privacy and Security Culture. While data guardians recognize their responsibility to care, we found that their organization's culture does not always support them in enacting that care. Therefore, establishing a strong privacy/security culture at all levels of the organization, although non-trivial, is essential for supporting data guardians. This may be especially important in educational institutions, where there are current gaps impacting data guardians. Organizational leadership can outwardly recognize the value of the data guardian role and ensure adequate resources to support these workers. IT and security staff should model desired security and policy behaviors by consistently following organizational policies. Privacy and security champions can also play a significant role in improving their organization's security and privacy culture, for example, through targeted discussions about the importance of privacy/security, gaining management support for privacy functions and tools, and facilitating communication between teams [13,14,33].

Communicate Expectations. Our participants were sometimes uncertain about specific actions they were required to take. To minimize uncertainty, organizational expectations about online security/privacy should be clearly and consistently communicated, including why these policies are in place and the consequences when rules and policies are not followed. In particular, data guardians should understand how their security and privacy actions relate to the ethical and legal responsibilities of their jobs. In this regard, organizations can appeal to data guardians' strong motivation of responsibility to care to impart on them the importance of acting diligently to protect data.

Provide Targeted and Ongoing Awareness and Training. We found that security and privacy awareness training varied greatly in quantity and quality. Training and reference documentation should be meaningful for the data guardians and customized to the specific work they do within the organization. For example, training could identify common types of personal data encountered in the daily work, risks, mitigations, misconceptions, and challenges faced by data guardians within a specific domain. Training and documentation should include not just awareness of privacy and security issues, but also actionable and achievable steps to take [14] that empower guardians to engage in best practices while also being successful in their primary tasks. Furthermore, beyond the typical, once-a-year training common in many organizations, training should be engaging, relatable, and reinforced throughout the year via a variety of communication media tailored to the preferences and needs of the data guardians within an organization [4]. Furthermore, providing information that makes a "work-home" connection can encourage the building of sustainable and consistent online security and privacy habits [8].

Procure and Develop Usable Systems and Processes. Complexity and lack of usability was a common challenge noted in our interviews, often resulting in frustration or less-secure workarounds. To counter this challenge, organizations should work toward developing or selecting usable systems and processes for use by data guardians. Interfaces, applications, and tools must be adapted to the specific needs and constraints of these workers and avoid placing too great a burden on data guardians as they try to accomplish their primary tasks. There also needs to be greater integration between systems to minimize the burden on data guardians, for example, by enacting single sign-on authentication. Data guardians should be involved in the requirements gathering and piloting of these systems and processes to voice questions or issues they encounter.

6.4   Limitations and Future Work

Our study has several limitations. Participants' self-reported responses might have been influenced by social desirability or recall biases. For example, participants may have been hesitant to talk about negative security behaviors or attitudes. Additionally, since the concept of a data guardian role is emergent, we relied on traditional domains where employees typically work with others' personal data, specifically focusing on just three domains as a starting point. Coupled with the smaller number of participants common to qualitative research, the study cannot be generalized to all professional roles and domains. However, unlike quantitative research, generalizability is not the goal of exploratory qualitative work, which strives to provide rich descriptions that allow for understanding of the phenomenon under study, the identification of future research areas, and the transferability of findings to other contexts [32]. Additional research may extend our study to include other domains or do a deep-dive into a particular domain to gather sector-specific insights. Finally, we did not consider the size or type (e.g., private, public) of organizations in the selection of participants. This may be a focus for future research that could explore how data guardians are supported in different categories of organizations.

7   Conclusion

Through an interview study of professionals in the education, finance, and healthcare domains, our research identifies the motivations, behaviors, and challenges of taking on a data guardian role. Data guardians, while not security or privacy experts, are unique from general public users in their sense of responsibility and care for safeguarding other people's data. Although this role is in support of their primary profession, it is nonetheless essential for their jobs and supporting their students, clients, and patients. Our identification of current security and privacy misconceptions and the challenges faced by data guardians can aid organizations in the improvement of organizational awareness and training programs. Study insights can also help designers of systems that store, process, and protect personal data to better understand the perspectives of prospective system users (the data guardians) so that interfaces, applications, and tools can be adapted to user needs and constraints. Our investigation, though focused on professionals in only three domains, may also be transferable and adapted to other populations of workers responsible for sensitive data.

Disclaimer

Certain commercial companies or products are identified in this paper to foster understanding. Such identification does not imply recommendation or endorsement by the National Institute of Standards and Technology, nor does it imply that the companies or products identified are necessarily the best available for the purpose.

References

1. 106th Congress: S.900 - Gramm-Leach-Bliley Act (1999). https://www.congress.gov/bill/106th-congress/senate-bill/900
2. 113th Congress: S.607 - Electronic communications privacy act amendments act of 2013 (2013). https://www.congress.gov/bill/113th-congress/senate-bill/607/text
3. Alotaibi, M., Furnell, S., Clarke, N.: Information security policies: a review of challenges and influencing factors. In: 2016 11th International Conference for Internet Technology and Secured Transactions (ICITST), pp. 352–358 (2016)
4. Bada, M., Sasse, M.A., Nurse, J.R.: Cyber security awareness campaigns: why do they fail to change behaviour? (2019). https://arxiv.org/ftp/arxiv/papers/1901/1901.02672.pdf
5. Barbour, R.S.: Checklists for improving rigour in qualitative research: a case of the tail wagging the dog? BMJ **322**(7294), 1115–1117 (2001)
6. Barth, S., de Jong, M.D., Junger, M., Hartel, P.H., Roppelt, J.C.: Putting the privacy paradox to the test: online privacy and security behaviors among users with technical knowledge, privacy awareness, and financial resources. Telematics Inform. **41**, 55–69 (2019)
7. Busse, K., Schäfer, J., Smith, M.: Replication: '...no one can hack my mind' - revisiting a study on expert and non-expert security practices and advice. In: Fifteenth Symposium on Usable Privacy and Security (SOUPS 2019), pp. 117–136 (2019)
8. Caldwell, T.: Making security awareness training work. Comput. Fraud Secur. **6**, 8–14 (2016)
9. Congressional Research Service: Financial services and cybersecurity: The federal role (2016). https://crsreports.congress.gov/product/pdf/R/R44429
10. D'Arcy, J., Teh, P.L.: Predicting employee information security policy compliance on a daily basis: the interplay of security-related stress, emotions, and neutralization. Inf. Manag. **56**(7), 103151 (2019)
11. Department of Health and Human Services: The HIPAA privacy rule (2021). https://www.hhs.gov/hipaa/for-professionals/privacy/index.html
12. European Union: General data protection regulation (2016). https://gdpr.eu/
13. Gabriel, T., Furnell, S.: Selecting security champions. Comput. Fraud Secur. **8**, 8–12 (2011)
14. Haney, J.M., Lutters, W.G.: "It's scary...it's confusing...it's dull": how cybersecurity advocates overcome negative perceptions of security. In: Fourteenth Symposium on Usable Privacy and Security (SOUPS 2018), pp. 411–425 (2018)
15. Herley, C.: So long, and no thanks for the externalities: the rational rejection of security advice by users. In: 2009 Workshop on New Security Paradigms, pp. 133–144 (2009)

16. Ion, I., Reeder, R., Consolvo, S.: '...no one can hack my mind': comparing expert and non-expert security practices. In: Eleventh Symposium on Usable Privacy and Security (SOUPS 2015), pp. 327–346 (2015)
17. Kang, R., Dabbish, L., Fruchter, N., Kiesler, S.: "My data just goes everywhere:" user mental models of the internet and implications for privacy and security. In: Eleventh Symposium on Usable Privacy and Security (SOUPS 2015) (2015)
18. Kirlappos, I., Parkin, S., Sasse, M.A.: "Shadow security" as a tool for the learning organization. Comput. Soc. 45(1), 29–37 (2015)
19. Lee, C., Lee, C.C., Kim, S.: Understanding information security stress: focusing on the type of information security compliance activity. Comput. Secur. 59, 60–70 (2016)
20. McDonald, N., Schoenebeck, S., Forte, A.: Reliability and inter-rater reliability in qualitative research: norms and guidelines for CSCW and HCI practice. In: ACM on Human-Computer Interaction, p. 72. ACM (2019)
21. Merriam, S.B., Tisdell, E.J.: Qualitative Research: A Guide to Design and Implementation, 4th edn. Wiley, San Francisco (2016)
22. Petersen, R., Santos, D., Smith, M.C., Wetzel, K.A., Witte, G.: NIST Special Publication 800-181 Revision 1: Workforce Framework for Cybersecurity (NICE Framework) (2020). https://nvlpubs.nist.gov/nistpubs/SpecialPublications/NIST.SP.800-181r1.pdf
23. Pfleeger, S.L., Caputo, D.D.: Leveraging behavioral science to mitigate cyber security risk. Comput. Secur. 31(4), 597–611 (2012)
24. Post, G.V., Kagan, A.: Evaluating information security tradeoffs: restricting access can interfere with user tasks. Comput. Secur. 26(3), 229–237 (2007)
25. Prettyman, S.S., Furman, S., Theofanos, M., Stanton, B.: Privacy and security in the brave new world: the use of multiple mental models. In: Tryfonas, T., Askoxylakis, I. (eds.) HAS 2015. LNCS, vol. 9190, pp. 260–270. Springer, Cham (2015). https://doi.org/10.1007/978-3-319-20376-8_24
26. Racine, E., Skeba, P., Baumer, E.P., Forte, A.: What are PETs for privacy experts and non-experts. In: Sixteenth Symposium on Usable Privacy and Security (SOUPS 2020) (2020)
27. Seberger, J.S., Llavore, M., Wyant, N.N., Shklovski, I., Patil, S.: Empowering resignation: there's an app for that. In: 2021 CHI Conference on Human Factors in Computing Systems, pp. 1–18 (2021)
28. Smith, S.W., Koppel, R., Blythe, J., Kothari, V.: Mismorphism: a semiotic model of computer security circumvention. In: 2015 Symposium and Bootcamp on the Science of Security, pp. 1–2 (2015)
29. Stanton, B., Theofanos, M.F., Prettyman, S.S., Furman, S.: Security fatigue. IT Prof. 18(5), 26–32 (2016)
30. State of California: SB-327 Information privacy: connected devices (2018). https://leginfo.legislature.ca.gov
31. Stickland, R., Haimson, L.: The state student privacy report card: grading the states on protecting student data privacy. Technical report, Network for Public Education (2019)
32. Swedberg, R.: Exploratory research. In: Elman, C., Gerring, J., Mahoney, J. (eds.) The Production of Knowledge: Enhancing Progress in Social Science, pp. 17–41. Cambridge University Press (2020)
33. Tahaei, M., Frik, A., Vaniea, K.: Privacy champions in software teams: understanding their motivations, strategies, and challenges. In: Proceedings of the 2021 CHI Conference on Human Factors in Computing Systems, pp. 1–15 (2021)

34. Theofanos, M., Stanton, B., Furman, S., Prettyman, S.S., Garfinkel, S.: Be prepared: how US government experts think about cybersecurity. In: Workshop on Usable Security (USEC) (2017)
35. Verizon: 2021 data breach investigations report (2022). https://www.verizon.com/business/resources/reports/2021-data-breach-investigations-report.pdfx
36. Wash, R.: Folk models of home computer security. In: Sixth Symposium on Usable Privacy and Security (SOUPS 2010), pp. 11–26 (2010)
37. West, R., Mayhorn, C., Hardee, J., Mendel, J.: The weakest link: a psychological perspective on why users make poor security decisions. In: Social and Human Elements of Information Security: Emerging Trends and Countermeasures, pp. 43–60 (2009)

A Privacy-Orientated Distributed Data Storage Model for Smart Homes

Khutso Lebea and Wai Sze Leung[(✉)]

University of Johannesburg, Johannesburg, South Africa
{klebea,wsleung}@uj.ac.za

Abstract. With the wide adoption of smart home devices, users are concerned with what sensitive data these devices may be collecting and what that data may be used for. This paper proposes a way to reduce the level of dis-trust between the end-users and the companies that offer smart home hard-ware and/or personalised software services by allowing end-users to retain an optimal degree of control over their personal data (such as voice and video recordings) which is typically collected by the service provider and stored on the service provider's cloud platform.

Keywords: Privacy · Smart Devices · User Data Collection · IoT

1 Introduction

The Internet of Things (IoT) refers to physical devices that are connected to the Internet [1]. According to statista.com, the number of devices connected to the Internet in a typical United States home stands at an average of 10.37 devices in the year 2020. The list of devices includes but is not limited to mobile phones, computers, tablets, televisions and television smart boxes, video game consoles, smart speakers, smartwatches, and virtual reality devices [2]. These smart devices create, analyze, and store an abundance of user data in order to provide what the service providers deem the best possible end-user experience [3].

The creation of smart home devices that are capable of learning and processing information as close to human capacity is one of the core ambitions of Artificial Intelligence (AI) and Machine Learning (ML). To achieve this aspiration, AI and ML have had to make progress in numerous domains, with the aforementioned connected devices leveraging advancements such as object recognition, image processing, speech recognition, robotics, and natural language processing to learn and understand the environments they are designed to function in [4].

To train and perfect these AI concepts, one requires a considerable amount of data for training and testing purposes. Smart home industry giants such as Amazon, Google, and Apple all boast devices designed to make the lives of their end-users simpler and more efficient through smart assistance, a feat only achievable when the various AI

The original version of the chapter has been revised. A correction to this chapter can be found at https://doi.org/10.1007/978-3-031-35822-7_45

A. Moallem (Ed.): HCII 2023, LNCS 14045, pp. 184–193, 2023.
https://doi.org/10.1007/978-3-031-35822-7_13

technologies have the means to learn the habits, traits, likes, and dislikes of the user. This effectively equates to the need to collect data about the user for the smart devices to continuously improve in how they do their job [4].

The issue identified with the creation, processing, and collection of user data is mainly in *how* this data is collected, *who* has access to this data, and for what *purpose* is the data collected. For owners of smart home devices such as a Google Home product, an Amazon Alexa-enabled product, or an Apple Home- Kit device, there exists the privacy concern that said devices are listening and constantly creating, processing, and sending data back to the manufacturer for different reasons [5].

This research topic is a by-product of a research Master's focused on Context- Driven Authentication in which users' physical access patterns were extracted and applied in the decision-making powering an alternative to the existing two- factor authentication mechanism in place [6]. Surveying related literature, it is clear that many researchers have realized that the advancements in AI or any smart or learning system depend largely on the availability of a large number of input data, without which, would prove difficult to determine the future or success of AI projects [4, 6].

This paper proposes a multi-tier, privacy-orientated distributed data storage model, that will allow users who do not wish to share data with the service provider to do so for a fee. The approach is multi-tier, meaning users should be allowed to customize their sharing of information with service providers according to their privacy appetite. The multi-tier approach should increase the level of trust between end users and service providers, whilst increasing the adoption of smart home devices.

The rest of this paper is therefore structured as follows: Sect. 2 unpacks the objectives of this paper, followed by a discussion of the necessary background in Sect. 3 in the form of related work and a literature study. Section 4 then details the reasons behind user data collection while Sect. 5 discusses the legal approaches to solving user privacy issues. Finally, the proposed solution is presented in Sect. 6 before concluding the paper in Sect. 7.

2   Objective

The collection of user data by smart home companies is a problem for all users of smart home devices, regardless of the user's knowledge of Information Technology. This is because while data collected by a single device may be inconsequential, the combination of data collected by several devices can potentially expose patterns about the end-user [7].

The objective of the paper is thus to develop a framework that not only strikes an appropriate balance between allowing the end-user to retain control of the data being collected by smart devices, and the ability for the smart device to collect sufficient user data to function optimally; but serves as a viable solution to decreasing the level of distrust between end-users and smart home companies. To achieve this, the following section provides the necessary context by providing the background into the underlying problem.

3 Background

In 1984, the American Association of house builders officially announced the first version of a smart home. The term "Smart Home" is not restricted to the home, and it has a broader meaning that encompasses any technological environment, including smart cities and smart factories [3, 8, 9].

A smart home is defined as a cyber-physical system built on the IoT, computers, and smart appliances, along with human interactions through communication networks and the Internet [8, 9]. These devices typically communicate with each other and the service provider servers over the Internet via Wi-Fi [10].

3.1 Internet of Things

The architecture of IoT is as layered as follows [1, 11]:

1. Physical devices and controllers
2. Connectivity
3. Edge computing
4. Data accumulation
5. Data abstraction
6. Application
7. Collaboration and processes

Developed by the IoT World Forum in October of 2014 [11], the above architectural layers provide a common framework for the deployment of an IoT solution, with data in such a setup typically bidirectional in nature [12]. This research focuses on the 4th layer where data collected by the physical layer is stored, analyzed, and processed, before being made available to the other layers [3].

Currently, there are two ways to store data collected by the physical layer. The data can be stored and processed, either locally, or on the cloud. When it comes to cloud storage, the data can be stored on a public cloud, a private cloud, or using a hybrid approach with cloud storage [5, 13].

Industry-leading organizations typically prefer storing data using the private cloud approach [5] as this grants the organization complete control over the data and it is not publicly accessible. Under such an arrangement, the organization can set up any security management and day-to-day operation internally. Where third parties access the data, this is generally done through a service level agreement (SLA) contract which typically stipulates what rights the third party has to the data.

One of IoT's security and privacy issues is that end-users are not always aware of the data that the physical layer devices collect [14]. Since the data collected is stored on the organization's private cloud, it is often not possible to see what data the organization is collecting, or for how long it will be kept. As a result, the role of user privacy in IoT has remained largely unexplored in IoT, more so in a smart home context [3].

IoT is a relatively new field in the Information technology space. Much re- search has been done on the privacy and security issues that come with IoT on all of the various layers. However, solutions that are concerned with the use and access of data stored in the data accumulation layer are scarce. In the data accumulation layer, research on privacy and security is conducted mainly to ensure that nodes only have access to the data when authenticated and authorized to do so [15]. Mainly the research done looks at security threats such as a denial- of-service attack or a man-in-the-middle attack [11, 12, 16]. These vulnerabilities have more to do with the architecture of the IoT solution, keeping the data secure within the system.

3.2 User Concerns

The collection of personal data combined with the increased number of Internet- connected devices exposes the user to privacy and security risks. Furthermore, the data collected is generally processed and analyzed by the service provider offsite and not locally within the device containing the data. This fear of privacy risk adds to the potential barrier to adopting smart home devices [3].

Due to the increase in devices and sensors collecting data, there is a need to find an increasingly accurate method of measuring information privacy concerns [11, 15]. While smart home devices are meant to make life easier, they do come at a price. Several reports have shown that the convenience of smart home devices comes at the expense of privacy and cyber security [17]. According to an ADT consumer privacy survey, about 93% of consumers with smart devices in their homes are concerned about how the service providers use and share user data. Respondents say that smart home companies need to take measures to protect their personal data [17, 18].

Consumer concerns go beyond the protection of their personal data and what these companies do with that data. Consumers are afraid of unauthorized data collection and the sharing of their data with third parties. These concerns are over and above the threat of hackers gaining access to these data vaults and using the data stored there for nefarious purposes [17].

Hackers aside, smart home devices are capable of collecting so much information and have so many capabilities. It becomes very difficult to know what information is being collected by the service provider and with whom the service provider shares that information. Furthermore, it can be difficult for the user to know when a device is collecting data or when that specific feature is turned off. In essence, the only time anyone can know for certain that the device is not collecting information is when the device is currently not powered on [17, 18].

The recent uptake in smart home devices has ushered in several new service providers and brands that come onto the market at relatively lower prices as compared to the mainstream smart home service providers. These brands typically hit lower price points for their hardware because they prioritize convenience above privacy, exposing the end-user to a heightened degree of risk [18]. A re- cent example of new smart home service providers taking shortcuts to penetrate the market is Wyze, a company that sells inexpensive smart home cameras. It has recently come to light that Wyze knew for several years that hackers could remotely access its camera feeds, but said nothing to customers [19].

Despite such a concern, most service providers do allow their users to determine what data is collected by smart devices. The power to determine what data is collected is typically found in the permission settings of the smart device. With this, a user can deny permissions that they deem to be too intrusive. However, restricting the device's access to certain data may result in the device not working to its full potential. Another concern is that most such permission settings are set to some default that may or may not favour a more data-driven gathering profile. To counter this, the user is then expected to follow additional, sometimes cumbersome steps to deactivate permissions for a more liberal and relaxed data gathering profile [17].

3.3 Terms and Conditions

One of the consumer issues highlighted in the ADT survey is the fact that 40% of the respondents admitted that they do not feel knowledgeable about privacy, and this issue is made worse by the terms and conditions put up by the service providers. These documents, along with the transparency reports, tend to be lengthy, typically written using technical and legal jargon, which a normal person may not necessarily understand [20, 21]. One approach that can be viewed as a step in the right direction of addressing the legal information overload and making it more accessible to the typical user, has been employed by Apple, making use of pop-up prompts that inform the user to opt-in to a service, and explaining what the purpose of that service is and how it works.

The data collected by smart devices, the purpose of the data collection, the duration of the data storage, along with third parties with whom this data will be shared are usually buried in these terms and conditions. There are typically no alternative routes or agreements that can be made with the service provider unless the product is a business or enterprise version [17]. Companies like Apple, for example, have since identified that certain data collecting and sharing permissions should not be set by default. With their iOS 14.5 update, Apple's mobile operating system has introduced a pop-up that asks iOS users to opt-in to the tracking of their activities within each individual app [22].

To understand why smart home companies go to such lengths to collect user data, one should look at the reasons that drive data collection and data sharing among companies.

4   Why is Data Collected?

One of the reasons why smart home companies or anyone interested in building a learning system needs to collect data is simply to make the system better at what it is designed to do, the better the system is, the more potential to make money.

4.1 Making Money

In 2007, it was estimated that the global market for smart home services was about $38.50 billion. This forecast is set to increase to an estimated $125.07 billion by 2023. At this point, the global market penetration will be at an estimated 19.5% [11], with a large number of devices and appliances following a one-time purchase transactional revenue model.

Such a revenue model is however something of a misnomer - rather than only benefit from the proceeds of the sale of the device alone [23], vendors are also potentially capable of tapping into additional revenue models once the user connects their device to the Internet and is presented with a bevy of subscription services. Some vendors may, for example, opt to supplement the one-time purchase revenue with an advertisement-based revenue model [23, 24].

Advertisement-based revenue models typically include sharing user data with third parties. In this way, information that contributes to building up customer profiles of the end-users could be collected, opening the user up to targeted advertisements [24].

4.2 Improving the Service

In general, smart devices that are designed to learn about their end-users tend to improve their functionality the more they are used. It would therefore be beneficial for smart devices that are already deployed in a household to share what it already knows of the inhabitants' habits with newly-introduced smart home devices to provide an overall smart home experience that is consistent and capable of providing smart assistance [25].

Such a notion is not novel - in 2017, iRobot, a smart home company that manufactures smart cleaning robots admitted that they were considering sharing the floor plan data collected by their smart vacuums with companies such as Google and Amazon. The reason behind this, as said by the CEO of iRobot, was for these companies to develop and provide products and services that would be suited to the end-users' home [23].

Such sharing of users' information is a contentious topic - the problem lies in the fact that service providers are generally not very transparent with their customers concerning what they do with the customer's personal information. This problem is particularly problematic given that service providers appear to be operating in a lawless territory, with most cases bringing scandalous and non- ethical behaviors of the service providers to light while the law appears to have no way of dealing with it [20].

5   A Legal Approach

Another concern linked to the opaque nature of how smart devices share personal data is linked to elements of government spying through the use of in-home cameras and smart speakers [26]. Although the more established smart home service providers (such as Apple, Amazon, Facebook, and Google) have indicated that they disclose when and if governments demand customer data in their transparency reports, the process is not always satisfactory. Apple, for ex- ample, claims that because the data they turn over is anonymized, there is no need to disclose or report with whom the data is shared with [26]. The argument is that Since the data is stored on the cloud, law enforcement agencies, and government agencies are lawfully able to request the data from these service providers if they believe this data could assist in a criminal investigation [17].

To address such concerns, several governments have created regulations and policies that are aimed at assisting smart home service providers in reassuring their customers that their data is not at risk. These policies include The EU General Data Protection (GDPR), the California Consumer Privacy Act (CCPA), and in South Africa, the Protection of Personal Information Act (POPIA) [20, 21]. Such initiatives have, however, not necessarily lived up to their expectations as some of the minimal laws contain ambiguous provisions that tend to blur and complicate data protection issues [17].

It has been estimated that the law is typically about five years behind developing technologies [20]. One reason legislation is not the solution to technological problems is that it is difficult and often impossible for technology industry leaders, not to mention the government and lawmakers, to predict new technologies before they emerge. This leaves the law to constantly play a game of catch-up after the fact [20]. In South Africa, POPIA assented in parliament on the 19th of November 2013 but only commenced on the first of July 2020, with the expectation of compliance one year later [21]. Given the slow turn of the law, it is clear that technological problems cannot be solved by legislation alone. Rather, technological solutions to technological problems should be a more realistic approach [20].

6   A Technical Approach

With smart home devices as established as they currently are, any solution aimed at identifying an optimal middle ground between privacy concerns and functionality should build on the use of existing technology and methods that are already established. One aspect that should be considered is the fact that later iterations of smart home devices are getting smarter, with increased capacity for local storage (local data abstraction according to the IoT architecture) [1]. This allows for service providers such as Amazon to shift the processing of user data to its local environment. In this way, the smart device is potentially capable of processing commands and building up the user's profile without ever having to connect to the Internet [27]. Such an approach will however lead to an increase in manufacturing costs as such offline-capable devices must have the hardware specifications that ensure it is capable of performing the computations independently.

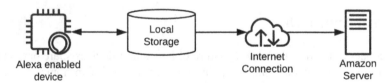

Fig. 1. Architecture of the proposed framework

Figure 1 illustrates the proposed framework. Using Amazon as the example, the framework should ideally work for different smart home service providers and their platforms. Ideally, all devices will have access to a local storage facility, where all the collected data will be stored. Each service provider's devices should be linked to their own service provider shared storage facility. In other words, all devices from a particular service provider will have access to the same storage facility. This decision is based on the fact that not all service providers need the same data for their devices, and in instances where the data may be the same, the processing could be different.

Within each local storage facility, there should be permissions that are in the control of the end-user. In this way, end-users should have the ability to grant access to service providers, determine the level of access, and duration of that access, as well as the power to revoke access to personal data. The storage facility should ideally restrict any party from copying or modifying the data stored for data accuracy reasons.

Devices in the same household should be able to communicate over a local network and share data if needed and if the end-user permits such action to be taken. The smart device will still be connected to other devices but not directly to the Internet. Thus, any data that is to be transferred to the service provider will have to first be authorized by the end-user.

Different users tend to have different thresholds and appetites for various things, and privacy is no exception. This research categorizes end-users into three different categories, with room for other categories to exist in between, depending on the need for granularity. The three categories can be described as follows:

Overly Concerned with all User Data: Users should be allowed to share little to no information with the service provider. In this scenario, all data should be created, processed, and stored locally. Because service providers make money from the data they collect, the user should be comfortable moving from an advertisement-based secondary revenue model to a monthly service subscription or a higher one-time purchase price. The user also needs to acknowledge that some of the functions of the device may not be fully operational due to the limitations of sharing little or no data with the service provider.

Moderately Concerned with Some User Data: Users should be allowed to use parts of the software that they are comfortable with while leaving out and not agreeing to parts they feel are too invasive. In this category, the user should be allowed to choose what information they are comfortable sharing with the service provider. Based on the number of data points the two parties are in agreement with, a monthly subscription for the omitted data could be arranged.

Not Concerned with User Data at All: For security and general awareness concerns, the user should at least be made aware of what information is being collected from them and for what reason. This information should be put in layman's terms and be easy to understand.

Regardless of the category of user, they should not be bombarded with all the terms and conditions when they install an app or buy a new smart home device. The setup should be quick and easy, with each level or feature of the software educating the user on what that feature requires from the user and what granting the feature access to the requirements means for the end-user.

7 Conclusion

This paper looked at the processing and storage of user data created by smart home devices, highlighting that advancements in IoT, AI, and ML have relied on the availability of data for improvements while noting the issues related to user data collection by service providers. Related work in this field was examined, leading to the conclusion that there is a lack of literature in the field of IoT with an emphasis on smart homes and user data storage.

An alternative approach to storing user data, which follows a distributed data storage model, is proposed. This approach would make it possible to bridge the gap between upholding user privacy and the need for access to personal data to provide the convenience of smart home devices.

References

1. Atlam, H.F., Wills, G.B.: Technical aspects of blockchain and IoT. In: Advances in Computers, pp. 1–39. Elsevier (2019). https://doi.org/10.1016/bs.adcom.2018.10.006
2. Average number of connected devices residents have access to in U.S. households in 2020. https://tinyurl.com/mpfte866
3. IoT Architecture: the Pathway from Physical Signals to Business Decisions. https://tinyurl.com/2p93wjhc
4. Adadi, A.: A survey on data-efficient algorithms in big data era. J. Big Data **8**(1), 1–54 (2021). https://doi.org/10.1186/s40537-021-00419-9
5. Rosado, D.G., Gomez, R., Mellado, D., Fernandez-M.E.: Security analysis in the migration to cloud environments. Future Internet **4**, 469–487 (2012). https://doi.org/10.1109/EST.2013.13
6. Lebea, K., Leung, W.S.: A model for context-driven authentication in physical access control environments. In: Kim, K.J., Kim, H.-Y. (eds.) Information Science and Applications. LNEE, vol. 621, pp. 319–328. Springer, Singapore (2020). https://doi.org/10.1007/978-981-15-1465-4_33
7. Smart home privacy: How to avoid data paparazzi. https://tinyurl.com/3t9tkccr
8. Wang, P., Ye, F., Chen, X.: Smart devices information extraction in home Wi- Fi networks. Internet Technol. Lett. 42 (2018). https://doi.org/10.1002/itl2.42
9. Wang, P., Chen, X., Ye, F., Sun, Z.: A smart automated signature extraction scheme for mobile phone number in human-centered smart home systems. EEE Access **6**, 30483–30490 (2018). https://doi.org/10.1109/ACCESS.2018.2841878
10. Hashizume, K., Rosado, D.G., Fernández-Medina, E., Fernandez, E.B.: An analysis of security issues for cloud computing. J. Internet Serv. Appl. **4**, 1–13 (2013)
11. Bertino, E.: Data security and privacy in the IoT. In: EDBT (2016)
12. Tabassum, M., Kosinski, T., Lipford, H.R.: "I don't own the data": end user perceptions of smart home device data practices and risks. In: Fifteenth Symposium on Usable Privacy and Security, pp. 435–450. SOUPS (2019). https://doi.org/10.1109/ISSA.2016.7802925
13. Choosing a Smart Home Hub?—Why Cloud vs Local Matters. https://tinyurl.com/sex5rpcm
14. Guhr, N., Werth, O., Blacha, P.P.H., Breitner, M.H.: Privacy concerns in the smart home context. SN Appl. Sci. **2**, 1–12 (2020)
15. Smart Home and Data Protection: Between Convenience and Security. https://tinyurl.com/399fkt6u
16. Suresh, S., Sruthi, P.V.: A review on smart home technology. In: 2015 Online International Conference on Green Engineering and Technologies (IC-GET), pp. 1–3. IEEE (2015)
17. What are the benefits of home automation?. https://tinyurl.com/tbazmxem
18. ADT Survey Reveals Strong Consumer Expectations for Smart Home Privacy Protections. https://tinyurl.com/5yf3hrxx
19. Wyze knew for years that hackers could remotely access its cameras, but didn't tell anyone. https://tinyurl.com/t5nmk7b8
20. A Losing Game: The Law is Struggling to Keep Up With Technology. https://tinyurl.com/ynz4ce3n
21. Information Regulator in South Africa. https://tinyurl.com/36h7hp2v
22. Apple Says its Updated, Opt-In Prompts for User Data Tracking on iOS will Come into Effect. Next Week. https://tinyurl.com/4kdjyzhh

23. What you should know about smart home data collection. https://tinyurl.com/2tdjh4xn
24. Revenue Model Types in Software Business: Examples and Model Choice. https://tinyurl.com/fm882rbp.
25. The case for building a data-sharing culture in your company. https://tinyurl.com/mwa4kste
26. Many smart home device makers still won't say if they give your data to the government. https://tinyurl.com/336s9sa5
27. New Amazon Echo devices will have local voice processing, giving users more privacy. https://tinyurl.com/mwtfp3fc

A Question Answering Tool for Website Privacy Policy Comprehension

Luca Mazzola[1]([✉])(iD), Atreya Shankar[1](iD), Christof Bless[1](iD),
Maria A. Rodriguez[1](iD), Andreas Waldis[1](iD), Alexander Denzler[1](iD),
and Michiel Van Roey[2]

[1] School of Information Technology, HSLU - Lucerne University of Applied Sciences
and Arts, Suurstoffi 1, 6343 Rotkreuz, Switzerland
{luca.mazzola,atreya.shankar,christof.bless,maria.anduezarodriguez,
andreas.waldis,alexander.denzler}@hslu.ch
[2] Profila GmbH, Seeburgstrasse 45, 6006 Luzern, Switzerland
info@profila.com

Abstract. Everyday we interact with online services from companies that ask for our permission to use our personal information. Nowadays it is common practice for websites and apps to collect big amounts of data which are mainly used for revenue optimization based on user analytics. This customer data collection and usage is regulated by legal agreements (i.e., privacy and cookie policies) which we are required to accept (multiple times a day), but which are generally very long and formulated in a way that makes their interpretation difficult for the general public. An average privacy policy takes 15 min to read and includes lots of legal jargon (e.g., including words like "data controller" and "legal basis for processing"). In this research project, we are developing a support system where users can search for concrete answers in the privacy policies of companies or websites, by formulating their questions in natural language. Instead of blindly accepting a privacy policy, a user could first query the system for answers to a potential concern. The system will return a ranked list of phrases and documents matching the query. In case the generated answer is not sufficient for the user, an extension will allow them to forward complex requests to best-matching legal professionals, specialized in privacy legislation, which can process them for a small fee. We present different aspects of the internal implementation, including the identification of relevant spans in unstructured privacy policies and the selection of the best-suited NLP model for this specific task. The initial results of a user evaluation are presented, showing promising directions. Eventually, some future research directions for the extension of the system conclude our contribution.

Keywords: Privacy · Personally Identifiable Information · Policy Comprehension · Websites' Privacy Regulation · Sentence Boundary Detection · Question to Document Matching · Natural Language Processing · Question Answering

A. Moallem (Ed.): HCII 2023, LNCS 14045, pp. 194–212, 2023.
https://doi.org/10.1007/978-3-031-35822-7_14

1   Introduction

Online privacy and data protection is a trending topic, both in research and within the political agenda [27]. In fact, many countries or geographical regions enforced regulations [8] to oversee the scope and the rights of this personal data collection and usage by companies. These privacy laws provide a significant level of privacy guarantees to people [33] and obligations on brands that process people's personal data [29].

The regulations and their enforcement have to deal with balancing between the level of protection for individuals' privacy and the legitimate and necessary usage of data as part of the information age (e.g. as protection under the Freedom of Information [1], which is generally guaranteed in the constitution of liberal countries). This is even more relevant in sectors such as social care [2] and health, where the quality of the cures and the advancements in medicine can be directly affected by the possibility to collect, manipulate and interpret medically-relevant parts of patients' personal data [13], at different levels of aggregation [28].

The problem is even more pervasive and hard to control in an online setting, where tracking technologies and information collection tools can be seamlessly embedded into web browsers and apps. In fact, everyone is affected by the phenomenon of the usage of personal data by online companies running websites and online services. As a demonstration, you are constantly asked to accept agreements to be able to access the information or application requiring you to give your "consent" to the processing of your personal information, even though you do not exactly know what you are consenting to [32].

Despite the fact that strict new regulations have been put into place in Europe (starting with the General Data Protection Regulation or GDPR) and other regions in the world, which protect the collection and use of customer's personal data, the biggest obstacle to their effectiveness remains people's inability to understand their legal rights and the lack of transparency from companies collecting data [4].

In our research project [15], we aim at supporting customers to understand practically the terms of a website's privacy policy before accepting it. In that direction, we are proposing a system that can identify relevant parts of an official website privacy policy, based on users' queries formulated in natural language. Instead of blindly accepting a privacy policy, a website user could first get a response to a concern he/she might have (e.g., *"I don't want to be targeted by email after reading an article on your site. Can you please confirm that I will not receive any marketing or promotional emails after I accept the privacy policy?"*).

This is a first step towards better awareness and a higher comprehension rate regarding the permitted usage of the collected personal data by companies, and how customers can more effectively defend themselves whenever the terms and conditions are not fully respected [12].

2   Relevant Works

In this section, we present the main relevant works for the different subcomponents of our solution. First, we shortly introduce approaches for *Sentence Boundary Detection* followed by solutions for *Question to Document matching*.

2.1   Sentence Boundary Detection

Proposed by [11], *NLTK Punkt Tokenizer* is an unsupervised model that relies on the identification of abbreviations in a sentence. The authors argue that abbreviations can disambiguate sentence boundaries as the assumption is that an abbreviation is a collocation of the truncated word and its period. This collocational system has also shown efficiency in detecting initial and ordinal numbers. The method is very straightforward as it only needs the sentence itself and is not dependent on the context or language, an ideal feature when applied in a multilingual setting.

[22] proposed a rule-based sentence boundary disambiguation toolkit, *PySBD*, that has both universal rules shared across languages and language-specific rules. These rules for segmentation go from common rules (i.e. identification of main sentence boundaries, periods, single/multi-digit numbers, parentheses, time periods, etc.) to rules that handle geolocation references, abbreviations, exclamations, etc.

Another toolkit proposed by [19], *Stanza*, offers a fully neural pipeline for natural language processing (NLP) including tokenization, lemmatization, named entity recognition, and more. The tokenization model, in particular, combines tokenization and sentence segmentation by treating text as a tagging problem and predicting if a given character is the end of a word, a sentence or a multi-word token.

In the legal domain, [23] examined several models as legal text presents problems in terms of punctuation, structure and syntax, that common language does not have. Three models were considered: NLTK Punkt Tokenizer, Conditional Random Field (CRF) [14], and a neural network such as Word2Vec [16]. The author observed that a simple model such as NLTK Punkt Tokenizer might be a good choice in general but needs further training to give acceptable results in the legal domain. The best performance was given by the CRF approach since it resulted to be the most practical and simple model to train. As for the neural network, the author suggested to use more sophisticated word embeddings such as BERT [3] to obtain better and competitive results.

A legal dataset was created by [25] to help NLP models to segment US decisions into sentences. The dataset has sentence boundaries annotations made by human annotators and is composed by 80 US court decisions from four different domains resulting in more than 26000 annotations.

2.2   Question to Document Matching

IDF-Based. Usually adopted as a baseline for Question to Documents (Q2D) matching, *BM25-Okapi* [21] is an Inverse Document Frequency-based (IDF)

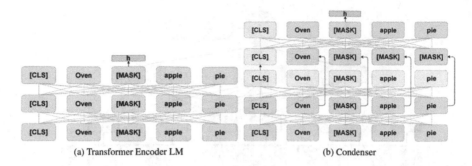

Fig. 1. A general Transformer LM architecture (a) vs. Condenser architecture (b) [7].

model that relies on rare words to match a query with documents by ranking their relevance. It is a computationally lightweight method reported in many scientific works, as in some cases it can still outperform heavier deep learning models. In addition to BM25-Okapi, several other variants of the BM25 algorithm have been proposed such as BM25-L and BM25+ [31].

Keyword-Based. Proposed by [26], *KeyBERT*[1] is a method for extracting keywords and keyphrases and find similarities between a sentence and a given document. It uses BERT word embeddings to extract document and sentence representations paired with cosine similarity to get the most similar documents to a given sentence. It is a quick, simple but powerful method that can be considered state-of-the-art in the keyword extraction domain.

Bi-encoders. The idea is to use pre-trained Transformer language models to extract the representations from queries and documents in an independent manner and compute their similarity with the dot product. However, pre-trained models, such as BERT, are not specifically trained to do retrieval out of the box so what most of the bi-encoder models try to do is fine-tuning. Furthermore, pre-trained models do not have an attention structure ready for bi-encoders, that is, they are not capable of aggregating complex data into single dense representations. In this regard, [6,7] argue that bi-encoder fine-tuning is not efficient as pre-trained models lack *structural readiness*. Thus, they proposed *Condenser*[2], a novel pre-training architecture that not only tries to fine-tune towards a retrieval task but, more importantly, is pre-trained towards the bi-encoder structure by generating dense representations (Fig. 1).

Cross-Encoders. As opposed to bi-encoders, cross-encoders compute the score between a query and documents by encoding them together. This enables, when using Transformers, full self-attention between queries and documents. However,

---

[1] https://maartengr.github.io/KeyBERT/index.html.
[2] https://github.com/luyug/Condenser.

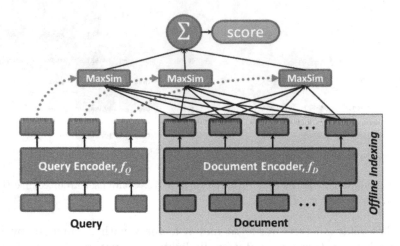

Fig. 2. Architecture of ColBERT given a query and a document [10].

such a powerful structure requires significant computational power as it has to do a forward pass through the model to obtain a score for each document. To reduce the computational burden, cross-encoders are usually combined with re-ranking. [17] proposed a cross-encoder combined with $BM25$[3] to narrow the searching space. Firstly, they retrieve a fixed number of relevant documents to a given query by using $BM25$. Secondly, they re-rank the retrieved documents by using BERT as a binary classification model. Finally, the top-k documents will be chosen as the candidate answers.

Hybrids. Hybrid architectures can be considered as a composition of bi-encoders and cross-encoders. Some models such as *ColBERT* [10][4], introduce a new ranking method, *late interaction*, to adapt language models, such as BERT, for retrieval (Fig. 2). The model encodes independently query and documents using BERT, re-ranks documents offline through pre-computation and computes the relevance between query and documents via late interaction that the authors define as a summation of maximum similarity. Santhanam et al. [24] then proceeded to enhance the model by producing *ColBERTv2*. It consists of the same architecture as *ColBERT* but with advances in quality and space efficiency of vector representations. This method is state-of-the-art.

Another method, *LaPraDoR*[5], proposed by [34], uses an unsupervised dual-tower model for zero-shot text retrieval that iteratively trains query and document encoders with a cache mechanism. Unlike supervised methods, this model combines lexical matching with semantic matching, achieving state-of-the-art results. Our own investigations of transformer model performances in the pri-

---

[3] https://github.com/nyu-dl/dl4marco-bert.
[4] https://github.com/stanford-futuredata/ColBERT.
[5] https://github.com/JetRunner/LaPraDoR.

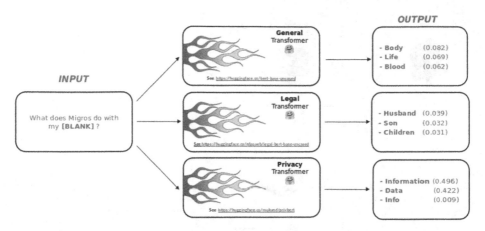

Fig. 3. A simple example of the effect of a domain-specific corpus in the training/fine-tuning of deep learning models. The same input query is matched with different words. This is explained by the different frequencies of co-occurrence in the specific realms.

vacy text domain are summarized in Fig. 3. We show that using a domain-specific corpus for training and/or fine-tuning of deep learning models leads to increased performance, thus justifying the need for a specialized model in privacy policy comprehension tasks.

3   Technical Solution

The design of the current demonstrator was based on recent approaches for serving deep learning (DL) models on the web. Figure 4 present the three-layer architecture orchestrated by *docker-compose* which also manages efficiently all the dependencies. The first layer (back-end supporting services) is composed of three parts.

1. A performant, flexible and easy to use tool for serving Machine (ML) models, called TorchServe[6]: here different DL models are served in a RESTful way. In particular, we plan to embed there the following models: BERT, SBERT, PrivBERT.
2. A vector database QDrant[7] able to store all the vector representations of the sentences and documents. This allows providing real-time answers to users, without the need to recompute the documents and sentence embeddings for every request.
3. A DBMS to store information, such as the TF-IDF representations of the documents.

---

[6] https://pytorch.org/serve/.
[7] Vector Search Engine QDrant, see https://qdrant.tech/.

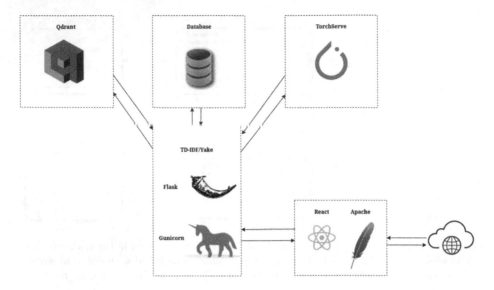

Fig. 4. The architecture of the solution in development. Everything is implemented as a multi-container Docker application, thus the orchestration and dependencies can be managed effectively.

The second layer is the core of the service, composed of a python-based RESTful interface relying on the library flask, Gunicorn, and Yake, while the third layer is the frontend, implemented as a web-based interface using the Apache2 web server and the React JavaScript library.

In the following subsections, we present two main technical aspects affecting the quality of results from our initial demonstrator. On one side, the identification of spans representing valid sentences, as the basic building blocks for the matching and, on the other side, the matching approach between the user query and the documents existing in our library.

3.1   Sentence Boundary Detection

To benchmark SBD for our project, we first proceed to find annotated SBD datasets which may be relevant to our case. One relevant dataset was proposed by [25] and consists of annotated sentence boundaries for legal US documents (hereby referred to as *Legal*). We find this useful for us since privacy documents could be considered as special legal documents. To construct another dataset, we sample 10 privacy policies crawled from [15] and perform SBD annotation on these policies. For this, we utilize five independent annotators who are familiar with privacy policies and conduct specialized annotation using the Label Studio community edition software [30]. We gather all annotations and resolve annotator conflicts using the majority decision. This produces a dataset hereby referred to as *Annotation*, where the Inter-Annotator Fleiss κ metric [5] is 0.707.

Table 1. Summary of SBD tokenizers, datasets, performances and runtime per sentence (in milliseconds)

Model	Dataset	Macro-F_1	Runtime (ms)
nltk	Legal	0.729	0.014
	Annotation	0.867	0.014
pysbd	Legal	0.656	1.571
	Annotation	0.689	0.944
spacy	Legal	0.682	1.894
	Annotation	0.681	2.189
stanza	Legal	**0.927**	3.221
	Annotation	**0.938**	4.606

With the legal and annotation SBD data sets, we proceeded to choosing competitive sentence tokenizers to benchmark. For this, we select the NLTK Punkt, PySBD, SpaCy and Stanza sentence tokenizers, hereby referred to as

Table 2. Tabular results of Q2D with models, datasets MRR@N metrics, precompute runtime per document (in milliseconds) and search runtime per query (in milliseconds).

Model	Dataset	MRR@1	MRR@5	MRR@10	Precompute runtime (ms)	Search runtime (ms)
TF-IDF	PrivacyQA	0.068	0.082	0.089	2.433	100.165
	Profila	0.577	0.639	0.647	2.433	93.153
BM25-L	PrivacyQA	0.047	0.055	0.062	2.345	0.509
	Profila	0.471	0.572	0.585	2.345	0.547
BM25-Okapi	PrivacyQA	0.079	0.097	0.106	2.297	0.486
	Profila	0.654	0.714	0.720	2.297	0.516
BM25+	PrivacyQA	0.076	0.093	0.103	2.354	0.496
	Profila	0.692	0.740	0.747	2.354	0.525
Db-Tas	PrivacyQA	0.079	0.108	0.120	323.305	17.358
	Profila	**0.712**	**0.762**	**0.766**	323.305	17.834
Db-Dot	PrivacyQA	0.074	0.101	0.113	309.471	17.183
	Profila	0.538	0.639	0.651	309.471	16.239
Rb-Ance	PrivacyQA	**0.089**	**0.114**	**0.123**	546.367	21.224
	Profila	0.615	0.688	0.695	546.367	21.972
ML-4	PrivacyQA	0.084	0.109	0.117	19.775	255.300
	Profila	0.673	0.746	0.756	19.775	265.205
ML-6	PrivacyQA	0.082	0.105	0.114	20.041	357.514
	Profila	0.654	0.728	0.739	20.041	372.114
ML-12	PrivacyQA	0.085	0.107	0.117	21.039	663.972
	Profila	0.663	0.744	0.752	21.039	690.180

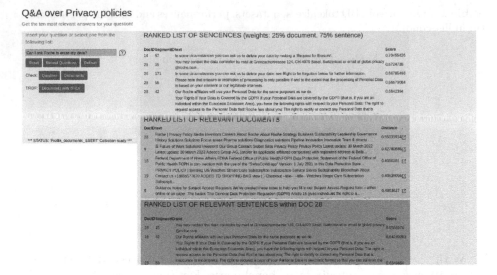

Fig. 5. The current prototype that implements the Architecture presented in Fig. 4.

nltk, pysbd, spacy and stanza respectively. The nltk, pysbd and stanza sentence tokenizers have been described in Sect. 2.1. spacy [9] is an additional sentence tokenizer which works by segmenting sentences using a dependency parser. Table 1 provides a summary of results from our SBD benchmarking process. To calculate the Macro-F_1 metric, we use a similar BIL character-token framework as per [23] and only use the statistic from the B and L character tokens, so as to prevent over-representation from I tokens. Our results show that the stanza sentence tokenizer outperforms all other tokenizers by a margin between 5% and 20% F_1 score. Additionally to Table 1, we provide visualizations of the results in Appendix A.

3.2   Question to Document Matching

The next pertinent technical problem in our project is finding relevant documents for each query. We refer to this problem as Q2D or Question to Documents. This is a well-known problem in NLP and falls under the general domain of Information Retrieval (IR), as described in Sect. 2.2. To benchmark Q2D, we start off by selecting appropriate datasets. We use *PrivacyQA* [20] and convert the dataset into a Q2D format, since its original format was designed for query-to-sentence tasks. Next, we select annotated data from [15] for Q2D and refer to this as *Profila*.

Based on Sect. 2.2, we select the following sparse Q2D models: TF-IDF, BM25-L, BM25-Okapi, BM25+ [31]. For dense models, we utilize bi-encoders and cross-encoders. The bi-encoders are Db-Tas, Db-Dot and Rb-Ance with the following Huggingface tags: sentence-transformers/msmarco-distilbert-base-tas-b, sentence-transformers/msmarco-distilbert-base-dot-prod-

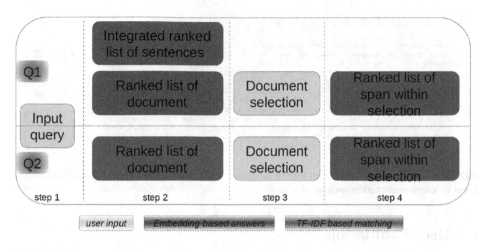

Fig. 6. The two pathways envisioned for the interaction with the GUI: the upper one is purely based on DL embedding, while the other uses the TF-IDF approach, as a first initial to match relevant documents.

v3 and `sentence-transformers/msmarco-roberta-base-ance-firstp`. Cross-encoders consist of a BM25+ layer which minimizes the search space to the top 100 documents. These top documents are then fed into the cross-encoder to re-rank. The selected cross-encoders are ML-4, ML-6 and ML-12 which correspond to the following huggingface tags: `cross-encoder/ms-marco-MiniLM-L-4-v2`, `cross-encoder/ms-marco-MiniLM-L-6-v2` and `cross-encoder/ ms-marco-MiniLM-L-12-v2`.

We report the results of the Q2D benchmark in Table 2. We utilize the Mean Reciprocal Rank (MRR) metric with a cutoff for the top K documents. We utilize cutoffs of 1, 5, and 10 and, therefore, report the MRR@1, MRR@5 and MRR@10 metrics. We observe Db-Tas performs the best overall on the Profila dataset. Correspondingly, we observe Rb-Ance performs the best in the PrivacyQA dataset. Additionally to the Table 2, we visualize these results in Appendix A.

3	Toyota Privacy Notice | Privacy Notice | Toyota Motor Corporation Official Global Website Toyota Privacy Notice Web site privacy policy Last updated on Oct. 25, 2021 1. Introduction Toyota ("we", "our", or "us") is committed to protecting your privac...	0.5429595	
13	Tesla.info | Privacy Policy • TVs • Home Appliances • Air Conditioning • Monitors • Domestic appliances • English – Bosnian – Bulgarian – Croatian – Greek – Macedonian – Romanian – Serbian – Slovenian – Hungarian – Montenegrin – Polish – Russian – Cy...	0.46252915	
26	Privacy Notice Auto Trader cars Skip to content Skip to footer Auto Trader Logo Open / close Menu Sell Saved Search Sign in Cars Vans Bikes Motorhomes Caravans Trucks Farm Plant Main site menu Sign up or sign in Vehicle types Cars Vans Bikes Motorhom...	0.44856954	
	4.5.2016 EN Official Journal of the European Union L 119/1 I (Legislative acts) REGULATIONS REGULATION (EU) 2016/679 OF THE		

Fig. 7. A mockup that adopts the semaphore metaphor to represent the match level between the requested query and the presented documents.

RANKED LIST OF RELEVANT DOCUMENTS

DocID	text	Distance
33	PRIVACY NOTICE FOR CLIENTS – SWITZERLAND DATA PROTECTION UNDER THE SWISS DATA PROTECTION LAW To run our business, UBS processes information about natural and legal persons ("Personal Data"), including information about our prospective, current and fo...	0.14509618
45	Amazon.com Help: Amazon.com Privacy Notice Skip to main content .us Deliver to Switzerland All Select the department you want to search in All Departments Audible Books & Originals Alexa Skills Amazon Devices Amazon Pharmacy Amazon Warehouse Applianc...	1.4142134
52	Gap Inc. Privacy Policy LAST UPDATED: July 1, 2022 Available Languages English Español Français Canada Français France Italiano Deutsch Nederlands 1. Introduction At Gap Inc., we strive every day to build the world's most popular, authentic, and icon...	1.4142134
31	Privacy Policy - Airbnb Help Centre Skip to content We're sorry, some parts of the Airbnb website don't work properly without JavaScript enabled. Help Centre – home page Search Suggestions will show after typing in the search input. Use the up and do...	1.4142134
49	4.5.2016 EN Official Journal of the European Union L 119/1 I (Legislative acts) REGULATIONS REGULATION (EU) 2016/679 OF THE EUROPEAN PARLIAMENT AND OF THE COUNCIL of 27 April 2016 on the protection of natural persons with regard to the processing of ...	1.4142134

Fig. 8. Another proposal for the representation of the trustworthiness and authoritative level of each reported resource.

4   User Evaluation

In order to have an initial feedback on the current prototype we designed and ran an online survey, with a restricted set of potential users. In the survey we check different aspects of the prototype such as the quality of the proposed query to document matches, and the proposed design prototypes.

4.1   Questionnaire Design

The questionnaire is composed of 3 different parts. The first one is about the perceived ease of interaction with the demonstrator (see Fig. 5), in particular with respect to the two different pathways envisioned (see Fig. 6) namely the pure Deep Learning and the TF-IDF pathway. The second part is about the usage of graphical scales to report the trustworthiness (see Fig. 7) and the relevance of the match (see Fig. 8). The third one is about the next steps in the project: first, the type of information that seems to be relevant and important for creating the expert profile (see Fig. 10), and second, a different organization of information in the GUI, that seamlessly embed also the expert advice (see Fig. 9).

In Fig. 7, the semaphore metaphor is used to represent the relevance of the documents with respect to the query. The scale is dynamically applied to show groups with comparable relevance levels. The top group (in this case a single resource) is marked as green, while the next group is yellow and all the remaining matches are associated with a red semaphore, indicating that they are less relevant. An alternative approach we would like to explore could be to assume the score follows a standard distribution, and then compute the mean m and the standard deviation σ of the relevance score on the top-k resources. Thus, green could be assigned to resources with a value larger than $m + 2 * \sigma$ and red to resources with a score lower than $m - 2 * \sigma$ while all the other ones will be marked as yellow.

Table 3. Survey responses: quantitative (top) and qualitative part (bottom)

Code	Question	Scale	Mean	Std	Ref
Q1	Please, rate the intuitiveness of the service (pure embeddings)	1..5	2.82	1.17	Figure 6, top
Q2	Please, rate the intuitiveness of the service (TF-IDF + embeddings)	1..5	2.91	1.22	Figure 6, bottom
Q3 1	The semaphore metaphor is self-explanatory	1..10	7.36	1.45	Figure 7
2	I prefer the semaphore over the numerical value	1..10	8.09	1.73	
3	For me, it is easier to grasp the ranking using ONLY the semaphore icon	1..10	6.73	1.29	
4	I would prefer the semaphore icon AND the numerical value	1..10	5.18	1.20	
5	I would like a solution with the semaphore icon and the numerical value, ON MOUSE-OVER	1..10	6.45	1.10	
6	I would like a solution with the semaphore icon and the numerical value, ON CLICK	1..10	3.82	1.45	
Q4 1	The Nutri-Score metaphor is self-explanatory	1..5	3.27	0.84	Figure 8
2	I find the interface with the two icons overwhelming	1..5	3.27	1.10	
3	I would prefer a scale with only 3 values (trustable - partially trustable - user-generated/doubt)	1..5	3.91	2.86	
4	I would simply use a color scale, without a letter	1..5	3.91	2.81	
5	I find this information valuable	1..5	3.27	1.30	
Q6	How would you rate this proposal	1..5	4.6	0.7	Figure 9

Q5 (ref: Figure 10)	Relevance			Importance			
	Not	*Partial*	*Very*	*Not*	*Partial*	*Somehow*	*Very*
document edited	0%	45%	55%	0%	27%	18%	55%
document contributed to	0%	36%	64%	0%	9%	27%	64%
answer provided	0%	9%	91%	0%	9%	9%	82%
activity on the platform	36%	55%	9%	9%	27%	45%	18%
self-declared knowledge	9%	82%	9%	18%	45%	18%	18%

Another proposition for the representation of the trustworthiness and authoritative level of each reported resource is presented in Fig. 8. This builds on top of the presented semaphore metaphor from Fig. 7. The scale work as follows: Dark Green (A) means those are (national or international) laws, where *Light Green (B)* matches with regulations, court, administrative cases, and privacy-oriented associations recommendations, with *Yellow (C)* official privacy policies or law-regulated agreements from institutions/companies are identified, while the two final categories Light (D) and Dark Red (E) indicate the resources that are user-generated (UGC) or found online on not-vetted resources, such as in public fora or non-professional new groups about legal and privacy issues.

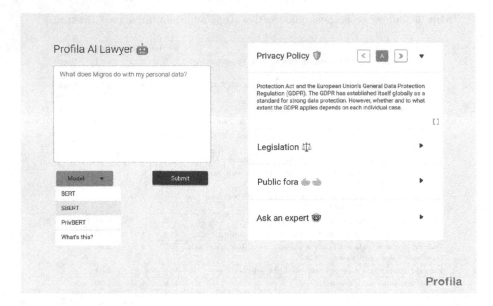

Fig. 9. A mockup of the potential Web-based GUI for the initial release of the "*Profila AI Lawyer*" service. Here, the user is guided by the responses' headers to understand the trustworthiness and authoritativeness level of each proposed resource.

4.2   Data Analysis

We collected 16 valid responses in the time span of a week from individual participants. Their profiles are heterogeneous, as they cover multiple roles and responsibilities within members of the project team, but also marketing, communication, and product engineering on the company side. A limited number of potential users were also included.

Table 3 presents a synoptic view over this initial survey. The first two questions (current demonstrator intuitiveness) show average values with significant variability, thus demonstrating the need for improvement in the way of presenting information and in the proposed interaction pathways. The third question, dealing with the semaphore metaphor, explores it in contrast to the current similarity values. The participants rated positively the intuitiveness of this analogy as a replacement for the numeric value, with the possibility to reveal it using a mouse-over approach. This question also exposes the participants' preference for a simpler and minimalist interaction approach (Q3.4 and, particularly, Q3.6). In question Q4 we proposed to use the additional metaphor of the Nutri-Score as the information carrier [18] for the trustworthiness and authoritativeness level of each reported resource. Its intuitiveness is rated quite positively, even if its simplification to a limited set of three values (see Q4.2) represented by a single color without an alphabetical label could be even preferred by some users (even if with a significantly larger variability, see Q4.4). The use of the two icons is anyway almost constantly not perceived as overwhelming. Another aspect covered in the survey, even if in a purely qualitative way, is the sources relevant and

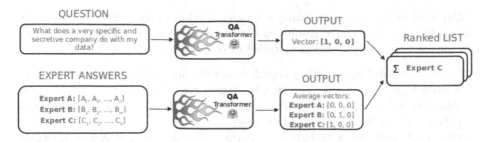

Fig. 10. The envisioned solution for matching the best-suited scholars (in terms of expertise and correct level of knowledge) to a privacy-oriented user query that did not receive a satisfactory answer through the Q&A self-help approach presented in Fig. 9.

important to be included in the experts' profile (see Table 3, bottom). Here it seems pretty evident that the document edited and contributed to, together with answers provided to customers' queries form the most relevant part. It is very important that these aspects are considered by future iterations of the platform, in order to obtain an accurate and reliable profiling process.

Other activities in the platform, including also the event of self-declaring skills, knowledge and/or competencies are perceived as less or not relevant and should be less or not at all included in the profiling process at run-time. Nevertheless, even if not perceived by the average user of this platform, this information can be relevant to solve the cold-start problem, where data about experts' contributions are very limited or absent. Eventually, the last question Q6 explores an alternative approach to display the trustworthiness and authoritativeness level of resources matching a user query, by grouping them into the categories of legislation, official privacy policies, and public fora/user-generated content. Additionally, the function to forward the customer request for support to one or more relevant legal scholars is presented as an additional option, then having a seamless integration into the remainder of the platform demonstrator. This mock-up was rated as very appealing by all the participants in the survey. We are planning to refine the questionnaire and extend its panel of participants, to obtain even more insights in the continuation of the project.

5   Conclusions and Future Work

Supporting consumers' comprehension of privacy policies and usage of their personal information collected online is an open problem. Legal agreements regulating this subject are usually difficult to interpret for the general public, due to their length and their domain-specific language and formulation.

This work presents a first prototype for an interface to extract relevant sections from privacy policies based on user queries in natural language. This contribution details the aims, the current status and the immediate future steps of a joint research project aimed at solving these issues by means of question answering within existing legislation and privacy policies, with the possibility to seamlessly obtain inexpensive professional punctual support for the more complex issues. In particular, the two aspects of *Sentence Boundary Detection* and of *Question to Document matching* were identified as particularly important for the quality of the provided results, and their effects were initially explored. To sum up, our main contributions detailed in this work are as follows.

1. We compare different SBD approaches specifically in the domain of privacy-related legal documents. The results demonstrate that the *stanza* sentence tokenizer delivers the best results in our use case clearly outperforming competing tools such as *nltk*, *pysbd* or *spacy*.
2. Our work features a technical evaluation of different automatic information retrieval models of different complexity, ranging from pure IDF- and keywords-based to bi-encoder and cross-encoder solutions, which indicates that a relatively light-weight and sparse IDF-based model (BM25+) practically outperforms other approaches when considering accuracy and efficiency aspects.
3. We present a user interface and architecture for delivering the results of the presented IR algorithms on privacy policy documents of potential customers.
4. We provide a user evaluation of the presented user interface which gives insights into the user comprehension of specific design decisions of our first prototype and sets a baseline to measure improvements of further iterations of the tool. This initial survey showed some promising results about the users' perception but also definitive areas of improvement that we need to tackle in order to make the service effective.

Based on these results and the general objective detailed, the list of next research steps is the following.

- We will realize the second part of the application, which will feature the transfer of queries to legal professionals based on multifaceted expert profiles (see Fig. 10). Here we will test different options, mainly based on the perception of relevance and importance of different user activities within the platform, as indicated by the survey results.
- Further experiments with the best-performing Q2D models will be carried out. One key point will be to explore why sparse lexical approaches outperform dense NN-based ones, and to use this information to reduce the complexity of the search while maintaining acceptable performances in the matching process.
- The user interface will be improved based on user evaluation. We will implement the mock-up (Fig. 9) of the next version presented in the user evaluation.

With these points, we aim at providing an effective solution to the presented problem, while advancing the state of the art in the area of domain-specific question answering for privacy policies and of heterogeneous profiling for similarity matches.

Acknowledgements. The research leading to this work was partially financed by *Innosuisse* - Swiss federal agency for Innovation, through a competitive call. The project 50446.1 IP-ICT is called *P2Sr Profila Privacy Simplified reloaded: Open-smart knowledge base on Swiss privacy policies and Swiss privacy legislation, simplifying consumers' access to legal knowledge and expertise* (https://www.aramis.admin.

ch/Grunddaten/?ProjectID=48867). The authors would like to thank all the people involved on the implementation side at Profila GmbH (https://www.profila.com/) for all the constructive and fruitful discussions and insights provided about privacy regulations and consumers' rights.

Appendix A - SBD and Q2D Graphs

In this appendix, we provide the reader with the graphical representations of the data from Table 1 and from Table 2. Effectiveness of *nltk* is demonstrated with a good F1 measure and a very limited runtime.

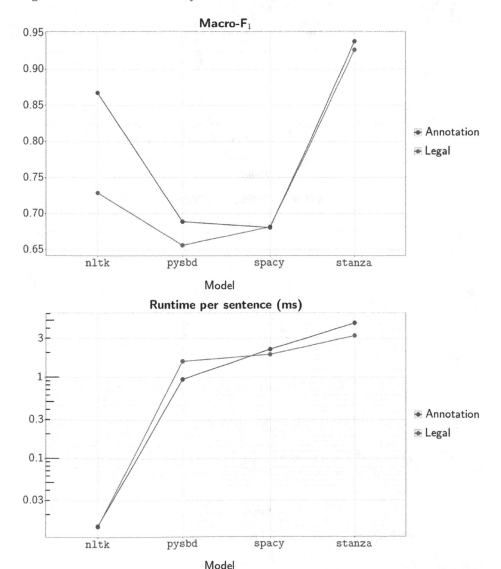

BM25+, a relatively simple and sparse IDF-based model, practically outperforms other approaches when considering accuracy and runtime.

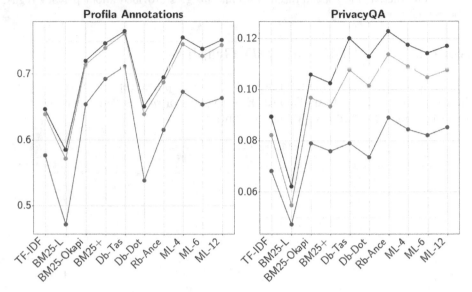

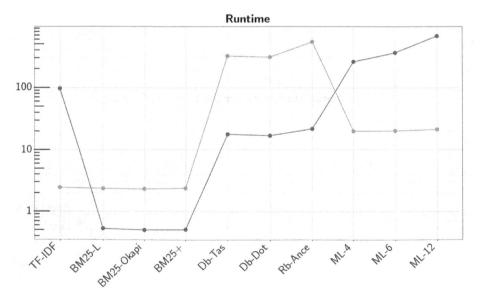

References

1. Abela, S.: Data protection and freedom of information. In: Abela, S. (ed.) Leadership and Management in Healthcare, pp. 103–107. Springer, Cham (2023). https://doi.org/10.1007/978-3-031-21025-9_10
2. Crook, M.: The Caldicott report and patient confidentiality (2003)
3. Devlin, J., Chang, M.W., Lee, K., Toutanova, K.: BERT: pre-training of deep bidirectional transformers for language understanding. arXiv preprint arXiv:1810.04805 (2018)
4. Fabian, B., Ermakova, T., Lentz, T.: Large-scale readability analysis of privacy policies. In: Proceedings of the International Conference on Web Intelligence, pp. 18–25 (2017)
5. Fleiss, J.L.: Measuring nominal scale agreement among many raters. Psychol. Bull. **76**(5), 378 (1971)
6. Gao, L., Callan, J.: Condenser: a pre-training architecture for dense retrieval. arXiv preprint arXiv:2104.08253 (2021)
7. Gao, L., Callan, J.: Is your language model ready for dense representation finetuning. arXiv preprint arXiv:2104.08253 (2021)
8. Goddard, M.: The EU general data protection regulation (GDPR): European regulation that has a global impact. Int. J. Mark. Res. **59**(6), 703–705 (2017)
9. Honnibal, M., Montani, I., Van Landeghem, S., Boyd, A., et al.: Spacy: industrial-strength natural language processing in Python (2020)
10. Khattab, O., Zaharia, M.: ColBERT: efficient and effective passage search via contextualized late interaction over BERT. In: Proceedings of the 43rd International ACM SIGIR Conference on Research and Development in Information Retrieval, pp. 39–48 (2020)
11. Kiss, T., Strunk, J.: Unsupervised multilingual sentence boundary detection. Comput. Linguist. **32**(4), 485–525 (2006)
12. Korunovska, J., Kamleitner, B., Spiekermann, S.: The challenges and impact of privacy policy comprehension. arXiv preprint arXiv:2005.08967 (2020)
13. Leatherman, S., Berwick, D.M.: Accelerating global improvements in health care quality. JAMA **324**(24), 2479–2480 (2020)
14. Liu, Y., Stolcke, A., Shriberg, E., Harper, M.: Using conditional random fields for sentence boundary detection in speech. In: Proceedings of the 43rd Annual Meeting of the Association for Computational Linguistics (ACL 2005), pp. 451–458 (2005)
15. Mazzola, L., Waldis, A., Shankar, A., Argyris, D., Denzler, A., Van Roey, M.: Privacy and customer's education: NLP for information resources suggestions and expert finder systems. In: Moallem, A. (ed.) HCII 2022. LNCS, vol. 13333, pp. 62–77. Springer, Cham (2022). https://doi.org/10.1007/978-3-031-05563-8_5
16. Mikolov, T., Sutskever, I., Chen, K., Corrado, G.S., Dean, J.: Distributed representations of words and phrases and their compositionality. In: Advances in Neural Information Processing Systems, vol. 26 (2013)
17. Nogueira, R., Cho, K.: Passage re-ranking with BERT. arXiv preprint arXiv:1901.04085 (2019)
18. Peters, S., Verhagen, H.: An evaluation of the nutri-score system along the reasoning for scientific substantiation of health claims in the EU—a narrative review. Foods **11**(16), 2426 (2022)
19. Qi, P., Zhang, Y., Zhang, Y., Bolton, J., Manning, C.D.: Stanza: a Python natural language processing toolkit for many human languages. arXiv preprint arXiv:2003.07082 (2020)

20. Ravichander, A., Black, A.W., Wilson, S., Norton, T., Sadeh, N.: Question answering for privacy policies: combining computational and legal perspectives. In: Proceedings of the 2019 Conference on Empirical Methods in Natural Language Processing and the 9th International Joint Conference on Natural Language Processing (EMNLP-IJCNLP), Hong Kong, China, pp. 4949–4959. Association for Computational Linguistics (2019). https://doi.org/10.18653/v1/D19-1500. https://www.aclweb.org/anthology/D19-1500

21. Robertson, S.E., Walker, S., Jones, S., Hancock-Beaulleu, M.M., Gatford, M., et al.: Okapi at trec-3. NIST Special Publication Sp **109**, 109 (1995)

22. Sadvilkar, N., Neumann, M.: PySBD: pragmatic sentence boundary disambiguation. arXiv preprint arXiv:2010.09657 (2020)

23. Sanchez, G.: Sentence boundary detection in legal text. In: Proceedings of the Natural Legal Language Processing Workshop 2019, Minneapolis, Minnesota, pp. 31–38. Association for Computational Linguistics (2019). https://doi.org/10.18653/v1/W19-2204. https://aclanthology.org/W19-2204

24. Santhanam, K., Khattab, O., Saad-Falcon, J., Potts, C., Zaharia, M.: ColBERTv2: effective and efficient retrieval via lightweight late interaction. arXiv preprint arXiv:2112.01488 (2021)

25. Savelka, J., Walker, V.R., Grabmair, M., Ashley, K.D.: Sentence boundary detection in adjudicatory decisions in the United States. Traitement automatique des langues **58**, 21 (2017)

26. Sharma, P., Li, Y.: Self-supervised contextual keyword and keyphrase retrieval with self-labelling (2019). https://www.preprints.org/manuscript/201908.0073/v1

27. Sivan-Sevilla, I.: Varieties of enforcement strategies post-GDPR: a fuzzy-set qualitative comparative analysis (FSQCA) across data protection authorities. J. Eur. Public Policy 1–34 (2022)

28. Subrahmanya, S.V.G., et al.: The role of data science in healthcare advancements: applications, benefits, and future prospects. Irish J. Med. Sci. (1971-) **191**(4), 1473–1483 (2022)

29. Tikkinen-Piri, C., Rohunen, A., Markkula, J.: EU general data protection regulation: changes and implications for personal data collecting companies. Comput. Law Secur. Rev. **34**(1), 134–153 (2018)

30. Tkachenko, M., Malyuk, M., Holmanyuk, A., Liubimov, N.: Label Studio: Data labeling software (2020–2022). Open source software https://github.com/heartexlabs/label-studio

31. Trotman, A., Puurula, A., Burgess, B.: Improvements to BM25 and language models examined. In: Proceedings of the 2014 Australasian Document Computing Symposium, pp. 58–65 (2014)

32. Vail, M.W., Earp, J.B., Antón, A.I.: An empirical study of consumer perceptions and comprehension of web site privacy policies. IEEE Trans. Eng. Manag. **55**(3), 442–454 (2008)

33. Vanberg, A.D.: Informational privacy post GDPR-end of the road or the start of a long journey? Int. J. Hum. Rights **25**(1), 52–78 (2021)

34. Xu, C., Guo, D., Duan, N., McAuley, J.: LaPraDoR: unsupervised pretrained dense retriever for zero-shot text retrieval. arXiv preprint arXiv:2203.06169 (2022)

Perception of Privacy and Willingness to Share Personal Data in the Smart Factory

Luisa Vervier⬤, Philipp Brauner(✉)⬤, and Martina Ziefle(✉)⬤

Chair of Communication Science, RWTH Aachen University, Aachen, Germany
{vervier,brauer,ziefle}@omm.rwth-aachen.de

Abstract. By optimising data-driven processes and improving automation, the digital transformation in production aims to increase effectiveness, efficiency and improve the working conditions of employees. In such a networked working environment, the performance and actions of workers need to be captured in form of digital data. However, the collection of personal data is a sensitive issue. More research, not only from a techno-centric but also from a human-centric perspective, is needed. Using a multi-method approach, this study examines the motives, barriers and acceptance of technologies that use personal data in a production context. A qualitative pre-study ($n = 7$) identified motives (e.g. data offering personal benefit) and barriers (e.g. privacy concerns) of personal data disclosure. In the subsequent quantitative main study ($n = 152$), these key elements were operationalised in a scenario-based online survey, and two different working scenarios – cobot and chatbot – were additionally assessed using the Technology Acceptance Model (TAM and UTAUT2). The results show: The more fun it is to use and the higher the expected performance, the higher the acceptance of technology using personal data. Trust in automation followed by expected effort were important. Views on the disclosure of personal data and the expected benefit to the organisation varied widely. Out of seven categories, work-related and demographic data were considered to be disclosable, while five categories were considered important to the organisation. The article concludes with actionable recommendations on how the collection and use of personal data can be well aligned with stakeholder interests.

Keywords: Smart Factory · Industry 4.0 · User-centered Design · Data Sensitivity · Information Privacy · Acceptance

1 Introduction

Rapidly changing market demands, increasing competitive pressure as well as an increased demand in fair working conditions and a competition for qualified personnel require innovative industries. One of the key concepts to address these challenges is the digitized and connected factory, where data-based processes are optimised and automated to increase the effectiveness and efficiency of production and improve working conditions [5, 22, 23].

A. Moallem (Ed.): HCII 2023, LNCS 14045, pp. 213–231, 2023.
https://doi.org/10.1007/978-3-031-35822-7_15

In addition to machine data, smart sensors in the Internet of Things can collect data from human workers, such as the performance of a worker, his or her actions in the factory, movement data, or possibly even their well-being through camera systems. The collection and use of this personal data can have both advantages and disadvantages: On the one hand, the data can be used to make work safer, more ergonomic or more comfortable, for example by tailoring tasks to the individual's abilities or automatically adjusting workstations to the individual's height. On the other hand, there is a risk of workers being exploited by identifying and cancelling break times, or of sensitive personal data being shared with third parties. This involves collecting and processing not only machine data but also real-time data about an employee's activities or movements, such as work speed to assess performance or body height to adjust machines ergonomically. The collection and use of personal data is therefore a sensitive issue that can invade employees' privacy and be perceived by them as a risk [36].

Although employee acceptance of data-based technologies is an essential prerequisite for the successful implementation, current research often has a technocentric perspectives and neglects the employees' perspective [27,28]. Therefore, this study contributes to a better understanding of the acceptance, perception, and willingness to share personal data in the smart factory. The article concludes with a research agenda and actionable guidelines on how to incorporate the social perspective into the design of monitoring systems in smart factories.

1.1 Human Perspective is Key to Industry 4.0 Adoption

Recent technological innovations led to significant changes in many areas, including production, with the emergence of Industry 4.0 and Industry 5.0 [15,22]. These advances have the potential to improve efficiency and productivity, but their success depends on the acceptance and adoption by organizations and the individuals [48]. In this context, acceptance is defined as a positive adoption of an idea in the sense of active willingness to use it and not only in the sense of reactive acquiescence [12]. So far, a rather techno-driven approach has been taken, neglecting the human perspective, even though they are precisely the counterpart of a cyber-physical technology. However, one key factor influencing acceptance is the consideration of the human perspective. Considering the human perspective can lead to a more user-friendly and easy-to-use technology development [33]. In addition, by listening to people and meeting their needs, trust can be built between the user and the technology. This is particularly important in the context of Industry 4.0 and Industry 5.0, where the adoption of new technologies may require significant changes to existing processes and practices. This approach recognizes that technology should not be imposed on people, but developed in partnership with them [47].

It is more important than ever to understand attitudes and personal concerns about the use of personal data and perceptions of privacy, especially in the connected digital industry, where using employees' data can help optimise the work process. What exactly is meant by data privacy in the context of the smart factory is clarified as follows.

1.2 Information Privacy and Data Sensitivity in the Smart Factory

First, it is important to have a general idea of the multifaceted and complex construct of data privacy. The number of approaches to define privacy are huge and alter referring to its discipline. Privacy was explained as the right to be "undisturbed" in the late 18th century, or a century later defined as a state of limited access or isolation [37, 46]. Altman referred to privacy as a kind of control over access to one's self and disclosure of information [2]. With digitization, where privacy is no longer purely physical but a person's data and information becomes relevant, privacy has been transferred to the online context and called *information privacy*.

Information Privacy. According to Bhave [4], information privacy is about perceived control over the collection, storage, use, disclosure and dissemination of employee information. In other words, it is about control over the information that could be made available to others. The willingness to share data depends on the context and the audience with which the information is shared [31]. Furthermore, because data in the smart factory is stored digitally and is therefore persistent, easily replicated, scaled, and may be shared with third parties, employees are concerned about how it is used, which may have a negative impact on trust, productivity, and efficiency.

Smart factory research has mainly taken a technology-centric perspective. Hence, the human perspective in general and the attitudes to privacy and willingness to share data in particular are insufficiently understood. A definition of the term *Digital Shadow* has been established, which aggregates, links, and abstracts human data about physical objects [5, 27]. It integrates data directly related to the human production environment, such as their behavioural patterns, data on work patterns and performance, physiological and cognitive parameters, as well as socio-demographic data [27]. Sensor-based data collection has been explored with the aim of increasing safety at work, improving employee health and satisfaction, or identifying inefficiencies caused by over- or underworking. Wearables, such as watches or sensors integrated into clothing, can collect physiological data such as heart rate or blood pressure to detect stress, physical inactivity, fatigue or physically demanding work [28].

Perceived Data Sensitivity. Data sensitivity refers to the level of risk associated with disclosing certain types of information. This is particularly relevant because, according to several studies, perceived sensitivity correlates with the willingness to share data. The higher the perceived sensitivity of data, the lower the willingness to share data [30, 39, 41].

In the context of the adoption of fitness wearables, the perceived sensitivity and importance of different types of personal data was empirically investigated by Lidynia [25]. Both the perceived sensitivity and the perceived importance of tracking varied across the available parameters. GPS data, weight, and sleep analysis were perceived as more sensitive, whereas UV radiation, number of stairs, or hours spent standing were perceived as less sensitive. Heart rate, steps and GPS position were perceived as particularly important, whereas current UV exposure, outdoor temperature and blood glucose levels were not perceived as important in the fitness context.

For workplace monitoring, Tolsdorf and others investigated the perceived sensitivity of certain types of data and employees' willingness to disclose their data [41]. The study found that the perceived sensitivity of data for workplace monitoring differs from other contexts. In addition to considering the employee perspective on workplace monitoring, the expectations and concerns of other stakeholders are also relevant, but have not been sufficiently explored. Pütz addressed this gap in a study with over 700 managers [34] and found that most managers expect improved well-being and workplace design. Still, privacy concerns are seen as a key barrier to the adoption of monitoring systems.

In summary, using personal data in the smart factory offers many opportunities for both the companies as well as the employees. However, this potential can only be exploited if the employees' willingness to disclose personal information and the social acceptance of these approaches is well understood. This study contributes to this understanding by evaluating the willingness to disclose various types of information in two different contexts: First for using a cobot (collaborative robot) in human-robot collaboration and second for using a chatbot. Both context have in common that they build on an autonomous agent of future smart factories. Yet, the first stands for a human-technology interface from the factories' shopfloor ("Blue Collar" work) while the latter is envisioned to support managers of the companies in the form of conversational agents ("White Collar" work). In both contexts the use of automated agents will likely gain in relevance in the near future and both approaches may profit from using personal data for improved adaptation and personalisation.

1.3   Empirical Approach and Logic of Procedure

To gain insights into the willingness to disclose personal data in the context of smart factories, we chose a two-method approach. Figure 1 shows an overview of the research process.

First, we used focus groups for gathering qualitative insights into peoples' motives and barriers, as well as a ranking of the perceived sensitivity of different types of personal data. The following guiding questions facilitated the group discussions to get the different opinions and viewpoints of the participants:

- What are the benefits or motives of sharing personal data in a smart working scenario?
- What are the barriers you associate with collecting personal data in the smart factory?
- What personal data are you willing to share and what data do you consider too sensitive to share?

Second, building on the results of the focus groups, we included all relevant factors in an online survey to empirically model the peoples' attitudes. We developed two scenarios to measure the preconditions and overall acceptance of

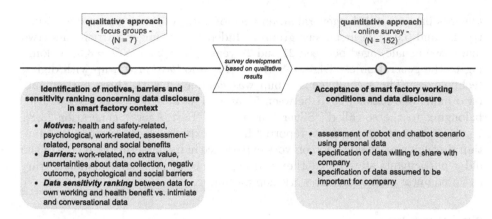

Fig. 1. Overview of the research process showing the qualitative and quantitative measures to address the research questions.

a cobot and a chatbot that builds on the use of personal data. The research questions of the study were:

- What data is considered sensitive in the context of the smart factory?
- What data is associated with being of interest to the company from an employee's perspective?
- Which acceptance relevant factors have an impact on the intention to use smart technologies requiring personal data, exemplified by a cobot and chatbot scenario?

The following section is structured according to our study process. First, we present the procedure and results of the pre-study (focus groups). Second, we illustrate the design of the main study (scenario-based online survey).

2   Qualitative Focus Groups (Pre-study)

The aim of the focus groups was to identify and discuss the potentials, motives, and barriers of younger and older adults for the use of personal data in smart factories. The advantage of the qualitative approach is the possibility to gain new insights in an exploratory way by generating opinions and ideas that serve as a basis for an extended acceptance analysis. For this purpose, two focus groups were conducted as part of a bachelor thesis at RWTH Aachen University in winter 2021/22. The participants participated voluntarily and were not compensated. The sample, procedure and results are briefly outlined below.

2.1   Sample

Participants were recruited from the authors' social circles. The inclusion of different age groups allowed for the consideration of age effects regarding attitudes towards privacy and the general acceptance of data collection and use in Industry 4.0 and 5.0. The first focus group included four younger participants (two male, two female) aged between 21 and 29 years ($M = 23.3$, $SD = 3.9$), belonging to the generation of "Digital Natives" [29] who have grown up with digital technologies. The second focus group was conducted with three participants (two male, one female) aged between 58 and 61 years ($M = 59.7$, $SD = 1.5$), belonging to the so-called "Silver Surfers" or "Best Agers" generation [3,8]. 75.0% of younger respondents reported having experience of industrial production through a mechanical job or work experience in manufacturing. 66.6% of the older participants stated that they had experience of industrial manufacturing as an engineer or as a former workshop mechanic.

2.2   Procedure

First, participants were informed about data protection and the voluntary nature of the focus groups. As an introduction to the topic of general data collection, participants were encouraged to brainstorm about data collected by technologies such as apps in everyday life. As a next step, participants were introduced to the idea of a smart factory and brainstormed about data that is already needed and collected by technologies and that could be of interest in future smart factory scenarios. A short video clip presented a possible human-robot interaction in production. Subsequently, possible personal data of interest for such a collaboration were collected and divided into possible advantages and disadvantages. Finally, the associated data was ranked as most useful and most sensitive. After the discussion, participants completed a short paper-and-pencil questionnaire covering demographics, industry experience and technical affinity. The focus groups were audio recorded and a verbatim transcript was made. Conventional content analysis was used to identify key motivators and barriers to willingness to share personal data in the context of the smart factory.

2.3   Main Results

The analysis focused on the identification of motives and barriers, as well as a ranking of the use of personal data in Industry 4.0 from the perspective of employees. Figure 2 gives an overview of the main issues mentioned.

What are the Benefits or Motives of Sharing Personal Data in a Smart Working Scenario? The motives associated with data sharing in the context of smart factories could be categorised into five themes. The specific motivation to provide personal data is based on the benefits derived from health-related, psychological, work-related, assessment-related and social benefits.

Which are the Barriers you Associate with Capturing Personal Data in the Smart Factory? Barriers to sharing personal data were identified in five themes: uncertainty about data collection, psychological reasons, work-related reasons, negative consequences for oneself, and lack of value of data collection.

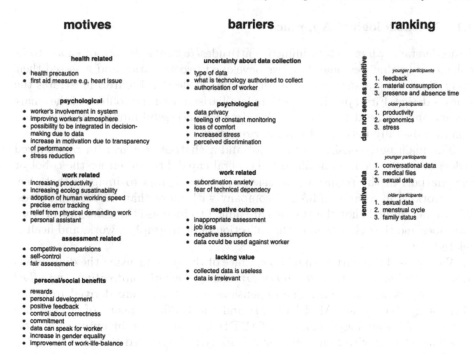

Fig. 2. The main motives, barriers and data ranking by sensitivity identified in the pre-study (n = 7).

Which Personal Data are you Willing to Disclose and Which Data Seems to be too Sensitive for Disclosure? A total of three types of data were asked to be ranked from the brainstorming results. Participants ranked the data differently according to their sensitivity and especially according to their generation. Younger participants are willing to share data about personal feedback, material consumption and information about attendance and absence times. Older participants categorised information about productivity, ergonomics and stress as disclosable data. Conversational data, medical records and sexual data were classified as sensitive by younger participants. Older participants classified sexual data, menstrual cycle and marital status as very sensitive data.

3 Quantitative Scenario-Based Survey (Main Study)

Based on the results from above, we developed a scenario-based online survey. Our goal was to empirically model the willingness to disclose personal information towards autonomous agents in the smart factory and how that relates to the overall acceptance of a cobot or chatbot scenario.

3.1 Methodological Approach

To understand what factors influence attitudes towards the use of smart technologies requiring personal data, we developed two scenarios and assessed their evaluations using a survey with a within-subject design. Figure 3 illustrates the study's design. First, participants were familiarised with the context of the smart factory and the need to collect worker data for successful human-robot interaction in a digitally networked work environment.

The main part consisted of a cobot and a chatbot scenario (in randomized order) and each scenario outlined the general capabilities of either the cobot or the chatbot. In the scenarios, we asked the participants to imagine that they were working in a large industrial company with more than 32,000 employees. We further argued that the systems are aimed to increase the efficiency of work processes and that they require the collection of demographic, work, and health-related data.

We assessed the participants' acceptance of the systems using the dimensions overall *intention to use, performance expectancy, hedonic motivation*, and *effort expectancy* using ten items. The dimensions and items were derived from the Technology Acceptance Model (TAM) and the Unified Theory of Acceptance and Use of Technology2 model (UTAUT2) [11,44]. Trust in automation was added as a factor with four items, as it is likely to be related to acceptance [24]. We also let the participants evaluate the scenarios on a semantic differential consisting of 20 opposing word pairs adapted from Hassenzahl's AttrakDiff [18] (e.g., *"The possibility of using a cobot and the AI behind it that can access all the necessary personal data, I would find ... " important—unimportant, controllable—uncontrollable, etc.*).

The requirement for a smooth personalised workflow was the disclosure of different types of personal data in both scenarios, such as name, age, height, date of birth, error rate and speed of workflows for the cobot scenario, and name, age, working days, attendance records, sick days, holidays and overtime worked in the chatbot scenario. Prior to the demographic section at the end, participants were asked to evaluate seven data categories (work-related, demographic, movement profile, health-related, biometric, expressive behaviour and personal data) regarding their perceived sensitivity and potential interest to the company on a five-point Likert item.

3.2 Sample Description and Statistical Analysis

A total of 152 surveys were fully completed, consisting of 39% male and 61% female participants aged between 18 and 81 ($M = 31.5$, $SD = 14.8$). The current activity was widely spread across different fields (e.g. health (36%), IT (15%), engineering (29%)). Due to the small sample size, non-parametric tests were calculated: Spearman's rank correlation r_s, Friedman's test to analyse differences in means, and Cohen's d to determine effect sizes. The significance level was set at $\alpha = .05 = 5\%$.

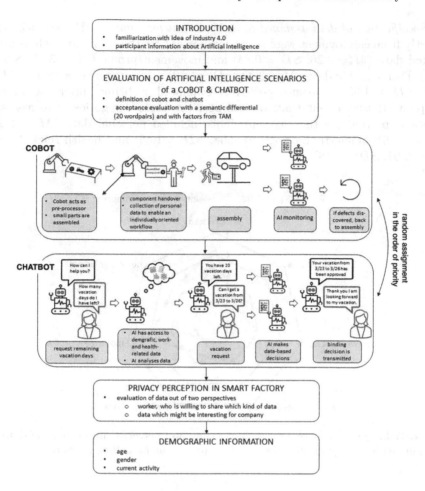

Fig. 3. Process of scenario-based online survey. Order of cobot and chatbot scenario is randomly assigned (within-subject design).

4   Results

The results are presented guided by the research questions. *Specification of data willing to share with company.* Seven categories were ranked according to its sensitivity as can be seen in Fig. 4. With an average value rating above three (min. 1, max. 5), work related ($M = 3.51$, $SD = 0.88$) and demographic data ($M = 3.35$, $SD = 1.08$) were positively evaluated and considered as disclosable data. Data about movement profile turned out to be just under average ($M = 2.71$, $SD = 1.11$). Evaluated as not disclosable at all were the four remaining categories: biometric data ($M = 1.84$, $SD = 1.09$), health related data ($M = 1.84$, $SD = 0.88$), expressive behavior ($M = 1.68$, $SD = 1.14$) and finally personal data ($M = 1.37$, $SD = 0.67$).

Specification of data assumed to be important for company. Data which arise directly from employment were seen as important for the company such as work related data ($M = 4.26$, $SD = 0.84$) and movement profile ($M = 3.97$, $SD = 1.07$). Demographic data ($M = 3.39$, $SD = 1.12$) and expressive behavior ($M = 3.02$, $SD = 1.38$) were also positively evaluated as being important for the company. It turned out that, on average, the three categories were assessed as not important for the company. This included personal data ($M = 2.20$, $SD = 1.16$), biometric data ($M = 2.58$, $SD = 1.46$) and health related data ($M = 2.92$, $SD = 1.18$).

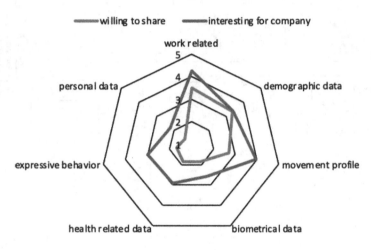

Fig. 4. Willingness to share data with company and perceived importance of data to company with 1 = *not at all willing to share* to 5 = *totally willing to share* (n = 152).

Acceptance Relevant Factors for the Intention to Use a Cobot or Chatbot in an Interconnected Digital Working Scenario. As Table 1 shows, acceptance ratings were on average high and relatively similar in both scenarios.

Regarding the acceptance of the two scenarios, a small significant difference was found between the cobot and the chatbot scenario with $U = 1951.5$, $Z = -3.442$, $p < .001$. The relationships between the acceptance-relevant factors and the intention to use such concepts of an smart factory (cobot vs. chatbot) differed slightly: The strongest relationship to the use of a cobot is described by hedonic motivation, followed by performance expectation, trust and effort expectancy. Conversely, the likelihood of using a chatbot is strongly related to performance expectancy, hedonic motivation, trust and effort expectancy (see Fig. 5). Figure 6 shows the acceptance ratings of the cobot and chatbot scenarios.

Table 1. Descriptive statistics and difference in mean value of TAM, UTAUT2 factors and trust regarding the evaluated cobot and chatbot scenario (min. = 1, max. = 6).

	Cobot	Chatbot	p
	M (SD)	M (SD)	
Performance expectancy	4.37 (0.87)	4.25 (1.21)	n.s
Hedonic motivation	3.82 (1.06)	3.82 (1.27)	n.s
Effort expectancy	4.48 (0.84)	4.69 (0.87)	<.001
Trust	4.14 (0.77)	3.91 (0.92)	n.s
Intention to use	4.18 (1.07)	3.98 (1.21)	n.s

In general, the chatbot scenario was associated with more positive attributes than the cobot scenario. For the chatbot, attributes such as fair, transparent, intuitive, welcome, exciting to use and generally positive stood out. The most positive attributes for the cobot were that it is trustworthy, fast, and accelerating. However, the evaluation of the semantic differential was associated with more negative attributions such as being inhibiting, disruptive, disconnected, and negative. Similarities were that both technologies are neither bad nor good, neither discouraging nor motivating, and more difficult to use than easy, but still more controllable than uncontrollable.

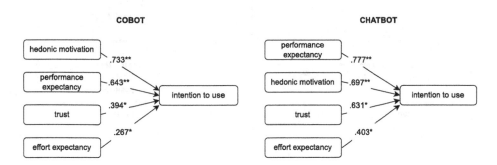

Fig. 5. Correlations between the queried acceptance factors and intention to use the chatbot or cobot ($n = 152$).

5   Discussion

Data is driving the digital transformation of production, bringing huge changes to shop floor operations, production planning and management. In addition to increasing the efficiency and effectiveness of existing production systems, new applications are emerging, such as interactive agents in the form of collaborative robots (to support shop floor operations) or chatbots (to support management activities). However, as soon as workers are involved in a socio-technical

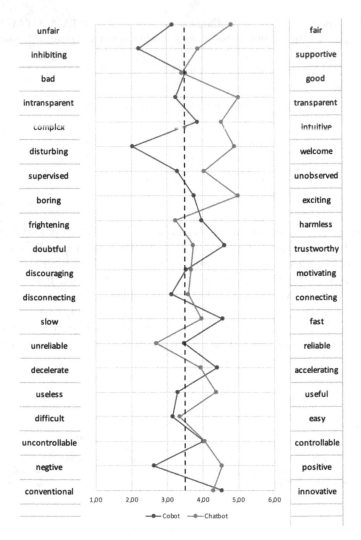

Fig. 6. Results of acceptance assessment of cobot and chatbot scenario with semantic differential ($n = 152$).

production system, the collection and use of data can affect the right to self-determination and perceived autonomy of individuals. In particular, when systems collect and build on workers' personal data, the expected benefits need to be carefully weighed against individuals' motives, barriers and perceptions of privacy.

As these trade-offs are currently not sufficiently understood, this study investigated the motives, barriers and acceptance of technologies that use personal data in a manufacturing context. We used a two-method approach: A qualitative pre-study identified the motives and barriers for personal data sharing in the context of smart factories. In a next step, a scenario-based survey quantified the acceptance and its predictors of the willingness to disclose personal data, exemplified by a cobot and chatbot scenario.

Motives of Data Sharing. The motives for sharing data were drivers. Health-related reasons were highlighted with the possibility of alerting a worker, health precaution and conducting quick first aid measures by wearing wearables. The results were in line with the state of scientific research that the more the technologies are increasing the worker's health, the higher the acceptance to share personal data [20,40]. The same results were found for psychological motives, such as reducing workers stress and uncertainties as well as worker's fear. Even more positive associations were found according to work related aspects. This study could also validate that the willingness to disclose data goes hand in hand with the personal arising benefits concerning work or assessment related or even personal reasons: knowing, that the own productivity will increase [16], that a relief from physical demanding work could be assured [42], or motivating factors such as competing the own performance with colleagues for fun and real could be enabled [35] are some examples. It can be stated that sharing personal data is linked to many motives that increase the willingness to share data. Further research should examine the identified motives in more detail and provide incentives with regard to privacy concerns.

Barriers of Data Sharing. Barriers of data sharing were associated with uncertainties about data collection and privacy concerns. Workers may be hesitant to share their personal data due to concerns about how it will be used and who will have access to it. Privacy concerns have particularly been studied in different domains such as i.e. in the digital health care context: by using mhealth apps [45] or in the context of ambient assisted living [38]. In either way, the intention to share data with the offered technology could technically be achieved by guaranteeing, that data is collected and stored securely and by transparently informing the user about the single stages the data is passed onto and with witch provider. Moreover, the decision to share data and with who they want to share should be adjustable. In the context of the Internet of Production (IoP) with cyber-physcial workplaces the possibility of voluntarily sharing data with whomever workers want could turn out to be challenging. However, transparency of data sharing needs to be considered as a prerequisite for positive acceptance [21]. Further concerns were mentioned regarding fear of negative feedback, unnecessary data collection, the feeling of being monitored all the time or fear of job loss among others. Taking these concerns seriously is very important and communicating transparently about the benefits, the new technology might bring already relieves these severe fears. An empirically investigated phenomena which describes a difference between the attitude and actual behaviour is known as the *privacy paradox*: Although people generally express concern about their data, want to protect it, and want to have control over who accessibility, they nevertheless disclose a great amount of personal information [1] due to a risk-benefit-analysis [13]. This assumption indicates that the intention to provide data depends on the trade-off between personal benefit and the perceived privacy risk. Thus, further research needs to be done on possible benefits taking the mentioned motives of this study into account.

Perceived Sensitivity of Data Sharing. Our main study gave further information about data sensitivity meaning the associated level of risk and willingness to disclose personal data. Only demographic data and work related data were seen as less sensitive and thus shareable within the working context. These findings are congruent with the results from Tolsdorf et al. [41] that found that data groups related to the employment context show a significantly lower perceived sensitivity and a higher willingness to share. According to Tolsdorf, hair color, occupation, language skills, shift schedules, and business trips were the least sensitive data. Further research should focus on the assessment of personal data and pursue a classification of different data clusters [41]. For the actual use of sensitive data in the work context, communication concepts need to be developed that transparently explain the use of the data and the processing of the data to the worker. Moreover, further research should also investigate on influencing factors such as culture and age which have been shown to have an influence on the perception of data sensitivity [6, 26]. Asked the other way around, which data is associated as being important for the company, work related, movement profile, demographic data and expressive data were stated; data, which were personally too sensitive to share. Further research is needed which firstly identifies concrete data types needed in cyber-physical work environment and secondly evaluates the data according to its perceived sensitivity.

Acceptance of Chatbot and Cobot-scenario. In this study participants evaluated two scenarios which included several kinds of personal data on whose basis a working interaction between human and technology could take place. Both, the chatbot- and cobot-scenario were rated positively. It was found that four factors were prominent in measuring the acceptance of both scenarios: hedonic motivation, performance expectancy, trust and effort expectancy.

Cobot Scenario. The strongest influence on intention to use was found for the hedonic motivation factor. Fun as a motivating factor for sharing data and interacting with a cobot is also reflected in current empirical research [10]. In order to achieve an active willingness to interact with a networked cyber-physical system that requires personal data, playful and motivational elements need to be considered in its design. In order to identify adequate motivational factors, the user must be involved in the empirical development according to user-centred design. Performance expectation, understood as utility, was the second most important factor. As cobots are designed to work side-by-side with the human operator, fluent interaction and high performance based on worker data such as location, height, etc. are essential for successful joint task performance. A clear understanding and predictability in terms of their movement, speed, acceleration and others, taking into account the required personal data of the worker, needs to be elaborated [32]. Trust in automation, as generated by the expected predictability, credibility and usefulness of the technology [24], was also considered important in relation to the intention to work with a cobot. Similar to the need for high performance, the worker needs to be able to trust the technological functions of the cobot for a successful collaboration. Once again, the clusters of personal data required for the specific collaborative work context need to be specifically explored and the benefits transparently explained to the user in order to achieve a positive roll-out for Industry 4.0. Effort expectancy is defined as the extent to which a user perceives the interaction with the cobot as user-friendly and easy. In this study, effort expectancy was rated significantly lower compared to the chatbot scenario. A smooth collaboration requires not only personal user data, but also knowledge and experience in working with robots. The very idea of working with a cobot can give an indication of the importance of effort expectancy. However, this result should only be taken as an indication. Therefore, user studies need to be conducted with real interaction and focus on the required user data.

Chatbot Scenario. Here, performance expectancy showed the strongest correlation with intention to use. It is defined as the degree to which a person believes that using the chatbot will help them achieve gains in job performance [43]. The chatbot acts as a conversational agent which, in this study, provides information about a holiday request based on personal and work-related data. This study provided insights into the general evaluation of two technological innovations through the advancement of Artifical Intelligence and machine learning. As the implementation of conversational agents such as chatbots will increase in general and specifically in the context of smart factories, deeper insights into the willingness to disclose personal data and privacy concerns when interacting with chatbots need to be conducted [19]. Hedonic motivation was seen as a second important factor and underlines the fact that the interaction with the chatbot needs to be designed with joyful elements [9]. On a conversational basis, it would be interesting to study the impact and practical use of humour within the chatbot. In addition, privacy concerns and the willingness to share personal data depending on the human-like characteristics of the chatbot may influence adoption and require further research [14]. Trust in automation was seen as reliance on the actions of the chatbot. Effort expectancy was found as an important explanation for the intention to use a chatbot. It reflects the extent to which the potential user thinks that much or little effort is necessary to use an appropriate chatbot and to learn how to deal with it. Since they are programmed to have a human-like dialogue with natural language understanding, the chatbot is perceived as human-like or anthropomorphic [17] which promotes the usage intention.

Both contexts were rated on a semantic differential and again, the chatbot was described with more positive attributes than the cobot which can be derived from the fact, that interactions with chatbots are common in i.g. booking contexts and therefore a higher experience is given [7].

The following key findings and actionable recommendation have emerged from this study:

- Employees' willingness to share personal data increases with personal benefits.
- Transparent communication and detailed information about data processing is very important.

- High acceptance of technology of either the cobot or chatbot can be reached by considering factors such as fun, performance, trust and effort expectancy.
- Playful, joyful and motivational elements need to be considered in their design.
- A clear understanding and predictability regarding the cobot's movement, speed, acceleration are important.
- Cobots need to be designed trustfully,
- Human-like and anthropomorphic patterns are relevant.

Furthermore, the results show that the perception of sensitivity differs according to the context of use and the type of data. This indicates that there is no one-size-fits-all solution for the use of personal data in smart factories, but that data use must be negotiated individually with the affected employees.

The study can be seen as an initiation of various research projects towards the acceptance of cobots and chatbots. Understanding individual privacy concerns and trust in automation are prerequisites for the development of practical guidelines that should serve as a benchmark for the implementation of such technologies in industry for a successful roll-out.

It is foreseeable that the collection and use of personal data, in addition to machine and production data, will increase in the near future. As this has affects the employees' self-determination, autonomy, and perceived privacy responsible (research and) innovation (R(R)I) mandates to taken this into account when designing future work environments. As privacy perceptions in smart factories are currently insufficiently understood, further research needs to integrate the perspectives of all stakeholders affected by the digital transformation of production (e.g. employees, managers, or trade unions). The different perspectives on the motives and barriers for data sharing can then be integrated and translated into a socially and collectively negotiated protocol for the use of personal data in smart factories. In the face of skills shortages caused by demographic change, the participatory integration of workers' perspectives is gaining importance beyond responsible research and innovation: Creating smart, fair, and accepted work environments that promote self-determination and autonomy can become a key competitive advantage in attracting and retaining talent.

Acknowledgments. The authors would like to thank all the participants for sharing their personal views. We would also like to thank Lena Herrmann and Tim Schmeckel for their valuable research assistance. Funded by the Deutsche Forschungsgemeinschaft (DFG, German Research Foundation) under Germany's Excellence Strategy - EXC-2023 Internet of Production - 390621612.

References

1. Acquisti, A., Brandimarte, L., Loewenstein, G.: Privacy and human behavior in the age of information. Science **347**(6221), 509–514 (2015)
2. Altman, I.: The environment and social behavior: privacy, personal space, territory, and crowding (1975)

3. Auer-Srnka, K.J., Meier-Pesti, K., Grießmair, M.: Ältere menschen als zielgruppe der werbung: Eine explorative studie zu wahrnehmung und selbstbild der "best ager" sowie stereotypen vorstellungen vom alt-sein in jüngeren altersgruppen. der markt **47**(3), 100–117 (2008)
4. Bhave, D.P., Teo, L.H., Dalal, R.S.: Privacy at work: a review and a research agenda for a contested terrain. J. Manag. **46**(1), 127–164 (2020)
5. Brauner, P., et al.: A computer science perspective on digital transformation in production. ACM Trans. Internet Things **3**(2), 1–32 (2022). https://doi.org/10.1145/3502265
6. Van den Broeck, E., Poels, K., Walrave, M.: Older and wiser? Facebook use, privacy concern, and privacy protection in the life stages of emerging, young, and middle adulthood. Soc. Media+ Soc. **1**(2), 2056305115616149 (2015)
7. Buhalis, D., Cheng, E.S.Y.: Exploring the use of chatbots in hotels: technology providers' perspective. In: Neidhardt, J., Wörndl, W. (eds.) Information and Communication Technologies in Tourism 2020, pp. 231–242. Springer, Cham (2020). https://doi.org/10.1007/978-3-030-36737-4_19
8. Choudrie, J., Vyas, A.: Silver surfers adopting and using Facebook? A quantitative study of Hertfordshire, UK applied to organizational and social change. Technol. Forecast. Soc. Chang. **89**, 293–305 (2014)
9. Chung, M., Ko, E., Joung, H., Kim, S.J.: Chatbot e-service and customer satisfaction regarding luxury brands. J. Bus. Res. **117**, 587–595 (2020)
10. Dammers, H., Vervier, L., Mittelviefhaus, L., Brauner, P., Ziefle, M., Gries, T.: Usability of human-robot interaction within textile production: insights into the acceptance of different collaboration types (2022)
11. Davis, F.D.: User acceptance of information technology: system characteristics, user perceptions and behavioral impacts. Int. J. Man Mach. Stud. **38**(3), 475–487 (1993). https://doi.org/10.1006/imms.1993.1022
12. Dethloff, C.: Akzeptanz und Nicht-Akzeptanz von technischen Produktinnovationen. Pabst Science Publ. (2004)
13. Dinev, T., Hart, P.: An extended privacy calculus model for e-commerce transactions. Inf. Syst. Res. **17**(1), 61–80 (2006)
14. Epley, N., Waytz, A., Cacioppo, J.T.: On seeing human: a three-factor theory of anthropomorphism. Psychol. Rev. **114**(4), 864 (2007)
15. European Commission: Industry 5.0 (2022). https://ec.europa.eu/info/research-and-innovation/research-area/industrial-research-and-innovation/industry-50_en. Accessed 12 Dec 2022
16. Greco, A., Caputo, F., Caterino, M., D'Ambra, S., Fera, M., Laudante, E.: Composite parts assembly operational improvements. In: Macromolecular Symposia, vol. 389, p. 1900098. Wiley Online Library (2020)
17. Han, M.C.: The impact of anthropomorphism on consumers' purchase decision in chatbot commerce. J. Internet Commer. **20**(1), 46–65 (2021)
18. Hassenzahl, M., Burmester, M., Koller, F.: Attrakdiff: ein fragebogen zur messung wahrgenommener hedonischer und pragmatischer qualität. In: In: Szwillus, G., Ziegler, J. (eds.) Mensch & Computer 2003. Berichte des German Chapter of the ACM, vol. 57, pp. 187–196. Springer Vieweg+Teubner Verlag (2003). https://doi.org/10.1007/978-3-322-80058-9_19
19. Ischen, C., Araujo, T., Voorveld, H., van Noort, G., Smit, E.: Privacy concerns in chatbot interactions. In: Følstad, A., et al. (eds.) CONVERSATIONS 2019. LNCS, vol. 11970, pp. 34–48. Springer, Cham (2020). https://doi.org/10.1007/978-3-030-39540-7_3

20. Jacobs, J.V., et al.: Employee acceptance of wearable technology in the workplace. Appl. Ergon. **78**, 148–156 (2019)
21. Jandl, C., Zafari, S., Taurer, F., Hartner-Tiefenthaler, M., Schlund, S.: Location-based monitoring in production environments: does transparency help to increase the acceptance of monitoring? Prod. Manuf. Res. **11**(1), 2160387 (2023)
22. Kagermann, H.: Change through digitization—value creation in the age of industry 4.0. In: Albach, H., Meffert, H., Pinkwart, A., Reichwald, R. (eds.) Management of Permanent Change, pp. 23 45. Springer, Wiesbaden (2015). https://doi.org/10.1007/978-3-658-05014-6_2
23. Lasi, H., Fettke, P., Kemper, H.-G., Feld, T., Hoffmann, M.: Industry 4.0. Bus. Inf. Syst. Eng. **6**(4), 239–242 (2014). https://doi.org/10.1007/s12599-014-0334-4
24. Lee, J.D., See, K.A.: Trust in automation: designing for appropriate reliance. Hum. Factors **46**(1), 50–80 (2004)
25. Lidynia, C., Brauner, P., Ziefle, M.: A step in the right direction – understanding privacy concerns and perceived sensitivity of fitness trackers. In: Ahram, T., Falcão, C. (eds.) AHFE 2017. AISC, vol. 608, pp. 42–53. Springer, Cham (2018). https://doi.org/10.1007/978-3-319-60639-2_5
26. Markos, E., Milne, G.R., Peltier, J.W.: Information sensitivity and willingness to provide continua: a comparative privacy study of the united states and Brazil. J. Public Policy Mark. **36**(1), 79–96 (2017)
27. Mertens, A., et al.: Human digital shadow: data-based modeling of users and usage in the internet of production. In: 2021 14th International Conference on Human System Interaction (HSI), pp. 1–8. IEEE (2021)
28. Mettler, T., Wulf, J.: Physiolytics at the workplace: affordances and constraints of wearables use from an employee's perspective. Inf. Syst. J. **29**(1), 245–273 (2019)
29. Millward, P.: The'grey digital divide': perception, exclusion and barriers of access to the internet for older people. First monday (2003)
30. Milne, G.R., Pettinico, G., Hajjat, F.M., Markos, E.: Information sensitivity typology: mapping the degree and type of risk consumers perceive in personal data sharing. J. Consum. Aff. **51**(1), 133–161 (2017)
31. Nissenbaum, H.: Privacy in context. In: Privacy in Context. Stanford University Press (2009)
32. Paliga, M.: Human-cobot interaction fluency and cobot operators' job performance. the mediating role of work engagement: a survey. Robot. Auton. Syst. **155**, 104191 (2022)
33. Pfeiffer, S., Lee, H., Held, M.: Doing industry 4.0-participatory design on the shop floor in the view of engineering employees. Cuadernos de Relaciones Laborales **37**(1), 293–311 (2019)
34. Pütz, S., Rick, V., Mertens, A., Nitsch, V.: Using IoT devices for sensor-based monitoring of employees' mental workload: Investigating managers' expectations and concerns. Appl. Ergon. **102**, 103739 (2022). https://doi.org/10.1016/j.apergo.2022.103739
35. Salvatore, M., Stefano, R., et al.: Smart operators: how industry 4.0 is affecting the worker's performance in manufacturing contexts. Procedia Comput. Sci. **180**, 958–967 (2021)
36. Schall, M.C., Jr., Sesek, R.F., Cavuoto, L.A.: Barriers to the adoption of wearable sensors in the workplace: a survey of occupational safety and health professionals. Hum. Factors **60**(3), 351–362 (2018)
37. Schoeman, F.: Privacy: philosophical dimensions. Am. Philos. Q. **21**(3), 199–213 (1984)

38. Schomakers, E.M., Biermann, H., Ziefle, M.: Users' preferences for smart home automation-investigating aspects of privacy and trust. Telematics Inform. **64**, 101689 (2021)
39. Schomakers, E.M., Lidynia, C., Ziefle, M.: All of me? Users' preferences for privacy-preserving data markets and the importance of anonymity. Electron. Mark. **30**(3), 649–665 (2020)
40. Stefana, E., Marciano, F., Rossi, D., Cocca, P., Tomasoni, G.: Wearable devices for ergonomics: a systematic literature review. Sensors **21**(3), 777 (2021)
41. Tolsdorf, J., Reinhardt, D., Iacono, L.L.: Employees' privacy perceptions: exploring the dimensionality and antecedents of personal data sensitivity and willingness to disclose. Proc. Priv. Enhanc. Technol. **2022**(2), 68–94 (2022)
42. Turner, C.J., Oyekan, J., Stergioulas, L., Griffin, D.: Utilizing industry 4.0 on the construction site: challenges and opportunities. IEEE Trans. Ind. Inform. **17**(2), 746–756 (2020)
43. Venkatesh, V., Davis, F., Morris, M.G.: Dead or alive? The development, trajectory and future of technology adoption research. J. Assoc. Inf. Syst. **8**(4), 267–286 (2007)
44. Venkatesh, V., Thong, J.Y., Xu, X.: Consumer acceptance and use of information technology: extending the unified theory of acceptance and use of technology. MIS Q. 157–178 (2012)
45. Vervier, L., Ziefle, M.: A meta-analytical view on the acceptance of mhealth apps. In: ICT4AWE, pp. 322–329 (2022)
46. Warren, S.D., Brandeis, L.D.: The right to privacy'. Harv. Law Rev. **4**, 193 (1890)
47. Yao, X., Ma, N., Zhang, J., Wang, K., Yang, E., Faccio, M.: Enhancing wisdom manufacturing as industrial metaverse for industry and society 5.0. J. Intell. Manuf. 1–21 (2022)
48. Yavari, F., Pilevari, N.: Industry revolutions development from industry 1.0 to industry 5.0 in manufacturing. J. Ind. Strateg. Manag. **5**(2), 44–63 (2020)

Multi-ledger Coordinating Mechanism by Smart Contract for Individual-Initiated Trustworthy Data Sharing

Yenjou Wang[1] , Ruichen Cong[1] , Yixiao Lin[1] , Kiichi Tago[2] , Ruidong Li[3] ,
Hitoshi Asaeda[4] , and Qun Jin[5(✉)]

[1] Graduate School of Human Sciences, Waseda University, Tokorozawa, Japan
[2] Department of Information and Network Science, Chiba Institute of Technology, Narashino, Japan
[3] Faculty of Electrical, Information and Communication Engineering, Institute of Science and Engineering, Kanazawa University, Kanazawa, Japan
[4] National Institute of Information and Communications Technology (NICT), Tokyo, Japan
[5] Faculty of Human Sciences, Waseda University, Tokorozawa, Japan
jin@waseda.jp

Abstract. With the development of the Internet of Things (IoT) and sensors, personal health data can be collected by wearable devices. However, one of the biggest concerns about the storage and use of sensitive personal health data is privacy. To address this issue, we propose a new Multi-Ledger Coordinating Mechanism (MLCM) with blockchain for trustworthy data sharing under the control of each individual data owner. MLCM, enabled by smart contracts, lets an individual user control and manage all his/her own data in a flexible way and enhances data security and privacy preservation in user authentication and management. Also, all activities related to data access are monitored and further recorded in blockchain. The evaluation experiment is designed to demonstrate the feasibility of the proposed mechanism, and the result shows that the prototype implementation of one smart contract based on Hyperledger Fabric is stable.

Keywords: Blockchain · IPFS · Smart Contract · Privacy Protection · Data Sharing · Personal Health Data

1 Introduction

With the rapid development of Internet of Things (IoT) technology, sensors make it possible to collect a large amount of data for higher levels of services through data sharing, such as personalized healthcare services. In particular, the health data collected for a person by wearable devices is called Personal Health Data (PHD), which may include privacy. Privacy protection is a complex and sensitive issue, which is a big challenge for data sharing [1]. Therefore, many countries have enacted laws to address privacy concerns. On the other hand, two complex issues should be considered, which are "who owns the data" and "what rights does ownership imply" [2]. For example,

A. Moallem (Ed.): HCII 2023, LNCS 14045, pp. 232–243, 2023.
https://doi.org/10.1007/978-3-031-35822-7_16

medical service providers, such as hospitals, create medical records about patients as the data owner, but do not allow data sharing with patients. However, medical records are more related to patients in essence, and they should also be the data owner to control, manage and decide who can share and use the data. Therefore, practical solutions are necessary to secure personal data sharing and ensure individuals' data ownership.

In recent years, blockchain with decentralization and immutability has been used to be a helpful solution for implementing data privacy protection and secure data transmission. As mentioned above, PHD involves privacy and is sensitive, therefore, they are unsuitable for recording on blockchain in plaintext. An Individual-Initiated Auditable Access Control (IIAAC) mechanism was proposed in [3], which is based on a consortium blockchain, CP-ABE (Ciphertext-Policy Attribute-Based Encryption) and IPFS (InterPlanetary File System) to share encrypted PHD and enable data owners to define the access policy on their data initiatively.

Currently, many studies focus on using smart contracts or traditional access mechanisms to define access permissions [4, 5]. These authentication methods are preset when a user accesses blockchain for the first time, and the authentication data is recorded on the CA (Certificate Authority) or cloud server [6]. Since we target to provide an individual-initiated system for health and medical data sharing, it is necessary to consider the third-party certificates that can be used to authenticate the identity of different hospitals or different types of users. There must be a trusted manager as the authenticator to avoid identity forgery in each node when the users first register. We design a mechanism based on blockchain, in which the certification information and access logs are recorded to allow secure data sharing between hospitals and individual users and ensure that the information cannot be tampered with. In addition, recorded access logs on blockchain can also be used for subsequent discriminant analysis of illegal accesses.

To share PHD securely, this study proposes a Multi-Ledger Coordinating Mechanism (MLCM) for individual-initiated trustworthy data sharing enabled by smart contracts. Smart contracts are taken as the coordinator of ledgers, defining which actions can be performed by different types of users on which ledgers through MLCM. In MLCM, the access policy of personal data can be set by individuals flexibly, and the ownership of their data can be kept to individuals by smart contracts, even if others create the data. In addition, user authentication information can also be recorded and shared safely through smart contracts. Then MLCM, with the blockchain as a surveillance zone, is used to automatically record the access log to prevent not-targeted users from tampering with it for subsequent analysis. The major contributions of this study are summarized as follows.

- An individual-initiated system for health and medical data sharing based on blockchain ensures the ownership of data to individuals who can manage all their own data in a flexible way and enhances privacy protection.
- The multi-ledger coordinating mechanism allows different types of users to access different related ledgers, and to share and use data securely.
- The recordability of access enables illegal access to be monitored and analyzed.

The rest of this paper is organized as follows. In Sect. 2, we overview related work on data sharing and access control based on smart contracts. In Sect. 3, how to coordinate each ledger through smart contracts is explained in detail. In Sect. 4, we describe the experiment environment for performance evaluation and discuss the results to demonstrate the feasibility and stability of the proposed mechanism. Finally, Sect. 5 concludes this work and highlights future directions.

2 Related Work

This section describes data sharing and access control by smart contracts based on blockchain platforms. A smart contract is a program that can be executed automatically after certain conditions are satisfied. It was initially introduced by Nick Szabo [7]. It can receive, store, send messages, and perform operations with predetermined rules. In addition, the integration of smart contracts and IoT with significant benefits are discussed, such as transaction management, distributed computing, data traceability, access control, etc. [8].

To enable secure sharing of sensitive data, such as PHD, many frameworks and approaches using smart contracts in blockchain have been proposed [9–13]. In previous studies, smart contracts have been used to achieve access control of medical data by using policies to remain patient centricity across the system. Saini et al. [9] developed an access control model based on smart contracts for smart healthcare services to secure sharing of electronic medical records (EMRs). The EMRs are encrypted and stored in the cloud, while the hash-values corresponding to the EMRs are stored on blockchain. However, the integration of blockchain and cloud incurs challenges of security, scalability, and performance, in which the attack and latency may occur in the centralized-cloud server. Putra et al. [10] use the Ethereum smart contract and re-encryption method to provide a safe electronic medical record data sharing method between hospitals and provide a reward mechanism to encourage data sharing. However, patients have no control over their PHD. Kumar and Dakshayini [11] proposed secure sharing of health data using Hyper ledger Fabric, a consortium blockchain platform, among medical organizations. However, there is a limitation on on-chain storage, which is the inefficiency of storing large size of data on blockchain.

Besides the utilization in access control, smart contracts are also used to register staff members of medical institutions before they request access to patients' electronic health records. Zaghloul et al. [12] proposed a security and privacy enhanced medical record sharing and management scheme. Two smart contracts are deployed for staff member registration (SMR) and access verification and permission announcements (AVPA). After verifying the attributes of staff members, which are physically certified by a registering institution first, the transaction between the SMR contract and the registering institution is executed. The attributes of staff members are stored on blockchain. In addition, patients can develop and deploy the AVPA contract to define who can obtain the electronic health record through blockchain initiatively. However, since user registration and access verification are performed by smart contracts, and the attributes data are stored in the smart contracts, it is necessary to optimize on-chain storage to improve the overall performance.

This study focuses on a new multi-ledger coordinating mechanism (MLCM), in which we design four ledgers as multi-ledger to let individuals manage their own data initiatively and further design three smart contracts for multi-ledger coordination. In our proposed mechanism, different types of users are permitted to access different ledgers, and all access activities on blockchain are monitored and recorded.

3 Coordinating Multi-ledger by Smart Contracts

In this section, we first introduce the system architecture, which combines multi-ledger in blockchain, IPFS, and a client application that connects blockchain and IPFS. Then, we describe four ledgers in the system in terms of functions and their relationships with each other. Finally, we describe how the ledgers coordinate with each other through smart contracts and explain the detailed procedures in the system.

Trustworthy Data Sharing with Multi-ledger Coordinating Mechanism. To achieve trustworthy data sharing, a multi-ledger coordinating mechanism is proposed, which coordinates four ledgers to record users' PHD, electronic medical records, access logs and authentication data through three smart contracts. In this system, users are classified into three types: a general user (patient) who creates the PHD, the medical staff (doctor) who creates the electronic medical records, and the manager who perform user authentication and management. In this study, we focus on defining and constructing smart contracts for data sharing and access monitoring. CP-ABE, an attribute-based encryption scheme, lets users customize and manage the accessor attributes of their PHD reliably and flexibly. The system architecture is shown in Fig. 1, which mainly consists of four components: consortium blockchain, off-chain storage (IPFS), CP-ABE encryption mechanism, and a client application that connects blockchain and IPFS.

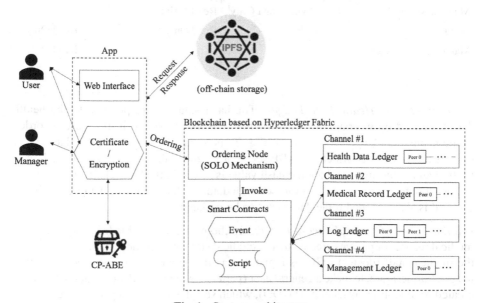

Fig. 1. System architecture

Multi-ledger for Encrypted Multi-Source Data. In this study, the users in the blockchain vary in attributes and organization, resulting in inconsistent content and purpose for the stored data. Dividing the blockchain into multiple ledgers according to storage content and purpose can increase the efficiency of data sharing and access. Therefore, we design four ledgers for individual-initiated trustworthy data sharing. The membership service provider (MSP) is used to set the access permission for different user types on each ledger as shown in Table 1. The general user (patient) who owns the health data collected by wearable devices can read and write on the health data ledger. They can also have ownership to read their electronic medical records created by a medical staff through smart contracts. In the same way, the medical staff (doctor) who generates the electronic medical records can read and write on the medical record ledger and read permitted data in the health data ledger. General users and medical staffs have no permission to access the management ledger. In contrast, the manager has no permission to access the health data ledger and medical record ledger. However, the manager can read and write on the management ledger to record the authentication data. Furthermore, all blockchain users have read right on the log ledger to check if there is illegal access by malicious users. The data structure of each ledger is represented in JSON and is described as follows.

Table 1. Access permissions for different user types on each ledger by MSP

	General User (Patient)	Medical Staff (Doctor)	Manager
Health Data Ledger	Read/Write	Read Permitted Data Only	–
Medical Record Ledger	Read Owned Data Only	Read/Write	–
Log Ledger	Read Only	Read Only	Read Only
Management Ledger	–	–	Read/Write

Data Structure of Health Data Ledger. The hash values corresponding to the health data generated by wearable devices or other sensors and stored in IPFS are recorded in the health data ledger. As shown in Fig. 2, the data owner in the health data ledger records the user's GID, which CP-ABE sets. Furthermore, the action in which reading or writing and timestamp in which the hash value is stored in the blockchain are recorded. In addition, to ensure the correlation between data, the hash value of data before being updated is also recorded if the data needs to be updated.

Data Structure of Medical Record Ledger. In the medical record ledger, the electronic medical records of patients created by the medical staff are recorded. As shown in Fig. 3, the medical staff (doctor)'s GID is registered as the data owner in the medical record ledger. Furthermore, to make a general user (patient) own his/her data, a smart contract is created for doubling ownerships (SCDO), which sets the doctor and patient as co-owner of the electronic medical records and the ownership information is stored in the medical record ledger.

Data Structure of Log Ledger. In the log ledger, for traceability on the blockchain, a smart contract monitors the blockchain and records all access events, actions, and reasons

```
{"healthdata_ledger:{
    "key": {
        "data_owner": GID_User,
    }
    "value" {
      "operation": {
          "action": "read"/"created"...
      },
      "hash": "jei273891wheu...",
      "prv_hash": "jeiqwejiq280391ejiqu...","none",      # if update/revised
      "timestamp": 3728042
}}
```

Fig. 2. Data structure of health data ledger

```
{"medicalrecord_ledger":{
    "key": {
        "data_owner": GID_Doctor, GID_USER,
    }
    "value" {
      "operation": {
          "action": "read"/"created"...
      },
      "hash": "jei273qejodiaseu...",
      "prv_hash": "jeiqwejiq280391ejiqu...","none",      # if update/revised
      "creator": GID_Doctor/ GID_Nurse/ GID_Officer,
      "timestamp": 3728042
}}
```

Fig. 3. Data structure of medical record ledger

to the log ledger. As shown in Fig. 4, the GID of the data owner and requestor, and the smart contract, which is used to execute the request, and the access token are recorded. In addition, the ID of the target data on IPFS, the hash value of target data returned from IPFS, and the metadata corresponding to the target data are also recorded in the log ledger. These data can be used for future analysis of user behaviors to detect illegal access.

Data Structure of Management Ledger. In the management ledger, the authentication data of the users' identities are recorded. Hyperledger Fabric, a consortium blockchain that allows one manager in each organization in the blockchain network, is used in the system. The manager is responsible for the initial identity authentication of the blockchain node. The authentication data on blockchain are shared through the management ledger to improve the efficiency of initial authentication. Since authentication is related to the security of the blockchain network, the management ledger can only be accessed by the manager as shown in Fig. 5, and the GID of the user, the action in which

```
{"log_ledger":{
    "value" {
      "data_owner": GID_USER/GID_Doctor/ GID_Supervisor,
      "controller": GID_SC,                #smartcontract's GID
      "creator": GID_USER/ GID_Doctor/ GID_Supervisor
      "access_token": "qwjieo23j1ioeqw",
      "access_number": 123456,
      "status": "approved"/"rejected",
      "Target_hash": "jei27389qwereu...",
      "dataID_number": "123489",           #Data ID on IPFS
      "index":"heartbeat, weight, CA....",          #keywords
      "operation":"read","created"....,
      "reason": "Daily upload"/"Medical records"/
                "Required for diagnosis and treatment"/"Authorize"....,
      "timestamp": 3728042
}}
```

Fig. 4. Data structure of log ledger

reading or writing, and the CA name which authenticates the identity of the target user are recorded.

```
{"management_ledger":{
    "key": {
        "target_user": GID_USER,       #data_owner/CA authorized target
        "creator": GID_Supervisor    #CA's GID
    }
    "value" {
      "operation":{
          "action": "authorize","read"
      },
      "CA_name":"A hospital"/"B hospital"/"Root CA", #Where did user get the CA
      "number":234567,
      "access_transaction_no": 123456,    #log_ledger_access_number
      "timestamp": 3728042
}}
```

Fig. 5. Data structure of management ledger

Smart Contracts for Multi-ledger Coordination. To enhance the protection of privacy and data security, MLCM is proposed and designed, and it is enabled by smart contracts, namely smart contracts for doubling ownerships (SCDO), smart contracts for managing users (SCMU), and smart contracts for monitoring accesses (SCMA). The relationship between smart contracts and ledgers is shown in Table 2, and the detailed functions of each smart contract are described as follows.

Table 2. Multi-ledger coordination by smart contracts

	Smart Contracts for Doubling Ownerships (SCDO)	Smart Contracts for Managing Users (SCMU)	Smart Contracts for Monitoring Accesses (SCMA)
Health Data Ledger		✓	✓
Medical Record Ledger	✓	✓	✓
Log Ledger	✓	✓	✓
Management Ledger	✓	✓	✓

Smart Contracts for Doubling Ownerships (SCDO). To ensure the patients to have their own medical data ownership, SCDO is responsible for coordinating the medical records ledger, management ledger, and log ledger to let a specified medical record be owned by both the creator (doctor) and the patient. The process sequence of SCDO is shown in Fig. 6.

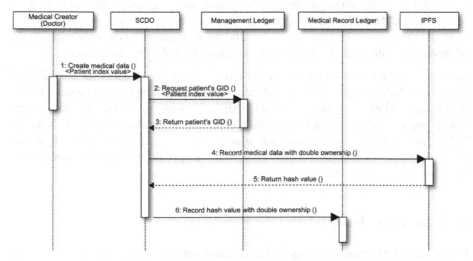

Fig. 6. The process sequence of smart contract for doubling ownerships (SCDO)

When the doctor generates a medical record for a patient, the SCDO requests the patient's GID from the management ledger based on the patient information provided by the doctor and records the GID to the medical data. Medical record data with double-owners is recorded in IPFS. When the SCDO receives the hash value returned by IPFS, it creates a new transaction that records the double-owners' GIDs and hash value.

Smart Contracts for Managing Users (SCMU). To allow that the user's authentication data can be recorded in a private way and resolve the issue of repeated authentication. The manager records and shares the user's authentication with other nodes through SCMU. The process sequence of SCMU is shown in Fig. 7.

In SCMU, the authentication process is divided into two cases. (1) a new user has never registered in blockchain before, and (2) a user was authenticated in other nodes (e.g., hospitals). When the manager confirms that the authentication case is (1) from SCMU, the user needs to provide GID and attributes to the manager for authentication by the CP-ABE server. The authentication data is recorded to IPFS through SCMU. SCMU also sets the visitor list in the corresponding ledger through the user's attribute to ensure the user to access different ledgers which match his/her attributes. Finally, SCMU records the hash value returned by IPFS in the management ledger and notifies the manager that the identity authentication was succussed.

When the manager confirms that the user authentication case is (2) from the management ledger, SCMU can send an authentication request to the previous authentication node (manager of the old node) through the information on the management ledger record. SCMU records the information of a new authorization node (manager of the new node) to IPFS, so that the manager of a new node can access the authentication data. Next, SCMU sends the authorization success message to the manager of the old node and the manager of a new node. Finally, the manager of a new node requests the authentication information from IPFS to complete the authentication process.

Smart Contract for Monitoring Accesses (SCMA). To enable all data to be shared trustworthily, SCMA is used to monitor and record all the access logs in blockchain. SCMA coordinates and monitors the health data ledger, medical record ledger, management ledger, and log ledger. These ledgers are represented as "Ledger" in Fig. 8. Through SCMA, all blockchain users' access activities are monitored and recorded to log ledger, e.g., a user uploads a new PHD, or a doctor views a case profile, etc. The process sequence of SCMA is shown in Fig. 8.

4   Experiment Result

To verify MLCM proposed in this study, we constructed a prototype of SCDO. We ran a workstation with Ubuntu 20.04, 48 logical CPUs, 140 GB main memory and 1TB storage capacity, and built the experiment environment based on Hyperledger Fabric 1.4.4. We used the docker version 20.10.12. The Go version is 1.13.8 Linux/amd64, and the tool for evaluating performance is Tape, which is a lightweight tool that can be used to measure TPS (Transactions Per Second) on Hyperledger Fabric.

In our experiment, we mainly evaluate the stability of smart contracts based on blockchain. Therefore, we replaced the hash value and other information returned by off-chain storage (IPFS) or application out of blockchain into a fixed string. The experiment is conducted with two actions, write, and read. Write is that the doctor creates the electronic

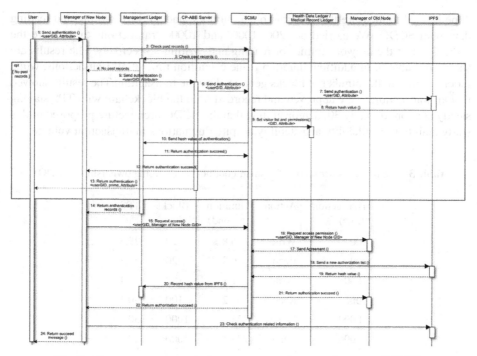

Fig. 7. The process sequence of smart contract for managing users (SCMU)

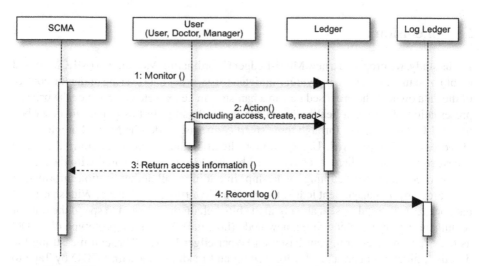

Fig. 8. The process sequence of smart contract for monitoring accesses (SCMA)

medical records, and then SCDO is used to copy the electronic medical records to create a transaction that includes the patient's GID. Read fetches the medical records containing the patient's GID and doctor's GID and records the result to the log ledger by SCDO.

Tape is used to measure the duration, block number, and TPS for writing and reading data with SCDO. We carried out 200, 1000, and 10000 transactions to measure the throughput of the network traffic for reading and writing respectively. The results are shown in Table 3. In addition, duration is the execution time of all transactions, while blocks represent the number of blocks generated by the transaction. The results showed that all transactions were approved and recorded onto the blockchain with TPS staying steady at approximately 30, demonstrating that the SCDO architecture proposed in this study maintains availability and stability despite fluctuations in transaction volume.

Table 3. Transactions per second for smart contract for doubling ownerships (SCDO)

Transaction (time)	Action	Duration (second)	Blocks	TPS
200	Write	6.8	20	29.3
200	Read	6.8	20	29.1
1000	Write	31.1	100	32.1
1000	Read	33.2	100	30.1
10000	Write	325.2	1000	30.7
10000	Read	338.1	1000	29.6

5 Conclusion

In this study, we proposed a new Multi-Ledger Coordinating Mechanism (MLCM) based on blockchain that enables individual-initiated trustworthy data sharing under the control of the data owner. The proposed new mechanism can be expected to enhance the privacy preservation of personal health data in sharing and using. In this paper, we described how MLCM coordinates through three smart contracts. Under the MLCM architecture, all accesses are monitored. Users are more flexible and secure in defining their data access rights. The medical records created by the doctor can be shared with the patient by smart contracts for doubling ownership. In addition, all authentication information is recorded by a management ledger to ensure trustworthy data sharing. With sharing of data between hospitals, users already in the blockchain do not need to spend the time of re-authentication when entering a new node (hospital). We built a prototype of SCDO as the experiment environment based on Hyperledger Fabric. Through measuring the duration, block number, and TPS for writing and reading data with SCDO by Tape to evaluate the stability of MLCM. The result showed that the prototyping implementation based on Hyperledger Fabric is stable.

In future works, we plan to investigate illegal access on a blockchain and improve the access control mechanism through feature analysis utilizing machine learning techniques, aiming to effectively resolve the problem of consortium blockchain attacks initiated by malicious users.

Acknowledgement. The work was supported in part by 2020–2021 Waseda University-NICT Matching Funds Program, 2020–2025 JSPS A3 Foresight Program (Grant No. JPJSA3F20200001), 2022 Waseda University Grants for Special Research Projects (Nos. 2022C-225 and 2022R-036), 2022–2024 Masaru Ibuka Foundation Research Project on Oriental Medicine, 2022 JST SPRING (Grant No. JPMJSP2128), and 2022 Waseda University Advanced Research Center for Human Sciences Project (Grant No. BA080Z000300).

References

1. Data Revolution Group: A World that counts. https://www.undatarevolution.org/report/. Accessed 05 Feb 2023
2. Wry, T., Cobb, J.A., Aldrich, H.E.: Personal data: The emergence of a new asset class. World Economic Forum, Swiss (2011)
3. Cong, R., Liu, Y., Tago, K., Li, R., Asaeda H., Jin, Q.: Individual-initiated auditable access control for privacy-preserved IoT data sharing with blockchain. In: 2021 IEEE International Conference on Communications Workshops (ICC Workshops), Montreal, QC, Canada, pp. 1–6. IEEE (2021)
4. Griggs, K.N., Ossipova, O., Kohlios, C.P., Baccarini, A.N., Howson, E.A., Hayajneh, T.: Healthcare blockchain system using smart contracts for secure automated remote patient monitoring. J. Med. Syst. **42**(7), 1–7 (2018)
5. Zhang, X., Chen, X.: Data security sharing and storage based on a consortium blockchain in a vehicular ad-hoc network. IEEE Access **7**, 58241–58254 (2019)
6. Ur Rahman, M., Baiardi, F., Ricci, L.: Blockchain smart contracts for scalable data sharing in IoT: a case study of smart agriculture. In: 2020 IEEE Global Conference on Artificial Intelligence and Internet of Things (GCAIoT), Dubai, United Arab Emirates, pp. 1–7. IEEE (2020)
7. Szabo, N.: Formalizing and securing relationships on public networks. First Monday **2**(9) (1997). https://doi.org/10.5210/fm.v2i9.548
8. Peng, K., Li, M., Huang, H., Wang, C., Wan, S., Choo, K.-K.R.: Security challenges and opportunities for smart contracts in internet of things: a survey. IEEE Internet Things J. **8**(15), 12004–12020 (2021)
9. Saini, A., Zhu, Q., Singh, N., Xiang, Y., Gao, L., Zhang, Y.: A smart-contract-based access control framework for cloud smart healthcare system. IEEE Internet Things J. **8**(7), 5914–5925 (2021)
10. Putra, F.A., Febriansyah, H., Sari, R.F.: Blockchain-based data owner rating in medical record data sharing using ethereum. In: 2022 20th International Conference on ICT and Knowledge Engineering (ICT&KE), Bangkok, Thailand, pp. 1–9. IEEE (2022)
11. Kumar S.N., Dakshayini, M.: Secure sharing of health data using hyperledger fabric based on blockchain technology. In: 2020 International Conference on Mainstreaming Block Chain Implementation (ICOMBI), Bengaluru, India, pp. 1–5. IEEE (2020)
12. Zaghloul, E., Li T., Ren, J.: Security and privacy of electronic health records: decentralized and hierarchical data sharing using smart contracts. In: 2019 International Conference on Computing, Networking and Communications (ICNC), Honolulu, HI, USA, pp. 375–379. IEEE (2019)
13. Cong, R., et al.: Secure interoperation of blockchain and IPFS through client application enabled by CP-ABE. In: Moallem, A. (ed.) HCI for Cybersecurity, Privacy and Trust. HCII 2022. Lecture Notes in Computer Science, vol. 13333, pp. 30–41. Springer, Cham (2022). https://doi.org/10.1007/978-3-031-05563-8_3

Cybersecurity Challenges and Approaches for Critical Infrastructure and Emerging Technologies

Privacy Awareness Among Users of Digital Healthcare Services in Saudi Arabia

Hebah A. Albatati[1,2]($\boxtimes$), John A. Clark[1], and Maysoon F. Abulkhair[2]

[1] The University of Sheffield, Sheffield, UK
{halbatati1,john.clark}@sheffield.ac.uk
[2] King Abdulaziz University, Jeddah, Saudi Arabia
{halbatati,mabualkhair}@kau.edu.sa

Abstract. With the emergence of the Internet of Things (IoT) technology over the past few years, many sectors have developed services that depend on it. One of them is healthcare. Healthcare services based on the IoT depend on users' personal and sensitive data, and users' awareness of privacy issues is essential when using these systems. Therefore, this study aims to discover current privacy awareness of users of healthcare services in Saudi Arabia to determine if they can manage their privacy within IoT-based healthcare services by themselves. First, the factors that affect users' privacy awareness were obtained from the literature. Then, a questionnaire that focused on discovering users' privacy awareness regarding the collection, use, and sharing of their personal and identifiable data when using digital services, especially healthcare services, was designed and developed. The survey was conducted, and the data were collected and analyzed to establish the results. The results found that the majority (61.8%) of respondents subjectively believe they have medium privacy awareness, 27.7% believe they have low awareness, and 10.5% believe they have high awareness. Regarding the objective assessment, where questions have right and wrong answers and do not depend on participants' opinions, the majority (72.3%) of respondents have medium awareness, and 23.1% have low awareness; however, only 4.6% have high awareness.

Keywords: Privacy awareness · Privacy measures · Digital healthcare · IoT-based healthcare · Questionnaire

1 Introduction

Healthcare is a critical area where many services and applications depending on Internet of Things (IoT) have been developed recently, for example, remote patient monitoring, telenursing and medicine reactions monitoring [1]. People are drawn to IoT-based healthcare technology because it allows them to automatic tracking of their vital indicators, such as heart rate and body temperature. Also, they can receive health services remotely at their homes. However, IoT-based healthcare solutions depend on users' health data, which is sensitive and critical [2]. Moreover, medical data are considered more sensitive than many other sectors' data [3].

© The Author(s), under exclusive license to Springer Nature Switzerland AG 2023
A. Moallem (Ed.): HCII 2023, LNCS 14045, pp. 247–261, 2023.
https://doi.org/10.1007/978-3-031-35822-7_17

In the near future, most people will be able to configure and utilize healthcare equipment and an IoT-based healthcare system without professional assistance. However, users of IoT-based healthcare systems must be aware of the many factors related to their privacy to be able to make an appropriate decision regarding the collection, use and sharing of their data and to avoid performing inappropriate actions. Privacy awareness is one of the factors that affect users' privacy concerns, which consequently affects their data disclosing behaviour [4]. Moreover, users' awareness is one of the factors that affect their decisions and behaviours when giving consent in IoT systems [3]. However, IoT-based healthcare technology is considered a new research area, and it is unclear how aware users are of the technology and related privacy issues.

This study aims to discover current privacy awareness among users of Saudi digital health systems, especially the "Sehatty" application, to find out if regular users are ready and aware enough to make informed decisions when using IoT-based healthcare services soon. First, the factors affecting users' privacy awareness when their personal and identifiable data are collected, used and shared, especially in healthcare services, were extracted from the relevant literature. Then, a questionnaire-based survey to determine users' privacy awareness was conducted, and the results analysed.

Section 2 of this paper gives background on some existing privacy awareness measurements. Section 3 describes the methodology for designing and developing the questionnaire and conducting the survey. Section 4 presents and discusses the results. Section 5 concludes the study and presents future work.

2   Related Work

Many available academic and non-academic questionnaires focus on users' information security awareness. For example, the human aspects of the information security questionnaire (HAIS-Q) assesses seven areas, namely, password management, email use, internet use, social media use, mobile devices, information handling and incident reporting [5]. Most available questionnaires focus on a specific area of information security, such as security awareness of smartphone use and security awareness of behaviour on social media. In addition, most questionnaires focus on two types of users: employees and students.

Most studies on privacy focus on privacy concerns, privacy paradox and privacy calculus [6]. Regarding measuring privacy concerns, Smith et al. [7] developed a scale to measure privacy concerns regarding information privacy practices. Their instrument has four dimensions: collection, errors, unauthorized secondary use, and unauthorized access to information. Moreover, Malhotra et al. [8] proposed a multidimensional scale of Internet users' information privacy concerns (IUIPC), including control, awareness, and collection. Xu et al. [9] measured Information privacy concerns using the MUIPC (Mobile Users' Information Privacy Concerns).

Many survey studies concerning privacy in different areas focus on the privacy calculus theory. For example, based on the privacy calculus theory framework, Krasnova et al. [10] examined the role of culture in individual self-disclosure decisions on social networks and, Kim et al. [11] surveyed the factors influencing users of IoT regarding the sharing of private information in different contexts such as smart homes and healthcare.

Extant studies that focus on measuring users' privacy awareness are limited. Some of these studies focus on social networks, e.g.[12, 13]; and others focus on one privacy aspect, such as privacy policy e.g. [12, 14].

Regarding the surveys and questionnaires that are concerned with privacy awareness, Bergmann [15] developed two questionnaires, completed before and after an experiment. The pre-questionnaire included questions that gathered statistics and privacy concerns using a Likert scale, while the post-questionnaire contained questions about the privacy policy that the user agreed to during the experiment, which focused on disclosing data. Pelet and Taieb [12] study focus on privacy policy. They developed a multidimensional scale to measure users' attitudes towards privacy policies. The participants in their study were from France and the USA, and most of them were students and employees. In their questionnaire, they used a seven-point Likert scale to measure users' attitudes, which may have led the participants to portray themselves positively or over/underestimate themselves. A study conducted by Sim et al. [14] proposed an Information Privacy Situation Awareness (IPSA) scale which focuses on the effect of situational awareness on users' privacy behaviour and decision making.. Their experiment was conducted with Facebook users, but they clarified that the IPSA could be applied to other social networks. Regarding the questions, they designed 16 items using a seven-point Likert scale (Strongly Disagree to Strongly Agree). However, their questions focused on Facebook's privacy policies despite the IPSA's applicability to other social networks. In [16], Alani designed a survey to measure Android users' privacy awareness about application permissions. The survey consists of thirteen items, varying between open questions and yes/no questions. Moreover, the survey uncovered what users consider to be their most private data.

Some studies concerned with measuring the user's privacy awareness used other techniques. For example, Braunstein et al. [17] proposed techniques using indirect questions to measure privacy concerns in different contexts such as email, news, online calendar, online photos, online documents, online purchases, online bank records and web history. They did not use it in the healthcare area. They explained that indirect questions help to mitigate any emotional response's impact. These questions depend on self-reported behaviours in an imaginary situation using a 5-point Likert scale. Their research also examines the effect of the language used in the questionnaire. They used the same questions in three questionnaires but modified the language in the instruction section to examine its impact on users' responses.

Currently, many studies focus on developing healthcare services and systems that depend on IoT. These systems depend on users' sensitive medical data and personal information. However, the current users' privacy awareness regarding the healthcare system is unclear. Furthermore, there is no specific tool to measure users' privacy awareness in healthcare. Therefore, there is a need to design a questionnaire that measures users' awareness of healthcare and which will help the designers and developers of healthcare systems to understand their target users.

3 Methodology

First, the factors that affect users' privacy awareness were obtained from the literature. Then, the conceptual framework was designed, followed by the design of questions to measure user knowledge and understanding of each factor. After that, a pilot study was conducted before the questionnaire was distributed to collect data.

3.1 Identifying Factors that Affect Users' Privacy Awareness

Concerning the factors that affect users' privacy awareness, Correia and Compeau [6] conducted a review of privacy awareness in information systems. They found that regulation, common practice, and technology affect users' privacy awareness. Moreover, the Antecedents, Privacy Concerns, Outcomes Model (APCO Macro Model) illustrates that regulations affect users' privacy concerns, consequently affecting their data-disclosing behaviour [4]. Thus, knowing and understanding the privacy regulations can affect users' awareness and consequently assist them in making appropriate decisions regarding their sensitive and personal data when interacting with any system that handles it.

Correia and Compeau [6] observe that common practices refer to service providers' policies in managing personal user data, while technology is concerned with the devices and software used to collect, transfer, and use users' personal data and the security and privacy measures used to protect personal user data. However, the privacy policy is the most appropriate means to inform any system user about how their personal information is collected, processed, and saved [18]. Thus, technology information is usually clarified in any service's privacy policies. Also, as mentioned previously in the related work section, many studies concerned with privacy awareness focus on privacy policies due to their importance in users' decisions regarding the data. Therefore, users' knowledge and understanding of the service provider's privacy policy is one factors that affects users' privacy awareness.

Privacy calculus theory suggests that individuals' behavioural responses, including disclosing their data, are determined by trade-offs between costs (risk) and benefits [4]. However, there is a need to discover the effect of users knowing and understanding of potential risks and perceived benefits on their privacy awareness. Many studies in the literature, such as [19] and [20], are concerned with users' privacy risk awareness in IoT. Udoh and Alkharashi [20] conducted an exploratory study to find the level of privacy risk awareness among smartwatch users in Indiana in the USA. They found that users preferred to use the Apple smartwatch over other brands because Apple does not have serious privacy violation issues. Thus, experience with privacy violations can be considered one of the factors that affect users' privacy awareness. In an experimental study by Aleisa et al. [21] user privacy awareness was enhanced by observing some privacy violations that appear in network traffic analysis reports when using IoT services that collect non-personal data. They investigated users' trust and privacy concerns before and after an experiment that aimed to raise privacy awareness; trust decreased and privacy concerns increased. From the above, it can be concluded that regulation, privacy policy, potential risks, perceived benefits and user experience with previous privacy violations are essential factors that affect users' privacy awareness.

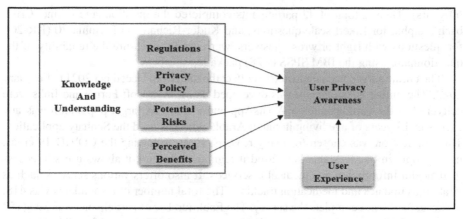

Fig. 1. The conceptual framework.

3.2 Designing and Developing Questions

The second stage was to develop questions for each factor to measure user knowledge and understanding. In the context of this study, users' privacy awareness can be defined as a combination of the user's knowledge and understanding of specific factors. Figure 1 illustrates the conceptual framework of this study. A set of questions has been designed for each factor. Some were designed to measure users' knowledge, such as if the user knows what regulations are used to protect personal data. In contrast, others were designed to measure understanding, e.g. of such regulations. Experience questions focus on users' experience with healthcare devices and privacy violations.

According to Sim et al. [14], situation awareness measures can be classified into subjective and objective measures. Subjective measures rely on users' self-assessment of their knowledge or skills, whilst objective measures usually rely on the observer's judgment to assess a subject's abilities by studying their responses to an actual situation. Moreover, Braunstein et al. [17] observed that self-reporting behaviours could produce unreliable estimates, leading to errors in the results. Thus, to avoid the limitation of using self-assessment and self-reported behaviours, where users might be affected by their emotions or have an inaccurate memory when evaluating themselves, two types of assessments were used: subjective measures and objective measures. In this questionnaire, a five-point Likert scale was used as a self-assessment measure, while score scaling was deployed for objective assessment. The questionnaire consisted of 57 questions, not including demographic questions, divided into five major categories: regulations (6 questions), privacy policies (16 questions), risks and benefits (19 questions) and user experience (16 questions).

3.3 Pilot Study and Data Collection

First, a pilot study was conducted to investigate the validity and reliability of the survey. The questionnaire was tested on three participants from different age groups: young adults (18–35 years), middle-aged adults (36–60 years), and older adults (above

60 years). Then, a total of 42 participants completed the questionnaire online. Cronbach's alpha, for Likert scale questions, and Kuder-Richardson Formula 20 (KR-20), for questions with right or wrong answers, were used to measure the reliability of the questionnaire using the IBM SPSS (v.28) package.

The online survey was conducted to collect the data from December 2021 to February 2022. The online questionnaire was developed using Microsoft Forms and links were delivered to the participants via WhatsApp and e-mail. Its target population was any user over 18 years of age living in Saudi Arabia who has used the Sehhaty application. This application was chosen for many reasons. First, following the COVID-19 crisis, most people in Saudi Arabia have used it regularly. Second, it allows users to access their health information and medical e-services. It also offers various services such as vital signs updates and medication tracking. The total number of respondents was 418; of these, 28 did not complete the survey. The final number of participants was 390 (152 male and 238 female). Ethical approvals for this survey were obtained from The Ministry of Health in Saudi Arabia and The University of Sheffield in the UK.

4   Results and Discussion

4.1   Demographic Profile

A total of 390 participants returned valid surveys to be analysed, consisting of 61.0% females and 39.0% males, with ages ranging from 18 to 70 years. The average age was 39.03. Most responses were from either Jeddah (66.4%) and Riyadh (12.3%). Respondents seemed well-educated; 53.6% held at least a Bachelor's degree, with 32.3% holding a Master's degree or a PhD. See Table 1 for more information.

4.2   Regulation

The respondents self-assessed their knowledge of the laws and regulations relating to data privacy in Saudi Arabia with a mean score of 3.07 out of 5 and a standard deviation (SD) of 1.102, indicating that they assess their level of knowledge of regulations is on average (61.4%). However, the percentage of respondents who really knew the current state of personal data protection in Saudi Arabia was 53.6% (at the time of conducting the survey), which indicates to the need to enhance the people awareness of regulations that protect their personal data.

When the respondents, who really knew the current state of personal data protection in Saudi Arabia, self-assessed their understanding of the regulations they demonstrated a relative level of understanding of 64.2%, with a mean score of 3.21 and SD of 1.007. The result of the objective assessment of these respondents' understanding of personal data regulation can be aggregated and is illustrated in Fig. 2. It is indicated that the majority, 51.7%, of respondents have a good level of understanding of personal data regulation in Saudi Arabia and nearly 8% have excellent understanding of personal data regulation.

Table 1. Sample demographic profile.

Demographics	N	Percent
Age		
Mean = 38.03, SD = 10.478, Minimum = 18, Maximum = 70		
Gender		
Male	152	39.0%
Female	238	61.0%
City		
Aldamam	6	1.5%
Almadenah	12	3.1%
Jeddah	259	66.4%
Makkah	20	5.1%
Rabigh	11	2.8%
Riyadh	48	12.3%
Yanbu	10	2.6%
Other	24	6.2%
Education		
Below high school level	2	0.5%
High school or diploma	52	13.3%
Bachelor degree	209	53.6%
Higher education	126	32.3%
Pharmacist fellowship	1	0.3%

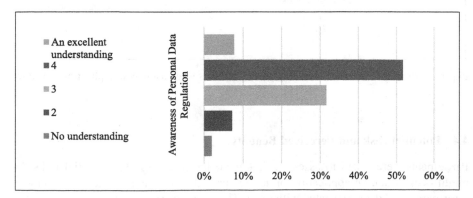

Fig. 2. Total awareness of personal data regulation.

4.3 Privacy Policy

Participants were asked if they read the privacy policy when using a new application or system. A low number indicated that they read the privacy policy (25% rarely read and 33% sometimes read), while 27% stats that they never read the privacy policy. Respondents who said that they read the privacy policies indicated their motivations to do so. These can be summarised in five categories, as illustrated in Fig. 3.

Regarding the Ministry of Health's (MOH) "Acceptable Use Policy", which defines the acceptable use of information resources by employees, including patients' information, to protect their data privacy, the majority (74.9%) of respondents stated that they did not know about its existence.

All participants were Sehhaty application users. However, most (74.4%) were unaware of its privacy policy's existence, while 25.6% were aware of it and had read it. This result agrees with most previous studies' results, which confirm that users agree to the privacy policy without reading it. For the participants who said they had read the Sehhaty application privacy policy, three aspects were used to measure their satisfaction: ease of access, the clarity of the language and length of text. Respondents were most satisfied with the clarity of the language used in the privacy policy, as the relative satisfaction was 75.6%. The second aspect that respondents were satisfied with is the ease of access to the privacy policy (relative satisfaction of 73.4%). Finally, 70.6% respondents were satisfied with the length of the privacy policy text. Overall, respondents demonstrated a good level of satisfaction.

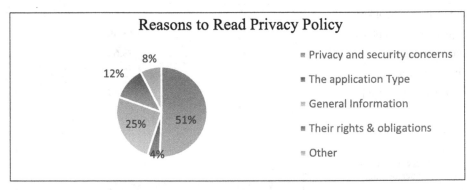

Fig. 3. Participants' reasons for reading privacy policies when using new application or service.

4.4 Potential Risk and Perceived Benefits

Participants were asked to assess their knowledge regarding the potential risks that might occur when an application or service provider collects and uses their personal information and data associated with them. The mean score was 3.11 with SD of 1.170.

However, 34.6% of respondents know that new E-health systems in Saudi Arabia are designed to reduce potential privacy risks. Those who were aware of this were assessed for their awareness of some of the potential privacy risks that they expect the new E-health systems will reduce (unauthorized access, collecting unnecessary data, and personal data leakage). It was found that the largest proportion of respondents (44.4%) have medium awareness.

Of the respondents, 48.7% know that the new E-health system offers many benefits to users (patients), while 60.5% of the respondents that know that there are benefits have a medium understanding of some of the benefits of the new E-health systems for the users (patients). The benefits for the users (patients) include: the ease of finding health services requested through the internet services, reducing the need to revisit service providers resulting from lack of correct information or difficulties resulting from setting appointments, and the ability to view the patient's health information at any time, and who can access it and for what purpose. The overall relative knowledge is 55.3%, which can be regarded as a medium level of knowledge.

4.5 User Experience

It was found that 38.5% of respondents use medical devices at home, such as a Blood Glucose Monitor and a Blood Pressure Monitor, and 27.3% of respondents use a mobile application related to the medical device they use. The majority 51.3% of respondents had no concern at all about privacy when using their devices. As shown in Fig. 4, 32.3% of respondents do not have any privacy concerns when using the Sehhaty application, while 21.0% have little concern. However, 46.7% have at least a medium level of concern.

Regarding privacy breaching, only 9.5% of respondents indicated that their data privacy had been previously breached. Of those respondents who had their data privacy breached, 45.9% did not take any action, 37.8% reported the breach to the authorities, and 16.2% solved the problem by themselves, i.e. they contacted the person or entity who exposed their data and asked them to stop (see Fig. 5).

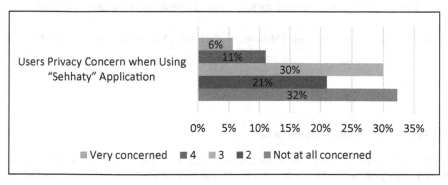

Fig. 4. Users' concern about user privacy when using the Sehhaty application.

4.6 Overall Self-assessed Awareness

Based on the level of self-assessed awareness on the topics of Data Regulations, Privacy Policy, Risks and Benefits, and User Experience, an overall level of awareness was calculated using the mean of all these aspects and performing the Visual Binning procedure

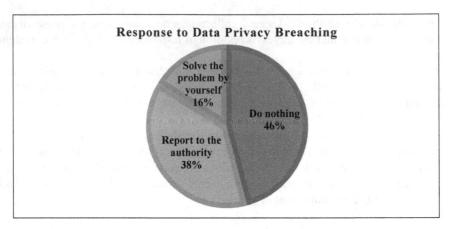

Fig. 5. Participants' responses to data privacy breaches.

in SPSS to create a new variable that represents the three levels of awareness: (1) low, (2) moderate, and (3) high. First, these four scores were averaged and a new variable was created, as summarized in Table 2 and in Fig. 6. Then, three bins (classes) were created using the Visual Binning procedure to create three levels of awareness. The bin size was calculated by dividing the range (5.00–1.00) by 3 to reflect three levels of awareness, yielding a bin size of 1.33. The first bin starts at 1.00 to 2.33, the second bin starts at 2.34 to 3.67, and the third bin starts at 3.68 to 5.00. The results show that the majority (61.8%) of respondents believe they have medium awareness, 27.7% believe they have low awareness, and 10.5% believe they have high awareness.

Table 2. Descriptive statistics for self-assessed awareness calculated mean score.

Mean	Median	Std. Deviation	Skewness	Kurtosis	Minimum	Maximum	Bin Size
2.73	2.68	.802	.229	.302	1.00	5.00	1.33

4.7 Overall Objective Assessment

Based on the level of awareness (objective assessment) on the topics of Data Regulations, Privacy Policy, Risks and Benefits, and Risks and Benefits in Healthcare, an overall level of awareness was calculated using the mean of all these aspects and performing the Visual Binning procedure in SPSS to create a new variable that represents the three levels of awareness: (1) low, (2) moderate, and (3) high. First, these four scores were averaged, and a new variable was created, as summarized in Table 3 and the histogram in Fig. 7. Then, three bins (classes) were created using the Visual Binning procedure to create three levels of awareness. The bin size was calculated by dividing the range (5.07–1.57) by 3 to reflect three levels of awareness, yielding a bin size of 1.17. The first bin has range 1.57 to 2.74, the second has range 2.75 to 3.90, and the third bin has range 3.91

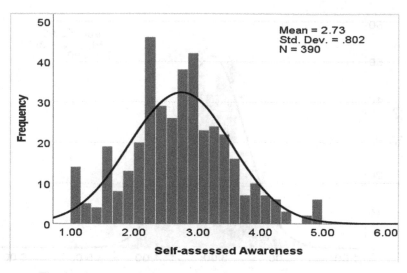

Fig. 6. Histogram of self-assessed awareness calculated mean score.

to 5.07. The majority (72.3%) of respondents have medium awareness, 23.1% have low awareness, and only 4.6% have high awareness.

Table 3. Descriptive statistics for objective awareness calculated mean score.

Mean	Median	Std. Deviation	Skewness	Kurtosis	Minimum	Maximum	Bin Size
3.06	3.05	.508	.120	.446	1.57	5.07	1.17

4.8 The Relationship Between Users' Objective Privacy Awareness and Ages

Spearman's rho correlation coefficient was used to measure the relationship between age and the awareness criteria, as shown in Table 4. The Spearman's rho values indicate that there is no significant relationship between overall objective awareness level and age, $r = -0.054$, $p = 0.283$. There was a significant weak negative relationship between age and Risk and Benefits Awareness, $r = -0.116$, p-value $= 0.022$. That is, older users would have slightly lower levels of awareness in terms of Risk and Benefits. On the other hand, there was a significant weak positive relationship between age and Risk and Benefits in Healthcare Awareness, $r = 0.133$, $p = 0.009$. The result indicate that older users would have higher levels of awareness of Risk and Benefits when they use healthcare systems and applications.

4.9 The Relationship Between Users' Objective Privacy Awareness and Gender

As the awareness variables are measured on an ordinal scale, a Mann-Whitney test was used to find significant differences between males and females in terms of their levels

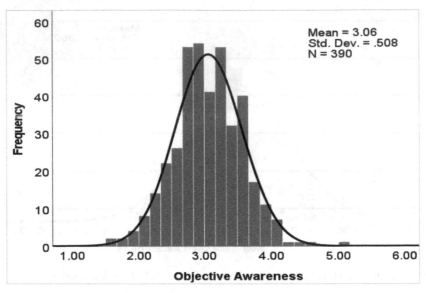

Fig. 7. Histogram of objective awareness calculated mean score.

of awareness. The test results are presented in Table 5, showing a significant difference between males and females in the levels of Privacy Policy Awareness and Risk and Benefits in Healthcare Awareness (p-value < 0.05). As shown in the Mean Rank section of Privacy Policy Awareness, females have a higher level of awareness about Privacy Policy. Similarly, females have a higher level of awareness of Risk and Benefits in Healthcare Awareness.

4.10   The Relationship Between Users' Objective Privacy Awareness and Education

Post hoc multiple comparisons Mann-Whitney tests were used to determine which groups have significant differences in Privacy Policy, Risk and Benefits in Healthcare, and overall objective awareness levels. The results are presented in Table 6. The results revealed that for Privacy Policy, Risk and Benefits in Healthcare Awareness, and objective awareness, users with postgraduate degrees (Masters or PhD) had significantly higher mean rank than users with a high school award or diploma, p-value < 0.005 (the Bonferroni corrected significance level, calculated as an alpha level divided by the number of Mann-Whitney tests conducted, i.e. 0.05/10). That is, users with postgraduate degrees had higher awareness of Privacy Policy, Risk and Benefits in Healthcare, and overall objective awareness than users with High school or diploma. Post hoc analysis also revealed that for Privacy Policy and Risk and Benefits in Healthcare Awareness, users with postgraduate degrees had higher mean rank than users with Bachelors degrees, p-value < 0.005. That is, users with postgraduate degrees had higher awareness of Privacy Policy and Risk and Benefits in Healthcare than users with a Bachelors degrees.

Table 4. Spearman's rho Correlation Coefficients for Objective Awareness vs. Age.

Awareness Criteria	Age
Personal Data Regulation Awareness	−.093
Privacy Policy Awareness	−.024
Risk and Benefits Awareness	−.116*
Risk and Benefits in Healthcare Awareness	.133**
Objective Awareness	−.054

*. Correlation is significant at the 0.05 level (2-tailed).
**. Correlation is significant at the 0.01 level (2-tailed).

Table 5. Mann-Whitney Test Results for Awareness vs. Gender.

Awareness Criteria	Mean Rank		Test Statistics[a]	
	Male	Female	Mann-Whitney U	Sig.
Personal Data Regulation Awareness	104.18	105.50	5070.50	.871
Privacy Policy Awareness	179.79	205.53	15700.00	.012*
Risk and Benefit Awareness	205.79	188.93	16523.50	.128
Risk and Benefits in Healthcare Awareness	181.97	204.14	16031.50	.036*
Objective Awareness	188.71	199.84	17056.00	.223

a. Grouping Variable: Gender
*. Significant at 0.05.

Table 6. Post hoc multiple comparisons Mann-Whitney tests [Education].

Awareness	Category (J)	Category (Y)	Mean Rank Difference (J-Y)	M-W U	Sig.
Privacy Policy	Postgraduate degrees	High school or diploma	31.12	2130.50	<.001*
		Bachelor degree	31.62	10681.50	.001*
Risk and Benefits in HC	Postgraduate degrees	High school or diploma	31.26	2125.00	<.001*
		Bachelor degree	30.97	10732.50	.002*
Objective Awareness	Postgraduate degrees	High school or diploma	23.20	2422.00	<.001*

*. Significant at 0.005 [Bonferroni Corrected]

5 Conclusion and Future Work

A quantitative questionnaire to measure users' privacy awareness was designed with questions focused on factors drawn from the extant literature. These factors were: regulation, privacy policies, potential risks and benefits, and the user experience. For each factor, questions were used to assess users in both subjective and objective ways, apart from the "user's experience" subjective assessment. The data were collected using an online survey. The results of subsequent analysis show that most users of health apps have an average awareness of the five factors tested.

This study aimed to discover the current levels of privacy awareness of healthcare service users in Saudi Arabia. This helps researchers interested in designing digital healthcare services, especially IoT-based systems in Saudi Arabia and other countries with similar cultures, to understand their target users.

The results show that most users of health applications show an average privacy awareness of the five factors tested in both ways, objective and subjective assessments. Considering these results when designing healthcare services, especially IoT-based healthcare systems that depend on users' personal and sensitive data, will help design and develop services that fit these users' needs. At the same time, they help enhance users' privacy awareness so they can manage their data and decisions when using these systems without professional assistance. This questionnaire focused on users' privacy awareness in the healthcare context. However, most of these questions can be used to assess users in Saudi Arabia's privacy awareness in other contexts (with some modification), such as privacy policies and user experiences.

The next step of this research will be to investigate suitable consent mechanisms for IoT-based healthcare systems and then investigate the users who have different privacy awareness levels of behavior when deciding on the collection, use and sharing of their personal and sensitive data.

Acknowledgements. The study is part of the primary author's PhD work, which is concerned with investigating the actual behavior of users when their informed consent is sought in IoT-based healthcare systems. An experiment will investigate the effects of specific consent mechanisms upon users' actual behavior when their sensitive data are being collected, used, and shared in IoT-based health systems. Approval to publish the paper was obtained from The Ministry of Health in Saudi Arabia. The work is sponsored by King Abdulaziz University (KAU), Jeddah, Saudi Arabia.

References

1. Bellini, P., Nesi, P., Pantaleo, G.: IoT-enabled smart cities: a review of concepts, frameworks and key technologies. Appl. Sci. **12**(3), 1607 (2022)
2. Awotunde, J.B., et al., Privacy and security concerns in IoT-based healthcare systems. In: Siarry, P., Jabbar, M., Aluvalu, R., Abraham, A., Madureira, A. (eds.) The Fusion of Internet of Things, Artificial Intelligence, and Cloud Computing in Health Care. Internet of Things, pp. 105–134. Springer, Cham (2021). https://doi.org/10.1007/978-3-030-75220-0_6
3. Tanczer, L., et al.: IoT and Its Implications for Informed Consent. PETRAS IoT Hub, STEaPP: London (2017)

4. Smith, H.J., Dinev, T., Xu, H.: Information privacy research: an interdisciplinary review. MIS Q. **35**(4), 989–1016 (2011)
5. Parsons, K., et al.: The human aspects of information security questionnaire (HAIS-Q): two further validation studies. Comput. Secur. **66**, 40–51 (2017)
6. Correia, J., Compeau, D.: Information privacy awareness (IPA): a review of the use, definition and measurement of IPA. In: Proceedings of the 50th Hawaii International Conference on System Sciences (2017)
7. Smith, H.J., Milberg, S.J., Burke, S.J.: Information privacy: measuring individuals' concerns about organizational practices. MIS Q. 167–196 (1996)
8. Malhotra, N.K., Kim, S.S., Agarwal, J.: Internet users' information privacy concerns (IUIPC): the construct, the scale, and a causal model. Inf. Syst. Res. **15**(4), 336–355 (2004)
9. Xu, H., et al.: Measuring mobile users' concerns for information privacy (2012)
10. Krasnova, H., Veltri, N.F., Günther, O.: Self-disclosure and privacy calculus on social networking sites: the role of culture. Bus. Inf. Syst. Eng. **4**(3), 127–135 (2012)
11. Kim, D., et al.: Willingness to provide personal information: perspective of privacy calculus in IoT services. Comput. Hum. Behav. **92**, 273–281 (2019)
12. Pelet, J.-É., Taieb, B.: Privacy protection on social networks: a scale for measuring users' attitudes in France and the USA. In: Rocha, Á., Correia, A., Adeli, H., Reis, L., Costanzo, S. (eds.) WorldCIST 2017. Advances in Intelligent Systems and Computing, vol. 570, pp. 763–773. Springer, Cham (2017). https://doi.org/10.1007/978-3-319-56538-5_77
13. Zlatolas, L.N., et al.: Privacy antecedents for SNS self-disclosure: the case of Facebook. Comput. Hum. Behav. **45**, 158–167 (2015)
14. Sim, I., Liginlal, D., Khansa, L.: Information privacy situation awareness: Construct and validation. J. Comput. Inf. Syst. **53**(1), 57–64 (2012)
15. Bergmann, M.: Testing privacy awareness. In: Matyáš, V., Fischer-Hübner, S., Cvrček, D., Švenda, P. (eds.) Privacy and Identity 2008. IFIP Advances in Information and Communication Technology, vol. 298, pp. 237–253. Springer, Heidelberg (2008). https://doi.org/10.1007/978-3-642-03315-5_18
16. Alani, M.M.: Android users privacy awareness survey. Int. J. Interact. Mob. Technol. **11**(3) (2017)
17. Braunstein, A., Granka, L., Staddon, J.: Indirect content privacy surveys: measuring privacy without asking about it. In: Proceedings of the Seventh Symposium on Usable Privacy and Security (2011)
18. Kuznetsov, M., Novikova, E., Kotenko, I.: An approach to formal desription of the user notification scenarios in privacy policies. In: 2022 30th Euromicro International Conference on Parallel, Distributed and Network-based Processing (PDP). IEEE (2022)
19. Psychoula, I., et al.: Privacy risk awareness in wearables and the internet of things. IEEE Pervasive Comput. **19**(3), 60–66 (2020)
20. Udoh, E.S., Alkharashi, A.: Privacy risk awareness and the behavior of smartwatch users: a case study of Indiana University students. In: 2016 Future Technologies Conference (FTC). IEEE (2016)
21. Aleisa, N., Renaud, K., Bongiovanni, I.: The privacy paradox applies to IoT devices too: a Saudi Arabian study. Comput. Secur. 101897 (2020)

Threat Actors and Methods of Attack to Social Robots in Public Spaces

Yonas Zewdu Ayele[1]($\boxtimes$), Sabarathinam Chockalingam[1], and Nathan Lau[2]

[1] Department of Risk and Safety, Institute for Energy Technology, 1777 Halden, Norway
{yonas.ayele,sabarathinam.chockalingam}@ife.no
[2] Grado Department of Industrial and Systems Engineering, Virginia Tech, Blacksburg, VA 24061, USA
nkclau@vt.edu

Abstract. The use of social robots in critical domains such as education and healthcare, as well as in public spaces, raises important challenges in ethics, information governance, cybersecurity, and privacy. Studies have shown that commercial social robots can be compromised, highlighting the need for manufacturers, code developers, operators, and users to prioritize cybersecurity and privacy in the design and development, as well as operational phases. However, anticipating exact sources of cyber-attacks and various attack vectors is very difficult. As a starting point, this study aims to identify and analyze potential threat actors to social robots operating in public spaces, methods of attack that they might use, and vulnerable aspects of social robots to these threats. This study also examines social engineering attacks, and successful methods cybercriminals might use to install various forms of malware on social robots in public spaces.

Keywords: Attack vectors · Social engineering · Social robots · Threat actors · Threat landscape

1 Introduction

In recent years, technological innovations in Artificial Intelligence (AI), Machine Learning (ML), and robots are redefining and enhancing the way in which we work and live. In addition, our reliance on these technologies makes us more vulnerable to cyber-attacks. Therefore, in today's technology-driven world, protecting against cyber-attacks is a major concern for organizations and governments. The integration of social robots into public spaces to perform different tasks, such as guiding people, raises important discussions about the security impact of AI on society and social interactions.

"Social robot" can be defined as an autonomous physically embodied robot that interacts and communicates with humans or other autonomous agents by following social behaviour and rules attached to its role [1]. This disruptive breakthrough will have a significant impact on society, once social robots acquire a degree of autonomy, AI, safety, and security for their widespread application [2]. However, introducing robots into the public and private spheres [3] presents a challenge in assuring safety and security

to those who interact with the robots. Public spaces are more complex and unpredictable than a private space, especially given more stakeholders and interactions.

Social robots operating in public spaces have the potential to gather and analyze enormous amounts of personal information, like social media platforms and digital assistants found on smartphones. However, users have the option to choose not to use such social media platforms or digital assistants, refusing consent to terms of use and controlling the information permitted to share in a much higher degree. Social robots in public spaces can be difficult to avoid while pedestrians may not have the necessary configuration privileges to disable data gathering. Additionally, interactions with the robot become essential to express non-consent to data collection, and if the robot is designed to remember this preference to avoid nuisance for future interactions, data storage and privacy represents a serious concern. Furthermore, the robot may initiate interactions without the user's knowledge. Social robots would need to access increasing amount of personal information to become more useful and integrated into the routines of our daily lives, thereby increasing the concerns on cybersecurity and privacy issues. Therefore, both robot manufacturers and code developers must consider cybersecurity and privacy during the design and development phase. In addition, operators and users must consider cybersecurity and privacy during the operational phase when robots are in use by the public.

The introduction of social robots in society, especially in public space fuels various discussions ranging from the dark side of AI to the future of public space and its security impact on social interactions. In addition, social robots possess the interaction capabilities to meet a wide range of diverse individuals in public spaces and to solicit personal information that would pose a bigger threat landscape to citizens as well as companies designing and operating the robots. However, anticipating the exact sources and methods of cyber-attacks can be difficult for robot manufacturers, code developers, operators, and users of these robots. Therefore, this study aims to identify potential security incidents that operators and users of social robots in public spaces may face, classify these incidents, and analyze how potential threat actors may conduct attacks. Cybersecurity incidents, in the context of this paper, refer to events that affect the Confidentiality, Integrity, and Availability (CIA) of information, Information Technology (IT) systems, and other infrastructures. Examples of such incidents are disclosure of confidential information to unauthorized parties, unauthorized modification of information, and a critical system not being operable.

For this paper, we will use ARI as a reference social robot for discussing the potential threat actors to social robots operating in public spaces. Figure 1 shows ARI[1], which is an advanced AI-powered humanoid social robot and its components. ARI is intended to be a socially assistive companion which can be used as a receptionist. It stands 1.65 m tall and features a moveable base, touchscreen on the torso, an onboard PC, moving arms, and a head with LCD eyes that can perform gaze behaviour. Furthermore, ARI has a 360-degree field of view with several cameras. Four digital microphone array is installed on the front of the belly for audio capture and processing. Finally, ARI has both wired (ethernet) and wireless connectivity (Wi-Fi).

---

[1] ARI is PAL Robotics' humanoid platform specifically created for Human-Robot-Interaction and to perform front-desk activities.

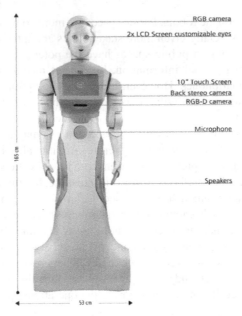

Fig. 1. ARI's Components (c) PAL Robotics

The rest of this paper is organized as follows: Sect. 2 provides an overview of malware, including several types and methods of installation. Section 3 covers a general overview of attack methods. Section 4 examines the vulnerabilities of social robots. Lastly, Sect. 5 present conclusions.

2 Malware

As organizations strengthen their defenses against cyber-attacks, cybercriminals are turning to more advanced methods. The most usual form of attack is installing malware on targeted systems, including social robots. Malware is a broad term that encompasses several types of harmful software that take advantage of vulnerabilities in program code, enabling attackers to compromise other software and cause damage. Once malware is installed, attackers can use it to steal sensitive information, disrupt the system's operation, or even gain control of the targeted social robot. Attackers commonly use six types of malwares.

2.1 Types of Malwares

2.1.1 Viruses

Viruses are harmful strings of code that attach themselves to other programs [4]. When the infected program is run, the virus is installed on the targeted social robot [5]. They spread by being transferred from one machine to another through the infected file. A study by [6] found that about 40% of people interacting with ARI are willing to share their personal information with the robot. However, this trust in the robot presents a potential and significant risk if the security and privacy measures of the robot are compromised. The ARI has an onboard Personal Computer (PC) that could be vulnerable to several types of malwares and viruses. This malicious software can exploit vulnerabilities in the onboard PC, giving attackers access to the personal information shared with the robot, as well as control of the robot's functionality. This can lead to serious security breaches, such as identity theft, financial fraud, and even physical harm. Therefore, it is crucial for the organizations who are deploying ARI in public spaces to have robust security measures in place to protect people's personal information and prevent malware attacks on the robot's onboard PC.

Worms. A worm functions like a virus. It can also infect a PC that runs the social robot via an infected file. However, worms can also spread independently without the need for any users triggering the activation of the initial infected file [7]. Worms can self-propagate by identifying and taking advantage of weaknesses in computer networks, which the social robot is part of [4]. In other words, they spread by exploiting vulnerabilities in the network connected the social robot. This can include things like unpatched software, weak passwords, or open ports that allow unauthorized access to the network. Once they have access to the network, they can move laterally to other devices and continue to spread, potentially causing damage to the network or stealing sensitive information.

Rootkits. A rootkit is a type of malware that grant attackers administrative access to a targeted social robot [5]. Unlike viruses, rootkits are manually installed on a computer's application layer and cannot replicate through infected files shared between computers [5]. However, rootkits are challenging to detect and eliminate as they are designed to stay hidden. Rootkits could exploit the onboard PC that runs and controls its functionality of the ARI social robot. This computer system could be targeted by attackers, who want to install rootkits. Once installed, a rootkit can then take control of the social robot and use it to gain access to the network to which it is connected. It can also hide its presence from the system administrator, making it harder to detect and remove. This is a serious security concern because rootkits allow attackers to steal sensitive information, disrupt operations, or even take control of the ARI for malicious purposes.

Spyware. Spyware refers to software that tracks a user's internet activity, collecting data such as browser history, browsing habits, and personal information without the user's consent. This data is then shared with third parties. Spyware is often used by websites and applications to show advertisements tailored to the user's web activity.

ARI robots operating in public spaces will interact with a large number of people [6]. This indicates that the impact of a spyware attack on ARI operating in public spaces could be much more severe on the scale of spying than if it is operating in a private setting. This is mainly because many people are willing to trust the robot with their personal information [6], making it easier for attackers to steal sensitive information, and cause damage. Additionally, ARI robots being in public spaces enable personal information of a large group of people to be targeted.

Ransomware. Ransomware is a type of malware that blocks access to a system or threatens to reveal sensitive information unless a ransom is paid [8]. Unlike other forms of cybercrime, attackers using ransomware inform the victim of the attack and provide instructions for payment, usually in digital currency to preserve the attacker's anonymity. There are two main types of ransomware: crypto ransomware which encrypts files on the victim's computer, and locker ransomware which denies access to the victim's computer without encrypting files [8]. The frequency of ransomware attacks has significantly increased in recent years, making it one of the most used forms of malware attacks (e.g., [9] and [10]).

A ransomware attack could be particularly challenging for social robots operating in public spaces, as they interact with a diverse group of people who may have their own mobile devices. These mobile devices are often connected to personal and business networks vulnerable to attack. During a ransomware attack, the attacker will typically encrypt the data on a device or network to make access impossible to the owner. The cybercriminals will then demand payment, usually in the form of cryptocurrency in exchange for the decryption key. In the case of a social robot operating in public spaces, an attacker could target the mobile devices of the people interacting with the robot. This could lead to the encryption of personal and work data on those devices, causing significant disruption and potentially costing the affected individuals or organizations a significant amount of money to regain access to their data. Additionally, since the social robot interacts with diverse people, attackers could target different individuals with different ransomware attack impacting many people.

Furthermore, the social robot operating in public spaces may not be under the direct control of a single organization, challenging any coordinated response to a ransomware attack. At the same time, as social robots aim to provide an array of public services, such as guiding people with different routes in city ferries operated by municipality, ransomware attacks on such robots could cause public service disruptions in addition to financial and reputational damage to the municipality.

Trojans. A Trojan is a type of malware that disguises itself as a harmless application, but once downloaded and executed, it grants an attacker direct access to the targeted computer [12]. The attacker can then monitor all activity on the computer, such as internet activity, keystrokes, and mouse movements, or even make copies of the computer screen [13]. In some cases, Trojans give attackers an ability to take control of the infected machine.

For social robots, such as ARI that are operating in public spaces, a Trojan attack can be serious because these robots often store sensitive data such as personal information, passwords, and credit card numbers. An attacker who can gain access can use the information for fraudulent activities or identity theft. Additionally, a Trojan attack could allow an attacker to take control of the robot for conducting further attacks. This could include spreading malware to other systems, stealing data from other connected devices, or even physically damaging the robot or its surroundings.

2.2 Methods of Installing Malware

Cybercriminals use different techniques to ensure that social robot maintenance operators and users remain unaware that malware has been installed on social robots. Attackers have been most successful with three methods.

Drive-by Download. Drive-by download method refers to downloading malware onto a computer without the user's knowledge [11]. It can happen in two ways: when the user visits a website embed with malicious code, or when the user unknowingly downloads infected software [11]. For the former, the visited website initiates a network probe on the user's computer, exploiting a hidden vulnerability to download malware without the user's permission. For the latter, the user unknowingly downloads malware.

Drive-by download method would be easy to execute on an ARI social robot that is operating in public spaces, as the robot embodies an onboard PC. An attacker could target the onboard PC by compromising the website that the ARI robot uses to download updates or access information. This could allow the attacker to install malware on the robot, giving them control over the robot's functionality and allowing them to steal sensitive information from the people interacting with the robot. Additionally, the attacker can easily access ARI in public spaces to employ drive by download. Furthermore, the robot being in public space could easily connect to many people, which could make the impact of drive-by download more severe.

Phishing and Baiting. Social engineering is a tactic that uses psychological manipulation to trick individuals into performing actions that lead to systems and networks being infected with malware [14]. Phishing and spear-phishing attacks are common social engineering techniques used by attackers to infect targeted computers or gather personal information [15]. These attacks disguise malicious software as a protected attachment or a trustworthy link in an email. When an email is opened, malware is automatically installed on the targeted computer. In the context of ARI, phishing email opened in the onboard PC could infect the robot by downloading the malware, which can then lead to negative consequences, such as personal data leak, disruption in the operation of ARI.

Baiting attacks exploit human curiosity by leaving infected flash drives in places where targeted operators are likely to find them, in the hopes that they will insert the flash drives into their system, thereby initiating the automatic download of malware onto the organization's networks [15]. Social engineering not only enables malware to be transferred to targeted systems, but also facilitates a broader range of cyber-attacks. In the context of ARI, USB port is available and is susceptible to baiting attacks and subsequent installation of malware. The consequences of such attacks could be like phishing.

Using Non-Secure Wi-Fi. Once connected to a Wi-Fi network, new devices may view and interact with the network's PCs and servers in accordance with your network sharing settings. This implies that any compromised computer or device on the network can launch attacks against other computers on the network to infect and compromise connected devices. It may easily infect every device linked to the network. Operating in public places, the ARI robots which possess Wi-Fi capability would have immense opportunities to connect to non-secure Wi-Fi networks that would mitigate the challenges for an attacker to compromise the robot by installing the malware. ARI can be hacked to connect to unsecure Wi-Fi and provide conduits for other devices to connect to insecure ones via P2P.

3 Types of Attacks

This section examines the various other types of cyber-attacks that are commonly employed by attackers to steal sensitive data or gain unauthorized access to social robots operating in public spaces and organizational information systems. The methods used in these attacks can vary depending on attackers' goals.

3.1 Social Engineering

Social engineering, as previously mentioned, uses psychological manipulation to deceive individuals into downloading malware or unknowingly assisting attackers with cyber-attacks. When conducting a cyber-attack, attackers may manipulate people with access to secure data by establishing trust with them, and then use that trust to gain sensitive information or help bypass security measures [16]. For social robots operating in public spaces, attackers can use social engineering techniques to establish trust with people who interact with the robot [6]. This can include people who use, as well as those who are responsible for maintaining and operating the robots. Once the trust is established, the attackers can then use that trust to exploit any vulnerabilities, such as onboard PC that may exist in the robot. For example, an attacker may use social engineering tactics to trick an operator into downloading malware that is disguised as a legitimate software update. Once the malware is installed, the attacker can gain access to the robot's system and steal sensitive information or control the robot's actions. Additionally, an attacker may use social engineering tactics to trick an operator into providing their login credentials, which can then be used to gain unauthorized access to the robot or the organization's information systems.

Four types of social engineering attacks are particularly relevant for compromising social robots' cybersecurity measures.

Phishing Attacks. Phishing is a type of social engineering attack where an attacker uses email, text message, or social media to trick a user into providing sensitive information or clicking on a malicious link [17, 18]. In the case of social robots, an attacker may use phishing tactics to trick an operator into providing their login credentials or personal information, which can then be used to gain unauthorized access to the robot or the organization's information systems.

Avoiding and preventing phishing attacks on social robots is also difficult, as these robots are typically designed to interact with human users and may not have the same level of access control as traditional computers or servers. However, it is important for organizations and users to be aware of the potential risks and to take steps to protect against phishing attacks, such as education on the social robots being the target or facilitator phishing tactics and implementing security measures such as multi-factor authentication.

Spear-phishing Attacks. A spear-phisher may use personal information, such as the robot's name, manufacturer and its functions, to create a convincing message that tricks the user into providing sensitive information or clicking on a malicious link [19]. Avoiding and preventing spear-phishing attacks on social robots is also challenging, as detecting spear-phishing requires constant and conscientious monitoring of the personal information of the robot, such as its name, manufacturer, and its functions, as well as educating the operators and users, on how to identify spear-phishing attempts. Additionally, it is important for organizations to implement security measures such as multi-factor authentication and regular security audits to detect and prevent spear-phishing attacks.

Quid Pro Quo Attacks. Quid pro quo attacks involve offering a service in exchange for a user's login information or sensitive data [20]. The method of impersonating IT staff to gain access to sensitive information or perform malicious actions on social robots is also known as "pretexting" [21]. In this type of attack, attackers often impersonate IT staff and request login details or direct access to a social robot's information system, claiming that they need to install software or perform updates. This method is particularly effective because users are often more likely to trust IT staff and may not question their requests for sensitive information or access.

Operators and users may also be prompted to perform specific actions to aid the attack, such as disabling antivirus software or alert notifications. These actions help attackers to bypass security measures and gain access to sensitive information. These types of attacks can happen remotely, such as through a user interface that prompts users to enter their login credentials, over the phone, or in person with the attacker.

Pretexting attacks can be particularly difficult to detect and prevent because they rely on social engineering tactics to trick users into providing sensitive information or taking specific actions. Social robot operators can take steps to protect against pretexting attacks by educating users about the risks and warning signs of pretexting, implementing strict security policies, and monitoring for suspicious activity. Additionally, it is important for the social robot operators to have an incident response plan in case of a pretexting attack, and to ensure that users are aware of and know how to respond to such an attack.

Tailgating. Tailgating, also known as *"piggybacking"*, is a type of security breach in which an attacker gains unauthorized access to a building or secure area by following an authorized person through an entrance without being challenged [22]. This method can be particularly effective when the social robot is operating in a reception/public space because the attackers can easily blend in and gain access to the secured building or area. The attacker, for instance, may pretend to be a maintenance operator, delivery person, or a member of the public who is visiting the area, and then follows the authorized person/social robots through the entrance. The attacker may also use the opportunity to gain access to sensitive information or steal valuable data from the robot or organization's server rooms or networks.

Tailgating is a serious security threat, allowing attackers to bypass security measures and gain access to sensitive information. To prevent tailgating, social robots' operators should implement strict security protocols, such as requiring all employees, contractors, and visitors to show identification before entering the building or secure area and installing security cameras to monitor the entrances. Additionally, it is important for the operators to regularly train employees to recognize tailgating attempts and how to respond to them.

3.2 Denial-of-Service Attacks

A Denial-of-Service (DoS) attack aims to make a system unavailable by sending an excessive amount of traffic or data to overwhelm the network or specific equipment [23]. For social robots operating in public spaces, DoS attacks can have a significant negative effect on their ability to function properly. This is because DoS attacks can cause the robot's network to become overwhelmed with traffic that hinders the robot to communicate with its control center or other systems [23]. This can cause the robot to become unresponsive or even malfunction, leading to disruptions in service and a poor user experience.

DoS attacks can also cause damage to the robot's or robot operator's reputation, as users may lose trust in the robot and the operator ability to protect their information and provide a reliable service. Another negative effect of DoS attacks on social robots operating in public space would be the financial impact on the organization. DDoS attacks can be costly to mitigate, as operators may need to invest in additional hardware and software to protect against them, or even pay for specialized DoS protection services. In addition, DoS attacks can also cause revenue losses for the operators, as the robot's service may be unavailable to users during the attack.

To mitigate the negative effects of DoS attacks on social robots operating in public spaces, social robot operators should have a robust incident response plan in place. This plan should include measures to detect and respond to DoS attacks, as well as procedures to minimize the impact of the attack on the robot's network and service [24]. Additionally, organizations should also invest in DoS protection solutions such as firewalls, intrusion prevention systems, and cloud-based DoS protection services, to prevent DoS attacks from happening in the first place [24]. Regularly monitoring network traffic for unusual activity and keeping software updated can also help prevent DoS attacks.

3.3 Advanced Persistent Threats

An Advanced Persistent Threat (APT) is a type of cyber-attack that is typically carried out by a group of highly-skilled attackers, such as nation-state actors, who are focused on gaining unauthorized access to an organization's network and stealing sensitive data over an extended period of time [25]. APTs are known for their ability to evade detection and maintain access to a network for long periods, often months or even years [25].

When it comes to social robots operating in public spaces, APTs can be particularly dangerous because they allow attackers to gain access to the robot's computer networks and steal sensitive data over extended period. This can include information about the users of the robot, such as personal details, login credentials, and even credit card information. Additionally, APTs can also allow attackers to gain access to the control systems of the robot, allowing them to take control of the robot and use it for malicious purposes, such as surveillance or data exfiltration [26]. APTs can also have a negative effect on the reputation of the social robot operator and the social robot, as users may lose trust in the robot and the organization's ability to protect their information. This can lead to a decline in the use of the robot and a negative impact on the operator's revenue.

To prevent and mitigate the effects of APTs on social robots operating in public spaces, organizations should implement a comprehensive security strategy that includes a combination of technical and non-technical measures [27]. Technical measures include implementing firewalls, intrusion prevention systems, and antivirus software, as well as keeping software updated [27]. Non-technical measures include educating employees on the dangers of APTs, and implementing security policies that require the use of strong passwords, regular security awareness training and incident response plans [28].

Monitoring of network traffic and performing vulnerability assessments and penetration testing regularly can also help prevent and detect APT attacks. Additionally, social robot operators should also have incident response plans in place to quickly detect and respond to APT attacks.

3.4 Brute-Force Attacks

A brute-force attack is a technique that uses repetitive attempts to guess the correct password for accessing a system [29]. For social robots operating in public spaces, brute-force attacks are more likely due to the exposure to many people including maintenance operators, users, pedestrians. In case of a successful brute-force attack, this allows attackers to gain access to the robot's computer networks and steal sensitive data in addition to gain access to the control systems of the robot. To prevent and mitigate the effects of brute-force attacks on social robots operating in public spaces, organizations should implement a comprehensive security strategy that includes a combination of technical and non-technical measures, lockout policy, and incident response plans.

4 Concluding Remarks

As social robots are becoming increasingly prevalent in public spaces, operators and users of these robots must have a deep understanding of the various methods that attackers use to gain access to their systems. Cybersecurity is a critical concern for social robot operators and users, as malware can take many forms and can cause considerable damage to systems, networks, and data.

One of the most critical aspects of cybersecurity for social robot operators and users is preventing malware from reaching their critical information systems. Malware can take many forms such as viruses, worms, Trojans, and ransomware. Each type of malware has the potential to cause considerable damage to systems, networks, and data. However, attackers do not solely rely on technology to infiltrate targeted systems. They also employ social engineering tactics that exploit human negligence and error. Social engineering is the use of psychological manipulation to trick people into giving away sensitive information or taking actions that can compromise security.

To effectively safeguard social robots from these types of attacks, it is essential to be aware of the common methods employed by cybercriminals and to take the necessary measures to protect against them. This includes educating users and operators on how to identify and prevent social engineering attacks and implementing robust security protocols and software. Regularly monitoring systems for unusual activity is also important for detecting and responding to cyber-attacks. This can include monitoring network traffic for unusual patterns, monitoring system logs for signs of unauthorized access, and conducting regular security audits. It is also important to train different stakeholders of social robots on cyber security.

Acknowledgments. This research is funded by the Research Council of Norway (RCN), under the projects *"User-centred Security Framework for Social Robots in Public Space (SecuRoPS)"*, with the project number #321324, and *"Reinforcing Competence in Cybersecurity of Critical Infrastructures: a Norway – US Partnership"*, with the project number #309911. These projects are facilitated at the Institute for Energy Technology, Halden.

References

1. Kirby, R., Forlizzi, J., Simmons, R.: Affective social robots. Robot. Auton. Syst. **58**(3), 322–332 (2010)
2. Chui, M., Chung, R., van Heteren, A.: Using AI to help achieve sustainable development goals (2019)
3. Schmiedel, T., Zhong, V.J., Jäger, J.: Value-sensitive design for AI technologies: proposition of basic research principles based on social robotics research. Appl. Med. Manuf. 74
4. Leavitt, N.: Mobile phones: the next frontier for hackers? Computer **38**(4), 20–23 (2005)
5. Abraham, S., Chengalur-Smith, I.: An overview of social engineering malware: trends, tactics, and implications. Technol. Soc. **32**(3), 183–196 (2010)
6. Rødsethol, H., Ayele, Y.Z.: Social robots in public space: use case development. In: Proceedings of the 32nd European Safety and Reliability Conference (ESREL 2022) (2022)
7. Szor, P.: The Art of Computer Virus Research and Defense: Art Comp Virus Res Defense _p1. Pearson Education (2005)
8. Kolodenker, E., Koch, W., Stringhini, G., Egele, M.: Paybreak: defense against cryptographic ransomware. In: Proceedings of the 2017 ACM on Asia Conference on Computer and Communications Security, pp. 599–611 (2017)
9. Genç, Z.A., Lenzini, G., Ryan, P.: The cipher, the random and the ransom: a survey on current and future ransomware. Adv. Cybersecur. **2017** (2017)
10. Cabaj, K., Mazurczyk, W.: Using software-defined networking for ransomware mitigation: the case of cryptowall. IEEE Netw. **30**(6), 14–20 (2016)
11. Lu, L., Yegneswaran, V., Porras, P., Lee, W.: Blade: an attack-agnostic approach for preventing drive-by malware infections. In: Proceedings of the 17th ACM Conference on Computer and Communications Security, pp. 440–450 (2010)
12. Roseline, S.A., Geetha, S.: A comprehensive survey of tools and techniques mitigating computer and mobile malware attacks. Comput. Electr. Eng. **92**, 107143 (2021)
13. Mosteanu, N.R.: Artificial intelligence and cyber security–a shield against cyberattack as a risk business management tool–case of European countries. Qual.-Access Success **21**(175) (2020)
14. Moallem, A.: Social engineering. In: Human-Computer Interaction and Cybersecurity Handbook, pp. 139–156. CRC Press (2018)
15. Krombholz, K., Hobel, H., Huber, M., Weippl, E.: Advanced social engineering attacks. J. Inf. Secur. Appl. **22**, 113–122 (2015)
16. Harnish, R.: Cybersecurity in the world of social engineering. Cybersecur. Our Digit. Lives **2**, 143 (2015)
17. Stanton, J.M., Stam, K.R.: The Visible Employee: Using Workplace Monitoring and Surveillance to Protect Information Assets–Without Compromising Employee Privacy or Trust. Information Today, Inc. (2006)
18. Frye, D.W.: Email, instant messaging and phishing. In: Frye, D.W. (ed.) Network Security Policies and Procedures, vol. 32, pp. 131–152. Springer, Boston (2007). https://doi.org/10.1007/978-0-387-47955-2_13

19. Jasper, S.: Strategic Cyber Deterrence: The Active Cyber Defense Option. Rowman & Littlefield (2017)
20. Prasad, R., Rohokale, V.: Cyber Security: The Lifeline of Information and Communication Technology. Springer, Cham (2020). https://doi.org/10.1007/978-3-030-31703-4
21. Scales, P., Aycard, O., Auberge, V.: Studying navigation as a form of interaction: a design approach for social robot navigation methods. In: 2020 IEEE International Conference on Robotics and Automation (ICRA), pp. 6965–6972. IEEE (2020)
22. Fan, W., Kevin, L., Rong, R.: Social engineering: IE based model of human weakness for attack and defense investigations. IJ Comput. Netw. Inf. Secur. 9(1), 1–11 (2017)
23. Yan, Q., Yu, F.R.: Distributed denial of service attacks in software-defined networking with cloud computing. IEEE Commun. Mag. 53(4), 52–59 (2015)
24. Cheema, A., Tariq, M., Hafiz, A., Khan, M.M., Ahmad, F., Anwar, M.: Prevention techniques against distributed denial of service attacks in heterogeneous networks: a systematic review. Secur. Commun. Netw. 2022 (2022)
25. Sood, A.K., Enbody, R.J.: Targeted cyberattacks: a superset of advanced persistent threats. IEEE Secur. Priv. 11(1), 54–61 (2012)
26. Virvilis, N., Vanautgaerden, B., Serrano, O.S.: Changing the game: the art of deceiving sophisticated attackers. In: 2014 6th International Conference On Cyber Conflict (CyCon 2014), pp. 87–97. IEEE (2014)
27. Goode, S., Lacey, D.: Detecting complex account fraud in the enterprise: the role of technical and non-technical controls. Decis. Support Syst. 50(4), 702–714 (2011)
28. Saxena, N., Hayes, E., Bertino, E., Ojo, P., Choo, K.-K.R., Burnap, P.: Impact and key challenges of insider threats on organizations and critical businesses. Electronics 9(9), 1460 (2020)
29. Owens, J., Matthews, J.: A study of passwords and methods used in brute-force SSH attacks. In: USENIX Workshop on Large-Scale Exploits and Emergent Threats (LEET) (2008)

Supporting Small and Medium-Sized Enterprises in Using Privacy Enhancing Technologies

Maria Bada[1]([✉]) [iD], Steven Furnell[2] [iD], Jason R. C. Nurse[3] [iD], and Jason Dymydiuk[4] [iD]

[1] Queen Mary University of London, London, UK
Maria.Bada@qmul.ac.uk
[2] University of Nottingham, Nottingham, UK
Steven.Furnell@nottingham.ac.uk
[3] University of Kent, Canterbury, UK
J.R.C.Nurse@kent.ac.uk
[4] University of Wolverhampton, London, UK
J.Dymydiuk@wlv.ac.uk

Abstract. Small and Medium-sized Enterprises (SMEs) are a critical element of the economy in many countries, as well as being embedded within key supply chains alongside larger organisations. Typical SMEs are data- and technology-dependent, but many are nonetheless ill-equipped to protect these areas. This study aims to investigate the extent to which SMEs currently understand and use Privacy Enhancing Technologies (PETs), and how they could be supported to do so more effectively given their potential constraints in terms of understanding, skills and capacity to act. This was studied via a mixed method approach collecting qualitative and quantitative data. Survey responses from 239 participants were collected and 14 interviews conducted. Participants were SME owners as well as experts working with SMEs. The findings clearly demonstrate that SMEs generally tend not to think about privacy, and if they do so it is mainly because of risk, potentially after a cyber attack, with the main drivers for implementing privacy being the potential of being fined by regulators, reputational damage, the demands of customers, and legal or regulatory compliance. The main reasons for the lack of attention are lack of skills and necessity. On this basis, the findings were taken forward to inform the initial design of an SME Privacy Starter Pack, which aims to assist SMEs in understanding that privacy and PETs are relevant to them and their industry in a simple and facilitated manner.

Keywords: Small business · SMEs · Privacy · PETs · Data protection

1 Introduction

Small and Medium-sized Enterprises (SMEs) are a critical element of the economy in many countries, as well as being embedded within key and critical supply chains with larger organisations. Typical SMEs are data- and technology-dependent, but many are nonetheless ill-equipped to protect these areas. Very little is definitively known about their security strategies and day-to-day security challenges [1], but they are frequently

A. Moallem (Ed.): HCII 2023, LNCS 14045, pp. 274–289, 2023.
https://doi.org/10.1007/978-3-031-35822-7_19

viewed as easy targets by attackers [2]. Indeed, there is clear evidence to suggest that SMEs face a corresponding share of privacy incidents and data breaches [3]. At the same time, the challenges of understanding privacy and applying appropriate measures can be significant. For example, SMEs often do not fully appreciate the importance of the threats they can face and are limited in the attention that these can be given due to the need to maintain day-to-day business operations. Prior research has indicated that many struggle to engage even with conducting privacy impact assessments [4].

Organisations and users face numerous occurrences of privacy incidents and data breaches. In many cases, the challenges of understanding privacy and applying appropriate measures can be significant. SMEs often face numerous occurrences of privacy incidents and data breaches [5]. However, as owners and staff are immersed in day-to-day activities they may lack the time or expertise to fully understand the importance of, and protect themselves against, privacy threats. The Cisco Data Privacy Benchmark Study 2023 [6] clearly illustrates the importance of privacy for organisations globally. The findings of the report show that: most organisations say they need to do more to reassure customers about how their data is used; global providers are better able to protect their data compared with local providers; and all their employees need to know how to protect data privacy. Our study aims to understand more about the situation facing SMEs and seeks to provide additional support to help them move forward with greater understanding and confidence. Specifically, it investigates:

- the extent to which SMEs currently understand and use Privacy Enhancing Technologies (PETs); and
- how they could be supported to do so more effectively given their potential constraints in terms of understanding, skills and capacity to act.

This research has led to the initial design and development of an SME Privacy Starter Pack (SPSP) aiming to: a) promote awareness about privacy tailored to the unique needs of SMEs, companies with fewer than 250 personnel; b) support SMEs in identifying how privacy may relate to them (targeted at the organisational level but also guidance provided at an employee level) and how it plays a critical role in determining long-term performance and competitiveness; and c) develop a series of case studies and scenarios that will provide practical guidance to SMEs in order to identify which privacy harms and concerns are most important to them (e.g., these may be based on the types of privacy threats, relevant regulations and technologies already being used). The resulting guidance aims to assist all SMEs in understanding that privacy and privacy enhancing technologies are relevant to them and their industry in a simple and facilitated manner. The resulting value of the work is the development of new ways to engage with SMEs on privacy issues and enable them to improve their position. On a broader scale, it also offers a basis to build trust and to utilise privacy as a means to open a wider discussion on data protection and enhancing the cyber resilience of SMEs.

This paper begins with the literature review of this field. Following, an outline of the data collection methodology for interview and survey activities is presented in Sect. 3, leading to discussion for the results obtained in each case in Sect. 4. Section 5 then discusses how the findings help to inform the approach that has been taken in designing the proposed SME Privacy Starter Pack and presents the work to date on the associated prototype. Section 6 then highlights the conclusions of this study.

2   Literature Review

As context for the research undertaken with the SMEs, this section examines the related background in terms of the Privacy Enhancing Technologies (PETs), followed by tools and frameworks that have been established to support organisations in the pursuit of privacy issues, and finally the extent of specific support available to SMEs.

2.1   Privacy Enhancing Technologies

PETs have been characterised in various ways. Based on the work by the Royal Society [7] PETs '*are an umbrella term covering a broad range of technologies and approaches that can help mitigate security and privacy risks*'. According to the Centre for Data Ethics and Innovation [8] PETs are '*any technical method that protects the privacy or confidentiality of sensitive information*'. This is quite a broad definition, covering from simple browser extensions to anonymous communication via Tor. These technologies are mainly categorised as traditional or emerging PETs. Examples of traditional PETs are encryption schemes that will secure data in transit and at rest, and de-identification techniques such as tokenization and k-anonymity. Emerging PETs are mainly solutions such as: homomorphic encryption, trusted execution environments, secure multi-party computation, differential privacy and systems for federated data processing.

ENISA [9] classified privacy enhancing technologies as the special type of technology tailored for supporting pseudonymous identity for data, anonymity of data and minimising data. The definition of ENISA also suggests that PETs have been tailored for supporting core data protection and privacy principles. Examples are: a) cryptographic algorithms: encryption; b) data masking techniques: pseudonymisation and c) with the help of AI & ML algorithms: data minimisation by reducing the amount of data that must be retained on a centralised server or in cloud storage.

Previous work from the Royal Society [7] sought to explain and scope some of the available PETs alongside their current development and potential through case studies and a sample of some technologies, that are ready for use and others in prototype phases.

Further work from ENISA [10] outlined the criteria required of online privacy tools with the aim of increasing trust and assurance in their use by the general public. ENISA divided them into three categories: basic, quality, and functionality. PETs are also frequently linked to the notion of Privacy by Design, because their development usually implicitly takes into account some related principles, in particular privacy by default and end-to-end security [11], and more recently also respect for user privacy.

2.2   Frameworks and Tools with a Privacy Component

Having established that there are issues to be addressed, organisations need support and guidance in how to do so. A number of existing frameworks include components in relation to privacy. A representative set of these is discussed below.

ENISA defined the PETs control matrix [12], an assessment framework and tool for the systematic presentation and evaluation of online and mobile privacy tools for end users. The term 'PET' is used in the context of this work with a narrow focus, addressing standalone privacy tools or services (and not the broader concept of privacy enhancing technologies). In addition, the NIST Privacy Framework [13] can support organisations in: a) building customers' trust by supporting ethical decision-making in product and service design or deployment; b) fulfilling current compliance obligations, and c) facilitating communication about privacy practices with individuals, business partners, assessors, and regulators. More recently, the NIST Special Publication 800-53A [14] provides a methodology and set of procedures for conducting assessments of security and privacy controls employed within systems and organisations within an effective risk management framework.

The UK's ICO [15] has released an awareness campaign 'Think Privacy Toolkit' with training resources for businesses, providing messages about the importance of data and phishing, responsibility, reputation, and respect. However, it does not provide guidance on how to comply with GDPR and DPA 2018 or how to implement PETs. In addition, the Centre for Data Ethics and Innovation (CDEI) developed a PETs Adoption Guide [8]. The CDEI PETs Adoption Guide is a question-based flowchart to aid decision-makers in thinking through which of the PETs may be useful in their projects. The guide seeks to support decision-making around the use of PETs by helping the user explore which technologies could be beneficial to their use case.

In addition, a number of existing resources offer guidance and support such as the Reset the Net [16] resource which under the 'Privacy Pack', offers free software tools covering different privacy areas like instant messaging, anonymous browsing or email encryption, the Best Privacy Tools website [17] which offers help for preserving privacy online and the Internet Privacy Tools [18] a website that identifies some of the major areas of interest regarding the protection of private data and communications, such as encrypted email, file and disk encryption and wiping, anonymous browsing. Additionally, a concept of a tool [19] for the GDPR-compliant handling of personal data by employees was created that supports employees in data management and data protection compliance. Also, AMBIENT Automated Cyber and Privacy Risk Management Toolkit [20] has been designed to be used in the healthcare domain for a variety of use case scenarios related to health data exchange.

ENISA [21] developed a tool on Privacy Enhancing Technologies (PETs) knowledge management and maturity assessment and provided recommendations on how to build and maintain an online community for PETs maturity assessments, which is assisted by ENISA's tool [22]. In addition, ENISA [23] developed a web application prototype, the 'PET maturity assessment online repository' which supports the maturity assessment methodology by implementing a systematic collaborative process.

2.3 Existing Tools for SMEs

Various tools and guidelines have also been developed specifically targeting SMEs. Some relevant examples are presented and discussed below in order to give a sense of the resources available to those that look for it.

The ICO self assessment checklist [24] has been created with small business owners and sole traders in mind. The checklist provides information on how understanding data protection can build a business's reputation, but also enhance the confidence for employees and customers by ensuring that personal information is accurate and relevant. Once an organisation completes the checklist a short report is created suggesting some practical actions SMEs can take and providing links to additional guidance for them to read that will help them improve their data protection knowledge and compliance.

The Global Cyber Alliance (GCA) [25] developed the GCA Cybersecurity Toolkit for Small Business, a free online resource simple, accessible and engaging that falls into a cybersecurity trend of indirectly engaging in entry level privacy issues without acknowledgement.

ENISA [26] aimed to support SMEs, through practical guidelines on the security of personal data processing, on how to calculate the risks for personal data processing and adopt appropriate security measures. The approach undertaken is an attempt to bridge the gap between the legal provisions and SMEs understanding and perception of risk.

Sangani et al. [27] designed a framework that brings out a Security & Privacy Architecture as a service for SMEs (SPAaaS) pertaining to Web Applications which can be offered by various security vendors. SPAaaS aims to assist the SMEs to evaluate the security requirements pertaining to host their data and services on the cloud.

Although these tools and frameworks aim to support SME privacy practises they can quickly become complicated to follow, and often lack a direct recognition of Privacy Enhancing Technologies and potential benefits to SMEs. Additionally, privacy and PETs specific tools are often targeted at developers, those with prior knowledge, or more technical backgrounds in data processing. Therefore, the barriers to begin the process for novices and SMEs without technical officers are increased. They may need to invest in technical knowledge or in contracting companies greatly increasing the upfront cost. Another common gap is that the tools tend not to distinguish privacy from information security, leaving SMEs with a potentially confused message on the privacy-specific issues.

3 Methodology

Our main objective is to understand the drivers that SMEs have, and unique obstacles that they face, in making privacy-aware decisions (e.g., about actions, requirements, and technologies), and to subsequently provide a suite of support to aid them in understanding and implementing appropriate PETs. To fulfil the above objective, we collected qualitative and quantitative data using a mixed-methods approach [28]:

- Online survey (quantitative data): A survey was conducted to enable us to reach a wide sample of micro, small, and medium organisations. The results of the survey enabled us to collect data on the situation and understanding of privacy across different sectors.

- Interviews (qualitative data): The importance of the interviews was to gain an in-depth understanding of what SMEs currently comprehend and what they actually need to know around privacy issues. This was achieved through interviewing different stakeholders such as SME owners as well as experts working with SMEs. We are supplementing this data with interviews conducted with persons involved in supporting SMEs through their information and privacy processes. Their understanding of the regulations and how to engage businesses and individuals, let alone getting them to act, means that they hold key information that can help to inform our findings and the subsequent the privacy starter pack.

Participants in this study were different stakeholders such as SME owners as well as experts working with SMEs. This includes third-party support SMEs – companies and personnel who help business meet regulation – as well as bodies that administer and assess certification schemes in the UK. Throughout the process of recruiting participants, data collection and analysis, all necessary steps to ensure anonymisation of data was followed. Personal information such as names were not collected or stored. Consent forms were collected prior to participation informing participants about the aim of the project and the data handling and storing process.

The participants of the online survey were given the opportunity to enter a raffle to win one of the three Amazon vouchers (£50 each) at the end of their participation. A separate survey was created to direct participants if they wished to participate in the Amazon voucher raffle. This ensured no contact details are linked to a specific survey response. Also, ethics approval for this project was granted from the Psychology Department Research Ethics Committee (Ref: PSY2022-41) at Queen Mary University of London and the National Research on Privacy, Harm Reduction and Adversarial Influence Online (REPHRAIN) Ethics Board [29]. The latter being the funding body for this research.

4 Results

This section presents and discusses the main findings of the two data collection phases, focusing firstly upon the quantitative data from the survey, and then considering the accompanying qualitative insights from the interview sessions.

4.1 Quantitative Data

In total, 296 participants responded to the online survey. Of these, 239 responses were fully completed. The results are based on the complete 239 responses. The data collected for the online survey are analysed producing descriptive statistics. A total of 36 questions comprised the online survey.

In terms of the role of the participants in their organisation, the majority are a programme manager (28%), researcher (23%) or in IT support (17%) (see Fig. 1). In addition, 3% indicated a different role (Other) such as head of business unit, risk advisor or security assurance manager.

The majority of organisations are a small (10–49 employees) (54%) or medium business (50–99 employees) (32%). In terms of the sector, participants mainly belong to an

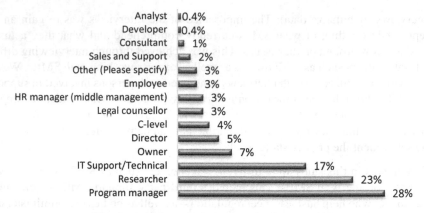

Fig. 1. Participant Role in Organisation (n = 239)

organisation focusing on Information Technology, professional scientific and technical activities, and public administration. The majority of participants claim that they somewhat consider privacy in their day-to-day business (40%), 25% responded that they do so very little, 21% not at all, while 14% to a great extent.

The main drivers for implementing privacy controls are: a) a perceived threat of losing an important customer (40%); b) gaining new business (21%); c) being part of the 'license to operate' perception (15%); d) the demands of customers (13%); e) compliance (8%); f) the potential for reputation damage (2%); g) the desire to avoid potential loss (1%) (see Fig. 2). From what we observe, the majority of motivations are mainly customer-driven, either because they directly search for new customers, or because their business could be lost because of losing existing ones.

Fig. 2. Main drivers for implementing privacy – Multiple answer (n = 239)

The main practises followed to keep data secure are: a) physical security measures (keeping documents secure in lockable storage) (51%); b) logging off computers when not at use (40%); c) encrypting mobile devices & use passwords (6%); d) using external storage devices (2%); e) back-ups (1%); f) other (0.4%) such as encrypting the data or using cloud services to retain data i.e. CRM. The results illustrate a lack of best practise use such as backing up data and using best practise for data encryption.

In addition, the majority of participants (93%) stated that privacy is an essential component of the overall strategy of their organisation, and they do have a data governance strategy as well (88%). Also, most organisations consider privacy an essential component for developing a culture of accountability and responsibility. The results indicate that the majority of participants understand the distinction between personal and sensitive data and have a record of what personal data they hold, such as email addresses, names and medical information. In addition, participants know what personal data are used for and they only keep personal data for as long as it is needed.

In terms of being targeted by cybercriminals, most participants perceive their organisation as being an attractive target and have also been attacked in the past. However, the majority of participants consider that there would be very little harm in the event of a data breach. Lastly, participants mentioned that during internal exercises they would consider the cost of a data breach.

The main sources of information on privacy used by study participants are: a) the ICO (46%); b) ENISA (22%); c) Data Protection Officer (9%); d) NIST (6%); e) Federation of Small Businesses (FSB) (6%); f) legal department (5%); g) Information security colleagues (2%); h) professional training (2%); and i) Internet sources (1%). The results show that the ICO is a go-to platform for information and guidance for SMEs. However, the Federation of Small Businesses (FSB) [30], a UK business organisation representing small and medium-sized businesses offering a wide range of vital business services including advice, financial expertise, support, is a source less visited for privacy related information.

The main responsibility for privacy related decisions is placed upon the: a) CIO or equivalent (35%); b) CFO (20%); c) CISO (12%); d) data protection officer (8%); e) IT director (8%); f) CEO (6%); g) the departmental manager (5%); h) all employees (3%); and i) HR manager (2%). The results show that privacy related matters are mainly handled by the chief information officer (CIO) or the CFO (Chief Financial Officer). The CIO usually plays a key leadership role in the critical strategic, technical and management initiatives—from information security and algorithms to customer experience and leveraging data—that mitigate threats and drive business growth, while the CFO has substantial input into a company's investments, capital structure, money management and long-term business strategy. However, in the case of SMEs we often see the role of a Fractional Chief Information Officer (CIO) as a part-time executive who usually works for more than one primarily small- to medium-sized enterprise (SME) [31].

Participants were asked how they consider and discuss topics of privacy internally. Some of the responses collected indicate that usually such discussions will emerge during a Management Board, an Infosec Committee meeting or the biannual trainings. In addition, privacy would come into discussion during internal audits, bidding for work, or due to customer requirements. Some participants also mentioned that they would consider privacy requirements during the development of their products.

The majority of participants (86/%) were aware of PETs, 8% were not aware of PETs (34%), while 6% were not sure. From those organisations who are aware, the majority also engage with these practises. The main reasons for organisations not utilising PETs are the lack of a PET catalogue (43%), the requirements being covered by the internal implementation (29%), the lack of skills (14%) and the fact that PETs are not available for purchase by a 3rd party (14%). In addition, the majority of participants stated that they develop PETs in house based on reusable patterns. The main privacy tools used by participants are the GDPR (53%) and Fair Information Practice Principles (FIPPs) (25%).

In terms of decision-making processes followed when implementing PETs or making privacy related decisions, the majority of participants indicate that decisions are based on perceptions of leaders in the organisation (86%) but also they use external expert advice (35%). Additionally, internal expert advice (21%) and online resources (24%) are used to make such decisions. Participants seem to base their decision-making process less on using technology (11%) or on the support of internal support communities (1%). These results agree with the findings showing that privacy related decisions are usually made at a senior level within an organisation. It is also common for SMEs to ask for advice from an external consultant or search the Internet for related information.

Some of the challenges faced in relation to implementing PETs are: a) reusability issues (34%); b) the use of legacy projects (21%); c) lack of a PET catalogue (14%); d) the lack of detailed requirements (10%); e) difficulty in differentiating sensitive data (8%); f) high computational cost (4%); g) lack of training (2%); h) lack of resources or regulatory oversight (2%); i) the immaturity of implementations (2%); j) the difficulty to avoid sensitive data leakage (2%).

Finally, participants provided their suggestions for being best supported to use PETs. These are: a) provision of tools for implementing PETs (41%); b) the provision of clear instructions on how personal data may be processed (20%); c) provision of templates for data inquiries (13%); d) the use of a PETs catalogue (10%); e) the provision of clear requirements on obtaining personal data (8%); f) low computational cost (6%) and g) skilled employees (1%).

4.2 Qualitative Data

To complement the survey data, 14 semi-structured interviews were conducted to explore the SME views and constraints in more detail. The interviews were audio-recorded, and transcriptions were then analysed using thematic analysis [28]. An iterative process was followed to first identify preliminary codes of the qualitative data collected. Then a further analysis was conducted to identify themes in our codes across the different interviews. These are collated and summarised as follows:

– **Perceptions and attitudes of SMEs about privacy:** According to interviewees, SMEs overall do not think about privacy and if they do it is mainly because of risk, potentially after an attack. Another interesting observation during interviews is that SMEs face the same risks and need to follow the same practices as larger organisations. However, the GDPR language is too difficult to understand. In addition, SMEs have a number of organisations telling them what to do, without necessarily explaining them why. Given the perception barriers around cybersecurity and technology, it was suggested that perhaps the best way to approach SMEs is by asking SMEs what they feel their most valuable assets are and whether they fell they need to protect these: *'We don't exist without data....Some small businesses have realised the issues and seek to be certified with Cyber Essentials'*. In addition, interviewees mentioned that people choose not to make privacy a priority, because there are other priorities, for which SMEs know what they need to do, know deadlines and know what will happen if they do not fulfil these. In terms of incentives, interviewees claimed that SME owners are also worried of being fined by the ICO. For this reason, they would follow a risk versus benefit approach. As an incentive, for SMEs it is suggested to promote that *'having Cyber Essentials will give you a lower fine'*. Supply chain expectations could also be another useful factor - i.e. that those using the SME as a supplier having an expectation of measures being in place.

- **Risk Perception:** According to interviewees, SMEs overall do not think that they are an attractive target for cybercriminals. As stated, *'I assume that organisations of high value would be a target. We don't have a lot of reserve in the bank. So we are not an attractive target. So, criminals would not attack us'*. It was further suggested that *'SMEs know that they might get in trouble with the ICO if they share data accidentally, but they don't know in how much trouble and they believe that by apologizing they will not be fined. And this impacts how they perceive risk'*. In addition, we have identified a sense of 'blind trust' from both clients and SME owners: *'Most of our clients trust us to be sensible. Similarly, we trust our developers to take measures so that we avoid an attack'*.

- **Information on PETs and use for SMEs:** Our findings indicate that forcing SMEs to meet best practices or in case of supply chains the practices of the lead, and often cyber mature, organisations is not effective. In addition, employing internal measures to meet frameworks such as ISO27000 is not feasible for many small companies that possess small budgets and minimal personnel. Because of this, organisations having SMEs in their supply chain ignore basic security requirements especially when it comes to SMEs. This has not only become apparent through our qualitative data collection but is also evident through the research conducted by agencies – such as the National Cyber Security Centre and the Research Institute for Socio-Technical Cyber Security (RISCS) [32]. One interviewee stated that in the case of charities, advocacy, and the social clubs, such demands on smaller organisations to meet legislation and regulation could shut down the entire sector. The dream resolution would be a device set up to meet the requirements of privacy – encryption of data at rest, access protocols such as 2FA, and timed notifications of data to ensure unnecessary data is not stored beyond requirement or a stated timeframe. Such a device would have a certified 'stamp of approval'.

- **Recognising constraints:** Another aspect which emerged in our interviews is the lack of focus on privacy due to many organisations being very small in size, which do not have someone working specifically on privacy. As mentioned by an interviewee *'We make use of 'pro bono' information and advice. This is how I became a member of the London Digital Security Centre..... It's like health and safety, people don't like to go to the authority, because they think that the authority is making them do more that they have to. This is why they are not looking at the information provided by the ICO'*.

The first step, then, is toward basic practices, understanding and processes. Money is often key to the discussion and to the uptake of privacy in any business. Is it worth the cost? This brought up numerous discussions during the interviews revolving around regulatory fines, fine reduction systems (when a breach inevitably occurs), insurance, and tone of our privacy starter pack pitch – that is, it should not be demanding, but should be persuasive and helpful for SMEs to recognise why PETs are useful. Finally, SMEs and specifically for charities, information and advice is being sought through the official bodies '*there is the official body for each aspect such as the ICO for data, and then you can join a group such as the charity finance group, and you can find advice from such groups*'.

- **SMEs Privacy Starter Pack (SPSP) Specifications:** In relation to the development of the SPSP interviewees suggested the following: a) provide simple advice; b) prioritise 2–3 main basic steps SMEs need to follow; c) inform SMEs why it is important to follow best practise and privacy related guidance; and d) provide information in digital and physical form. In addition, interviewees suggested the SPSP to be designed in multiple accessible formats. First, to provide basic guidance, demonstrating to everyone that privacy is a concern to their business, no matter what sector. It would also include a section entitled: '*what to ask your...*' with questions to ask a cloud service provider, an accountant, payroll, or payment service provider on data protection. Second, provide guidance with core considerations with a focus on different sectors. This would have more sector specific questions and guidance. Our initial results have already demonstrated that one-size approach is unlikely to fit all. This guidance too would include a '*questions to ask...*' section. However, unlike the above guidance, these would be aligned to a sector. Third, guidance on privacy and what SMEs might require. Interviewees also referred to the need for SMEs to understand why they need to consider privacy, how they need to consider it and clear channels for them to find useful advice. In terms of the approach '*Less is more. Everything you need to know is on the ICO website, but people don't have the time to go through all this information. It looks too complicated. You need to provide the top 5 priorities they need to do*'. And also '*Is there a clear path? If you can walk people through, you have a better chance*'. Telling stories about real people has been suggested as the beast approach. That would help because a lot of the time it is thought that the advice is for someone else, SMEs do not relate to that information or existing templates do not match to their needs. As stated, '*Templates, enough examples so that people can find something they can start with. You can find similar information, but it is different colour, you need to trick people into thinking that this is the right one*'.

The points from the latter theme feed into the next phase of our research, which is the design and development of a proposed Starter Pack to support SMEs in understanding and addressing their privacy needs (which in turn provides a foundation for their adoption of PETs).

5 Toward an SME Privacy Starter Pack

The findings from the quantitative and qualitative analysis conducted provided us with some basic understanding of current practices SMEs follow in relation to privacy. In addition, challenges and gaps have been identified which feed into the work towards the development of an SME Privacy Starter Pack (SPSP). Based upon the findings to date, such a tool is considered to require:

- **A tiered or level approach to encourage manageable and measurable steps.** A level approach will guide businesses to identify the steps needed to advance from baseline privacy related information to adoption of PETs. Such an approach is key to increase the number of entry points into PETs to take into account existing information security or data handing knowledge.
- **Physical guide and resource.** Within the qualitative research phrase the requirement to provide physical resources became clear. Suggestions in the interviews included decision tables, templates, delegation packs, printer friendly information sheets, posters, and reports. In other words, taking into account the fact that each person has preferred learning style or condonation of kinetic, visual, and auditory.
- **Interactive, logged, and specific interface.** The information provided must be simple and accessible. Overwhelming displays or avenues of decision making might produce accurate results, but are often at the cost of losing engagement. However, the starter pack needs to provide bitesize information to guide businesses to efficient adaptation of data processing of PII or sensitive information. A likely aspect once the benefits beyond a decreased risk to processes already in place.
- **Relevant information matching the needs of SMEs.** Information that provides guidance that SMEs consider relevant and confident to use. Interviewees discussed the difficulty in deciding which information to use since there are multiple resources providing basic steps for organisations to ensure they protect their data. However, that information is often off-putting due to the fact that it is difficult to follow or not relevant to them. It is therefore imperative to provide relevant information that matches each SME's needs.

The findings emphasised the severe lack of understanding of the basic principles around privacy. As such, the core of the Starter Pack is intended to address two main areas, namely Information Audit and Data Handling, each of which will be implemented in the form of decision trees that the SMEs navigate in order to identify their related data usage and protection needs.

As the Information Audit begins, users are directed through a decision tree to identify whether their collection of data potentially infringes privacy, before suggesting possible solutions. The audit gives specific consideration to sensitive and personally identifiable information, and considers the need for it to be collected and how it is used. This serves to determine which branches of the Data Handling decision tree are then required by that specific SME. Directing the user to the appropriate branches of the Data Handling tree is where the SPSP begins to support the implementation of PETs. This approach is similar to the CDEI PETs adoption tool discussed earlier, although addressing an audience with a lower target knowledge level.

At the time of writing the work on the Starter Pack remains a work in progress, and the authors intend to document the outcome and related findings within a future publication.

6 Conclusions

The overall findings from the data collection demonstrate that SMEs generally tend not to think about privacy, or do so at a less extent. For those who do so it is mainly because of risk, potentially after a cyber attack. The main reasons for the lack of attention are lack of necessity and the lack of skills. By highlighting the need for organisations to understand the nature of the risk and the probability of an event occurring, the security approaches highlight the need to address both the threats and actions in the event of an incident to reduce the risk to privacy [33].

In relation to privacy decision-making, the majority of participants indicated that they use internal expert input, and online resources to make such decisions. Our findings also identified several drivers for implementing privacy, including the potential of being fined, reputation damage, the demands of customers, the desire to avoid potential loss, legal or regulatory compliance, and gaining new business. Forcing SMEs to meet best practices (or, in case of supply chains, follow the practices of a lead, and often cyber mature organisation) is not effective. In addition, the language, demands, and expectations are too technical and therefore easily misunderstood and then misapplied. These findings agree with research conducted by [34] showing that the drivers for implementing security and privacy in SMEs are the demands by customers, the perceived threat of losing an important customer, regulatory compliance requirements and the desire to avoid reputation damage.

Along the lines of promoting an understanding of risks emerging from incidents such as a data breach, the actions necessary to allow SMEs to benefit from and use of PETs is needed. Previous work from the Royal Society [7] sought to explain and scope some of the available PETs alongside their current development and potential through case studies and a sample of some technologies, that are ready for use and others in prototype phases. The application of the technologies chosen in the study either are only relevant to individuals or would require a dedicated expertise within an organisation, or significant outside support.

As shown in previous studies in relation to security [35] skilled personnel, technology readiness, data security concerns, data privacy concerns, legal compliance, and trust in cloud service providers are essential determinants of the intention to adopt cloud computing by SMEs. Our results in relation to privacy showed that to best support the use of PETs requirements such as the provision of clear instructions on how personal data may be processed, the provision of clear requirements on obtaining personal data and tools for implementing PETs as well as skilled employees, are needed.

Our findings also identified a number of drivers for implementing privacy, mainly the potential for reputation damage, the demands of customers, the desire to avoid potential loss, being part of the 'license to operate' perception, compliance, avoiding the threat of losing a customer and gaining new business. These can be factors that need to be better communicated to SMEs in order to change their perceptions and attitudes around privacy.

On this basis, the findings were taken forward to inform the development of an SME Privacy Starter Pack, which includes pathways for contextualising privacy requirements through scenarios, and real case studies. This aims to provide SMEs with guidance that takes into account the local business environment and cyber threat landscape, raise awareness of the scale of the threat facing these organisations, encourage and incentivise them to invest the time needed to make best use of the available tools such as PETs, and improve their overall privacy posture.

Acknowledgements. This work is supported by REPHRAIN: National Research centre on Privacy, Harm Reduction and Adversarial Influence online (EPSRC Grant: EP/V011189/1).

References

1. Bada, M., Nurse, J.R.C.: Developing cybersecurity education and awareness programmes for small- and medium-sized enterprises (SMEs). Inf. Comput. Secur. **27**(3), 393–410 (2019). https://doi.org/10.1108/ICS-07-2018-0080
2. European Union Agency for Cybersecurity, ENISA. Cybersecurity for SMEs (2021). https://www.enisa.europa.eu/publications/enisa-report-cybersecurity-for-smes. Accessed 11 July 2022
3. DCMS. Cyber Security Breaches Survey. Department for Digital, Culture, Media and Sport (2022). https://www.gov.uk/government/statistics/cyber-security-breaches-survey-2022/cyber-security-breaches-survey-2022. Accessed 11 July 2022
4. Sirur, S., Nurse, J. R.C., Webb, H.: Are we there yet? Understanding the challenges faced in complying with the general data protection regulation (GDPR). In: Proceedings of the 2nd International Workshop on Multimedia Privacy and Security (MPS 2018), pp. 88–95. Association for Computing Machinery, New York (2018). https://doi.org/10.1145/3267357.3267368
5. The Department for Digital, Culture, Media and Sport, Cyber Security Breaches Survey (2022). https://www.gov.uk/government/statistics/cyber-security-breaches-survey-2022/cyber-security-breaches-survey-2022#chapter-5-incidence-and-impact-of-breaches-or-attacks. Accessed 11 July 2022
6. Cisco. Data Privacy Benchmark Study (2023). https://www.cisco.com/c/en/us/about/trust-center/data-privacy-benchmark-study.html. Accessed 11 July 2022
7. The Royal Society. Protecting privacy in practice: The current use, development, and limits of Privacy Enhancing Technologies in data analysis, 5 (2019)
8. Centre for Data Ethics and Innovation. PETs Adoption Guide. https://cdeiuk.github.io/pets-adoption-guide/adoption-guide/. Accessed 27 Sept 2022
9. European Union Agency for Cybersecurity, ENISA. https://www.enisa.europa.eu/publications/pets. Accessed 11 July 2022
10. European Union Agency for Cybersecurity, ENISA. Study on the availability of trustworthy online privacy tools for the general public (2015). https://www.enisa.europa.eu/publications/privacy-tools-for-the-general-public. Accessed 11 July 2022
11. Danezis, G., et al.: Privacy and data protection by design – from policy to engineering. CoRR (2015). http://arxiv.org/abs/1501.03726
12. European Union Agency for Cybersecurity, ENISA. PETs controls matrix - A systematic approach for assessing online and mobile privacy tools (2016). https://www.enisa.europa.eu/publications/pets-controls-matrix/pets-controls-matrix-a-systematic-approach-for-assessing-online-and-mobile-privacy-tools. Accessed 11 July 2022

13. NIST Privacy Framework. https://www.nist.gov/privacy-framework/privacy-framework
14. NIST Special Publication 800-53A1. Assessing Security and Privacy Controls in Information Systems and Organizations (2022). https://csrc.nist.gov/publications/detail/sp/800-53a/rev-5/final
15. ICO, E-Learning, posters and stickers. https://ico.org.uk/for-organisations/posters-stickers-and-e-learning/. Accessed 27 Sept 2022
16. Reset the Net: Privacy Pack. www.resetthenet.org. Accessed 27 Sept 2022
17. Best Privacy Tools, bestprivacytools.com. Accessed 27 Sept 2022
18. Internet Privacy Tools privacytools.freeservers.com. Accessed 27 Sept 2022
19. Tolsdorf, J., Dehling, F., Iacono, L.L.: Data cart – designing a tool for the GDPR-compliant handling of personal data by employees. Behav. Inf. Technol. **41**(10), 2084–2119 (2022). https://doi.org/10.1080/0144929X.2022.2069596
20. AMBIENT-Automated Cyber and Privacy Risk Management Toolkit. https://www.mdpi.com/1424-8220/21/16/5493. Accessed 27 Sept 2022
21. European Union Agency for Cybersecurity, ENISA. A tool on Privacy Enhancing Technologies (PETs) knowledge management and maturity assessment (2018). https://www.enisa.europa.eu/publications/pets-maturity-tool. Accessed 11 July 2022
22. European Union Agency for Cybersecurity, ENISA. Privacy Enhancing Technologies: Evolution and State of the Art (2017). https://www.enisa.europa.eu/publications/pets-evolution-and-state-of-the-art. Accessed 11 July 2022
23. European Union Agency for Cybersecurity, ENISA. PETs Maturity Assessment Repository (2017). https://www.enisa.europa.eu/publications/enisa2019s-pets-maturity-assessment-repository. Accessed 11 July 2022
24. ICO. Self assessment checklist. https://ico.org.uk/for-organisations/sme-web-hub/checklists/assessment-for-small-business-owners-and-sole-traders/. Accessed 27 Sept 2022
25. GCA Cybersecurity Toolkit for Small Business. https://gcatoolkit.org/smallbusiness/?utm_source=IFA&utm_medium=Website. Accessed 11 July 2022
26. European Union Agency for Cybersecurity, ENISA. Guidelines for SMEs on the security of personal data processing (2016). https://www.enisa.europa.eu/publications/guidelines-for-smes-on-the-security-of-personal-data-processing. Accessed 11 July 2022
27. Sangani, N.K., Velmurugan, P., Vithani, T., Madiajagan, M.: Security & privacy architecture as a service for small and medium enterprises. In: Proceedings of the International Conference on Cloud Computing Technologies, Applications and Management (ICCCTAM), Dubai, United Arab Emirates, pp. 16–21 (2012). https://doi.org/10.1109/ICCCTAM.2012.6488064
28. Corbin, J., Strauss, A.: Grounded theory research: Procedures, canons, and evaluative criteria. Qualit. Sociol. **13**, 3–21 (1990)
29. National Research on Privacy, Harm Reduction and Adversarial Influence Online (REPHRAIN). https://www.rephrain.ac.uk. Accessed 11 July 2022
30. The Federation of Small Businesses (FSB). https://www.fsb.org.uk. Accessed 11 July 2022
31. Kratzer, S., Drechsler, A., Westner, M., et al.: The fractional CIO in SMEs: conceptualization and research agenda. Inf. Syst. E-Bus. Manage. **20**, 581–611 (2022). https://doi.org/10.1007/s10257-022-00557-4
32. RISCS, About US. Research Institute for Socio-technical Cyber Security. https://www.riscs.org.uk/about/. Accessed 27 Sept 2022
33. Allison, I., Strangwick, C.: Privacy through security: policy and practice in a small-medium enterprise. In: Subramanian, R. (ed.) Computer Security, Privacy and Politics: Current Issues, Challenges and Solutions, pp. 157–179 (2008)

34. Lacey, D., James, B.E.: Review of availability of advice on security for small/medium sized organisations. ICO (2010). https://ico.org.uk/media/about-the-ico/documents/1042344/review-availablility-of-security-advice-for-sme.pdf
35. Nagahawatta, R., Warren, M., Salzman, S., Lokuge, S.: Security and privacy factors influencing the adoption of cloud computing in australian SMEs. In: PACIS 2021 Proceedings, Dubai, p. 7 (2021). https://aisel.aisnet.org/pacis2021/7

Cybersecurity Compliance Requirements for USA Department of Defense Contractors - Dragons at the Gate

Gordon J. Bruce[✉]

Department of Cyber Compliance, GjB and Associates, Honolulu, HI, USA
gordon.bruce@gjbandassociates.com

Abstract. Dragons at the Gate provides you with insightful details about those who continue to exploit our intellectual expertise, and technical expertise and take advantage of our trust. Your life and your family's lives will and are being impacted. This paper is intended to wake you up and realize you have already been attacked and who and what you do not matter to those that attack us. This paper will not solve the problem but will provide you with an insight into how you might influence those you count on to protect you or what you might do to protect yourself, those around you, and the rest of us. These collectively will help in protecting us against the problem (cybersecurity attacks). It is still up to you. We will look at the cause and effect of the attackers, the cause and effect of defending against them, and the restrictions that prevent us from attacking back.

With over 50 years of hands-on experience in the computer industry, I provide a perspective from the coding, configuration, and large-scale computing systems to the cloud. I have worked in this industry from the private sector, healthcare, and government. I understand the legislative and front-line business perspectives. I have felt and continue to feel your pain. You have no idea what is coming next, and neither do I. If you are a front line, IT professional, or senior IT executive this paper is intended to help you get the message across to all senior executives, and employees that the Dragon is at the Gate and has already broken through the walls! The Department of Defense has placed and is increasing the requirements and the penalties for DoD contractors not complying with existing and future cybersecurity laws. It's the senior executive that will be confronted by the DoD, not the IT professional! But are our laws good enough when our laws do not pertain to our adversaries?

Keywords: cybersecurity · NIST · CMMC · hacker · hacking · DFARS · SPRS · SSP · POAM · CUI · cyber

1 Introduction

There are Dragons at the Gate! Your world is no longer safe! What should you do? Escape – find a safer place to live (impossible). Defend – strengthen the Gates (you have no choice). Attack – take on the dragons before they get stronger (the private sector is prohibited from doing this in the USA). One thing is for sure the status quo is not working.

© The Author(s), under exclusive license to Springer Nature Switzerland AG 2023
A. Moallem (Ed.): HCII 2023, LNCS 14045, pp. 290–308, 2023.
https://doi.org/10.1007/978-3-031-35822-7_20

We depend on others to ensure that all of our needs are met and that we are safe and secure. Pipe dreams! You are in charge of defending yourself from the Dragon at the Gate. This is a wake-up call. No rule, no law, and no guidance from others can protect us. Not even those in power whom we depend on to protect us from our adversaries. The front-line defenders, those on the ground may be whom we will have to count on. You may have to be one of those on the ground.

1.1 Attacks in 2022

To set the stage... a few attacks from 2022 [1].

October 2022. Hackers targeted a communications platform in Australia, which handles Department of Defense data, in a ransomware attack. The government believes hackers breached sensitive government data in this attack.

October 2022. Hackers targeted several major U.S. airports with a DDoS attack, impacting their websites. A pro-Russian hacking group promoted the attack before its execution.

October 2022. Pro-Russian hackers claimed responsibility for an attack that knocked U.S. state government websites offline, including Colorado's, Kentucky's, and Mississippi's.

October 2022. CISA, the FBI, and NSA announced that state-sponsored hacking groups had long-term access to a defense company since January 2021 and compromised sensitive company data.

August 2022. Hackers used phishing emails to deploy malware in government institutions and defense firms throughout Eastern Europe in January 2022. A report by Russian-based company Kaspersky linked the campaign to a Chinese hacking group.

July 2022. A hacker claimed to acquire records on 1 billion Chinese from a Shanghai police database and posted the data for sale online.

July 2022. China stated the United States stole 97 billion pieces of global internet data and 124 billion pieces of telephone data in June, specifically blaming the National Security Agency (NSA)'s Office of Tailored Access Operations (TAO).

June 2022. The FBI, National Security Agency (NSA), and CISA announced that Chinese state-sponsored hackers targeted and breached major telecommunications companies and network service providers since at least 2020.

June 2022. Hackers targeted municipal public address systems in Jerusalem and Eliat, triggering the air raid siren systems throughout both cities. An Israeli industrial cybersecurity firm attributed the attack to Iran.

May 2022. A Chinese hacking group stole intellectual property assets from American and European companies in 2019 and went largely undetected. Researchers believe the group is backed by the Chinese government.

April 2022. The United States removed Russian malware from computer networks around the world, a move made public by Attorney General Merrick B. Garland. While it is unclear what the malware's intention was, authorities noted it could be used for anything from surveillance to destructive attacks. The malware created a botnet controlled by the Russian GRU.

March 2022. The U.S. Department of Justice charged four Russian government employees involved in hacking campaigns that took place between 2012 and 2018. The hacks targeted critical infrastructure companies and organizations largely in the energy sector. The hackers sought to install backdoors and deploy malware in the operational technology of their targets.

March 2022. Hackers linked to the Chinese government penetrated the networks belonging to government agencies of at least 6 different U.S. states in an espionage operation. Hackers took advantage of the Log4j vulnerability to access the networks, in addition to several other vulnerable internet-facing web applications.

February 2022. A U.N. report claimed that North Korean hackers stole more than $50 million between 2020 and mid-2021 from three cryptocurrency exchanges. The report also added that in 2021 that amount likely increased, as the DPRK launched 7 attacks on cryptocurrency platforms to help fund their nuclear program in the face of a significant sanction regime.

February 2022. An investigation led by Mandiant discovered that hackers linked to the Chinese-government compromised email accounts belonging to Wall Street Journal journalists. The hackers allegedly surveilled and exfiltrated data from the newspaper for over two years beginning in at least February 2020.

These are just a few from 2022. This list is larger and goes on and on. Feel better?

1.2   Who Are the Dragons? The Top Five

1. *CHINA – A HOTBED OF HACKERS*

China has continued to wage large-scale cyber-attacks, and this includes stealing intellectual property. More than a third of all cyber-attacks are instituted in China, where the People's Liberation Army (PLA) even employs military units that are specialized in network attack and defense.

A *Foreign Policy* magazine estimate from 2017 suggested that China's "hacker army" could be upwards of 100,000 personnel strong, larger than the size of many nations' actual military force. According to Venafi's research, APT groups like APT41 use cyber espionage to support China's long-term economic, political and military goals, often targeting carefully selected victims.

"In China, there are myriad state-sponsored groups, and we see evidence of the nation's cyber offensive capabilities on a near-constant basis," said Blachman. "Recently, as the threat of war in Taiwan has escalated, we've witnessed attacks on Taiwan's infrastructure, which could be a precursor to invasion."

Given how it continues to train the next generation, the threat from China is likely only to increase.

2. *NORTH KOREA – SMALL NATION WITH A STRONG HACKING FORCE*

2021 was seen as a banner year for North Korean hackers, who reportedly stole $400 million in cryptocurrency – and 2022 will certainly be even better, as cyber agents operating from the Hermit Kingdom allegedly lifted some $600 million from a cryptocurrency gaming startup this past March.

Hacking is increasingly important for North Korea, and it now seeks to increase its efforts.

"It has been reported that North Korea, gives aptitude tests and starts training as young as 11 years old," said Tim Morris, technology strategist at cybersecurity firm Tanium.

"Then those skills are used for ransomware and/or cryptocurrency theft to finance other programs for the government or military," Morris told Clearance Jobs.

North Korea is also notable in that it is now the only nation in the world whose government is known to conduct such open criminal hacking for monetary gain.

"Infamous North Korean cybercrime groups such as Lazarus and APT38 are renowned for their links to the state. Lazarus is particularly prolific and has made a name for itself with attacks on Sony, the Bangladesh Bank cyber heist, WannaCry and recently targeting US energy companies," Blachman continued. "Our research shows that North Korean state-employed hackers help to circumvent the international sanctions placed on DPRK, with the proceeds of cybercrime funneled directly into the nation's nuclear weapons program."

3. IRAN – QUASI-GOVERNMENT GROUP

The Islamic Republic's Iranian Cyber Army has a known connection with Tehran, and it has even pledged its loyalty to the nation's Supreme Leader. It is also believed that the Islamic Revolutionary Guard initiated plans for the group as early as 2005, while it was possibly commanded by Mohammad Hussein Tajik until his death in early 2020.

The Islamic Revolutionary Guard has also stated that it had the fourth largest cyber power among the world's cyber armies. Hackers tied to the Iranian government have recently been targeting individuals specializing in Middle Eastern affairs, nuclear security, and genome research as part of a new social engineering campaign designed to hunt for sensitive information.

However, Iran's hacking efforts could now be used against the government – as the country's state broadcaster was recently hacked as protests for reform, and greater rights for women, grip the Middle Eastern nation. It seems that Iran could have a hard time controlling the beast it created.

4. RUSSIA – A HACKER SUPERPOWER

Even as the mighty Russian bear appears to be more of a paper tiger on the battlefield, its cyber capabilities shouldn't be underestimated. Moscow has been focused on STEM (science, technology, engineering, math) skills for longer than the United States, and it has paid off.

"Russia has half of our population and churns out six times the number of engineering graduates, many of whom use their skills for state-sponsored cyber attacks on America," Gunn explained to ClearanceJobs. "If some of the battles of the future will be fought online, we could end up woefully outmanned and the gap is growing every year."

This puts Russia among the greatest cyber threats – even as it faces setbacks in its so-called "Special Military Operation" against Ukraine.

"Russia will increase its use of cyber warfare to gain a better foothold in Ukraine," said Henry Collier, program director for Norwich University's online Master of Science in Cybersecurity program. "Russia has previously used cyber attacks against its adversaries, including Ukraine, with some degree of success."

More worrisome is what it could mean for the upcoming U.S. midterm elections.

"Russia has worked to coordinate cyber attacks to try and undo the political process of their intended target," Collier told ClearanceJobs. "The threat of Russia trying to influence the outcome of the elections is real, especially as they continue to spread misinformation across social media sites."

In addition, Russia could target NATO countries' infrastructure like electricity or gas in a pointed effort to make the supporting countries concentrate on their well-being, rather than supporting Ukraine, Collier warned.

"There's already strong evidence that cyber espionage groups such as Sandworm and Fancy Bear are associated with the Russian armed forces (GRU)," added Blachman. "Famous attacks by these groups include the Ukrainian power grid attacks in 2015 and the NotPetya attacks of 2017, as well as numerous attempts to derail political processes across the globe. These targets suggest the motives of these groups are aligned to Russia's political and military goals."

5. *UNITED STATES – READY FOR THE CYBER DOMAIN*

Cyberattacks aren't just something the "bad guys" conduct. The United States maintains its wide-reaching cyber warriors. This includes the United States Cyber Command, which is one of the 11 unified combatant commands of the United States Department of Defense. While created with a defensive mission in mind, Cyber Command has increasingly been viewed as an offensive force.

"The U.S. has its programs that do the reconnaissance, defensive, and offensive operations," said Morris.

In just the past month, China alleged that U.S. cyber operatives have conducted cyberattacks against its interests. Beijing accused the National Security Agency of infiltrating China's telecommunication infrastructure to steal user data by intercepting digital communication between multiple parties [2].

Those also worth noting are Brazil, India, Germany, Vietnam, Thailand, Indonesia, Turkey, and the Netherlands.

1.3   Recent Infrastructure Attacks

The dragons are attacking! The dragons are attacking! The sky is falling! This is not Chicken Little. With hundreds of attacks occurring daily, you better watch out. Your sky may be falling all around you. In this chapter, I will provide some insight into a few of the varieties of attacks that have reaped havoc. This is a gnat on the butt of an elephant when considering all the attacks. These attacks are the testing grounds. With special thanks to Wikipedia.

The Solar Winds Attack [3].
In 2020, a major cyberattack suspected to have been committed by a group backed by the Russian government penetrated thousands of organizations globally including multiple parts of the United States federal government, leading to a series of data breaches. The cyberattack and data breach was reported to be among the worst cyber-espionage incidents ever suffered by the U.S., due to the sensitivity and high profile of the targets and the long duration (eight to nine months) to which the hackers had access. Within days of its discovery, at least 200 organizations around the world had been reported to be affected by the attack, and some of these may also have suffered data breaches. Affected organizations worldwide included NATO, the U.K. government, the European Parliament, Microsoft, and others.

The attack, which had gone undetected for months, was first publicly reported on December 13, 2020, and was initially only known to have affected the U.S. Treasury Department and the National Telecommunications and Information Administration (NTIA), part of the U.S. Department of Commerce. In the following days, more departments and private organizations reported breaches.

The cyberattack that led to the breaches began no later than March 2020. The attackers exploited software or credentials from at least three U.S. firms: Microsoft, SolarWinds, and VMware. A supply chain attack on Microsoft cloud services provided one way for the attackers to breach their victims, depending upon whether the victims had bought those services through a reseller. A supply chain attack on SolarWinds's Orion software, widely used in government and industry, provided another avenue if the victim used that software. Flaws in Microsoft and VMware products allowed the attackers to access emails and other documents, and to perform federated authentication across victim resources via single sign-on infrastructure. *Makes you feel so comfy, doesn't it?*

The Colonial Pipeline Attack [4].
The Colonial Pipeline carries gasoline, diesel, *and* jet fuel from Texas to as far away as New York. About 45% of all fuel consumed on the East Coast arrives via the pipeline system. The attack came amid growing concerns over the vulnerability of infrastructure (including critical infrastructure) to cyberattacks after several high-profile attacks, including the 2020 SolarWinds hack that hit multiple federal government agencies, including the Defense, Treasury, State, and Homeland Security departments.

The primary target of the attack was the billing infrastructure of the company. The actual oil pumping systems were still able to work. According to CNN sources in the company, the inability to bill the customers was the reason for halting the pipeline operation. Colonial Pipeline reported that it shut down the pipeline as a precaution due to a concern that the hackers might have obtained information allowing them to carry out further attacks on vulnerable parts of the pipeline. The day after the attack, Colonial could not confirm at that time when the pipeline would resume normal functions. The attackers also stole nearly 100 gigabytes of data and threatened to release it on the internet if the ransom was not paid. It was reported that within hours after the attack the company paid a ransom of nearly 75 Bitcoins ($5 million) to the hackers in exchange for a decryption tool, which proved so slow that the company's business continuity planning tools were more effective in bringing back operational capacity.

Stuxnet – Cyberweaponry [5].
Experts believe that Stuxnet required the largest and costliest development effort in malware history. Developing its many abilities would have required a team of highly capable programmers, in-depth knowledge of industrial processes, and an interest in attacking industrial infrastructure. Eric Byres, who has years of experience maintaining and troubleshooting Siemens systems, told *Wired* that writing the code would have taken many man-months, if not man-years. Symantec estimates that the group developing Stuxnet would have consisted of between five and thirty people and would have taken six months to prepare. *The Guardian*, the BBC, and *The New York Times* all claimed that (unnamed) experts studying Stuxnet believe the complexity of the code indicates that only a nation-state would have the ability to produce it. The self-destruct and other safeguards within the code implied that a Western government was responsible, or at least is responsible for

its development. However, software security expert Bruce Schneier initially condemned the 2010 news coverage of Stuxnet as hype, stating that it was almost entirely based on speculation. But after subsequent research, Schneier stated in 2012 that "we can now conclusively link Stuxnet to the centrifuge structure at the Natanz nuclear enrichment lab in Iran".

2   Holding Off the Dragons

We have all the rules, we have all the laws. All DoD contractors are following the rules? I feel safer already…NOT! Our adversaries do not play by these rules. They like that we get bogged down in the rules. More rules, more laws, more delays. Keep the rules coming they say.

2.1   Leading up to Stopping the Dragons

Over 170 Dragons are pounding at your gate! What are you doing to stop them? Are you going to pay to be protected? Who are you going to pay? How will you pay? How much are you willing to pay? Your taxes fund the local first responders. Your taxes fund our military complex. Is it working? Is there enough of our money to fund protecting us from international cyber-attacks? Many industries are impacted. The Defense Industrial Base, Healthcare, Utilities, Government (local, state, federal), Supply Chain, Communications, Transportation, and Education to name a few. One of the most important in my opinion is the Defense Industrial Base. The DIB is the foundation for all our safety. The DIB uses all of the industries earlier mentioned. Without the DIB our "leaders" and local First Responders, all industries, and possibly our military will be overwhelmed.

As mentioned earlier our Department of Defense depends on small contractors to create the technologies and weaponry needed to protect us and defeat our adversaries. Do these contractors understand and realize how important it is to practice not only good but the best cyber hygiene? The DFARS law was set up to ensure that contractors maintained proper cyber hygiene. Up until the Interim Rule (see below) DoD contractors self-attested to meeting the cybersecurity requirements in DFARS. The facts show that this was not the case.

Now there is a Department of Defense Interim Rule (the law), that all DoD contractors (up to 300,000) must legally abide by. How do you think they are doing? Analysis shows that approximately 70% of DoD contractors are not meeting the cyber standards dictated by law.

Some hacks that led up to the interim rule include: [1].

August 2020. Hackers for hire suspected of operating on behalf of the Iranian government were found to have been working to gain access to sensitive information held by North American and Israeli entities across a range of sectors, including technology, government, defense, and healthcare.

August 2020. U.S. officials announced that North Korean government hackers had been operating a campaign focused on stealing money from ATMs around the world.

August 2020. The Israeli defense ministry announced that it had successfully defended against a cyberattack on Israeli defense manufacturers launched by a suspected North Korean hacking group.

August 2020. An Iranian hacking group was found to be targeting major U.S. companies and government agencies by exploiting recently disclosed vulnerabilities in high-end network equipment to create backdoors for other groups to use.

August 2020. Seven semiconductor vendors in Taiwan were the victim of a two-year espionage campaign by suspected Chinese state hackers targeting firms' source code, software development kits, and chip designs.

June 2020. The most popular of the tax reporting software platforms China requires foreign companies to download to operate in the country was discovered to contain a backdoor that could allow malicious actors to conduct network reconnaissance or attempt to take remote control of company systems.

June 2020. Suspected North Korean hackers compromised at least two defense firms in Central Europe by sending false job offers to their employees while posing as representatives from major U.S. defense contractors.

May 2020. Businesses in Japan, Italy, Germany, and the UK that supply equipment and software to industrial firms were attacked in a targeted and highly sophisticated campaign by an unknown group of hackers.

May 2020. The NSA announced that Russian hackers associated with the GRU had been exploiting a bug that could allow them to take remote control of U.S. servers.

April 2020. U.S. officials reported seeing a surge of attacks by Chinese hackers against healthcare providers, pharmaceutical manufacturers, and the U.S. Department of Health and Human Services amidst the COVID-19 pandemic.

February 2020. The U.S. Department of Justice indicted two Chinese nationals for laundering cryptocurrency for North Korean hackers.

February 2020. The U.S. Defense Information Systems Agency announced it had suffered a data breach exposing the personal information of an unspecified number of individuals.

January 2020. An Iranian hacking group launched an attack on the U.S.-based research company Wesat as part of a suspected effort to gain access to the firm's clients in the public and private sectors.

January 2020. The FBI announced that nation-state hackers had breached the networks of two U.S. municipalities in 2019, exfiltrating user information and establishing backdoor access for future compromise.

April 2007. The Department of Commerce had to take the Bureau of Industrial Security's networks offline for several months because its networks were hacked by unknown foreign intruders. This Commerce Bureau reviews confidential information on high-tech exports.

2007. Chinese hackers breached the Pentagon's Joint Strike Fighter project and stole data related to the F-35 fighter jet. An Australian contractor was also hacked for F-35 data. China built the J-31 fighter jet which is a striking resemblance to the F-35.

December 2006. NASA was forced to block emails with attachments before shuttle launches out of fear they would be hacked. Business Week reported that the plans for the latest U.S. space launch vehicles were obtained by unknown foreign intruders.

November 2006. Hackers attempted to penetrate U.S. Naval War College networks, resulting in a two-week shutdown at one institution while infected machines are restored.

August 2006. A senior Air Force Officer stated publicly that, "China has downloaded 10 to 20 terabytes of data from the NIPRNet (the unclassified military network)."

May 2006. The Department of State's networks were hacked, and unknown foreign intruders downloaded terabytes of information. If Chinese or Russian spies had backed a truck up to the State Department, smashed the glass doors, tied up the guards, and spent the night carting off file cabinets, it would constitute an act of war. But when it happens in cyberspace, we barely notice.

April 2005. Chinese hackers infiltrated NASA networks managed by Lockheed Martin and Boeing and exfiltrated information about the Space Shuttle Discovery program.

2005. Chinese hackers infiltrated U.S. Department of Defense networks in an operation known as "Titan Rain." They targeted U.S. defense contractors, Army Information Systems Engineering Command; the Defense Information Systems Agency; the Naval Ocean Systems Center; and the U.S. Army Space and Strategic Defense installation.

2003. Chinese hackers exfiltrated national security information from Naval Air Weapons Station China Lake, including nuclear weapons test and design data, and stealth aircraft data.

2.2   Stopping the Dragons – More on the Interim Rule

What is and how effective is the Interim Rule? *We cannot survive by rules alone, they must be implemented. My comments are in italics.*

On September 29, 2020, the Defense Acquisitions Regulation System released a new Interim Rule to supplement current DFARS regulations.

The purpose of this Interim Rule is to increase DoD contractor security in existing DFARS 7012 requirements while the process of Cybersecurity Maturity Model Certification (CMMC) implementation is still in development. It will ensure that DFARS requirements are being followed by creating a DoD Assessment Methodology and Cybersecurity Maturity Model Certification framework.

While the Department of Defense is working to get the CMMC program completed in record time, the process is taking longer than anticipated, and CMMC is now slated to be rolled out over several years. But over the past few years, the current method of self-assessment used in DFARS standards has proved insufficient as the DoD supply chain continues to be subjected to cyber-attacks, leading to the necessity of more immediate improvements to security.

This rule enacts new requirements, such as a self-scoring methodology and reporting, as well as the announcement of increased audits at the three levels of Basic, Medium, and High levels of scrutiny.

Key Takeaways.
Although there are many takeaways from the new interim rule, we identified the following five items that we think will affect many contractors right away:

1. This new requirement takes effect on December 1, 2020, for all contractors that are subject to the DFARS 252.204-7012 clause based on their handling of Controlled

Unclassified Information (CUI). *Contractors are confused about what constitutes CUI.*

2. Contractors that handle CUI will need to complete a new NIST 800-171 Self-Assessment based on a new scoring methodology and then post their score in the Supplier Performance Risk System (SPRS) before a contract will be awarded. *Many who have submitted a score of 110 have not even prepared a Systems Security Plan (SSP). If they billed the government, they may be in breach of contract and subject to fines. This does not stop the dragons.*

3. The Self-Assessment must also include the completion of a System Security Plan (SSP) with a Plan of Action and Milestones (POAM) describing the current state of their systems, and their plan to achieve 100% compliance with the NIST 800-171 requirements along with supporting evidence such as written Policies and Procedures. *POAMs are non-existent in many submissions. Policies and procedures are inadequate and have not been adopted.*

4. Prime Contractors must flow this requirement down to their subcontractors/suppliers that handle CUI as well. *The BIG primes are starting to get more aggressive in what their subs are doing. Do they have the resources to assess their subs?*

5. The Defense Contract Management Agency (DCMA) will be conducting random audits to ensure companies have not only completed the self-assessment but have scored themselves accurately, have an SSP, and are working towards completing a realistic POAM. *There is not enough staff to do this! This is to be the role of the CMMC ecosystem... not available till 2023 and even then, not be enough assessors.*

New Interim Rule Self-assessment Scoring and Reporting.
DoD contractors who handle controlled unclassified information (CUI) may not be familiar with the NIST SP 800-171 security requirements, which require contractors to self-assess their cybersecurity preparedness. One Hundred and Ten (110) controls must be put into place that supports over three hundred (300) objectives.

The NIST SP 800-171 DoD Assessment Scoring Methodology detailed in the Interim Rule is supposed to help contractors grade themselves with a standardized score that reflects the NIST SP 800-171 security requirements they do not yet have in place. *Scores will range from negative 203 to positive 110. Many do not understand the 300 objectives that need to be achieved if you handle CUI.*

How NIST SP 800-171 DoD Assessment Methodology Scoring Works.

- The NIST SP 800-171 DoD Assessment Methodology enables DoD to strategically assess a contractor's implementation of NIST SP 800-171 on existing contracts which include DFARS clause 252.204-7012, 7019, and 7020, and to provide DoD components with visibility to the summary level scores of strategic assessments completed by DoD, thus providing an alternative to the contract-by-contract approach.
- The NIST SP 800-171 DoD Assessment consists of three levels of assessments. These three types of assessments reflect the depth of the assessment and the associated level of confidence in the assessment results. Those levels are Basic, Medium and, High.
- Assessment of contractors with contracts containing DFARS clause 252.204-7012 is anticipated to be once every three years unless other factors, such as program

criticality/risk or a security-relevant change, drive the need for a different assessment frequency.

SPRS Reporting.
To submit your basic assessment to SPRS, you must fill out:

- Your system security plan name, and latest updated date
- The CAGE code associated with the plan
- A brief description of the planned architecture
- The date the assessment was completed
- Your total score
- The date that a score of 110 will be achieved – over 300 objectives must be met

Increased Audits.
To ensure the legitimacy of reported results, increased, random audits will be conducted. These check-ups will evaluate companies' compliance with NIST and the accuracy of their self-assessment score posted on SPRS.

Contractors will receive one of three assessment levels—Basic, Medium, or High—depending on the depth of the assessment and the level to which the contractor has implemented the security measures outlined.

What the Interim Rule Means for DoD Contractors.
Get an Assessment Immediately.

Even if they had an assessment recently, they probably need to update that assessment to incorporate the new scoring methodology. And this needs to happen quickly, as starting December 1, 2020, this will be required for all contractors with a 252.204-7012 clause in their agreement. Whistleblowers are financially incentivized to notify the Federal government about contractors who have submitted false scores. *DFARS 252.204-7012 Isn't Going Away.*

DFARS 7012 was created three years ago to better protect the DoD supply chain. CMMC has become the new focus as companies prepare to meet the new standards, but the announcement of the Interim Rule emphasizes that the Cybersecurity Maturity Model Certification (CMMC) is building on the foundation of DFARS 7012 and acting as the enforcement mechanism for cybersecurity standards already in place.

Think of CMMC as a continuation of DFARS, and the Interim Rule as a procedure that helps bridge the gap between the two while CMMC is still being enacted. *CMMC is expected to be codified in the summer of 2023.*

2.3 Cyber Security Maturity Model Certification

We see that under NIST and the Interim Rule that DoD contractors must self-assess, submit their Supplier Performance Risk System (SPRS) Score, a Systems Security Plan (SSP), and a Plan of Action and Milestones to develop Policies and Procedures to address gaps and provide evidence that supports the implementation of the objects. As of this writing, the average score of those who submitted is a positive 66 (+66). *There is some doubt about the validity of this average.*

History showed that self-assessments could not be trusted. The result is an attempt to legalize (codify) this process by not only implementing the interim rule but establishing an independent entity to oversee and ensure that DoD contractors comply with the law. The Cybersecurity Maturity Model Certification ecosystem is intended to be that mechanism.

The Cyber AB is the official accreditation body of the Cybersecurity Maturity Model Certification (CMMC) Ecosystem and the sole authorized non-governmental partner of the U.S. Department of Defense in implementing and overseeing the CMMC conformance regime.

Founded in January 2020 as The CMMC Accreditation Body, Inc., The Cyber AB is a Maryland-based, nonprofit, 501(c)(3) tax-exempt organization. They exist to further the successful implementation of CMMC within the Defense Industrial Base to reduce digital risk to DoD's supply chains and contractor support infrastructure.

The Cyber AB does not receive any funding from the Department of Defense, nor any other governmental taxpayer resources. Their contract with DoD is a "no-cost" contract, and their primary sources of revenue are the application and renewal fees that they receive from participants within the CMMC Ecosystem.

In short, the primary mission of The Cyber AB is to authorize and accredit the CMMC Registered Practitioner Organizations, Registered Practitioners, and Third-Party Assessment Organizations (C3PAOs) that conduct CMMC Assessments of companies within the Defense Industrial Base (DIB). As CMMC is being brought into full operational status, however, their roles and responsibilities have been more expansive than just that.

Currently, Cyber AB also manages the professional certification and training aspects of the CMMC Ecosystem, working with partners to develop the curricula and examination protocols for CMMC Assessors and CMMC Instructors. This responsibility, however, will soon be "spun-out" from The Cyber AB as the Cybersecurity Assessor and Instructor Certification Organization (CAICO), which will become a separate legal entity.

The Cyber AB is operated by a full-time professional staff that is accountable to and overseen by, the organization's Board of Directors. Members of the Board serve in a voluntary, uncompensated capacity. The Cyber AB's support to CMMC is through a direct contract with the CMMC Program Management Officer (PMO) within the Department of Defense [6].

Accreditation.
Under the International Organization for Standardization (ISO) definition, accreditation is the "third-party attestation related to a conformity assessment body conveying formal demonstration of its competence to carry out specific conformity assessment tasks." In simpler terms, and specific to CMMC, accreditation is the formal standard and validation process to ensure that C3PAOs are qualified to conduct CMMC Assessments of DIB companies. There is a lot at stake for organizations seeking CMMC Certification- -first and foremost, the ability to bid and win Department of Defense procurement and acquisition contracts. It is imperative for the success of CMMC that every organization seeking CMMC certification be assessed impartially, accurately, and with consistency and integrity. The Department of Defense, in establishing the CMMC program, has imposed eligibility, authorization, and accreditation requirements for all C3PAOs. It is

the responsibility of Cyber AB to enforce these requirements and administer the requisite processes.

The process of accreditation is rigorous. It culminates with an assessment conducted by a team of experienced and qualified professionals to affirm the standards are satisfied. Once accreditation is achieved, it is in force for a set term and requires periodic renewal to ensure standards are maintained [7].

The Cyber AB is in the process of pursuing recognition as an international accreditation body that meets ISO/IEC requirements under the 17011 standards. Upon attaining that recognition, The Cyber AB will begin to accredit CMMC Third-Party Assessment Organizations under the ISO standards for conformity assessment bodies [8].

- The updated CMMC Rule has been submitted to OMB. It is expected to be an Interim Final Rule that is estimated to be released in March '23 and implemented in May of '23

  - We will have to see but so far, they have met their rule projections

- There will be some kind of CMMC implementation plan, but that is baked into the rule and has not been shared. It will *not be* a requirement for instant certification of companies in the DIB that are estimated to need a CMMC Cert by DoD

  - No matter what the plan, rapid certification of everyone cannot be executed with the number of assessors we have. As of this writing, there are 175 listed assessors. It is unclear though how many of those people are planning to work full-time as assessors once the C3PAO assessments start. Probably a significant percentage are not. For example, I run a company. I plan to do some assessments, but it is not going to be as a Certified Third Party Assessor (C3PAO) but as a Registered Practitioner (RP) helping contractors prepare for the official C3PAO. This will further lower the number of assessments per year that can reasonably be accomplished.

3 The Struggle to Secure the Nation

The character of war is changing. Our adversaries no longer have to engage the United States kinetically. They have shifted their strategy to engage our nation asymmetrically, exploiting the seams of our democracy, authorities, and even our morals. They can respond to a kinetic action non-kinetically and often in misattributed ways through blended operations that take place through the supply chain, cyber domain, and human elements.

Today, various parts of the Department of Defense (DoD) and the Intelligence Community (IC) are generally aware of cyber and supply chain threats, but intra- and inter-government actions and knowledge are not fully coordinated or shared. Few if any holistically consider the entire blended operations space from a counterintelligence perspective and act on it.

There is no consensus on roles, responsibilities, authorities, and accountability. Responsibilities concerning threat information are "siloed" in ways that frustrate and delay fully informed and decisive action, isolating decision makers and mission owners from timely warning and opportunity to act.

DoD must make better use of its existing resources to identify, protect, detect, respond to, and recover from network and supply chain threats. This will require organizational changes within the DoD, increased coordination, and more cooperation with the Department of Homeland Security and other civilian agencies.

It will also require improved relations with contractors, new standards and best practices, changes to acquisition strategy and practice, and initiatives that motivate contractors to see active risk mitigation as a "win." Risk-based security should be viewed as a profit center for the capture of new business rather than a "loss" or an expense harmful to the bottom line.

While DoD cannot control all the actions of its numerous information system and supply chain participants, it can lead by example and use its purchasing power and regulatory authority to move companies to work with DoD to enhance security by addressing the threat, vulnerabilities, and consequences of its capabilities and adapt to dynamic, constantly changing threats.

Improved cyber and supply chain security requires a combination of actions on the part of the Department and the companies with which it does business. Through the acquisition process, DoD can influence and shape the conduct of its suppliers. It can define requirements to incorporate new security measures, reward superior security measures in the source selection process, include contract terms that impose security obligations, and use contractual oversight to monitor contractor accomplishments. Of course, there are limitations on what DoD can accomplish. DoD is not so large a customer that it can control all parts of its supplier base.

DoD has the strongest influence over companies with which it contracts directly. Nonetheless, DoD spending is a principal source of business for thousands of companies. The Department can reward the achievement, demonstration, and sustainment of cyber and supply chain security [9].

3.1 Protecting Controlled Unclassified Information in Nonfederal Systems and Organizations

The protection of Controlled Unclassified Information (CUI) resident in nonfederal systems and organizations is of paramount importance to federal agencies and can directly impact the ability of the federal government to successfully conduct its essential missions and functions. There are recommended security requirements for protecting the confidentiality of CUI when the information is resident in nonfederal systems and organizations; when the nonfederal organization is not collecting or maintaining information on behalf of a federal agency or using or operating a system on behalf of an agency; and where there are no specific safeguarding requirements for protecting the confidentiality of CUI prescribed by the authorizing law, regulation, or governmentwide policy for the CUI category listed in the CUI Registry. The requirements apply to all components of nonfederal systems and organizations that process, store, and/or transmit CUI, or that protect such components. The security requirements are intended for use by federal agencies in contractual vehicles or other agreements established between those agencies and nonfederal organizations [10].

3.2 NIST Requirements

There are fourteen families of recommended security requirements for protecting the confidentiality of CUI in nonfederal systems and organizations. The security controls from [SP 800-53] are associated with the basic and derived requirements.

Organizations can use the NIST publication to obtain additional, nonprescriptive information related to the recommended security requirements (e.g., explanatory information in the discussion section for each of the referenced security controls, mapping tables to [ISO 27001] security controls, and a catalog of optional controls that can be used to specify additional security requirements, if needed). This information can help clarify or interpret the requirements in the context of mission and business requirements, operational environments, or assessments of risk.

Nonfederal organizations can implement a variety of potential security solutions either directly or using managed services, to satisfy the security requirements and may implement alternative, but equally effective, security measures to compensate for the inability to satisfy a requirement.

Nonfederal organizations describe, in a system security plan, how the security requirements are met or how organizations plan to meet the requirements and address known and anticipated threats. The system security plan (SSP) describes the system boundary; operational environment; how security requirements are implemented; and the relationships with or connections to other systems. Nonfederal organizations develop plans of action (POAMs) that describe how unimplemented security requirements will be met and how any planned mitigations will be implemented. Organizations can document the system security plan and the plan of action as separate or combined documents and in any chosen format. Additional supporting evidence such as policies and procedures, network drawings, and data governance is also required.

The recommended security requirements listed below are only applicable to a nonfederal system or organization when mandated by a federal agency in a contract, grant, or other agreement. The security requirements apply to the components of nonfederal systems that process, store, or transmit CUI, or that provide security protection for such components. For more detail on these requirements see NIST Special Publication 800-171 Revision 2 [10].

3.1 Access Control
3.2 Awareness and Training
3.3 Audit and Accountability
3.4 Configuration Management
3.5 Identification and Authentication
3.6 Incident Response
3.7 Maintenance
3.8 Media Protection
3.9 Personnel Security
3.10 Physical Protection
3.11 Risk Assessment
3.12 Security Assessment
3.13 Systems and Communications Protection

3.14 System and Information Integrity

A total of 320 objectives must be met to support a contractor's implementation of these controls. For example,

3.1 There are 22 objectives to be met under Access Control. Access Control includes some of the following objectives.

3.1.1[a]: authorized users are identified.

3.1.1[b]: processes acting on behalf of authorized users are identified.

3.1.1[c]: devices (and other systems) authorized to connect to the system are identified.

3.1.1[d]: system access is limited to authorized users.

3.1.1[e]: system access is limited to processes acting on behalf of authorized users.

3.1.1[f]: system access is limited to authorized devices (including other systems).

3.1.2[a]: the types of transactions and functions that authorized users are permitted to execute are defined
Up to:
3.1.22 [a,b,c,d]

3.3 CMMC 2.0 Requirements

CMMC 2.0 is currently under the rulemaking process. This rulemaking process is expected to be completed by the summer of 2023. The Cybersecurity Maturity Model Certification (CMMC) framework is the Department of Defense's (DoD) unifying standard for the implementation of cybersecurity measures within the Defense Industrial Base (DIB).

The CMMC Assessment Guides that are developed, maintained and published by DoD provide the objectives, specific criteria, and technical guidelines for assessing the conformance of DIB organizations seeking CMMC Certification to the applicable cybersecurity practices of the CMMC standard, which is grounded in the National Institute of Standards and Technology (NIST) Special Publication 800-171. These guides serve as the controlling technical authority to assess the implementation of CMMC practices. The CMMC-AB has drafted the CMMC Assessment Process (CAP) draft which is currently under review. They have identified four phases of the CAP process. They are:

- Phase 1: "Plan and Prepare the Assessment";
- Phase 2: "Conduct the Assessment";
- Phase 3: "Report Assessment Results"; and

- Phase 4: "Close-Out POA&Ms and Assessment" *(if necessary)*

For more detail on the CMMC CAP see CMMC Assessment Process (CAP) Version 1.0 Publication dated July 2022 [11].

4 How Can the Contractor Comply?

Contractors have a choice. One, they can elect not to comply. Two, lie and submit false statements that they are complying. Three start the compliance process (they should be at least here already). Four, elect not to participate in DoD contracts. We venture to say some contractors fall into one of these categories.

There are five functions in the Cybersecurity Framework that contractors must address. They are Identify, Protect, Detect, Respond, and Recover.

These five Functions were selected because they represent the five primary pillars of a successful and holistic cybersecurity program. They aid organizations in easily expressing their management of cybersecurity risk at a high level and enabling risk management decisions.

Identify

The Identify Function assists in developing an organizational understanding of managing cybersecurity risk to systems, people, assets, data, and capabilities. Understanding the business context, the resources that support critical functions, and the related cybersecurity risks enables an organization to focus and prioritize its efforts, consistent with its risk management strategy and business needs.

Examples of outcome Categories within this Function include:

- Identifying physical and software assets within the organization to establish the basis of an Asset Management program
- Identifying the Business Environment the organization supports including the organization's role in the supply chain and the organization's place in the critical infrastructure sector
- Identifying cybersecurity policies established within the organization to define the Governance program as well as identifying legal and regulatory requirements regarding the cybersecurity capabilities of the organization
- Identifying asset vulnerabilities, threats to internal and external organizational resources, and risk response activities as a basis for the organizations' Risk Assessment
- Identifying a Risk Management Strategy for the organization including establishing risk tolerances
- Identifying a Supply Chain Risk Management strategy including priorities, constraints, risk tolerances, and assumptions used to support risk decisions associated with managing supply chain risks

Protect

The Protect Function outlines appropriate safeguards to ensure the delivery of critical infrastructure services. The Protect Function supports the ability to limit or contain the impact of a potential cybersecurity event.

Examples of outcome Categories within this Function include:

- Protections for Identity Management and Access Control within the organization including physical and remote access
- Empowering staff within the organization through Awareness and Training including role-based and privileged user training
- Establishing Data Security protection consistent with the organization's risk strategy to protect the confidentiality, integrity, and availability of information
- Implementing Information Protection Processes and Procedures to maintain and manage the protection of information systems and assets
- Protecting organizational resources through Maintenance, including remote maintenance, activities
- Managing Protective Technology to ensure the security and resilience of systems and assets are consistent with organizational policies, procedures, and agreements

Detect

The Detect Function defines the appropriate activities to identify the occurrence of a cybersecurity event. The Detect Function enables the timely discovery of cybersecurity events.

Examples of outcome Categories within this Function include:

- Ensuring Anomalies and Events are detected, and their potential impact is understood
- Implementing Security Continuous Monitoring capabilities to monitor cybersecurity events and verify the effectiveness of protective measures including network and physical activities
- Maintaining Detection Processes to provide awareness of anomalous events

Respond

The Respond Function includes appropriate activities to take action regarding a detected cybersecurity incident. The Respond Function supports the ability to contain the impact of a potential cybersecurity incident.

Examples of outcome Categories within this Function include:

- Ensuring Response Planning processes are executed during and after an incident
- Managing Communications during and after an event with stakeholders, law enforcement, and external stakeholders as appropriate
- An analysis is conducted to ensure effective response and support recovery activities including forensic analysis, and determining the impact of incidents
- Mitigation activities are performed to prevent the expansion of an event and to resolve the incident
- The organization implements Improvements by incorporating lessons learned from current and previous detection/response activities

Recover

The Recover Function identifies appropriate activities to maintain plans for resilience and to restore any capabilities or services that were impaired due to a cybersecurity incident. The Recover Function supports timely recovery to normal operations to reduce the impact of a cybersecurity incident.

Examples of outcome Categories within this Function include:

- Ensuring the organization implements Recovery Planning processes and procedures to restore systems and/or assets affected by cybersecurity incidents
- Implementing Improvements based on lessons learned and reviews of existing strategies
- Internal and external Communications are coordinated during and following the recovery from a cybersecurity incident

5 Epilogue/Conclusion

Cyber attacks are real and continue. It is up to the government, individuals, and organizations to protect people, places, and things. We documented what the American government expects from its Defense Industrial Base. We detailed what needs to be done and we provided insight on how to meet these requirements. Not only do defense contractors have to meet these requirements, but it should also be ingrained in all that we as nations do.

Acknowledgments. Thanks to Kapu Technologies, High Tech Hui, our clients, and other business partners who continue to guide and support us through this compliance journey.

References

1. CfSI Studies. "CSIS" (2022). https://www.csis.org/programs/strategic-technologies-program/significant-cyber-incidents
2. Suciu, P.: https://news.clearancejobs.com/2022/10/17/the-not-so-secret-cyber-war-5-nations-conducting-the-most-cyberattacks/
3. Various. "Wikipedia". https://en.wikipedia.org/wiki/2020_United_States_federal_government_data_breach
4. "Wikipedia". https://en.wikipedia.org/wiki/Colonial_Pipeline_ransomware_attack
5. "Wikipedia". https://en.wikipedia.org/wiki/Stuxnet
6. Cyber-AB. https://cyberab.org/About-Us/Overview
7. Cyber-AB. https://cyberab.org/Accreditation/General-Accreditation
8. Cyber-AB. https://cyberab.org/Accreditation/ISO-IEC-17011
9. Nissen, C., Gronager, J., Metzger, R., Rishikof, H.: "Deliver Uncompromised". https://www.mitre.org/sites/default/files/2021-11/prs-18-2417-deliver-uncompromised-MITRE-study-26AUG2019.pdf
10. Ross, R., Pillitteri, V., Dempsey, K., Riddle, M., Guissanie, G.: https://nvlpubs.nist.gov/nistpubs/SpecialPublications/NIST.SP.800-171r2.pdf
11. CMMC-AB. "CMMC Assessment Process (CAP)" (2022)
12. PreVeil. https://www.preveil.com/resources/zero-trust-a-better-way-to-enhance-cybersecurity-and-achieve-compliance/

Behavioral Biometrics Authentication in Critical Infrastructure Using Siamese Neural Networks

Arnoldas Budžys$^{(\boxtimes)}$ [ID], Olga Kurasova[ID], and Viktor Medvedev[ID]

Institute of Data Science and Digital Technologies, Vilnius University,
Akademijos str. 4, 08412 Vilnius, Lithuania
arnoldas.budzys@ieee.org

Abstract. Cybersecurity is a crucial issue in today's critical infrastructure to ensure a secure connection between the administrator and the session. Detecting insiders is a difficult task for cybersecurity professionals, as insiders are hard to detect and identify and thus require advanced techniques to prevent their activities. These users may be current or former employees with access to the organization's data. A methodology for authenticating users of critical infrastructure systems using deep learning networks is proposed in this paper. Behavioral biometric data or user behavioral characteristics are converted into an image and used in the proposed methodology for authentication. The keystroke data obtained from the login password is transformed into a more acceptable format for deep neural networks. Siamese neural networks can be used for image similarity detection to distinguish a real user from an insider. In the current investigation, numerical keystroke data has been transformed into graphical representations. The transformed data are then subjected to comparative analysis, leading to the determination of similarities between the biometric keystroke profiles. The experiments have shown there is a tendency for the accuracy of a Siamese neural network with a triplet loss function to decrease with increasing margin size. The results obtained are promising, showing that using a deep learning-based approach to analyze images derived from user keystroke data can improve intrusion detection accuracy and perform user authentication more efficiently.

Keywords: Cybersecurity · Keystroke biometrics · User authentication · Siamese neural network · Non-image to image · Triplet loss function

1 Introduction

Securing critical infrastructures from cyber threats, such as data breaches, cyber-attacks, and unauthorized access to confidential information, is crucial for critical infrastructures and businesses. These types of threats can result in severe repercussions for companies, including financial losses, harm to reputation, and loss of customer trust. In critical infrastructure systems, the use of cameras is

© The Author(s), under exclusive license to Springer Nature Switzerland AG 2023
A. Moallem (Ed.): HCII 2023, LNCS 14045, pp. 309–322, 2023.
https://doi.org/10.1007/978-3-031-35822-7_21

not permitted, and when working with command line-based software, system administrators frequently use keyboard commands instead of a mouse. The Federal Bureau of Investigation's Internet Crime Report estimates that in 2021, the potential losses from cybercrime in the US reached 6.9 billion dollars [10].

Traditionally, authentication methods for computer users and IT professionals have included passwords, smart cards, and fingerprint scanning. However, keystroke dynamics is a newer development in authentication technology. It is becoming a leading contender for the next generation of authentication tools on the market, which means we now need to add another category, "what you do" (signature, voice, keyboard biometrics) to the existing types of authentication methods, "what you know" (passwords, hints, questions) and "what you have" (smart cards, PIN generator) and "who you are" (facial recognition, fingerprints).

The shortcomings of traditional authentication methods are well known. In the case of passwords, it comes with problematic issues. They are easy to overlook and can often be compromised, especially with recent improvements in hacking tools and processor performance. Finally, passwords and passphrases are certainly vulnerable to social engineering attacks.

The use of biometric solutions such as fingerprint scanners, voice authentication, and iris recognition has become popular for providing a high level of security. However, implementing these solutions can require the installation of new and potentially expensive hardware, and in some cases, someone may be able to force a person to authenticate to the system. As new cybersecurity threats emerge, scientists are searching for new methods of authenticating user access to digital resources that are less intrusive and more convenient. One such method is keystroke dynamics, which analyzes a user's keystroke patterns using behavioral biometrics to identify them. This technology dates back to the 19th century when telegraph operators were able to identify who was on the other end of the line based on their typing style [11]. It is important to note that new and better ways to authenticate user access to digital resources are being looked into, especially when it comes to preventing illegal actions of an insider who pretend to be employees or partners and use other people's credentials to leak the company information, causing financial loss to the company.

Keyboard behavior biometrics are divided into two categories: static authentication (SA) and dynamic authentication, also known as continuous authentication (CA). The static authentication method requires the user to enter a password or passphrase only once. On the other hand, continuous authentication focuses on monitoring the user throughout the entire session. This method involves collecting data in real-time, analyzing it, and creating a profile of the user based on their behavioral characteristics during the session [17].

The study in question will not examine various machine learning methods utilized for static authentication as reported in previous studies (see [15,20,25]), but will concentrate on deep learning techniques that are based on fixed-text keystroke features.

The aim of this research is to develop a methodology for authenticating critical infrastructure system administrators on their biometric behavioral data leveraging the deep learning-based Siamese neural network. For this purpose, a Siamese neural network with branches of Convolutional neural networks is used to enhance the accuracy of the user's static authentication. Considering the specificities of Convolutional neural networks, the study focuses on identifying users based on the image representation of their keyboard inputs through a non-image to image method.

The paper is organized as follows. Section 2 summarises related works on fixed-text keystroke dynamics for user authentication. Section 3 describes the proposed methodology. Section 4 presents the experimental setup and discusses the results obtained. Finally, Sect. 5 concludes the paper and discusses future work.

2 Related Works

Keystroke biometrics is a method of identifying and authenticating individuals based on their unique typing patterns and habits [6]. This can include factors such as typing speed, rhythm, and the amount of pressure applied to keys. Keystroke biometrics can be used as an additional security measure in combination with traditional authentication methods such as passwords or fingerprints. It is non-intrusive, cost-effective, and can be used in a variety of settings, such as computer systems, mobile devices, and ATMs. However, it can be affected by certain factors, such as physical impairments or the use of typing aids, and some users may be able to mimic others' typing patterns.

Keystroke biometrics can be classified into two groups: those that require a fixed sequence of keystrokes, such as a username or password, and those that allow for any sequence of keystrokes, such as writing an email or transcribing a sentence with mistakes. Research on these types of biometric authentication algorithms, which are based on keystroke dynamics for desktop and laptop keyboards, has mostly focused on fixed-text scenarios, where accuracy rates of over 95% are often achieved [23]. Researchers have demonstrated that the most successful outcomes in fixed-text scenarios are produced by Dynamic Time Warping [23], Manhattan distance [22], and statistical models (e.g., Hidden Markov Models [1]). These methods involve comparing the timing of keystrokes between different samples, such as those from a user's training session and their actual authentication attempt, to determine if the person typing is the same.

Static keystroke dynamics focuses on confirming the identity of a person by analyzing their typing technique when entering a pre-determined password. These data are collected by recording the keystrokes of an individual during a typing task, such as typing a password or a passage of text. The data are then used to create a unique "keystroke profile" for the individual, which can be used for authentication and identification purposes. Among the publicly available databases that can be used for this purpose (see [12, 15, 18]), the Carnegie Melon University (CMU) dataset [15] has been extensively examined due to its large number of samples per person. The creators of the dataset evaluated the basic performance of the system and found that the average Equal Error Rate (EER) across all individuals was 9.6%. EER is a commonly used evaluation metric that represents the balance between the False Rejection of legitimate samples and the False Acceptance of imposter samples.

Many researchers in their studies have also used this dataset (see [15]) and have achieved better results than the baseline. However, it should be noted that these studies used different experimental methods, which may not be directly comparable. The current research focuses on methods that are based on neural networks. DeepSecure [19] achieved an EER of 3% by using a 4-layer Multi-Layers Perceptron (MLP) that was trained separately for each user. The model was trained using 200 legitimate samples and 5 imposter samples from each other individual. In another study, a single multi-class Convolutional neural network (CNN) model was trained with a specialized data augmentation technique and using 80% of the samples, resulting in an EER of 2.3% [5].

Furthermore, Siamese neural networks (SNN) [27] have been effectively used with other forms of biometric identification. Siamese neural networks are a specific type of neural network architecture that consists of two or more identical sub-networks or branches, which share the same parameters and are trained together. These branches process different inputs but are optimized to produce similar or correlated outputs. The main idea behind SNN is to learn a similarity or distance metric between the inputs by comparing the output representations of the branches. SNN firstly used a contrastive loss function during training [13], which encourages the network to produce similar representations for similar inputs and dissimilar representations for dissimilar inputs. This helps the network to learn a robust similarity metric between the inputs. In recent years, researchers introduced the use of SNN for intrusion detection systems (see [2,14,24]). More specifically, Siamese networks are examined in [2] to address the problem of class imbalance in network intrusion detection systems. Both studies address the multi-class classification task by combining attack classification with intrusion detection. The method of FaceNet [28] uses a triplet loss function for a Convolutional neural networks. It aims to preserve the difference between each pair of faces belonging to one person and all other faces. The triplet loss function [28] is a type of loss function that is commonly used in training Siamese neural networks to produce similar representations for similar inputs, and dissimilar representations for dissimilar inputs. Triplets consisting of an anchor, positive and negative images are needed to train the network. The comparison is performed in latent space.

SNNs are used for image recognition tasks because of their ability to learn a robust similarity metric, perform one-shot learning [16], generalize well to new unseen data, and handle variations in the input images. Time series data are directly fed into CNN, which only takes into account one-dimensional information. The authors of [9] utilize image encoding techniques to convert the data into a two-dimensional format in the first layer, resulting in improved accuracy. Therefore, the keystroke biometrics pattern can be transformed into images by well-known methods such as Markov Transition Field (MTF), Gramian Angular Summation Field (GASF), Gramian Angular Difference Field (GADF) or Recurrence Plot (RP) [7]. Convolutional neural networks have been proven to perform well on image-based tasks, such as image classification, object detection, and segmentation. The transformation of numerical data into images is necessary to enable CNN to extract and learn features from the visual representation of data, leveraging its ability to identify patterns and perform mathematical operations on them. This can result in improved performance compared to using only textual or numerical data, as CNN can extract higher-level representations from the image representation of the text.

3   Methodology

Our suggestion is to incorporate the use of Siamese neural networks in combination with Convolutional neural networks for time series (biometric keystroke profile) transformed into image formats. When SNN and CNN are combined, the SNN can be used to learn a similarity or distance metric between images, while the CNN is used to extract features from the images. This allows the network to effectively compare and recognize patterns in images, making it well-suited for password authentication tasks.

In the context of password authentication, the passwords can be transformed into images by well-known methods (see Sect. 2). By utilizing the triplet loss function, triplets are created and fed into Siamese neural networks. The triplets are composed of an anchor example, a positive example, and a negative example. The anchor represents the input sample, and the positive and negative examples are chosen such that they belong to the same and different users, respectively. The goal is to learn a feature representation such that the distance between the anchor and the positive example is minimized, and the distance between the anchor and the negative example is maximized. The triplet loss function is a commonly used loss function in deep learning, particularly in the field of face recognition and speaker verification. The aim of triplet loss is to learn a mapping that reduces the variance between the anchor and positive images while increasing the variance between the anchor and negative images, based on a specified margin. The margin is a hyper-parameter that determines the minimum distance between anchor and positive examples and anchor and negative examples in the embedding space. This helps the model develop a feature representation that effectively separates different classes, making it ideal for user identification tasks like password verification. The comparison of the distance between two passwords transformed into images determines if they belong to the same person.

3.1   Data Preparation

This paper focuses on the CMU dataset [15], which includes 51 individuals who typed the password "tie5Roanl" 400 times, generated by a publicly available password generator, during 8 collection sessions. Each input is represented by a 31-dimensional vector that contains keydown-keydown times, keyup-keydown times, and hold times for all keys in the password.

It is well established that everyone has their own unique typing patterns. By analyzing these patterns, it is possible to create a biometric profile of an individual that is unique to them, much like a fingerprint. Using multidimensional data reduction methods [4, 8, 21], it is possible to represent the typing behavior of all 51 users in a visual format (see Fig. 1). This visualization using the t-SNE method shows that each person has a unique typing pattern, which is evident from the distinct clusters in Fig. 1. This confirms that every one of us is unique in the way we type on the keyboard. The t-SNE method allows for the high-dimensional data of the keystroke dynamics to be reduced to a 2D space, making it easier to visualize and observe the uniqueness of each user's typing pattern.

Fig. 1. Visualizing users' data using t-SNE (CMU dataset).

To train an SNN, the data, in our case images, must be properly prepared. For this purpose, data are converted into images using GADF (see Sect. 2) for several reasons (see [26, 29, 30]):

– The GADF method captures the time-dependent dynamics of the time series by using the angular information of the phase space trajectory. This results in improved robustness against noise and other variations in the time series data.

- GADF is able to extract both linear and non-linear features from the time series, making it more versatile than other non-image to image methods.
- GADF is able to produce a 2D representation of the time series, which allows the use of CNN and other image-based models for further processing and analysis. This can improve the overall performance of the system.
- GADF is not affected by the length of the time series, this means that it can be applied to time series of different lengths without any change in the final representation.

The process of creating a GADF image is illustrated in Fig. 2. The time-series (non-image data) is an input for the GADF method (see Fig. 2(a)), which is then transformed into a polar coordinate (see Fig. 2(b)). Finally, the GADF image is calculated to obtain the final image representation of the time-series data (see Fig. 2(c)). For more detail, see [29].

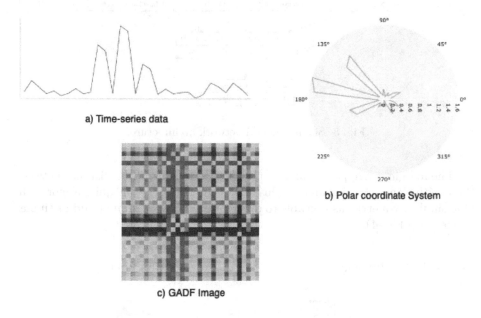

a) Time-series data

b) Polar coordinate System

c) GADF Image

Fig. 2. Conversion of time-series data into the GADF method representation.

3.2 Siamese Neural Network Architecture

Siamese neural networks are an effective solution for image recognition tasks, this is due to their capability to learn a strong similarity metric between inputs. This study uses the Euclidean distance as a similarity metric, but other metrics may also be used (see [3]). SNNs are designed to evaluate the similarity or dissimilarity between two images by encoding them into a feature space using a shared neural network and then comparing the encodings.

In order to measure the similarity, the proposed methodology employs a Siamese neural network architecture based on a triplet loss function. The structure comprises three identical branches that share weights and parameters. Each branch of the architecture includes a Convolutional neural network consisting of a series of convolutional layers, rectified linear units (ReLU), batch normalization and other parameters. During the training process, triplets consisting of anchor (A), positive (P), and negative (N) images are input into the branches (see Fig. 3). The network is trained to minimize the dissimilarity between the anchor image and the positive image, and to maximize the dissimilarity between the anchor image and the negative image. This is typically done by using a contrastive loss function or a triplet loss function, which compares the anchor, positive and negative images, and enforces a margin between them.

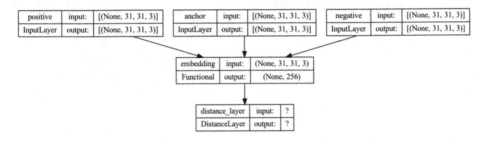

Fig. 3. Siamese neural network architecture.

The margin is a hyper-parameter that is used to control the distance between the positive and negative image. This allows the network to acquire a more reliable similarity metric, as it is able to differentiate between similar and dissimilar images (see Fig. 4).

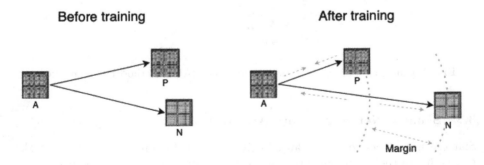

Fig. 4. An example of a triplet before and after SNN training.

This SNN input consists of triplets of anchor, positive and negative images. These images are fed into the network and processed by three convolutional layers at the top of the SNN. The parameters of the neural network are shown in Table 1. These layers take the output of the previous layer as input. After every convolutional layer, batch normalization and max pooling are applied. This is followed by a flatten layer, whose output is the input to a dense layer. The final layer of the network was designed with 256 outputs. A high number of outputs in the dense layer allows the network to learn more fine-grained distinctions between the anchor, positive, and negative images. The network has a total of 172,224 parameters and is 12 layers deep.

Table 1. Convolutional neural network branches parameters for triplet network

Parameters	Options
Convolutional layers	3
Kernel number	64
Kernel size	6, 4, 2
MaxPooling filter size	5, 1, 1
Dense	256
Output activation function	ReLu, Sigmoid

After the dense layer, we used the Lambda function to normalize the input tensor (output from the dense layer) by applying the l2_normalize function along the specified axis. This helped in achieving a stable and optimal feature representation of the input pairs.

4   Experiments

In order to create triplets for training the Siamese neural network, the dataset of converted images from the typed passwords of each user was split into two groups. The first 200 typed passwords of each user were considered as positive examples, and the next 200 were considered as anchor examples. This was done because it was assumed that after the first 200 tries, the users had already learned how to type the password, and their typing behavior would be more consistent. By using the last 200 typed passwords as anchor examples, the network would be able to learn more robust and generalizable representations of the users' typing behavior. This strategy of selecting the positive and anchor examples can be useful for training the network to recognize the typing behavior of users even if they are not perfectly consistent in their typing. When building triplets for training the network, the anchor and positive images were taken from the same user, and the negative sample was chosen randomly from a different user. During the training process, 70% of the created triplets were utilized; the other 30% were set aside for validation purposes.

While training a Siamese neural network, enlarging the margin size can impact the Euclidean distance between the anchor and positive images and the anchor and negative images. Nevertheless, a larger margin provides the network with more room to distinguish between positive and negative images relative to the anchor, which can result in improved accuracy. Increasing the margin makes it easier for the network to differentiate between image samples, but it also means that the network has to learn fewer subtle differences, potentially leading to decreased accuracy. Accuracy in this context refers to the ability of the Siamese neural network to correctly predict the outcome of the validation data. It measures the proportion of correct predictions made by the model and provides an indication of how well the network is able to distinguish between positive and negative images. It is determined by dividing the number of correct predictions made by the model by the total number of predictions.

The choice of the optimal margin is therefore a balance between the dissimilarity of the negative and anchor images and the similarity of the positive and anchor images, and the accuracy of the network. Experimentation may be necessary to find the optimal margin value for a given dataset and task.

Increasing the margin size increases the difference between the Euclidean distance of the negative and anchor images and the Euclidean distance of the positive and anchor images, so the network would be more stringent in determining the relationship between the inputs. Thus, the network's ability to accurately recognize the connections between inputs may be hindered, resulting in a decrease in its accuracy. We experimented with different margin sizes and activation functions for the dense layer, such as ReLu and Sigmoid, in order to determine which combination results in larger distances between negative and anchor images and positive and anchor images and higher accuracy based on the margin value. Accuracy dependencies on margin size and activation functions are shown in Fig. 5. Figure 5(a) presents dependencies between the margin size, accuracy and Euclidean distance among Anchor and Positive (AP_ED) and among Anchor and Negative (AN_ED) when the ReLU activation function is set in the dense layer. Figure 5(b) shows the dependencies between the margin size, accuracy and Euclidean distance among Anchor and Positive (AP_ED) and among Anchor and Negative (AN_ED), when the Sigmoid activation function is set in the dense layer.

The analysis of the data reveals that as the margin size increases, the Euclidean distances between the vectors expand, however, the accuracy, which is contingent upon the margin, decreases. Using the ReLU activation function in combination with L2 normalization in the dense layer can lead to higher accuracy on the CMU dataset. However, the optimal parameters may vary depending on the dataset and the problem being solved. In this specific dataset, the best results in terms of accurately predicting positive and negative images with respect to the anchor were achieved when the margin was set between 0.1 and 0.5, resulting in an accuracy of approximately 92% (see Fig. 5). The accuracy of the network in distinguishing between positive and negative images with respect to the anchor image ranges from 93.3% to 91.5%, depending on the margin size, which is set between 0.1 to 0.5. However, this may not always be the case, and other factors, such as the specific dataset and problem, play a role in determining the optimal model architecture. The example of triplets shown in Fig. 6 involves comparing typed passwords of the same user (positive and anchor) to a typed password of a different user (negative) using the optimal margin value in the triplet loss function.

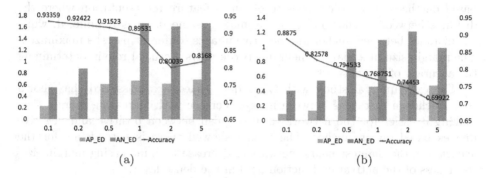

(a)   (b)

Fig. 5. The dependencies of accuracy and Euclidean distance on margin size using different activation functions in the dense layer: (a) ReLU, (b) Sigmoid.

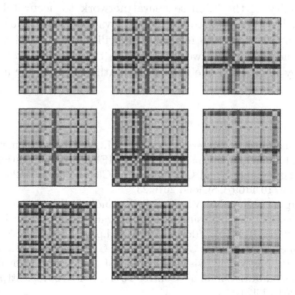

Fig. 6. Triplets: positive (left), anchor (center), negative (right).

5   Discussion and Conclusions

This paper proposes a deep learning-based methodology to authenticate users of critical infrastructure systems. The approach involves transforming behavioral keystroke biometric data into an image format for use in static authentication.

The keystroke data of the login password is transformed into a visual representation that is more suitable for the use as input to Convolutional neural networks. Using Siamese neural networks to determine the similarity of images, it is possible to distinguish the real user from the insider. The methodology involves using a triplet loss function to generate triplets and training Siamese neural networks based on them. The objective is to obtain a feature representation where the distance between anchor and positive images (same user) is minimized, while the distance between anchor and negative images (different users)is maximized. The margin size in a Siamese neural network plays a crucial role in determining the accuracy of the network.

The experimental study with CMU data (fixed-text password) has shown that Euclidean distances between images increase with increasing margin size, making it easier for the network to distinguish between positive and negative images based on an anchor. The results showed there is a tendency for the accuracy of the Siamese neural network to decrease with increasing margin size, regardless of the activation function used in the dense layer.

The results are promising, showing that using a deep learning-based approach to analyze images obtained from user keystroke data can improve intrusion detection accuracy and perform user authentication more efficiently. In order to enhance the ability of the Siamese neural network to accurately identify the legitimate user, it is essential to thoroughly evaluate the various methods for converting non-image data into images. This will allow extending the functionality of the Siamese neural network to address this specific problem in critical infrastructure by identifying the insider and authenticating the user.

References

1. Ali, M.L., Thakur, K., Tappert, C.C., Qiu, M.: Keystroke biometric user verification using hidden Markov model. In: 2016 IEEE 3rd International Conference on Cyber Security and Cloud Computing (CSCloud), pp. 204–209. IEEE (2016). https://doi.org/10.1109/CSCloud.2016.23
2. Bedi, P., Gupta, N., Jindal, V.: Siam-IDS: handling class imbalance problem in intrusion detection systems using Siamese neural network. Procedia Comput. Sci. **171**, 780–789 (2020). https://doi.org/10.1016/j.procs.2020.04.085
3. Bernataviciene, J., Dzemyda, G., Bazilevicius, G., Medvedev, V., Marcinkevicius, V., Treigys, P.: Method for visual detection of similarities in medical streaming data. Int. J. Comput. Commun. Control **10**(1), 8–21 (2015). https://doi.org/10.15837/ijccc.2015.1.1310
4. Bernataviciene, J., Dzemyda, G., Kurasova, O., Marcinkevicius, V., Medvedev, V.: The problem of visual analysis of multidimensional medical data. In: Torn, A., Zilinskas, J. (eds.) Models and algorithms for global optimization, Springer Series in Optimization and Its Applications, vol. 4, pp. 277–298. Springer, Boston, MA (2007). https://doi.org/10.1007/978-0-387-36721-7_17
5. Çeker, H., Upadhyaya, S.: Sensitivity analysis in keystroke dynamics using convolutional neural networks. In: 2017 IEEE Workshop on Information Forensics and Security (WIFS), pp. 1–6. IEEE (2017). https://doi.org/10.1109/WIFS.2017.8267667

6. Chen, J., et al.: Personalized keystroke dynamics for self-powered human-machine interfacing. ACS Nano **9**(1), 105–116 (2015). https://doi.org/10.1021/nn506832w
7. Dias, D., Dias, U., Menini, N., Lamparelli, R., Le Maire, G., Torres, R.D.S.: Image-based time series representations for pixelwise eucalyptus region classification: a comparative study. IEEE Geosci. Remote Sens. Lett. **17**(8), 1450–1454 (2019). https://doi.org/10.1109/LGRS.2019.2946951
8. Dzemyda, G., Sabaliauskas, M., Medvedev, V.: Geometric MDS performance for large data dimensionality reduction and visualization. Informatica **33**(2), 299–320 (2022). https://doi.org/10.15388/22-INFOR491
9. Estebsari, A., Rajabi, R.: Single residential load forecasting using deep learning and image encoding techniques. Electronics **9**(1), 68 (2020). https://doi.org/10.3390/electronics9010068
10. Federal Bureau of Investigation: Internet crime report 2021 (2022). https://www.ic3.gov/Media/PDF/AnnualReport/2021_IC3Report.pdf
11. Giancardo, L., Sánchez-Ferro, A., Butterworth, I., Mendoza, C., Hooker, J.M.: Psychomotor impairment detection via finger interactions with a computer keyboard during natural typing. Sci. Rep. **5**(1), 1–8 (2015). https://doi.org/10.1038/srep09678
12. Giot, R., El-Abed, M., Rosenberger, C.: Greyc keystroke: a benchmark for keystroke dynamics biometric systems. In: 2009 IEEE 3rd International Conference on Biometrics: Theory, Applications, and Systems, pp. 1–6. IEEE (2009). https://doi.org/10.1109/BTAS.2009.5339051
13. Hadsell, R., Chopra, S., LeCun, Y.: Dimensionality reduction by learning an invariant mapping. In: 2006 IEEE Computer Society Conference on Computer Vision and Pattern Recognition (CVPR'06), vol. 2, pp. 1735–1742. IEEE (2006). https://doi.org/10.1109/CVPR.2006.100
14. Jmila, H., Ibn Khedher, M., Blanc, G., El Yacoubi, M.A.: Siamese network based feature learning for improved intrusion detection. In: Gedeon, T., Wong, K.W., Lee, M. (eds.) ICONIP 2019. LNCS, vol. 11953, pp. 377–389. Springer, Cham (2019). https://doi.org/10.1007/978-3-030-36708-4_31
15. Killourhy, K.S., Maxion, R.A.: Comparing anomaly-detection algorithms for keystroke dynamics. In: 2009 IEEE/IFIP International Conference on Dependable Systems & Networks, pp. 125–134. IEEE (2009). https://doi.org/10.1109/DSN.2009.5270346
16. Koch, G., Zemel, R., Salakhutdinov, R., et al.: Siamese neural networks for one-shot image recognition. In: ICML Deep Learning Workshop, vol. 2. Lille (2015)
17. Krishnamoorthy, S., Rueda, L., Saad, S., Elmiligi, H.: Identification of user behavioral biometrics for authentication using keystroke dynamics and machine learning. In: Proceedings of the 2018 2nd International Conference on Biometric Engineering and Applications, pp. 50–57 (2018). https://doi.org/10.1145/3230820.3230829
18. Li, Y., Zhang, B., Cao, Y., Zhao, S., Gao, Y., Liu, J.: Study on the BeiHang keystroke dynamics database. In: 2011 International Joint Conference on Biometrics (IJCB), pp. 1–5. IEEE (2011). https://doi.org/10.1109/IJCB.2011.6117485
19. Maheshwary, S., Ganguly, S., Pudi, V.: Deep secure: a fast and simple neural network based approach for user authentication and identification via keystroke dynamics. In: IWAISe: First International Workshop on Artificial Intelligence in Security, vol. 59 (2017)
20. de Marcos, L., Martínez-Herráiz, J.J., Junquera-Sánchez, J., Cilleruelo, C., Pages-Arévalo, C.: Comparing machine learning classifiers for continuous authentication on mobile devices by keystroke dynamics. Electronics **10**(14), 1622 (2021). https://doi.org/10.3390/electronics10141622

21. Medvedev, V., Dzemyda, G.: Optimization of the local search in the training for SAMANN neural network. J. Glob. Optim. **35**(4), 607–623 (2006). https://doi.org/10.1007/s10898-005-5368-1
22. Monaco, J.V.: Robust keystroke biometric anomaly detection. arXiv preprint arXiv:1606.09075 (2016). 10.48550/arXiv.1606.09075
23. Morales, A., et al.: Keystroke biometrics ongoing competition. IEEE Access **4**, 7736–7746 (2016). https://doi.org/10.1109/ACCESS.2016.2626718
24. Moustakldls, 3., Papandilanos, N.I., Chilstodolou, E., Papageorglou, E., Tsaopoulos, D.: Dense neural networks in knee osteoarthritis classification: a study on accuracy and fairness. Neural Comput. Appl. 1–13 (2020). https://doi.org/10.1007/s00521-020-05459-5
25. Muliono, Y., Ham, H., Darmawan, D.: Keystroke dynamic classification using machine learning for password authorization. Procedia Comput. Sci. **135**, 564–569 (2018). https://doi.org/10.1016/j.procs.2018.08.209
26. Oh, S., Oh, S., Um, T.W., Kim, J., Jung, Y.A.: Methods of pre-clustering and generating time series images for detecting anomalies in electric power usage data. Electronics **11**(20), 3315 (2022). https://doi.org/10.3390/electronics11203315
27. Oh Song, H., Xiang, Y., Jegelka, S., Savarese, S.: Deep metric learning via lifted structured feature embedding. In: Proceedings of the IEEE Conference on Computer Vision and Pattern Recognition, pp. 4004–4012 (2016). https://doi.org/10.1109/CVPR.2016.434
28. Schroff, F., Kalenichenko, D., Philbin, J.: FaceNet: a unified embedding for face recognition and clustering. In: Proceedings of the IEEE Conference on Computer Vision and Pattern Recognition, pp. 815–823 (2015). https://doi.org/10.1109/CVPR.2015.7298682
29. Wang, Z., Oates, T.: Imaging time-series to improve classification and imputation. In: Twenty-Fourth International Joint Conference on Artificial Intelligence (2015)
30. Yang, C.L., Yang, C.Y., Chen, Z.X., Lo, N.W.: Multivariate time series data transformation for convolutional neural network. In: 2019 IEEE/SICE International Symposium on System Integration (SII), pp. 188–192. IEEE (2019). https://doi.org/10.1109/SII.2019.8700425

Trust and Blame in Self-driving Cars Following a Successful Cyber Attack

Victoria Marcinkiewicz[1] and Phillip L. Morgan[1,2(✉)]

[1] Centre for AI, Robotics and Human-Machine Systems (IROHMS), Human Factors Excellence Research Group (HuFEx), School of Psychology, Cardiff University, Cardiff, UK
{marcinkiewiczv,morganphil}@cardiff.ac.uk
[2] Division of Health, Medicine and Rehabilitation, Luleå University of Technology, Luleå, Sweden

Abstract. Even as our ability to counter cyber attacks improves, it is inevitable that threat actors may compromise a system through either exploited vulnerabilities and/or user error. Aside from material losses, cyber attacks also undermine trust. Self-Driving Cars (SDCs) are expected to revolutionize the automotive industry and high levels of human trust in such safety-critical systems is crucial if they are to succeed. Should adverse experiences occur, SDCs will be particularly vulnerable to the loss of trust. This paper presents findings from an initial experiment which is part of an ongoing study exploring how fully autonomous Level 5 SDCs would be blamed and trusted in the event of a cyber attack. To do this a future thinking-based methodology was used. Participants were presented with a series of randomly ordered hypothetical news headlines about SDC-cyber incidents. After reading each headline, they were required to rate their trust and assign blame. Twenty different hypothetical SDC-cyber incidents were created and manipulated between participants through the use of cyber security specific terminology (e.g. hackers) and non-specific cyber security terminology. This was manipulated to investigate whether the wording – i.e. being explicitly or overtly cyber (versus non explicitly or covert) of a reported incident affected trust and blame. Overall trust ratings in SDC technology in the context of a cyber incident were low across both conditions which has the potential to impact uptake and adoption. Whilst there was no significant overall difference in trust between the overtly and covertly cyber conditions, indications for further lines of inquiry were evident – including differences between some of the scenarios. In terms of blame, attribution was varied and context dependent but across both conditions the SDC company was blamed the most for the cyber incidents.

Keywords: Self-Driving Cars · Cyber Security · Trust

1 Introduction

Road vehicles driven entirely by humans have existed for ~150-years. However, the goal of designing, developing and deploying self-driving cars (SDCs) was established ~50 years ago - when even then, many believed that computing technology was not

© The Author(s), under exclusive license to Springer Nature Switzerland AG 2023
A. Moallem (Ed.): HCII 2023, LNCS 14045, pp. 323–337, 2023.
https://doi.org/10.1007/978-3-031-35822-7_22

sophisticated enough for such vehicles to become a reality. Factors such as cyber security and potential cyber-attacks on SDC systems were perhaps science fiction at best. Despite numerous efforts, a significant surge in the development of SDCs did not happen until the early 2000s - a time which welcomed many technological advancements that became quite sophisticated in the years that followed aiding the development of SDCs. However, even with far more sophisticated technology than ever before – e.g. vehicles designed and manufactured that can self-drive some of the time or in certain locations such as airports - are still not deployed on a mass scale. This provides a vital yet possibly short window of opportunity to address, through rigorous research, factors that may negatively impact not only the technology being developed but also the potential users – in terms of their perceptions, attitudes and behaviors including their willingness to consider adoption such intelligent mobility solutions.

The Society of Automotive Engineers (SAE) defines 6 levels of driving automation ranging from Level 0 (no automation) to Level 5 (fully autonomous). As the levels increase so does the cars' ability to drive itself under more (complex) conditions and circumstances with less need for human interaction [1].

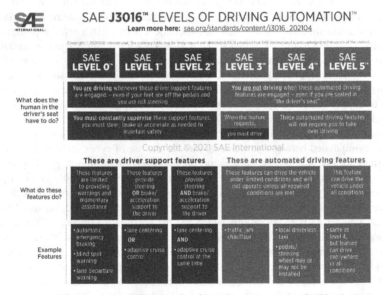

Fig. 1.   SAE (2021) *Levels of Driving Automation.*© [2].

Figure 1 illustrates the requirements of a (human) driver and features of a car according to its level of automation. A Level 0 car has no automated capabilities whilst a Level 1 car has one automated feature (e.g. Adaptive Cruise Control – ACC or Automated Lane Keeping System – ALKS). Level 2 cars have semi-automated systems often working in tangent to control e.g. steering, speed and braking whereas a Level 3 car is able to self-drive some of the time without interaction from a human (i.e. should allow hands and feet off controls and *possibly* eyes off the road). A Level 4 SDC should be able to drive itself under most conditions with minimal need for human intervention whereas a Level

5 SDC would be able to drive itself under all conditions with (and perhaps arguably) absolutely no human intervention required. Most vehicles on e.g. UK roads today are Level 0 or Level 1 (i.e. they have one automated system). However, we are beginning to see far more cars with Level 2 capabilities and some at Level 3, although the latter are not yet deemed legal to be operated at that level. By 2035, it is estimated that self-driving technologies (Level 3+) will be present in 40% of all new UK car sales [3] however, this is not referring to Level 5 SDCs. This is because drivers will be expected to stay alert and takeover control when requested - a criteria of Level 3 (more so) and Level 4 (less so) SDCs.

The anticipated introduction of SDCs has made them an interesting area of discussion and research – not only for engineers, computer scientists and vehicle designers, but also for psychologists (including human factors experts) interested in human-machine interface (HMI) design, human-computer interaction (HCI), driving and non-driving behaviors, and, somewhat crucially factors such as barriers or enablers to adoption. This includes factors such as trust in the system(s), blame (e.g. if and when something goes wrong – i.e. prototyping and testing for failure to minimize it in the future) and any potential handover and hand-back of driving functions between the vehicle and the user. Governments, industrial organizations (including vehicle manufacturers), legal experts and researchers in areas such as engineering, computer science, law, and psychology are invested in better understanding the future of SDC technology - and determining – through e.g. research, testing, policy, and legislation – whether e.g. Level 3 SDCs could be safe and efficient to operate on roads and whether Level 4 and Level 5 SDCs could one day become a commercial reality to be deployed on a mass scale.

SDC technology (particularly at higher levels of automation) is expected by many to bring a host of benefits including, but not limited to, increased road safety and improvements to shared transportation [4]; more accessible mobility [5]; and positive environmental impacts [6]. Despite the anticipated benefits, it is important to remember that as cars become more connected and intwined into our Critical National Infrastructures (CNIs) there are a number of concerns that need to be adequately addressed with potential consequences mitigated. One major – though to date under-researched – concern relates to the potential for SDC technology (and connected infrastructure) to be cyber attacked and to what extent potential future users understand and perceive this to be a negative factor that could, for example, affect their willingness to adopt and use SDCs.

Cyber security considerations across the automotive industry are already becoming a growing concern. Currently, regulations, guidelines and standards such as: UN R155 [7] and UN R156 [8], UNECE WP29 [9] and ISO/SAE 21434:2021 [10] are being developed and implemented. Many questions are being asked across industry in the realms of cyber security including:

- In the event of a cyber attack, who is accountable?
- Will individuals need training – including cyber – on how to use an SDCs system?
- How do we update entire fleets of SDCs to have an acceptable level of cyber security protection?
- How will user Personally Identifiable Information (PII) be managed; by whom?
- How do we ensure cyber security across an SDCs whole lifecycle?

• How do manufacturers know third-party supplier parts meet cyber security requirements?

There is however also a dearth of research – especially experimental - on SDCs and cyber security which is further generating research questions that have not yet been tackled or sufficiently investigated. The emerging questions are further complicated by the vast scale and connected nature of SDC technologies (and connected infrastructure) which could be vulnerable to being attacked. Ensuring best practice in cyber security across an entire dispersed network of SDCs presents a unique challenge that is currently hindered by the vast and unanswered nature of many emerging questions.

Various studies have projected different types of cyber attacks an SDC (and/or connected infrastructure) could fall victim to [11]. Concerns about the consequences of such attacks for e.g. users, other road users, manufacturers, legislators, legal experts, and governments have been raised. Procedural and technical solutions have also been proposed to tackle the SDC-cyber security challenge, including the proposition of a cyber-risk classification model capable of ranking the risk of a CAV GPS system [12]. However, cyber security is an issue that also encompasses people. Any adverse experiences with an SDC (e.g. cyber attack, system failure, accident) are likely to erode human trust in the technology with negative and potential catastrophic consequences for the acceptance, adoption, use, and continued use of such technology. Parasuraman and Riley (1997) seminally noted such concerns (albeit not focused on cyber security), over 25-years ago [13], with many others including Lee and See (2004) stressing that automation must be designed for appropriate reliance and reliance – especially when considered that humans *will have to be* in the loop [14]. (This could even be the case for Level 5 SDCs – e.g. a user will need to interact with the vehicle in terms of setting and possibly changing destination information, and so on.) In fact, such concerns echo back to the early 1980s where researchers such as Bainbridge (1982) stressed some of the then unintended consequences or ironies of automation [15], with many of these – and others such as cyber security still being major concerns. To achieve acceptance of and trust in these systems, optimal human factors considerations, including HCI factors are likely to play a key role – both before (i.e. design for failure) and after (i.e. design so that failure can be investigated for improvements) a cyber attack.

Trust can be defined as "a characteristic of an entity that indicates its ability to perform certain functions or services correctly, fairly and impartially, along with assurance that the entity and its identifier are genuine" (NIST, SP 800-152) [16]. It is a critical component in people's willingness to adopt SDCs and a lack of trust - or indeed factors and incidents that lead to trust erosion – could subsequently inhibit the publics uptake and adoption [17]. This could have severe consequences for this already major area of innovation that is set to grow exponentially over the coming years bringing with it many jobs including for HCI experts. This is crucial in an area such as SDC technology where to date, the potential adoption of such road vehicles would be based on choice rather than other factors such as environmental concerns and constraints (e.g. atmospheric damage, fuel resource limitations, and so on).

With cyber security concerns mounting, it is therefore important to understand the factors that influence trust and blame in an SDC following a *successful* cyber attack – i.e. when and where a cyber attack has infiltrated at least one system within or linked to an

SDC(s). Such incidents (when rather than if they occur) will likely be communicated to nations e.g. via news channels, and the way such news is reported is likely to be very important in terms of how they are perceived and potentially acted upon. For example, false or even exaggerated information that exceeds the actual threat society is facing can create a moral panic [18] leading to an erosion of trust. Noting that some information (facts or otherwise) concerning incidents can be exaggerated through the choice of certain words over other alternatives (e.g. describing a financial market as being in *turmoil* is likely to result in exaggerated emotional and other reactions than there being *instability*, say). The current experiment sets out to address some of these concerns – i.e. over the way in which news regarding cyber incidents involving SDCs are communicated and how this impacts trust and could even influence the assignment of blame. The main aim of the experiment is to:

- Determine whether an explicitly communicated (overt – involving the use of cyber security language) cyber security incident causes a Level 5 SDC to be trusted and blamed differently in comparison to a implicitly communicated (covert – not involving the use of cyber security language) cyber security incident;

  It is hypothesised that:

- H1 - Overt reporting of a cyber attack on an SDC (i.e. using words and/or terminology directly associated with cyber security) will lead to lower trust ratings compared to covert reporting (i.e. using words and/or terminology that does no not specifically indicate a cyber security issue *per se*).
- H2 - Headlines that contain overt reporting of a cyber attack are more likely to have blame attributed to cyber criminals (or similar wording – e.g. hackers) than those that are written and framed covertly.

2 Methodology

2.1 Participants

The total sample consisted of 283 participants who were all Psychology students at Cardiff University. The age of the participants ranged from 18 to 36 years (M 19.90, SD 2.20). All participants were registered students on the Cardiff Universities Experient Management System (EMS) Portal run by the School of Psychology; had normal/normal-corrected vision and spoke English as a first language or were fluent in English as a second language. No other requirements were specified in order for participants to have taken part. The experiment took ~20–30 min to complete.

2.2 Design and Materials

Attitudes such as trust and acceptability of SDCs cannot always be measured after a real interaction – Level 4 and Level 5 vehicles are largely in the design phase and many trials currently do not involve human interaction - especially on the scale required for robust psychological research studies with human participants. Therefore, not only is it currently (at least in most cases) impractical; but in terms of initiating a cyber attack, depending on the attack type and consequence, it could also be unethical to subject a participant to a potentially adverse incident. Nevertheless, it is crucial to explore potential factors that could (are likely to) occur before it happens so that systems (including humans with machines) can be better prepared and developed in readiness. To overcome this challenge, various methodologies have been used in SDC research including:

- Virtual Reality (VR) animations of future SDC-driving scenarios e.g. [19] - a video elicited testing methodology using animations created with VR.
- Simulation Software Generated Animations e.g. [20] - a video elicited testing methodology using scenarios developed within a driving simulator.
- Immersing a participant into a driving simulation experience - in person experiments using a driving simulator e.g. [21–23].
- Having participants experience journeys in prototype autonomous vehicles – in person experiments using real road vehicles e.g. [24–26].

Vignette-based studies are another commonly-used method when researching human perceptions of and attitudes towards SDCs and related factors [27]. Vignettes are (usually) hypothetical descriptions of a situation, event or person (or combinations of), often embedded into questionnaire-based experiments. Given that cyber attacks on Level 5 SDCs remain both a hypothetical and (perhaps very near) future event and that many people have not experienced being driven by a SDC with far fewer still having experienced a cyber attack when being a passenger in one, this future-thinking style approach was adopted for the current experiment.

Twenty pairs of SDC-cyber attack vignettes in the form of news headlines were created. Both headlines in each pair had identical subtext varying in length from ~20–30 words that gave the participants more detail about the event (see Fig. 2).

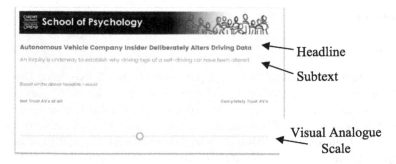

Fig. 2. Example of an Overt Hypothetical SDC-Cyber News Headline

To generate the headlines, an internet search to identify recent SDC news or automotive cyber security news was conducted. The true, reported news stories, formed the basis of the hypothetical incidents and were adapted for the conditions operationalised within the current experiment - overtly cyber (OC) and covertly cyber (CC) – the between participants independent variable (IV). In the OC condition cyber-specific terminology was used – i.e. the incident was unambiguously cyber. In the CC condition, non-specific cyber language was used illuding to the incident being caused by 'something else'. The experiment deployed a two-group randomised design (see Fig. 3). The experiment was also designed to be able to draw comparisons between similar headlines within each condition. The order in which the scenarios were presented was randomized.

Fig. 3. Two-Group Randomised Design Using Vignette-Based Methodologies

A preliminary questionnaire was included with questions on gender; age; driving experience; how likely participants were to use an SDC in the future and to what extent they currently trust SDC technology. A key question was included to measure to what extent participants' trust an SDC based on each news headline from 'Not at all' to 'Completely Trust'. This was gauged by moving a slider on a 100-point Visual-Analogue Scale (VAS) situated beneath each headline. Often participants are asked to rate, typically on a Likert scale (e.g. 5, 7, 9-point), 'How much do you trust X?'. Unlike a Likert scale, VAS offer greater granularity and the 'number' that the participants selects is not visible to them, only the researcher. This prevents certain uncontrollable bias such as participants only picking even/odd numbers; rounding to the nearest e.g. 5 or 10 or always choosing the same number. The headlines were embedded into Qualtrics© – a free online software package used to build and distribute surveys - and disseminated on EMS. No other materials were required to run this study. The experiment was programmed to be completed online on any device with materials scaled accordingly.

2.3 Procedure

At the outset, participants were presented with an online participant information sheet explaining the aims; requirements; anonymising of data process and their right to withdraw. Should they decide that they wished to partake, they were asked to read the consent form. Once satisfied with the information on both the participant information sheet and consent form, participants were then required to tick a box on the CF which stated that they freely gave their consent to taking part in the experiment. They were also asked to generate a memorable code to be used in the event should they wish to have their data withdrawn, which was possible from up to 10-working days from having taken part in the experiment.

Having understood the requirements and consented, participants were asked to complete a short preliminary questionnaire which consisted of tick-box questions on demographics, with prefer not to say options. Following these questions, the main part of the experiment began. Participants in each condition were asked to read each headline one-by-one and rate to what extent they would trust an SDC following the specified incident. Having moved the slider to their chosen trust rating, participants were then asked to state – using free text – who or what was to blame for the incident that occurred.

Finally, there was a short closing questionnaire about the level of familiarity of cyber security words/phases. Participants were asked to select how familiar they were with a variety of cyber-specific terms ranging from 'Very Unfamiliar' to 'Very Familiar'. In the interests of brevity and focus, data on this measure are not reported in the current paper. Having completed this section, participants were then appropriately debriefed about the experiment and were provided with more specific information on e.g. predictions as well as being given links to related news stories and articles to read if interested.

3 Results and Discussion

Before undergoing analysis, the data was screened for completeness resulting in a usable sample of $N = 192$. On forty-three occasions, participant trust-ratings were missing. Rather than omit the participants dataset, their mean value was calculated providing the predefined criteria - performing the calculation for ≤ 2 ratings (or ≥ 18) - was met. If this criteria was not met, the participant's dataset was excluded from analysis. For blame data, unambiguous spelling mistakes were rectified (commonly misspelt words included manufacturer and autonomous) and where necessary responses were streamlined (e.g. car/SDC/autonomous vehicle (AV)).

3.1 Trust

Before conducting statistical analyses, histograms for both conditions were produced for the overall trust rating across the twenty headline pairs. Histograms are a useful way to visually display data and can provide indications about normality. The histogram for the CC condition indicated a normal distribution, however, for the OC condition it suggested that there was a right skew. A Shapiro-Wilk normality test, $S = 0.0007958$ $p < 0.05$, confirmed the OC condition was skewed. Therefore a Wilcoxon-Rank sign test, $w = 10573, p = 0.42$, was used to determine whether overall trust ratings between the OC and CC conditions were different - overall rust ratings in the OC condition were not significantly different from overall trust ratings in the CC condition. The effect of using cyber-specific terminology compared to using non-specific cyber terminology when reporting SDC-cyber incidents had no overall effect. A Welch's two sample t-test, $t = 0.372, df = 274.66, p = 0.71$, conducted after a Box-Cox transformation using the *optimal lambda* $= 0.697326407$ also revealed that the effect of using cyber specific terminology (OC versus the CC condition) was not significant.

Despite a non-significant main effect, Wilcoxon tests were conducted to determine whether individual significant differences existed across each of the twenty pairs of headlines – with the analyses justified given the use of 20 new scenarios that have not been used experimentally prior to the current experiment. For eighteen of the scenario pairs, explicit knowledge of a cyber attack in the OC condition did not cause an SDC to be trusted differently in comparison to an incident that seemingly appears to be caused by 'something else' in the CC condition. Interestingly, two headlines did yield significantly different trust ratings:

- 'Autonomous Vehicle Sensors Fooled by Individuals Projecting Road Signs' (CC) and 'Autonomous Vehicle Sensors Fooled by Hackers Projecting Road Signs (OC), $w = 11540, p = 0.03$.

- 'Autonomous Vehicle Firms Under Global Espionage Attacks (CC) and 'Autonomous Vehicle Firms Under Global Cyber Attacks (OC), $w = 11914, p = 0.01$.

The experiment had also been designed with a secondary aim to draw comparisons between certain headlines within each condition in order to give an indication into potential future research. Of interest was the difference in trust ratings and blame assignment when the cyber attack had a more or less severe outcome or when its cause was accidental (non-malicious) versus deliberate (malicious). Significant differences existed for both severity of attack ($w = 4465, p = 2.2e-16$) and malicious/accidental intent ($w = 8454, p = 0.03$) although these findings are based on isolated headlines and therefore shall not be discussed in detail further in this paper. Experiments exploring these and other boundary conditions are currently in progress. It should also be noted that overall, trust ratings were low - on a scale from $0 - 100$ the mean value for each headline was in all cases lower than 50. This is perhaps indicative of the negative news headlines themselves. It is however important to note that rarely would a cyber attack result in a positive outcome. It is also the case that SDC technology is still very new for many people and this possible lack of knowledge may have also impacted the findings on trust.

3.2 Blame

Blame assignment varied depending on the headline however, in both conditions the SDC company was blamed the most for the cyber attack. In the OC condition there was a greater use of cyber-specific terminology such as 'hackers' and 'attackers'. A granular breakdown of the five most blamed entities in each condition across all of the headlines is displayed in Table 1.

Table 1. The Five most Blamed Entities within the CC and OC Conditions (Frequency Max = 3061)

Ranking	CC Condition	Frequency	OC Condition
1	SDC Company	493–489	SDC Company
2	SDC Manufacturer	380–421	Hackers
3	SDC itself	301–269	Attackers
4	Employee	200–223	SDC itself
5	Internet	88–197	Security

A WordCloud[1] displaying the full lexicon of blame data was produced for each condition. The frequency of words is reflected in the WordCloud by the size of the writing - larger words/terms were more frequently blamed for the SDC-cyber incident than the smaller words (see Figs. 4 and 5).

---

[1] https://www.wordclouds.com/

Fig. 4. WordCloud of Blame Assignment in Covertly Cyber Condition.

Fig. 5. WordCloud of Blame Assignment in Overtly Cyber Condition

4   General Discussion

As SDCs continue to gain traction, one emerging area of major concern with this technology is cyber security. With cyber attacks becoming increasingly sophisticated and prominent across the automotive industry, there is a fear that SDCs and their infrastructure – due to the vast connectivity and number of potential entry points - will be vulnerable to both malign and benign cyber attacks. Should such events – cyber attacks – occur, trust in SDCs is highly likely to be impacted. The current experiment set out to investigate and better understand whether the use of cyber-specific terminology impacts trust ratings, and blame assignment on SDCs – positioned in the context of news-type reports that people (e.g. the public) would be exposed to following such an incident. Headlines containing explicit cyber security language and/or terminology (the *overtly cyber* condition/*OC*) were compared with those where cyber security was not mentioned explicitly (the *covertly cyber* condition/*CC*). This methodology was developed to determine whether the simple change of a word and/or phrase is powerful enough to impact participant perception(s) of the event and consequently how they process and respond to the information. (Much in the same way as media outlets with different views and approaches report on news stories where the events and outcome(s) are essentially the same but the language used to describe these is different in some way – e.g. explicitly one thing vs implicitly the same thing.) It was predicted that trust would be lower when cyber-specific terminology was used to report a cyber incident (i.e. in the OC vs the CC condition) and blame in the OC condition would be more attributed to cyber criminals such as hackers than in the CC condition.

The findings indicate that the use of cyber-specific terminology (i.e. in the OC condition) when reporting, second-hand, an SDC-cyber incident did not have an overall impact trust ratings – i.e. the between participants main effect was non-significant. This suggests that a confirmed cyber incident (compared to one that is not specifically confirmed to be cyber) does not influence trust in an SDC at least when that information is communicated via text-based news headlines with some subtext. One reason for this could that the wording of headlines was identical other than the manipulation of one word/phrase in the headline. Perhaps the manipulation was not strong enough to capture an effect, at least with a respectable sample size recruited to detect a medium effect size based on the design of the experiment. Interestingly, there were two headlines where the choice of wording -'cyber espionage' as oppose to 'global espionage' and 'hackers' as opposed to 'individuals' did affect trust – i.e. trust was significantly lower in the OC compared to the CC condition. However, there were other headlines using the same (or highly similar) manipulation but did not yield the same significant differences. As a result, the explanation for this finding remains ambiguous and future research is required – for example – by further drilling into aspects of the headlines that might be driving differences whilst being mindful that the overall main effect across all headlines was non-significant. Caution must be taken before drawing any firm conclusions at this stage. It is however crucial to determine what other characteristics of a cyber incident – reported second hand as news stories (or similar) may reliably affect trust. Other studies exploring, for example, automation in Level 2 SDCs found that trust was not affected by driving conditions or conflicts between driver and advocated that dynamic aspects of trust-in-automation should be examined situationally [28].

To determine blame assignment, an open-ended question (per headline) allowed participants to provide detailed and unrestricted responses. This style of question was deemed most appropriate because if a drop down list of options had been available, participants may for example, have been inclined to choose only one option despite others being important as well, or even to have chosen an option(s) at random. There was also a risk that including cyber related terms could have been perceived as priming a response in this experiment as the options presented could have been something that the participant had otherwise not thought of. This could have also led to carryover (including priming) effects for subsequently presented scenarios/trials. In terms of blame, assignment was varied and context dependent. In both conditions the SDC company was blamed the most for the incident. In the OC condition blame was far more frequently attributed to, in participants self-reported statements, 'hackers' and 'attackers', as was predicted. There were also occurrences of joint blame where participants blamed more than one entity e.g. some responses involved blaming parts of the SDC system; some involved blaming the physical environment; and others involved blaming a specific entity or person such as the manufacture or individual. Although and overall, this exercise provided an interesting insight into the type of entities being blamed with findings being able to inform future research, one potential downside – mainly due to the open ended nature of the question – was the inability to determine blame weighting – e.g. the degree to which one factor was blamed vs another/others. This is a future line of enquiry.

The findings regarding blame are largely as predicted although the overall non-significant differences in trust between the OC and CC conditions were not (apart from between two of the twenty headlines). However, there are other potential limitations to the current experiment that can speak to the latter non-significant findings. One possible limitation in this experiment is the measurement of trust. Trust is a complex phenomenon - it is not only impacted by through personal experiences but it is also influenced by environmental factors – e.g. what is seen and heard on a day-to-day basis and what is read via news outlets as well as social media. To determine trust ratings, there are two main approaches: self-report questionnaires or physiological monitoring. Due to the subjective and context-dependent nature of trust, physiological measures can be preferred. This is largely because with self-report methods, there is a risk that participants will answer in one way but think and/or act in another and is not possible to judge the accuracy of their rating (especially with an online questionnaire where there is even less potential to follow-up). However, given the online nature of this experiment, trust was measured via self-reported means but this is not withstanding the notion that future research could triangulate both self-reported and physiological measures. For example, capturing eye tracking data could help determine whether and to what extent 'keywords' within the headlines are focussed on and whether this is enough to elicit deep semantic processing in the brain.

When it came to choosing a suitable and established trust scale, there are a vast array available, each with advantages and disadvantages – including appropriateness for contexts as well as e.g. validity and reliability. Different trust scales are more or less suited for different studies depending on their design. In terms of measuring trust in an SDC, it has been recognized by Holthausen et al. (2020) that there is not a standardized method. Subsequently, Holthausen et al. (2020) developed the Situational Trust Scale for Automated Driving (STS-AD) [29]. The scale is based on the Trust Model pro-posed by Hoff & Bashir [30], who conducted an extensive literature review to elaborate trust-influencing factors. The need for a bespoke and separate SDC-trust scale can be questioned. An SDC could be regarded as a (complex) IoT device or cyber-physical system, through the lens of an ICT specialist; a robot through the lens of an Roboticist or it could be argued that an SDC is an entity in its own right. If SDCs are regarded as entities in their own right, then it is logical to use a separate scale to measure trust. How-ever, should an SDC be regarded as e.g. a robot or IoT device, then this raises questions as to why there is a need for a new questionnaire when there are already existing and established questionnaires measuring trust in relation to robots and IoT devices. There-fore, choosing a suitable questionnaire is largely dependent on how an SDC is defined. Given the operationalization of the news headlines, it would not have been appropriate to opt for the STS-AD and therefore instead a bespoke questionnaire was used. Whilst it is common for researchers to devise bespoke questionnaires based on their specific research question, they are often less reliable and can make comparing data difficult.

Implications for HCI. The context, methodology and in some cases – the findings – of the current experiment have important HCI implications. One key reason to conduct human factors and applied psychology research on SDCs – especially in relation to factors impacting (and likely to impact) their acceptance, adoption and usage (or indeed potential misuse and abandonment) – is the sheer value of the marketspace including GDP, expansion of current companies, development of new companies and employment in general – including specialist jobs for tens of thousands of current and future HCI experts. For example, Allied Market Research asserted that the worldwide SDC market was valued at $76.13b in 202; set to rise to $2,161.79b by 2030 [31]. Trusting SDC technology especially after an adverse event – including a cyber attack – will play a key role in the markets growth, or indeed decline and potential failure. Quality research focused on optimal human interaction with and experiences of SDC technology is key to maximizing trust as well as restoration if it is degraded – e.g. in the event of a cyber attack.

In addition, SDCs above Level 2 irrespective of their degree of automation, will require human-machine interfaces (HMIs) with features and functions that support and enhance user experience, including trust. It is likely that the HMIs will provide some degree of explainability about what the vehicle is doing/planning to do e.g. to support situation awareness [32, 33] and help maintain trust. Having such information optimally communicated via interfaces might help to mitigate loss of trust as well as support restoration of trust if and when an incident occurs – such as a cyber attack attempt. Understanding the characteristics of a cyber attack most affecting trust will help with the information likely to be relayed through the HMI.

Such interfaces could also be used by SDC manufacturing companies (and/or companies who develop interfaces for SDCs) to in real-time (or close to real time) communicate important information to users to help keep them in the loop and to demonstrate high standards in terms of how such companies respond to factors that are in some cases inevitable – including e.g. bringing vehicles to a safe stop in the event of a suspected/potential/actual incident such as a cyber attack.

5 Conclusion

The current experiment sought to understand the effect that the wording of a reported cyber incident on a SDC(s) has on trust and blame assignment. The findings indicated that a reported incident worded using cyber specific terminology (i.e. overtly cyber condition) was not trusted any differently to an incident that had been reported using non-cyber specific terminology (i.e. covertly cyber condition). Other than in two instances, there was no difference in trust between the overtly and covertly cyber worded conditions. Blame assignment varied depending on the headline – where cyber terminology had been used, blame was more frequently attributed using such words. Based on indications from this experiment, future research has been proposed to investigate whether other characteristics of a cyber attack such as severity and intentionality impacts trust ratings and blame assignment in SDCs following an incident.

Acknowledgments. A warm thank you goes to Dr Christopher D. Wallbridge for your assistance in discussions for some aspects of this experiment.

Funding. This PhD project is funded by the EPSRC DTP Hub in Cyber Security Analytics awarded to Cardiff University.

Ethical Statement. This experiment has been reviewed and approved by The School of Psychology Research Ethics Committee (SREC), Cardiff University and has also undergone and passed a risk assessment.

References

1. SAE Levels of Driving Automation. Warrandale, PA, SAE (2021). https://www.sae.org/standards/content/j3016_202104/
2. SAE Levels of Driving Automation [graphic] (2021). https://www.sae.org/blog/sae-j3016-update. Accessed 10 Oct 2022
3. UK on the Cusp of a Transport Revolution (2021). https://www.gov.uk/government/news/uk-on-the-cusp-of-a-transport-revolution-as-self-driving-vehicles-set-to-be-worth-nearly-42-billion-by-2035. Accessed 06 Dec 2022
4. Litman, T.: Autonomous vehicle implementation predictions. Implications for Transport Planning. Victoria Transport Policy Institute, Canada (2023). https://vtpi.org/avip.pdf. Accessed 14 Oct 2022
5. Milakis, D., Arem, B.V., Wee, B.V.: Policy and society related implications of automated driving: a review of literature and directions for future research. J. Intell. Transp. Syst. 21(4), 324–348 (2017). https://doi.org/10.1080/15472450.2017.1291351
6. Milakis, D., Arem, B.V., Wee, B.V.: The ripple effect of automated driving. In: 2015 BIVEC-GIBET Transport Research Day. BIVEC-GIBET, Eindhoven, The Netherlands (2015)
7. UNECE UN Regulation No. 155. https://unece.org/transport/docments/2021/03/standards/un-regulation-no-155-cyber-security-and-cyber-security. Accessed 07 Jan 2023
8. UNECE UN Regulation No. 156 - Software update and software update management system. https://unece.org/transport/documents/2021/03/standards/un-regulation-no-156-software-update-and-software-update. Accessed 07 Jan 2023
9. UNECE WP.29 – Introduction. https://unece.org/wp29-introduction. Accessed 07 Jan 2023
10. ISO/SAE 21434:2021 - Road vehicles—Cybersecurity engineering. https://www.iso.org/standard/70918.html. Accessed 07 Jan 2023
11. Phama, M., Xiongb, K.: A survey on security attacks and defense techniques for connected and autonomous vehicles. Comput. Secur. 109(1), 1–29 (2021)
12. Sheehan, B., Murphy, F., Mullins, M., Ryan, C.: Connected and autonomous vehicles: a cyber-risk classification framework. Transp. Res. Part A: Policy Pract. 124(1), 523–536 (2019). https://doi.org/10.1016/j.tra.2018.06.03
13. Parasuraman, R., Riley, V.: Humans and automation: use, misuse, disuse, abuse. Hum. Factors 39(2), 230–253 (1997). https://doi.org/10.1518/001872097778543886
14. Lee, J., See, K.A.: Trust in automation: designing for appropriate reliance. Hum. Factors: J. Hum. Factors Ergon. Soc. 46, 50–80 (2004)
15. Bainbridge, L.: Ironies of automation. Automatica 19(6), 775–779 (1983)
16. NIST Glossary. https://csrc.nist.gov/glossary. Accessed 15 Dec 2023
17. Kim, P.H., Dirks, K.T., Cooper, C.D.: The repair of trust: a dynamic bilateral perspective and multilevel conceptualization. Acad. Manag. Rev. 34(3), 401–422 (2009). https://doi.org/10.5465/AMR.2009.40631887
18. Cohen, S.: Folk Devils and Moral Panics. MacGibbon and Kee, London (1972)
19. Kallioinen, N., et al.: Moral judgements on the actions of self-driving cars and human drivers in dilemma situations from different perspectives. Front. Psychol. 10, 2415 (2019). https://doi.org/10.3389/fpsyg.2019.02415

20. Zhang, Q., Wallbridge, C.D., Morgan, P., Jones, D.M.: Using simulation-software-generated animations to investigate. Procedia Comput. Sci. **207**, 3516–3525 (2022). https://doi.org/10.1016/j.procs.2022.09.410

21. Eriksson, A., Stanton, N.A.: Takeover time in highly automated vehicles: noncritical transitions to and from manual control. Hum. Factors **59**(4), 689–705 (2017). https://doi.org/10.1177/0018720816685832

22. Parkin, J., Crawford, F., Flower, J., Alford, C., Morgan, P., Parkhurst, G.: Cyclist and pedestrian trust in automated vehicles: an on-road and simulator trial. Int. J. Sustain. Transp. 1–13 (2022). https://doi.org/10.1080/15568318.2022.2093147

23. Merat, N., Jamson, A.H., Lai, F.C.H., Daly, M., Carsten, O.M.J.: Transition to manual: driver behaviour when resuming control from a highly automated vehicle. Transport. Res. F: Traffic Psychol. Behav. **27**, 274–282 (2014). https://doi.org/10.1016/j.trf.2014.09.005

24. Stephenson, A.C., et al.: Effects of an unexpected and expected event on older adults' autonomic arousal and eye fixations during autonomous driving. Front. Psychol. **11** (2020). https://doi.org/10.3389/fpsyg.2020.571961

25. Morgan, P.L., Alford, C.A., Williams, C., Voinescu, A., Parkhurst, G.: Venturer Trial 1: Planned Handover, Technical report (2017)

26. Flower, J., Williams, C., Alford, C., Morgan, P., Parkin, J.: Venturer Trial 2: Interactions Between Autonomous Vehicles and Other Vehicles on Links at Junctions (2017)

27. Awad, E., et al.: Drivers are blamed more than their automated cars when both make mistakes. Nat. Hum. Behav. **4**(2), 134–143 (2019). https://doi.org/10.1038/s41562-019-0762-8

28. Stapel, J., Gentner, A., Happee, R.: On-road trust and perceived risk in level 2 automation. Transport. Res. F: Traffic Psychol. Behav. **89**, 355–370 (2022). https://doi.org/10.1016/j.trf.2022.07.008

29. Holthusen, B., Wintersberger, P., Walker, B., Riener, A.: Situational trust scale for automated driving (STS-AD): development and initial validation. In: 12th International Conference on Automotive User Interfaces and Interactive Vehicular Applications, Washington DC, USA (2020)

30. Hoff, K.A., Bashir, M.: Trust in automation: integrating empirical evidence on factors that influence trust. Hum. Factors **57**(3), 407–434 (2015). https://doi.org/10.1177/0018720814547570

31. Autonomous Vehicle Market Size, Share, Value, Report, Growth. (n.d.). Allied Market Research. https://www.alliedmarketresearch.com/autonomous-vehicle-market. Accessed 09 Feb 2023

32. Endsley, M.R.: Measurement of situation awareness in dynamic systems. Hum. Factors **37**(1), 65–84 (1995)

33. Endsley, M.R.: Situation awareness in future autonomous vehicles: beware of the unexpected. In: Bagnara, S., Tartaglia, R., Albolino, S., Alexander, T., Fujita, Y. (eds.) IEA 2018. AISC, vol. 824, pp. 303–309. Springer, Cham (2019). https://doi.org/10.1007/978-3-319-96071-5_32

I Just Want to Help: SMEs Engaging with Cybersecurity Technology

Brian Pickering[1]([✉]) [iD], Stephen C. Phillips[1] [iD], and Gencer Erdogan[2] [iD]

[1] Electronics and Computer Science, IT Innovation, University of Southampton, Southampton SO17 1BJ, UK
{j.b.pickering,s.c.phillips}@soton.ac.uk
[2] Sustainable Communication Technologies, SINTEF Digital, Oslo, Norway
gencer.erdogan@sintef.no

Abstract. The cybersecurity landscape is particularly challenging for SMEs. On the one hand, they must comply with regulation or face legal sanction. But on the other, they may not have the resource or expertise to ensure regulatory compliance, especially since this is not their core business. At the same time, it is also well-attested in the literature that individuals (human actors in the ecosystem) are often targeted for cyber attacks. So, SMEs must also consider their employees but also their clients as potential risks regarding cybersecurity. Finally, it is also known that SMEs working together as part of a single supply chain are reluctant to share cybersecurity status and information. Given all of these challenges, assuming SMEs recognise their responsibility for security, they may be overwhelmed in trying to meet all the associated requirements. There are tools to help support them, of course, assuming they are motivated to engage with such tooling. This paper looks at the following aspects of this overall situation. In a set of four studies, we assess private citizen understanding of cybersecurity and who they believe to be responsible. On that basis, we then consider their attitude to sharing data with service providers. Moving to SMEs, we provide a general overview of their response to the cybersecurity landscape. Finally, we ask four SMEs across different sectors how they respond to cybersecurity tooling. As well as providing an increased understanding of private citizen and SME attitudes to cybersecurity, we conclude that SMEs need not be overwhelmed by their responsibilities. On the contrary, they can take the opportunity to innovate based on their experience with cybersecurity tools.

Keywords: SME · Cybersecurity · Awareness · Training ·
Self-Efficacy · Innovation · Mixed Methods · Secure System Modelling

1 Introduction

Small-to-medium enterprises (SMEs) reportedly constitute 99% of businesses worldwide, employing 70% of the workforce [1]. As a sector and similar to larger,

---

This work was supported by the EU H2020 project CyberKit4SME (Grant agreement: 883188).

more resource-rich enterprises, they are subject to many regulations in addition
to their day-to-day business: mandatory in the case of data protection [2] and
highly desirable for cybersecurity not least for reputational reasons [3]. At the
same time, SMEs suffer multiple attacks [4–7], lack resource or skill [8,9] or
budget [10,11] to address them, and may not even have access to appropriate
information to mitigate such risks [12,13]. The risk perception literature identifies behavioural factors about cybersecurity attitudes and activities which need
to be taken into account as well. Bada et al [14], for instance, highlight the need
to consider perceptions and beliefs, whilst Beldad and colleagues [15] emphasise
trust, and Siegrist [16] affect. Others have highlighted that overoptimism [17],
lack of confidence [18,19] (low self-efficacy [20]), of feeling personal responsibility [21], or even the attraction of doing nothing [22] may be inhibitors to
risk-mitigation behaviours. Finally, Geer and his colleagues suggest that cyber
risks change depending on the operational context [23]. In the empirical work
presented here, we explore factors such as context, self-efficacy and responsibility from the perspective of different stakeholders in the actor network ecosystem
around SMEs.

1.1 Background

The situation outlined above is exacerbated by the direct involvement of human
agents for everything the SME undertakes including their employees, their clients
and those they collaborate with [24,25]. SMEs may be more vulnerable to cybersecurity threats because of their relationships with these stakeholders. For these
relationships are built on mutual assumptions and dependencies: all enterprises,
for example, rely on their employees to adhere to cybersecurity policy which may
depend on awareness as well as willingness to conform to such policies [26]; and
on their clients to respect and comply with controls [14,27]. Figure 1 summarises
some of the pressures on SMEs to engage with risk-mitigation strategies, including the main stakeholder types: human agents such as *clients* and *employees*,
and institutions like *other enterprises* and *regulators*.

Notwithstanding providing advice, regulators exert an influence on SMEs
to comply without the SME being able to influence behaviours of the regulator directly. With all other stakeholders, this is not the case. Employees work
toward common *business objectives* to ensure the success of that SME. They
are responsible, therefore, for following company policy and implementing what
measures are required. At the same time, they expect the SME to provide a
secure environment for them to operate and to keep any personal data about
them secure. By contrast, when a client *interacts with* an SME for goods or services, they expect their data to be processed appropriately and kept secure. But
at the same time, and especially in cases where a client accesses SME infrastructure such as placing an order or using a fault reporting system, the SME must
equally rely on them to act in such a way as to avoid exposing the infrastructure to attack. They expect adherence to security policies, though may not have
direct visibility of what clients do or of what they know. One example would
be a requirement in the terms of service that the client protect their credentials

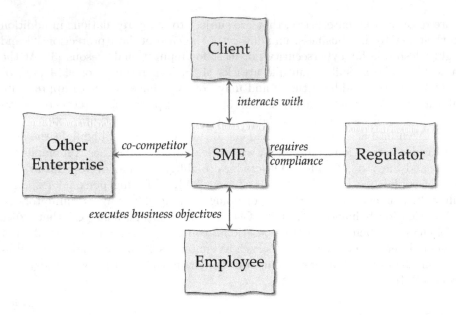

Fig. 1. Cybersecurity Landscape for SMEs

or check for malware embedded in any communication they send. Finally, *other enterprises* must co-operate across a supply chain, including other SMEs, whilst at the same time exposing only limited information about cybersecurity threats and controls.

The specific purpose of this study, therefore, is to investigate cybersecurity awareness and practice amongst the stakeholders where there is a mutual expectation of security-appropriate behaviours as summarised in Fig. 1.

2   Method

Against this background, we report empirical findings from three related quantitative studies exploring the attitudes and behaviours of different stakeholders in Fig. 1; and a complementary qualitative study regarding SME readiness to engage with cybersecurity tooling to meet these expectations.

In addition to regulatory requirements (e.g., [2], Art 25), individuals - Clients or Employees - expect their data to be processed securely, though their own practices and lack of knowledge may be maladaptive and in turn represent a risk to the SME. Further, since an SME rarely operates alone, they must protect information exchange with Other Enterprises, and protect themselves from vulnerabilities coming from those enterprises.

Providing cybersecurity technology to support SMEs may be contextualised in technology adoption terms [28]. In this sense, the main focus has been on perceived easy-to-use (PEOU) and perceived usefulness (PU). This would allow the

SME to satisfy their security obligations whilst reducing their resource commitments and lack of skill (PEOU). Part of PU would include identifying the effect of the maladaptive behaviours from these groups, namely *Clients, Employees* but also *Other Enterprises*. Providing usable and useful technology to identify threats, knock-on effects and mitigations should be enough to guarantee tool adoption, therefore. However, our own previous work has concluded that developing a narrative around *Self-Efficacy* and motivational factors like *Innovation* may be just as significant [29].

Table 1. Summary of Participants in each Study

Study	N	Participants	Instrument	Ethics Approval
1	800	Private Citizens (UK)	Anonymous Survey	FEPS 67628 and 69107
2	470	Private Citizens (UK)	Anonymous Survey	FEPS 71408
3	141	SMEs (UK & Norway)	Anonymous Survey	FEPS 61721
4	4	SMEs (Europe)	Semi-structured Interviews	FEPS 73328

Table 1 summarises the participants in each of the four studies (numbered from 1 to 4 as in the first column of the table). Note that respondents to the anonymous surveys were principally UK based. The Private Citizens represent the *Client* type from Fig. 1, whilst the SMEs represent the *Employee* as well as *Other (SME) Enterprises*. The three surveys in 2 were run via crowdsourcing platforms: *Studies 1* and *2* used *Prolific.co*, and *Study 3* used *Norstat*. Participants were self-selecting.

Table 2. Summary of Survey Instruments

Study	Description	Reference
1	Based on instrument developed and validated in [30]	Pickering & Taylor [31]
2	Derived from focus group discussions; see [32]	Pickering et al. [33]
3	Derived from cybersecurity experts; see [34]	Erdogan et al. [35]

Study 1 sought to identify cybersecurity awareness and competence among private individuals. Participants were balanced across gender identity, age group and ethnicity. They were randomly assigned to one of four conditions: ranking cybersecurity threats, ranking potential controls, matching threats and controls, and identifying who they believed responsible for implementing those controls. They were then asked to respond to assertions (*Strongly Agree* to *Strongly Disagree*) from a model derived from Protection Motivation Theory and previously validated by [30]. Of the 800 respondents, approximately 46% identified themselves as technology experts and 53% as comfortable with technology.

Whilst *Study 1* looked at cybersecurity attitudes, *Study 2* turned to the practical implications of such attitudes. Specifically, within the context of secure services, how do private individuals feel about sharing their data? Again, participants were balanced across gender identity, age group and ethnicity, and were asked to respond to 48 assertions (a 6-point Likert scale from *Strongly Agree* to *Strongly Disagree*) derived from focus group discussions and divided arbitrarily into four sections. Each section began with a general question followed by 12 assertions. Each of the general questions had three choices for participants to identify when or how comfortable they felt about that particular issue. The four such questions were:

1. **Data Sharing**: who they would share their data with;
2. **Decision Making**: how they would make a data sharing decision;
3. **Privacy Concerns**: general issues around privacy;
4. **Jurisdiction**: what regulations apply.

One of each - *Data Sharing, Decision Making, Privacy Concerns*, and *Jurisdiction* - introduced each of the four groupings of 12 assertions, therefore.

Both Study 1 and 2 were contextualised in terms of health data. But whereas Study 1 explicitly asked about security threats and controls, Study 2 asked participants to consider what they expect when they share their data, that is more specifically privacy expectations. Although not wishing to conflate privacy and security, we maintain that they are related [36]. Individual behaviours around privacy and data sharing, for instance, identify the circumstances under which individuals might engage with security measures. We therefore believe Study 1 and 2 to be complementary.

Study 3 turned to SMEs themselves. Based on the results from *Studies 1* and *2*, the aim here is to understand where SMEs stand on issues of security and data handling. They may feel overwhelmed by their legal responsibilities under data protection laws, for instance, or be ill-equipped to deal with client expectations regarding responsibility. Understanding how private individual expectations map to SME capabilities would be an important finding, of course. The survey for *Study 3* consisted of 27 questions with a mixture of closed response questions allowing either single or multiple responses, and free-form text input. The questions were developed based on discussion with cybersecurity experts. They were grouped into five categories:

1. General information **about the SME** (5 questions);
2. General information **about the respondent themselves** (4 questions);
3. Information about **the ICT infrastructure** (4 questions);
4. **Cybersecurity Awareness** (8 questions); and
5. **Cybersecurity Practices** (5 questions)

Study 3 in this context is, therefore, about providing a perspective both of *Employees* and *Other Enterprises* in Fig. 1.

Study 4 extends the findings of *Study 3*, focusing on *Employees* and *Other Enterprises* from a slightly different perspective. Given our previous work on SME engagement supporting the use of qualitative methods rather than just traditional technology acceptance methods [29], semi-structured interviews with

SMEs across four sectors (automotive, finance, healthcare and utilities) were conducted exploring their attitudes towards a specific modelling technology [37] to support them with their cybersecurity responsibilities in terms of other SMEs/enterprises, and with respect to individuals, be they *Clients* or *Employees*. Following previous experience, participants were simply asked to describe their attitude to cybersecurity prior to using the technology and then their experience of using the technology. Based on the three previous studies, we decided to explore indications of *Responsibility* and whether they accept such obligations; in response, whether they may feel *Overwhelmed* or alternatively believe themselves capable of meeting all demands (i.e., *Self-Efficacy*). Finally, if SMEs respond to the technology not only in terms of meeting specific needs but also in encouraging future engagement and *Innovation*. To facilitate a thematic analysis [38,39] of the interviews, an initial coding schema was developed therefore as follows:

1. **Responsibility**: since individuals need to feel responsible before they will engage; see [20,21];
2. **Overwhelmed**: to identify adaptive and maladaptive behavioural attitude; see the Extended Parallel Process Model [18,22];
3. **Self-efficacy**: the belief that the individual is capable of taking action; see Protection Motivation Theory [40];
4. **Innovation**: to represent an affective aspect, having previously identified evidence that technology acceptance advantageously includes creative thinking in potential SME-based adopters [29].

Items 1, 2 and 3 relate to constructs from the Theory of Planned Behavior, of course. For instance, *Responsibility* for implementing controls derives from the construct *Normative beliefs*: what is expected by and from others. Feeling *Overwhelmed* or capable (*Self-Efficacy*) are reminiscent of the construct *Perceived Behavioral Control*: they represent the two sides of a cost-benefit analysis in deciding to act. As such, we maintain that these codes are well supported in the behavioural science literature [41]. The final code, *Innovation*, is intended to capture perceptions which go beyond the specific feeling that the SME can and should act. In the context of motivational factors [42], we believe the successful adoption of a technology should encourage feelings of autonomy, at least, an *intrinsic* motivator, which will therefore tend to be more persistent. Further, consistent with Uses and Gratifications theory [43,44], we would expect adoption intention to be moderated by enjoyment.

3   Results

In this section, we begin by summarising the main outcomes of the quantitative studies (*Studies 1, 2* and *3*). Conclusions from these three studies then inform the interpretation of the outcomes from the final study, *Study 4*.

3.1   Study 1

Respondents ranked *If I lost my phone or laptop, or someone got my password, someone getting at my medical records* 1 or 2 (most worrying) 55% of the time; and *If the hospital gets hacked, my medical records falling into the wrong hands* 51% of the time. They were reasonably consistent, therefore, in identifying unauthorised access to data as a significant threat. Regarding controls, 71% ranked *Adding protection (encryption) to all medical data wherever it's stored, sent or viewed, so it can't be tampered with* as 1 or 2 (most effective; the next closest being *Making sure that my medical data are protected and can only be looked at by medical staff* with 40% 1 or 2 rankings). Protecting the data itself via encryption, therefore, was perceived to be the most effective control. As far as responsibility for implementing controls is concerned, overwhelmingly, participants identified the NHS or the Hospital as responsible; only in the case of *Having an automatic lock on a phone or computer app, so my data stays safe even if the phone or computer is stolen* did they see themselves as responsible.

It is clear, therefore, that private individuals *can* make decisions about threats, controls and indeed about who is responsible. In consequence, we may generalise this to say that private individuals (*Clients* in Fig. 1) only see themselves responsible for implementing a control for a device they own. Otherwise, they perceive responsibility to lie with the service provider, that is the SME offering a service. In the survey [31], neither an equipment manufacturer nor service developer was regarded as responsible for the controls.

3.2   Study 2

Study 1 sought to identify a baseline of what private individual perceptions around cybersecurity might be. *Study 2* provides a complementary viewpoint: namely, is this awareness reflected in data sharing attitudes? Responding to general attitudinal questions, participants reported that they make decisions about sharing their data based on trust in the data steward (73% of the time) rather than any published privacy notice. This is important because *trust* in behavioural sciences is regarded as a willingness to expose oneself to risk [45], not reliance on rights or contract as imposed by regulation. Indeed, 84% disagree with the statement *I feel I make informed choices about privacy and data sharing*. Further, in response to the assertion *If I agree to let a company or researcher use my data, I no longer have any rights to it*, 95% agree; and for the assertion *I share responsibility for my data with whoever I release it to*, 88% disagree. whatever rights data protection affords ([2], Chap. 3) clearly do not inform decisions or empower data subjects [46].

Private individuals do not therefore necessarily understand their own rights and what these allow them to do. Data sharing decisions are based on trust in the recipient (data steward). Further, trust in that recipient seems to be influenced by what they perceive to be the likelihood of third party (onward) sharing. SME clients (see Fig. 1), therefore, may not respond to assurances from the SME about how they claim to secure the data, even if they do read privacy notices or understand their data protection rights. The expectation is that the SME assumes responsibility. This is consistent with the expectations from *Study 1*.

3.3 Study 3

Study 1 showed a reasonable level of awareness among private individuals, but an assumption that responsibility lies with the service provider. *Study 2*, primarily focused on privacy aspects of cybersecurity, reinforced the belief that service providers are responsible, but also that engagement (in this case for data sharing) is predicated on trust not regulation. With that in mind, *Study 3* looks specifically at whether SMEs report the ability to be able to provide the necessary cybersecurity context to meet private individual expectations.

Although 80% of respondents report a moderate to high degree of cybersecurity awareness, only 19% report they provide ongoing training, and 73% that they provide none. Further, 15% reported that they were aware of an attack, and 77% were not. Whether this reflects the actual situation is difficult to judge. The SMEs in question may not have been attacked (though see [47], for instance), or whether there is no internal communication of security incidents. Finally, only 16% reported that they use specific tools to identify and mitigate against cyber attacks; 62% do not, and 23% reported they didn't know. Overall, and despite reporting a reasonable level of understanding, there is a lack of training and tool implementation to mitigate against cyber threats should they occur.

In *Study 1*, it was clear that clients almost always expect a service provider to assure the security of their data, and *Study 2* that they believe themselves at the mercy of service providers, having no control once they have shared their data. The onus therefore is perceived to be on SMEs to protect data, but this third study highlights that they are not necessarily in a position to assume this responsibility. More importantly, though, is that if engagement with the SME is based on *trust* as suggested by *Study 2* rather than policy or regulation and shared responsibility, then there is a significant reputational risk to the SME. In the context of the SME collaborating with Other Enterprises, although the assumption is that working together will be subject to compliance with a service-level agreement, non-disclosure agreements, or other contractual instruments - rather than trust - this reputational risk needs to be addressed.

3.4 Study 4

The first two studies indicate that responsibility for security and associated privacy rests with the SME. The third highlights a concern that training and tools are not used sufficiently, and therefore the SME may not be in a position to assume such responsibility. In the fourth and final study, we engaged directly with SMEs whose business was largely dependent on maintaining the trust of their end-user clients and the security of their data. For the interviews, we asked the SMEs to describe their experience with a specific security modelling tool. As outlined above, a coding scheme was used to identify relevant themes from the interviews. (Note that the SMEs are referred to as P1 to P4; there were two employees involved for P1 and P4, and one for P2 and P3).

Starting with *Responsibility*, the SME interviewees report an awareness that they are responsible for the data from their clients, but also to support their non-technical staff members in appreciating the importance of security:

(P2)... we collect some sensitive data ... we should protect them and also, [control] access to... to our servers ... and also [help] understand that our nontechnical employees how to protect them [*sic.*] data and so... so our customers data

They recognise, therefore, and accept that they are responsible for their infrastructure (*our servers*), the data they process (*we should protect them*), and have an obligation to train or raise awareness with their own staff (*[help]...* *our nontechnical employees to protect ... data*).

(P4) Sometimes there are some sensitive data and sensitive projects and they just want it [*sic.*] to be 100% sure that everything is secured from our side. So we should spend a lot of money on this.

They appreciate, though, that such obligations demand resource, in this case, financial. Notwithstanding the financial implications, in attempting to meet these obligations, they can become *overwhelmed*. Without training and tooling (see *Study 3*), it may not be possible to move beyond this state:

(P4) We didn't know how to handle [an] attack from the outside if something is... not safe in our office.

further:

(P1) it's complex and the models are getting huge and complex really quickly

and

(P2) Maybe it's a bit difficult to manage all threats that we found because sometimes there are a lot of all of them

Feelings of being *overwhelmed* mean that the SME may fail to provide the level of service security that their clients and enterprise partners expect. However - and remembering that the SMEs were simply asked to describe their experience as opposed to respond to specific questions on the security tool – the SMEs also report an increase in *Self-Efficacy*:

(P1) we have to model the overall architecture of the infrastructure and [with this tool] we can see where are the caveats of this infrastructure ... where we need to intervene

and

(P2) I think in the future we can understand how... how to apply..., for example, these are risk reports

If they use appropriate tools, therefore, the SMEs in *Study 3* who do not use tools are missing out, especially given that clients expect them to be responsible, and despite a possible lack of resource as reported in the literature, would nevertheless be in a better position to meet the expectations of their clients with appropriate tooling.

Beyond that, with increasing familiarity with such tooling, the SMEs interviewed began to identify other uses that they were not necessarily aware of originally. Although task-orientated, there is nevertheless a sense that it's not just about utility (PU), but also a sense that they are looking for other opportunities to use the tools, and to extend their own understanding:

(P1) What can come out of the model that we we create ... the [threat] path ... that we can see once we finish the model and we sort out all the threats and we can see the threat paths where an attacker might steal information or we have information leak. But for us, I think it will be *great advantage.*"

(our emphasis), and:

(P3) there is [the] GDPR compliance issue and possible modelling errors. So, this part of the tool it's very... important and interesting

What emerges from our interviews is that the SMEs in *Study 4* are aware of their responsibilities and can feel over-faced: cybersecurity is too complex and beyond their core competence. However, with suitable tooling (which is often missing, as in *Study 3*), the SME is not only able to meet their commitments (their *Self-efficacy* increases), but they begin to see other and more generalised potential with the tooling (*Innovation*). We suggest that this actually influences cybersecurity technology acceptance, which complements its importance for risk perception and adaptive behaviours in individuals [48–50].

Close collaboration from tool vendors with the SMEs, including encouraging them to explore the potential of cybersecurity tools rather than simply check that the tools meet *a priori* requirements, means that they are able to fulfil the expectations of their clients as well as comply with regulation. Such narratives take them beyond feeling overwhelmed to self-efficacy and the development of innovation [29]. And this is in parallel with their basic business, even though SMEs are generally assumed to lack (and report, see (P4)'s comments above on money implications) the resource to support anything beyond their core business.

4   Discussion

The four studies reported here had been run independently. There had been no overall plan to develop a coherent research approach to identify the challenges for the SME security landscape and expectations of their stakeholders. It is perhaps all the more remarkable that there is an emerging narrative from SMEs who engage with cybersecurity tooling that they not only meet their obligations but can also start to see ahead for other opportunities for security technologies to support their business and reputation. Despite confused client expectations, for instance, their lack of understanding of their rights under data protection and the abdication of responsibility to others when sharing their data, even just thinking about appropriate tools can expand SME self-efficacy and their ability to meet their obligations while maintaining their reputation vis-à-vis their stakeholders.

Our findings are not inconsistent with what has already been documented regarding private individuals. It is well-attested, for instance, that regulation does not necessarily empower private individuals [46]: they feel overwhelmed. In that context, it is no surprise in *Study 2* to discover that private individuals do not believe themselves to retain control over their data, even though they may be aware of cyber threats and suitable controls to mitigate them (*Study 1*). Further, even though regulation imposes responsibilities on those who process personal data [2], if SMEs are not completely aware of the threats they are exposed to, do not provide the training, and do not exploit predictive or preventative tooling (*Study 3*), there is a serious risk to multiple players, not least given the pervasiveness of SMEs [1]. What we have found in bringing the results from these studies together is that engagement with tooling can encourage *Self-efficacy* but also *Innovation* within the SME.

The project developing the security tools focused on close collaboration and support for the SMEs who took part in *Study 4*. Significantly, though, the interviews reported here were not about checking that requirements had been met with the tools in questions. Instead, they were given free rein to describe whatever their experience had been. Their response, as reported above, in developing the appropriate *Self-Efficacy* to meet their responsibilities has led them to think creatively (*Innovation*): seeing additional potential in the tools [29], without reporting any concerns about the resource implications of engaging with them. This seems to meet a significant need. Whatever the data subject rights are that regulation foresees, private individuals do not appear to be reassured and still believe their data are at the mercy of service providers. This imposes an obligation on the SMEs, though, which is more about reputation and the ongoing negotiation around mutual trust. To enable SMEs to go beyond their statutory regulatory obligations and focus on the trust of their clients, they need to be supported to understand how tools work with and for them, not simply tick a box: *Study 3*, for example, highlights that awareness does not necessarily translate into action. The aim of tool vendors shifts therefore away from compliance towards enabling the SMEs to feel empowered to handle cyber security.

Study 4 shows that a disparate set of SMEs across finance, healthcare, automotive and utilities can be helped along this path. So, even though private individuals do not understand their rights or responsibilities, SMEs can nonetheless develop and maintain their trust.

5   Limitations and Future Directions

The studies reported here were not part of a coherent research plan, as stated above. Further, the SMEs in *Study 4* were collaborators on a common project.

It is not clear, therefore, how representative they are of the SME cohort in *Study 3*. The connection between the first three studies and the final one may not be self-evident, therefore. That being said, that a narrative is developing of how SMEs can meet the expectations beyond what they are required to do suggests that in future a coordinated set of studies focused on the various aspects covered here may identify what support needs to be delivered to SMEs above and beyond generic awareness and training programmes. In so doing, a set of concrete recommendations can be generated to encourage SMEs faced with their responsibilities regarding security to engage with cybersecurity tools not just from ensuring preparedness for possible cyber attacks but also as a starting point to think innovatively about how they use tools in-house. Intrinsic motivation is known to be more robust than short-term extrinsic motivators like rewards and sanctions [42]. Encouraging a sense of self-fulfilment which seems to lead to innovation may encourage employees to assume responsibility for security compliance rather than imposing it on them. This would need further investigation.

6 Conclusion

Our research has examined different aspects of the SME cybersecurity landscape from different, stakeholder perspectives, and highlights different expectations and actual behaviours. Whatever regulation is in place which imposes obligations on SMEs, such regulation does not necessarily correspond with the expectations of private individuals. Further, SMEs themselves may be ill-equipped to meet their regulatory obligations but also to address customer expectation. Exploring how they use and could use cybersecurity tools can encourage self-efficacy, and therefore enable the SME to satisfy both. The interviews conducted here – based just on a generalised description of benefit to the individual – provides further evidence for introducing qualitative methods into our understanding of technology adoption.

Ethics. The various studies reported here were provided separate approval from the Faculty of Engineering and Physical Sciences (FEPS) Research Ethics Committee at the University of Science. The reference numbers are shown in the final column of Table 1 above.

References

1. Lin, D.-Y., Rayavarapu, S.N., Tadjeddine, K., Yeoh, R. : Beyond financials: helping small and medium-sized enterprizes thrive. In: McKinsey & Company, Public & Social Sector Practice (2022). https://www.mckinsey.com/industries/public-and-social-sector/our-insights/beyond-financials-helping-small-and-medium-size-enterprises-thrive
2. European Commission: Regulation (EU) 2016/679 of the European Parliament and of the Council of 27 April 2016 (2016)

3. International Organization for Standardization: ISO/IEC 27000:2018, in Information technology - Security techniques - Information security management systems - Overview and vocabulary. 2018

4. Wilson, M., McDonald, S., Button, D., McGarry, K.: It won't happen to me: surveying SME attitudes to cyber-security. J. Comput. Inf. Syst. 1–13 (2022). https://doi.org/10.1080/08874417.2022.2067791

5. Khan, M.I., Tanwar, S., Rana, A.: The need for information security management for SMEs. In: 2020 9th International Conference System Modeling and Advancement in Research Trends (SMART), pp. 328–332. IEEE, Moradabad, India (2020)

6. Bell, S.: Cybersecurity is not just a 'big business' issue. Gov. Dir. **69**(9), 536–539 (2017)

7. Sharma, K., Singh, A., Sharma, V.P.: SMEs and cybersecurity threats in E-commerce. EDPACS EDP Audit Control Secur. Newsl. **39**(5–6), 1–49 (2009)

8. Blythe, J.: Cyber security in the workplace: understanding and promoting behaviour change. In: Bottoni, P., Matera, M. (eds.) Proceedings of CHItaly 2013 Doctoral Consortium, vol. 1065, pp. 92–101. Trento, Italy (2013)

9. Alahmari, A., Duncan., B. : Cybersecurity risk management in small and medium-sized enterprises: a systematic review of recent evidence. In: 2020 International Conference on Cyber Situational Awareness, Data Analytics and Assessment (CyberSA), pp. 1–5. IEEE, Dublin, Ireland (2020)

10. Saleem, J., Adebisi, B., Ande, R., Hammoudeh, M.: A state of the art survey-impact of cyber attacks on SME's. In: Proceedings of the International Conference on Future Networks and Distributed Systems, ACM, Cambridge, UK (2017). https://doi.org/10.1145/3102304.3109812

11. Blythe, J.M., Coventry. L.: Costly but effective: comparing the factors that influence employee antimalware behaviours. Comput. Hum. Behav. **87**, 87–97 (2018)

12. Gafni, R., Pavel, T.: The invisible hole of information on SMB's cybersecurity. Online J. Appl. Knowl. Manag. (OJAKM) **7**(1), 4–26 (2019)

13. Wachinger, G., Renn, O., Begg, C., Kuhlicke, C. : The risk perception paradox - implications for governance and communication of natural hazards. Risk Anal. **33**(6), 1049–1065 (2013). https://doi.org/10.1111/j.1539-6924.2012.01942.x

14. Bada, M., Sasse, M.A., Nurse, J.R. : Cyber security awareness campaigns: why do they fail to change behaviour? In International Conference on Cyber Security for Sustainable Society, pp. 118–131. Coventry, UK. (2015)

15. Beldad, A., de Jong, M., Steehouder., M.: How shall i trust the faceless and the intangible? A literature review on the antecedents of online trust. Comput. Hum. Behav. **26**(5), 857–869 (2010). https://doi.org/10.1016/j.chb.2010.03.013

16. Siegrist, M.: Trust and risk perception: a critical review of the literature. Risk Anal. **41**(3), 480–490 (2021). https://doi.org/10.1111/risa.13325

17. De Kimpe, L., Walrave, M., Verdegem, P., Ponnet, K.: What we think we know about cybersecurity: an investigation of the relationship between perceived knowledge, internet trust, and protection motivation in a cybercrime context. Behav. Inf. Technol. **41**(8), 1796–1808 (2022). https://doi.org/10.1080/0144929X.2021.1905066

18. Witte, K.: Putting the fear back into fear appeals: the extended parallel process model. Commun. Monogr. **59**(4), 329–349 (1992)

19. Witte, K., Allen, M.: A meta-analysis of fear appeals: implications for effective public health campaigns. Health Educ. Behav. **27**(5), 591–615 (2000). https://doi.org/10.1177/109019810002700506

20. Rimal, R.N., Real, K.: Perceived risk and efficacy beliefs as motivators of change. Hum. Commun. Res. **29**(3), 370–399 (2003)

21. Paek, H.-J., Hove, T.: Risk Perceptions and Risk Characteristics. In: Oxford Research Encyclopedia of Communication. Oxford University Press, Oxford (2017)
22. Bax, S., McGill, T., Hobbs, V.: Maladaptive behaviour in response to email phishing threats: the roles of rewards and response costs. Comput. Secur. **106**, 102278 (2021). https://doi.org/10.1016/j.cose.2021.102278
23. Geer, D., Jardine, E., Leverett, E.: On market concentration and cybersecurity risk. J. Cyber Policy **5**(1), 9–29 (2020). https://doi.org/10.1080/23738871.2020.1728355
24. Öğütçü, G., Testik, Ö.M., Chouseiniglo, O. : Analysis of personal information security behavior and awareness. Comput. Secur. **56**, 83–93 (2016). https://doi.org/10.1016/j.cose.2015.10.002
25. Lewis, R., Louvieris, P., Abbott, P., Clewley, N., Jones, K.: Cybersecurity information sharing: a framework for information security management in UK SME supply chains. In: Twenty Second European Conference on Information Systems, Tel Aviv, Israel (2014)
26. D'Arcy, J., Hovav, A., Galletta, D.F.: User awareness of security countermeasures and its impact on information systems misuse: a deterrence approach. Inf. Syst. Res. **20**(1), 79–98 (2009). https://doi.org/10.1287/isre.1070.0160
27. Morrow, B.: BYOD security challenges: control and protect your most sensitive data. Netw. Secur. **2012**(12), 5–8 (2012). https://doi.org/10.1016/S1353-4858(12)70111-3
28. Davis, F.D.: Perceived usefulness, perceived ease of use, and user acceptance of information technology. MIS Q. **13**(3), 319–340 (1989). https://doi.org/10.2307/249008
29. Pickering, B., Phillips, S., Surridge, M.: Tell me what that means to you: small-story narratives in technology adoption. In: Kurosu, M. (eds.) Human-Computer Interaction. Theoretical Approaches and Design Methods. HCII 2022. LNCS, vol. 13302, pp. 274–289. Springer, Cham (2022). https://doi.org/10.1007/978-3-031-05311-5_19
30. Ifinedo, P.: Understanding information systems security policy compliance: an integration of the theory of planned behavior and the protection motivation theory. Comput. Secur. **31**(1), 83–95 (2012). https://doi.org/10.1016/j.cose.2011.10.007
31. Pickering, B., Taylor, S.: Cybersecurity Survey. https://zenodo.org/record/7589508
32. Boniface, M., et al.: DARE UK PRiAM Project D4 Report: Public Engagement: Understanding private individuals' perspectives on privacy and privacy risk. https://zenodo.org/record/7107487
33. Pickering, B., Baker, K., Boniface, M., McMahon, J.: Privacy Perspectives Survey. https://zenodo.org/record/7589522
34. Erdogan, G., Halvorsrud, R., Boletsis, C., Tverdal, S., Pickering, J.B.: Cybersecurity awareness and capacities of SMEs. In: 9th International Conference on Information Systems Security and Privacy. Lisbon Portugal (2023)
35. Erdogan, G., Halvorsrud, R., Boletsis, C., Tverdal, S., Pickering, J.B.: Cybersecurity awareness and capacities of SMEs. In: International Conference on Information Systems Security and Privacy (ICISSP), Lisbon, Portugal (2022). https://doi.org/10.5281/zenodo.7443048
36. Edelman, S., Peer, E.: Predicting privacy and security attitudes. ACM SIGCAS Comput. Soc. **45**(1), 22–28 (2015). https://doi.org/10.1145/2738210.2738215
37. Chakravarthy, A., Chen, X., Nasser, B., Surridge, M.: Trustworthy systems design using semantic risk modelling. In: 1st International Conference on Cyber Security for Sustainable Society, Coventry, UK (2015)

38. Braun, V., Clarke, V.: Using thematic analysis in psychology. Qual. Res. Psychol. **3**(2), 77–101 (2006). https://doi.org/10.1191/1478088706qp063oa
39. Braun, V., Clarke, V.: Reflecting on reflexive thematic analysis. Qual. Res. Sport Exerc. Health **11**(4), 589–597 (2019). https://doi.org/10.1080/2159676X.2019.1628806
40. Chenoweth, T., Minch, R., Gattiker, T.: Application of protection motivation theory to adoption of protective technologies. In: 42nd Hawaii International Conference of System Sciences. IEEE, Walkoloa, HI, USA (2009)
41. Ajzen, I.: The theory of planned behaviour: reactions and reflections. Psychol. Health **26**(9), 1113–1127 (2011). https://doi.org/10.1080/08870446.2011.613995
42. Deci, E.L., Ryan, R.M.: The "what" and "why" of goal pursuits: human needs and the self-determination of behavior. Psychol. Inq. **11**(4), 227–268 (2000). https://doi.org/10.1207/S15327965PLI1104_01
43. Ruggiero, T.E.: Uses and gratifications theory in the 21st century. Mass Commun. Soc. **3**(1), 3–37 (2000). https://doi.org/10.1207/S15327825MCS0301_02
44. Camilleri, M.A., Falzon, L.: Understanding motivations to use online streaming services: integrating the technology acceptance model (TAM) and the uses and gratifications theory (UGT). Span. J. Mark. ESIC **25**(2), 217–238 (2021). https://doi.org/10.1108/SJME-04-2020-0074
45. Mayer, R.C., Davis, J.H., Schoorman, F.D.: An integrative model of organizational trust. Acad. Manag. Rev. **20**(3), 709–734 (1995). https://doi.org/10.5465/AMR.1995.9508080335
46. Acquisti, A., Brandimarte, L., Loewenstein, G.: Privacy and human behavior in the age of information. Science **347**(6221), 509–514 (2015). https://doi.org/10.1126/science.aaa1465
47. Jahankhani, H., Meda, L.N.K., Samadi, M.: Cybersecurity challenges in small and medium enterprise (SMEs). In: Jahankhani, H., V. Kilpin, D., Kendzierskyj, S. (eds.) Blockchain and Other Emerging Technologies for Digital Business Strategies. Advanced Sciences and Technologies for Security Applications. Springer, Cham (2022). https://doi.org/10.1007/978-3-030-98225-6_1
48. Slovic, P., Peters, E.: Risk perception and affect. Curr. Dir. Psychol. Sci. **15**(6), 322–325 (2006)
49. Van Schaik, P., Renaud, K., Wilson, C., Jansen, J., Onibokun, J.: Risk as affect: the affect heuristic in cybersecurity. Comput. Secur. **90**, 101651 (2020). https://doi.org/10.1016/j.cose.2019.101651
50. Slovic, P., Finucane, M.L., Peters, E., MacGregor, D.G.: Risk as analysis and risk as feelings: some thoughts about affect, reason, risk, and rationality. Risk Anal. **24**(2), 311–322 (2004). https://doi.org/10.1111/j.0272-4332.2004.00433.x

Business Continuity Planning (BCP) for Election Systems

David Stevens[✉] [iD] and Richard Halverson

Kapiʻolani Community College, University of Hawaiʻi, Honolulu, HI, USA
{david.stevens,richardh}@hawaii.edu

Abstract. Governments are embracing IT at an ever-increasing pace, incorporating technology into their critical infrastructure, and bringing cybersecurity to the forefront as policymakers balance system availability and convenience with privacy and security. However, achieving this balance can be challenging when planning for unforeseen circumstances during an election. In the United States, although there is guidance at the national level, plans to deliver election services during a cyber or physical attack or disaster are left up to each state and local jurisdiction. This paper covers a brief history of disaster recovery and business continuity planning. We then examine election systems as a critical system in the United States and discuss the status of each state's ability to respond to and plan for election system emergencies or failures during an election. Finally, we recommend promoting a more unified approach to business continuity planning (BCP) for election systems.

Keywords: Business Continuity Planning · Cybersecurity · Secure Election Systems

Acronyms

BCP	Business Continuity Planning
C3PAO	Certified third-party auditing organization
CCPA	California Consumer Privacy Act
CFITF	Countering Foreign Influence Task Force
CISA	The Cybersecurity and Infrastructure Security Agency
CMMC	Cybersecurity Maturity Model Certification
CMMC-AB	CMMC Accreditation Board
CSF	NIST Cybersecurity Assessment Framework
CUI	Controlled unclassified information
DDoS	Distributed denial of service
DHS	Department of Homeland Security
DIB	Defense Industrial Base
DR	Disaster Recovery
DoD	Department of Defense
EAC	US Election Assistance Commission
EI-ISAC	Election Infrastructure Information Sharing and Analysis Center

A. Moallem (Ed.): HCII 2023, LNCS 14045, pp. 353–367, 2023.
https://doi.org/10.1007/978-3-031-35822-7_24

EIS-GCC	Election Infrastructure Subsector Government Coordinating Council
ESI	Election Security Initiative
ETF	Election Task Force
FEMA	Federal Emergency Management Association
HAVA	Help America Vote Act of 2002
HIPAA	Health Insurance Portability and Accountability Act
ISA	International Federation of the National Standardizing Associations now known as the ISO
ISO	International Standards Organization
IT	Information Technology
ITAR	International Trafficking of Arms
NASS	National Association of Secretaries of State
NCSL	National Conference of State Legislatures
NEMA	National Emergency Management Association
NIPP	National Infrastructure Protection Plan
NIST	National Institute of Standards and Technology
OSINT	Open-source intelligence
PCI DSS	Payment Card Systems Data Security Standard
PII	Personally Identifiable Information
PPD-21	Presidential Policy Directive 21 established strategic imperatives for the national critical infrastructure
SSA	Sector Specific Agency in charge of structuring and managing the sector
TGDC	EAC Technical Guidelines Development Committee
UNSCC	United Nations Standards Coordinating Committee
UOCAVA	The Uniformed And Overseas Citizens Absentee Voting Act
USA PATRIOT	Uniting and Strengthening America by Providing Appropriate Tools Required to Intercept and Obstruct Terrorism Act of 2001
USPS	United States Postal Service
VVSG	Voluntary Voting System Guidelines Version 2.0

1   Introduction

We expect any critical system in which we place our faith to be well-managed, somewhat efficient, and, most importantly, reliable. Availability and security play integral roles in the acceptance and success of any system, and those systems that provide for reliable elections should be no different. Therefore, it is imperative to prepare for unforeseen circumstances during elections by developing contingency plans to ensure seamless election experiences for voters [1].

2   Background

2.1   What is a System?

We can define a system as a group of interacting or interrelated entities forming a unified whole for a purpose. We place our faith in systems every day. We have utilities such as water, power, and waste systems. We place our trust in emergency response systems such as police, fire, and ambulance services. We depend on transportation systems for freight and travel, such as shipping, airlines, rail, buses, and automobiles. We rely heavily on computers, telecommunications, and the Internet. Unfortunately, not everyone trusts in our election systems, but to preserve a democratically elected government, we should. A sound and trustworthy election system is critical to the survival of a democracy and encourages citizens to participate in the democratic process.

2.2 What is a Critical System?

We can characterize a system as critical by defining the consequences associated with its failure. The more damage possible attributed to the system failure, the more critical we consider the system. An example of a critical system would be emergency services, including law enforcement, fire/rescue services, and emergency medical services. If any of these systems were to fail, human lives would likely be lost.

Similarly, our modern civilization's dependence on technology makes our computer systems critical. Consider air traffic control, nuclear command, or the power grid. Damage to these systems would have the capacity to cause considerable loss of life and great financial loss. This dependence can lead to the targeting of critical systems by cyber, military, or terrorist attacks [2].

Recent evidence of critical systems being high-value targets for cyber-attacks appeared in the news (May 2021), when a primary US oil pipeline system stretching from New Jersey to Texas and transporting almost one-half of the fuel products used on the US East Coast, was the victim of a ransomware attack. As a result, Colonial Pipeline, the company that runs this pipeline, shut down operations for six days while recovering from the attack and experienced losses in the millions of dollars [3].

2.3 Are Election Systems Critical?

We can answer this question by researching the policies and laws related to election systems in the US. On Jan. 6, 2017, the United States Dept. of Homeland Security (DHS) designated US election systems as critical infrastructure [4]. DHS used language from the USA Patriot Act of 2001 as guidance for categorizing election systems as critical infrastructure. The USA Patriot Act defines critical infrastructure as "…systems and assets, whether physical or virtual, so vital to the United States that the incapacity or destruction of such systems and assets would have a debilitating impact on security, national economic security, national public health or safety, or any combination of those matters [5]".

The National Infrastructure Protection Plan (NIPP) further defined critical infrastructure and established a process roadmap by which the nation's critical infrastructure sectors can be identified and created. The plans developed by the NIPP set a process to identify and create national critical infrastructure sectors [6].

The DHS used the USA Patriot Act and the NIPP as the foundational documents for developing sector-specific critical infrastructure contingency plans.

US presidential policy prioritized critical infrastructure definition and supported the Patriot Act and NIPP, adding a critical infrastructure governing authority with Policy

Directive 21 (PPD-21). This directive, released in 2013, established "strategic impera-
tives" to guide the Federal Government's approach to the national critical infrastructure.
It also established sector-specific agencies (SSAs) charged with managing their critical
infrastructure sectors [7].

3 How Can We Protect Critical Systems?

3.1 Disaster Recovery Planning

Up to the 1950s, organizations planned for disasters by instituting fire prevention strategies and purchasing insurance. In the 1960s, with the implementation of computers in
organizations, the disaster recovery dogma began to adapt to cover electronic data storage. As a result, organizations created policies and procedures to preserve critical data
offsite and recover vital technology infrastructure and services after a natural or human-
caused disaster, allowing them to resume operations at a new location if necessary [8].
These policies and procedures form the organization's disaster recovery (DR) plan.

While the term disaster recovery may seem to be synonymous with the term business
continuity, they have some fundamental differences.

The key difference is that disaster recovery focuses on restoring human operations,
information technology (IT) infrastructure, and access to data after a disaster. Business
continuity, however, also focuses on providing continuous business operations during a
disaster.

3.2 Evolution of Business Continuity Planning

Because business continuity planning (BCP) is more comprehensive than disaster recovery and includes considerations such as high availability and continuous operations,
organizations routinely have DR plans in their BCP. In addition, business continuity
planning contains contingencies for every aspect of the business that might be affected,
including human resources, corporate assets, business processes, and other business
stakeholders, such as the supplier network.

BCP emerged in the 1970s when financial organizations invested in alternative sites,
mainframe cooling systems, backup tapes, etc., and became more popular in the 1980s
with the growth of commercial recovery sites offering computer services on a shared
basis.

Dependency on computers, and the growing need for access to digital resources, led
to an increase in the available tools allowing people to rapidly recover from many natural
and human-caused disasters [9].

Corporate globalization in the 1990s increased the pervasiveness of data access,
and companies saw that the loss of service time could mean the loss of customers and
competitive market advantage.

During this time, BCP became more complex with the addition of clustered server
environments [10], later known as 'the cloud', which hosted distributed applications,
data processing, and data storage. However, BCP still had not yet become pervasive
throughout civilian and government organizations.

3.3 When did BCP Become Important?

In the late 1990s, the projected threat of critical system failures associated with the 'Year 2000' coding deficiencies, brought business continuity to the forefront. Companies struggled to update their software and firmware to a four-digit date to prevent systems from failing completely at midnight on Dec. 31, 1999.

BCP came into stronger focus when, on Sept. 11, 2001, organizations saw first-hand the impact of unmanaged risk, forever changing the breadth of organizational resources included in BCP, now commonly referred to as the "risk landscape."

The risk landscape continued to grow, shift, and become more unpredictable in the early years of the new millennium with the Madrid Train Bombing and the Indian Ocean Tsunami in 2004, hurricanes Katrina and Wilma in 2005 [11], the Deepwater Horizon oil rig explosion and oil spill in 2010, and Hurricane Sandy in 2012.

3.4 What's Happening Now?

Today, the organizational risk landscape includes cyber-attacks that can destroy IT infrastructure and permanently cripple businesses. As many as seventy-five percent of small and medium-sized companies lacking effective business continuity plans could fail within three years after a disaster [12].

BCP must now incorporate resilience against cyber-attacks, intrusion, and illegal exfiltration of confidential data. In addition, enterprise data storage requirements grow an average of forty to seventy percent, which means there is an ever-increasing amount of data to backup or recover [13].

Organizations must balance the necessity to be up and running with the potential damage from attacks such as ransomware, trojans, viruses, phishing scams (social engineering), distributed denial of service (DDoS), physical attacks, and natural disasters.

3.5 How Can We Achieve a Balance?

This balance is difficult to achieve, considering that most people now expect $24 \times 7 \times 365$ service from any system. The lack of system availability is not an option for most organizations and makes preventing attacks targeting a system's availability a serious threat and a top priority.

However, BCP promotes a holistic approach to keeping a system running and includes considerations for all organizational components during disruptions caused by attacks or natural disasters which adversely affect technology, physical assets, and people.

BCP also includes defense-in-depth, a layered approach to cyber and physical security that manages risk with diverse defensive tactics.

Defense-in-depth addresses circumstances when a security device or application fails to stop an intruder, with deeper defensive layers to stop the attack. However, this approach can often be expensive, and some organizations must plan this implementation over months or sometimes years.

4 BCP and Election Systems

4.1 Applying the Balance to Election Systems

Because election systems are considered critical infrastructure in the US, national cyber-security and continuity planning guidance is provided to local and state jurisdictions by federal agencies such as the Election Assistance Commission (EAC), the Department of Homeland Security (DHS), the Election Infrastructure Information Sharing and Analysis Center (EI-ISAC), the Cybersecurity & Infrastructure Security Agency (CISA), and the Election Infrastructure Subsector Government Coordinating Council (EIS-GCC).

4.2 What are the Barriers to Success?

Barriers to success often include issues related to complex bureaucracies. For example, creating an effective contingency plan includes advanced planning and practice scenarios. In addition, it requires comprehensive networking, information sharing, autonomy, and flexibility, which are not typical attributes of most government organizations.

The power to conduct elections in the US rests with the states and the national government. The federal government plays an advisory role and has no real authority in elections administration. State and local government compliance is mostly voluntary outside voter registration administration.

Adding to that complexity, the US has over 8,000 local election jurisdictions. Some of these jurisdictions have conducted elections since colonial times, and there are currently no required national-level reviews of local election office operations or effectiveness. Election officials also fear that the philosophy of administrative transparency combined with the freedom of the press could allow open-source intelligence (OSINT) operations by bad actors, primarily nation-states, to facilitate interference in US elections [1].

4.3 State-Level Barriers

The National Association of Secretaries of State report of the Task Force on Emergency Preparedness for Elections [14] provided information on state laws relating to the postponement or relocation of an election, the executive branch's role in election emergencies, and suggestions on potential mitigation strategies that state governments can take.

States differ in their ability to respond to election emergencies. Barriers can include the ability of state officials to suspend state statutes or for state officials to relocate or reschedule an election due to emergency circumstances such as weather-related events.

The Coronavirus pandemic tested how well states could respond to an emergency that interrupted the nation's ability to conduct the 2020 elections at the local, state and national level.

Allowing mail-in ballots greatly reduces vulnerability to interruption from situations in which voters are required to go to a physical location to cast their vote. All states provide absentee mail-in ballots for military personnel overseas and for illness, but voting by mail was not guaranteed for all voters and depended largely on how willing

Table 1. Accommodations by State for Mail-In Voting for the November 2020 Election

All-mail elections		No-excuse absentee voting		Coronavirus Accommodation		Minimal/No Accommodation	
1	California	9	Alaska	37	Alabama	47	Indiana
2	Colorado	10	Arizona	38	Arkansas	48	Louisiana
3	Hawaii	11	District of Columbia	39	Connecticut	49	Mississippi
4	Nevada	12	Florida	40	Delaware	50	Tennessee
5	Oregon	13	Georgia	41	Kentucky	51	Texas
6	Utah	14	Idaho	42	Missouri		
7	Washington	15	Illinois	43	New Hampshire		
8	Vermont	16	Iowa	44	New York		
		17	Kansas	45	South Carolina		
		18	Maine	46	West Virginia		
		19	Maryland				
		20	Massachusetts				
		21	Michigan				
		22	Minnesota				
		23	Montana				
		24	Nebraska				
		25	New Jersey				
		26	New Mexico				
		27	North Carolina				
		28	North Dakota				
		29	Ohio				
		30	Oklahoma				
		31	Pennsylvania				
		32	Rhode Island				
		33	South Dakota				
		34	Virginia				
		35	Wisconsin				
		36	Wyoming				

states were to allow voting by mail during an emergency. Table 1 below lists each state's accommodations for mail-in voting before the pandemic [15].

At the beginning of the pandemic, only eight states allowed all mail-in voting (where the state proactively mails each voter a ballot), while another twenty-eight states allowed no-excuse absentee voting (where voters apply to vote by mail). The remaining 15 states required a state-defined valid reason to vote absentee, such as a service member stationed overseas or an illness. During the 2020 election season, just 5 states provided no accommodation for mail-in ballots for those who feared of contracting the coronavirus.

Despite these barriers, all states were able to make adjustments to elections voting periods and deadlines either by emergency powers by the governor or secretary of state, or by enacting legislation. From this experience, it would seem that state governments would be able to react reasonably well in the event of a natural disaster.

Guidance must sufficiently accommodate the potential for cybersecurity issues. Legislators could recommend that state agencies review options for DHS support, including pre-event emergency preparedness training. Plans should focus on the effects of an emergency instead of the types of emergencies.

4.4 What Progress Have We Made?

To help coordinate federal security support for the election community, in 2018, the DHS established the Election Task Force (ETF) and the Countering Foreign Influence Task Force (CFITF). Both are now part of the Election Security Initiative (ESI) within the CISA.

The CISA promotes services such as vulnerability scanning, physical security assessments, remote penetration testing, and phishing campaign assessments for the election community.

As of 2020, CISA has provided policy and planning guidance to over one thousand election jurisdictions. But only fifteen states completed customized cybersecurity plans with the help of the CISA. Another twenty states expressed interest in CISA assistance for the 2020 elections [16].

To assist election jurisdictions in normalizing election system implementation, reliability, and security, the Federal Election Commission created the first two revisions of the federal voting standards in 1990 and revised them in 2002.

Created by the Help America Vote Act of 2002 and formed as an independent agency of the United States government, the Election Assistance Commission (EAC) serves as a national resource for election administration information.

The Technical Guidelines Development Committee (TGDC) of the EAC, with assistance from the National Institute of Standards and Technology (NIST), adopted and updated the standards and published the Voluntary Voting System Guidelines (VVSG) in 2005.

The EAC produced revisions to the VVSG in 2015 and 2021. In version 2.0, the VVSG is a set of election system specifications and requirements that allow testing to determine if the systems provide functionality, accessibility, and security.

The VVSG provides instructions to implement and improve consistent voter experiences, enabling all voters to vote independently and in private, while also ensuring all votes are marked, verified, and cast as intended, and the final vote count is accurate [17].

Some US State agencies also provide guidance for contingency planning and can include support for emergencies other than cyber-attacks, such as natural disasters.

Following Hurricane Sandy in 2012, the National Association of Secretaries of State (NASS) created a task force to study US states' election contingency planning and preparedness.

NASS held discussions with key stakeholders to highlight shared concerns with the Florida Division of Emergency Management, the National Emergency Management Association (NEMA), the Emergency Management Assistance Compact, the United States Postal Service (USPS), and the Federal Emergency Management Association (FEMA).

NASS then conducted a survey of the US States to assess emergency readiness. The results were released in 2014, then updated in 2017.

Only thirty-seven states replied to the task force survey. The survey included questions that covered state laws authorizing the postponement of elections in an emergency, legislative activity regarding election contingency plans and other election emergency plans, voting by individuals responding to or impacted by an emergency, the intersection of state election officials, state emergency officials, and the federal government in an emergency affecting an election, and general security planning.

The results of the NASS survey provided data highlighting the need for contingency planning improvement for all responding US states. Especially regarding the second topic, legislative activity regarding election contingency plans and other election emergency plans.

Out of thirty-seven states responding regarding legislative activity for *both* cybersecurity *and* contingency planning, none had a state election statute containing a section related to both topics. Three have an election statute that mentions both topics, and none had legislation (not specifically election-related) introduced with the mention of the topic [18]. Fifteen states have no legislation containing even the mention of either topic (See Table 2).

Table 2. Voting System Security Rules and Guidance by State

Activity	Number of States	Cybersecurity *and* Contingency
State election statute contains section(s) related to both topics	0	n/a
Election statutes mentioning both topics	3	IN, MO, ND
Legislation introduced with mention of both topics	0	n/a
Missing both cybersecurity and contingency planning	15	AL, AK, AR, DC, MA, MI, MS, NE, NH, NM, RI, SC, TN, WA, WY

Much of the NASS survey data focused on delays or postponement of elections and voting by individuals impacted by or responding to an emergency.

Many responding states have contingencies for first responders and emergency workers who had to leave the jurisdiction during an election. These workers can use other voting methods, including mail-in and early voting, if available in those states. However, most alternate voting methods are contingent upon an emergency declaration by the Governor or State courts.

However, when it came to requiring contingency planning for elections, the results varied. Eleven of the thirty-seven states responding required state and/or local officials to develop specific election-related emergency plans.

Of the thirty-seven NASS survey responding states delivering contingency planning information to state election offices, seventeen states provide general resources, eleven provide broad election administration information documentation, six provide official public statements relating to election security, and seventeen states don't have any information publicly available on the topic.

Delivering cybersecurity planning information to state election offices, of the thirty-seven responding states, sixteen states provide general resources, seven provide broad election information administration documentation, twenty-four provide official public statements relating to election security, and four don't have any information publicly available on the topic.

Wide gaps in preparedness appear when survey results of the thirty-seven responding states reveal that states provide information regarding both cybersecurity and contingency planning to state election offices; nine provide general resources, four provide broad election administration information documentation, and only two states provide official public statements relating to election security. Two states don't have any publicly available information on either topic. Surprisingly, Washington, DC, falls into the last category (counted as a state in the NASS survey).

It is important to emphasize that the absence of evidence does not ensure the evidence of absence. For example, some states could very well have election system cybersecurity and/or contingency planning and just choose not to make those plans public. Further details are shown in Table 3.

Table 3. Contingency and Cybersecurity Planning by State Election Offices

Activity	Number of States	Cybersecurity *and* Contingency planning
General resources provided	9	CA, CO, CT, KY, MN, NJ, VA, WA, WI
Broad election administration information documentation	4	AZ, IA, NH, NM
Public Official statements relating to election security	2	HI, NC
Nothing found	2	DC, WY

5 BCP for Similar Critical Systems

5.1 Private Industry Frameworks

By comparison, organizations administering systems other than election systems use different accepted security and contingency planning frameworks. For example, some non-governmental standards with certification programs include the NIST Cybersecurity Assessment Framework (CSF) [19], the Payment Card Systems Data Security Standard (PCI DSS) [20], and the International Standards Organization (ISO) standards 22301, 22313, and 27001 [21].

In February 2013, Presidential Executive Order 13636 directed NIST to develop a cybersecurity assessment framework (CSF), consisting of standards, guidelines, and practices for protecting critical infrastructure from cyber-attacks. The NIST CSF presented critical infrastructure operators with a cost-effective, flexible, repeatable, and prioritized approach to managing cyber risk. This standard is now used by many disparate organizations, from banks to cloud providers, to plan and execute their cybersecurity strategy [19].

Originally founded as the International Federation of the National Standardizing Associations (ISA) in the 1920s, then reformed as the International Organization for Standardization in 1946 by the United Nations Standards Coordinating Committee (UNSCC), and now recognized as the International Standards Organization, the ISO is a non-governmental, independent organization with members representing 165 countries and is the world's largest developer of voluntary international standards covering technology, agriculture, food safety, and manufactured products. Some of the ISO standards covering cybersecurity and business continuity are in publications 22301, 22313, and 27001 [21].

The Payment Card Systems Data Security Standard (PCI DSS) is a set of standards mandated and regulated by major credit card companies to increase the controls for cardholder data to reduce the risk of credit card fraud. Major credit card companies impose these standards on financial institutions that accept credit cards. Compliance is verified quarterly or annually by varying methods based on the company's volume of transactions. If a company that handles credit card data suffers a data breach, the major credit card companies can impose significant fines that can amount to millions of dollars. Additionally, companies that suffer a data breach will usually be required to purchase insurance at higher rates [22].

5.2 Government-Mandated Frameworks

Some examples of security standards and certifications mandated by Federal legislation are the Health Insurance Portability and Accountability Act (HIPAA) [23], the Cybersecurity Maturity Model Certification (CMMC) [24], the California Consumer Privacy Act (CCPA) [25], and the (NIST) special publications 800-34, 800-171, and 800-53 [26].

Signed into law on Aug. 21, 1996, the Health Insurance Portability and Accountability Act (HIPAA) ensures health insurance coverage for US workers and their families when they change employers or lose their jobs. Other focus areas of HIPAA were to specify how healthcare insurance industries protect personally identifiable information (PII) from fraud and theft and to correct healthcare insurance limitations [23].

As a unifying standard to ensure that DoD contractors properly protect controlled unclassified information (CUI), the US government has provided cybersecurity guidance to contractors for decades. However, there was no way for contractors to demonstrate the efficacy of their cybersecurity programs. To remedy this, the Department of Defense (DoD) created a cybersecurity program for the Defense Industrial Base (DIB) contractors called the Cybersecurity Maturity Model Certification (CMMC). Before the contract award, all DoD contractors and vendors will require this new certification by late 2024 [24].

Signed into law in 2018 and intended to enhance consumer protection and privacy rights, the California Consumer Privacy Act (CCPA) lets California residents know what personal data the vendor is collecting about them and whether their personal data is sold or disclosed, and to whom. The CCPA also lets residents of California access their collected personal data and allows them to say no to the sale of that data. California residents can also request that businesses delete their personal information without being discriminated against for exercising their privacy rights. [25].

5.3 Compliance Audit and Verification

Companies requiring these and similar standards, both government-mandated and non-government security standards, can implement the requirements for compliance in a way that uniquely addresses the organization's needs and still achieve compliance.

A third-party certification organization validates organizational compliance with the security standard after thoroughly auditing the security requirements for the specified framework.

Despite the vast number of frameworks that exist, and despite the government mandated compliance by government entities and government contractors against certain frameworks, there is no clear nationally applicable required election system threat analysis and resiliency framework certification.

Additionally, there are challenges in verifying specific framework requirements for organizations. Currently, the PCI DSS is the only framework with certified training provided by the governing organization, the PCI Standards Council. In addition, the CMMC Accreditation Board CMMC-AB certifies organizations as having met the requirements of the CMMC. However, the CMMC-AB provides training standards for third-party auditing organizations (C3PAOs) that perform the actual audits.

The International Trafficking of Arms (ITAR) requirements require organizational compliance according to the NIST 800-53 controls. Unfortunately, there is no ITAR compliance certification, and no organizations are currently performing audits to ensure ITAR compliance [27]. An organization's leaders may believe they are compliant against a given framework, but only an audit by a third party can provide assurance that an organization is protected from an attack.

6 Conclusions

There is no current framework with a holistic approach to BCP for election systems. However, we can find the foundational elements for a new standardized BCP framework for election systems in the VVSG and the CMMC.

The US Government should create a new election system BCP framework by combining these foundational elements. Then adding specific language allowing states to implement secure election systems that fit their specific needs.

This requirement would not adversely affect the disparate election systems because jurisdictions could each choose their own unique approach to implement the standard yet still achieve the goal of compliance.

This compliance standard would also be essential to enforce on election systems vendors and would be much the same as the new Department of Defense (DoD) vendor compliance standard, the CMMC.

For this Federal standard, vendors in contracts with the DoD must comply with a security model based on the NIST special publications 800-171 and 800-172. The vendor must choose how to implement the required security controls, then go through an audit performed by a third party to obtain the CMMC certification every three years.

No two vendor compliance implementations are the same, yet they all comply with the CMMC model. Additionally, the details of how the vendor complied with the requirements are only shared with the third-party auditor and the DoD organization on the contract and are never to be made public. This security measure protects the organization from those attempting to plan an attack on specific systems.

Even though fragmentation between election jurisdictions exists, the US Government could implement a security and continuity standard, and tie grant funding to the adherence to the standard. Thus, also providing jurisdictions a financial incentive to comply.

Acknowledgments. "This material is based upon work supported by the National Science Foundation under Grant No. 1662487. Any opinions, findings, and conclusions or recommendations expressed in this material are those of the authors and do not necessarily reflect the views of the NSF."

References

1. Brown, M., Forson, L., Hale, K., Smith, R., Williamson, R.D.: Capacity to address natural and man-made vulnerabilities: the administrative structure of US election system security. Election Law J.: Rules Polit. Policy **19**(2), 180–199 (2020). https://doi.org/10.1089/elj.2020.0626
2. Dekker, A.H.: Simulating network robustness for critical infrastructure networks. In: Proceedings of the Twenty-Eighth Australasian Conference on Computer Science, vol. 38, pp. 59–67 (2005)
3. U.S. pipeline system, Washington Post (2021). https://www.washingtonpost.com/business/2021/05/08/cyber-attack-colonial-pipeline/

4. US Election Assistance Commission, "Starting Point: US Election Systems as Critical Infrastructure" (n.d.). https://www.eac.gov/sites/default/files/eac_assets/1/6/starting_point_us_election_systems_as_Critical_Infrastructure.pdf
5. H. R. 3162, 107th Cong., "Uniting and Strengthening America by Providing Appropriate Tools Required to Intercept and Obstruct Terrorism (USA Patriot) Act" (2001). https://www.congress.gov/107/plaws/publ56/PLAW-107publ56.pdf
6. Department of Homeland Security, "National Infrastructure Protection Plan (NIPP) 2013: Partnering for Critical Infrastructure Security and Resilience", p. 12 (2013). https://www.dhs.gov/sites/default/files/publications/National-Infrastructure-Protection-Plan-2013-508.pdf
7. Presidential Decision Directive 63, "SUBJECT: Critical Infrastructure Protection" (1998). https://fas.org/irp/offdocs/pdd/pdd-63.htm
8. Hayhoe, G.F.: Managing in a post-9/11, post-Katrina world: an introduction to disaster-recovery planning for technical communicators, pp. 34–36 (2006). https://doi.org/10.1109/IPCC.2006.320367
9. Fong, K.: Contingency planning and disaster recovery. In: Proceedings of the 1984 Annual Conference of the ACM on the Fifth Generation Challenge, p. 256 (1984). https://doi.org/10.1145/800171.809643
10. Landry, B.J.L., Koger, M.S.: Dispelling 10 common disaster recovery myths: lessons learned from Hurricane Katrina and other disasters. J. Educ. Resour. Comput. 6(4), 6-es (2006). https://doi.org/10.1145/1248453.1248459
11. Saleem, K., Luis, S., Deng, Y., Chen, S.-C., Hristidis, V., Li, T.: Towards a business continuity information network for rapid disaster recovery. In: Proceedings of the 2008 International Conference on Digital Government Research, pp. 107–116 (2008)
12. Blythe, B.: Blindsided: A Manager's Guide to Catastrophic Incidents in the Workplace. Portfolio (2002)
13. IBM Services. "Adapt and respond to risks with a business continuity plan (BCP)" (2021). https://www.ibm.com//services/business-continuity/plan
14. National Conference of State Legislatures. "Election Emergencies" (2017). https://www.nass.org/sites/default/files/Election%20Cybersecurity/report-NASS-emergency-preparedness-elections-apr2017.pdf
15. National Conference of State Legislatures. "Voting Outside the Polling Place: Absentee, All-Mail and other Voting at Home Options" (2020). https://www.justia.com/covid-19/50-state-covid-19-resources/elections-during-covid-19-50-state-resources/
16. Cybersecurity and Infrastructure Security Agency (CISA). "Protect2020 Strategic Plan" (2020). https://www.cisa.gov/sites/default/files/publications/ESI%20Strategic%20Plan_FINAL%202.7.20%20508.pdf#page=1&zoom=auto,-271,798
17. Election Assistance Commission. "Requirements for the Voluntary Voting System Guidelines 2.0" (2021). https://www.eac.gov/sites/default/files/TestingCertification/Voluntary_Voting_System_Guidelines_Version_2_0.pdf
18. Merrill, et al.: "State Laws & Practices for the Emergency Management of Elections: Report of the NASS Task Force on Emergency Preparedness for Elections, Released February 2014; Updated April 2017" (2017). https://www.nass.org/sites/default/files/surveys/2019-07/report-NASS-emergency-preparedness-elections-apr2017.pdf
19. National Institute of Standards and Technology (NIST) Cybersecurity Assessment Framework (CSF) (n.d.). https://www.nist.gov/itl/smallbusinesscyber/nist-cybersecurity-framework
20. Payment Card Industry Security Standards Council. "Payment Card Industry Data Security Standard (PCI DSS)" (n.d.). https://www.pcisecuritystandards.org/document_library
21. International Standards Organization (ISO). "ISO standards 22301, 22313, 27001" (n.d.). https://www.iso.org/standards.html

22. US Securities and Exchange Commission. "Settlement Agreement Between Heartland Payment Systems, Inc. and Mastercard" (2010). https://www.sec.gov/Archives/edgar/data/1144354/000119312510124368/dex101.htm
23. US Department of Health and Human Services (HHS). "Health Insurance Portability and Accountability Act (HIPAA)" (n.d.). https://www.hhs.gov/hipaa/for-professionals/security/laws-regulations/index.html
24. Cybersecurity Maturity Model Certification Accreditation Board (CMMC-AB). "The Cybersecurity Maturity Model Certification" (n.d.). https://cmmcab.org/cmmc-standard/
25. California Consumer Protection Act (CCPA) (2018). https://www.oag.ca.gov/privacy/ccpa
26. National Institute of Standards and Technology (NIST). "special publications 800-34, 800-171, 800-53" (n.d.). https://csrc.nist.gov/publications
27. US Department of State Directorate of Trade Controls International Trafficking of Arms Requirements (ITAR) (n.d.). https://www.pmddtc.state.gov/?id=ddtc_kb_article_page&sys_id=24d528fddbfc930044f9ff621f961987

Cybersecurity as Part of Mission Assurance

Joel Wilf[✉] [iD]

Jet Propulsion Laboratory (JPL), California Institute of Technology, 4800 Oak Grove Dr,
Pasadena, CA 91109, USA
Joel.m.wilf@jpl.nasa.gov

Abstract. In this paper, we examine the development of Cybersecurity Assurance
(CSA) as a new Mission Assurance role at NASA's Jet Propulsion Laboratory
(NASA/JPL). Our purpose is to better understand how space flight organizations
are responding to the growing cybersecurity threat to their space and ground systems – with a focus on Mission Assurance. We begin by considering the traditional
role of Mission Assurance: to independently assess and report the risks to mission
success, throughout the mission lifecycle. We note that in recent years, the cybersecurity threat to space and ground systems has been increasing; and we describe
how space flight organizations have been responding. Among the responses at
NASA/JPL has been the creation of Cybersecurity Assurance (CSA) as a new
Mission Assurance role. We describe how CSA has combined aspects of traditional software assurance, risk analysis, and the assessment of security controls
into a new discipline. We show how the CSA role (and mission-based cybersecurity roles, in general) differ from the established Information Technology (IT)
security roles. We review the current state of the CSA role, and the challenges
faced in creating this new mission assurance discipline. Finally, we look forward
at the possible future of the CSA role at NASA and other space flight organizations.

Keywords: Cybersecurity assurance · mission assurance · space systems · risk

1 Introduction

This paper is a study of organizational change under pressure. Even in the best of
circumstances, Space flight is a complex and risky endeavor. Commonly known risks
include navigational errors, loss of communication, failure of unreliable parts, damage
from radiation, and software defects. Over the decades, space flight organizations have
developed engineering practices, testing regimes, risk analyses, and many other strategies
to mitigate those risks. Yet even with those in place, there are still mishaps, sometimes
resulting in the failure of the mission. For example, one study observed that between the
years of 2000 to 2016, 41.3% of all small satellites launched failed or partially failed
[1].

In recent decades, a new type of risk has become an ever-larger concern to space flight
organizations: the risk of cybersecurity attacks. These are attacks though the information
and communications technology, which is relied upon by every system used in space

missions, including: mission operations systems, ground data systems, science data systems, spacecraft (whether Earth-orbiting satellites, rovers on Mars, or deep space probes), and the communication links between them [2].

Unlike traditional space risks – such as those arising from radiation or random part failures – cybersecurity-attacks are the deliberate acts of a human adversary, often with powerful nation states behind them. Space is a contested domain, and Russia and China are competing with US interests [2]. Space flight organizations have seen the need to adapt to this new and ever-changing threat landscape. Space systems still need to operate safely and reliably, as they always have. Now they also need to operate securely.

This paper describes one organization's response to the emergence of cybersecurity risk to space systems. It focuses on JPL's Mission Assurance organization, and its creation of a new Cybersecurity Assurance (CSA) role. It is hoped that this will prove to be a useful organizational case study and that the CSA may be adapted by other space flight organizations.

2   The Traditional Role of NASA/JPL Mission Assurance

Since this is a study of organizational change, it is important to understand the "before" state, how NASA/JPL Mission Assurance worked in the decades prior to the expansion of the space cybersecurity threat.

2.1   Mission Assurance and Mission Success

A good starting point for understanding Mission Assurance at NASA and JPL is knowing its overarching goal. The current homepage for NASA's mission assurance organization declares: "The Office of Safety and Mission Assurance (OSMA) assures the safety and enhances the success of all NASA activities" [3].

But focusing on missions, it would be reasonable to recast this sentence as: "OSMA assures the safety of missions and increases the odds of mission success." That would bring the statement into alignment with JPL's emphasis on safety and mission success. If fact, JPL's mission assurance organization is named the "Office of Safety and Mission Success (OSMS)."

What does mission success mean? One past Director of Mission Assurance at JPL defined it succinctly as: "Meeting Level 1 Requirements, within cost and schedule, with acceptable risk, and doing it safely" [4].

This gets us closer to the actual Mission Assurance practice at NASA and JPL. Throughout the Mission lifecycle, Mission Assurance independently assesses and reports on risks to mission success, enabling missions to lower that risk to an acceptable level.

2.2   Mission Assurance Domains

Mission assurance provides an aggregate view to the projects of all the risks that threaten mission success. But where do these risks come from? The answer is from specific elements of the mission that are needed for mission success – and may pose risks to mission success if they don't work as required. For example, the mission depends on its hardware. But if that hardware has quality defects, it may pose a risk to the mission.

Hardware Quality Assurance (HQA) assesses and reports on that risk. HQA inspects the quality of the hardware (and often assess the process by which the hardware was manufactured), thus assuring that the hardware meets the required standard of quality. Think of Mission Assurance as having domains, each of which is assigned to a potential source of risk, particular to that domain, which needs to be assured through domain-specific techniques (e.g., hardware inspection, software testing, and so on).

Figure 1, below, shows the Mission Assurance domains [4] as they are usually visualized: as being on the same level, and reporting upward to the Mission Assurance organization:

Fig. 1. JPL's traditional Mission Assurance domains, with the addition of Cyber Security Assurance (CSA).

Table 1, below, shows the Mission Assurance domains at JPL [4], with an example of a domain-specific risk and a domain-specific technique for identifying and assessing that risk:

Table 1. Mission Assurance Domains

Domain	Example risk source	Assurance technique
Hardware Quality Assurance	Bad workmanship	Inspect using checklist
Software Quality Assurance	Undiscovered defect in code	Static code analysis
Cybersecurity Assurance	Misconfigured router	Router config-checking
Reliability	Unknown failure modes	Fault tree analysis
Safety	Hazard may not be controlled	Hazard analysis
Electronic Parts	Part may be counterfeit	Trace part to manufacturer

At first glance, CSA clearly fits in with the traditional Mission Assurance domains. There are domain-specific risks that CSA covers, which the other domains do not. There are also cybersecurity-specific assurance techniques available to assess the risk.

But the converse question is also interesting: If we took CSA out of the domain table, would another assurance domain or another mission role find that particular risk? Here the answer isn't so certain. A Ground Data Systems (GDS) or IT Security engineer could certainly find a misconfigured router. But they might miss it. They might be too busy to check. Or they might not think it's needed, assuming that the router settings haven't been changed. In this case, the assurance function provides a "second set of eyes" to assess the cybersecurity control, independent from the engineer who implemented the control.

3 Response to Increased Cybersecurity Risk

By the early 2010s, every defense, commercial, and civilian space flight organization was aware of the changing cybersecurity threat landscape. Cybersecurity became a serious national security concern, with top-level cybersecurity declarations issued directly from the President of the United States. "Space Policy Directive 5 (SPD-5)" from President Donald Trump in 2020, focused on space [5], while the "Executive Order on Improving the Nation's Cybersecurity," from President Joseph Biden in 2021 [6], addressed all government systems.

These declarations flowed down to influence new cybersecurity policies and standards for organizations such as NASA and JPL. Significantly, Biden's executive order frequently invoked the National Institute of Standards and Technology (NIST), implying that organizations should view NIST as an official source for cybersecurity standards. The Executive Order went so far as levying requirements on the Director of NIST to provide these standards, stating for example, "the Director of NIST shall publish preliminary guidelines" on criteria for evaluating software security [6].

3.1 Initial Technical Response at JPL

In the 2013–2016 timeframe – even before the first presidential cybersecurity declaration – NASA and JPL were already responding to the new cybersecurity threat landscape. These responses included:

Adoption of NIST Standards. The JPL IT security organization began applying NIST standards for cybersecurity controls (NIST SP 800-53 and related publications) [7] and the NIST risk management framework (NIST SP 800-37) [8]. An inventory of systems on JPL networks was created. System security plans were being developed and internally assessed.

NASA Blue Team Assessments. In 2015, NASA established a Blue Team Vulnerability Assessment Program to evaluate the security posture of critical mission systems and networks [9]. JPL ground systems were assessed, vulnerabilities revealed, and networks were consequently hardened.

Exploring Static Code Analysis for Security. JPL Software Quality Assurance (SQA), began exploring static code analysis, scanning software source codes for defects and vulnerabilities [10]. This was the first Mission Assurance domain to get involved with an aspect of cybersecurity. It was a natural step to take, since many of the static code analysis tools supported scanning for both reliability-related defects and security-related vulnerabilities.

3.2 Initial Organizational Response at JPL

Even more important than the technical response, discussed in the previous section, was JPLs organizational response, which demonstrated a long-term strategic commitment to mission cybersecurity.

Starting at the executive level, JPL formulated cybersecurity strategic goals, funded the strategic hiring of well-known cybersecurity experts, and created a Cybersecurity Council (CSC) for JPL Directors to discuss the issues amongst themselves. The CSC and its advisory group then created an institutionally funded, multi-year Cybersecurity Improvement Project (CSIP). CSIP was chartered to coordinate cybersecurity improvement activities across JPL and meet JPL's cybersecurity goals. In a presentation in 2016, CSIP laid out an ambitious program for building mission cyber security, spanning the following areas [11]:

Risk Assessment and Planning. Risk assessment included threat and vulnerability assessments, architecture reviews, and forensics improvement. Planning included the prioritization of CSIP's improvement activities.

Development of Institutional Assets. This covered requirements, design and operations principles, policies and procedures, standards, policies, and acquisition guidelines.

Training, Coaching, and Communication. This addressed cybersecurity awareness, classes, certifications, providing experts for consultation, infusion/compliance advice, distributing actionable information, and information sharing exercises.

Implementation and Metrics. This last area collected activities that weren't covered above. Some were research-oriented, such as cyber verification and validation (V&V) in the Cyber Defense Laboratory (CDL), then being built, and investigation of "sensor mesh" technology. It also covered metrics specification, gathering and analysis in various forms. Interestingly, "assurance" was also dropped into this category.

Looking back, one can see a broad desire to make progress across the board, with a roadmap still taking shape. Various approaches to cybersecurity risk assessment were tried, and institutional assets were created – notably a first set of Flight Project Cybersecurity Requirements (FPCR). Internal training classes, lectures, and mentoring spread mission cybersecurity knowledge throughout the organization.

3.3 Steps Towards a CSA Role

CSIP provided an opportunity for the Mission Assurance organization to collaborate with the Engineering and IT Security on common goals. Mission Assurance worked on risk assessments, requirements, Project Protection Plans (PPPs), and research proposals, mainly supporting others. However, the first steps were also being taken towards defining its CSA role.

As mentioned above, CSIP developed a set of Flight Project Cybersecurity Requirements, which gave Mission Assurance a set of requirements that could be assured (or verified), and so these were used to define initial CSA activities. There were enough activities to assign to a role statement, which was then accepted as part of the standard work breakdown structure (WBS) for Flight Projects. This meant that a CSA could now be hired by missions.

Meanwhile, there was a cadre of potential CSA engineers, who had hired into the SQA group, but had expressed an interest in a future CSA role. This was important since there wasn't anything exactly like CSA in industry. The knowledge and skills needed were at an intersection of three areas:

1. Cybersecurity engineering
2. Software assurance
3. How missions worked throughout the NASA/JPL project lifecycle

SQA engineers were already immersed in the second and third areas, above. All that remained was to provide the future CSA engineers with solid training in cybersecurity. This was done by bringing in commercial training classes from the SANS Institute [12]. The SANS training was augmented by internal JPL cybersecurity classes, mentoring. In addition, two CSA engineers enrolled in online master's programs in Cybersecurity, offered by Georgia Tech [13].

The elements were falling in place. With CSA activities in hand, mission requirements were drafted, cost models and briefings on CSA for Mission Assurance managers were created. CSA engineers began working on real missions.

3.4 Focusing on Cybersecurity Risk

So far, in the sections above, it was established that: Mission Assurance independently assessed and reported risks to mission success; cybersecurity was identified as a growing risk to mission success; and CSA was established as the Mission Assurance discipline assigned to cybersecurity. It is worth asking, then, how is cybersecurity risk assessed on missions? And what is the role of CSA in that assessment?

Part of the NASA/JPL response to cybersecurity risk was to adopt a standard process for characterizing risk to individual mission systems, using that information to select and implement the right set of protective cybersecurity controls, then assessing whether the protected system is secure enough to approve for operations. The process adopted is called "Assessment and Authorization (A&A) and is based on the NIST Risk Management Framework (NIST SP 800-37) [8]. It is shown in Fig. 2, below:

All NASA mission systems go through the A&A process shown in Fig. 2, in order to obtain an Approval to Operate (ATO), granted in the "Authorize" step. The process starts with "Characterize," evaluating the impact if the system were compromised – characterized as high, moderate, or low. Based on that characterization, the appropriate cybersecurity controls (from NIST SP 800-53) are selected, then implemented, then assessed to see if they were all implemented correctly.

Once the system is authorized (given an ATO), the process is not over – it continues for as long as the system is in operations. The final "Monitor" step requires a partial re-assessment for every first and second year following an ATO, and a full one every three-years, which if successful, leads to a renewal of ATO.

As of this writing, CSA is developing its role in the A&A process as an independent security control assessor, supporting the "Assess" and "Monitor" steps, shown in Fig. 2,

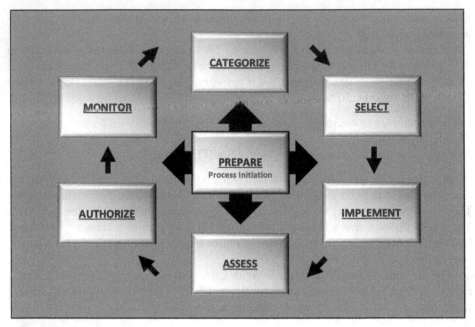

Fig. 2. The NASA Assessment and Authorization (A&A) process is based on the NIST Risk Management Framework (NIST SP 800-37 rev2) shown above [8].

above. CSA has currently been approved to pilot the first-year assessment, mentioned above, for several missions.

4 Conclusions

The final sections, below, summarize the current state of the CSA role, key challenges encountered along the way, and finally a brief look at the future of the CSA role.

4.1 Current state of the CSA Role

As of this writing, CSA is established as a Mission Assurance discipline at JPL. CSA is a defined role on flight projects. CSA team members are working on active flight projects, including JPL's two current flagship missions, Mars Sample Return (MSR) and Europa Clipper.

As mentioned above, CSA is piloting the role of independent security control assessor for NASA A&A process and signed-up to perform annual A&A assessments on several missions.

The program infrastructure that supports the CSA engineers is progressing. CSA requirements are included as part of JPL's Safety and Mission Assurance Requirements (SMAR). Role statements are in place, as are cost models, statements-of-work (SOWs), processes, procedures, and a CSA Project Plan Template. Due to the rapidly evolving cybersecurity environment, the infrastructure in place is still evolving. [These documents are not cited here, publicly, as they are currently considered proprietary.]

Within JPL, collaboration with cybersecurity colleagues in Engineering and IT Security is proceeding well, with roles and responsibilities settling into official status. Within NASA and other NASA centers, there is interest in the CSA role, and meetings, presentations, and discussions have begun. But the CSA role is new, and much socialization work remains to be done.

4.2 CSA Challenges

CSA faces challenges, some of which are technical in nature, some organizational, some both:

Moving CSA from an Information Technology (IT) to an Operational Technology (OT) Perspective. Most cybersecurity standards and practices were originally designed for an Information Technology (IT) environment – networks of purely digital, interconnected computing devices. But in an Operational Technology (OT) environment, computing devices are used to sense and control aspects of the real, physical world. As the *National Cybersecurity Strategy*, released in 2023 by the White House, states: "Next-generation interconnectivity is collapsing the boundary between the digital and physical worlds, and exposing some of our most essential systems [including space assets] to disruption." [14] For NASA/JPL and other space flight organizations, mission control, ground data systems, and space-based assets form an interconnected OT environment. CSA and space flight organizations, in general, need to better understand mission cybersecurity risk in this environment.

Integrating CSA More Completely into the Mission Lifecycle and Risk Processes. Work has begun at JPL in integrating OT-oriented mission cybersecurity into the NASA/JPL mission lifecycle. Mission Assurance is included in the NASA/JPL lifecycle, and CSA activities are defined with respect to standard mission phases and reviews. But there is still work to be done in integrating CSA into the mission requirements flowdown from NASA, into mission processes, and to become part of risk-informed decision-making. Cyber risk assessment, itself, is an evolving practice, and a focus of current CSA efforts. CSA is also exploring this through NIST SP 800–160, the NIST standard for Engineering Trustworthy Secure Systems – a systems engineering/lifecycle view of cybersecurity standards [15].

Increasing the Rigor of Cybersecurity Assurance. As mentioned in Sect. 2.1, above, Mission Assurance practice is primarily based on independent risk assessment throughout the mission lifecycle. However, there is a more rigorous definition of assurance, based on formally assuring the validity of cybersecurity claims – e.g., claims that a mission system truly has cybersecurity properties such as confidentiality, integrity, and availability. The formal method of assessing these claims is called an "assurance case," and an accessible description of security assurance cases can be found in Saydjari [16].

4.3   Looking to the Future of CSA

As cybersecurity threats to space missions increase, there will be an increasing need for the Mission Assurance domain in cybersecurity. CSA will assure that missions are compliant with the appropriate requirements and standards, and it will improve the assessment of actual cybersecurity risk to mission systems. CSA will help the missions manage and control risk. As integration into the mission lifecycle proceeds, CSA will be part of space flight organizations' mission cybersecurity strategy, as well as being a domain in Mission Assurance.

Funding Acknowledgment. The research was carried out at the Jet Propulsion Laboratory, California Institute of Technology, under a contract with the National Aeronautics and Space Administration (80NM0018D0004).

References

1. Jacklin, S.: Small-satellite mission failure rates. No. NASA/TM-2018-220034 (2019)
2. Defense Intelligence Agency (DIA): Challenges to security in space. https://www.dia.mil/Portals/110/Documents/News/Military_Power_Publications/Challenges_Security_Space_2 022.pdf. Accessed 10 Feb 2023
3. NASA OSMA. https://sma.nasa.gov/. Accessed 10 Feb 2023
4. Brace, R.: Mission assurance at the Jet Propulsion Laboratory. In: Northrop Grumman Mission Assurance Summit (2005). JPL Technical Report Server. https://trs.jpl.nasa.gov/handle/2014/39497. Accessed 10 Feb 2023
5. Trump, P.D.J.: President Donald J. Trump is establishing America's first comprehensive cybersecurity policy for space systems. FAS Intelligence Resource Program. https://irp.fas.org/off docs/nspm/spd-5-fs.pdf. Accessed 10 Feb 2023
6. Biden, J.: Executive order on improving the nation's ybersecurity. Whitehouse.gov site. https://www.whitehouse.gov/briefing-room/presidential-actions/2021/05/12/executive-order-on-improving-the-nations-cybersecurity. Accessed 10 Feb 2023
7. Joint Task Force: Security and Privacy Controls for Information Systems and Organizations (NIST SP 800-53 rev 5). National Institute of Standards and Technology (NIST), Gaithersburg, MD (2020)
8. Joint Task Force: Risk Management Framework for Information Systems and Organizations (NIST SP 800-37 rev 2). National Institute of Standards and Technology (NIST), Gaithersburg, MD (2020)
9. NASA Office of Inspector General: Final Memorandum, Review of NASA's Information Security Program (IG-16-016; A-15-005-01). https://oig.nasa.gov/docs/IG-16-016.pdf. Accessed 10 Feb 2023
10. Barner, L.: Application software security scanning. In: Hawaii International Conference on System Sciences, Atlanta, Georgia, pp. 7353–7362. AIS (2019)
11. Morgan, S.: JPL's cyber security improvement project. In: IV&V Secure Coding Summit, Fairmont, West Virginia, 27 June 2016. JPL Technical Report Server. https://trs.jpl.nasa.gov/handle/2014/46828. Accessed 10 Feb 2023
12. SANS Cybersecurity Training. https://www.sans.org/. Accessed 10 Feb 2023
13. Georgia Tech Online Masters in Cybersecurity. https://pe.gatech.edu/degrees/cybersecurity. Accessed 10 Feb 2023
14. House, W.: National Cybersecurity Strategy. White House, Washington, D.C. (2023)

15. Ross, R., et al.: Engineering Trustworthy Secure Systems (NIST SP 800-160v1r1). National Institute of Standards and Technology (NIST), Gaithersburg, MD (2022)
16. Saydjari, S.: Engineering Trustworthy Systems. McGraw Hill, New York (2018)

User-Centered Perspectives on Privacy and Security in Digital Environments

Investigating Mobile Instant Messaging Phishing: A Study into User Awareness and Preventive Measures

Rufai Ahmad[1,5]($\boxtimes$) (iD), Sotirios Terzis[1] (iD), and Karen Renaud[1,2,3,4] (iD)

[1] Department of Computer and Information Sciences, University of Strathclyde, Glasgow, UK
{rufai.ahmad,sotirios.terzis,karen.renaud}@strath.ac.uk
[2] Rhodes University, Makhanda, South Africa
[3] University of South Africa, Pretoria, South Africa
[4] Abertay University, Dundee, UK
[5] Sokoto State University, Sokoto, Nigeria

Abstract. Users of mobile instant messaging (MIM) applications (apps) are increasingly targeted by phishing attacks. MIM apps often lack technical counter-measures for protecting users from phishing. Thus, users need to take preventive measures against phishing threats. Measures include awareness of the threat and the adoption of phishing preventive behaviours. This study adds to the literature by exploring these measures. Using an online survey, we collected data from 111 users of MIM apps and examined their awareness of the phishing attacks targeting them and the preventive measures they take. Previous studies showed that smartphone users exhibit poor security behaviour, which was mostly not the case in our sample, as we have found moderate awareness of phishing and the adoption of preventive measures by the participants. The results also showed several correlations between the participants' adoption of preventive measures and their phishing self-efficacy, knowledge, and concern about phishing. These findings may be useful in developing user awareness strategies for combating phishing in MIM apps.

Keywords: Phishing · Phishing Awareness · Mobile Instant Messaging

1 Introduction

Mobile Instant Messaging (MIM) apps allow users to communicate with each other in real-time. They provide a cheap way for individuals to stay connected and maintain distanced social relationships. Applications such as WhatsApp, Telegram, Signal and Viber facilitate MIM are prevalent means of communication. According to recent data by Statista, 3.09B mobile phone users communicated via MIM in 2021 [1]. Their popularity has triggered their adoption by electronic commerce, a phenomenon known as "instant messaging social commerce" [2].

As the popularity of MIM applications surges amongst smartphone users, protection from cyber threats becomes crucial. Though these apps claim to protect users' data through end-to-end encryption, there are instances where they can serve as vectors for

© The Author(s), under exclusive license to Springer Nature Switzerland AG 2023
A. Moallem (Ed.): HCII 2023, LNCS 14045, pp. 381–398, 2023.
https://doi.org/10.1007/978-3-031-35822-7_26

cybersecurity threats [3]. One of the most common threats facing users of MIM applications is phishing [4]. Phishing is an internet crime where cyber criminals attempt to obtain sensitive details from internet users by tricking them into visiting fraudulent websites, providing personal information, or downloading malware. According to recent data from Kaspersky, cybercriminals currently use MIM applications to propagate phishing campaigns [4], with most of the phishing links shared on WhatsApp (89.6%), followed by Telegram (5.6%) and Viber (4.7%). Although phishing is moving to MIM applications, recent research has shown that such applications lack automated countermeasures to protect users from phishing [5]. Thus, user awareness is a key priority.

The large user base of MIM applications, and the fact that users of these apps have widely varying levels of computer experience, educational backgrounds, cultures, and languages, can facilitate phishing. Furthermore, built-in functionalities, such as sharing and forwarding links and joining private and public instant messaging groups, can increase user susceptibility to phishing [6]. It has already been shown in [6] that MIM application users frequently click on and forward links via instant messaging applications. The consequences may be that MIM applications' users fall victim to a phishing attack.

This study explores the phishing awareness of MIM application users and their adoption of phishing prevention behaviours and practices using an online survey. We pose the following research questions: 1) Are MIM application users aware of phishing attacks targeting them on these platforms? 2) Do MIM application users adopt phishing preventive behaviours and practices? 3) Does the adoption of phishing preventive behaviours differ by phishing self-efficacy, knowledge of phishing and phishing concerns?

This paper proceeds as follows. First, we review related work. After that, we detail our research methodology. This is followed by an analysis of the data and a discussion of the findings. We conclude by providing recommendations for future research.

2 Background

2.1 Smartphone Security Behaviour

The growing popularity of smartphones and their integration into many aspects of our lives has made mobile security vital [7]. Similar to desktop computers, smartphones attract the attention of many bad actors [8]. The biggest threat to smartphone users is the loss of their personal information, which can occur via phishing attacks [9].

Phishing prevention measures fall into two categories: automated technical solutions and user-focused awareness/training drives [10]. Automated solutions aim to detect and block phishing links and contents with minimum or no user intervention [11, 12], while user awareness/training aims to train users to recognise phishing campaigns [13]. However, neither of these approaches is sufficient in and of itself as a solution to the phishing problem, which is why researchers argue that both solutions are needed to reduce the success rate of phishing [14].

Phishing awareness campaigns aim to help internet users spot deceptive attempts to protect themselves from phishing scams. Prudent behaviour is essential in phishing prevention since the success of a phishing attack relies on the user taking an ill-advised action, such as clicking on a fraudulent link or opening a malicious attachment. However, despite ongoing phishing awareness campaigns, recent studies have found that smartphone users still exhibit poor security behaviour, including clicking on links from unknown sources [6, 15, 16]. This unwise online behaviour can render smartphone users more susceptible to phishing attacks [16].

Findings from prior studies have demonstrated that individual characteristics could predict security-related behaviour and attitudes. Using the Human Aspects of Information Security Questionnaire (HAIS-Q), McCormac et al. (2017) [17] examined the relationship between individuals' information security awareness and their personality traits, age and gender. They found that age and gender did not predict online security behaviour. However, personality traits, including being open, conscious, agreeable and having the propensity to take fewer risks, predicted online security behaviours. Also, [15] showed that gender and age did not affect individuals' cyber hygiene behaviours. However, the studies by Whitty et al. [18] and Merdayan and Petrie [19] show that younger participants were more likely to share their passwords.

Self-efficacy, defined as an ability to implement safeguarding measures to protect oneself from cyber threats [20], predicts behaviour. Researchers have confirmed that phishing self-efficacy is essential in preventing phishing success, which is important when technical measures fail [21, 22].

Current studies tend to explore the influence of self-efficacy on users' general information security behaviours. These studies have found that self-efficacy significantly affects performing security-conscious behaviour [21, 23, 24]. A more recent study by [22] with mobile device users delivers similar results with phishing self-efficacy positively affecting mobile phishing avoidance motivation and behaviour. Verkijika (2019) study revealed that gender moderated the effect of phishing self-efficacy on mobile phishing avoidance motivation and behaviour, with women being more cautious than men.

2.2 Research Gap

While current studies have explored the security-related practices and attitudes of internet users and how they relate to phish detection, the extant literature lacks an understanding of the security-related behaviours of MIM app users. With evidence of phishing attacks moving to these apps and the fact that the apps themselves currently lack technical countermeasures to protect users from phishing, there is a need for user security-related behaviour studies that target the users of these apps. Such studies are essential because even though users may be aware of online threats such as phishing, they might still exhibit poor cyber hygiene behaviour during communication in MIM apps. Furthermore, the informal nature of communication in MIM Apps might affect how users view and practiced security behaviour in them. Herein, we extend the analysis presented in [6] by investigating MIM Apps users' knowledge of phishing scams, the measures they take to protect themselves from such scams and to determine whether their phishing self-efficacy and knowledge of phishing influence these behaviours.

3 Methodology

Our study utilised a web-based survey to collect self-reported data from users of MIM apps aged 18 years and above. The survey was hosted on Qualtrics and ran from October 12, 2021, to November 5, 2021. Our department's ethics review board approved the survey. The survey focused on user behaviour towards links shared through MIM apps during one to one and group communication and the factors influencing these behaviours. Specifically, we collected data about users' 1) frequency of clicking links, 2) frequency of forwarding links, 3) knowledge and awareness of phishing, 4) security behaviours relating to phishing in the MIM App, 5) phishing self-efficacy and 6) perceived protection from phishing by MIM platforms. All questions in the survey were based on either Likert-type or multiple-choice answers.

3.1 Survey Instrument

The study utilised a quantitative approach to data collection. The survey questions were not forced responses. Thus, participants were allowed to skip questions they didn't wish to answer. The survey contained the following sections:

Demographic Questions: We asked about the participants' age group, gender, education, and country of residence.

Device and MIM Apps Usage: This section asked participants about their current ICT devices. Participants were also asked to indicate which MIM apps they currently used from a list of selected apps, their frequency of usage and with whom they use such apps to communicate. Questions in this section were both Likert-type and multiple - choice.

Link Clicking Behaviour: This part of the survey measured the participant's link-clicking behaviour while communicating in MIM Apps. Participants were asked to indicate how frequently they click links during one-to-one and group-based communication. We also measured their click behaviour concerning different communicating parties such as friends, family, work/business colleagues and other communicating parties. All questions in this section were Likert-type.

Link Forwarding Behaviour: This section measured the participants' link forwarding behaviour. We asked them how frequently they forward link to others. We also asked them to indicate how frequently they forward link that others share in public or private MIM groups. All questions in this section were Likert-type.

Phishing Preventive Behaviour: We measured the phishing preventive behaviours of the participants during instant messaging using behaviours such as 1) checking the link before clicking, 2) considering the sender of a message before clicking it, 3) considering the sender of a link before forwarding it to others and 4) following links before forwarding them to others. We believe these behaviours highlight users' phishing safety behaviour when communicating in these apps. We consider these behaviours preventive because checking the link before clicking is among the most popular anti-phishing advice security professionals give users [25, 26]. The message forwarding functionality of MIM apps allows users to forward messages they receive during either one-two-one or group-based communication, making it possible for messages to reach a large audience very quickly. This behaviour can aid in propagating fraudulent messages rapidly across the network. Evidence has shown that cybercriminals currently use this functionality to reach more targets by directing users to send fraudulent links to several other users before they can claim prizes [27]. Thus, an essential precautionary behaviour would be for users always to consider whether those sending them messages have the skills to differentiate between fraudulent and legitimate links. We also believe that security-minded users will likely follow and evaluate links before forwarding them to others. All questions in this section were Likert-type.

Knowledge and Concern About Phishing in MIM Apps: In this section, we first asked the participants to indicate if they know what phishing is using Likert-scale answers from strongly disagree to strongly agree. We also asked them whether they were aware of general phishing and MIM-based phishing scams using yes/no responses. Participants were asked to indicate how concerned they were about phishing scams on MIM Apps, with response options from not at all to extremely concerned. Furthermore, participants were asked to indicate from a list of options how they respond to the problem of phishing in MIM Apps. Options include 1) I look for suspicious links, 2) I check the link preview, 3) I do not click on a link from unfamiliar senders, 4) I search google for further information before giving out my details, and 5) I do nothing.

Phishing Self-efficacy: We developed a phishing self-efficacy scale for MIM app users. The scale contains five questions, three adapted from [28], and we created the remaining. This study refers to phishing self-efficacy as the participants' confidence in implementing a security measure to protect themselves from phishing threats [29]. The phishing self-efficacy questions measured the participants' belief in their abilities to protect themselves from phishing and that of their friends and MIM platforms.

Phishing Protection: Participants were asked their views on who should be responsible for protecting users of MIM apps from phishing scams.

3.2 Recruitment

Participation required users to be 18 years or above and be able to complete a survey in English. Furthermore, we limited our participants to those using Signal, Slack, Telegram, Viber, Line, and WhatsApp, due to their popularity and the features that they provide, such as group communication, link previews, link sharing, messages/links forwarding, and the ability to join public groups via links shared by group admins online. These features can increase the phishing susceptibility of their users.

We utilised snowball sampling and social media to recruit participants. Snowball sampling is a non-random sampling method appropriate for recruiting research participants that are hard to reach or unknown [30]. Recruitment starts with the first author sharing the link to the survey with contacts on his current MIM Apps, including those in his private and public groups. The survey link was also posted on various social media groups, including r/SampleSize on Reddit, samplesize on Facebook and SurveyCycle. Finally, we emailed our colleagues, asking them to take part and forward the survey to others. At each stage of the recruitment, we asked participants to invite others to participate in the study by sharing the survey link with them. A total of 129 participants accessed the survey. However, after data cleaning, we excluded 18 participants for failing to meet our screening criteria, including 1) Declining to participate in the study after reading the consent and participants' information note (n = 2), 2) Not using any mobile instant messaging applications mentioned in the study (n = 6), 3) Failing to provide sufficient data (n = 8). We also excluded participants who consented to the survey but did not answer any survey questions (n = 2). Thus, our analysis is based on 111 participants who have provided sufficient data and met all our screening requirements. The survey took an average of 15 min, and participation was voluntary.

3.3 Participants

The highest age group in the sample was 18–30 (54, 48.6%), followed by 31–45 (51, 45.9%) and 46+ (6, 5.4%). The sample was skewed with respect to gender (73, 65.8%) male, (37, 33.3%) female, and one participant preferred not to disclose their gender. Most of the participants had a postgraduate qualification (60, 54.1%), followed by undergraduate (33, 29.7%), further education (13, 11.7%), and secondary education (5, 4.5%). Geographically, most of the participants resided in the UK (64, 58.7%), followed by Nigeria (18, 16.5%), and (29, 26.1%) other countries, including Germany, Canada, the USA, Malaysia, the Netherlands, France, Singapore, Saudi Arabia, Finland, Russia, and Libya. Most participants used WhatsApp (106, 95.5%), followed by Telegram (40, 36.0%), Signal (19, 17.1%), Slack (13, 11.7%), Viber (6, 5.4%) and Line (4, 3.6%).

3.4 Data Analysis

The data collected from the survey was purely nominal or ordinal. Thus, we calculated each response's frequencies and percentages and presented the data visually using frequency graphs. We tested for significance using non-parametric tests like Wilcoxon signed-rank, Friedman, and Spearman's rank-order test as they are considered appropriate for this type of data [31]. However, we acknowledge the ongoing discussion on the appropriateness of parametric or non-parametric tests [32]. The phishing self-efficacy scale was analysed at the interval measurement scale as it is the recommended analysis method for the Likert scale [33].

All survey questions were optional. Therefore, missing values exist, but these have been excluded from the analysis. In these cases, the actual number of participants is reported. We used SPSS software for the statistical analysis.

4 Results

The results presented in this paper extend the findings presented in [6], where we examined the link-clicking and forwarding behaviours of users of MIM apps. Herein, we present our findings on the participants' awareness of phishing in MIM Apps and their phishing prevention behaviours. We also investigated the relationship between these behaviours and the participants' concerns about phishing, phishing knowledge, and phishing self-efficacy.

4.1 Phishing Awareness, Concerns, and Response

As phishing in MIM apps is relatively new, it is essential to understand users' awareness of such scams and how they respond. Thus, we asked participants to indicate their understanding of the term phishing. As Fig. 1 illustrates, most participants felt they know what phishing is. This is not surprising, considering the effort from academia and industry to educate users about phishing scams. Phishing also tends to receive significant media attention, so participants may likely have read about it.

While the participants may be familiar with the term, this awareness is likely for email-based phishing as this is the oldest and most popular form. To investigate participants' awareness of MIM-based phishing scams, we asked them to indicate if they were aware of such scams. As illustrated in Fig. 2, most participants (n = 85) are aware of such scams. However, a significant number (n = 19) said they were not aware. We expect some users to be unaware of this scam because phishing in MIM apps is quite a new phenomenon. In addition, the fact that mobile instant messaging tends to be with those we trust may mean that if users receive such messages, they may likely not flag them as phishing. Further analysis shows that the participants were very concerned about phishing in MIM apps. Specifically, most participants (n = 32, 28.8%) said they were quite concerned, followed by (n = 26, 23.4%) who said they were extremely concerned (see Fig. 3).

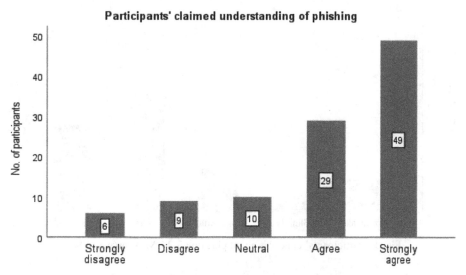

Fig. 1. Claimed understanding of the term phishing (n = 103)

Having accessed the participants' claimed awareness of phishing and their concerns, it was also essential to consider the extent to which the participants were taken measures to protect themselves from such scams. Therefore, we asked them to indicate from a list of options how they respond to the problem of phishing in MIM Apps. The options reflect the current advice given by security professionals to internet users on how to react to phishing [25, 26]. Specifically, the options included: 1) looking for suspicious

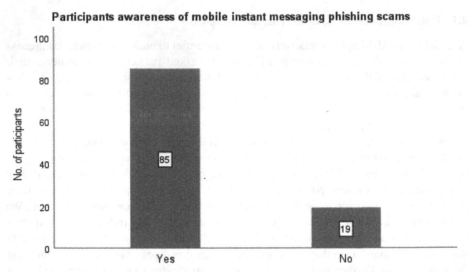

Fig. 2. Awareness of phishing in MIM apps (n = 104)

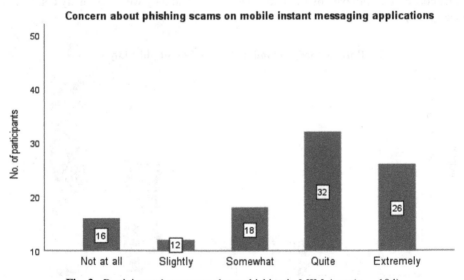

Fig. 3. Participants' concerns about phishing in MIM Apps(n = 104)

links, 2) not clicking on a link from unfamiliar senders, 3) searching google for further information before giving out my details, 4) checking the link preview and 5) doing nothing. As this question allows participants to select all that apply, we expect security-conscious users to choose options 1–3 as these behaviours tend to be the recommended safety behaviour when dealing with phishing. As illustrated in Fig. 4, option 1) not clicking on a link from unfamiliar senders, was the most selected option by participants (n = 78, 75.0%). This strategy is in line with current anti-phishing advice and therefore suggests that the participants were aware of phishing and are taking the proper prevention mechanism. Participants also indicated that they look for suspicious links (n = 53, 51%). However, since we didn't ask what elements, they used to classify links as suspicious, the effectiveness of their strategy cannot be established. Moreover, a recent study has found that even advanced computer users find it challenging to classify fraudulent links [34].

Many participants indicated they checked the link preview (n = 48, 46.2%). The preview adds extra information, including an image/logo, hostname, title, and summary of the webpage's content. The main goal of the preview is to provide users with a sense of the content they are visiting. We anticipated that the participant would likely use the preview to decide on the legitimacy of the link. However, a recent study by [5] discovered that cybercriminals could manipulate link previews to lure users into visiting fraudulent pages making those relying on this strategy susceptible to phishing scams. Only a few participants (n = 4, 3.8%) indicated that they do not take any action to prevent themselves from phishing in MIM apps.

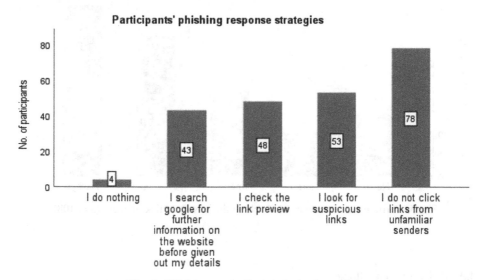

Fig. 4. Phishing prevention strategies (n = 104)

4.2 Phishing Preventive Behaviours

Our findings show that the participants practised preventive behaviours while communicating in MIM apps. These behaviours include checking the link before clicking, considering the sender of a message before clicking the links in that message, considering the sender of a link before forwarding it to others and following links before forwarding them to others. Figure 5 shows that the rating levels for the participant's frequency of checking links before they click them were above the midpoint of the scale (Mdn = 4), implying that most participants very often or always check on links before clicking them. Thus, the participants are cautious of their link-clicking behaviour during instant messaging.

When asked if they consider a message's sender before clicking links, most participants stated that they performed this behaviour, as seen in Fig. 6.

Results from the participants' link-forwarding behaviour revealed that most participants (n = 43, 38.7%) always consider a link's sender before forwarding it to others (see Fig. 7). This behaviour can aid in detecting phishing scams by encouraging systematic evaluation of messages. Similarly, most participants (n = 35, 31.5%) indicated that they always follow links before forwarding them to others, (n = 26, 23.4%) said they very often do so, (n = 19, 17.1%) said sometimes, (n = 9, 8.1%) said rarely and (n = 3, 2.7) said they never follow links before sharing.

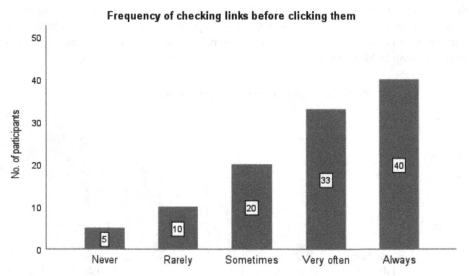

Fig. 5. Participants' frequency of checking links before clicking them (n = 108)

4.3 Phishing Self-efficacy

The phishing self-efficacy constructs contained items relating to the participants' confidence in; 1) having the knowledge and skills to identify phishing scams when they are presented to them, 2) protecting their personal information from being stolen by phishers, 3) having the skills to implement security measures to stop cybercriminals from stealing their confidential information. In addition, the construct also measured the participants' beliefs in the skills of their contacts to protect them and their trust in the MIM apps to protect them.

We measured the internal consistency of the construct using the Cronbach reliability test. The Cronbach's alpha value of phishing self-efficacy was 0.733. Previous research has shown that a minimum Cronbach's alpha value of 0.7 is required for a construct's items to be internally consistent [35, 36].

Table 1 shows the mean scores and standard deviation for each phishing self-efficacy construct item. The first three items, which measure an individual's belief in their abilities

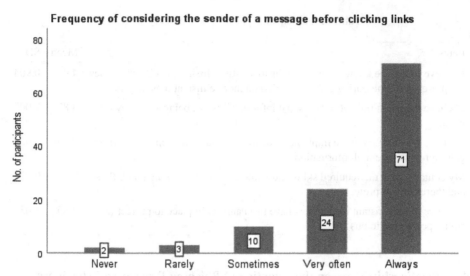

Fig. 6. Participants' frequency of considering the sender of a message before clicking links (n = 111)

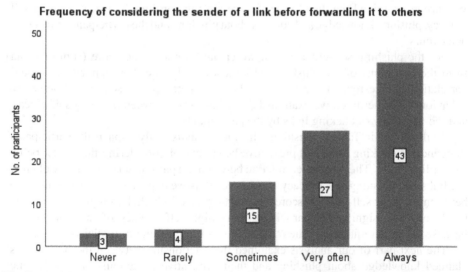

Fig. 7. Participants' frequency of considering the sender of a message before forwarding links (n = 92)

to protect themselves, have high mean scores, implying that most responses are at the high end of the scale. However, the last two items, which measure participants' perception of the ability of both their contacts and the platforms to protect them from phishing scams, have mean scores of 2.91 and 2.81, which implies low confidence in the ability of others to protect the participants.

Table 1. Participants' phishing self-efficacy scores

Items	Mean	SD
I believe I have the knowledge and skills to identify phishing URLs when they are presented to me during communication on mobile instant messengers	4.08	0.904
I believe that I can protect my personal information from being stolen by phishers	3.82	1.007
I believe I have the skills to implement security measures to stop people from getting my confidential information	3.64	1.064
My contacts have the required skills and knowledge to detect phishing URLs and therefore can protect me	2.91	0.971
I believe mobile instant messengers have mechanisms in place to protect me from opening malicious URLs	2.85	1.038

4.4 Relationship Between the Adoption of Phishing Preventive Behaviours and Phishing Self-efficacy, Phishing Knowledge, and Concern About Phishing

We further examined the data to see if there are relationships between phishing self-efficacy, phishing knowledge and concern about phishing and the participants' preventive behaviours.

For the phishing self-efficacy test, we created a composite score (sum or mean) from the five items of the phishing self-efficacy scale. We then applied Spearman's correlation to investigate the relationship between participants' scores and preventive behaviours. Furthermore, we examined the relationship between phishing self-efficacy and the frequency of clicking links by the participants.

As illustrated in Table 2, phishing self-efficacy statistically impacts the participants' frequency of clicking links and preventive behaviour of considering the sender before forwarding a link. The positive correlation between the participants' frequency of clicking links and phishing self-efficacy is unexpected as we expected negative relationship between phishing self-efficacy scores and participants' link click ratings. However, this result may also signify that participants with high self-efficacy often click on links because of their confidence in their ability to identify phishing or malicious links.

The next part of our analysis examined the relationship between the participants' claimed knowledge about phishing and their preventive behaviours. This self-belief of understanding phishing was found to have a statistically significant impact on the participants' preventive behaviours during instant messaging, positively affecting these behaviours, as seen in Table 3.

Finally, we examined if the participants' concern about phishing in MIM Apps impacts their preventive behaviours during communication in MIM Apps. Table 4 shows the participants' concern about phishing in MIM apps influencing some of their preventive behaviours during instant messaging, positively affecting them, as seen in the table.

Table 2. Spearman's correlation coefficient (rs) between participants' phishing self-efficacy in MIM Apps and statistically significant frequency of engaging in specific behaviours towards links. Correlation values with a double asterisk indicate significance at 0.01, while a single asterisk indicates significance at 0.05

	Clicking links df = 101	Consider sender before clicking df = 100	Check the link before clicking df = 100	Follow the link before forwarding df = 90	Consider sender before forwarding df = 90
Phishing self-efficacy	.212*, p = .031	−.001	.068	.143	.312**, p = .002

Table 3. Spearman's correlation coefficient (rs) between participants' claimed knowledge of phishing and statistically significant frequency of engaging in specific behaviours towards links. Correlation values with a double asterisk indicate significance at 0.01, while a single asterisk indicates significance at 0.05

	Clicking links df = 101	Consider sender before clicking df = 100	Check the link before clicking df = 100	Follow the link before forwarding df = 89	Consider sender before forwarding df = 89
Phishing knowledge	.221*, p = .025	.376**, P < .001	.257**, p = .009	.217*, p = .038	.408**, p < .001

Table 4. Spearman's correlation coefficient (rs) between participants' concern about phishing in MIM Apps and statistically significant frequency of engaging specific behaviours towards links. Correlation values with a double asterisk indicate significance at 0.01, while a single asterisk indicates significance at 0.05

	Clicking links df = 102	Consider sender before clicking df = 100	Check the link before clicking df = 101	Follow the link before forwarding df = 89	Consider sender before forwarding df = 90
Level of concern	.023	.197*, p = .046	.206*, p = .037	.101	407**, p < .001

5 Discussion and Limitations

This study investigated the phishing awareness of users of MIM apps and their preventive behaviours against such attacks. Overall, we found that most participants were aware of phishing scams targeting them and were highly concerned about the prevalence of such scams in MIM apps. This finding is similar to the results of [37], who tested the online security attack experience of young adults in the UK and found that 55.6% experienced phishing attacks.

Our results also show that most participants (n = 78, 75.0%) try to reduce their susceptibility to phishing in MIM apps by not clicking on links from unfamiliar senders. Participants also reported looking for suspicious links as a strategy to prevent phishing in MIM apps. This finding reinforces our earlier findings as it confirms that the participants were highly aware of phishing scams and were taking recommended measures to protect themselves. However, our results contrast with the study by [15], where 96% of participants said they had indeed clicked on embedded links from unknown senders. Similarly, the study by [16] found that smartphone users from India exhibited poor online security behaviour, including clicking on links from unknown sources.

While the participants in our study reported not clicking on links from unfamiliar senders, we cannot claim that they were more security aware than the participants in previous studies since the present study focused on users of MIM apps. Furthermore, a study by [6] showed that communication in these apps tends to be between users with offline associations. Hence, users will likely receive links from familiar contacts in most instances. However, the group functionality of these apps, which allows users to communicate with those they do not know, makes it possible for links to be shared by unknown contacts.

To investigate the phishing preventive behaviours of participants during communication in MIM apps, we created a set of questions to measure the frequency at which the participants performed a set of behaviours. Our results show that most participants self-reporting that they performed these behaviours frequently, as evidenced by their rating levels above the midpoint of the scale (Mdn = 4).

Our examination of the phishing self-efficacy of the users revealed that the participants rated themselves highly regarding their ability to protect themselves from phishing scams in MIM apps. However, we found that the participants did not trust their contacts and the platforms to protect them. This low rating might be due to their experience of seeing these scams circulating on MIM apps, as that shows a lack of protection measures by the platforms and skills by those spreading the scams. This result, however, contradicts findings in [6] that show that the participants try to reduce their susceptibility to phishing in MIM apps by clicking links from their friends, family and work/business colleagues.

In line with prior studies, we investigated the relationship between the participants' phishing self-efficacy and their phishing preventive behaviours. Our findings show that phishing self-efficacy statistically impacts the participants' frequency of clicking links and preventive behaviour of considering the sender before forwarding a link to others. Specifically, we found a weak correlation between participants' phishing self-efficacy scores and the frequency of clicking links and a moderate correlation between phishing self-efficacy scores and the frequency of considering the sender before forwarding a link to others. We expected a negative correlation between participants' link clicking frequency and phishing self-efficacy. However, the positive result may signify that participants with high phishing self-efficacy often click on links because of their confidence in their ability to identify phishing links. Although the phishing self-efficacy score didn't predict all the preventive behaviours, however, our result is in agreement with the findings in [21, 23, 24] where self-efficacy was found to significantly affect performing security-conscious behaviour.

There were also interesting results on the relationships between the participants' claimed knowledge of phishing and their preventive behaviours during instant messaging. We found that the participants' claimed knowledge of phishing had a statistically significant impact on their preventive behaviours during instant messaging, positively affecting them. This finding shows that participants that strongly agree that they know what phishing is were more likely to perform phishing preventive behaviours.

Finally, our investigation revealed that the participants' concern about phishing in MIM Apps positively affected adoption of preventive behaviours. This finding shows that those worried about phishing in MIM apps are more likely to take precautions when communicating in these apps.

The limitation of this study is that our sample is relatively small. In addition, we used the snowball sampling method for recruiting participants. Snowball sampling often results in participants with higher interconnectivity than would be seen in the general population. This effect can be seen in our sample as many of our participants have undergraduate or postgraduate qualifications. Furthermore, most participants were male, young, and residing in Nigeria or the UK. All these limitations may have an impact on the measured behaviours. This study relies on self-reported data; as such, the data may not accurately reflect how the participants behave in real life.

6 Conclusion

Phishing attacks remain a cyber threat to both individuals and organisations. One reason these attacks remain successful is because they exploit human vulnerabilities. The popularity of MIM apps and the functionalities they offer their users, such as the ability to share links or join groups, have made them an attractive medium for phishers. Recent findings reveal that MIM Apps lack countermeasures to protect users from phishing scams. Thus, user awareness remains a key priority. As a first step, this study used an online survey to investigate MIM apps users' knowledge of phishing scams, the preventive measures they take from such scams and whether their phishing self-efficacy and knowledge about phishing influence these behaviours. The survey revealed that most participants were aware of phishing scams targeting them. The participants also expressed concerns regarding the prevalence of such scams. Our findings show that participants try to reduce their susceptibility by following recommended anti-phishing advice. However, one of the approaches they used, which relied on checking the link preview, is flawed, and could be used by phishers to direct them to fake websites. The survey also shows that phishing self-efficacy, knowledge and concern about phishing predicted the adoption of preventive behaviours. In addition to revealing that user awareness contributes to adopting phishing preventive behaviours in MIM apps, this study shows that users relied on a vulnerable approach when deciding the legitimacy of links. Thus, calling for the development of phishing awareness intervention to help protect users of MIM apps. Furthermore, since this study relied on self-reported data, future work could measure actual behaviour by conducting simulated phishing campaigns against the users of these apps and comparing their actual and reported responses.

Acknowledgment. This work is part of a PhD research sponsored by the Petroleum Technology Development Fund (PTDF)-Nigeria. There were no conflicts of interest in this study.

References

1. Statista. Number of mobile phone messaging app users worldwide from 2018 to 2022 (2021). https://www.statista.com/statistics/483255/number-of-mobile-messaging-users-wor ldwide/. Accessed 13 Apr 2021
2. Cao, H., Chen, Z., Cheng, M., Zhao, S., Wang, T., Li, Y.: You recommend, I buy: how and why people engage in instant messaging based social commerce. Proc. ACM Hum.-Comput. Interact. **5**(CSCW1), 1–25 (2021). https://doi.org/10.1145/3449141
3. Ramamoorthi, L.S., Peko, G., Sundaram, D.: Information security attacks on mobile messaging applications: procedural and technological responses. In: 2020 International Conference on Computational Science and Computational Intelligence (CSCI), pp. 275–281 (2020). https://doi.org/10.1109/CSCI51800.2020.00053
4. Kaspersky. "Phishing in messenger apps – what's new?" (2021). https://www.kaspersky.com/about/press-releases/2021_phishing-in-messenger-apps-whats-new. Accessed 04 Jan 2022
5. Stivala, G., Pellegrino, G.: Deceptive Previews: A Study of the Link Preview Trustworthiness in Social Platforms (2020)
6. Ahmad, R., Terzis, S.: Understanding phishing in mobile instant messaging: a study into user behaviour toward shared links. In: Clarke, N., Furnell, S. (eds.) HAISA 2022. IFIPAICT, vol. 658, pp. 197–206. Springer, Cham (2022). https://doi.org/10.1007/978-3-031-12172-2_15
7. Becher, M., Freiling, F.C., Hoffmann, J., Holz, T., Uellenbeck, S., Wolf, C.: Mobile security catching up? Revealing the nuts and bolts of the security of mobile devices. In: 2011 IEEE Symposium on Security and Privacy, pp. 96–111 (2011). https://doi.org/10.1109/SP.2011.29
8. Parker, F., Ophoff, J., Van Belle, J.-P., Karia, R.: Security awareness and adoption of security controls by smartphone users. In: 2015 Second International Conference on Information Security and Cyber Forensics (InfoSec), pp. 99–104 (2015). https://doi.org/10.1109/InfoSec.2015.7435513
9. Kim, D., Shin, D., Shin, D., Kim, Y.-H.: Attack detection application with attack tree for mobile system using log analysis. Mob. Netw. Appl. **24**(1), 184–192 (2019)
10. Khonji, M., Iraqi, Y., Jones, A.: Phishing detection: a literature survey. IEEE Commun. Surv. Tutor. **15**(4), 2091–2121 (2013). https://doi.org/10.1109/SURV.2013.032213.00009
11. Netcraft. "Phishing protection, in your favourite browse" (2020). https://netcraft.app/bro wser/. Accessed 15 Mar 2020
12. Rao, R.S., Vaishnavi, T., Pais, A.R.: CatchPhish: detection of phishing websites by inspecting URLs. J. Ambient. Intell. Humaniz. Comput. **11**(2), 813–825 (2019). https://doi.org/10.1007/s12652-019-01311-4
13. Kumaraguru, P., Sheng, S., Acquisti, A., Cranor, L.F., Hong, J.: Teaching johnny not to fall for phish. ACM Trans. Internet Technol. (2010). https://doi.org/10.1145/1754393.1754396
14. Kumaraguru, P.: PhishGuru: A System for Educating Users about Semantic Attacks. Carnegie Mellon University (2009)
15. Cain, A.A., Edwards, M.E., Still, J.D.: An exploratory study of cyber hygiene behaviors and knowledge. J. Inf. Secur. Appl. Appl. **42**, 36–45 (2018). https://doi.org/10.1016/j.jisa.2018.08.002
16. Shah, P., Agarwal, A.: Cybersecurity behaviour of smartphone users in India: an empirical analysis. Inf. Comput. Secur. **28**(2), 293–318 (2020). https://doi.org/10.1108/ICS-04-2019-0041

17. McCormac, A., Zwaans, T., Parsons, K., Calic, D., Butavicius, M., Pattinson, M.: Individual differences and information security awareness. Comput. Hum. Behav. **69**, 151–156 (2017). https://doi.org/10.1016/j.chb.2016.11.065

18. Whitty, M., Doodson, J., Creese, S., Hodges, D.: Individual differences in cyber security behaviors: an examination of who is sharing passwords. Cyberpsychol. Behav. Soc. Netw. **18**(1), 3–7 (2015). https://doi.org/10.1089/cyber.2014.0179

19. Merdenyan, B., Petrie, H.: Generational differences in password management behaviour. In: Proceedings of the 32nd International BCS Human Computer Interaction Conference 32, pp. 1–10 (2018)

20. Verkijika, S.F.: Understanding smartphone security behaviors: an extension of the protection motivation theory with anticipated regret. Comput. Secur. **77**, 860–870 (2018). https://doi.org/10.1016/j.cose.2018.03.008

21. Arachchilage, N.A.G., Love, S.: Security awareness of computer users: a phishing threat avoidance perspective. Comput. Hum. Behav. **38**, 304–312 (2014)

22. Verkijika, S.F.: 'If you know what to do, will you take action to avoid mobile phishing attacks': self-efficacy, anticipated regret, and gender. Comput. Hum. Behav. **101**, 286–296 (2019). https://doi.org/10.1016/j.chb.2019.07.034

23. Safa, N.S., Sookhak, M., Von Solms, R., Furnell, S., Ghani, N.A., Herawan, T.: Information security conscious care behaviour formation in organizations. Comput. Secur. **53**, 65–78 (2015). https://doi.org/10.1016/j.cose.2015.05.012

24. Torten, R., Reaiche, C., Boyle, S.: The impact of security awarness on information technology professionals' behavior. Comput. Secur. **79**, 68–79 (2018). https://doi.org/10.1016/j.cose.2018.08.007

25. Reeder, R.W., Ion, I., Consolvo, S.: 152 simple steps to stay safe online: Security advice for non-tech-savvy users. IEEE Secur. Priv. **15**(5), 55–64 (2017). https://doi.org/10.1109/MSP.2017.3681050

26. Indiana University. "Phishing Education & Training" (2022). https://phishing.iu.edu/tips-and-strategies/index.html

27. Dassanayake, D.: WhatsApp users warned not to trust fake Amazon anniversary free gift message (2021). https://www.express.co.uk/life-style/science-technology/1415675/WhatsApp-message-warning-Amazon-free-gift-scam. Accessed 15 Sept 2022

28. Li, L., He, W., Xu, L., Ivan, A., Anwar, M., Yuan, X.: Does explicit information security policy affect employees' cyber security behavior? A pilot study. In: 2014 Enterprise Systems Conference, pp. 169–173 (2014). https://doi.org/10.1109/ES.2014.66

29. Liang, H., Xue, Y.L.: Understanding security behaviors in personal computer usage: a threat avoidance perspective. J. Assoc. Inf. Syst. **11**(7), 1 (2010). https://doi.org/10.17705/1jais.00232

30. Rashidi, Y., Vaniea, K., Camp, L.J.: Understanding Saudis' privacy concerns when using WhatsApp. In: Proceedings of the Workshop on Usable Security (USEC 2016), pp. 1–8 (2016)

31. Jamieson, S.: Likert scales: how to (ab) use them? Med. Educ. **38**(12), 1217–1218 (2004)

32. Norman, G.: Likert scales, levels of measurement and the 'laws' of statistics. Adv. Heal. Sci. Educ. **15**(5), 625–632 (2010)

33. Boone, H.N., Boone, D.A.: Analyzing likert data. J. Ext. **50**(2), 1–5 (2012)

34. Albakry, S., Vaniea, K., Wolters, M.K.: What is this URL's destination? Empirical evaluation of users' URL reading. In: Proceedings of the Conference on Human Factors in Computing Systems, pp. 1–12 (2020) https://doi.org/10.1145/3313831.3376168

35. Cronbach, L.J.: Coefficient alpha and the internal structure of tests. Psychometrika **16**(3), 297–334 (1951)

36. Pallant, J.: SPSS Survival Manual: A Step by Step Guide to Data Analysis Using SPSS for Windows, 3rd edn. McGraw Hill Open University Press, New York (2007)

37. Aldaraani, N., Petrie, H., Shahandashti, S.F.: Online security attack experience and worries of young adults in the United Kingdom. In: Clarke, N., Furnell, S. (eds.) HAISA 2022, pp. 300–309. Springer, Cham (2022). https://doi.org/10.1007/978-3-031-12172-2_24

Look Before You Leap! Perceptions and Attitudes Towards Inferences in Wearable Fitness Trackers

Abdulmajeed Alqhatani[1,2(✉)] and Heather R. Lipford[2]

[1] Najran University, Najran 61441, Kingdom of Saudi Arabia
aaalqhatni@nu.edu.sa
[2] University of North Carolina at Charlotte, Charlotte, NC 28223, USA
{aalqhata,Heather.Lipford}@uncc.edu

Abstract. Users of fitness trackers regularly share their data with a variety of people and entities and do not consider this data as very sensitive. Yet, this data could be used to infer additional information, such as mood, health status, or even identity. We conducted interviews and a survey with fitness tracker users to examine their awareness and attitudes towards multiple inference scenarios. Our results demonstrate that participants have a higher willingness to share individual primary data over information inferred from that data, providing evidence that users are not considering potential inferences in their sharing decisions. Our findings also identify a number of factors related to users' attitudes towards inferences.

Keywords: Fitness trackers · Privacy · Inferences

1 Introduction

Internet of Things (IoT) devices that collect fitness data have been widely adopted, with increasing sales over the past few years [1]. Depending on the device, today's fitness trackers are laden with sensors, such as GPS, accelerometers, and gyroscopes to capture a variety of data. Many of these devices also have mobile applications and web services that allow users to view and share updates about their personal activities with other users through social platforms and with third parties. Thus, sharing data outside of the fitness tracker platform is commonly done.

Compared to other IoT devices, fitness trackers are unique in that they can be worn by users continuously, which enables the collection of massive amounts of personal, and frequently, health-related data. The pervasive and often invisible collection of data by these sensor devices and the sharing of it can expose users to privacy risks. One major risk is the possibility of inferring information from the data collected by devices or that shared by users. For example, in January 2018, reports revealed that fitness tracker data shared by users on Strava, a social fitness service, showed accurate locations of U.S. military sites [2].

A. Moallem (Ed.): HCII 2023, LNCS 14045, pp. 399–418, 2023.
https://doi.org/10.1007/978-3-031-35822-7_27

Traditional privacy awareness protocols and application features may not be sufficient to communicate what data an IoT device company collects from users, including what might be inferred from their data [3,4], resulting in potential privacy intrusions. In this paper, we expand prior work by examining fitness tracker users' perceptions and attitudes about inferences, and how those attitudes could relate to users' sharing decisions. We conducted semi-structured interviews and an online survey with users of wearable fitness devices regarding the information that can be inferred from their tracker data by other individuals, device manufacturers, and external parties. Our main findings include:

- Additional evidence that users of fitness trackers lack awareness that personal information can be inferred from the primary data their devices capture and share.
- Analysis demonstrating that users are less comfortable sharing inferred information than primary information with all kinds of recipients, indicating that users are likely not considering the potential for inferences in disclosing fitness tracker data.
- Identification of factors related to users perceptions of inferences, including notice and consent, likelihood and trade-offs of risk, accuracy and anonymity of data, and trust.

2   Related Work

Prior studies have examined users' concerns regarding the accumulation of personal information on a wide range of online services [5–7], including exploration of inferences [6,8]. However, inferences in the context of wearable fitness trackers have not been fully explored, particularly from an end-user's perspective. Concerns toward inferences in wearable fitness devices can be linked to users' knowledge and attitudes regarding privacy [3,4,9–13]. We first discuss the potential inferences that can occur with wearable fitness devices before turning to research on users' awareness and attitudes.

2.1   Inferences in Fitness Trackers

Researchers have defined inferences as any information that can algorithmically be inferred about users from the data collected online and offline [14]. Wearable fitness trackers are one common category of IoT devices that has a number of embedded sensors, such as accelerometers, altimeters, temperature sensors and others that collect and report a range of data to their users. We refer to this data as *primary data*, and includes things such as step count, heart rate, miles covered, and sleep patterns. In addition to sensed data, users also typically provide personal information, such as gender, weight, and age, to a device's mobile or online platform to take advantage of certain tracking or application features, such as reporting calories consumed.

Researchers have demonstrated that such primary data can be used to infer other information with high accuracy; for example, eating moments [15], moods

[16], places [17,18], and sexual activity [19]. In addition, there is wide concern that data generated by fitness trackers might be used in the future for undesirable decisions, such as to disqualify users for employment, insurance, or loans [20]. Studies have noted that current regulations do not protect personal data collected by wearable devices, or that such regulations are outdated and cannot cope up with the increasing legal challenges created by such IoT devices [9,20]. For example, unlike common sensors, such as cameras and GPS on mobile phones, fitness tracker sensors do not always require permission to operate, and can thus collect data automatically and continually [16,21].

The greatest privacy concern is that data collected by IoT fitness trackers might be unexpectedly associated with a user's real identity [9]. The accumulation of data provided by a user (e.g., birth date), along with activity data (e.g., exercise route), contextual data (e.g., timestamps), and online data has been demonstrated to accurately infer users' real identities [9,11]. Aktypi et al. [9] stated that their study participants underestimated the risks associated with the usage of their fitness trackers. Users are not aware of the differences between raw data and the information inferred from that data [4]. However, what contributes to users' lack of awareness, or their apathy, towards inferences in the context of wearable fitness devices has not been explored deeply.

Finally, while much of the research on inferences is concerned with information that can be derived algorithmically, studies have also demonstrated that users can be concerned with what people infer about them based on information shared socially. For example, users who do not have much time to exercise may choose to not share fitness tracker data on social media so friends would not think they were lazy [10].

2.2   Awareness of Inferences

Apart from IoT devices, researchers have examined peoples' awareness about inferences in a wide range of services, such as behavioral advertising and social media [6,18,22]. In general, users are aware that their data is processed and stored by service providers [5]. Users can also be aware of online tracking [23], but they may not know that their data could be aggregated and even shared with third parties [5]. Individuals who have greater awareness of data aggregation have greater likelihood of concerns towards undesirable inferences [22]. Awareness increases when users link inferences to their own past actions [8], and this also influences users to take protective actions [23]. Nevertheless, users sometimes have misconceptions about inferences, and their beliefs about how companies use their data differ from reality [18].

In terms of wearable devices, researchers have examined users' understanding about the information that can be inferred from data collected by these devices [3,4,9]. For example, Rader and Slaker [3] investigated the impact of folk theories on users' reasoning about data collected by fitness trackers. The findings reveal that users' conceptions helped them reason about dependencies among data types, but did not support users in understanding what additional information can be inferred from their data. Alqhatani and Lipford [10] indicated that their study participants believed that private information could potentially be inferred from their tracker data, but the participants did not provide concrete examples of how such inferences could be done.

There is considerably less work on how awareness of inferences can impact users' behaviors with wearable fitness devices. In an online survey, Schneegass et al. [4] examined how information collection representation in fitness trackers could impact users' willingness to disclose information. More specifically, when data is requested at the sensor level (e.g., accelerometer) versus when it is requested at the information level (e.g., step count). The authors reported that users have inconsistent preferences between these representation levels- participants showed higher willingness to share labeled information in certain contexts than sensor data and vice versa. We are investigating potential inconsistencies between primary information, such as step count, and inferred information. As people become more aware of potential inferences over time, this may discourage them from sharing their personal fitness tracking data. Gorm and Shklovski [24] showed evidence of this, where participants in a workplace campaign discovered how shared step count can reveal additional personal information, and as a result they renegotiated their personal disclosure boundaries with colleagues.

Overall, prior work has indicated that users are unaware about inferences based on data collected by IoT sensor devices [9,20,25]. Yet, little research has investigated the factors that contribute to that lack of awareness. Gabriele and Chiasson [11] found that users may not believe that certain inferences are possible, leading them to discount the threats. Other studies have attributed the lack of awareness about inferences by users to the absence of interface cues that help users to speculate about possible inferences [3,26].

2.3   Attitudes

A number of researchers have investigated users' attitudes about the collection and sharing of fitness tracker data. Attitudes towards this data have been shown to be dependent on data sensitivity [10,12,24], risk perception [9], trust [9,27] and comfort with recipients [10,11]. However, we have seen little research examining attitudes towards inferences in this domain. Users' reactions to inferences have been studied in online tracking and advertising [5–7,23]. These studies reported that users have mixed feelings about such inferences, considering them "useful" and "creepy" [6,7]. For example, inferences that are relevant to users' interests are perceived as useful [6,7], but users can be uncomfortable that they are being monitored [6]. Inferences related to certain data, such as gender, financial information and online behavior are regarded as sensitive [5], but people's comfort was found to be correlated with the accuracy of inferences regardless of sensitivity [5].

The personal nature of fitness tracker data may also result in inferences that users would consider sensitive, such as mood, health status, or location. Yet, researchers report that users do not consider much of the primary data as sensitive [10,27], and are generally willing to widely disclose information, such as step count and heart rate. The primary concern users have is with location data captured by wearable devices with GPS [12]. Users are worried that location data can be abused; for example, by criminals to know where they live. Studies have also reported that fitness tracker users trust the companies who collect their data and feel that the risk of disclosing their information is low [9,27]. Finally, users' concerns about the disclosure of their personal data is greatly dependent on who receives the data. Several studies have indicated that users are generally comfortable disclosing their fitness tracker data to friends and family members but are less comfortable providing it to strangers and advertisers [10,11].

3 Methods

We utilized mixed methods to examine users' perceptions and comfort regarding inferences. In total, we have 23 interview participants and 159 survey respondents. The study was approved by our university Institutional Review Board (IRB).

3.1 Semi-Structured Interviews

We recruited our participants by advertising in the Reddit communities that are related to IoT and fitness trackers. The research team contacted the participants through email to schedule a phone interview. The interview participants live in the United States (17), the United Kingdom (2), Argentina (1), Australia (1), Belgium (1), and Canada (1). We did not deliberately sample participants from different locations. However, since Reddit has users from around the world, we chose not to restrict participants based on a country. The interviews lasted between 17 and 40 min. Each participant received a $10 Amazon gift card after completing the interview.

We recruited a total of 23 users (13 M & 10 F) with an average age of 33 years old, ranging from 18 to 52 years old. The participants are well educated; all the participants except two attended a university and have a degree. The interviewees utilized a wide range of devices for tracking health and fitness, most commonly the Apple Watch, followed by Fitbit. Most of these devices enable users to track a variety of sensor-based data, including movement, vital signs, and location. Most of the devices used by our participants are also paired with that device's mobile app or web service that provides users with a variety of tracking features and allows them to share their data with others. Many participants also reported connecting their device data to external platforms, such as Strava, mainly to access metrics or features not offered by their devices. In addition, a few participants utilized fitness trackers for other reasons that include tracking sleep and monitoring medical conditions.

The interview began with behavioral questions, such as what data participants think is collected by their devices, who can access it, and what concerns they have about their information. The main part of the interview focused on the information that can be inferred about participants based on their data. We then provided our participants with seven brief hypothetical scenarios to examine their reactions to sharing their information if inferences could be made about them by the device company, third parties, or by other individuals. Our scenarios are similar to other studies about privacy preferences and data collection awareness, such as for online services [5] and IoT [3,28]. We designed these scenarios based on potential inferences described in previous related work [20]. Users' sharing comfort is dependent on who receives the data [10,11], and so we assume that this might also be true for inferred information. Thus, we designed our study scenarios to investigate users' comfort regarding sharing data with different individuals and parties (see Table 3). We chose to explore inferences from these different angles because data use and sharing decisions can involve multiple kinds of overlapping considerations.

We audio recorded and transcribed all the interviews. The transcripts were analyzed using qualitative data analysis software and an inductive coding approach. First, two coders independently and iteratively coded three transcripts to identify a list of common themes and patterns. The coders then compared and merged their themes into one codebook. The resulting codebook consisted of 32 codes that were conceptually grouped into: use and sharing, inference perceptions and comfort, and protection. The remaining interview transcripts were coded by the two coders using the same codebook. The researchers kept track of their disagreements and the calculated inter-rater agreement was 81.25%. The coders then discussed and resolved their disagreements.

3.2   Online Survey

We then conducted an online survey to further examine fitness tracker users' perceptions and comfort regarding inferences across a fuller set of data and audiences. We utilized Amazon Mechanical Turk (MTurk) to recruit our survey participants, and the survey was hosted on Qualtrics. We recruited participants who are English speakers, aged 18 or older, current or former users of wearable fitness trackers, and had at least a 98% HIT approval rate on MTurk. We first conducted a pilot test of our survey questions with 5 users to ensure the appropriateness of wording and to estimate the duration to complete the survey. The final survey consisted of 45 questions. Of the 206 participants who answered a pre-screening question, 159 met our participation criteria. The participants took, on average, 10 min to complete the survey and received $1.50 USD as compensation.

Our sample consisted of 65.4% males and 34.6% females. Their ages ranged from 19–64 years old with an average of 33.5 (SD = 8.1). In terms of education, 71.7% had a bachelor's degree or attended some college, 20.1% held a master or a doctoral degree, and 8.2% had not attended college.

We first asked the participants to select all the fitness trackers they used, to identify if they shared their information with other individuals or parties, and to indicate their goals for sharing fitness tracker information. To examine our participants' attitudes about inferences, we first provided them a list of ten recipients and asked about their comfort with sharing different types of primary data (e.g., step count and heart rate), which is collected by common wearable devices. The recipients included both other people, such as friends and acquaintances, as well as organizations, such as insurance companies and workplaces. We then presented our respondents with six short statements where personal information might be inferred from the primary data that was already provided (e.g., stress level, as suggested by heart rate data) and asked them to specify their sharing preferences with the same group of recipients. This allowed us to also explore users' sharing preferences of different fitness tracker data with different audiences. We also asked them to choose "likely", "unlikely", or "not sure" that a given scenario would happen.

Our results are presented primarily as descriptive statistics and graphical representations, which we use to draw a conclusion about the participants' knowledge and comfort regarding inferences. However, we performed inferential statistics using McNemar's and Cocheran's Q tests (the latter for a comparison involving three types of information) to compare participants' comfort with sharing primary data and inferred information with multiple groups of recipients.

4   Results

In the following, we present the interview and survey results together. Note that any numbers reported in the interview results are merely to reflect prevalence of themes in our sample. We use the following words in characterizing the results: a few (2–4), some (5–10), many (11–18), and most (19–22).

4.1   General Sharing and Concerns

Our interview participants described a wide variety of data they believe is collected by their trackers. For example, P12 said: *"Everything, and I think it also collects log activity, like how many times I use it, what features I chose, how much time with the app has been opened, when I chose it. Everything"*. We asked our survey participants to rate their level of confidence on a scale from 1 ("not at all confident") to 5 ("very confident") about: how their fitness tracker collects data; and how the data is used and stored. Respondents had higher confidence in their knowledge of how their data is collected than in their knowledge of how it is used and stored. However, 58% of respondents did not read their fitness tracker company's privacy policy and terms of service or were unsure. Taken together, our participants seemed to have a good understanding about the primary data collection capabilities of their devices, although are less sure of how it is used.

We asked our participants if they ever shared their fitness information, why, and with whom. The majority of the interview participants said that they shared their information. Friends were the most common, where goals include competition and accountability. Some people reported sharing information openly with significant others or family members for mutual encouragement towards health and fitness goals. The participants also disclosed their data on external health and wellness platforms, such as Strava and MyFitnessPal, where they mostly connect with strangers. Other reported recipients include healthcare providers and a pharmacy. Sharing was less also common for survey participants, where almost half (47%) reported sharing their information with other individuals, most commonly with friends (68%) and family (35%). Only 30% reported sharing with companies and third parties, connecting their data to external wellness apps (46%), health insurance companies (25%), or health providers (6%). Similar to the interview, the survey participants shared their information mainly to stay fit and accountable towards their fitness goals, track medical conditions, or receive incentives based on activity.

We also asked our interviewees about their concerns with sharing primary data, particularly step count, sleep patterns, and heart rate. Similar to prior studies (e.g., [10]), more than half of our interview participants were not concerned about fitness tracker data because they did not consider it risky. In contrast, some of the interview participants did express discomfort, indicating that while their information is not identifiable, it is personal, and thus they only shared with people known to them in real-life. A few reported concerns about adjusting insurance premiums; while a few others said they were primarily concerned about location information, mainly because it may compromise their physical safety.

4.2   Sharing Comfort with Recipients

In this section, we report our survey participants' comfort regarding sharing primary data with a list of audiences, as well as their comfort sharing the information that is inferred from that primary data with those same audiences. Figure 1 summarizes the responses for several scenarios.

Primary Data. Overall, the respondents were more comfortable sharing their primary data (e.g., step count, heart rate) with family members and friends, followed by significant others and health providers. Respondents were least comfortable sharing with third parties, and most data with workplaces. Across all kinds of recipients, respondents were more comfortable sharing step count, and less comfortable sharing their friends list. In addition, the sharing comfort with health providers increases with data that has health connotations, such as heart rate and height and weight. These patterns are similar to those found in other studies on fitness trackers [10,11].

Inferences Based on Primary Data. We presented participants with the following six statements where information can be inferred based on some of the primary data, and the participants were asked to choose all the recipients that they would be comfortable sharing with:

- Body Mass Index (BMI), as calculated based on the weight and height.
- A record of sexual activity, as calculated by the heart rate and movement data.
- Home location, as suggested by an exercise map/route.
- Stress level, as suggested by the heart rate data.
- A sedentary lifestyle, as suggested by the average step count.
- Personal connections, as shown by the user competition in fitness challenges.

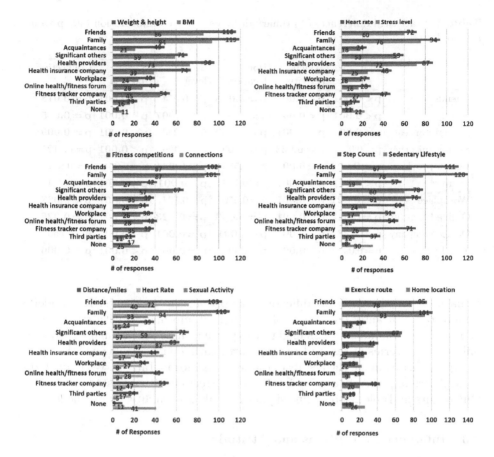

Fig. 1. Users' comfort with sharing primary data vs. inferred information.

For most information, patterns are similar to the primary data. Respondents were most comfortable sharing with family members and friends, followed by significant others and health providers. Third parties were chosen least often, especially for location information.

Figure 1 shows a comparison between the percentage of respondents who were comfortable with sharing primary data and the related inferred information. Across all scenarios and audiences, fewer respondents were comfortable sharing inferred information than primary. This suggests that at least some of the participants were not considering the potential for these inferences in their initial comfort responses.

We also conducted a series of McNemar's tests, as well as Cocheran's Q tests for sexual activity, to examine statistical differences ($p < .05$) regarding users' comfort with sharing primary data versus inferred information with the same group of recipients. The results show significant differences across most audiences in each scenario, with a few exceptions. As Table 1 shows, only the sexual activity

Table 1. Statistical differences of primary data Vs. inferred information (sig. p-values are bolded).

	BMI	Sexual activity	Home location	Stress level	Sed. lifestyle	Connections
Friends	p < 0.001	p < 0.001	p = 0.015	p = 0.074	p < 0.001	p = 0.018
Family	p < 0.001	p < 0.001	p = 0.268	p = 0.007	p < 0.001	p = 0.035
Acquaintances	p < 0.001	p < 0.001	p = 0.009	p = 0.203	p < 0.001	p = 0.009
Significant other	p = 0.074	p = 0.034	p = 1.000	p = 0.429	p < 0.001	p = 0.112
Health provider	p = 0.002	p < 0.001	p = 0.532	p = 0.041	p = 0.064	p = 0.511
Insurers	p < 0.001	p < 0.001	p = 0.719	p < 0.001	p < 0.001	p = 0.064
Workplace	p = 0.021	p < 0.001	p = 0.556	p = 0.124	p < 0.001	p = 0.038
Online fit. group	p = 0.012	p < 0.001	p = 0.003	p = 0.023	p < 0.001	p = 0.026
Device company	p = 0.137	p < 0.001	p < 0.001	p = 0.001	p < 0.001	p = 0.556
Third party	p = 0.092	p < 0.001	p < 0.001	p = 0.006	p < 0.001	p = 0.006

scenario revealed significant differences across all the recipients. Respondents were also significantly uncomfortable sharing all information with strangers on online fitness communities. As might be expected, there are not many statistical differences in terms of respondents' comfort sharing with significant others.

To further examine the results of the relationships in Table 1, we conducted a multiple testing correction using Bonferroni correction with adjusted $p < 0.0008$. Our results in Table 2 show some significant values even after adjustment.

4.3 Inference Perceptions and Attitudes

The survey results establish reduced comfort in the sharing and use of inferred information. The interview results provide deeper insights into user perceptions of these inferences. Our interviewees indicated that inferences are possible, but many of them were uncertain about what can be inferred and how. Several were aware of widely reported incidents; for example, P7 indicated: *"I remember when some soldiers where they were recording their training runs on Strava, and because of their unique positions in the world, it was very easy to track and identify who they are even that was uploaded anonymously"*. P16 distinguished between individuals and companies in their ability to make inferences. Unlike companies, this participant believed that people are unlikely to be able to infer his information because he can control the sharing of it with them.

Three interview participants showed advanced understanding by pointing out that information can be aggregated from multiple sources, which increases the chance of inferring precise information: *"I use a variation on my date of birth just to not make it easy if any one of those services leaks information so I can't easily be linked from cross-tabulation to other services, and that's something I've always done since the 90s. I was always cautious about leaking my identity"* [P18].

Table 2. Significant values after correction (bolded).

	BMI	Sexual activity	Home location	Stress level	Sed. lifestyle	Connections
Friends	**p < 0.001**	**p < 0.001**	p = 0.015	p = 0.074	**p < 0.001**	p = 0.018
Family	**p < 0.001**	**p < 0.001**	p = 0.268	p = 0.007	**p < 0.001**	p = 0.035
Acquaintances	**p < 0.001**	**p < 0.001**	p = 0.009	p = 0.263	**p < 0.001**	p = 0.009
Significant other	p = 0.074	p = 0.034	p = 1.000	p = 0.429	**p < 0.001**	p = 0.112
Health providers	p = 0.002	**p < 0.001**	p = 0.532	p = 0.041	p = 0.064	p = 0.511
Health insurers	**p < 0.001**	**p < 0.001**	p = 0.719	**p < 0.001**	**p < 0.001**	p = 0.064
Workplace	p = 0.021	**p < 0.001**	p = 0.556	p = 0.124	**p < 0.001**	p = 0.038
Online fit. group	p = 0.012	**p < 0.001**	p = 0.003	p = 0.023	**p < 0.001**	p = 0.026
Device company	p = 0.137	**p < 0.001**	**p < 0.001**	**p = 0.001**	**p < 0.001**	p = 0.556
Third party	p = 0.092	**p < 0.001**	**p < 0.001**	p = 0.006	**p < 0.001**	p = 0.006

To go beyond these generic perceptions, we provided our interview participants with seven scenarios (Table 3), each with different levels of sensitivity that implicitly or explicitly suggest some information could be inferred from their fitness tracker data. We first discuss specific reactions to each scenario before describing more general themes.

Table 3. Interview scenarios

Level	Summary
Device & Third Parties	1# Your device company shares your data with a background screening company who offers background check for different parties including employers, insurers, and banks
	2# Your wearable device records a history of your sexual activity
	3# A health insurance company classified you as overweight based on your wearable fitness data
	4# Your employer uses your device data to predict your mood (e.g., if you are stressed)
Socially	5# You joined a public fitness group where all members share fitness data collected by their trackers with each other
	6# A friend asked you to share your fitness data collected by your device with friends on one of your social media accounts (e.g., Facebook)
	7# Strangers infer your social connections based on fitness tracker data you share over the app

Background Screening. The survey results indicate that users are generally not comfortable with external parties being able to access personal fitness data. As shown in Fig. 1, respondents were least comfortable sharing both primary data and inferred information with third parties. The interview scenario provided several examples of third parties for one particular purpose. Participants indicated that they had never heard of such data being used for background screening, and most of them were uncomfortable sharing with insurance companies, employers, and banks because they believed that the data would mostly be used by these parties in a negative way (e.g., insurance rate increase, promotion discrimination, or loan application rejection). The participants demanded detailed information, which may suggest a lack of trust about the purpose of sharing their information with external parties. However, a considerable number of the participants said that they will be less uncomfortable if there were some benefits. For instance, P19 stated in response to this scenario: *"I wouldn't necessarily be concerned if I was going to be rewarded for good behavior"*.

Sexual Activity. We expected to find a large number of people uncomfortable with the second scenario due to the sensitivity of the inferred information. This seemed to be the case in the survey, where few participants were comfortable sharing this information across all audiences, except with significant others. Surprisingly, a considerable number of interview participants seemed indifferent and considered recording sexual activity as another interesting metric to track. Many participants also said that they would not mind their device inferring this information if it is anonymized. P5 stated: *"If it's only stored and seen by me, then I wouldn't have a problem with it. If it was anything that got to, like, the people in my family whom I'm okay with sharing other information, I definitely don't think that's something I would be comfortable with."*. However, P15 pointed out that she did not want even the device to store a record such data because it will be embarrassing if the device gets hacked and the information was leaked.

Health Insurance. The third scenario presents a clear threat to the participants, with an insurance company classifying someone as overweight. A common response by our participants is that they would probably not mind if a notice describing how their information will be used for that purpose is provided in advance, and they optionally agreed to it. Some other interview participants also said that they will feel less uncomfortable sharing their information if they were actually overweight. Our survey participants were also unwilling to share information about their overall health with insurance companies, but they seemed indifferent about sharing other information, such as location information, which is likely to already be known by one's insurance company.

Employer Predicting Mood. All interview participants, except two, were extremely uncomfortable that an employer can predict their mood or stress level. Participants considered this an invasion of their personal privacy, because they could be judged in their workplace based on irrelevant information. Many participants felt that if employers request this type of information, they will always use it to harm employees. One participant indicated: *"I would not like that at* *all because I think that it's a private thing that shouldn't affect your work life."* [P22]. Similarly, only 11% of survey respondents were comfortable sharing this type of information with a workplace, but the results do not show a significant difference between sharing stress level and the primary data inferred from it.

Online Fitness Group. This scenario elicits participants' comfort regarding potential inferences made by other people, in particular if the information is shared with strangers. Overall, our participants were more comfortable with this scenario than any other scenario, because they anticipated value from sharing their information. For example, P7 pointed out that sharing fitness data with other people has helped him to move from being obese to normal weight. The participants were also comfortable since the sharing in this scenario is reciprocal. A few people noted that their decision will also depend on the type of data being requested, indicating that they would be comfortable disclosing fitness data they deemed insensitive, such as step count. The survey shows similar results, as the respondents were more comfortable sharing step count than any other data with online fitness communities, although most of them were unwilling to disclose additional information. Those few interview participants who were not comfortable to share with strangers expressed concerns as to what other people would think about them based on their information.

Social Media. The sixth scenario examines users' sharing comfort of fitness tracker data socially with people they know, but the participants also discussed sharing with a third party (e.g., Facebook). In the survey, participants were comfortable sharing a wide range of information with friends, without regard to how that information was shared. Yet, our interview participants showed some discomfort with this scenario for two reasons. First, participants expressed a general distrust of social media because they consider these platforms *"wide open"*, and thus their information can be subject to risks, such as data leakage and targeted ads. For example, P18, a Twitter user, stated that he would create a secondary account with a new username if he decided to share his fitness information there to hide his identity. Secondly, the participants felt that social media platforms are not the right place to share fitness data, as it went against their norms of what they consider appropriate to share on those platforms.

Social Connections. Lastly, we examined users' comfort if their social connections (i.e., friends) were inferred. Overall, our participants were uncomfortable if strangers infer their social connections because that could then expose their connections to privacy risks. The survey results are similar, as the respondents were more comfortable sharing their connections with friends, family, and significant other than with other audiences. The interview participants struggled to figure out how this information could be inferred from their fitness tracker data.

4.4 Emerging Factors

Our interview participants' reactions to the given scenarios provided insights into their set of considerations regarding inferences. We then asked about several of these factors within the survey, rating the importance of those factors on their comfort with sharing inferred information in each scenario using a five-point Likert Scale. Figure 3 presents a heatmap of the survey results. We will refer to this heatmap throughout the results below.

Likelihood of a Risk. While participants provided examples of the potential threats for each given scenario, some of them believed that certain risks are less likely to happen. P23 explained: *"I haven't heard of data being used in that way, but if it's used in that way then definitely I'd have to re-evaluate it"*. P12 said that some risks are possible but will not occur in the near future. However, many participants initially considered the data collected by fitness trackers insignificant but changed their opinions after discussing the scenarios, indicating that many scenarios were credible.

Figure 2 presents our survey respondents' perceptions regarding the likelihood that the six scenarios described in the survey would occur. The participants are asked to select "likely", "unlikely", or "unsure" in response to each scenario. As can be seen, users thought BMI and lifestyle inferences were most likely, with 82% and 84% respectively. In contrast, only about half of the respondents (53%) thought it was likely that a device can infer sexual activity based on heart rate and movement data. Similar to our interview participants, the respondents were "unsure" whether personal connections can be inferred based on competition in fitness challenges.

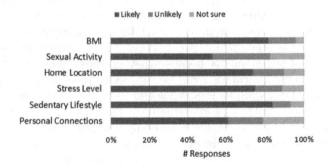

Fig. 2. Survey: likelihood that each inference can occur.

Notice/Consent. Many participants brought up in the discussion of scenarios 3 and 4 that notice and consent were factors that would make them more comfortable with sharing information with insurance companies and workplaces. Our survey results also indicate the importance of this, particularly for third parties. As Fig. 3 shows, notice and consent, as well as the ability to control sharing, were the two most important aspects for survey respondents.

To ensure that their information will not be used against them, participants demanded a clear and full explanation of data usage. For example, P8 stated: *"I would always ask how the company [a health insurance company] gets my data and if I authorize data how they use it, where it goes, and how it is stored"*.

Benefit-Risk Tradeoff. Our results are in line with much privacy research that disclosure decisions are impacted by the perceived benefits [5,10]. Some of our interview participants indicated in response to some of the scenarios that they may be willing to share their information if there is a value. For some of them, the obtained benefits from sharing their information outweigh the potential risk. In addition, the participants felt that they have limited control, but they *"have to give something to get something back"*. However, the perceived benefit was rated as the least important factor by survey respondents (Fig. 3).

Accuracy of Data. Some participants stated that the data recorded by wearable fitness devices can be inaccurate, and that measurements could have multiple causes. For example, P9 commented about the ability of a device to infer sexual activity: *"It wouldn't know if your heart rate goes up for a workout, if your heart rate goes up because you're sleeping and you have a nightmare, you're watching a movie or something like that, even if you have drugs, there's no way to say why your heart rate went up, so it would be a lot more difficult to determine if you had sexual activity versus if you didn't"*.

Our participants had two views regarding accuracy of inferences. Because they believed the inferred information would not be reliable, it would not likely to be used by insurance companies or employers, for example, making those scenarios less likely. However, lack of accuracy did raise concerns that someone might be unfairly judged based on incorrect information if those inferences were done.

Anonymization. Our findings provide evidence of the interplay between people's comfort and anonymization in the context of fitness tracker data sharing. The expectation that information is anonymized when shared with the device or third parties was mentioned by interview participants, indicating that they will be uncomfortable and most likely will not share their information in certain scenarios if the information is connected with their real identity. Our survey supports this finding. As shown in Fig. 3, anonymization of sexual activity was the most important factor in that particular scenario. Thus, assurances that identity is protected would be important for users to feel comfortable with inferences.

Trust. Our findings suggest that high-level trust can decrease privacy concerns and vice versa. For example, three participants, who are Apple Watch users, were comfortable about certain scenarios because, according to them, Apple will not jeopardize its reputation by abusing users' data:
"With Apple overall as a company with many instances over the years, especially toward encryption, that does alleviate some of those initial lack of trust that would be with other companies, lets' say [some fitness tracker company], for instance, doesn't necessarily have that record of fighting to keep the keys to the kingdom locked up and not pass it over" [P13].

In contrast, three other interview participants were uncomfortable sharing their information, noting that they generally disbelieve companies regarding their data practices. One participant mentioned that she had grown more concerned over time with the data practices of fitness tracker companies.

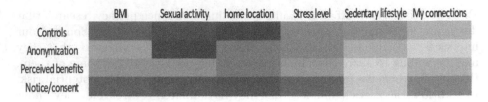

Fig. 3. Survey: heatmap that represents the importance of specific factors regarding users' comfort with sharing inferred information.

5 Study Limitations

As with many interview and survey studies, our sample is not representative of the broader population of fitness tracker users. We attempted to recruit participants from diverse age, gender, education, and technical backgrounds. However, 95.6% of the survey respondents were between 19 and 49 years old, and thus the perceptions of older users is not represented. The survey sample also skewed toward male participants (65.4%). In addition, interview participants are on average more educated. Lastly, self-reported data may not necessarily be accurate.

6 Discussion

The overarching finding of our study is that users are less comfortable sharing personal details that can be inferred from primary data collected by fitness trackers than they are with the primary data. This was demonstrated by comparing interview participants' pre- and post-reactions to different scenarios, as well as by comparing survey participants' comfort with sharing primary data vs. information inferred from that data with the same recipients. Given this discrepancy, our results continue to suggest a lack of awareness of the potential for inferences.

Many of our participants were comfortable sharing a variety of data with other people and organizations. However, interview participants' opinions changed after we presented them with different scenarios—they were, in general, less willing to share their information after considering what could be inferred. Similarly, comfort sharing inferred information in the survey was reduced for all kinds of data and recipients.

6.1 Reasons for Lack of Awareness

While we did not ask participants directly about why they may lack awareness, our data provides several indications. First, the lack of awareness about inferences can partially be attributed to the limited knowledge about wearable device company data practices, understandably because privacy policies that describe these practices are generally not usable. For example, more than half of our survey respondents were unaware of their fitness tracker's privacy policy. Prior research has also shown that there is generally a mismatch between what fitness tracker companies report through their privacy policies and what users need to know about data practices [29].

In addition, most of our interview participants indicated that they had not experienced any risks from sharing their data, and thus they felt unthreatened- a mental bias known as "optimistic bias". While a few people recalled well-publicized previous incidents, such as Strava's leakage of location information [2], none provided examples of incidents related to other common types of information. For example, Fitbit was in the news years ago when details of sexual activity were inferred from information found on Google searches [30]. However, our participants expressed doubts of the likelihood of the various scenarios, which aligns with Gabriele and Chiasson's study results that users found many potential threat scenarios unlikely [11].

Users were quite aware of the primary data collected by their fitness trackers, as they can easily view and interact with such information within their fitness applications. This is not the case for inferences. Rader and Slaker identified the importance of visibility for informing users' mental models of the relationships between fitness tracker data [3]. Therefore, another issue that might contribute to the problem of users' lack of awareness about inferences is the lack of privacy nudges that provide some visibility into the inferences that are possible. We believe that nudges, in particular, could stimulate users' reasoning about potential inferences. Currently, users can only rely on what they learn from privacy policies or the news media to learn about inferences that are possible and probable.

6.2   Comfort with Inferences

Our participants' comfort sharing inferred information shows patterns similar to that of primary information– comfort varies with the type of information and the audience [10,11], with people being most comfortable sharing information with those closest to them. Our interview participants' reactions to the scenarios also suggest that their comfort with inferences are dependent on the perceived benefits, data accuracy, and anonymization.

Users' willingness to obtain a benefit even though a risk is knowingly involved can be described by the "Privacy Calculus" theory, which posits that users balance the perceived benefits (e.g., monetary or health benefit) against the privacy risks; if the benefits outweigh the risks, then users are likely to disclose personal information [31]. In both studies, our participants reported little value in sharing inferred information with workplaces and insurance companies, for example. However, as prior studies have shown, many people currently do share their sensed data with such organizations to gain discounts or participate in workplace health campaigns [10]. When users consider much of the primary information not sensitive, they see few risks involved in gaining those benefits. Yet, greater awareness of what information could be inferred from such information may change that privacy calculus.

Interestingly, interview participants expressed willingness to share information if done anonymously. Several participants mentioned strategies they already take or would take to protect their identities, such as providing fake information on accounts. Thus, users may not be against inferences being used in situations where they can remain anonymous. However, only a few of our interview participants recognized the possibility of combining and de-anonymizing data. Therefore, users may not recognize the risks of sharing what they think is non Personally Identifiable Information (PII).

Finally, users also raised the issue of accuracy. Many participants believed that wearable technology is not smart enough to predict certain information (e.g., mood and sexual activity), thus impacting their judgements on the likelihood of the inference. A few of those participants who considered inferences useful seemed to value the accuracy of those inferences. Yet, accuracy perceptions also impact comfort, as users do not want people or organizations to draw judgements or use information about them that is inaccurate. Accuracy is especially important if data is used to determine consumer eligibility for benefits, for example. Yet, there are currently few mechanisms for reviewing the information that could be inferred from fitness tracker data.

7   Conclusion

Our findings provide evidence that users may not be considering all of the potential privacy consequences of inferences before they leap into sharing personal information. While many of our interview participants were initially unconcerned about sharing fitness tracker data in general, they became more concerned after considering inferences. This finding was confirmed by our survey results, which show that the participants were less comfortable sharing inferred information across a range of audiences. Thus, user decisions to disclose information may go against their desires should their data be used to infer additional information. Our findings also highlight important aspects that users do consider, including the probability that an inference can happen, the accuracy of data being used to make inferences, the benefit obtained in return for sharing information, and the belief that their real identity is anonymized. Overall, we conclude that wearable device interfaces and privacy notices need to include additional awareness mechanisms to help users think about inferences.

References

1. CCS Insight (2018). https://www.ccsinsight.com/press/company-news/3695-succ ess-of-apple-watch-means-more-growth-in-sales-of-wearable-technology/
2. Hern, A. (2018). https://www.theguardian.com/world/2018/jan/28/fitness-track ing-app-gives-away-location-of-secret-us-army-bases
3. Rader, E., Slaker, J.: The importance of visibility for folk theories of sensor data. In: Thirteenth Symposium on Usable Privacy and Security ({SOUPS} 2017), pp. 257–270 (2017)

4. Schneegass, S., Poguntke, R., Machulla, T.: Understanding the impact of information representation on willingness to share information. In: Proceedings of the 2019 CHI Conference on Human Factors in Computing Systems, pp. 1–6 (2019)
5. Bilogrevic, I., Ortlieb, M.: "If you put all the pieces together..." attitudes towards data combination and sharing across services and companies. In: Proceedings of the 2016 CHI Conference on Human Factors in Computing Systems, pp. 5215–5227 (2016)
6. Dolin, C., et al.: Unpacking perceptions of data-driven inferences underlying online targeting and personalization. In: Proceedings of the 2018 CHI Conference on Human Factors in Computing Systems, pp. 1–12 (2018)
7. Ur, B., Leon, P.G., Cranor, L.F., Shay, R., Wang, Y.: Smart, useful, scary, creepy: perceptions of online behavioral advertising. In: Proceedings of the Eighth Symposium on Usable Privacy and Security, pp. 1–15 (2012)
8. Rader, E., Hautea, S., Munasinghe, A.: "I have a narrow thought process": constraints on explanations connecting inferences and self-perceptions. In: Sixteenth Symposium on Usable Privacy and Security ({SOUPS} 2020), pp. 457–488 (2020)
9. Aktypi, A., Nurse, J.R., Goldsmith, M.: Unwinding Ariadne's identity thread: privacy risks with fitness trackers and online social networks. In: Proceedings of the 2017 on Multimedia Privacy and Security, pp. 1–11 (2017)
10. Alqhatani, A., Lipford, H.R.: "There is nothing that i need to keep secret": sharing practices and concerns of wearable fitness data. In: Fifteenth Symposium on Usable Privacy and Security ({SOUPS} 2019) (2019)
11. Gabriele, S., Chiasson, S.: Understanding fitness tracker users' security and privacy knowledge, attitudes and behaviours. In: Proceedings of the 2020 CHI Conference on Human Factors in Computing Systems, pp. 1–12 (2020)
12. Motti, V.G., Caine, K.: Users' privacy concerns about wearables. In: Brenner, M., Christin, N., Johnson, B., Rohloff, K. (eds.) FC 2015. LNCS, vol. 8976, pp. 231–244. Springer, Heidelberg (2015). https://doi.org/10.1007/978-3-662-48051-9_17
13. Vitak, J., Liao, Y., Kumar, P., Zimmer, M., Kritikos, K.: Privacy attitudes and data valuation among fitness tracker users. In: Chowdhury, G., McLeod, J., Gillet, V., Willett, P. (eds.) iConference 2018. LNCS, vol. 10766, pp. 229–239. Springer, Cham (2018). https://doi.org/10.1007/978-3-319-78105-1_27
14. Hautea, S., Munasinghe, A., Rader, E.: 'That's not me': surprising algorithmic inferences. In: Extended Abstracts of the 2020 CHI Conference on Human Factors in Computing Systems, pp. 1–7 (2020)
15. Thomaz, E., Essa, I., Abowd, G.D.: A practical approach for recognizing eating moments with wrist-mounted inertial sensing. In: Proceedings of the 2015 ACM International Joint Conference on Pervasive and Ubiquitous Computing, pp. 1029–1040 (2015)
16. Kröger, J.L., Raschke, P., Bhuiyan, T.R.: Privacy implications of accelerometer data: a review of possible inferences. In: Proceedings of the 3rd International Conference on Cryptography, Security and Privacy, pp. 81–87 (2019)
17. Meteriz, Ü., Yıldıran, N.F., Mohaisen, A.: You can run, but you cannot hide: using elevation profiles to breach location privacy through trajectory prediction. arXiv preprint arXiv:1910.09041 (2019)
18. Warshaw, J., Taft, N., Woodruff, A.: Intuitions, analytics, and killing ants: inference literacy of high school-educated adults in the {US}. In: Twelfth Symposium on Usable Privacy and Security ({SOUPS} 2016), pp. 271–285 (2016)
19. Lupton, D.: Quantified sex: a critical analysis of sexual and reproductive self-tracking using apps. Cult. Health Sex. **17**(4), 440–453 (2015)

20. Peppet, S.R.: Regulating the internet of things: first steps toward managing discrimination, privacy, security and consent. Tex. L. Rev. **93**, 85 (2014)
21. Kröger, J.: Unexpected inferences from sensor data: a hidden privacy threat in the internet of things. In: Strous, L., Cerf, V.G. (eds.) IFIPIoT 2018. IAICT, vol. 548, pp. 147–159. Springer, Cham (2019). https://doi.org/10.1007/978-3-030-15651-0_13
22. Rader, E.: Awareness of behavioral tracking and information privacy concern In Facebook and Google. In. 10th Symposium on Usable Privacy and Security ({SOUPS} 2014), pp. 51–67 (2014)
23. Weinshel, B., et al.: Oh, the places you've been! User reactions to longitudinal transparency about third-party web tracking and inferencing. In: Proceedings of the 2019 ACM SIGSAC Conference on Computer and Communications Security, pp. 149–166 (2019)
24. Gorm, N., Shklovski, I.: Sharing steps in the workplace: changing privacy concerns over time. In: proceedings of the 2016 CHI Conference on Human Factors in Computing Systems, pp. 4315–4319 (2016)
25. Ziegeldorf, J.H., Morchon, O.G., Wehrle, K.: Privacy in the internet of things: threats and challenges. Secur. Commun. Netw. **7**(12), 2728–2742 (2014)
26. Wagner, I., He, Y., Rosenberg, D., Janicke, H.: User interface design for privacy awareness in eHealth technologies. In: 2016 13th IEEE Annual Consumer Communications & Networking Conference (CCNC), pp. 38–43. IEEE (2016)
27. Zimmer, M., Kumar, P., Vitak, J., Liao, Y., Chamberlain Kritikos, K.: 'There's nothing really they can do with this information': unpacking how users manage privacy boundaries for personal fitness information. Inf. Commun. Soc. **23**(7), 1020–1037 (2020)
28. Naeini, P.E., et al.: Privacy expectations and preferences in an IoT world. In: Thirteenth Symposium on Usable Privacy and Security ({SOUPS} 2017), pp. 399–412 (2017)
29. Paul, G., Irvine, J.: Privacy implications of wearable health devices. In: Proceedings of the 7th International Conference on Security of Information and Networks, pp. 117–121 (2014)
30. Rao, L.: (2011). https://techcrunch.com/2011/07/03/sexual-activity-tracked-by-fitbit-shows-up-in-google-search-results/
31. Smith, H.J., Dinev, T., Xu, H.: Information privacy research: an interdisciplinary review. MIS Q. 989–1015 (2011)

User Motivations of Secure Web Browsing

Umai Balendra[1](✉) and Sana Maqsood[2]

[1] Carleton University, Ottawa, ON, Canada
umaibalendra@cmail.carleton.ca
[2] York University, Toronto, ON, Canada
smaqsood@yorku.ca

Abstract. Users regularly use the web to complete various tasks, which can expose them to security and privacy risks. One mechanism to protect them is Secure Web Browsing (SWB), which provides complete anonymity to the user's browsing activities. Given the security and privacy advantages of Secure Web Browsing, it is important to explore users' motivations, perceptions, and mental models of using SWB. Our work addresses these research questions. We conducted an online questionnaire study with 30 Canadian participants, and analyzed the data using statistics and thematic analysis. We found that users' primary motivations for using SWB was to protect their personal information from unauthorized parties. We also found that users often have incomplete mental models of SWB, which can lead to security and privacy concerns, and potentially affect the adoption of SWB. We use our findings to provide recommendations for the design of SWB tools to improve their usability.

Keywords: Usable Security · Secure Web Browsing · User Study · Questionnaire

1 Introduction

Web browsing is considered an essential skill in the 21st century, having been used by diverse users (e.g., children, adults, seniors) to complete daily tasks such as work, entertainment, and shopping. While helpful in completing regular activities, web browsing also exposes users to additional security and privacy risks. For example, a 2017 Global Commission on Internet Governance survey found that users from twenty-four countries were particularly concerned about cybercrime, in addition to their personal information being accessed by unauthorized users, such as Internet Service Providers (ISPs) and the Government [14].

Given users' online security and privacy concerns, it is important to explore their protection strategies, the accuracy of these strategies, and their motivations for using them. Secure Web Browsing (SWB) tools are a mechanism for offering users some protection against online risks, but the level of protection offered varies by tool. Our work seeks to understand users' perceptions and mental models of SWB, and their motivations for using them. Having this understanding can help us design more tailored SWB tools to protect users' security and privacy. In our work, we define SWB as users having complete anonymity online, with none of their personal information being tracked by any entity, including ISPs [6,40]. Prior work related to SWB has focused on exploring users' mental models of one particular SWB tool [1,20,21,38,45], and does not explore the concept of SWB holistically, as understood by the user. Our work is tool agnostic and uses a broader definition of SWB to explore different tools and techniques utilized by users to meet their SWB needs. Specifically, our work explores the following research questions:

RQ1: What are users' motivations for using secure web browsing?
RQ2: What are users' perceptions and mental models of secure web browsing?

To answer our research questions, we conducted an online questionnaire study with 30 Canadian participants using a broader definition of SWB. Data from the questionnaire was analyzed using statistics and thematic analysis [7,10]. We found that users primarily engaged in SWB in an effort to protect their personal information from unauthorized parties (e.g., hackers and ISPs), especially during activities which involved financial transactions, such as banking. SWB was also used to avoid targeted advertisements. With regard to mental models, we found that users had experience and knowledge of different SWB tools, however they were most familiar with the Private Browsing/Incognito mode of web browsers, despite it offering less privacy compared to other tools. We also found that participants had incomplete or incorrect mental models of SWB tools, which can affect their trust and adoption of these tools. We use our findings to provide recommendations for improving the design of SWB tools to make them more accessible to users, especially those who may be novice.

2   Background

We begin by discussing SWB and related tools. We then provide a review of research on users' motivations of SWB and their mental models.

2.1   Secure Web Browsing (SWB)

We define SWB as users having complete anonymity online, with none of their personal information being tracked by any entity, including ISPs [6,40]. SWB can be accomplished using various tools (Table 1), such as the Private Browsing/Incognito feature on major web browsers, browser extensions, the HTTPS protocol, and VPNs [3,4,11,13,29,30,34]. These tools vary in terms of the level of anonymity they provide to users.

For example, the Private Browsing/Incognito browsing mode and the HTTPS protocol provide users partial anonymity. Specifically, the Private Browsing/Incognito mode does not save users' cookies, browsing or download history [11,23,33]. However, in this mode user activities are visible to their ISP, which in turn could make this information accessible to employers or the Government [11,23,33]. Similarly, the HTTPS protocol ensures that users have encrypted communication with a website, but some of their data, such as their IP address, is accessible to unauthorized parties [17,32].

Table 1. Common tools for Secure Web Browsing (SWB)

SWB Tool	Description
Private Browsing	The Incognito or Private Browsing mode [23] of browsers enables users to discard their browsing data, such as browsing history, which files were downloaded, and cookies
Browser extensions	Provides additional security and privacy protection to users and are offered as add-ons to a browser [18]. Common extensions include Avast [4], which provides protection against invasive trackers, and Click&Clean [13] which allows users to delete their browsing data (e.g., cookies, history)
HTTPS protocol	Allows websites to communicate securely with users by encrypting their communication. Users are informed of this protocol being used through the presence of 'https' in the website's URL [31]
Virtual Private Network (VPN)	Downloadable software that provides users with increased online privacy and security by encrypting user data and masking users' virtual location [34].
Tor	Offers increased privacy to users by using a virtual tunnel network; this includes layered encryption and prevents other parties (e.g., ISPs) from accessing browsing information and activity while masking users' identities [41]
Brave	Provides a fast and secure browsing experience while protecting users' browsing data from unauthorized parties (e.g., ISPs) [8]. Also offers a Tor browsing mode which mirrors the Tor browser's network tunneling feature [8,9]

Alternatively, Secure Web Browsers (e.g., Tor [41] and Brave [8]) and VPNs provide users with complete anonymity. In addition to providing the privacy offered by Private Browsing mode, Tor and Brave also prevent ISPs from tracking user activities and data [8,41]. Similarly, VPNs such as Norton Secure VPN [34] and ExpressVPN [16] provide users with complete anonymity by masking IP addresses, encrypting data on public connections, and preventing tracking by ISPs [16,34]. However, both Secure Web Browsers and VPNs need to be downloaded and installed by the user, whereas some of the tools which offer partial anonymity are either built into the web browser or can easily be enabled by users. VPNs also often have an associated monetary cost, which could affect user adoption [38].

2.2 SWB Motivations

Since motivations can influence behaviours [37], it is important to explore users' motivations for engaging in SWB, so we can better understand how these motivations lead to security and privacy conscious behaviours online. Gao et al. [21] explored 200 participants' motivations for using SWB, and found the following motivators:

i) erasing browsing history and cookies, especially for pornographic and dating websites
ii) protecting personal information from malicious websites and users
iii) feeling safer while online shopping
iv) engaging in non-work related tasks

Other studies on users' Private Browsing usage and expectations [22] similarly found that users highly valued their online privacy [15,21,22,15]. Habib et al. noted that users utilized this SWB tool to prevent their searches and browsing activity from being saved on devices, especially on shared devices [22].

2.3 SWB Mental Models

Prior research has explored users' mental models of SWB tools, which offer partial to complete anonymity.

Partial Anonymity. Abu-Salma et al. [1], explored users' mental models of the Private Browsing mode on browsers. They found that users often had incorrect mental models of this tool, partially due to the UI of the tool violating well-established design heuristics [1]. Incorrect mental models were further influenced by the explanations of Private Browsing mode offered by the browsers [1]. Similarly, prior research [15,21,42,45] has found that users are often unaware of Private Browsing mode or do not fully understand the security and privacy advantages it provides. With regard to HTTPS, Krombholz et al. [25] found that users also have incorrect mental models of this tool, especially regarding the security and privacy advantages it offers and how encryption works.

Complete Anonymity. Gallagher et al. [20] explored users' mental models of Tor. They found that users had an incorrect understanding of the tool's functionalities and did not know how to configure it properly. These poor mental models could lead users to accidentally configure the tool in a way which compromises their privacy, such as deanonymizing the data.

Akgul et al. [2] examined VPN advertisements on YouTube, and found that influencers over-exaggerate the protection provided by VPNs. This communication could lead users to develop incorrect security and privacy mental models of VPNs. Ramesh et al. [38] examined users' mental models and perceptions of VPNs, and found that many participants had incorrect mental models of how VPNs worked. Specifically, misunderstandings were found with regard to how accessible user information could be to unauthorized parties [38].

2.4 Research Gap

Previous research on users' motivations, perceptions, and mental models of SWB have focused on a specific SWB tool, and has not explored them holistically. In our work, we allow the user to specify the tools that they use, and our goal is to understand what SWB means to them without specifying a particular tool.

3   Methodology

We conducted an online questionnaire to address our main research question. The research protocol was cleared by our university's research ethics board.

3.1   Participants

We recruited 30 participants through social media, including the researcher's personal social media and several groups associated with our university. Some were also recruited through snowballing.

All participants browsed the web daily. Most (60%) were between 18 24 years old, some (33%) were between 25–30 years old, and a few (6%) were between 31–50 years old. All participants had some form of higher education, by either enrolling in or completing a program. Over half (n = 17) had training or experience in a technical field such as computer science, information technology, software engineering, or web security. With regard to browser preference, most participants (n = 27) preferred using Google Chrome, and a few (n = 3) preferred Safari.

3.2   Questionnaire

The questionnaire was designed and distributed using Qualtrics [36]. The first page provided the informed consent, including details of the study. After obtaining consent, participants were presented with the questions associated with the study. This included questions about demographics and their SWB behaviours, understanding, and motivations.

Demographics: 10 closed-ended questions collected information about participants' background, such as their education, work experience, and level of comfort with technology and web browsing.

Secure Web Browsing: 19 questions, consisting of a mix of closed-ended and open-ended questions, collected information about users' motivations for engaging in SWB. 5 questions gathered details on users' web browsing activities, and how well they understood SWB in their own words. Next, participants were provided with our definition of SWB, created from consolidating dictionary definitions and definitions derived from research. This allowed participants who may have been unfamiliar with SWB to be able to respond to the remaining questions. After presenting our definition of SWB, 14 questions evaluated participants' usage of SWB tools, expectations, perceptions, and mental models.

3.3   Pilot Testing

Prior to distributing the questionnaire, we conducted two rounds of pilot testing with friends and family. Participant feedback from the pilot testing was used to improve existing questions and add new questions.

4 Results

Both qualitative and quantitative methods were used to analyze questionnaire responses to answer our research questions:

RQ1: What are users' motivations for using secure web browsing?
RQ2: What are users' perceptions and mental models of secure web browsing?

Qualitative data from open-ended questions was analyzed using thematic analysis [7,10]. This involved moving data from various questions into Microsoft Excel and iteratively categorizing the responses into themes emerging from the data.

Quantitative data was analyzed using descriptive statistics (e.g., mean, median, mode).

4.1 RQ1: User Motivations for Using Secure Web Browsing

We asked participants a closed-ended question about which activities they performed when using SWB. Activities included shopping (gifts, travel deals, etc.), entertainment (Netflix, YouTube, etc.), banking, social networking (Facebook, Instagram, Twitter, TikTok), and school/work tasks. Participants could select multiple options.

We found that participants used SWB to engage in all of the activities presented, which included entertainment, social networking, shopping, online banking, and school/work tasks. It is possible that participants may have used SWB for banking and shopping because they prioritize protecting their personal/private information and having secure online financial transactions.

We further evaluated users' motivations for using SWB by asking them the open-ended question: "Explain why you use SWB". We asked this question after presenting our SWB definition to participants. A thematic analysis of the responses revealed three main themes: protecting personal information, preventing targeted advertisements, and having secure financial transactions.

Protecting Personal Information. A number of participants (n = 11) indicated that they used SWB to protect their online privacy and anonymity. For example, one participant explained that they used Incognito mode as a SWB tool so that their information would not be saved on shared computers at work: *"It is essential for me to use incognito tabs on shared computers at work, to avoid having my information saved for the next user"* (p13).

SWB was also used to protect personal information from third parties such as malicious actors. For example, one participant explained *"I use secure browsing to give me peace of mind whenever I share information about myself. More than anything, I just want private information to be kept private and not to be misused in any way by other people"* (p6).

Another participant shared that they *"use SWB to ensure [their] safety and to ensure [their] personal information isn't used for malicious intentions... it's a huge amount of unnecessary stress"* (p21). This statement indicates that having to protect personal information from adversaries causes additional stress for users.

Preventing Targeted Advertisements. A few participants (n = 5) shared that they used SWB to avoid receiving targeted advertisements and unwanted content. As one participant explained: *"when I access streaming sites that are filled with ads, when I search up medical stuff, and just random things when I don't want a bunch of ads"* (p2). In addition to targeted advertisements that stem from Internet searches, another participant explained that their reason for using SWB was to *"hide interest tracking from travel agencies"* (p7). Our findings support previous research, which shows that users tend to find targeted ads 'invasive' because they cross a line in terms of personal privacy, exhibiting a 'creepiness' factor [24,27,28,43].

Financial Transactions. Some participants (n = 7) stated that they leveraged SWB for online financial transactions. One participant explained *"[I use SWB for] anything that uses my banking info. I try to be secure to ensure that no one else is buying/subscribing to things on my behalf"* (p10) and another participant shared that they use SWB to *"apply discount codes"* (p7). Overall, we found that participants used SWB to have an additional layer of security when dealing with sensitive information, such as credit card information used for personal banking.

4.2   RQ2: User Perceptions and Mental Models of Secure Web Browsing

We evaluated participants' perceptions and mental models of SWB using the following six open-ended questions:

1. Where did you hear about SWB
2. Describe what SWB means to you
3. Describe how you would use SWB
4. Explain why you use SWB
5. Describe a situation where using SWB did not work as expected
6. Do you have any concerns about SWB

Q1–Q3 evaluated participants' existing SWB mental models. We then presented our definition of SWB to participants, and asked them Q4–Q6. Data from all the questions was analyzed using thematic analysis [7,10], which revealed two main themes: Mental Models of SWB and Concerns about SWB.

Mental Models of SWB (Q1–Q3). When asked to describe what SWB meant to them, participants articulated various definitions. Some (n = 7) believed that SWB would prevent unauthorized access to their private data. For example, as one participant explained: *"Secure web browsing means data being* *kept safe from people that shouldn't have access to your information/without your permission"* (p2). Another participant shared their understanding: *"Information on browsing history cannot be retrieved even from your Internet Service Provider"* (p7).

A few (n = 2) explained that SWB would protect them from being hacked: *"[SWB is] a way of surfing the web while protecting your privacy and information from being hacked"* (p8). Some participants (n = 9) defined SWB as a way to prevent viruses. Additionally, participants (n = 6) also defined SWB as a general set of online safety practices: *"I think of secure web browsing as a set of good practices while on the internet. For example, making sure that you don't submit any valuable information (e.g. credit card data, login data) through sites using HTTP instead of HTTPS"* (p11).

Our analysis shows that participants found protecting personal data to be a key feature of SWB, which is built into most SWB tools. The type of personal information participants wanted to protect included their *"browser activity"* (p1), *"browser history"* (p7), and *"credit card data"* (p11). With regard to actors, participants wanted to protect this information from unauthorized parties, hackers, and viruses. We note that the use of the word secure in SWB may have primed participants to think more about the 'security' and 'privacy' issues associated with web browsing.

Accuracy of Mental Models. We found that participants had different mental models of SWB. Some had mental models which aligned with our definition of SWB (i.e., providing users with complete online anonymity), while others had incorrect mental models of SWB. For example, some believed that SWB would protect them from hackers, which is not necessarily true. Even if SWB is used, downloading malicious software could provide hackers access to a user's system and their personal data. Similarly, some participants believed that SWB was a term used to describe common online safety practices, which indicates that the participant may have a less developed mental model of SWB.

Sources of Mental Models. When asked to explain where they heard about SWB, participants identified various sources including the Internet, social media, work, and friends/family. Online resources, such as security/privacy blogs and articles, were common.

Some participants became aware of SWB from school or work. As one participant explained: *"While connected to the network at work, we are asked to use secure web browsing"* (p13). It is important to note that most of our participants had higher technical knowledge or worked in a technical field, so they may have had more opportunities to learn about SWB than the average user. One participant shared that they learned about SWB from their web browser: "Web browsers giving information on 'security updates'" (p4). Even within our technical participants, web browsers were not a commonly identified source. This indicates a missed opportunity by web browsers to proactively educate and improve users' understanding of the SWB tools they offer.

Social media was also identified as a source for learning about SWB. For example, one participant shared how they became aware of SWB from a social media influencer: *"I was tuning in to one of my favorite YouTubers and he shared about how VPN and secure browsers are helpful for him"* (p6). This shows that social media could influence users' mental models of SWB, and possibly other security and privacy concepts as well. These findings confirm previous research, which shows that media, such as TV shows, can influence both technical [2,5] and non-technical [2,19] users' mental models of security and privacy. However, when it comes to social media, it is important to note that the user-generated content on these platforms could also expose users to security and privacy misinformation/misconceptions. Thus, while social media can be beneficial for fostering correct security and privacy mental models, as was the case for our participant, it can also expose users to advice or information which may actually compromise their security and privacy.

Users were also motivated to use SWB from the experiences of others. Specifically, they used SWB to avoid security and privacy incidents experienced by their friends and family. For example, one participant shared that they use SWB to avoid getting hacked on Instagram: *"...[I have] had many friends who have fallen victim to those scandals [hacking]..."* (p21). Another participant shared similar sentiments with regard to using SWB to safeguard their personal information: *"Though I haven't experienced issues like identity theft, accounts getting hacked, or my information being misused, I have heard about people who had gone through this"* (p6).

Concerns About SWB (Q4–Q6). Participant concerns of SWB were primarily due to misconceptions of how SWB worked. A few concerns were due to usability issues with particular SWB tools that participants used.

Inaccurate Mental Models. Some participants had concerns regarding Private Browsing/Incognito mode. Many expected complete anonymity online with none of their data being saved during or after their Private Browsing session. However, that is not how Private Browsing/Incognito mode works. This browsing mode saves certain data (e.g., search queries) during the users' Private Browsing session, while discarding other types of data (e.g., browsing history, cookies, form input) at the end of the session [11,12,30], but these differences were not understood by users. For example, one participant was surprised to learn that they were being shown targeted advertising based on their Private Browsing session: *"When ads that are targeted toward you seem to "listen" to your conversations. Or if your phone remembers a sequence you've used only on secure web browsing, and it offers it as an option with predicted text"* (p1).

The Private Browsing/Incognito mode utilizes user activities in a private browsing session to prevent targeted advertising [12,23,30]. While the browser is working as designed, our results show that it does not meet participants' expectations and mental models, which could result in lack of user trust in SWB. Participants were also concerned with regard to how user credentials were treated by Private Browsing/Incognito mode. As one participant explained: *"There have been times where I have logged into something in a private browser and did not have to input my login info because it saved (I made sure I was actually in incog-*

nito mode here)? I'm not sure if this is normal though" (p10). Users being able to view their saved data while in Private Browsing is a normal feature. In fact, Google Chrome's documentation outlines that users can still view and access their password, contact, and payment information while in Private Browsing mode [12]. Thus, the participant's concerns were due to an incorrect mental model of how persistent credentials work in Private Browsing mode.

However, we argue that the participant's mental model of how personal data should be treated in Private Browsing mode is correct, and that browsers should be designed to support these mental models. For example, the user's expectation is that their personal information should not be saved in SWB. Thus, when they are presented with previously saved data, they are justly confused. By having access to previously saved data, they might question whether they are truly in Private Browsing mode, as was the case for our participant. Browsers should be designed to not provide previously saved data, such as passwords, to users in Private Browsing mode. The current implementation of this feature can be further confusing when users create new passwords in Private Browsing mode, which will not be saved by the browser, but the user may expect them to be saved, because they were able to access saved passwords from their non-Private Browsing mode sessions.

The HTTPS protocol is another SWB feature for which users had concerns due to incorrect mental models. A participant in our study described possessing an incorrect mental model of HTTPS: *"I thought that simply visiting websites that used the HTTPS protocol was enough to maintain web safety. However, recently I've learned that some infected websites can automatically download stuff onto your PC or fiddle with your browser's plugins even if they are HTTPS"* (p11). In this case, the participant incorrectly believed that using HTTPS would protect their browsing activities from all types of security and privacy risks. However, in reality that is not the case, as HTTPS offers a specific type of privacy protection to users, namely the encryption of communication between the user and the website [32]. In addition, this protocol can also be employed by malicious websites to gain user trust [32]. In our example, the participant corrected part of their mental model of HTTPS through more experience with the tool, but still believed that a legitimate website employing HTTPS would offer them complete protection online, which is not the case.

Overall, we found that users may possess incorrect mental models of SWB tools, and these mental models can further lead to concerns when it comes to using SWB. For example, users may be less likely to trust these tools when they do not work according to expectations, and this could reduce user adoption. We recommend that SWB tools should be designed to support users' mental models. Furthermore, they should provide mechanisms to develop and improve users' mental models, especially those of novice users.

Usability. Some users expressed usability and accessibility concerns related to SWB. For example, one participant explained that they found the user interface (UI) of Google Chrome's Incognito mode confusing, especially in relation to the browser's dark theme (i.e., colour and layout of the browser UI): *"Sometimes*

Chrome dark mode and incognito mode look very similar so sometimes I think I am in a private browser when I in fact am not" (p10). This indicates that the UI of Private Browsing mode should be redesigned to provide clear visual cues that show when Private Browsing has been enabled.

Some SWB tools, such as VPNs, have a monetary cost which can make them less accessible for users. For example, a user may have to weigh the costs and benefits of using a VPN to decide whether the protection it offers is worth the cost. One participant articulated this concern: *"I try to use VPN free trials but I never really cared enough to pay for it since I never felt that my data wasn't 'secure'"* (p2). This finding supports prior research which identified pricing as a main factor in users' decisions to adopt VPNs [38].

5 Discussion

5.1 Answering RQ1: Motivations of Using SWB

Maintaining Privacy. Similar to prior work, [26], our participants were most concerned about protecting their personal information (e.g., first name, phone number, address). With regard to online activities, we found that participants commonly used SWB for online banking and shopping, indicating that users are more protective of their financial information compared to other types of personal information. This shows that participants have different privacy requirements for different types of personal data. For example, they may consider their browsing history to be less private than their personal or financial information.

Participants were motivated to use SWB based on their own personal experiences or those of their friends and family members. Specifically, they chose to use SWB after hearing about friends getting hacked or reading about security and privacy incidents online. In some cases, participants were using SWB with hopes of gaining general protection from all security and privacy risks, indicating a gap in their mental models of SWB.

Avoiding Third Parties. Participants also used SWB to avoid security and privacy violations by third parties, including individuals unknown to users (e.g., malicious users, hackers, ISPs), as well as family members or friends. A context in which SWB was used to protect users' privacy was the use of shared devices, either at work or home. Specifically, some participants reported feeling the need to protect their information on shared devices by using their browser's Private Browsing/Incognito mode. In future work, it would be interesting to explore the types of activities for which SWB is used on shared devices.

Overall, we found that users' motivation for engaging in SWB was determined by their activity, the context of their activity, or the need to protect specific types of activities. Given this, we believe that SWB tools should be designed to allow users to easily switch between secure and non-secure browsing modes.

5.2   Answering RQ2: User Perceptions and Mental Models of SWB

Mental Models of SWB. We used a broader definition of SWB to understand what SWB meant to users, without constraining their responses by the definition or features of a specific SWB tool, which has been the case in prior work [1,2,20–22,25,38,45]. We found that some of our participants understood SWB as specified by our definition, so they had a broader understanding of the concept and did not associate it with a specific tool. Despite this, when it came to discussing the SWB tools used and challenges that users experienced, most of the discussion revolved around the Private Browsing/Incognito mode of web browsers. Tools which provide complete anonymity and privacy, such as VPNs and Secure Web Browsers (e.g., TOR, Brave) were less discussed. This indicates that Private Browsing mode was the most common SWB tool used by participants, despite it only offering partial anonymity compared to other tools. One reason for this may be due to it having better usability than other tools. Specifically, the Private Browsing mode is built-in to a web browser, making it relatively easy to access, even for novice users. In contrast, both VPNs and Secure Web Browsers, such as TOR and Brave, need to be downloaded and installed on the user's computer. This often requires higher technical knowledge, expertise, and overall effort compared to using the Private Browsing mode. We recommend that major web browsers should have improved integration for SWB tools which provide complete anonymity to users, to make them more accessible. For example, Mozilla Firefox could provide an option in the UI that allows users to easily launch the TOR browser, which is a modified version of Firefox [41]. VPNs present an additional challenge, which may impact their adoption. Most have a monetary cost which makes them less accessible to users, as some may not be able to afford them, and others might be unable to determine whether the privacy advantages they offer are worth the cost. To make VPNs accessible, we recommend that browsers provide a built-in option, which is easy to use for novice users.

Most of our participants reported having technical knowledge, thus being comfortable with web browsing and using technology. Despite this, we found that some participants had incorrect mental models of SWB tools and features. For example, some participants did not possess the correct understanding of how the HTTPS protocol worked, or were not aware of the privacy advantages it provided.

With regard to the formation of mental models, we found that media, the Internet, and social media were commonly used by participants to develop their SWB mental models. In addition to this, we found that these sources also motivated users to engage in SWB. However, given the prevalence of misinformation on social media, it is important to note that relying on it as a source of security and privacy advice could potentially put users' security and privacy at risk (e.g., in situations where a user follows incorrect or malicious security and privacy advice).

To foster improved SWB mental models, we recommend that browsers offer a built-in tutorial. With this tutorial, users could familiarize themselves with the various SWB tools offered by the browser, and learn how these tools can be used in conjunction with other browser-based security and privacy tools. For example, such a tutorial can educate users about the HTTPS protocol, and explain how it keeps communication between two parties secure, but does not erase the user's browsing history. We recommend that this tutorial be presented to users the first time they download and use a web browser, and it should be easily accessible from the browser's UI afterwards.

User Perceptions of SWB. We found several situations where participants reported usability issues with SWB tools, which affected their privacy. One situation involved the look-and-feel of Google Chrome's Private Browsing mode. When in Private Browsing mode, the colour of the browser's body (i.e., design elements outside of the content area) becomes darker, to provide visual feedback to the user that they are browsing in Private Browsing mode. This visual feedback is provided by most major web browsers including Mozilla Firefox and Opera [35]. However, a usability issue occurs with this visual feedback when the user manually changes their default browser setting to use a darker coloured theme. In this case, when users switch to Private Browsing mode, there are minimal changes in their UI, so there may be situations where users think they are browsing in Private Browsing mode, when in fact they are using the regular browsing mode. This usability issue is most concerning on shared devices, where the user who changed the browser UI to a darker theme may be different than the user who is interested in using Private Browsing as a SWB tool.

Some of our participants reported confusing the darker browser UI to being in Private Browsing mode, which could compromise their privacy. To address this usability issue, we recommend that browsers should offer clear user feedback to indicate that Private Browsing mode has been enabled. With regard to the colour, the UI should change to a different colour than the user's current layout settings, instead of always being defaulted to a darker theme. In addition, the browser UI should also offer clear visual or text indicators to improve the accessibility for users who may not be able to perceive colour. Currently, the primary indicator of Private Browsing mode is the change in the colour of the Chrome browser. A secondary visual cue is provided in the top-right corner of the browser UI, but this is located out of the main field-of-view, so users may miss seeing it.

5.3   Limitations and Future Work

In terms of limitations, our study had a small sample size of 30 participants. The majority also had higher technical expertise, and were young (between the ages of 18–24), which may have influenced our results. As a result, our participants may have had better understanding and experiences with SWB, and our findings may not be an accurate representation of the older demographic.

In future work, we will recruit a more diverse group of participants with regard to technical expertise and age to obtain a more representative sample of the general population. This may reveal new insights into users' SWB motivations and mental models, which were not considered in our work. Furthermore, we plan on using the *Protection Motivation Theory* framework [39,44] to contextualize findings from our preliminary study. We hope this will lead to a better understanding of the influences and motivations which impact users' decisions to engage in SWB and relevant tools.

6 Conclusion

We conducted an online questionnaire study with 30 Canadian participants to understand their motivations, perceptions, and mental models of SWB. We found that participants were motivated to protect their privacy and often employed the Private Browsing mode as the SWB tool of their choice, followed by the HTTPS protocol and VPNs. By analyzing their concerns of SWB, we noted that participants' incomplete mental models often led to security and privacy concerns. To address these concerns, we propose various improvements for SWB tools, especially to the UI.

References

1. Abu-Salma, R., Livshits, B.: Evaluating the end-user experience of private browsing mode. In: Proceedings of the 2020 CHI Conference on Human Factors in Computing Systems, CHI 2020, pp. 1–12. Association for Computing Machinery, New York (2020). https://doi.org/10.1145/3313831.3376440
2. Akgul, O., Roberts, R., Namara, M., Levin, D., Mazurek, M.L.: Investigating influencer VPN ads on YouTube. In: 2022 IEEE Symposium on Security and Privacy (SP), pp. 876–892 (2022). https://doi.org/10.1109/SP46214.2022.9833633
3. Apple: Use private browsing in safari on mac (2021). https://support.apple.com/en-ca/guide/safari/ibrw1069/mac
4. Avast: Browse with more privacy—install avast's security & privacy extension (2021). https://www.avast.com/en-ca/avast-online-security
5. Baig, K., Kazan, E., Hundlani, K., Maqsood, S., Chiasson, S.: Replication: effects of media on the mental models of technical users. In: Seventeenth Symposium on Usable Privacy and Security (SOUPS 2021), pp. 119–138. USENIX Association (2021). https://www.usenix.org/conference/soups2021/presentation/baig
6. Bell: Bell privacy policy (2021). https://www.bell.ca/Security_and_privacy/Commitment_to_privacy
7. Braun, V., Clarke, V.: Thematic Analysis. American Psychological Association, DC, USA (2012)
8. Brave: The best privacy online (2021). https://brave.com
9. Brave: What is a private window with tor connectivity? (2023). https://support.brave.com/hc/en-us/articles/360018121491-What-is-a-Private-Window-with-Tor-Connectivity-
10. Carvalho de, P., Fabiano, A.: Thematic analysis for interactive systems design: a practical exercise. In: Proceedings of the 2021 European Conference on Computer-Supported Cooperative Work. European Society for Socially Embedded Technologies, Zürich (2021)

11. Google Chrome: Browse in private (2021). https://support.google.com/chrome/answer/95464?hl=en&co=GENIE.Platform%3DDesktop
12. Google Chrome: How private browsing works in chrome (2023). https://support.google.com/chrome/answer/7440301?hl=en&co=GENIE.Platform%3DAndroid
13. Click&Clean: Click&clean - chrome web store (2021). https://chrome.google.com/webstore/detail/clickclean/ghgabhipcejejjmhhchfonmamedcbeod
14. De Nardis, L.: Introduction: security as a precursor to internet freedom and commerce. Cyber Security in a Volatile World (2017)
15. DuckDuckGo: A study on private browsing: consumer usage, knowledge, and thoughts (2017). https://duckduckgo.com/download/Private_Browsing.pdf
16. ExpressVPN: The VPN that just works (2023). https://www.expressvpn.com/
17. FAQ, U.C.I.O.: Introduction to HTTPS. https://https.cio.gov/faq/#what-information-does-https-not-protect
18. Mozilla Firefox: Manage add-ons (2023). https://support.mozilla.org/en-US/products/firefox/manage-preferences-and-add-ons-firefox
19. Fulton, K.R., Gelles, R., McKay, A., Abdi, Y., Roberts, R., Mazurek, M.L.: The effect of entertainment media on mental models of computer security. In: Fifteenth Symposium on Usable Privacy and Security (SOUPS 2019), pp. 79–95. USENIX Association, Santa Clara (2019). https://www.usenix.org/conference/soups2019/presentation/fulton
20. Gallagher, K., Patil, S., Memon, N.: New me: understanding expert and non-expert perceptions and usage of the tor anonymity network. In: Thirteenth Symposium on Usable Privacy and Security (SOUPS 2017), pp. 385–398. USENIX Association, Santa Clara (2017). https://www.usenix.org/conference/soups2017/technical-sessions/presentation/gallagher
21. Gao, X., Yang, Y., Fu, H., Lindqvist, J., Wang, Y.: Private browsing: an inquiry on usability and privacy protection. In: Proceedings of the 13th Workshop on Privacy in the Electronic Society, WPES 2014, pp. 97–106. Association for Computing Machinery, New York (2014). https://doi.org/10.1145/2665943.2665953
22. Habib, H., et al.: Away from prying eyes: analyzing usage and understanding of private browsing. In: Fourteenth Symposium on Usable Privacy and Security (SOUPS 2018), pp. 159–175. USENIX Association, Baltimore (2018). https://www.usenix.org/conference/soups2018/presentation/habib-prying
23. Johansen, A.G.: Is private browsing really private? Short answer: no (2019). https://us.norton.com/internetsecurity-privacy-your-private-browser-is-not-so-private-after-all.html
24. Kean, A., Dautlich, M.: A guide to online behavioural advertising. Internet Advertising Bureau, London (2009)
25. Krombholz, K., Busse, K., Pfeffer, K., Smith, M., von Zezschwitz, E.: "If HTTPS were secure, i wouldn't need 2FA" - end user and administrator mental models of HTTPS. In: 2019 IEEE Symposium on Security and Privacy (SP), pp. 246–263 (2019). https://doi.org/10.1109/SP.2019.00060
26. Lutaaya, M., Baig, K., Maqsood, S., Chiasson, S.: "I'm not a millionaire": how users' online behaviours and offline behaviours impact their privacy. In: Extended Abstracts of the 2021 CHI Conference on Human Factors in Computing Systems, CHI EA 2021. Association for Computing Machinery, New York (2021). https://doi.org/10.1145/3411763.3451603
27. Malheiros, M., Jennett, C., Patel, S., Brostoff, S., Sasse, M.A.: Too close for comfort: a study of the effectiveness and acceptability of rich-media personalized advertising. In: Proceedings of the SIGCHI Conference on Human Factors in Computing

Systems, CHI 2012, pp. 579–588. Association for Computing Machinery, New York (2012). https://doi.org/10.1145/2207676.2207758

28. McDonald, A., Cranor, L.F.: Beliefs and behaviors: Internet users' understanding of behavioral advertising. In: Proceedings of the 2010 Research Conference on Communications, Information and Internet Policy (2010)

29. Microsoft: Browse inprivate in Microsoft edge (2021). https://support.microsoft.com/en-us/microsoft-edge/browse-inprivate-in-microsoft-edge-cd2c9a48-0bc4-b98e-5e40-ac40c84e27c2

30. MozillaFirefox: Private browsing - use Firefox without saving history (2021). https://support.mozilla.org/en-US/kb/private-browsing-use-firefox-without-history

31. MozillaFirefox: Secure web certificates (2021). https://support.mozilla.org/en-US/kb/secure-website-certificate

32. MozillaFirefox: HTTPS and your online security (2022). https://blog.mozilla.org/en/products/firefox/https-protect/

33. MozillaFirefox: Incognito browser: what it really means (2022). https://www.mozilla.org/en-US/firefox/browsers/incognito-browser/

34. NordVPN: What is a VPN? (2023). https://nordvpn.com/what-is-a-vpn/

35. Opera: Private mode (2023). https://help.opera.com/en/touch/private-mode/

36. Qualtrics: Make every interaction an experience that matters (2023). https://www.qualtrics.com/about/

37. Rabideau, S.T.: Effects of achievement motivation on behavior. Rochester Institute of Technology (2005)

38. Ramesh, R., Vyas, A., Ensafi, R.: "All of them claim to be the best": multi-perspective study of VPN users and VPN providers (2022). https://doi.org/10.48550/ARXIV.2208.03505, https://arxiv.org/abs/2208.03505

39. Rogers, R.W.: A protection motivation theory of fear appeals and attitude change1. J. Psychol. **91**(1), 93–114 (1975)

40. RogersCanada: Rogers privacy policy (2020). https://www.rogers.com/consumer/privacy-policy

41. Tor: Browse privately.explore freely (2021). https://www.torproject.org

42. Tsalis, N., Mylonas, A., Nisioti, A., Gritzalis, D., Katos, V.: Exploring the protection of private browsing in desktop browsers. Comput. Secur. **67**, 181–197 (2017). https://doi.org/10.1016/j.cose.2017.03.006, https://www.sciencedirect.com/science/article/pii/S0167404817300597

43. Werbach, K., Staff: privacy on the web: Is it a losing battle? Wharton School of the University of Pennsylvania - Business Journal (2008)

44. Westcott, R., Ronan, K., Bambrick, H., Taylor, M.: Expanding protection motivation theory: investigating an application to animal owners and emergency responders in bushfire emergencies. BMC Psychol. **5**(1), 1–14 (2017)

45. Wu, Y., Gupta, P., Wei, M., Acar, Y., Fahl, S., Ur, B.: Your secrets are safe: how browsers' explanations impact misconceptions about private browsing mode. In: Proceedings of the 2018 World Wide Web Conference, WWW 2018, pp. 217–226. International World Wide Web Conferences Steering Committee, Republic and Canton of Geneva, CHE (2018). https://doi.org/10.1145/3178876.3186088

Working for Home – Privacy and Confidentiality Issues in University Education

Debasis Bhattacharya[1](✉) [iD] and Jodi Ito[2]

[1] University of Hawaii Maui College, Kahului, HI 96732, USA
debasisb@hawaii.edu
[2] Information Technology Services, University of Hawaii, Manoa, HI 96822, USA

Abstract. Since the start of the COVID-19 pandemic in Spring 2020 many institutions of higher secondary education have resorted to distance education, allowing courses to be taught in an online modality and allowing students, faculty, and staff to work from home or remote locations. Various educational and distance learning tools and technologies, such as electronic mail, learning management systems, video-teleconferencing systems and content management systems have evolved to support to support distant learners. This distributed nature of higher education has led to a greater reliance for authentication tools and processes to identify students and faculty. In addition, university researchers who conduct their research from home or remote locations have an increased threat or vulnerability to hackers and criminal organizations. Finally, the educational organization itself is under greater stress to comply with local, state, and federal regulations to conform to student confidentiality and privacy laws. This paper studies the impact that Working from Home (WFH) since the start of the COVID-19 pandemic has had to the workings of the Information Technology organization at a large public university in the State of Hawaii, with a focus on privacy and confidentiality issues and the resilience of the university.

Keywords: Cyber Hygiene · Cyberwarfare · Mitigation of insider threats · Ubiquitous computing

1 Introduction

The Covid-19 pandemic that impacted educational institutions since early 2020, had a major impact on the operations of Information Technology departments of higher education institutions. The University of Hawaii (UH) comprises of 10 campuses spread out across the Hawaiian Islands and caters to 40,000 or more students during any given academic year. The Information Technology Services (ITS) department at the UH is responsible for the information technology needs for all students and staff members across the island state. As the state's only public system of higher education, the UH system offers education opportunities to all island residents. This paper describes the impact to privacy and confidentiality from the Covid-19 pandemic and the resulting Work from Home (WFH) situation that prevailed during the pandemic and the current hybrid situation. The paper focuses on policies, procedures, and guidance from ITS.

A. Moallem (Ed.): HCII 2023, LNCS 14045, pp. 435–446, 2023.
https://doi.org/10.1007/978-3-031-35822-7_29

2 Privacy and Confidentiality Issues in Higher Education

The onset of the Covid-19 pandemic led to the rapid digitization of operations and modes of instruction at higher education institutions across the world. The University of Hawaii expedited the digitalization of its curriculum to an online format, adopted the widespread usage of video-teleconferencing technologies, partnered with online vendors of content and cloud storage services, and digitized its classroom content to an online format [1]. Much resistance to digitalization, from older practitioners to antiquated practices, were hastily removed, and set aside, thanks to the sudden onset of Covid-19 and the regulations that prevented in person activities in higher education facilities [2]. Many large-scale public universities such as the UH, also adopted Online Program Management (OPM) and Massive Open Online Course (MOOC) platform [3].

2.1 Privacy Issues

The European Union's General Data Protection Regulation (GDPR) was introduced on May 25, 2018 and has impacted all universities of higher education. This is especially relevant to research universities such as the UH, which relies on data science and the usage of 'Big Data' to conduct basic research. Related issues to privacy [4, 5] and security concerns [5]. While information privacy relates to the benefit or ability to exert control over how personal information is collected, stored, and used; information security involves the use of protection information using educational technology. The onset of the Covid-19 pandemic has led to an increase in usage of Big Data and cloud services from location outside the work environment or outside the secure network. This has immense ramifications on the privacy and security of the data collected, stored, and maintained for university operations.

2.2 Ethical Issues and Big Data

As research and teaching universities rely of Big Data, there are ongoing issue regarding the ethical usage of this data. Large amounts of data are collected by content providers of curriculum and education technology. In addition, cloud storage providers also store large amounts of data regarding students, courses, and other aspects of a university operations. While much of this data is stored in an "anonymized" manner, fragmented, and stored in silos across various databases of providers, there are great incentives to monetize the value of this data. As a result, the reliance on external vendors for content, educational tools and cloud storage could potentially result in the lack of privacy and confidentiality for students and the participants of research studies [6].

In relation to issues of privacy, anonymity and confidentiality are equally important issues to educators and students. Often, students are at the mercy of their instructors who often "mandate" students to sign up for "free" content and educational technology providers. These providers do not always require students to input their personal or confidential information, but there are common situations where students upload papers, videos and other learning materials that may identify their personal information.

3 Privacy and Confidentiality Issues During the Covid-19 Pandemic

Starting December 2019, the very foundations of privacy and confidentiality in higher education institutions was shaken up by the advent of the Covid-19 pandemic. Many assumptions and expectations about privacy and confidentiality were shaken up and changed due to the onset of this medical emergency and the new rules and regulations that were enacted for personal protection and safety [7]. Personal Identifiable Information (PII) according to the UH is the "type of information that needs to be protected because the inadvertent disclosure or inappropriate access requires a breach notification or is subject to financial fines" [8]. Table 1 below describes the various data classification categories and the minimum-security standards required [9].

Table 1. University of Hawaii Data Classification [9].

Public Data	Protected Data		
Public (No Risk)	**Restricted (Low Risk)**	**Sensitive (Medium Risk)**	**Regulated (High Risk)**
No privacy considerations	Data used internally within the UH community but not released to external parties without a contract or memorandum of agreement	Data subject to privacy considerations	Highly sensitive data that is subject to state breach notification requirements, financial fines, or other penalties
Definition: Institutional Data where access is not restricted and is subject to open records requests	**Definition:** Institutional Data used for UH business only. Restricted data will not be distributed to external parties except under the terms of a written memorandum of agreement or contract. Data is maintained in a physically secured location	**Definition:** Institutional Data subject to privacy or security considerations or any Institutional Data not designated as public, restricted, or regulated. Data is maintained in a physically secured location	**Definition:** Institutional Data where inadvertent disclosure or inappropriate access requires a breach notification in accordance with HRS §487N or is subject to financial fines. Social Security Number (SSN) and personal financial information fall within this category. Data is maintained in a physically secured location

The UH ITS organization adopts a minimum-security standard by device to ensure that each of the above categories of data (public, restricted, sensitive, and regulated) are managed in accordance with a subset of the Center for Internet Security's (CIS) Controls [9]. The key devices that are managed by the UH ITS are: 1) Endpoints: which includes desktops and laptops; 2) Servers: computer or a device on a network that manages network resources; and 3) Multi-function Devices (MFD) and Internet-of-Things (IoT) Devices: MFD includes printers, copies, scanners, and fax machines, while IoT includes tags, sensors, and devices that interact with people and other devices [9].

During the Covid-19 pandemic it was necessary to work from home, so a vast majority of students, staff, and other users at the UH used their "endpoints" or laptops and computers from a home location. It is important to note that the minimum-security policies for the endpoints were unchanged during the Covid-19 pandemic, despite the need to work from home. Table 2 displays the mandatory requirements for minimum-security standards for endpoints based on usage of a category of institutional data [10].

Table 2. Minimum Security Standards for Endpoint – Mandatory Requirements. [10]

Standards			Institutional Data Category		
Standards	Recurring Task	Public	Restricted	Sensitive	Regulated
Automatic Updates	Mostly	Yes	Yes	Yes	Yes
Firewall Configuration	No	Yes	Yes	Yes	Yes
Password Security	No	Yes	Yes	Yes	Yes
Data Management	Yes	No	Yes	Yes	Yes
Encryption	Yes	No	Mostly	Yes	Yes
Asset Management	Yes	No	No	Yes	Yes
Data Inventory	Yes	No	No	Yes	Yes
Removeable Media	No	Yes	Yes	Yes	Yes
Malware Protection	No	Yes	Yes	Yes	Yes
Session Locking	No	Yes	Yes	Yes	Yes
Backups	Rarely	No	No	Yes	Yes

As the above Table 2 indicates, it was required for all users from home environments to secure their laptops or computers to meet the minimum requirements for all sensitive and regulated data, based on the above standards. There were also many mandatory requirements for restricted data, as shown above. However, due to the nature of the pandemic and the restrictions in movement and collaboration, it was impossible for the UH ITS organizations to monitor and control the adherence of these minimum standards. Instead, the UH ITS adopted a policy of education and reinforcement training.

4   Covid-19 Resources, Guidelines and Training

In preparation for the transition to a Working from Home (WFH) environment, there was a need to educate and train users, especially those who accessed and used Sensitive and Regulated data [11] as part of their job duties. As shown in Table 3 below, the UH ITS organization launched a series of Webinars since March 2020 to May 2022 to educate users on security and private issues that revolved around a variety of job duties.

Table 3. UH ITS Education and Training during Covid-19 [11].

Date	Title of Training or Presentation
March 20, 2020	FERPA and Virtual Learning During Covid-19 by U.S. Department of Education Privacy Technical Assistance Center Presentation
April 17, 2020	Spring 2020 Security & Privacy Issues for Online & Remote Work Webinar
October 30 and November 9, 2020	Fall 2020 Data Governance & Information Security Webinars
December 3, 2020	Webinar on Protecting UH Research: Data Governance, Information Security, and Disclosure Requirements
March 23, 2021 April 28, 2021 October 20, 2021 October 27, 2021 November 17, 2021 April 12, 2022 April 27, 2022 May 11, 2022	Webinar: UH Research: Compliance, Governance & Security Spring 2021 Data Governance & Information Security Webinar Fall 2021 Data Governance & Information Security Webinar UH Digital Shred Day Presentation DGP and Other Vendor Management Processes Spring 2022 Data Governance & Information Security Webinar Webinar: Protecting Research at UH, Spring 2022 Briefing Webinar: Data Governance Process (DGP) Revision and Other Vendor Management Process

As the above Table 3 indicates there was a focused effort since the start of the pandemic in March 2020, to educate and inform users about the needs to ensure privacy and confidentially of student and research information, especially for those faculty and researcher who worked from home. Key areas included 1) the use of Video Conferencing tools, such as Zoom, to teach and learn remotely (both for faculty and students); 2) Connecting securely to UH servers and secure resources using Virtual Private Network (VPN) technology; 3) Installation and usage of LumiSight, a Covid-19 health tracking and contact tracing tool; and 4) Specific guidelines when using Sensitive or Regulated Data during video conferencing sessions on Zoom, document management, email transmission, file transmissions using secure File Drop, encryption of local hard drives for storage and using Multi Factor Authentication (MFA) to safeguard access to computers [12]. All these security training and education efforts led to a greater appreciation of the security issues and concerns amongst the faculty, staff, researchers, and students within the University of Hawaii System from the start of the Covid-19 pandemic to this day. This process has also spawned a greater reliance on hybrid work environments.

5   Protecting Research Activities Using Data Governance

A critical example of protecting sensitive and regulated data involves university researchers who routinely deal with research project data that involves sensitive topics such as illegal activities, identifying information such as first and last names, along with last four digits of a Social Security Number. Often, there are individual identifiable health information (IIHI) and other data protected by HIPAA regulations. As a result of these issues and concerns, the UH has instituted a Data Governance Process (DGP) that works in conjunction with the Institutional Review Board (IRB) process.

The DGP is required for research purposes when the project involves any of the following: 1) Health (medical record sourced or related) data is involved in the study; 2) Social Security Numbers are involved, even if the last four digits are collected; 3) student information that was originally collected by the UH for educational purposes; and 4) Surveys, interviews, focus groups or observations that collect personal identifiable information (PII) on high sensitive topics.

The purpose of the DGP is to identify and create an inventory of the protected data and track its source and destination. Another key component of the DGP is to secure the sensitive and regulated data by reviewing how the data will be collected, stored, and used. In addition, the legal agreements that bind UH to external organizations are reviewed for appropriate language to protect the interests of UH. Finally, a key value of the DGP process is to share good practices amongst the various campus locations of the UH and to provide notice to the data and IT providers of the need for security and vigilance. This DGP is relevant for many research projects and is applicable for researchers who work from home, in a hybrid environment, or in a university lab [13].

Due to the nature of the Covid-19 crisis, there was an urgent need to conduct annual Information Security Awareness Training (ISAT) within the UH. Table 4 displays the requirement for all UH employees to comply with this training requirement [14].

Table 4. Annual Information Security Awareness Training (ISAT) [14].

	Requirements
	Requirements
Who	Required for all UH employees, including student and graduate assistants; RCUH and UHF employees
What	Annual ISAT training, more than 1 h to complete
Where	Online format
When	On or before your anniversary date
Why	Federal compliance requirements, increased cybersecurity risk

As of Fall 2022, this ISAT was implemented or in progress at all 9 campus locations of the UH, UH Foundation (UHF), selected offices of Vice Presidents. This is a large section of the University, but is not yet complete within the flagship campus at UH Manoa, and the Research Corporation of UH (RCUH), select VP offices and student assistants.

6　Research Security, Key Regulations and Penalties

Researchers at the UH face specific restrictions and regulations governing their abilities to conduct research in safe and protected manner. These restrictions apply no matter where the research is conducted – in a secure research lab within the University firewall and perimeter, or when working from home or public locations such as hotels. While working outside the University firewall, any endpoint such as a laptop or computer, receives a public IP address before connecting to a UH network. This public IP address allows attackers to adopt brute force approaches to probe and infiltrate UH networks. Working from home environments provide a perfect opportunity for attackers to use several methods to infiltrate the endpoint – via ransomware, phishing, or other means.

Due to these threats from computers that access the UH network from outside areas using public IP addresses, the UH ITS team focuses on educating researchers on the guidance from the US Government on security for research and development. Issued in January 2021, NSPM-33 established a national security policy for research and development and was issued by the National Science and Technology Council (NSTC) Subcommittee on Research Security, Joint Committee on Research Environment [14]. This document provides guidance on five key areas addressed by NSPM-33 – 1) Disclosure Requirements and Standardization, 2) Digital Persistent Identifiers, 3) Consequences for Violation of Disclosure Requirements, 4) Information Sharing, and 5) Research Security Programs. The policy on standardization of Disclosure and Conflict of Interest was updated in August 2022 and established guidelines for disclosure of information and assigned the National Science Foundation (NSF) as the lead in this process [15].

The UH has identified several regulations that are critical for researchers to comply with and conform, to avoid penalties and other disciplinary measures. Table 5 below highlights the key regulations that are part of the training regimen for all researchers.

7　Trusted Cyberinfrastructure for University Research

With the advent of the Covid-19 pandemic in March 2020, through the writing of this paper, the authors have witnessed a dramatic change in the work habits of University researchers, as well as those faculty and staff who are not directly involved in research. This change involves working from home or collaboration sites such as We Work, or from hotels, airports, and other public locations. While there are guidelines to cyber hygiene and best practices to stay safe and secure in your official duties, there are many occasions when university researchers are conducting research outside the secure, network perimeter of the campus network. While these activities may be less impactful for instructional faculty who do not work on DoD or NSF contracts, there are several HIPAA and FEPRA requirements that need to be considered during online instruction.

However, for NSF-funded projects and other federally funded projects, there is a need for a secure cyberinfrastructure that enables Controlled Unclassified Information (CUI) to be handled in secure manner. The UH is in the process of adopting the Trusted CI Framework, a project from Indiana University [16]. Table 6 below highlights the framework core and the minimum-security requirements to manage CUI at UH. The table highlights four pillars (Mission Alignment, Governance, Resource, and Controls) along with 16 Musts that identify the minimum requirements for a secure program.

Table 5. Annual Information Security Awareness Training (ISAT) [15].

	Requirements
NIST SP 800-171	Federal DoD standards aimed at safeguarding Controlled Unclassified Information (CUI) – DFARS Clause 252.204-7012; 110 controls, 14 areas; Interim DFARS Clause 252.204-7020
Cybersecurity Maturity Model Certification CMMC v2	A tiered approach to audit contractor compliance with NIST SP 800-171 based on various levels of maturity expectation. Transition from CMMC v1 to v2
FAR 52.204-25; Sect. 889(a)(1)(B) of the NDAA	As of 8/13/2020, government agencies are prohibited from contracting or using telecommunication equipment or services from a variety of vendors from China including Huawei
National Industrial Security Program	DoD directive 5220.22-M – National Industrial Security Program Operating Manual, Classified data subject to regulation
Biological Safety	Governs all research, teaching, and testing activities involving infectious agents and recombinant materials
Export Control and ITAR	Federal regulations to impose access, dissemination or participation restrictions on the use or export of tech data, services

In addition to adopting the above Trusted CI framework, the UH is also considering the creation of a one-stop office or center to provide consulting and other resources to UH researchers along the model of SecureMyResearch from Indiana University [17]. Given that many UH researchers are unaware of their requirements for security, this center would provide an online website, a "cookbook" as well as personal guidance during the proposal writing phase, as well as during the initial and reporting stages of the project. This help and assistance will allow the researchers to focus on their domain of expertise, without running afoul of the various security rules and regulations that are required of them. This center would also facilitate the dissemination of best practices across UH.

To complement the in-house security guidance and consulting center, there may also be the need for a Research Security Operations Center (ResearchSOC) in some proposals generated by UH researchers. ResearchSOC, funded by the NSF in 2018, is a service offered by OmniSOC, higher education's only collaborative that provides online cybersecurity support for research program [18]. OmniSOC provides 24 × 7 assistance from an online team of security professionals and can also deploy decoy computers or honeypots on a UH facility to trap and detect intrusions. More importantly, OmniSOC can provide a hosted security information and event management (SIEM) software to

Table 6. Trusted CI – Framework Core [16].

Requirements	Description
Mission Alignment: Mission Focus	Organizations must tailor their cybersecurity program to the organization's mission
Stakeholders & Obligations	Organizations must identify and account for cybersecurity stakeholders and obligations
Information Assets	Organizations must establish and maintain documentation of information assets
Asset Classification	Organizations must establish and implement a structure for classifying information assets as they relate to the organization's mission
Governance: Leadership	Organizations must involve leadership in cybersecurity decision making
Risk Acceptance	Organizations must formalize roles and responsibilities for cybersecurity risk acceptance
Cybersecurity Lead	Organizations must establish a lead role with responsibility to advise and provide services to the organization on cybersecurity matters
Comprehensive Application	Organizations must ensure the cybersecurity program extends to all entities with access to or authority over information assets
Policy	Organizations must develop, adopt, explain, follow, enforce, and revise cybersecurity policies
Evaluation & Refinement	Organizations must evaluate and refine their cybersecurity programs
Resources: Adequate Resources	Organizations must devote adequate resources to address unacceptable cybersecurity risk
Budget	Organizations must establish and maintain a cybersecurity budget
Personnel	Organizations must allocate personnel resources to cybersecurity
External Resources	Organizations must identify external cybersecurity resources to support the cybersecurity program
Controls: Baseline Control Set	Organizations must adopt and use a baseline control set
Additional & Alternate Controls	Organizations must select and deploy additional and alternate controls as warranted

detect real-time analysis of security information, events, and anomalies. This online SOC covers several requirements of the above Trusted CI framework, especially for those projects that do not have the budget to pay for in-house security personnel, budget, external resources, and cybersecurity leadership.

The UH promotes community of practices (CoP) especially for researchers, which provides a forum for discussion and collaboration. This Regulated Research Community of Practice (RRCoP) of which UH is a member provides a forum for education, guidance, workshops and other in person conferences [19]. This collaboration allows for UH researchers to learn about the latest regulations and issues that are faced by other researchers and share best practices from UH. This forum allows for training and education on current and upcoming topics such as CUI Workflow, CMMC v2 training, as well as new and emerging topics such as using ChatGPT for regulatory compliance. The RRCoP also provides guidance on upcoming changes in federal regulations.

8   Evolution of Cybersecurity for WFH and Remote Users

As discussed in the above sections, since the advent of the Covid-19 pandemic and he WFH environment, an increasing number of users at the UH continue to access enterprise networks from outside the secure enterprise network zone. This includes access to CUI as well as non-controlled information that is accessed by instructional faculty to teach their courses in an online modality. This shift in work habits requires a shift in the security posture from UH Information Technology Services (ITS) to accommodate these new trends in workstyle and lifestyle. Based on the tenets of the Zero Trust Architecture (ZTA) as described in the NIST SP 800-207 [20], the UH is evaluating this concept, architecture, and approach in its planning for the post-Covid era. It should be noted that the Zero Trust concept did not arise during the Covid-19 pandemic but has been slowing evolving prior to the pandemic. The pandemic and the release of NIST SP 800-207 in August 2020 only precipitated the importance and need for this effort. Table 7 below highlights the significant events in the history of zero trust [21].

Table 7. Significant Events in the History of Zero Trust [21].

Date	Significant Events
2004	The Jericho Foundation introduces the concept of "de-perimeterization"
2010	John Kindervag introduces zero trust
2014	Google publishes the first BeyondCorp article about implementation
2018	Forrester releases the ZTX platform
2020	NIST publishes the SP 800-207 guidance on Zero Trust Architecture

As noted in the deployment scenarios/use cases in the NIST SP 800-207 publication, the UH is an enterprise with satellite facilities, on separate islands, given the island nature of Hawaii. The secure UH network covers all university locations across the state, but users also work from home or from non-enterprise location. In addition, the UH increasingly uses cloud providers to host applications, data, and many other services.

This provides a challenge in a multi-cloud environment, when different cloud providers, adopt a different security method for identification and authentication. This shift to users working outside the enterprise network perimeter, in conjunction with data and services residing on one or more cloud providers, has led to a re-evaluation of the security posture for UH users, and more emphasis on enhanced identity governance.

The UH is adopting the identity of the user as a key factor in determining access to enterprise resources and services. The identity of a user, as enforced by Multi-Factor Authentication (MFA) and the assigned attributes to the user, provides secure access to the enterprise network. Individual resources, such as HR applications or access to Learning Management System (LMS) provides access only to those identities that have appropriate access privileges. As result, university researchers involved with CUI, as well as instructional faculty and staff, use the same UH ID and MFA to access the common UH network for email and other common network resources. However, access to secure resources under the Applied Research Laboratory (ARL) is restricted based on the privileges granted to the identity of user [22]. The downside to this approach is that even getting network access allows an attacker to probe the network and try to launch denial of service attacks or implant malware in unpatched servers and resources such a printers and other devices. The UH is adopting new techniques, policies, and technology to monitor and respond to their abnormal or unusual behavior and respond to it before any adverse impact occurs. Overall, the UH is constrained by costs, resources, and skills to deploy various aspects of the ZTA, as most state universities.

9 Conclusions

The Covid-19 pandemic was a shock to the UH and it has dramatically changed the way that users in the university (as well as many other industries) approach the future of work. No longer is going to the office, or being secure in a networked environment, considered necessary or essential to productivity and work efficiency. This shift in work habits, work location and work hours has led to changes in the means of securing access to enterprise resources and services – with particular focus on identity and confidentiality of information. While this shift has impacted university researchers more than other segments of users, all users of university resources and services have changed their work habits and approach to work. A renewed effort at enhanced identity management, with the enforcement of MFA, and continued education and guidance on risks and regulations, is a balanced and cost-effective approach adopted by the UH. This ensures an incremental progress towards an implementation of Zero Trust architecture and mindset, without disrupting current practices and deployment activities.

References

1. Komljenovic, J.: The future of value in digitalised higher education: why data privacy should not be our biggest concern. High. Educ. **83**(1), 119–135 (2020). https://doi.org/10.1007/s10734-020-00639-7
2. Williamson, B., Hogan, A.: Commercialisation and privatisation in/of education in the context of Covid-19. Education International, Brussels (2020)

3. Thomas, D.A., Nedeva, M.: Broad online learning EdTech and USA universities: symbiotic relationships in a post-MOOC world. Stud. High. Educ. **43**(10), 1730–1749 (2018)
4. Mehmood, A., Natgunanathan, I., Xiang, Y., Hua, G., Guo, S.: Protection of Big Data Privacy. IEEE Access **4**, 1821–1834 (2016)
5. Sokolova, M., Matwin, S.: Personal privacy protection in time of big data. In: Matwin, S., Mielniczuk, J. (eds.) Challenges in Computational Statistics and Data Mining. SCI, vol. 605, pp. 365–380. Springer, Cham (2016). https://doi.org/10.1007/978-3-319-18781-5_18
6. Florea, D., Florea, S.: Big data and the ethical implications of data privacy in higher education research. Sustainability **12**(20), 8744 (2020)
7. Pandit, C., Kothari, H., Neuman, C.: Privacy in time of a pandemic. In: 2020 13th CMI Conference on Cybersecurity and Privacy (CMI) - Digital Transformation - Potentials and Challenges (51275), Copenhagen, Denmark, pp. 1–6 (2020). https://ieeexplore.ieee.org/abstract/document/9322737
8. University of Hawaii ITS AskUs. https://www.hawaii.edu/askus/1266. Accessed 12 Feb 2022
9. University of Hawaii ITS AskUs. https://www.hawaii.edu/infosec/minimum-standards/. Accessed 12 Feb 2022
10. University of Hawaii ITS Endpoints – Minimum Security Standards. https://www.hawaii.edu/infosec/assets/minimum-standards/endpoints/. Accessed 12 Feb 2022
11. University of Hawaii ITS Covid-19 Resources. https://www.hawaii.edu/its/covid-19-resources/. Accessed 12 Feb 2022
12. University of Hawaii ITS Working Remotely during an Emergency. https://www.hawaii.edu/infosec/working-remotely-during-an-emergency/. Accessed 12 Feb 2022
13. University of Hawaii UH Institutional Data Governance. https://datagov.intranet.hawaii.edu/dgp/. Accessed 13 Feb 2022
14. University of Hawaii NSPM-33 Guidance. https://go.hawaii.edu/25C. Accessed 14 Feb 2022
15. White House, Update on Research Security: Streamlining Disclosure Standards. https://www.whitehouse.gov/ostp/news-updates/2022/08/31/an-update-on-research-securitystreamlining-disclosure-standards-to-enhance-clarity-transparency-and-equity/. Accessed 14 Feb 2022
16. Trusted CI Framework. https://www.trustedci.org/framework. Accessed 18 Feb 2022
17. Center for Applied Cybersecurity Research – Secure My Research. https://cacr.iu.edu/projects/SecureMyResearch/index.html. https://cacr.iu.edu/projects/SecureMyResearch/index.html. Accessed 18 Feb 2022
18. ResearchSOC from OmniSOC. https://omnisoc.iu.edu/services/researchsoc/index.html. Accessed 18 Feb 2022
19. Regulated Research Community of Practice (RRCoP). https://www.regulatedresearch.org/home. Accessed 18 Feb 2022
20. NIST SP 800-207 Zero Trust Architecture. https://csrc.nist.gov/publications/detail/sp/800-207/final. Accessed 19 Feb 2022
21. Bush, F., Mashatan, A.: From zero to 100. Commun. ACM **66**(02), 48–55 (2023)
22. UH Applied Research Laboratory. https://arl.hawaii.edu/. Accessed 19 Feb 2022

Overcoming the UX Challenges Faced by FIDO Credentials in the Consumer Space

Francisco Corella[✉]

Pomcor, Sacramento, CA, USA
fcorella@pomcor.com
https://pomcor.com

Abstract. Cryptographic authentication using FIDO credentials promises to improve cybersecurity by preventing man-in-the-middle phishing attacks against traditional two-factor authentication. But the FIDO Alliance reported in a March 2022 white paper that FIDO authentication had not yet attained large-scale adoption in the consumer space, citing user experience challenges such as the burden of enrolling a new device to replace a lost or stolen device. Passkey syncing is now being implemented to eliminate the need to enroll a new device with the relying party, but it requires password-based, phishing-vulnerable enrollment with the platform provider. This paper proposes and shows how to implement two alternative user experiences that overcome these challenges. The first proposed UX lets the user log in on any browser, in any device, with on-the-fly device enrollment using an email verification link for authentication. The second UX frees the user from having to set up device locking, by using as a second factor a password submitted to the relying party, instead of a device-unlocking PIN or biometric. The password is protected against reuse at malicious sites and backend database breaches by being used together with an enhanced cryptographic credential in a joint authentication procedure. The same enhanced credential is replicated in all devices, without syncing, by regenerating it from a seed derived in an HSM from a master secret and the email address.

Keywords: User experience · Cryptographic authentication · Two-factor authentication · FIDO · WebAuthn

Patent Disclosure. Pomcor owns US patent 9,887,989, which is related to the joint authentication procedure described in Sect. 5.1.

1 Introduction

1.1 The Need for Cryptogaphic Authentication

Over the last decade, two-factor authentication (2FA) with a password and an authentication code has become the standard method for mitigating the well-known vulnerabilities of passwords. Revision 1 of the Electronic Authentication

© The Author(s), under exclusive license to Springer Nature Switzerland AG 2023
A. Moallem (Ed.): HCII 2023, LNCS 14045, pp. 447–466, 2023.
https://doi.org/10.1007/978-3-031-35822-7_30

Guidelines, published by NIST in December 2011, included 2FA as an option for authentication at Assurance Level 3, citing a code sent to the user's phone in a text message as an example of a second factor.

But traditional 2FA methods have been found to have their own vulnerabilities. Sending a code to a phone was "restricted" in Revision 3 of the Guidelines [4, §5.2.10] for being vulnerable to attacks such as "device swap, SIM change or number porting" [4, §5.1.3.3]. A one-time password (OTP) generated by an app was not restricted, but OTPs can be phished [19] just like passwords. Furthermore, a phishing attack against any authentication method based on sending secrets over the wire can be turned into a man-in-the-middle attack, allowing the attacker to log in by relaying the secrets, then observe and modify the traffic, capture the session cookie, and continue the session by importing the cookie "into a different browser, on a different computer, in a different country" [13]. Some of these vulnerabilities were reported to NIST in a response by the FIDO Alliance to a pre-draft call for comments on the forthcoming Revision 4 of the Guidelines [8].

The vulnerabilities of traditional 2FA can be avoided by using instead *cryptographic authentication*. In cryptographic authentication of a web user to a web site or web application (the "relying party" or RP), the JavaScript frontend of the RP running in the user's browser registers the public key with the backend, and later authenticates by proving possession of the private key. The private key cannot be phished because it is not sent to the backend, and a man-in-the middle phishing attack is prevented by restricting the use of the private key to JavaScript code of same web origin as the RP. FIDO authentication [15] is a method of cryptographic authentication.

1.2   FIDO2 and WebAuthn

Since its launch in 2012, the FIDO Alliance [10] has published a series of cryptographic authentication standards where a key pair called a *FIDO credential* is generated by a cryptographic module called a *FIDO authenticator*, and proof of possession of the private key is provided by a signature computed within the authenticator.

The World Wide Web Consortium (W3C) has endorsed FIDO authentication by specifying the *Web Authentication API (WebAuthn)* [20], which defines the interface that the RP frontend uses to ask the authenticator to generate a credential or compute a signature, while the *Client to Authenticator protocol (CTAP)* of the FIDO Alliance defines the communication protocol between the browser and the authenticator. Together, WebAuthn and CTAP comprise the *FIDO2 specifications* [9].

FIDO2 authenticators include *roaming authenticators*, implemented as *security keys* that communicate with the user's computing device over NFC, Bluetooth or USB, and *platform authenticators*, implemented within the device in secure storage, and made available by the operating system to the browsers running on the device. Original authenticators had a limited amount of storage and saved space by exporting the private key after encrypting it under a key-wrapping key. The wrapped private key serves as the *credential ID*, which is passed as an argument to the authenticator when requesting a signature, and is decrypted in the authenticator before signing. Platform authenticators have more space than security keys and may use *resident credentials*, a.k.a. *discoverable credentials*, which are not exported and are referenced by a randomly generated credential ID.

All OSes now provide platform authenticators, and all browsers support them. That makes FIDO2 a generally available web technology with the potential to greatly improve the security of web applications by providing phishing resistant authentication.

But as is the case for any new technology, adoption of FIDO credentials will require a favorable user experience (UX), and FIDO credentials face UX challenges, some of which were recognized in a FIDO Alliance white paper [11, 12]. While some of these UX challenges will no doubt be ironed out as the W3C publishes incremental revisions of the WebAuthn specification, two of them are major challenges that will require rethinking of the FIDO UX. This paper proposes two alternative user experiences that overcome those challenges, and two protocols that provide those experiences.

Complexity Issues in WebAuthn. Besides UX challenges, adoption of FIDO authentication is no doubt also impeded by a very complex and confusing specification [12].

A particularly complex aspect of WebAuthn is *attestation* [21]. Attestation is omitted by default [20, §5.4.7] and not recommended in consumer cases [17]. It is omitted in the protocols proposed here.

Another complexity issue is how signatures are computed and verified.

All WebAuthn signatures, including the "assertion signatures", called "authentication signatures" here for clarity, are computed on a signature base derived from a challenge, rather than on the challenge itself. As shown in [20, Figure 4], the signature base is the concatenation of authenticator data and a hash of client data comprising the challenge. The process used by the RP to verify such a signature takes as inputs the authenticator data and the client data. The RP verifies that the correct challenge is found in the client data, then it verifies the signature after reconstructing the signature base by concatenating the authenticator data and the hash of the client data.

In the figures, each signature should be understood as being supplemented by the authenticator and client data that the RP backend needs to reconstruct the signature base and verify the signature.

2   First Challenge: The Private Key is Bound to the Authenticator

The first challenge is not specific to FIDO credentials: it is faced by any key pair credential that is generated and used within a cryptographic module. It is a tenet of cryptography that the private key component of such a credential never leaves the module in the clear. This means that a FIDO credential can only be used in the authenticator where it was generated, and may be irrecoverably lost if the authenticator is lost.

A FIDO platform authenticator is accessible to every browser in the device and a FIDO credential can be used in any such browser. But it is not accessible to browsers in other devices, and this has been blamed for lack of adoption. The above-cited FIDO Alliance white paper [11] reported in March 2022 that FIDO2/WebAuthn "has not attained large-scale adoption in the consumer space", and attributed this to difficulties that users face with platform authenticators: "having to re-enroll each new device", and having "no easy ways to recover from a lost or stolen device".

As anticipated in the white paper, Apple, Google and Microsoft are addressing this challenge by syncing FIDO credentials across platform authenticators located in devices with operating systems from the same OS vendor [7]. A synced credential is called a "passkey", presumably because, like a password, it can be used on multiple devices.

2.1 Challenges Faced by Passkeys

But passkeys face their own challenges, with respect to both usability and security:

1. They weaken security by violating the cryptographic principle that a private key generated in a cryptographic module never leaves the module in the clear.
2. While a new device does not have to be enrolled with the RP, it must be enrolled with the platform provider for syncing, which may be just as onerous.
3. Enrollment with the platform provider requires authentication of the user to the platform provider with password-based, phishing-vulnerable, traditional 2FA,[1] which further weakens security and conflicts with the FIDO Alliance marketing message that FIDO authentication is passwordless and phishing resistant.
4. And credentials cannot be synced between devices with operating systems from different OS vendors.

3   First Alternative User Experience (UX 1): Multi-device Authentication Without Passkey Syncing

The loss of credential problem is not unique to cryptographic authentication. It also occurs when a user forgets a password, and a standard solution is used to recover from that in the consumer space: an email message is sent to a registered address with a password reset link containing an email verification code. This

---

[1] As documented, for example, in the section on "Synchronization security" of Apple's support article on the security of passkeys [2].

solution is phishing resistant: manually entering the code would be phishing-vulnerable, but clicking on the link is not. This solution can be adapted to construct a cryptographic authentication protocol, which we shall call *Protocol 1*, where the user can log in with any browser, on any device, without passkey syncing.

3.1 Summary of Protocol 1

To register with the RP, the user enters user data and an email address in the registration form of the relying party, shown on an initial browser. The email address is verified by a code contained in a link sent to the address, which the user opens, usually, in the initial browser.[2] The user unlocks the platform authenticator of the device where the browser is running with a biometric or a PIN, an initial FIDO credential is created by the authenticator, and the public key is registered with the RP backend. If the initial credential is a resident credential, the private key is stored in the authenticator; otherwise it is wrapped and exported as the credential ID; in either case we shall say that the browser *owns* the FIDO credential.

To log in on any browser, the user enters the email address in a login box. If the browser owns a FIDO credential, the user is authenticated by a signature computed by the platform authenticator using the private key. If not, the RP sends an email verification link to the address entered in the login box, and the user is authenticated by opening the link, usually in the same browser.[3] A new FIDO credential is created on the fly in the platform authenticator of the device where the browser is running, and a credential ID for the new credential is stored in the browser. Notice that different browsers in the same device create different credentials in the platform authenticator of the device, all with the same web origin as the RP, each referenced by a credential ID stored in the browser that owns the credential.

Figure 1 shows the resulting user experience.

3.2 RP Database Schema

Figure 2 illustrates the schema of the user database of the RP in Protocol 1.

The database comprises user records, credential records and session records. Each user record comprises the email address and the user data entered on the registration form. The email address is used as the unique identifier of the record. The user record is also used to record working data items such as the email verification code, the authentication challenge, and their issuance timestamps.

Different FIDO credentials are used to authenticate the user on different browsers, and there is a record for each of them, comprising the credential ID,

---

[2] If the link is opened is another browser, possibly on another device, the registration process continues on that other browser.

[3] If the link is opened in another browser, the user is logged in on that other browser, using an existing FIDO credential or a new one created on the fly.

REGISTRATION

A. User registers user data and email address
B. Email verification link is sent to address
C. User opens link in browser
D. User unlocks authenticator with biometric or PIN
E. User is now registered and logged in on browser,
   and browser owns a FIDO credential

LOGIN ON BROWSER THAT OWNS A FIDO CREDENTIAL

A. User submits email address
B. User unlocks authenticator with biometric or PIN
C. User is now logged in on browser

LOGIN ON BROWSER THAT DOES NOT OWN A FIDO CREDENTIAL

A. User submits email address
B. Email verification link is sent to address
C. User opens link in browser
D. User unlocks authenticator with biometric or PIN
E. User is now logged in on browser, and browser owns a FIDO credential

Fig. 1. UX 1

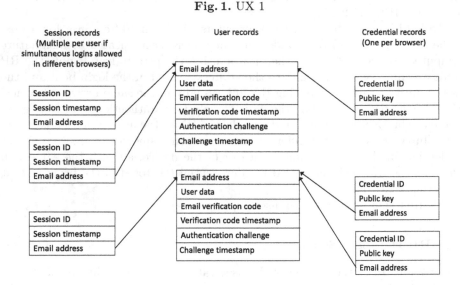

Fig. 2. Protocol 1: User database

the public key, and the user's email address, which is used as a reference to the user's record.

There may be multiple session records for a given user if simultaneous login sessions are allowed on different browsers. Each session record comprises the session ID used as the value of the session cookie, the session creation timestamp that determines expiration, and the user's email address, used as reference to the user's record.

3.3   Registration Phase

Figure 3 shows the steps of the registration phase of Protocol 1.

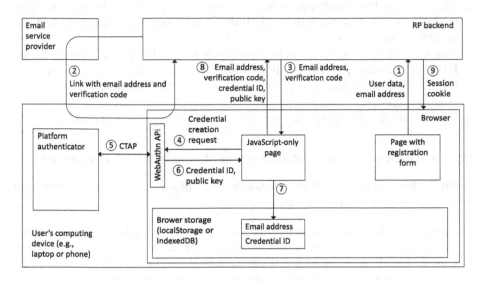

Fig. 3. Protocol 1: Registration

1. The user submits the RP's registration form with user data and the user's email address, and the RP backend creates a user record with the data and address, and a randomly generated email verification code.
2. The RP backend emails a link to the email address with the address and an email verification code. The user opens the link in the browser, causing the browser to send an HTTP request to the RP backend, containing the email address and the verification code. (All HTTP requests and responses should be understood as being sent over TLS).
3. The RP backend verifies the code against the user record referenced by the email address, and sends an HTTP response to the browser with a JavaScript-only page containing the email address and the verification code. The verification code is included in the response so that it can be used in step 8 to authenticate the browser to the backend; an alternative to using the verification code for this purpose would be to create a session (not yet a login session) and use the session ID.
4. The JavaScript code in the page calls the function navigator.credentials.create of the WebAuthn API to request the creation of a FIDO credential.
5. The browser communicates with the platform authenticator using the CTAP protocol, transmitting the request. The user is prompted to unlock the authenticator by supplying a biometric or a PIN. The authenticator creates a FIDO credential and returns the credential ID and the public key.

6. The browser asynchronously responds to the call to
   `navigator.credentials.create` with an object that contains the credential
   ID and the public key.
7. The code in the JavaScript-only page creates a record in browser storage
   (either LocalStorage or an IndexedDB database) containing the email address
   and the credential ID.
8. The code in the JavaScript-only page sends an HTTP POST request to the
   RP backend conveying the email address, the verification code, the credential
   ID and the public key. The RP backend verifies the code a second time and
   creates a credential record.
9. The RP backend creates a session record and sets the session cookie.

3.4   Authentication on a Browser that Owns a FIDO Credential

Figure 4 shows the steps of the authentication phase of Protocol 1 when the
browser already owns a credential.

1. The user visits an RP page containing a form with a text input field for entering an email address, enters his/her email address in the field, and requests
   submission of the form. A form submission event listener finds a record in
   browser storage containing the email address and a credential ID, and copies
   the credential ID to a hidden input of the form.
2. The form submission event listener submits the form, sending an HTTP
   POST request to the RP backend that conveys the email address and the
   credential ID.
3. The RP backend uses the email address to find the user's record, generates an
   authentication challenge that it records in the user's record, and responds to
   the HTTP request with a JavaScript-only page containing the email address,
   the credential ID and the challenge.
4. The JavaScript code in the page calls the function
   `navigator.credentials.get` of the WebAuthn API, passing as an argument
   an object that contains the credential ID and the challenge.
5. The browser communicates with the platform authenticator using the CTAP
   protocol, forwarding the credential ID and the challenge. The user is prompted
   to unlock the authenticator by supplying a biometric or a PIN. The authenticator computes the authentication signature and returns it along with authenticator data
6. The browser asynchronously responds to the call to
   `navigator.credentials.get` with an object that contains the signature,
   supplemented with the authenticator and client data (not shown in the figure)
   that the RP backend needs to reconstruct the signature base as explained in
   Sect. 1.2.
7. The code in the JavaScript-only page sends an HTTP POST request to the
   RP backend conveying the email address, the credential ID, and the supplemented authentication signature.

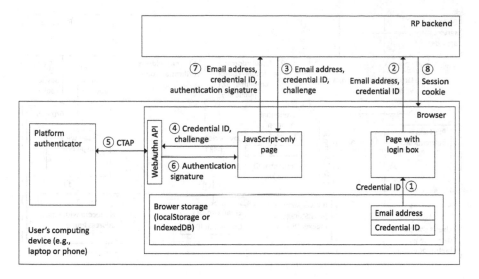

Fig. 4. Protocol 1: Authentication on browser owning a credential

8. The RP backend uses the email address to locate the user record, and the credential ID along with the user record to locate the credential record for the credential owned by the browser. It verifies the challenge found in the client data against the user record and authenticates the user by verifying the signature. Then it logs the user in by creating a session record and setting the session cookie.

3.5   Authentication on a Browser that Does Not Own a FIDO Credential

Figure 5 shows the steps of the authentication phase of Protocol 1 when the browser does not yet own a credential.

1. The user visits an RP page containing a form with a text input field for entering an email address, enters his/her email address in the field, and requests submission of the form. A form submission event listener cannot find a record in browser storage containing the email address.
2. The form submission event listener submits the form with the email address as-is, sending an HTTP POST request to the RP backend that conveys the email address.
3. The RP backend verifies that there is a user record with the submitted email address, then sends a link to the email address with the address and an email verification code, which the user opens as in step 2 of the registration phase.
4. Steps 4–10 are then as steps 3–9 of the registration phase.

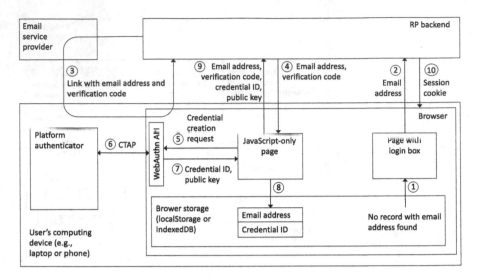

Fig. 5. Protocol 1: Authentication on browser not owning a credential

4   Second Challenge: Reliance on the Device Unlocking Mechanism

The second major UX challenge is specific to FIDO2 and WebAuthn. Crypto-graphic authentication needs a second factor for protection against theft of the hardware where the private key is stored, and FIDO2 uses as second factor the same biometric or PIN used to unlock the user's device; but many users do not set up the device unlocking mechanism. There is evidence, for example, that only about 30% of Windows users set up Windows Hello [1].

Large scale adoption of FIDO authentication would require convincing most users of setting up device unlocking, and that is going to be difficult. Recent user research [6] has shown that depending on biometrics as the sole authentication method for unlocking a device raises anxieties about being locked out of the device; therefore a PIN would have to be used instead of, or as backup for a biometric. But a PIN is a very weak and much reused password; and asking users to use a PIN for authentication conflicts with the "passwordless authentication" marketing campaign of the FIDO Alliance, and the decades of cybersecurity user education arguing against weak passwords and password reuse.

5   Second Alternative User Experience (UX 2): Cryptographically Protected Password as Second Factor

The second alternative UX uses a full-fledged password as a second factor instead of a PIN or a biometric. But the password is not submitted to the RP backend separately and independently from the cryptographic credential, which would make it vulnerable to reuse at malicious sites and backend database breaches. The password and the cryptographic credential protect each other by being used together in a joint authentication procedure.

5.1   Joint Authentication with an Enhanced Credential and a Password

While the UX of Sect. 3 can be implemented using ordinary FIDO authenticators and credentials, UX 2 requires several extensions to WebAuthn, as recapitulated below in Sect. 5.3.

One of those extensions is the option to generate an enhanced credential that can be combined with a password in a joint authentication procedure. An enhanced credential differs from an ordinary credential in two ways: (i) it has an additional component that is hashed with the password as a *secret salt*; and (ii) its public key is retained in the authenticator and is not stored in the backend database. In the joint authentication procedure, the RP frontend submits the authentication signature, the salted password and the public key to the backend. The backend uses the public key to verify the signature, then computes a *joint hash* of the salted password and the public key that it compares with a registered joint hash.

This protects the password against reuse at a malicious site, because different sites use different secret salts; and it protects both the password and the key pair against database breaches. In case of a database breach, the password is protected against a dictionary attack by being hashed first with the secret salt and then with the public key; and, by being hashed with the salted password, the key pair is protected against any weakness of its underlying cryptosystem that might be discovered by an adversary, and against a postquantum brute force attack that would attempt to derive the private key from the public key.

5.2   Replicating the Enhanced Credential Without Syncing

At first glance UX 1 and UX 2 are mutually exclusive. It would seem that an enhanced credential used to implement UX 2 could only be used on one device, because the same password must be used on all devices, and the public key of the credential generated in one device would not be available for computing the joint hash and verifying the password when creating a new credential in a different device.

This difficulty could be solved by syncing the enhanced credential across devices, as passkeys are now being synced. But that would negate the benefits of UX 1.

The protocol proposed here to implement UX 2, which we shall call *Protocol 2*, solves the difficulty instead by generating the enhanced credential using the same pseudo-random bit generation seed in all devices. The seed is computed by the RP backend in a hardware security module (HSM) from the email address and a master secret randomly generated in the module from a noise source. The seed can be derived, for example, as the PRK output of HKDF-Extract [16, §2.2], using the address as the HKDF salt, and the master secret as the IKM input. The seed is then included in the email verification link along with the email verification code at registration, and when creating a credential for a new device.

Using the same seed will result in having the same credential in all devices without syncing, provided that the same method is consistently used to generate the credential from the seed. This means that the credential creation options passed as input to `navigator.credentials.create` will have to determine not only the type of credential to be used (such as an ECDSA key pair suitable for use with COSE algorithm ES256 [14], or an RSA key pair usable with algorithm RS256) but also the procedure to be used for computing the key pair from the seed.

That can be done by specifying: (i) how to derive a stream of random bits from the seed; and (ii) how to compute one or more components of the credential from one or more portions of the stream. The bit stream can be derived, for example, using any of the DRBG algorithms of [3, §10] with specific parameters, or HKDF-Expand [16, §2.2] using the seed as the PRK input. The component computation is easy to specify for an ES256 credential: the private key d is a random number in the range $0 \ldots n$ where n is the order of the NIST P256 curve [5], which can be computed using, for example, the extra random bits method of [18, §B.1.1] by reducing modulo n the integer having as its binary representation the first $256 + 64 = 320$ bits of the stream. The public key is then the scalar product dG of the private key with the base point G of the curve. It would be more complicated to specify the computation of the p and q primes for an RS256 credential but, although RS256 is used by Windows Hello, it is not a recommended COSE algorithm [14] and may be replaced with ES256 in the future.

5.3 Required Extensions to WebAuthn

To recapitulate, the following modifications to WebAuthn are needed to implement Protocol 2:

- The function `navigator.credentials.create` used at registration must provide the option to create an *enhanced credential* that comprises a secret salt as an additional component and whose public key is retained by the authenticator.
- When an enhanced credential is requested, `navigator.credentials.create` must take a DRBG seed as an additional input and use it to generate the pseudo-random bits used to construct the credential.

– When creating an enhanced credential, `navigator.credentials.create` must take a password as an additional input, hash the password with the secret salt, and outputs the joint of hash the public key and the salted password instead of the public key.
– When authenticating with an enhanced credential, the function `navigator.credentials.get` must take the password as an additional input, compute the hash of the password and secret salt, and output the retained public key and the salted password in addition to the authentication signature.
– When creating or using an enhanced credential, the user must not be asked for a biometric or PIN to unlock the authenticator.

5.4   Summary of Protocol 2

To register, the user enters the email address and user data in a registration box. The RP backend creates a user record with the address and the data, then it derives a seed from the address and emails a link with the seed and an email verification code. The user opens the link and is prompted to register a password. The RP frontend inputs the seed and the password to the authenticator, which creates the enhanced credential and returns the credential ID and the joint hash of the public key and the salted password. The RP frontend creates a record with the email address and the credential ID in browser storage and sends the email address, the credential ID, and the joint hash to the RP backend. The backend adds the joint hash to the user record and logs the user in by creating a session record and setting a session cookie.

To log in, the user enters the email address in a login box. The RP frontend looks for a record containing the email address and a credential ID in browser storage.

If such a record is found, the email address and the credential ID are submitted to the backend, which generates a challenge and responds with a page containing a password submission box and JavaScript code containing the email address, the credential ID and the challenge. The user supplies the password and the RP frontend inputs the challenge, the credential ID and the password to the authenticator, which returns a signature, the salted password, and the public key. The RP frontend submits the email address, the salted password, the public key and the signature to the backend, which verifies the signature, computes the joint hash of the public key and the password, and verifies the joint hash against the user record referenced by the email address. The user is thus authenticated by possession of the private key and knowledge of the password. Then the backend logs the user in by creating a session record and setting a cookie with the session ID.

If no such record is found, the RP backend derives the seed from the email address and sends the seed to the address along with an email verification code in a link. The user opens the link and is prompted for the password. The authenticator creates an enhanced credential identical to the one that was created at registration. (The authenticator may have multiple replicas of the credential for multiple browsers installed in the device, each with a different credential ID). The authenticator computes the hash of the password and the secret salt and outputs the joint hash of the public key and the salted password, which is sent to the backend and verified against the registered joint hash. The user is thus authenticated by having received the email verification link and knowing the password. Then the backend logs the user in by creating a session record and setting a cookie with the session ID.

Figure 6 shows the resulting user experience.

```
REGISTRATION

A. User registers user data and email address
B. Link with email verification code and DRBG seed is sent to address
C. User opens link in browser and registers password
D. User is now registered and logged in on browser,
   and browser owns a credential

LOGIN ON BROWSER THAT OWNS A CREDENTIAL

A. User submits email address and is prompted for password
B. User submits password
C. User is now logged in on browser

LOGIN ON BROWSER THAT DOES NOT OWN A CREDENTIAL

A. User submits email address
B. Link with email verification code and DRBG seed is sent to address
C. User opens link in browser and is prompted for password
D. User submits password
E. User is now logged in on browser and browser owns a credential
```

Fig. 6. UX 2

5.5   RP Database Schema

Figure 7 illustrates the schema of the user database of the RP in Protocol 2.

Since the same enhanced credential is used for all browsers in all devices, there are no credential records. Instead, each user record stores the joint hash of the public key and the salted password. Notice how the public key is not stored in the database, as it is retained by the enhanced authenticator and submitted along with the salted password for authentication.

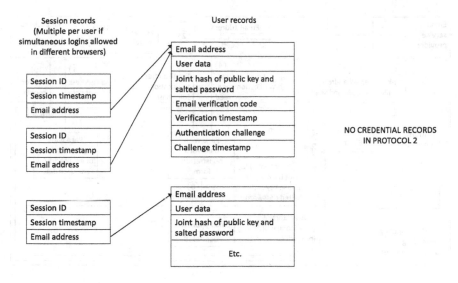

Fig. 7. User database of the RP

5.6   Registration Phase

Figure 8 shows the steps of the registration phase of Protocol 2.

1. The user submits the RP's registration form with user data and the user's email address; the RP backend creates a user record comprising the data, the address, and a randomly generated email verification code.
2. The RP backend inputs the email address to a hardware security module (HSM) containing a master secret. The HSM outputs a bit string to be used as a DRBG seed, computed as the PRK output of HKDF-Extract [16, §2.2] with the master secret as the IKM input and the email address as the salt input.
3. The RP backend sends a link to the email address with the email address, the verification code and the seed. The user opens the link in the browser, causing the browser to send an HTTP request to the RP with the contents of the link.
4. The RP backend verifies the code against the user record referenced by the email address, and sends an HTTP response to the browser with a password registration form. JavaScript code in the page contains the email address and the seed, as well as the verification code, which will be used in step 9 to authenticate the browser to the RP backend; an alternative to using the verification code for this purpose would be to create a session (not yet a login session) and use the session ID.
5. The user supplies a password. The JavaScript code in the page calls the function `navigator.credentials.create` of the extended WebAuthn API to request the creation of an enhanced credential, passing the seed and the password.

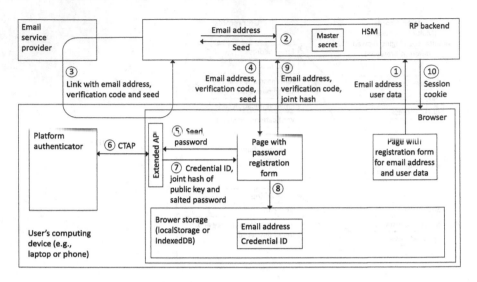

Fig. 8. Protocol 2: Registration

6. The browser communicates with the platform authenticator using an enhanced version of the CTAP protocol, and transmits the request. The user is NOT prompted to unlock the authenticator by supplying a biometric or a PIN. The authenticator creates an enhanced credential, computes the hash of the password and the secret salt, and returns the credential ID and the joint hash of the public key and the salted password.
7. The browser asynchronously responds to the call to `navigator.credentials.create` with an object that contains the credential ID and the joint hash.
8. The JavaScript code in the password registration page creates a record in browser storage (either LocalStorage or an IndexedDB database) containing the email address and the credential ID.
9. The JavaScript code in the password registration page sends an HTTP POST request to the RP backend conveying the email address, the verification code and the joint hash. The RP backend verifies the code again and adds the joint hash to the user record referenced by the email address.
10. The RP backend creates a session record and responds to the POST request with an HTTP response that sets a cookie with the session ID in the browser.

5.7   Authentication on a Browser that Owns a FIDO Credential

Figure 9 shows the steps of the authentication phase of Protocol 2, when the browser already owns a credential.

1. The user visits an RP page containing a form with a text input field for entering an email address, enters his/her email address in the field, and submits

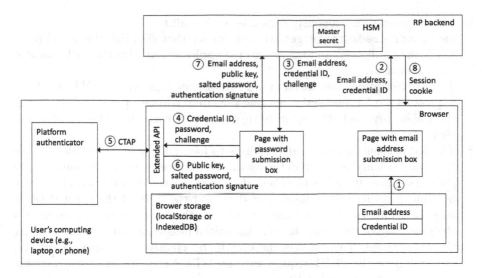

Fig. 9. Protocol 2: Authentication on browser owning a credential

the form. A form submission event listener finds a record in browser storage containing the email address and a credential ID, and copies the credential ID to a hidden input of the form.

2. The form submission event listener submits the form, sending an HTTP POST request to the RP backend that conveys the email address and the credential ID. The credential ID is not stored in the backend. It is sent in this step so that it can be returned in the next step and used in step 4.

3. The RP backend generates an authentication challenge, records it in the user's record along with a challenge creation timestamp, and responds to the HTTP request with a page for completing the login by entering a password. JavaScript code in the page contains the email address, the credential ID and the challenge.

4. The JavaScript code in the password submission page calls the function `navigator.credentials.get` of the extended WebAuthn API, passing as an argument an object that contains the challenge, the credential ID and the password.

5. The browser communicates with the platform authenticator using an enhanced version of the CTAP protocol, forwarding the challenge, the credential ID and the password. The user is NOT prompted to unlock the authenticator by supplying a biometric or a PIN. The authenticator computes the hash of the password with the secret salt, derives a signature base from the challenge as explained above in Sect. 1.2, signs it with the private key of the credential, and sends the signature, the salted password and the public key to the browser along with the authenticator data and the client data that the backend will need to reconstruct the signature base.

6. The browser asynchronously responds to the call to
   `navigator.credentials.get` with an object that contains the salted password, the public key, and the signature supplemented with the authenticator and client data.
7. The JavaScript code in the password submission page sends an HTTP POST request to the RP backend conveying the email address, the salted password, the public key, and the signature supplemented with the authenticator and client data.
8. The RP backend uses the email address to locate the user record and verifies that the challenge recorded in the user record is recent, and is the one found in the client data. It hashes the client data and reconstructs the signature base by concatenating the authenticator data and the hash of the client data. It uses the public key to verify the signature on the signature base. It computes the joint hash of the public key and the salted password and verifies it against the user record. Then it logs the user in by creating a session record and responding to the POST request with an HTTP response that sets a cookie with the session ID in the browser.

5.8 Authentication on a Browser that Does Not Own a FIDO Credential

Figure 10 shows the steps of the authentication phase of Protocol 2, when the browser does not yet own a credential.

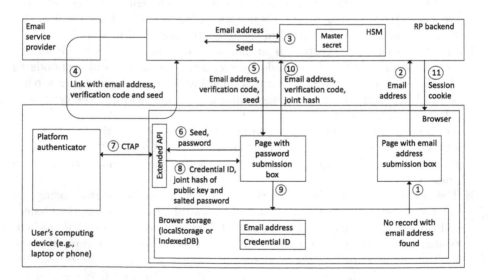

Fig. 10. Protocol 2: Authentication on browser lacking a credential

1. The user visits an RP page containing a form with a text input field for entering an email address, enters his/her email address in the field, and submits the form. A form submission event listener cannot find a record in browser storage containing the email address.
2. The form submission event listener submits the form with the email address as-is.
3. The RP backend verifies that there is a user record with the submitted email address, then inputs the email address to the HSM and obtains the seed as in Fig. 8.
4. Steps 4–11 are then as steps 3–10 of the registration phase, except that, at step 10, the RP backend verifies the joint hash against the user record instead of adding it to the user record.

6   Conclusion

This paper has proposed two protocols for two-factor cryptographic authentication to a web site or web application that overcome the user experience challenges of FIDO credentials. Both protocols allow the user to log in on any browser, in any device, with authentication by email verification and on-the-fly browser enrollment.

The first protocol uses ordinary FIDO credentials and authenticators. When a browser is enrolled, a key pair is generated for the browser in the platform authenticator of the device, and a record containing the public key, the credential ID and a reference to the user record is added to the backend database. The second authentication factor is provided by the biometric or PIN supplied by the user to unlock the authenticator.

The second protocol uses a cryptographically protected password as a second factor instead of a PIN or biometric, but requires an enhanced credential that comprises a secret salt in addition to the key pair. A two-factor joint authentication procedure protects the password against reuse at malicious sites and database breaches. If the database is compromised, it also protects the public key against exploitation of any cryptographic weakness that may be discovered by an adversary in the underlying cryptosystem, and against any postquantum brute force attempt to compute the private key from the public key. The use of the password and the credential in combination requires the same enhanced credential to be used in all devices. This is achieved, without passkey syncing, by using a pseudo-random bit generation seed derived in an HSM from the email address and a master secret to generate the credential.

References

1. Informal interview with a Geek Squad Agent on February 22, 2023
2. Apple Support: About the security of passkeys. https://support.apple.com/en-us/HT213305

3. Barker, E., Kelsey, J.: Recommendation for random number generation using deterministic random bit generators. NIST Special Publication 800-90A Revision 1 (2015). http://nvlpubs.nist.gov/nistpubs/SpecialPublications/NIST.SP.800-90Ar1.pdf
4. Burr, W.E., Dodson, D.F., Polk, W.T.: NIST SP 800-63-1 electronic authentication guideline (2011). http://csrc.nist.gov/publications/nistpubs/800-63-1/SP-800-63-1.pdf
5. Center for Research on Cryptography and Security: Standard curve database, P-256. https://neuromancer.sk/std/nist/P-256
6. Chuhan, S., Wojnas, V.: Designing and evaluating a resident-centric digital wallet experience. In: The Proceedings of HCI International (2023, to appear)
7. FIDO Alliance: Apple, Google and Microsoft Commit to Expanded Support for FIDO Standard to Accelerate Availability of Passwordless Sign-Ins, 5 May 2022. https://fidoalliance.org/apple-google-and-microsoft-commit-to-expanded-support-for-fido-standard-to-accelerate-availability-of-passwordless-sign-ins/
8. FIDO Alliance: FIDO Alliance Input to the National Institute of Standards and Technology (NIST) (2020). https://www.nist.gov/system/files/documents/2020/09/08/Comments-800-63-009.pdf
9. FIDO Alliance: FIDO2 Specifications. https://fidoalliance.org/fido2/
10. FIDO Alliance: Open Authentication Standards More Secure than Passwords, fidoalliance.org
11. FIDO Alliance: White Paper: Multi-Device FIDO Credentials (2023). https://fidoalliance.org/white-paper-multi-device-fido-credentials/
12. Firstyear (anonymous blogger): Exploring Webauthn Use Cases, 13 June 2022. https://fy.blackhats.net.au/blog/html/2022/06/13/exploring_webauthn_use_cases.html
13. Gretzky, K.: Evilginx 2 - Next Generation of Phishing 2FA Tokens, 26 July 2018. https://breakdev.org/evilginx-2-next-generation-of-phishing-2fa-tokens/
14. IANA: COSE algorithms. https://www.iana.org/assignments/cose/cose.xhtml#algorithms
15. Jen Easterly, Director, CISA: Next level MFA: FIDO authentication, 18 October 2022. https://www.cisa.gov/blog/2022/10/18/next-level-mfa-fido-authentication
16. Krawczyk, H., Eronen, P.: HMAC-based extract-and-expand key derivation function (HKDF), RFC 5869 (2010). http://tools.ietf.org/html/rfc5869
17. Langley, A.: Attestation not recommended in consumer cases. https://groups.google.com/a/chromium.org/g/security-dev/c/BGWA1d7a6rI/m/nwOt22fDBAAJ?pli=1
18. NIST: Digital Signature Standard (DSS). FIPS PUB 186-4 (2013). http://nvlpubs.nist.gov/nistpubs/FIPS/NIST.FIPS.186-4.pdf
19. Sachs, E., Dingle, P.: The cutting-edge: standards at work in Google's mobile-focused future. Presentation at Cloud Identity Summit (2015). https://www.youtube.com/watch?v=UBjEfpfZ8w0
20. W3C: Web Authentication: An API for accessing Public Key Credentials Level 3, W3C First Public Working Draft, 27 April 2021. https://www.w3.org/TR/webauthn-3/
21. Yubico: Attestation, WebAuthn Developer Guide. https://developers.yubico.com/WebAuthn/WebAuthn_Developer_Guide/Attestation.html

Understanding Older Adults' Safety Perceptions and Risk Mitigation Strategies when Accessing Online Services

Dandi Feng[1], Hiba Rafih[1], and Cosmin Munteanu[2]([⊠])

[1] University of Toronto, Toronto, ON, Canada
[2] University of Waterloo, Waterloo, ON, Canada
cosmin.munteanu@uwaterloo.ca

Abstract. Older adults increasingly adopt the Internet for general daily activities that improve their quality of life. At the same time, media reports and public safety campaigns are raising awareness of increases in digitally mediated scams that target this demographic. Without reliable access to information and support to manage risks, cybersecurity threats (actual or perceived) may consequently affect how older adults engage with essential online services such as online banking, e-health, or shopping, as well as further increase their vulnerability. We present an in-depth qualitative investigation aimed at uncovering how older adults' perceptions of and attitudes toward online threats, online safety behaviours, and risk mitigation strategies affect their willingness to adopt essential services involving financial transactions or personal information. We reflect on the consequences that these attitudes, strategies, and safety-related practices have for the age-inclusive design of online services such as banking or shopping.

Keywords: Older Adults · Online Safety · Privacy · Interfaces

1 Introduction

The number of adults over 65 or older who are active users of the Internet is constantly increasing – in a country such as Canada, 68% of these adults are using the Internet on a daily basis (Stats Canada, 2019). At the same time, law enforcement reports suggest older adults are a preferred target of frauds that exploit online services [7, 51, 53]. Previous research [4, 31, 52] has shown that mass-media is an important source of cybersafety- and privacy-related information for seniors, and often this information is presented in rather alarmist term – describing the online space as dangerous. At the same time, older adults (OAs) rely on their social network for support with Internet-related security problems [29]. As many older adults experience social isolation or shrinking social circles [32], the reduced contact with family or friends may limit opportunities that would allow seniors to learn about online safety from trusted or from competent sources to manage risks online. Research investigating OA's online practices with respect to safety reveal a lower rate of adherence to safe practices within this demographic, such as sharing geolocation data and using weaker passwords [57], or non-use of safety-oriented browser add-ons [29].

A. Moallem (Ed.): HCII 2023, LNCS 14045, pp. 467–491, 2023.
https://doi.org/10.1007/978-3-031-35822-7_31

While online connectivity for older adults means access to richer social and health resources that can aid in improving quality of life [13, 54, 55], we are increasingly witnessing a transition of other essential services from the physical space to the online space, such as online banking, shopping, prescription refills, and government services. The financial sector has seen one of the largest shifts, mainly represented by banks migrating from delivering services in person to an online model [11]. Yet, OAs are the least adopters of Internet banking – less than 20% use it 18. Several socioeconomic reasons explain this gap, some research notes concerns about financial losses or breaches targeting private data [1, 29] as factors limiting adoption.

Although the statistics on financial losses due to online scams of older adults seems alarming (10 million dollars lost every year in Canada 7), data collected by various agencies suggest that online fraud does not necessarily affect older adults at rates different than other age groups [33]. Prior research suggests that cybersecurity literacy and low-confidence partially explain older adults' skepticism towards security information gathered online and that OAs favour immediate available resources for security information and advice [31]. Therefore, we question whether OAs' perception of risks may be driven by social factors such as individual contexts, past experiences, and their immediate social network. In particular, we postulate that older adults' lower rates of engagement with online services such as banking may be in part attributed to their perceptions of and concerns with cybersafety threats (such as scams or fraud).

Prior research has shown that older adults' adoption of essential services online is affected by numerous complex factors [3]. A number of research studies have investigated many such factors, from accessibility [15] to mental models [1] and to caregivers' involvement [9]. While there is some research investigating older adults' knowledge of online threats, we still do not know whether OAs' concerns about actual or perceived security threats inherent to the use of online services contributes to any reluctance in using these services. We also do not know whether such concerns shape or change OA's strategies of mitigating potential safety risks. Within this context, in the research discussed in this paper, we aim to understand how older adults' knowledge, attitudes/beliefs, experiences, and information practices as related to online safety influence the engagement with essential Internet services, especially those involving financial transactions or disclosure of personal information. We do this by presenting the findings of an in-depth qualitative study with older adults, which brought to light cybersafety-related behaviours, perceptions, and risk mitigations strategies that older adult users engage in.

2 Related Work

2.1 Technology Adoption and Vulnerability

Internet use among older adults is increasing, with 68 percent of seniors being daily Internet users [16]. Most frequent activities include e-mailing, information searching, web browsing for entertainment, word processing, and accessing online health information [6, 10, 41].

Research showed attitudes and perceptions in particular may affect the use and adoption of new technologies [1, 2], including the use of online services that have a financial component such as banking, and e-commerce [4, 30] – a growing digital space as more services are transitioning from physical to online. Prior research on this topic also showed that family and friends may play an important role in guiding older adults to adopt technologies that handle personal finances online [4]. Prior work investigated older adults' information seeking behaviour related to the acquisition of cybersafety knowledge [31], however, studies about what older adults perceive as online safety threats are sparse. Within this context, we do not fully understand the relationship between older adults' perceived monetary and personal threats and the use of online financial services [29] – a barrier to adopting essential online services willingly or safely.

This raises several questions that help contextualize our research focus. What are the safety concerns perceived by older adults? Are OA's existing approaches to safety protecting them from becoming victims of malicious financial crimes online? How can designers and service providers promote greater safety for senior users through design improvements to online services?

Older adults are at greater risk from online threats than younger generations due to differences in digital literacy and limited experiences with identifying cybersecurity threats [23]; they also lose opportunities to maintain digital literacy skills post-retirement [19], making OAs more at risk of online scams such as email phishing attacks [23, 29]. Past studies attribute the cause to older adults' cybersafety vulnerability to a variety of social factors such as age, education, and attitudes [10, 46, 53]. Researchers such as Nicholson et al. also developed a cybersecurity information access framework to help identify older adults at risk of online threats based on cyberliteracy and social factors such as resource availability [31].

2.2 Risk Perception of Online Services

Research that studied online risk perception with a focus on the older adult population is scarce. Past approaches to understand how people perceive online risks concentrated at a broad, general public level [22], meaning how beliefs and attitudes form and shift information practices around cybersafety focused on the older adult population was not stressed. One research [28] noted that older adults are apprehensive of conducting transactions online; they are also fearful of risks associated with security breaches. Moreover, the perception of 'distrust' alone can make seniors reject technologies that they do not find essential or valuable [28, 48]. However, past research does not offer an explanation for the root cause of the objective behind older adults' perception of risks. Studies published on older adults' engagement with e-commerce (online shopping) and entertainment [10] discuss online safety issues primarily from a business and technology adoption viewpoint, with limited insights into how older adults' perception of online risks were formed. Such research did not cover perspectives on inclusive designs that may improve essential online services such as online banking for OAs.

In a study that compared the perception of risks across generations [27], older adult populations were more suspicious of online content and are highly aware of threats such as spam, e-mail scams and etc. This finding may require further research into connecting older adults' financial concerns and their perception of online risks. One research found a strategy which older adults prioritize for addressing security concerns is to use available social resources rather than cybersecurity expertise [31]. However, how older adults cope with cyber security concerns, especially in sudden, unexpected situations, is not well-studied and not yet documented in literature surveyed.

Past research discussed a few general criteria for which risks are accepted or not accepted. Non-identifiable, vague information such as interests and preferences are thought to be safe to share while financial information such as account details and credit card numbers are not [17]. The decision to transact depends highly on the confidence and trust older adults have in the online vendor [17]. Face-to-face trust signals are essential but these cannot be transferred to online communication, making the absence of human interaction a risk that is not accepted by older users [28]. This is not unexpected – a recent large-scale survey study found that older adults are extremely concerned with protecting their privacy when engaging in online activities [37].

2.3 Learning and Adoption Barriers

Several theoretical and empirical models have been proposed to explain the complex factors affecting adoption of technologies, such as the Diffusion of Innovation Theory [39] or the Technology Acceptance Model (TAM) [44]. Both these theories have been applied to understand older adults' technology adoption. These allow researchers to study technology adoption by older adults with consideration of individual contexts, personal beliefs about the value and complexity of the technology, and individual interests in trying the technology. Older adults do not always view technologies as compatible to their ingrained practices [6]; although this view varied between older adults who had exposure to computers at work and those who did not. Digital technology itself was perceived as a barrier because technology is usually explained in an unfamiliar language and many older adults believe technology is incomprehensibly complex [25]. Furthermore, there is a technical competency gap between presumed users and new older adult technology learners, and not all older adult learners are comfortable with acquiring technical skills independently, such as through trial-and-error 12. However, users with lower confidence in technology usage tend to seek help more frequently [58].

Motivation, combined with ease of learning, are key factors for adopting technology [44, 45]. While such factors may not be directly related to online safety, they represent heightened adoption barriers for older adults which likely contribute to new older adult learners' diminished motivation to learn how to use a new digital service, intensified fears towards technology, and strengthened misbeliefs about the safety of all technology.

3 Study Overview

Building on the context provided by the literature described earlier, we hereby explore the relationships between perceptions of risks and older adults' engagement with essential online services (such as banking). We do so by addressing three research questions:

RQ1: How do social and personal contexts, information practices, and mental models, contribute to older adults' cybersafety concerns and perceptions?

RQ2: How do older adults learn about online safety and how were their learning reflected in their everyday online (safety) practices, such as in balancing the risks and benefits of online activities?

RQ3: What are the consequences of adopting and engaging with online services given older adults' safety concerns, perceptions, practices, and knowledge?

The first question was answered using a combination of 1) responses from a demographic questionnaire (primarily focused on social isolation as a barrier to gaining cybersafety-related literacy) and 2) a thematic analysis of semi-structured interviews that incorporated prompts and scenarios of using various online services. The second and third questions were answered using the thematic analysis with direct quotes that highlight older adult participants' online behaviour, past experiences, safety practices and their attitudes towards online risks.

The most direct takeaway from this in-depth qualitative investigation is an understanding of how older adults approach online safety. In particular, we reflect on the effect this has on seniors' attitudes toward the engagement of essential online services where safety (particularly financial or of private data, e.g. banking, shopping) is a significant concern. By answering these research questions, we also reflect on the implications for the design of such online services, and for the development of appropriate support tools that may help older adults overcome cybersafety-related adoption barriers.

3.1 Instruments

Data were collected via several methods: A survey and questionnaire, a semi-structured interview, and prompted observation of scenarios related to online safety. The survey and social isolation questionnaire were paper-based.

Survey and Questionnaire. The survey asked participants background demographic info, as well as general details about their online use. With evidence suggesting in-person interaction being a signal for trust [28] and friends and family being a major resource for support [4, 29, 31, 52], social isolation may be a potential factor related to online safety due to limited access to a support network. Therefore, the survey was complemented by a social isolation questionnaire that combined the Duke Social Support scale and the Three-Item UCLA Loneliness scale. The questionnaire elicited data about social support and loneliness, measured through the abbreviated 10-item Duke Social Support Scale [49], and the Three-Item UCLA Loneliness Scale [26].

Interview. One-on-one semi-structured interviews were carried out by the investigator and guided by a set of prepared questions. The sessions averaged 2.1 h, with discussions of technology use, online safety practices and concerns, social support, and online shopping and banking practices.

Prompted Observations. Participants were shown a series of hypothetical online security scenarios as well as a banking website, each followed by a set of prepared questions. The scenarios showed phishing, identity theft, and banking scams posing as legitimate content. This was done by curating a collection of emails and browser pop-ups that were circulating in "real life" and presenting those to the participants, for example an email soliciting donations for a fraudulent charity, an email pretending to be from a legitimate bank that offered a refund for a transaction, etc. Six different scenarios were posed to each participant, where they were told a friend of theirs had received the email or exposed to the pop-up and asked how they would advise them to proceed. Participants were asked to elaborate on the rationale(s) driving their decisions.

The banking website (Fig. 1) was created for the purposes of this study using basic HTML. It did not record or store any data and was run locally on a laptop. The bank name shown was fabricated and held no resemblance to existing banks in Canada, where the study was conducted. However, it was created by a design expert under visual design specifications similar to what most banks would have for their websites.

Participants were asked to browse the website and think aloud while doing so. They were given the task of deciding whether they would register for a bank account online with this unknown bank. The registration form required sensitive information such as their current banking number, government ID, and insurance details; the investigator did not comment on these to avoid introducing bias. Participants were asked to elaborate on the rationale driving their decision and first impressions of the website content. The purpose of engaging with this banking interface was to better contextualize and prompt participants' reflections – we did not collect any quantitative metrics with respect to the information entered by participants.

Fig. 1. Banking website prototype used in the prompted observations.

3.2   Method

The survey was filled out by each participant before their interview began. The survey was followed by the semi-structured interview related to online activities. Prompted observation followed, where participants were shown the hypothetical online security scenarios and banking website. The session ended with the social isolation questionnaire.

Participants. Nine older adults participated (Table 1). Participants were recruited from our lab's mailing lists and through flyers distributed in the community (in a large urban area in Canada). Participants were compensated for their time (with an equivalent hourly rate that was in average 30% higher than minimum wage). Recruitment criteria were age (over 60 – the threshold for pension eligibility in Canada [50]), no diagnostic of dementia (not clinically verified), ability to consent, and language fluency that permits daily interactions. At this point we should note that we interchangeably use the terms "senior" and "older adult" (OA), as both our participants and direct surveys [42] indicate these to be the terms most commonly preferred.

Table 1. Participants' demographic data, and the aggregated social isolation data.

Participant	Age	Gender	Employment Status	Living Arrangement	Immediate Social Circle Size	Loneliness	Social Satisfaction
Mrs. A	60–64	Female	Retired	Alone	N/A	N/A	N/A
Mr. B	65–69	Male	Retired	With someone	2	Low	Satisfied
Mrs. C	60–64	Female	Retired	With someone	3	Moderate	Somewhat satisfied
Mrs. D	65–69	Female	Retired, casual work	Alone	4	Moderate	Satisfied
Mr. E	60–64	Male	Employed	With someone	4	High	Satisfied
Mrs. F	65–69	Female	Retired, casual work	With someone	2	Low	Satisfied
Mr. G	70–74	Male	Retired	Alone	0	Moderate	Satisfied
Mr. H	70–74	Male	Retired	With someone	5	Low	Satisfied
Mr. I	70–74	Male	Retired	Alone	3	Low	Very Satisfied

4 Data Analysis

Findings from this research are reported based on the results of the questionnaires and interviews conducted during the observations (scenarios). Interviews were transcribed in preparation for coding and thematic analysis. To minimize bias, and ensure validity and rigor, two researchers (one of which was not present during field data collection) independently coded the transcripts using inductive coding [5]. The codes were then independently clustered according to affinity and grouped into themes. The two investigators then jointly reviewed and compared their codes and clusters, merging themes through discussions and with the help of a third investigator who was further removed from the data.

4.1 Questionnaire Results

The demographic questionnaire results found our participants engaged in a variety of online activities (email, entertainment, etc.) similar to previous reports [2, 43]. The social isolation questionnaire results (Table 1) showed that most of our participants have a social network size that is in line with averages of their age groups, with the exceptions of Mr. E who reported high loneliness and Mr. G who does not have anyone to depend on within an hour distance of travel. As such, even if initially we anticipated that social isolation may be an aspect we need to consider in our analysis, the results presented in Table 1 indicated that this aspect was not a factor contributing to the findings of our study.

4.2 Interviews

The inductive thematic analysis produced seven themes (Fig. 2) that addressed the research questions. Each theme describes a cluster of 3 to 5 thematically cohesive subthemes (some being shared by two separate themes). The subthemes are based on codes which are directly attached to transcripts. The two coders identified 1344 and 1155 codes respectively.

5 Findings

We present here each of the seven themes identified in this research, supported by direct quotes from older adult participants. We follow the format of an analytic memo, with each subheading in this section corresponding to a theme as in (Fig. 2). Findings in the current research confirmed knowledge derived from previous research and contributed new knowledge to the field.

5.1 Perceived Differences Between Online and the Real World: Meaningful Engagement and Being in Control

The analysis of our coded data suggested that participants viewed the online world differently from the real world, indicating their day-to-day mental models of the real world cannot be directly applied to when they are online: a crucial context for our participants' perception of cybersafety concerns in response to RQ1.

By mental models of the real world we mean: the ways of conducting real-life daily activities understood by the participants (e.g. having a conversation with friends in-person, going to a bank); the relationship between a vendor and customers perceived by the participants (e.g. customer support, trust); and the rules used to govern how daily activities are carried out (e.g. having law and/or a regulatory body). In the current study, the participants spoke about their mental models covering these areas and compared the misalignments they saw in the online and real worlds.

We don't have Ownership of Our Online Personal Data or Privacy. Our participants expressed a major safety concern about losing control of their privacy and personal information online, demonstrating a desire for self-protection against information mishandling and the disclosure of personal information 56. This concern unfolded in a series of concrete situations where participants were worried about their personal data being misused, one of which involved losing control over how far information could travel on

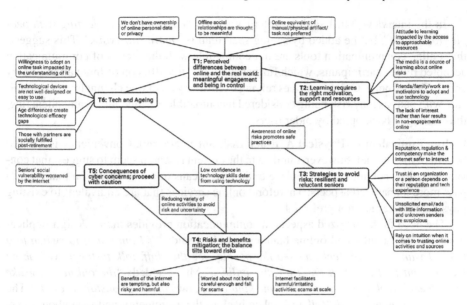

Fig. 2. Thematic network map visualizing the relationships between themes.

the internet. Mr. B commented: *"What about Facebook letting …people upload [personal and health issues] … where do they come from, where are they going?"* Another situation which participants were concerned about was online chat messages. Online conversation creeping has a haunting effect not only on privacy but also on older adults' emotional wellbeing. Mrs. C framed her concern through an analogy, she said: *"Emotionally, it bothers me that someone actually knows. […] the equivalent of you are keeping a diary and someone found your diary and read about all your thoughts that were just meant for you."*

Other participants shared similar views to Ms. C. Mr. I noted: *"Somebody can find anything they want about me. So, I don't believe there's any privacy at all."* All nine participants have mentioned losing control and privacy violation as their concerns 56; two participants in particular (Mr. B and Mr. G) held very strong desires to remain completely anonymous online as a strategy to retain control over their online activities and freedom. Autonomy and control over online engagement was both a strongly expressed preference – *"decide when I want to go online"* (Mr. E) – and a commonly observed privacy-related risk-mitigation strategy (thus providing an answer to **RQ2**).

Offline Social Relationships are Thought to be More Meaningful. Online and real world social relationships were viewed differently by research participants. Our data showed that participants perceived real world social relationships to be more authentic and meaningful than relationships established or maintained online. Four participants compared traditional, real-life communication means such as snail mail with e-mails and instant messaging. The same participants thought traditional means of communication are superior. They compared social relationships formed online to *"pen pals you've never met"* (Mr. B). They then said with letters *"you get excited and patient"*, *"it's a different connection"*, and *"more thoughts go into it"* (Mr. I, Mrs. C).

In the interview, Mr. I said the Internet affords *"ease of communicating with people from home"*, but he added by saying snail mail is *"more satisfying."* This suggests that online communication tools are not compatible with the means of communication accepted by our participants, which further supports the Diffusion of Innovation Theory and findings from 6. Online services relying exclusively on online channels to communicate with patrons may risk being considered incompatible, disingenuous, and alienating, thus failing to be adopted by older users.

Online Equivalent of Physical Artifact/Task not Preferred. Convenience is a major benefit of the internet, however, our data in the current research seem to suggest that convenience does not and cannot replace traditional means of communication that encompass more humanized aspects. Therefore, online services that are equivalent to existing physical services are not preferred.

The need for humanized aspects in communication provides major design implications for older adults and online banking, as Mr. I said: *"if I am going to switch to a bank, I want to go in, feel and see the people, see the staff, talk to them even about the account [...] and you can't do that online."* Mr. E added: *"the online thing like that, doesn't replace the need for some kind of trustworthy relationship to exist."* The *"seeing", "feeling"* and *"talking"* relate back to the aforementioned idea about physical communication being a *"different connection"*, suggesting participants perceived in-person banking to be safer and more trustworthy. This finding answered **RQ1** by indicating that an attitude favouring humanized technology and personal values may have a bigger impact on adoption than the potential benefits post-adoption.

5.2 Learning Requires the Right Motivation, Support, and Resources

Older adult participants often learn to use technology from and receive help for technical problems from media and family [4, 31, 52]. This theme summarizes the trusted learning resources older adults employ to acquire online safety knowledge and how they use this knowledge to assess the risk and benefits of various online activities in answering **RQ2**. In this research, we found older adult participants use online safety knowledge acquired through work, media sources, and friends and family to identify and cope with online safety concerns.

Attitude to Learning Impacted by the Access to Approachable Resources. Our study suggests that work is an important source of learning both in terms of technology adoption and online safety awareness, consistent with prior research [2]. Computer training at work helped participants (Mr. G, Mr. E, Ms. D, Mr. B and Mr. H) cultivate technology skills such as programming, Excel, and online banking.

Five out of nine participants were introduced to computers at work. The remaining participants did not use computers at work and were not required to learn computers by their employers. While we have not formally measured this, in our study we noticed a large difference in terms of computer skills and comfort level in trying out technology between participants who used computers at work and participants who did not. However, similar differences were not visible in terms of safety awareness across participants.

Lacking opportunities to interact with computers at work made two of our participants feel like they are left behind in a digital revolution. To quote, Ms. A said she *"didn't keep up."* Similarly, Mrs. C said she was "kicking and screaming to know more about the computer".

Having little exposure to computers early in life also seems to impact participants' fear of technology. Mrs. C repeated her fear of a computer *"blowing up"* six times during the interview. Ms. A felt extremely stressed about online safety, she noted: *"I wonder if he can get in my email" and "he (ex-boyfriend) is accessing my LinkedIn".* Other participants (more technically savvy or who received computer training at work) were concerned about data compromises and financial loss, but they did not show fears as strong as Ms. A and Mrs. C's. In addition, both Ms. A and Mrs. C were more de-motivated about learning computers, noting their incidents of *"giving up."* They also held the belief that they were *"not intelligent"* compared to their peers.

In addition, we found participants who had exposure to computers at work are comfortable with trial-and-error and practicing on the computer, albeit timidly. Both Mr. B and Mr. G said they were *"willing to try a few things."* Aside from the workplace being a catalyst for learning in agreement with prior finding [31], another approachable resource that benefited older adult participants' technology learning experience is having patient teachers. Six of nine participants in our research said they are more inclined to learn from *"someone there who knows and has lots of patience".*

The Media is a Source of Learning about Online Risks. All participants said they learned a lot about online safety from mass media, confirming prior research findings [31, 50]. Media that disseminated online safety information to our participants includes radio, television, newspaper and digital media such as newsletters from financial institutions, LinkedIn and YouTube. Mrs. C learned about email hacking through *"listening to the radio about Hilary Clinton's presidential campaign."*

Our data further answers **RQ2** by suggesting older adults learn about online safety from work, and mass media. In the current research, we found media to be a more accessible resource for older adult participants than work. However, given the nature of our research methods, we were unable to determine which resource created a more long-lasting impact on knowledge acquisition and retention in our participants. Future research examining the relationships between learning resources and knowledge retention in older adults, with a broader sample, may provide further understanding of adoption of technology.

Friends/Family/Work are Motivators to Adopt and Use Technology. Building on prior research of similar topics [4, 31, 40], we found that close family members and friends often adopt a teacher's role. In the current research, the teacher's role was adopted by the spouse/significant other, siblings, children, close friends of a participant, or an IT professional the participant has been visiting for many years. Different from the viewpoint established arguing that older adults being on the receiving end of cyber security information [31], we discovered the communication of cyber security knowledge is mutual; usually expressed in our participants teaching their children (Mr. G, Mr. H) about the meaning and importance of retaining privacy in an attempt protect their family [56].

Friends and family have a positive effect on our participants' technology adoption and use overall, especially for technology that has safety / security implications. They teach participants new technology and use it with them. For instance, Ms. D learned to transfer money electronically from her daughter *"I've been using e-transfers to get this kind of money back and forth with my daughter"*, which made her life more convenient. Family and friends provide technology assistance. Mrs. C often *"had to get [husband's name] to help."* Furthermore, family and friends provide online safety training to the participants. Mr. H's son educated him about privacy on Facebook: *"'dad you don't need this'"* and *"'don't do this'"*.

Close social relationships also impacted safety strategies and consumer choices in our study as our participants either followed their family/friend's advice on technology or they received new devices as gifts, similar to earlier research suggests [31]. To quote Ms. A: *"I've always been buying HP because [name], my brother, started buying the computers and it was always HP."* Although, following family and friend's advice may be dangerous especially if these family or friends follow unsafe online practices. As a result, the participants are also more likely to adopt unsafe behaviours [31]. Trust in family and friends' knowledge may reduce the propensity of participants conducting critical evaluations of safety practices.

The Lack of Interest Rather Than Fear Results in Non-Engagements Online. In our research, we found that a lack of interest also demotivates online engagements. In the interviews, all participants had some fears about the Internet and online scams, calling the internet as a *"monster thing"* (Mrs. C), Facebook and Google *"scary"* (Mr. H) and *"suspicious"* (Mr. B). However, in Mr. H and Mr. B's case, their fears did not stop them from participating in online activities, although these were mostly limited to familiar ones such as reading blogs and watching YouTube (weekly time spent online averaged at 20 h).

Instead, we found that having no interest in technology might be more demotivating than fear as Mrs. C noted: *"I don't find it a fun thing."* In addition, her comment on *"I figured I survived this long with a telephone and writing letters"* resonated with prior finding stating some older adults feel content with a pre-computer lifestyle [20].

5.3   Risk and Benefits Mitigation: The Balance Tilts Toward Risks (Avoidance)

Benefits of the Internet are Tempting, but also Risky and Harmful. To further answer **RQ 2**, participants did not have a one-sided view of the internet, rather they saw the Internet as a double-edged sword. Participants named benefits such as easy communication, entertainment, health information look-up, and online dating. However, cautious participants like Mrs. C think the benefits come with substantial risks: *"people find each other on Facebook after 20 years, [...], but I'm not willing to give up my privacy for that access."*

Two participants (Mr. G, Ms. D) use a website's degree of professional graphic design as an indicator for trust (which is not always a reliable indicator) in the hypothetical security scenarios. When Mr. G saw our coded banking site prototype Fig. 3 and Fig. 4 in a hypothetical online scenario, he said *"If you have good web design people [...] That's a fairly professional looking website [...] and its well done. So, I would be convinced that it's a real website."* Using good website designs and graphics as a risk assessment heuristic may be deceptive and lead older adults to misjudge the credibility of a website or an email. Mr. G had some difficulties differentiating credible websites from our observations of the hypothetical security scenarios. In response to our prototype he said, *"If I were inclined to do online banking, this looks real."* This finding indicates more education about deceptive visual design may be needed for older adults, especially when polished web design is made extremely accessible by service companies such as Webflow and Wix.com since the mid-late 2000s.

Aside from deceptive visual designs, sophisticated online chat messages (noted by Mr. I), romantic online dating matches (mentioned by Ms. A), the *"too good to be true"* (suggested by Mr. B) deals might also raise red flags alerting to potential harms.

Worried about not Being Careful Enough and Fall for Scams. Although our findings suggested that participants in the current research are cybersafety-aware and generally feel protected by antivirus software, they may still be at risk of online scams, sometimes by their own curiosity. Mr. B commented: "But sometimes, you are curious to read, what is it?" Staying safe online as an older person may be mentally demanding."

Internet Facilitates Harmful/Irritating Activities; Scams at Scale. Many participants (Mrs. C, Mr. H, Mr. E, Mr. G and Mr. B) believe that the Internet generates more risks than benefits as part of the response to RQ 2. Collectively, they believed that the openness of the internet creates more access for a data breach (Mr. H); social media worsens existing social issues such as oversharing and cyber bullying (Mr. B and Mrs. C); more misinformation spreads freely online (Mrs. C); there is not enough protection to children or women online (Mr. G); and the internet opens up another channel for aggressive advertisement campaigns and spam (Mr. E). Concerns raised by participants indicate the violation of longstanding societal values such as privacy and social responsibility [28].

In addressing **RQ 1**, there seems to be a particular concern about internet scams among research participants. Mr. E indicated that he often becomes nervous seeing a call-to-action in his email, he said: *"I don't wanna be prompted to do something. That's the best security thing, don't prompt me."* Both Mr. B and Mr. H are concerned about look-alike email scams that resemble emails from large, reputable institutions. Mr. B recounted an incident which he almost fell victim to a look-alike scam: *"The closest to attempt me to do something [...] it looked like it was coming from Google."* Mr. H said scammers often *"replicate the letter head and the logo of established companies, like IBM."* Providing access to peer-support that is trusted (e.g. through established entities such as seniors' associations or facilitated by financial institutions) and labelling look-alike scams may help improve older adults' confidence in online financial services and safety online.

5.4   Strategies to Avoid Risk: Resilient and Reluctant Seniors

Reputation, Regulation & Competency Make the Internet Safer. Participants were also concerned about how the Internet is governed. Mr.E said: *"if I come and take $20 off of you, then police would come, but if I go through internet (shrugs)...."* To our participants, the regulation of the Internet is opaque and insufficient, Mrs. C urged: *"someone has to manage it, someone has to take over and organize."*

Trust in an Organization or a Person Depends on their Reputation and Tech Experience. In our research, referring to the reputation of a company was a common practice for deciding whether it is safe to visit addressing the safety practice component in **RQ2**. Ms. D used the knowledge she learned from the CBC news to choose which website to visit, *"I am assuming because it was on a CBC article that it was safe."* CBC is Canada's national broadcast; therefore, its reputation made the participant trust the links recommended by the CBC as safe.

The importance of reputation carries into online transactional activities. Our participants followed two criteria to decide whether they should transact: 1) Do I have a pre-established relationship with this vendor? and 2) Is the vendor well-known and reputable? Mr. G shops on eBay because *"eBay I have established a relationship"* and *"PayPal has a good ongoing reputation."* Mr. B was not concerned about large companies such as Air Canada: *"[...] not concerned that they will see my bank account, that's where I trust Air Canada, the information is secure."* These participants entrust reputable companies with the responsibility to secure their personal and financial data and believe they are capable of keeping information safe and therefore are trustworthy data recipients [55].

Unsolicited Email/ad with Little info and Unknown Senders are Suspicious. Participants suggested e-mails delivered by a stranger is a major red flag. All participants told the investigator that they would not engage with an e-mail from whom they do not know personally. During the hypothetical online scenarios involving emails, our participants' first reaction was to check the sender information, often noting *"if I don't know who is from, I don't open a link" (Ms. D).*

Rely on Intuition for Trusting Online Activities and Sources. Our technically savvier participant Mr. H and novice participant Ms. A both mentioned relying on intuition as a risk avoidance strategy from time to time. While intuition in this context is difficult to formalize, our participants said they would stop proceeding further with an action when "something at the back of your mind says, 'this is not right'". An explanation for this may be that age-specific life experience (both in the digital space and in real life), combined with some of our participants' cautiousness in approaching online activities leads to a "I'll know it when I see it" attitude. Online service providers who are concerned about older adults not adopting their services due to safety concerns could however mitigate this haphazard approach through the development of appropriate learning resources.

Awareness of Risks Promote Safety Practices. Aside from Ms. D who was open to online banking or electronic billing and money transfers, and *"not worried"*, all other participants in our research showed high awareness of security risks especially for online financial services. Participants eagerly explained to the researchers that they know not to use *"123 and ABC"* (Mrs. F) as passwords, that public Wi-Fi is *"dangerous"* (Mr. G), to disable location tracking – *"took GPS off"* (Ms. A), and check for the "s" in the HTTPS from web links (Mr. G, Mr. E, Mr. I and Ms. A). It has been found in past research, not sharing geolocation and disabling GPS location tracker are important strategies older adults adopt to prevent physical crimes such as breaking-in [56]. Despite the varied levels of Internet knowledge our participants had, they demonstrated diligence and vigilance in their online safety practices (with the exception of Ms. D who is noticeably more relaxed with technology).

Under this theme, we found resources such as work, media, as well as family and friends are more valuable to participants when they are approachable and accessible, consistent with previous research findings [31]. This raises the concern that older adults without direct access to friends and family, who are more socially isolated, use technology in a home setting but had no prior training would be most vulnerable and susceptible to scams [21, 23].

Consequences of Cyber Concerns: Proceed with Caution. Our research data suggest some consequences to older adult's concerns about online safety, particularly having implication for financial, social, and technological aspects of their lives. To answer **RQ3**, we found that such consequences have the ability to extend into the real life, and impact older adults' day-to-day life.

Reducing Variety of Online Activities to avoid Risk & Uncertainty. Financial consequence from online internet scams (e.g. email phishing, credit card compromise) is the most commonly described consequence by research participants to answer **RQ3**. Although none of the participants fell for serious internet scams, all nine participants have experienced phone or email scams that targeted older adults in the past. In one case that involves online dating, Ms. A spoke about her close call with a scam artist: *"[...] He was short 40,000 euros, if I could lend it to him [...] and he kept pushing the euros and pushing for photos of my house."* Ms. C also recalled how her 80-year-old neighbour lost money to an online scam.

These negative experiences explain why six of the nine participants felt that they should refrain themselves from participating in online activities, particularly online banking. For them, the benefits of online services is *"not worth the risks"*. An additional answer for **RQ2**, withdrawal from technology is used to avoid online risk. Ms. A reported: *"I don't want to risk it. Something from Kijiji [a classified site] is not worth it."* This cyber safety strategy reflects one mental model of older adults: the cost of autonomy and privacy outweighs the benefits of online interaction and Internet usage [56]. Mr. H treated safety as the top priority: *"if there is even a perceived threat in my mind, I won't visit the site."* This can lead to refusal to use online financial services. Mrs. C said *"uh-uh. No. The thought of online banking makes me really, really nervous. If anything, it's better to get the [accessible] transit and go down to the bank"* This is quite telling, as accessible transit is notoriously inconvenient in our city, requiring booking by phone or online.

Seniors' Social Vulnerability Worsened by the Internet. The relationship between the perception of threats due to online scams and their social consequence for older adults is less discussed in literature. In this research, we explored through qualitative perspective social consequences such as embarrassment, stigmatization, alienation from friends, and anxiety in the context of online safety.

In response to **RQ3**, we derived that older adults' social vulnerability may be worsened by the use of the Internet. Ms. A reported to be terrified of friends finding out about her online dating: *"friends find it embarrassing."* The feeling of embarrassment may have been exacerbated by the negative view society has on seniors dating online. One known predictor of romantic scams is the fear of being socially excluded. [56] During the interview, Ms. A stressed multiple times that *"I don't want others to know I'm an* *old lady on Internet dating"* when Ms.A's online romantic interest had asked to see her house at this point, putting her in serious danger of online romance scam. Online romance scam deals a "double-hit" to its victims, causing not substantial monetary loss but also social loss [51]. Senior victims may have a harder time recovering from the relationship loss and social judgement, thereby making them more socially isolated.

The worrisome moment came when Ms. A revealed to the investigator that she went as far as gifting her IT technician at (an electronic store) a *"big Christmas present"* in order to secure her online dating secret. She instructed the IT technician who was now aware of her online dating to *"not let anyone touch"* her computer and emails. These detailed accounts of her anxiety suggest Ms. A has already been experiencing serious social consequences caused by her online activities. Not only does she worry about both her private information online, she also worries about her reputation socially in the real world. The aforementioned social concerns make it difficult for Ms. A to identify who she can or cannot trust her online data with. The same concern about "who gets to see the information" has also been reported by McNeil et al., supporting our finding in the current research [56].

Seniors' Social Vulnerability Worsened by the Internet. Participants who are less savvy did not feel confident using technology and had negative outlooks on their ability to improve. Low confidence is evident in behaviours such as: discomfort with using technology independently without help nearby: "I'll try to navigate it myself, but I know all that time I'm scared" (Mrs. C); an inability to respond to technical problems that are sudden and unfamiliar: "I'm following my steps…but something would pop up and I would not know what to do" (Mrs. C); also difficulties applying learnings in practice: "but when I have to go and apply it into action…" (Ms. A). Adding to RQ3, a consequence of low confidence in technological skills is that it may intensify older adults' fear and anxiety towards technology, thereby lowering their likelihood to interact with it. Mrs. C's reluctance to operate technologies when help is unavailable is consistent with the low confidence encourages help-seeking behaviour finding previously reported by Franz et al. [58].

5.5 Tech and Ageing

Willingness to Adopt an Online Task Impacted by the Understanding of it. In our research, Mrs. C struggled with comprehending how computers function in particular and is terrified of breaking electronic devices, as a consequence of media coverage about phones of the same model as her catching fire: *"I am terrified that I'd press the wrong button. It's gonna blow up."* Mrs. C's experience is consistent with earlier research finding about technological complexity being a major barrier of adoption 8; transform from a fear of breaking the technology into a fear about personal susceptibility to safety issues [25]; as well as with recent research that showed older adults' mental models of how digital technology (especially mobile and online) works does not align with how the technology is designed and built to be used, resulted in usage limitations at best, and lack of adoption at worst [1].

Technological Devices are not Well Designed or Easy to Use. Participants reported that they are frustrated when components and texts are small (Mrs. F, Mrs. C), passwords have different requirements across different sites (Ms. A); corrupted files (Mr. I) and general confusion about what to do: *"should I press backspace when I'm here"* (Mr. E). The consequences of unusable technology may increase personal anxiety [12] and when it is coupled with the (often amplified) concerns about online financial risks [4], it may lead to older adults avoiding engaging with such services as a result [30].

Technological Devices are not Well Designed or Easy to use. Past research indicates some older adults have the belief that younger generations are more proficient with technology growing up with technology and technology in return is designed and marketed to the younger demographic [6]. We saw this belief in our research as well. Mrs. C said she is *"envious"* towards the younger generations, fascinated that *"younger people can look at those things and make sense of it"* versus her situation of *"thinking of a paper way to do it"* and *"writing down step-by-step"* to use a computer.

However, our participants have also shared their concerns about the younger generations being too *"fearless"*, *"like devil may care"* (Mr. H) and *"don't necessarily pay as much attention [...]"* (Mr. E). Mr. E and Mr. G believed they have more online safety awareness than their children.

Those with Partners are Socially Fulfilled Post-Retirement. Our interview data revealed, expectedly, that participants who live with a partner post-retirement are more socially fulfilled. However, we did not observe any strong influence posed by this to concerns of online safety, although it is possible that social fulfillment in real life may reduce older adults' motivation to engage with online services.

5.6 Findings and Discussion

RQ 1: How do Social and Personal Contexts, Information Practices, and Mental Models, Contribute to Older Adults' Cybersafety Concerns and Perceptions?. Two major themes (5.1 "perceived differences between online and the real world" and 5.5 "tech and aging") and four subthemes (5.1–3 on privacy ownership, real-life social relationships, and online equivalence of physical artifacts, and 5.4.9 on low confidence in tech skills) suggest social and personal context such as favouring human-to-human interactions, perceiving online communication to be inauthentic, and the need of having control over data and privacy make participants wary of adopting online essential services. Participants expressed that online services relying exclusively on online channels for communications are incompatible, disingenuous, and alienating. Data from theme 5.1 "perceived differences between online and the real world: meaningful engagement and being in control" highlighted misalignments participants felt between the online world and the real world, noting mental models rooted in the real world cannot be easily transferred online. Surfaced from subthemes under 5.1, inauthenticity, data and privacy violation [59], malicious activities, and phishing scams [4] represent major online safety concerns older adult participants had. Moreover, participants saw a power shift in the control of data from individual to corporate entities such as Facebook. Adopting online services were at times seen as giving up control, which is concerning to our participants who believed they are the owner of their data and privacy.

Prior research shows a lower adoption of technology by older adults, often caused by age, low confidence in the uptake of electronic devices, self-efficacy, and technology literacy [2, 3]. In the current research, the theme 5.5 "tech and aging" also identified similar observations, with participants who were less comfortable with technology expressing greater concern over malicious activities online.

5.7 RQ 2: How Do Older Adults Learn About Online Safety and How Were Their Learning Reflected in Their Everyday Online (Safety) Practices, Such as in Balancing the Risks and Benefits of Online Activities?

The analysis of theme "5.2 learning requires the right motivation, support, and resources" provided the following insights that answered the second research question: older adult participants acquired safety knowledge through work, media sources, and friends and family. Within this, the sub-theme 5.2.1 "media is a source of learning about online risks" revealed that older adult participants acquire online safety knowledge from mass media such as the radio [31], family, friends, and/or work "5.2.2 friends/family/work are motivators to adopt and use technology." These findings connect with the social, community, and broadcast media constructs in the framework developed by Nicholson et al. to capture the source of OA's cybersecurity information. [31] Building on earlier findings, our research further suggests these resources' importance in shaping behavioural practices and informing risk mitigation strategies as related to older adults' engagement with online services.

In cases where technologies are adopted, either for essential services or broader use, participants use online safety knowledge acquired through work, media, and friends or family to inform and develop individual strategies to balance risks and benefits. These risk mitigation strategies include: selectively trust reputable organizations "5.4.2 Trust in an organization or a person depends on their reputation and tech experience", ignore emails from unfamiliar address "5.4.3 Unsolicited email/ad with little info and unknown senders are suspicious", restrict online activities to lower risk exposures "5.4.7 reducing variety of online activities to avoid risk & uncertainty", and rely on "gut feeling" as described by our participants in "5.4.4 Rely on intuition for trusting online activities and sources."

Our data showed older adult participants were aware of online safety threats and sought ways to react to cybersafety threats. Building on prior research that also identified older adults source of knowledge [4, 31, 40], the understanding of social and personal contexts of our participants allowed our research to suggest, through the lens of resource availability and approachability, that physical sources of knowledge such as mass media are more accessible than social sources of knowledge (e.g. family/friends/work). Despite friends and family playing a crucial role in offering safety information [4, 31, 40], the information may not always be accurate and instead lead older adults to unsafe practices and incorrect information about online safety as highlighted in theme 5.2.3 "friends/family/work are motivators to adopt and use technology".

5.8 RQ 3: What Are the Consequences of Adopting and Engaging in Online Services Given Older Adults' Safety Concerns, Perceptions, Practices, and Knowledge?

Sub-themes "5.4.6 Consequences of cyber concerns: process with caution", "5.4.7 Reducing variety of online activities to avoid risk and uncertainty", and "5.4.9 Low confidence in tech skills deter from using technology" highlighted financial, physical, and social consequences of engaging in online services. Given older adults' perception of online safety concerns and perception of risks, our participants' willingness to engage in essential services online can be characterized as "cautious". In addition to potential financial harm, older adults may also be at risk of social discrimination – a "double hit" (monetary loss and social consequences) as illustrated by Ms. A's concerns with the privacy of her online dating, which we have highlighted under theme 5.4.8 "seniors' social vulnerability worsened by the internet".

An underlying assumption we had prior to this research was that vulnerability to online threats would be amplified for older adults who are socially isolated [8, 14, 29, 31]. In the current research, we did not observe the impact of social isolation on the adoption of online essential services such as online banking and shopping. Linking individual's self-reported loneliness to their interviews did not reveal notable insights regarding social isolation and technological adoption. We speculate this may be due to both our sampling strategy and to the increased availability of mass media messaging warning older adults about online safety – which in itself has other negative consequences as we have found in other aspects of our research and as discussed by Boothroyd [4].

6 Recommendations: Online Service Design

An understanding of older participants' perception of risks and key practices around mitigating online safety risks could be utilized to define and refine design requirements of existing and future essential online services from a user-centred perspective that improve older adults' safety, well-being, and social connectivity. [30] We found that OA's use of essential online services is not confined to well-discussed factors such as access to technology [3], technology literacy [2], and usability [60]. Instead, older adult users' cybersafety beliefs, attitudes, and life values shape their perceptions of risks and contribute largely to their likelihood and willingness to adopt essential online services such as online banking. All research participants reported that they had access to devices that have the ability to connect to the Internet either at home or at local libraries, therefore, we did not observe access to technology devices as a barrier preventing participants' adoption essential online services. We should note that our participants come from a large metropolitan area in Canada that is above-median in income and education levels, and our recruitment of older adults was conducted through digital channels. We do not consider this to be a limitation, as our research data did not find participants' apparent or informally-disclosed education level to have a significant impact on our participants' perceptions of risks or risk mitigation strategy unlike work or media resources did.

Indeed, our study data suggests that, when the effect of technological access (established as a barrier to older adults' adoption of technology) is low, the perception of online risks and safety beliefs alone could impact decisions to adopt essential online services despite the benefits (5.3.1. Benefits of the Internet are tempting, but also risky and harmful). In addition, we found life values such as "5.2.4 The lack of interest rather than fear in results in non-engagements online" also affects learning [8], and, in order to take advantage of organized course programs and workshops, older adults must possess a general interest in technology first [31].

Grounded in this, we suggest here concrete steps that service designers may take to ensure that older adults' attitudes, concerns, and practices related to online service do not become barriers to their use of essential online services such as banking.

6.1 Automate Digital Services While Retaining the "HUMan Touch"

Prior research revealing that fewer than 20 percent of older adult users adopt online banking [18] could signal that the current designs of online essential services may not adequately accommodate older adult users' security needs and privacy beliefs when accessing such services. Our research data showed that, especially for seniors, complete removal of in-personal interactions results in online services that mismatch seniors' perception of authenticity [6], negatively affecting the engagement of online essential services that could provide significant benefits to older adult users. As we have seen in the research we described in this paper, this effect is amplified by older adults' concerns with or attitudes toward online safety. Thus, if a service provider is migrating to online service delivery, it is recommended that some forms of human-to-human interactions be preserved, for instance, **providing live chats with an agent or a customer representative** about services and/or technology related questions (grounded in our findings that older adults value in-person social interaction). If this is not possible, providing in a visible location where **verifiable and reachable contacts** can be found may be a good strategy to **prove legitimacy and encourage trust**.

Because **reputation is important for older adults** [56] to determine whether an online service or activity can be adopted, online service providers should communicate their corporate identity and where to find them in the real world clearly. It is important for such information to be clear, easily discoverable on organization's online presence, and embrace a voice of openness. Conversely, for a service that is migrating online (especially in the financial sector), the provider may consider facilitating this transition by **using in-person interaction as a starting point**.

6.2 Design Cybersafety Education into Service Tutorials

Using the hypothetical online scenarios, we found that older adult participants know about common online scams (i.e. look-alike email scams) and the key indicators of online security threats (i.e. links and pop-up windows). However, not all participants were equally knowledgeable or confident in their judgement when the design is deceptive. Our research findings confirm and enrich prior knowledge [27] about older adults being more suspicious about online security but less confident in their abilities to effectively protect themselves. Therefore, service designers should **not assume that older adults' awareness of these topics equates experience or comfort in handling online safety threats**. One potential service design solution to avoid falling victim is to **offer older adult users frequent and practical cybersafety tutorials or workshops**, especially on the topic of spotting counterfeits service providers. This may be particularly valuable for banking institutions that wish to convert their older adult clientele to online banking, especially if the tutorials are offered directly through these institutions as they already have an established trust with their older clients in the real world.

6.3 Appropriate and Personalized Learning Tools and Resources

In our research, older adult participants indicated what the appropriate and inappropriate resources are for them when they were learning to use new technologies. Requirements for appropriate resources depend largely on individual needs, learning styles, and the types of available help. We found resources that are conducive for learning could either be friends and family or approachable resources such as work and media (theme 5.4.5 "Awareness of online risks promotes safe practices, safety"). Our participants who identified as novice users stated that they would receive greater benefit from clear, procedural instructions and patient teachers. As participants suggested, teachers who are demanding and condescending were not useful resources even when they are a close family member or friend. Thus, service providers may wish to consider **cybersafety tutorials and educational materials that are produced / taught by people with experience in teaching seniors**. Additionally, trusted media sources (national news) and newsletters from reputable financial institutions may be leveraged to share cybersafety tips if done in a non-alarmist way. We should however note that our research was conducted in a country with a higher level of trust in financial and government-regulated institutions.

6.4 Provide Customized Technology Solutions that Match Older Adults' Expectations and Mental Models.

In our research we noted that access to technology in itself was not a barrier to the use of online services, but instead factors such as mental models were (which is line with prior research, e.g. 1), in particular with respect to how private data is used in online transactions. This suggests several service design implications. For example, grounded in our theme 5.1.1 "We do not have ownership of our online personal data or privacy", information may be communicated (online or in person) about the types of data that is collected online. This may also include instructions for older users on protecting online transactions. Additionally, based on the findings from our theme 5.4.2 "Trust in an organization or a person depends on reputation and experience", service providers such as bank may consider providing older adults with a **tested, branded browser with pre-built security features** that directly enable older adults' observance of the security practices recommended by the service provider.

7 Conclusion

Cybersecurity and privacy through design [57] is often an unfilled gap in current online service offerings. In this paper, we bring forward qualitative empirical evidence suggesting that such a gap may hinder the adoption of essential online services by older adult users. Participants in our study have concerns about data privacy, online financial scams, authenticity of online information, and the Internet's social responsibility. Concerns about these online security risks depend on participants' personal and social circumstances. By understanding these cybersecurity concerns in their context, service designers will be better equipped when creating online services that meet older adult users' privacy and safety needs, thereby removing some significant barriers to access.

In our study, when participants tried to decide whether or not to engage with an online service, they often rely on perceived risk-to-benefit ratios, magnitude of fears, the service provider's prior reputation, and friends and family's recommendations regarding risky online activities. Broadly, our participants were well aware of online safety risks, which reflected in their overly cautious approach to engaging with online services, particularly financial ones. Designers of online services should account for such factors in order to make their services more inclusive to older adults, in particular with respect to addressing older adults' concerns about and approaches to online safety.

This research was qualitative in nature and as such may not generalize to other socioeconomic categories within the same demographic. We invite future research to extent this research by employing different methods (e.g. participatory design, longitudinal studies of adoption) to gain more insights into how to effectively overcome older adults' low adoption of online services that is due to their online safety concerns.

Acknowledgements. This research was supported by a Mozilla Foundation Research Grant. The authors also wish to acknowledge the support received from AGE-WELL, Canada's technology and aging network federally-funded through the Networks of Centres of Excellence (NCE) program. Dr. Cosmin Munteanu also acknowledges the support provided through the Schlegel Research Chairship in Technology for Healthy Aging at the Schlegel-UW Research Institute for Aging.

References

1. Axtell, B., Munteanu, B.: Back to Real Pictures: A Cross-generational Understanding of Users' Mental Models of Photo Cloud Storage. Proc. ACM Interact. Mob. Wear. Ubiquit. Technol. **3**(3), 24 (2019). Article 74. https://doi.org/10.1145/3351232
2. Neves, B., Amaro, F., Fonseca, J.R.: Coming of (old) age in the digital age: ICT usage and non-usage among older adults. Sociol. Res. Online **18**(2), 1–14 (2013)
3. Neves, B.B., Waycott, J., Malta, S.: Old and afraid of new communication technologies? Reconceptualising and contesting the 'age-based digital divide.' J. Sociol. **54**(2), 236–248 (2018)
4. Boothroyd, V.: Older Adults' Perceptions of Online Risk (Master of Arts, Human Computer Interaction). Carleton University, Ottawa, Ontario, Canada (2014)
5. Braun, V., Clarke, V., Hayfield, N., Terry, G.: Thematic analysis. Handb. Res. Meth. Health Soc. Sci. **2019**, 843–860 (2019)
6. Buse, C.E.: E-scaping the ageing body? Computer technologies and embodiment in later life. Ageing Soc. **30**, 987–1009 (2010). https://doi.org/10.1017/S0144686X10000164
7. CAFC. A Brief History of the Canadian Anti-Fraud Centre (2015). http://www.antifraudcentre-centreantifraude.ca/about-ausujet/index-eng.htm. Accessed Sept 2019

8. Carpenter, B.D., Buday, S.: Computer use among older adults in a naturally occurring retirement community. Comput. Hum. Behav. **23**, 3012–3024 (2007). https://doi.org/10.1016/j.chb.2006.08.015

9. Cavenett, W., et al.: Deploying new technology in residential aged care: staff members' perspectives. In: Proceedings of the 30th Australian Conference on Computer-Human Interaction (OzCHI 2018) (2018)

10. Choudrie, J., Junior, C.-O., McKenna, B., Ritcher, S.: Understanding and conceptualising the adoption, use and diffusion of mobile banking in older adults: a research agenda and conceptual framework. J. Bus. Res. **88**, 449–465 (2018)

11. Citigroup Inc. Mobile Banking One of Top Three Most Used Apps by Americans, 2018 Citi Mobile Banking Study Reveals (2018). https://www.citigroup.com/citi/news/2018/180426a.htm

12. Conte, S., Munteanu, C.: Help! I'm Stuck, and there's no F1 Key on My Tablet! Presented at the MobileHCI 2019. ACM, Taipei, Taiwan (2019)

13. Czaja, S.J., Lee, C.C.: The impact of aging on access to technology. Univ. Access Inf. Soc. **5**, 341–349 (2007)

14. Czaja, S.J., Sharit, J., Nair, S.N., Lee, C.C.: Older adults and Internet health information seeking. In: Human Factors and Ergonomics Society Annual Meeting Proceedings, pp. 126–130 (2009)

15. Czaja, S.J., Boot, W.R., Charness, N., Rogers, W.A.: Designing for Older Adults: Principles and Creative Human Factors Approaches. CRC Press, Boca Raton (2019)

16. Davidson, J., Schimmele, C.: Evolving internet use among Canadian seniors. StatsCanada Analytical Studies Branch Research Paper Series. 11F0019M No. 427 (2019)

17. El Haddad, G., Aïmeur, E., Hage, H.: Understanding trust, privacy and financial fears in online payment. In: 2018 17th IEEE International Conference on Trust, Security and Privacy in Computing and Communications/ 12th IEEE International Conference On Big Data Science And Engineering. New York, USA (2018)

18. Federal Reserve System. Consumers and Mobile Financial Services 2016. Board of Governors of the Federal Reserve System. Washington, DC. (2016). https://www.federalreserve.gov/econresdata/consumers-and-mobile-financial-servicesreport-201603.pdf

19. Susannah Fox. Older Americans and the internet (2004). https://www.pewinternet.org/2004/03/28/older-americans-and-the-internet/. Accessed Sept 2019

20. Frissen, V.: Chapter 3: The myth of the digital divide. In: E-merging media: Communication and the Media Economy of the Future. Springer, Berlin (2005). https://www.dhi.ac.uk/san/waysofbeing/data/data-crone-frissen-2005.pdf

21. Furnell, S., Bryant, P., Phippen, A.D.: Assessing the security perceptions of personal Internet users. Comput. Secur. **26**(5), 410–417 (2007). https://doi.org/10.1016/j.cose.2007.03.001

22. Gabriel, I., Nyshadham, E.: A cognitive map of people's online risk perceptions and attitudes: an empirical study. In: Proceedings of the 41st Hawaii International Conference on System Sciences. Waikoloa, HI, USA: IEEE (2008)

23. Grimes, G.A., Hough, M.G., Mazur, E., Signorella, M.L.: Older adults' knowledge of internet hazards. Educ. Gerontol. **36**, 173–192 (2010). https://doi.org/10.1080/03601270903183065

24. Hall, A.K., Bernhardt, J.M., Dodd, V.: Older adults' use of online and offline sources of health information and constructs of reliance and self-efficacy for medical decision making. J. Health Commun. **20**, 751–758 (2015). https://doi.org/10.1080/10810730.2015.1018603

25. Hill, R., Betts, L.R., Gardner, S.E.: Older adults' experiences and perceptions of digital technology: (Dis) empowerment, wellbeing, and inclusion. Comput. Hum. Behav. **48**, 415–423 (2015). https://doi.org/10.1016/j.chb.2015.01.062

26. Hughes, M.E., Waite, L.J., Hawkley, L.C., Cacioppo, T.C.: A short scale for measuring loneliness in large surveys. Res. Aging **26**(6), 655–672 (2004). https://doi.org/10.1177/0164027504268574

27. Jiang, M., Tsai, H.S., Cotten, S.R., Rifon, N.J., LaRose, R., Alhabash, S.: Generational differences in online safety perceptions, knowledge, and practices. Educ. Gerontol. **42**(9), 621–634 (2016). https://doi.org/10.1080/03601277.2016.1205408

28. Knowles, B., Hanson, V.L.: Older adults' deployment of 'distrust.' ACM Trans. Comput.-Hum. Interact. (TOCHI) **25**(4), 1–25 (2018). https://doi.org/10.1145/3196490

29. Munteanu, C., Tennakoon, C., Garner, J.: Improving older adults' online security: an exercise in participatory design. In: Symposium on Usable Privacy and Security (SOUPS), Ottawa, Canada (2015)

30. Munteanu, C., Axtell, B., Rafih, H., Liaqat, A., Aly, Y.: Designing for older adults: overcoming barriers to a supportive, safe, and healthy retirement university of Pennsylvania press In: The Disruptive Impact of FinTech on Retirement Systems (2018)

31. Nicholson, J., Coventry, L., Briggs, P.: "If It's Important It Will Be A Headline": cybersecurity information seeking in older adults. In: CHI Conference on Human Factors in Computing Systems Proceedings, pp. 1–11. Glasgow, Scotland, U.K.: ACM, New York, NY, USA (2019). https://doi.org/10.1145/3290605.3300579

32. Nicholson, N.R.: A Review of Social Isolation: An Important but Underassessed Condition in Older Adults. The Journal of Primary Prevention, 33, 137–152 (2012). https://doi.org/10.1007/s10935-012-0271-2

33. Passy, J.: More millennials reported losing money to scam in 2017 than senior citizens (2018). https://www.marketwatch.com/story/more-millennials-reported-losing-money-to-scams-in-2017-th-an-senior-citizens-2018-03-02. Accessed Sept 2019

34. Passyn, K., Diriker, M., Settle, R.B.: Images of online versus store shopping: have the attitudes of men and women, young and old really changed? J. Bus. Econ. Res. **9**(1), 449–465 (2011)

35. Perrin, A., Anderson, M.: Tech Adoption Climbs Among Older Adults. Pew Research Center (2017). https://www.pewinternet.org/2017/05/17/technology-use-among-seniors/

36. Pride, J.: SEEFA policy panel on later life and ageing: Summary of the key issues on valuing the older population (2013). http://ageactionalliance.org/wordpress/wp-content/uploads/2014/05/SEEFA-key-issues-on-Valuing-the-Older-Population.pdf. Accessed 9 Sept 2019

37. Quan-Haase, A., Ho, D.: Online privacy concerns and privacy protection strategies among older adults in East York, Canada. J. Assoc. Inf. Sci. Technol. **71**(9), 1089–1102 (2020)

38. Robertson-Lang, L., Major, S., Hemming, H.: An exploration of search patterns and credibility issues among older adults seeking online health information. Can. J. Aging **30**(4), 631–645 (2011). https://doi.org/10.1017/S071498081100050X

39. Rogers, E.: Diffusion of Innovations, 5th edn. Free Press, New York. (2003)

40. Rosenthal, R.L.: Older computer-literate women: their motivations, obstacles, and paths to success. Educ. Gerontol. **34**(7), 610–626 (2008). https://doi.org/10.1080/0360127080194942

41. Taha, J., Sharit, J., Czaja, S.: Use of and satisfaction with sources of health information among older Internet users and nonusers. Gerontologist **49**(5), 663–673 (2009)

42. City of Toronto. TORONTO SENIORS STRATEGY 2.0. Seniors Transition Office Report (2018)

43. Van Ingen, E., Rains, S., Wright, K.: Does social network site use buffer against well-being loss when older adults face reduced functional ability. Comput. Hum. Behav. **70**, 168–177 (2017)

44. Venkatesh, V., Davis, F.D.: A theoretical extension of the technology acceptance model: four longitudinal field studies. Manage. Sci. **46**(2), 186–204 (2000)

45. Venkatesh, V.: Technology acceptance model and the unified theory of acceptance and use of technology Wiley Encycl. Manage., 1–92015). https://doi.org/10.1002/9781118785317.weom070047

46. Vroman, K.G., Arthanat, S., Lysack, C.: "Who over 65 is online?" Older adults' dispositions toward information communication technology. Comput. Hum. Behav. **43**, 156–166 (2014). https://doi.org/10.1016/j.chb.2014.10.018

47. Wagner, N., Hassanein, K., Head, M.: Computer use by older adults: a multi-disciplinary review. Comput. Hum. Behav. **26**, 870–882 (2010). https://doi.org/10.1016/j.chb.2010.03.029

48. Wang, S.W., Ngamsiriudom, W., Hsieh, C.-H.: Trust disposition, trust antecedents, trust, and behavioral intention. Serv. Ind. J. **35**(10), 555–572 (2015)

49. Wardian, J., Robbins, D., Wolfersteig, W., Johnson, T., Dustman, P.: Validation of the DSSI-10 to measure social support in a general population. Res. Soc. Work. Pract. **23**, 100–106 (2012)

50. Yosowich, M.: What age is someone considered a senior? (2019). https://elder.findlaw.ca/art icle/what-age-is-someone-considered-a-senior. Accessed Sept 2019

51. Das, S., Lo, J., Dabbish, L., Hong, J.I.: Breaking! a typology of security and privacy news and how it's shared. In: Proceedings of the 2018 CHI Conference on Human Factors in Computing Systems (CHI 2018). ACM, New York, NY, USA, pp. 1:1–1:12 (2018). https://doi.org/10. 1145/3173574.3173575

52. Witty, M.T.: Do You Love Me? Psychological characteristics of romance scams victims. Cyberpsychol. Behav. Soc. Netw. **21**, 105–109 (2018)

53. Lichtenberg, P.A., Sugarman, M.A., Paulson, D., Ficker, L.J., Rahman-Filipiak, A.: Psychological and functional vulnerability predicts fraud cases in older adults: results of a longitudinal study. Clin. Gerontol. **39**, 48–63 (2016)

54. Chopik, W.J.: The benefits of social technology use among older adults are mediated by reduced loneliness. Cyberpsychol. Behav. Soc. Netw. **19**(9), 551–556 (2016)

55. Cotten, S.R., Ford, G., Ford, S., Hale, T.M.: Internet use and depression among retired older adults in the United States: a longitudinal study. Comput. Hum. Behav. **2**, 496–499 (2012)

56. McNeil, A., Briggs, P., Pywell, J., Coventry, L.: Functional privacy concerns of older adults about pervasive health-monitoring Systems. In: The Pervasive Technologies Related to Assistive Environments (PETRA 2017). ACM, Island of Rhodes, Greece (2017)

57. Mentis, H.M., Madjaroff, G., Massey, A.K.: Upside and downside risk in online security for older adults with mild cognitive impairments. In: Proceedings of CHI Conference on Human Factors and Computer Systems (CHI 2019). Glasgow, Scotland, U.K.: ACM, New York, NY, USA (2019)

58. Franz, R.L., Findlater, L., Neves, B.B., Wobbrock, J.O.: Gender and help seeking by older adults when learning new technologies. In: Proceedings of ASSET Conference (ASSET 2019). Pittsburgh, PA, USA: ACM, New York, NY, USA (2019)

59. Ray, H., Wolf, F., Kuber, R., Aviv, A.J.: "Woe is me:" examining older adults' perception of privacy. In: CHI'19 Extended Abstracts, 4–9 May 2019, Glasgow, Scotland UK (2019)

60. Spinelli, G., Jain, S.: Designing and evaluating web interaction for older users. In: Yannacopoulos, D., Manolitzas, P., Matsatsinis, N., Grigoroudis, E. (eds.), Evaluating Websites and Web Services: Interdisciplinary Perspectives on User Satisfaction, (pp. 176–202). Hershey, PA: IGI Global. (2014). https://doi.org/10.4018/978-1-4666-5129-6.ch011

61. Toronto Seniors Strategy. Municipal survey report (2018). https://www.toronto.ca. Accessed May 2020

62. Stickdorn, M., Schneider, J., Andrews, K., Lawrence, A.: This is Service Design Thinking: Basics, Tools, Cases, vol. 1. Wiley, Hoboken, NJ (2011)

63. Interaction Design Foundation. The Principles of Service Design Thinking - Building Better Services. IDF Course Notes (2020). https://www.interaction-design.org/literature/article/the-principles-of-service-design-thinking-building-better-services. Accessed May 2020

Smart Home Device Loss of Support: Consumer Perspectives and Preferences

Julie M. Haney[✉][iD] and Susanne M. Furman[iD]

National Institute of Standards and Technology, Gaithersburg, MD 20899, USA
{julie.haney,susanne.furman}@nist.gov

Abstract. Unsupported smart home devices can pose serious safety and security issues for consumers. However, unpatched and vulnerable devices may remain connected because consumers may not be alerted that their devices are no longer supported or do not understand the implications of using unsupported devices. To investigate the consumer perspective on loss of manufacturer support, we conducted a survey of 412 smart home users. We discovered differences based on device category and provide insights into how user perspectives may relate to perceptions of smart home update importance, security, and privacy. Based on the results, we offer suggestions to guide the efforts of the smart home community to protect consumers from potentially harmful consequences of unsupported devices.

Keywords: smart home · internet of things · support · security · privacy

1 Introduction

The Internet of Things (IoT) industry is a fast-growing, constantly evolving tech sector. This growth can be especially observed in the consumer smart home device market, with about half of all United States (U.S.) households using at least one device [23] and a projected annual growth rate of 14% [27]. There is a constant churn of both products and companies coming in and out of the market [25,27], with manufacturers prioritizing their efforts on developing and releasing products with the newest technologies and features to maintain their competitive edge. This "planned obsolescence" – instilling in consumers the desire to own something newer, better, and sooner than necessary [16,20] – is common in the IoT market.

Given the focus on innovation, there may be few economic incentives for providing updates (functional and security) and long-term support to IoT devices, particularly those considered low-end and disposable [12,28]. Furthermore, because of the rapid evolution of technology and security threats and mitigations, manufacturers cannot "future-proof" products with long lifespans [14],

S. M. Furman—Designated as co-first authors.

A. Moallem (Ed.): HCII 2023, LNCS 14045, pp. 492–510, 2023.
https://doi.org/10.1007/978-3-031-35822-7_32

such as smart appliances, door locks, or even single-function devices like light-bulbs or smart plugs. For example, current encryption algorithms may eventually become obsolete, but devices may not be able to accommodate future advances due to processing or memory limitations. Therefore, it is likely that many smart home devices will outlast manufacturers' support commitments.

Unsupported devices can pose serious safety and security issues for consumers, especially since smart home devices may have access to sensitive data or directly make changes to the home environment. As new security threats evolve, unsupported, connected devices will remain unpatched and vulnerable. Consumers may not be alerted that their devices are no longer supported or may not understand the implications of using unsupported devices [15]. In addition, consumers may unknowingly buy discontinued products that are vulnerable from the moment they are connected or soon after as end-of-life, but new-in-box smart home devices are currently being sold on popular online marketplaces. For example, when this paper was written, there were two active listings on an e-commerce site for a new smart hub, which was discontinued in 2018. Multiple smart televisions listed as discontinued on the manufacturer's website were available for purchase on a popular electronics retailer site without any warnings.

Despite the potentially harmful impacts on consumers, little is known about consumers' perspectives on the loss of manufacturer support for smart home devices and how they might best be informed of the safety and security implications. Our study begins to address these unknowns. This paper presents a subset of results focused on manufacturer support from a broader survey study to explore consumers' perceptions of and experiences with smart home updates. The survey involved participants who were active users of smart home devices in five categories of interest: virtual voice assistants, smart thermostats, smart security devices, smart environment sensors, and smart lighting. Related to manufacturer support, we sought to answer the following research questions:

RQ1: What are consumers' concerns regarding loss of manufacturer support for their smart home devices?
   (a) How do responses differ among device categories?
   (b) How do consumers' perceptions of the importance of smart home updates relate to their concerns for loss of support?
   (c) How do consumers' concern levels for smart home security and privacy relate to their concerns for loss of support?
   (d) Is there a relationship between concerns and consumers having prior Information Technology (IT) job experience?
RQ2: What actions, if any, would consumers take if their devices were no longer supported?
   (a) How do responses differ among device categories?
RQ3: How would consumers prefer to be notified about loss of support?

Our study makes several contributions. We develop a better understanding of smart home device support loss from the perspective of consumers, discovering differences in consumers' perceptions and actions based on device category. We also provide insights into how these perspectives relate to perceptions of smart home security, privacy, and updates. Based on the results, we offer suggestions to guide efforts of smart home stakeholders - manufacturers, standards developers, regulators/oversight organizations, and consumer advocacy groups - to inform and protect consumers from physical safety and online security consequences of unsupported, connected devices.

This paper is organized as follows. In Sect. 2 "Methodology", we describe our survey development, data collection and analysis process, and limitations of the study. In Sect. 3 "Participants and Devices" we provide an overview of the survey respondents, their demographics, and the types of devices they owned. We present our findings in Sect. 4 "Results". Finally, in Sect. 5 "Discussion and Related Work", we situate our study within prior literature and other related industry and government efforts and offer suggestions on how consumers may be better informed and empowered when their smart home devices lose support.

2   Methodology

2.1   Survey Development

Because of the diversity of smart home devices, we focused the survey on five device categories of interest:

- *virtual voice assistants/smart speakers*, e.g., Amazon Echo/Alexa, Google Home, Apple HomePod
- *smart thermostats*, e.g., Nest, Ecobee
- *smart security devices*, e.g., cameras, door locks
- *smart environment sensors*, e.g., smoke/leak detectors
- *smart lighting*, e.g., light bulbs, lighting systems

We selected these categories since they are among the most popular in U.S. households [23,29], represented varying levels of sophistication, and were likely to elicit a range of consumer security and privacy concerns [30,34,35].

Survey questions were informed by our research questions and prior work on software and IoT updates (e.g., [9,17,31]). To ensure survey content and construct validity, an IoT security expert, a survey methodologist, and two individuals representative of our target survey population provided feedback used to refine the survey. Appendix A contains the survey questions relevant to this paper, which included select one answer, select all that apply, and Likert scale formats. To explore potential differences between device categories, for some survey items, participants answered the same question for all categories they owned. In these cases, a matrix of items was presented to the participant. Only those device categories the participant owned were displayed in the matrix. Figure 1 shows an example question of this type as displayed for a participant who owned devices in all categories.

Rate your agreement with the following statement for each category of smart home device: It is urgent that my smart home devices be updated when updates are made available.					
	Strongly Agree	Agree	Neither Agree nor Disagree	Disagree	Strongly Disagree
Virtual voice assistants/smart speakers	○	○	○	○	○
Thermostats	○	○	○	○	○
Home security devices	○	○	○	○	○
Home environment sensors	○	○	○	○	○
Lighting	○	○	○	○	○

Fig. 1. Example question with multiple device categories

2.2 Data Collection

The study was approved by our institution's Research Protections Office and was fielded for two weeks in April 2021. On the first screen of the survey, participants were provided with an information sheet describing the study and how their data would be protected. Survey responses were collected without personal or machine identifiers. After finishing the survey, participants received $12.50.

We hired an independent research company that utilized the Prodege non-probability, online opt-in sample panel to recruit a demographically diverse set of participants. With millions of panelists and thousands of demographic and behavioral attributes, Prodege allowed for granular demographic targeting and recruitment that could be adjusted on a daily basis to fill gaps in desired demographics as the survey timeframe progressed. Prodege also had a smart home ownership attribute that facilitated efficient sample targeting. To be eligible for the survey, participants had to be adults living in the U.S. who were active users and administrators of smart home devices in at least two of the five device categories of interest. A total of 412 participants completed the survey.

2.3 Data Analysis

We calculated descriptive statistics (percentages rounded to nearest whole numbers) to report response frequencies. We also conducted inferential statistics using non-parametric tests since the data were not normally distributed. To look for differences between device categories for ordinal (Likert scale) responses, we used the Kruskal-Wallis H test at the significance level $\alpha < 0.05$. For categorical responses, we used Chi-square tests of association as an initial test, with post-hoc Chi-square pairwise comparisons, applying the Bonferroni correction to counteract potential issues with multiple comparisons, with adjusted significance level $\alpha < 0.01$ (0.05 / 5 device categories). We report significant results by providing the Chi-square statistic (χ^2) and degrees of freedom (df).

In addition to understanding participants' views of potential loss of manufacturer support, since smart home updates are discontinued after manufacturers cease support, we wanted to know if those who placed more importance on updates were more concerned about the loss of manufacturer support. We also examined whether the level of security or privacy concern was related to concerns about loss of support, since unsupported products may become targets of cyber attacks if new vulnerabilities are discovered. Lastly, we looked for potential correlations between these various concerns and consumers' self-reported IT job experience since marked differences have been observed in the sophistication and accuracy of security and privacy mental models and risk understanding between experts and non-experts [19]. We calculated Kendall rank correlations to determine these relationships, with significant correlations ($\alpha < 0.05$) reported with the Kendall's Tau (τ) correlation coefficient.

2.4   Limitations

Our survey is limited in that responses only capture participant intentions and perceptions, which may not reflect actual behaviors. However, perceptions can and do influence behaviors [26]. Moreover, our results only represent the attitudes of a U.S. population, but individuals in other countries may have different perceptions. Finally, since we only included five device categories in the survey and the overarching study was primarily focused on updates (not manufacturer support), we did not include smart entertainment devices or smart appliances as categories of interest. However, we acknowledge that these categories represent a sizable share of the market and may be impacted by loss of support due to their higher costs and longer lifespans.

3   Participants and Devices

Participant were from 47 U.S. states and one U.S. territory and represented a wide range of age, race, education, and income groups. Only 16% (n = 65) reported having prior or current job experience in the IT, security, or privacy fields. Other participant demographics can be found in Table 1.

Among the categories of interest, voice assistants were owned by the most participants (83%, n = 341). Security devices were owned by 65% (n = 268), sensors 52% (n = 215), lighting 50% (n = 204), and thermostats 43% (n = 177). Including devices not in those categories (e.g., entertainment devices, appliances, and smart plugs), participants owned an average of 9 devices, with 34% having 2–5 devices, 31% with 6–9 devices, and 35% with 10 or more devices.

4   Results

Because questions could be skipped and the number of participants with each device category varied, we include the number of total responses (n) in our results.

Table 1. Participant Demographics (N = 412)

Demographic	Sub-category	n	%
Age Range (years)	18–24	35	9%
	25–34	55	13%
	35–44	107	26%
	45–54	37	9%
	55–64	71	17%
	65+	107	26%
Gender	Male	169	41%
	Female	241	58%
	Prefer to self-describe	2	<1%
Race*	White	301	73%
	Black	78	19%
	Asian	31	8%
	Pacific Islander	2	<1%
	No answer	3	<1%
Ethnicity	Hispanic or Latino	71	17%
	Not Hispanic or Latino	335	81%
	No answer	6	<2%
Education Level	Less than high school	11	3%
	High school	62	15%
	Some college	83	20%
	Associate's degree	47	11%
	Bachelor's degree	148	36%
	Graduate degree	60	15%
IT, Security, or Privacy Job Experience	No	347	84%
	Yes	65	16%
Household Income	Less than $50,000	145	35%
	$50,000 - $99,000	161	39%
	$100,000 - $149,999	68	17%
	$150,000+	34	8%
	No answer	4	1%
U.S. Region	Northeast	86	21%
	Midwest	71	17%
	South	167	41%
	West	84	20%
	U.S. Territory	1	<1%
	No answer	3	<1%
Urbanicity	Rural	68	17%
	Suburban	213	52%
	Urban	131	32%
Smart Home Experience	Less than 1 year	15	4%
	1 - 2 years	122	30%
	3 - 5 years	198	48%
	6+ years	76	18%
	No answer	1	<1%

* Participants could select more than one option.

4.1   Update Importance

We asked participants to rate their agreement that smart home device updates are important on a 5-point scale from strongly disagree to strongly agree for each of the device categories they owned (Fig. 2). Updates for security devices were rated as most important (strongly agree or agree) by 90% of participants, followed closely by sensors at 89%, voice assistants at 86%, and thermostats at 85%. Lighting devices were the lowest rated, although still viewed as important by 77%.

We found a significant but weak correlation between ratings of update importance and IT experience for the voice assistants category only ($\tau = 0.1642$). Those with IT experience rated voice assistant update importance higher.

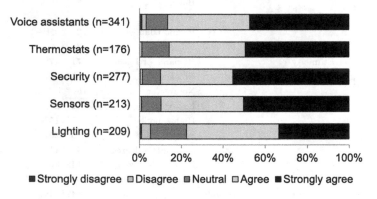

Fig. 2. Agreement with statement: "It is important for smart home devices to be updated"

4.2   Security and Privacy Concern

Participants rated their level of security and privacy concern on a 5-point scale from "not at all concerned" to "extremely concerned" (Fig. 3). They also could select an "I don't know/I'm not sure" option.

Smart security devices had the highest levels of security concern, with 43% of participants moderately or extremely concerned, followed by voice assistants (38%), sensors (35%), thermostats (33%), and lighting (28%). Depending on category, 37–55% were not at all or only slightly concerned about device security, with lighting devices eliciting the least concern. The level of security concern was higher for those with IT job experience for thermostats ($\tau = 0.2136$), sensors ($\tau = 0.1396$), and lighting ($\tau = 0.1686$).

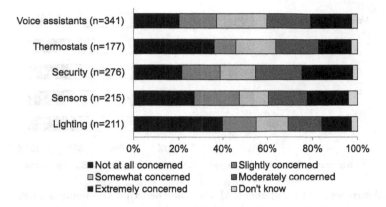

Fig. 3. Level of security concern with smart home devices

When rating their level of privacy concern (Fig. 4), 44% of participants were moderately or extremely concerned about voice assistants, 43% for security devices, 34% for thermostats, 32% for sensors, and 27% for lighting. Over half of participants were not at all or only slightly concerned about the privacy of data collected by their thermostats, sensors, and lighting devices. The level of privacy concern was higher for those with IT job experience for the thermostats ($\tau = 0.1428$) and lighting ($\tau = 0.1597$) categories only.

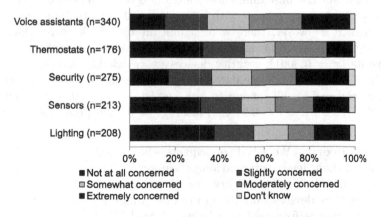

Fig. 4. Level of privacy concern for smart home devices

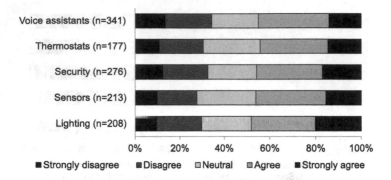

Fig. 5. Agreement with statement: "I am concerned that the manufacturer will eventually stop supporting my smart home devices."

4.3 Loss of Manufacturer Support

Level of Concern. Participants rated their level of agreement (5-point scale ranging from "strongly disagree" to "strongly agree") with the following statement: "I am concerned that the manufacturer will eventually stop supporting my smart home devices." For each of the device categories, less than half agreed or strongly agreed that they were concerned about loss of support (Fig. 5): 48% lighting, 46% security devices and sensors, 45% voice assistants, and 44% thermostats.

No significant response differences were found between device categories, and responses were not correlated with perceptions of update importance nor IT job experience. However, there were significant but weak correlations for the level of security concern for all device categories: voice assistants ($\tau = 0.2832$); thermostats ($\tau = 0.3001$); security devices ($\tau = 0.3002$); sensors ($\tau = 0.286$); and lighting ($\tau = 0.3112$). Similarly, there were significant correlations to level of privacy concern for all categories: voice assistants ($\tau = 0.2076$); thermostats ($\tau = 0.2227$); security ($\tau = 0.2182$); sensors ($\tau = 0.2206$); lighting ($\tau = 0.2437$).

Specific Concerns. We asked participants what specific concerns, if any, they might have if their devices were no longer supported. Figure 6 shows the percentages of responses by device category. For all device categories, the most common concern was that devices would stop working (ranging from 39–48%), followed by security updates/fixes no longer being released (31–42%).

We looked for differences among categories for each of the 7 response options. For the option "Updates containing non-security bug fixes no longer being released," there was a significant difference between security devices and lighting ($\chi^2 = 15.8483$, df $= 1$). For "New features no longer being added," there were differences between lighting and all other categories: voice assistants ($\chi^2 = 9.6008$, df $= 1$); thermostats ($\chi^2 = 7.0346$, df $= 1$); security devices ($\chi^2 = 14.8933$, df $= 1$); and sensors ($\chi^2 = 6.9937$, df $= 1$). Finally, for those selecting "I would not be concerned," there were significant differences between lighting

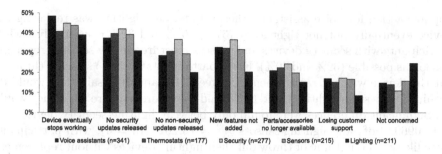

Fig. 6. Specific concerns if manufacturer support is lost

and the following categories: voice assistants ($\chi^2 = 8.0614$, df = 1); thermostats ($\chi^2 = 0.6971$, df = 1); and security devices ($\chi^2 = 16.3492$, df = 1).

Table 2. Significant correlations (τ) between support concerns and update importance, level of security concern, and level of privacy concern. "-" indicates a lack of significant correlation.

Concern Option	Update Importance	Security Concern	Privacy Concern
Device eventually stops working	Therm (0.1884) Sec (0.1211)	-	Sen (-0.1259)
No security updates released	Therm (0.1938) Sec (0.1318) Sen (0.1345)	Light (0.1744)	
No non-security updates released	-	Light (0.1974)	-
New features no longer added	Sec (0.1298)	-	-
Not concerned	-	Voice (-0.1383) Therm (-0.1478) Sec (-0.1707) Sen (-0.1863) Light (-0.3255)	Therm (-0.1974) Sec (-0.1395) Sen (-0.1558) Light (-0.217)

Voice = voice assistants; Therm = thermostats; Sec = security devices; Sen = sensors; Light = lighting

In exploring potential relationships between each response option and update importance, level of security concern, and level of privacy concern, we found several significant correlations (see Table 2), most notably a negative correlation between not being concerned and: level of security concern (all categories) and level of privacy concern (4/5 categories). In other words, those who selected the option that they did not have support concerns had lower levels of security and privacy concern.

Actions. Participants indicated what action they would take if their devices were no longer supported. Figure 7 shows responses by device category. The most popular action for voice assistants, thermostats, and lighting was replacing the device eventually but not right away (37%, 36%, and 32% respectively), while participants with security devices and sensors most frequently selected replacing as soon as possible (39% and 40%). Fewer participants (5–10%) selected throwing out the device without replacement. Between 11% and 20% said they would do nothing (highest for lighting), and 6–9% said they were not sure what they would do. Significant differences were found only between lighting-security devices (χ^2 = 15.0969, 4 df) and lighting-sensors (χ^2 = 13.2028, df = 4), with participants more likely to do nothing or throw out their lighting devices without replacement and less likely to immediately replace them.

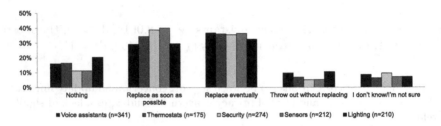

Fig. 7. Actions if manufacturer support is lost

Notification Preferences. We asked participants how they would prefer to be notified that their devices would no longer be supported. Of the 400 participants who answered this question, the most popular method was email (45%), followed by receiving a message in the smart home device companion app (31%) and a letter or postcard in the mail (19%). Only 6% said that they would prefer not to be notified.

5   Discussion and Related Work

While the majority of participants believed that it is important for smart home devices to be updated, their levels of concern for support loss were much lower. This contradiction implies that some consumers do not fully understand the implications of unsupported devices. Therefore, we offer suggestions on how manufacturers and third parties might better inform and empower consumers. We also situate our findings within related research literature. While prior studies have explored planned obsolescence and consumer responses (e.g., [16,20], none have specifically addressed smart home obsolescence.

5.1   Proactive Communications

Proactive communication by the manufacturer can be a first step towards consumer empowerment. In line with recommendations from U.S. Government agencies and researchers, manufacturers should provide consumers with information about their end-of-life support policy, expected lifespan, when security patches will no longer be provided, and how to sign up for notifications about changes to support [11, 13, 15, 20, 22].

Product labels are one way to provide pre-purchase support disclosure. Based on prior research [7], Carnegie Mellon proposed an IoT security and privacy label that includes how long security updates will be available and whether devices will automatically receive updates [3]. Other researchers found that security update labels, especially those focused on how long the manufacturer guarantees to provide updates, may have a significant impact on consumer product selection [21]. To that end, several governments have proposed IoT security labels that include an expiry date that specifies when security updates will no longer be available [4,6]. However, future work should be done to examine potential issues of including an expiry date on a label. For example, a study commissioned by the UK Government found that consumers were often confused about what the expiry date meant [18]. An Australian Government survey of 6,000 citizens revealed that a third of respondents mistakenly believed that a device with an expiry label came with an extended warranty up to the date on the label, and 20% thought the device would stop working on the date on the label [2]. In addition, it might be difficult for manufacturers to predict how long they will be able to maintain security updates given the speed at which technology and security threats change [14].

We found that many participants did care about security and privacy (particularly those with prior IT job experience) and indicated that loss of security updates was a major concern. However, participants with lower levels of security and privacy concern had less concern about loss of support. Therefore, we see a need to proactively raise awareness of smart home security, including the link between manufacturer support and security. This awareness is especially essential for device categories viewed as less important from a security/privacy and update perspective (e.g., thermostats, sensors, lighting devices) but which still have the potential to introduce vulnerabilities into the home network and affect higher-valued systems and information.

5.2 Aiding Consumers When Support Ends

To help consumers when device support ends, manufacturers should inform consumers of changes to device support in a timely manner, for example, via the notification methods most preferred by our participants (email or message in the device app). A dynamic, online product label that provides current security status may also help consumers keep abreast of support changes [22]. However, it should be noted that an appreciable number (19%) of consumers desired mail notification. This may be due to people being overwhelmed by electronic notifications and emails [32] and desiring more noticeable communication of support changes.

Support-related notifications are essentially a type of risk communication. Therefore, communicators (e.g., manufacturers) should follow security risk communication guidelines, including: using clear and concise language; being realistic about consequences (not downplaying the risk of negative impacts); providing clear and precise directions for action; and visually highlighting key information [24,36]. Translating those guidelines into the smart home context, consumers should be made aware of both the security and non-security (e.g., safety and functionality) implications of loss of support so they can make informed decisions about whether to continue using their devices and what additional protections should be enacted. Additionally, consumers should be told what options, if any, they have to safely continue using their unsupported devices. For example, if unsupported devices can still function without support outside the home network (e.g., cloud services), consumers could have the option of turning off connected capability or limiting operation of the device to the home network.

Options that allow consumers to safely continue using unsupported devices are especially desirable from a sustainability perspective to reduce waste of products that are discarded due to obsolescence [1]. Similar to prior research findings about how consumers respond to planned obsolescence [20], in our survey, a low percentage of participants said they would throw out the device without replacing it, but many said they would replace the device, leaving uncertainty about what will happen to the old devices. We acknowledge that this decision may be influenced by the state of the deprecated device, i.e., if device functionality is outwardly impacted after loss discontinuation. Global organizations are currently working on the problem of IoT sustainable development [33], with future user-centered research needed to determine how older products might continue to be easily updated and used by consumers (e.g., via modularization [14]).

Third parties (e.g., standards organizations, consumer advocacy groups, government agencies, and policymakers) may also play an important role in helping consumers navigate loss of support. These entities can encourage and set standards for manufacturers to document and communicate support issues (e.g., as in [5,8,10]), require organizations to purchase supported devices only and have a plan for loss for support, and engage retailers to pull unsupported devices from their stock.

Disclaimer

Certain commercial companies or products are identified in this paper to foster understanding. Such identification does not imply recommendation or endorsement by the National Institute of Standards and Technology, nor does it imply that the companies or products identified are necessarily the best available for the purpose.

Acknowledgements. We would like to thank our colleagues Yee-Yin Choong and Barbara Cuthill for their comments that helped improve the paper.

Appendix A: Survey Questions

The following are the survey questions related to the contents of this paper. These are a subset of a broader survey addressing smart home updates.

Throughout the survey, the following terms are used:

- **Smart home device** is a network-connected device (connected via Wi-Fi, Bluetooth, or similar protocols) that is used to remotely and/or more effectively and efficiently control functions or physical aspects of the home.
- **Smart home device app** is an application on your smartphone, computer, laptop, or tablet that is used to remotely control or access your smart home device.
- **Smart home updates** are incremental changes or improvements that manufacturers make to the software or firmware of smart home devices and device apps. Updates may be automatic in which updates are installed without you having to take any action or manual in which you may have to click a button or take some other action to install the update.
- The **security** of smart home devices refers to the prevention of damage to, unauthorized use of, and exploitation of smart home devices and the information they contain, in order to strengthen the confidentiality, integrity, and availability of these devices. In this survey, "security" is equivalent to "cybersecurity." Physical security related to the home or its occupants is different and will be referred to as "home security."
- The **privacy** of smart home devices refers to the right of a party to maintain control over and be assured confidentiality of personal information that is collected, transmitted, used, and stored during the use of smart home devices.

SMART HOME DEVICES

1) Which of the following smart home devices do you own? (Select all that apply.)

- ☐ Virtual voice assistants and smart speakers (e.g., Amazon Echo/Alexa, Google Nest Home Hub, Apple HomePod)
- ☐ Thermostats (e.g., Nest, Ecobee)
- ☐ Home security devices (e.g., video doorbells, cameras, door locks, garage door openers)
- ☐ Home environment sensors (e.g., smoke and leak detectors)
- ☐ Lighting (e.g., lightbulbs, lighting systems)
- ☐ Appliances (e.g., refrigerators, washing machines/dryers, ovens, coffee makers/espresso machines)
- ☐ Entertainment (e.g., TVs, streaming devices such as AppleTV or Roku)
- ☐ Plugs or outlets (e.g., Wemo Mini, Wyze Plug)
- ☐ Domestic robots that do household chores (e.g., robot vacuums such as iRobot Roomba, smart lawn mowers)
- ☐ Smart home hubs (e.g., Samsung SmartThings, Hubitat Elevation)*
- ☐ Other (e.g., smart windows solutions, smart watering system, smart pet feeder) (please specify):

2) Please indicate the number and types (including the brand) of smart home devices you own in each of the following categories.

[answer for each device category owned]

UPDATES

3) Rate your agreement with the following statement for each category of smart home device: It is important for smart home devices to be updated.

Strongly Disagree - Disagree - Neither Agree nor Disagree - Agree - Strongly Agree
  [answer for each device category owned]

MANUFACTURER SUPPORT

4) Please rate your agreement with the following statement: I am concerned that the manufacturer will eventually stop supporting my smart home devices.

Strongly Disagree - Disagree - Neither Agree nor Disagree - Agree   Strongly Agree
  [answer for each device category owned]

5) Which of the following would concern you if the manufacturer stopped supporting your smart home devices? (Select all that apply.)

☐ My devices eventually stop working
☐ Updates containing security bug fixes no longer being released
☐ Updates containing non-security bug fixes no longer being released
☐ New features no longer being added
☐ Parts or accessories no longer being available
☐ Losing online/call-in customer support from the manufacturer
☐ I would not be concerned

  [answer for each device category owned]

6) What would you do if your smart home devices were no longer supported by the manufacturer?

○ Nothing - leave it as is
○ Replace it with a new or different device as soon as possible
○ Replace it with a new or different device eventually but not necessarily right away
○ Throw the device out without replacing it

  [answer for each device category owned]

7) What would be your *preferred* method of notification from the manufacturer to inform you they were no longer supporting your smart home devices?

○ Email
○ Message/notification sent to the device app
○ Text message on my phone
○ Letter/postcard in the mail
○ I prefer not to be notified
○ Other (please specify):

SECURITY AND PRIVACY

8) Please rate your level of concern with the security of your smart home devices for each category:

Not at all concerned - Slightly concerned - Somewhat concerned - Moderately concerned - Extremely concerned

  [answer for each device category owned]

9) Please rate your level of concern with the privacy of your smart home devices for each category:

Not at all concerned - Slightly concerned - Somewhat concerned - Moderately concerned - Extremely concerned

[answer for each device category owned]

DEMOGRAPHICS

10) In which state or US territory do you live?

11) In which type of area is your home?

- o Rural
- o Suburban
- o Urban

12) How long have you been using smart home devices?

- o Less than 1 year
- o 3 - 5 years
- o 6 or more years

13) What is your age range?

- o 18 - 24
- o 25 - 34
- o 35 - 44
- o 45 - 54
- o 55 - 64
- o 65+

14) What is your gender?

- o Male
- o Female
- o Prefer to self-describe
- o Prefer not to answer

15) What is your race?

- ☐ American Indian or Alaska Native
- ☐ Asian
- ☐ Black or African American
- ☐ Native Hawaiian or Other Pacific Islander
- ☐ White
- ☐ Other
- ☐ Prefer not to answer

16) What is your ethnicity?

- o Hispanic, Latino/a, or Spanish Origin

o Not Hispanic, Latino/a, or Spanish Origin
o Prefer not to answer

17) What is your highest level of education?

o Less than high school degree
o High school degree or equivalent
o Some college
o Associate degree
o Bachelor's degree
o Master's degree
o Doctoral or Juris Doctoral degree
o Other:
o Prefer not to answer

18) Have you ever worked in a field/job related to information technology (IT) (for example, a system or network administrator, IT help desk, cybersecurity professional)?

o Yes
o No

References

1. ATT. End of life, unsupported IoT devices (2020). https://securityinnovation.att.com/stories/end-of-life-unsupported-devices/
2. Behavioral Economics Team of the Australian Government. Stay smart: Helping consumers choose cyber secure smart devices (2021). https://behaviouraleconomics.pmc.gov.au/sites/default/files/projects/beta-report-cyber-security-labels.pdf
3. Carnegie Mellow University. IoT security and privacy label (2020). https://iotsecurityprivacy.org/
4. Department for Digital, Culture, Media & Sport, United Kingdom. Consultation on the government's regulatory proposals regarding consumer Internet of Things (IoT) security (2020). https://www.gov.uk/government/consultations/consultation-on-regulatory-proposals-on-consumer-iot-security/consultation-on-the-governments-regulatory-proposals-regarding-consumer-internet-of-things-iot-security#the-top-three-guidelines
5. Department for Digital, Culture, Media and Sport. Code of practice for consumer IoT security (2018). https://www.gov.uk/government/publications/code-of-practice-for-consumer-iot-security
6. Department of Home Affairs, Commonwealth of Australia. Code of practice: Securing the Internet of Things for consumers (2020). https://www.homeaffairs.gov.au/reports-and-pubs/files/code-of-practice.pdf
7. Emami-Naeini, P., Dixon, H., Agarwal, Y., Cranor, L.F.: Exploring how privacy and security factor into IoT device purchase behavior. In: CHI Conference on Human Factors in Computing Systems. ACM (2019)
8. ETSI. ETSI EN 303 645 V2.1.1 CYBER; cyber security for consumer Internet of Things: Baseline requirements (2020). https://www.etsi.org/deliver/etsi_en/303600_303699/303645/02.01.01_60/en_303645v020101p.pdf

9. Fagan, M., Khan, M.M.H., Buck, R.: A study of users' experiences and beliefs about software update messages. Comput. Hum. Behav. **51**, 504–519 (2015)
10. Fagan, M., Megas, K., Watrobski, P., Marron, J., Cuthill, B.: NISTIR 8425 profile of the IoT core baseline for consumer IoT products. Technical report, National Institute of Standards and Technology (2022)
11. Fagan, M., Megas, K.N., Scarfone, K., Smith, M.: NISTIR 8259 foundational cyber-security activities for IoT device manufacturers (2020). https://nvlpubs.nist.gov/nistpubs/ir/2020/NIST.IR.8259.pdf
12. Federal Trade Commission. Internet of things privacy and security in a connected world (2015). https://www.ftc.gov/system/files/documents/reports/federal-trade-commission-staff-report-november-2013-workshop-entitled-internet-things-privacy/150127iotrpt.pdf
13. Federal Trade Commission. Careful connections: Keeping the internet of things secure (2020). https://www.ftc.gov/tips-advice/business-center/guidance/careful-connections-keeping-internet-things-secure
14. Furman, S., Haney, J.: Human factors in smart homes technologies workshop (2019). https://csrc.nist.gov/CSRC/media/Projects/usable-cybersecurity/images-media/Human%20Factors%20Smart%20Home%20Workshop%20Summary%20Report.pdf
15. Germain, J.M.: Unsupported IoT devices are cyber-trouble waiting to happen. Ecommerce Times (2021)
16. Guiltinan, J.: Creative destruction and destructive creations: environmental ethics and planned obsolescence. J. Bus. Ethics **89**(1), 19–28 (2009)
17. Haney, J.M., Furman, S.M.: Work in progress: towards usable updates for smart home devices. In: Proceedings of the 10th International Workshop on Socio-Technical Aspects in Security, pp. 107–117 (2020)
18. Harris Interactive. Consumer internet of things security labelling survey research findings (2019). https://assets.publishing.service.gov.uk/government/uploads/system/uploads/attachment_data/file/798543/Harris_Interactive_Consumer_IoT_Security_-Labelling_Survey_Report.pdf
19. Ion, I., Reeder, R., Consolvo, S.: "...no one can hack my mind": comparing expert and non-expert security practices. In: Proceedings of the 11th Symposium on Usable Privacy and Security, pp. 327–346 (2015)
20. Kuppelwieser, V.G., Klaus, P., Manthiou, A., Boujena, O.: Consumer responses to planned obsolescence. J. Retail. Consum. Serv. **47**, 157–165 (2019)
21. Morgner, P., Mai, C., Koschate-Fischer, N., Freiling, F., Benenson, Z.: Security update labels: establishing economic incentives for security patching of IoT consumer products. In: Proceedings of the 2020 IEEE Symposium on Security and Privacy (SP), pp. 29–446. IEEE (2020)
22. National Institute of Standards and Technology. Recommended criteria for cyber-security labeling for consumer internet of things (IoT) products (2022). https://nvlpubs.nist.gov/nistpubs/CSWP/NIST.CSWP.02042022-2.pdf
23. NPD Group. Half of U.S. consumers own at least one smart home device (2021). https://www.npd.com/news/press-releases/2021/half-of-u-s-consumers-own-at-least-one-smart-home-device-reports-npd/
24. Nurse, J.R., Creese, S., Goldsmith, M., Lamberts, K.: Trustworthy and effective communication of cybersecurity risks: a review. In: Workshop on Socio-Technical Aspects in Security and Trust (STAST), pp. 60–68 (2011)
25. Postscape. Closed IoT companies and devices: A directory of failed IoT startups (2019). https://www.postscapes.com/closed-iot-companies/

26. Powers, W.T.: Behavior: The Control of Perception, 2nd edn. Benchmark Publications Inc, California (2005)
27. Research on Investment. The IoT revolution: 5 industries that will change forever (2021). https://researchoninvestment.com/iot-revolution-5-industries-that-will-change-forever/
28. Bruce Schneier. The internet of things is wildly insecure - and often unpatchable. Wired Magazine (2014)
29. Statista. Smart home device household penetration in the United States in 2019 and 2021 (2021). https://www.statista.com/statistics/1247351/smart-home-device-us-household-penetration/
30. Tabassum, M., Kosinski, T., Lipford, H.R.: "I don't own the data": end user perceptions of smart home device data practices and risks. In: Proceedings of the 15th Symposium on Usable Privacy and Security (2019)
31. Vaniea, K.E., Rader, E., Wash, R.: Betrayed by updates: How negative experiences affect future security. In: Proceedings of the 2014 SIGCHI Conference on Human Factors in Computing Systems (CHI 14), pp. 2671–2674. ACM, Toronto, Canada (2014)
32. Westermann, T., Moller, S., Wechsung, I.: Assessing the relationship between technical affinity, stress and notifications on smartphones. In: Proceedings of the 17th International Conference on Human-Computer Interaction with Mobile Devices and Services, pp. 652–659 (2015)
33. World Economic Forum. IoT for sustainable development project (2021). https://widgets.weforum.org/iot4d/index.html
34. Zeng, E., Mare, S., Roesner, F.: End user security and privacy concerns with smart homes. In: Proceedings of the 13th Symposium on Usable Privacy and Security (2017)
35. Zheng, S., Apthorpe, N., Chetty, M., Feamster, N.: User perceptions of smart home IoT privacy. ACM Hum.-Comput. Int. 2(CSCW), 1–20 (2018)
36. Zou, Y., Danino, S., Sun, K., Schaub, F.: YouMight'Be affected: an empirical analysis of readability and usability issues in data breach notifications. In: Proceedings of the 2019 CHI Conference on Human Factors in Computing Systems, pp. 1–14 (2019)

Privacy, Safety, and Security in Extended Reality: User Experience Challenges for Neurodiverse Users

David Jones[1], Shiva Ghasemi[1], Denis Gračanin[1(✉)], and Mohamed Azab[2]

[1] Virginia Tech, Blacksburg, VA 24060, USA
{davidmj,shivagh,gracanin}@vt.edu
[2] Virginia Military Institute, Lexington, VA 24459, USA
azabmm@vmi.edu

Abstract. Neurodevelopmental disorders are a group of disorders that affect the development of the nervous system, leading to abnormal brain function, which may affect emotion, learning ability, self-control, and memory. Such disorders include Attention Deficit Hyperactivity Disorder (ADHD), Autism Spectrum Disorder, specific learning disorders such as dyslexia, traumatic brain injury, and others. The effects of neurodiversity tend to last for a person's lifetime. Neurodiversity (ND) has recently become a serious topic in cybersecurity because the perceived skills shortage has opened the door for ND candidates. However, ND introduces some cybersecurity challenges. For instance, in the educational domain, a minor manipulation of an online quiz design can have significant implications on the ability of students with ADHD to answer correctly. This type of manipulation can become a major vulnerability that can be exploited by skilled attackers and lead to a serious human-targeted Cyber-Physical System attack. Although the research community has dedicated significant research towards accessibility in the XR realm, there is still not a fair and adequate amount of research concerning potential immersive threats affecting neurodiverse users in XR. We need to shed light on a need for a revision in our collective understanding of risks brought on by XR technology.

Keywords: Accessibility · Cybersecurity · Extended Reality · Neurodiverse Users

1 Introduction

Neurodiversity (ND) is an umbrella term that represents the neurological variability of the human brain leading to abnormal brain function, which may affect emotion, learning ability, self-control, and memory. Such disorders include attention deficit hyperactivity disorder (ADHD), autism spectrum disorder (ASD), specific learning disorders, like dyslexia or dyscalculia, traumatic brain injury

A. Moallem (Ed.): HCII 2023, LNCS 14045, pp. 511–528, 2023.
https://doi.org/10.1007/978-3-031-35822-7_33

and others. ND emerged from self-advocacy and opposes the classification of neurotypes as having a deficit or impairment [8,70]. It can be argued that ND is the recognition that every person's brain develops uniquely, leading to differences in abilities and behavioral traits across the board. In the 1990s the word "neurodiversity" was initially coined in the online ASD community, and it has since gained popularity both offline and online [41]. It explains the notion that various brain developments and structures are present across the human population. The campaign for disability rights is expanded into the area of cognitive, affective, and perceptual difference by supporters of ND [46]. Autistic or "on the autism spectrum" individuals have been the most outspoken supporters of ND in the medical, psychiatric, and educational fields. The movement, however, also includes people with a wide range of neurological disorders, such as Tourette's Syndrome, Alzheimer's disease, bipolar disorder, dyslexia, dyspraxia, depression, and epilepsy [46].

ND individuals exist in every country in the world. They share commonalities regarding lack of employment opportunities, social stigma and challenging social interactions, that place strain on personal, romantic and professional relationships. Lastly, ND individuals with cognitive disabilities are typically prohibited from serving in the military, despite laws that advocate for the social inclusion of people with disabilities in all contexts that are a part of daily life in society. The occurrence of ND related disorders have steadily increased.

It is estimated that 1% of the world's population has been diagnosed with ASD [43,85]. In the United States 1 in 44 children have been diagnosed with ASD in 2022 which constitutes 178% increase since 2000 [85]. One quarter of ASD children are diagnosed with ADHD [20]. ND individuals diagnosed with ADHD similar to those with ASD have multiple mental health issues. Behavior and conduct problems occur in 50% of ADHD diagnosed individuals and 30% are diagnosed with anxiety and depression [43]. Like their ASD peers, ND individuals with ADHD experience difficulty retaining employment. Additionally, they experience poor academic outcomes. Males are 2.7 to 8.1 times more likely to drop out of school, while 7.5% fail their courses [29].

Extended Reality (XR) tools are being developed to help bring ND individuals into the mainstream by providing XR diagnosis tools for ADHD. The combined effect of recent studies suggests that a more sensible approach to treating mental disorders would be to abandon the "disability" or "illness" paradigm in favor of a"diversity" perspective, which considers both strengths and weaknesses as well as the notion that variation can be beneficial in and of itself [3].

The remainder of the paper is as follows. Section 2 discusses related work and summarizes the ND characteristic behaviors of three types; ADHD, ASD and Dyslexia. Neurodiversity specific Safety/Security/Privacy (Sa/Se/Pr) challenges in XR are described in Sect. 3. The corresponding defensive solutions are identified in Sect. 4. Section 5 discusses the findings while Sect. 6 concludes the paper.

2   Related Work

Due to high frequency, overlapping symptoms, and co-occurring nature, we focus on three ND conditions, ADHD, AST, and Dyslexia. The demand for research addressing the requirements of ND individuals has increased significantly in recent years, but there is still a dearth of such research in computer science and Human-Computer Interaction (HCI). The promising shift toward embracing ND has opened up new challenges and opportunities for XR developers.

First, XR developers were unaware of accessibility requirements and have trouble incorporating them into standard software development procedures. Second, ND individuals experience sensory overload when using XR technologies, these negative experiences are exacerbated by excessive multisensory stimulation. As XR technologies rely on immersive multi-modal simulations, it is uncertain how they may effect individuals with various patterns of sensory processing [42]. Third, there has been an ambiguity around this target population due to this fact that the recent studies contend that many mental or neurological illnesses are accompanied by both strengths and deficits which is a significant contributor to this ambiguity.

For instance, individuals with ASD appear to have abilities in working with systems (e.g., computer languages, mathematical systems, machinery), and in trials, they do better than control subjects at seeing minute details in intricate patterns [3]. In another example, it has been discovered that people with dyslexia have global visual-spatial talents, including the ability to recognize impossible objects [3,38] and perceive peripheral or diffused visual information more quickly and efficiently than participants without dyslexia [3,27].

ADHD is a prevalent neurobehavioral disorder affecting children and adolescents. Worldwide,up to 5% of adults and 6–9 % of children and adolescents suffer from ADHD [48,60,87]. There is up to a 91.5% chance of inheriting ADHD [86]. It affects more men than women globally, with an estimated incidence of 8% to 12% [1]. Compared to their neurotypical counterparts, adults with ADHD miss significantly more days of work [9,68], and they are more likely to be fired, change jobs, and have poor job performance evaluations [9].

Several studies have demonstrated that between 25 and 40 percent of people with ADHD also struggle with dyslexia, and vice versa [12]. Chronic inattention, hyperactivity, and impulsivity that interfere with functionality are the hallmarks of ADHD [51,83]. These core symptoms may negatively impact the academic and social performance of children throughout their school life [72] and may lead to low frustration tolerance which can obstruct a person to accomplish an activity or achieve a specified goal [54].

ASD is a complex disorder with a variety of etiologies, manifestations, and comorbidities that affect how it develops and is treated. Comorbidity, the term utilized for a dual diagnosis or multiple diagnoses use in medical literature, might signify an inability to provide a single diagnosis that fully explains all symptoms [65]. For instance, according to some estimates, between 30% and 50% of autistic people also have ADHD, especially in those who are younger than preschool age [40] and similarly, estimations indicate that two-thirds of people with ADHD have ASD-like characteristics [14, 40]. There is an indication that ASD is estimated to be 40–80% heritable [66] and it is estimated that approximately half of adults with ASD are unemployed [57].

It is believed that dyslexia affects between 5% and 15% of people worldwide [30, 63]. A child with an affected parent has a risk of 40–60% of developing dyslexia [67]. Dyslexia is a multifaceted cognitive disorder [44] that has effects on decoding and spelling fluency. In addition, it is marked by difficulty with accurate and, or fluent word recognition [4]. Dyslexics are more able to visually distinguish letters farther from the center and more diffusely around the edges compared to individuals without dyslexia.

ADHD, ASD and Dyslexia are susceptible to, and impact cybersecurity behaviours [45]. Accordingly, cybersecurity needs to become a primary level component on par with content, capability, functionality and delivery mechanism. If ND individuals are to have opportunities to use the unique skill sets they possess and to experience a more fulfilling life, then these individuals require safety, security, and environment acceptance assurance. Little XR research has been carried out so far about these ND conditions regarding cyber safe XR delivered content. Accordingly, further research is required to back up the effectiveness of these interventions in order to establish a strong foundation for supporting ND individual and the use of XR.

3   Neurodiversity Specific Privacy, Safety, and Security Challenges in Extended Reality

Cyber attacks are becoming prevalent and threaten IT systems used by businesses, governments, and individuals. According to a recent survey, the number of vulnerabilities exploited increased by 33% between 2020 and 2021 [7]. Therefore, as industries have adapted the use of XR technology, it is imperative to offer solutions to safety and security huddles faced by ND individuals. Each safety-critical XR system is required to adhere to safety standards as well as security and privacy standards. In order to provide insights into how XR developers address (Sa/Se/Pr) for ND individuals, it is crucial to highlight that (Sa/Se/Pr) might mean and measure differently depending on the industry.

The shift to inclusive security must be understood within the broader context of the development of accessible security and privacy technology. Cyber-physical systems require a higher level of security than standard information technology since the physical components and the data they provide to the system must be verified. While the allure of metaverse draws several industries into AR, VR, and MR technologies, numerous cybersecurity concerns have also surfaced. Consequently, there is a larger need for cybersecurity specialists as more businesses transition to metaverse.

In order to support (Sa/Se/Pr) in XR cybersecurity, a focus on educational goals should be first prioritized. Technical concepts that are necessary for grasping cybersecurity education may be difficult for individuals without a technical background to comprehend. In an effort to meet this demand, Jin et al. [33]

designed an XR experience with four unique cybersecurity games for high school students that covered subjects like social engineering, recognizing and handling phishing emails, as well as fundamental cybersecurity concepts.

Since Microsoft and the U.S. military teamed up in 2017 to use HoloLens to generate war game scenarios and give soldiers battlefield information through AR simulations [19], the demand of AR has been escalated in military service. With regard to the six domains of sensing, communication, maneuvering, attack, survival, and sustainability, HoloLens is meant to complement the military's objectives to increase close-combat effectiveness and survivability [19]. Cyber Affordance Visualization in Augmented Reality (CAVIAR) is another military project using Hololens to dynamically visualize cyber terrain within the user's immediate surroundings [19].

There are a few persuasive strategies to perform a target behavior to increase safety and security; rehearsal, self monitoring, rewards, reduction, reminder, simulation, praise, comparison, social learning, personalization, and liking [58]. Rehearsal and Self-monitoring are as the main persuasive strategies used in many systems in various industries. According to the World Health Organization, safety is the state in which hazards and conditions that lead to psychological, or material harm are controlled to preserve the health and well-being of individuals and the community [80]. In the field of information technology, cybersecurity, online theft, and identity theft can all be considered as aspects of safety [58]. The psychological perspective of safety focuses on how perceptual realism and immersive experiences may have the potential to traumatize and harm users in the long run and how we may prevent this [28].

3.1 Perceptual Manipulations

Perceptual Manipulation entails modifying users' multi-sensory (such as visual, auditory, and haptic) impressions of the outside world through XR content with an attempt to influence users' judgments and subsequent actions. Virtual-Physical Perceptual Manipulations (VPPMs) is a technique using XR-driven exploits that change how people perceive the multi-sensory aspects of our bodily activities and reactions in order to direct the user's physical movements (e.g., the position of body and hands) [2,73].

While current XR technology is sufficient to create such attacks, there is little research into accurate classification of attacks and how ND individuals perceive, react to, and defend against such potential manipulations. In VR, it is possible to create illusions that lead users to believe and act as though they have entered different settings and identities. Violent threats might seem more real in a virtual environment because they are not abstract; they are more than simply words on a screen because to active presence, embodiment, and the all-encompassing nature of immersive experiences [31].

VR is a fantastic tool for attackers in using perceptual manipulation. According to a recent study [84], people with ASD have a lower capacity to discern the distinction between the truth and lies, which makes them more susceptible to manipulation. Due to their difficulty detecting lies, they are vulnerable to manipulation [84]. Another vulnerability is advertisement. Exposure to manipulative advertising affect both ND and neurotypical individuals. There are concerns that the distinguishing characteristics of XR devices, such as the medium's immersion and the potential of XR devices to replicate reality, could be used to develop deceptive XR advertisements that persuade customers to buy things they do not need or that might damage them [49].

3.2 Immersive Attacks

Any attack that targets the distinctive characteristics of immersive VR and related immersed user vulnerabilities is referred to as an immersive attack [15]. A good model of immersive attacks is exemplified in [15] where OpenVR API is used to disorient users, activate their HMD camera without their knowledge, overlay undesired 2D pictures in their range of vision, and alter the VR environment so that users were compelled to strike walls and actual objects [56].

Another examples are malicious applications can take advantage of immersive feedback devices to deceive users about the real world. They can use some techniques to cause sensory overload in users. Applications that flash bright lights in the display, play loud sounds, or provide intense haptic feedback could physically harm users [64]. For instance, attackers have previously targeted epilepsy forums, posting messages containing flashing animated GIFs to cause headaches or seizures [64].

4   XR Defensive Solutions

Human-centered security design must take into account the three dimensions of 1) security; 2) usability; and 3) accessibility [62]. All three require receiving equal attentions in XR. The defensive requirements should be created to decrease cognitive load in order to increase usability because ND individuals are more prone to cognitive overload and its consequences are rather severe for them. All the attack categories listed below produce disorientation. To this extent, we formulated several recommendations to create a secure, privacy-aware XR system contributing to user experience.

Disorientation Attacks: Any attack that aims to make ND users feel dizzy and confused when they are fully immersed. This attack modifies the user's position and rotation within the virtual play area while they are immersed. Visually Induced Motion Sickness (VIMS) is a condition that can happen to users when they are exposed to visual motion signals without any actual movement [15].

Frame Rate and Human Joystick: While frame rate and human joystick attacks are quite different, the corresponding defense techniques are quite similar. Industry has already provided prevention measures for detecting anomalous activity, beyond digital signatures, based on user, machine, and network behavior in the form of end-point detection and response (XDR) software [34]. The behavior and events are correlated across an organization to determine the presence of cyber attacks [34]. Anomalous behavior detection occurs via predictive machine learning [34] and the software deployed is often referred to as an agent. The same considerations need to occur for XR devices.

In the framework rate and joystick attacks the computer connected to the XR devices requires prior compromise. Utilizing industry best practices for cyber defense and a defense in depth strategy, mitigation at the workstation and network layers are possible. However, the authors of this paper were unable to find research regarding XDR agents being available for installation on XR based devices. Therefore XDR for XR should be considered for future work.

The frame rate (refresh rate) in XR is defined as the rate in which images are rendered. Interactive and animated visualization rely the optimal frame rate to deliver the best end user experience [23]. Currently VR headsets 90 Hz [18]. Inadequate frame rates can induce sickness and disorientation within XR environments. Visually induced motion sickness (VIMS) specifically relates to nausea, oculomotor strain, and disorientation from the perception of motion while remaining still [35]. By attacking the frame rate of an XR user's experience, disorientation can be induced. Two methods provided demonstrated success at affecting a XR experience frame rate, graphical processing unit (GPU) and network based [56]. In the case of the GPU attack, the processor was attacked to slow the frame rate. The network based attack was conducted by a distributed denial of service (DDOS). Each attack was successful in lowering the frame rate of the VR environment.

Any attack used to force a user who is submerged to physically relocate to a specific spot without their knowledge. During an immersive session, this could be used to make a virtual space seem smaller or larger to a user who is immersed or to stop the chaperone from assisting users in recognizing their real-world boundaries (real walls) [15]. During an immersive session, the chaperone may be prevented from assisting users in recognizing their real world limits (actual walls) by making virtual space appear smaller or larger to them. Attackers intend to guide and control the XR user's movements without their knowledge, which leads to disorientation.

Cyberbullying: It is difficult to detect cyberbullying using algorithmic learning, especially when cyberbullying involves irony and sarcasm [50]. Additionally, cyberbullying can involve multi-modal approaches where text, images, and video are utilized. The multi-modal approach may not be abusive themselves, but when utilized together could provide abusive context. Lastly, cyberbullying by exclusion presents a challenge. One example is uploading pictures of a subset of people attending an activity and tagging the excluded individual [50]. One proposed defense is to utilize reflective messaging, that makes use of a deep neural network that creates a hate speech corpus [22] as part of a content development framework. Reflective messaging incorporates an interface design preventing users from posting harassing content by prompting the user to consider the content prior to posting [50]. Prompting allows a person to consider their actions and how those actions will affect others. However, if the post was intentional, the post could be flagged and removed. The goal is to teach and inform, but also prevent and protect those targeted from cyberbullying.

As cyberbullying occurs more frequently in social networks, it is crucial to automatically recognize it and take proactive action. Cyberbullying is defined as an individual's purposeful, planned, and repetitive acts of cruelty toward others through offensive posts, texts, or other types of social aggression using different digital technologies [6]. Additionally, cyberbullying is characterized by deliberately threatening, harassing, intimidating, or ridiculing an individual or group of individuals and is linked to increased depression and post traumatic stress disorder (PTSD) [74]. Lastly cyber bullying causes anxiety and stress and depression [32]. The most popular method for detecting cyberbullying is feature engineering, which enlarges the standard representation of text as a bag of words by adding new features using data domain expertise in an effort to enhance the performance of the classifier [6]. In case of ND individuals, since they have Internet addiction, they are more susceptible to cyberbullying. All of these disorders cause disorientation in ND people.

Eavesdropping Attacks: Contemporary mobile operating systems (MOS) are susceptible to speaker and microphone-based attacks since they do not control access to those devices [59]. Similarly, MOS cannot control untrusted application use or access. The lack of access control enables authorized apps to create exploitable communication channels. Three channels that can be targeted on mobile devices, speaker to microphone, speaker to external party, and third party to the microphone. Attacks may occur in real time or be replayed from recordings or by using text to speech.

Eavesdropping attacks are growing more widespread as voice interactions become more common in VR and AR and voice-based input has taken over as the main form of input in XR. Shi et al. [69] designed an eavesdropping method called Face-Mic that leverages speech-associated delicate facial dynamics acquired by zero-permission motion sensors in AR/VR headsets to deduce highly sensitive information from live human speech, such as speaker gender, identity, and speech content. Voice-based input, however, is vulnerable to numerous voice spoofing techniques. People with ADHD are hypersensitive to auditory stimulants such as multiple simultaneous conversations, loud music, or grating noises. Although there is a lack of proper research addressing how this type of attacks affect ND individuals, but we believe Dyslexics are more prone to this attack due to reliance on voice input for reading comprehension. Attackers could use AR/VR headsets with built in motion sensors to record subtle, speech-associated facial dynamics to steal sensitive information communicated via voice-command, including credit card data and passwords.

Overall, we need to consider that not not all XR defensive strategies will rely on technical solutions. Some challenges may necessitate social, policy, or legal solutions, such as potential policies for bystander opt-outs and compliant cameras [64].

5   Discussion

ND individuals are vulnerable to immersive attacks and perceptual manipulation by subtle and non-subtle changes to XR content not apparent to neurotypical users. Privacy and security-based immersive XR attacks include situations where the user's camera became active without knowledge or consent and, by overlaying images that obstructed users' vision along with XR environmental factors modification, XR users are induced into hitting or running into physical objects [15].

5.1   Vulnerabilities

Individual and relational vulnerabilities are due to diminished awareness or inattention, impulsivity, and poor decision-making, leading them into situations of possible compromise without thinking. XR vulnerabilities are not limited to physical or network access to the user's device [55] conducted a side-channel attack where keystrokes are inferred by casting a ray-cast orientation of the users' controllers and headsets. The attack allows the successful prediction of passwords. Individual vulnerabilities in XR are 1) immersive attacks; 2) perceptual manipulation; 3) violation of mental privacy due to the data derived from XR sensing; 4) lack of physical and psychological safety; 5) vestibular system degradation related to balance equilibrium, postural control, muscle tone, bilateral coordination, and field of vision stabilization; and 6) kinesthesia body's ability to sense its location, movements, and actions.

Conversely, relational vulnerabilities affect all parties involved in XR experiences, including ND users, bystanders, and the co-presence of other users involved in the same experience. Social difficulties, rejection, and interpersonal interaction issues are common in people with ADHD and ASD. XR environments make ND users feel more isolated and worsen their social capabilities. However, XR environments should provide the opposite experience and opportunities for interaction enrichment between ND and neurotypical users. Despite these vulnerabilities, there is a lack of standards for security, privacy, and behavioral data collection and usage within XR that delay the mass adaption of this technology for all users. Due to the nascence of XR technology mass adaptation, we currently have a limited grasp of what security, privacy, safety, and behavioral risks are present and yet to develop. As XR becomes ubiquitous, novel challenges emerged associated with (Sa/Se/Pr) have not been fully explored. The most frequent design factors influencing the degree of privacy features of XR technology are layout design, visibility, and accessibility levels. However, in-depth knowledge and subject-matter expertise are needed for evaluating design approaches.

Accessible Extended Reality (AXR) is a growing research area within HCI. Nascent research focuses on cybersecurity exploits targeting ND users within XR. XR technologies blur the distinctions between real and virtual environments through the subtle and unsubtle manipulation of user perception and interactions. As XR content researchers seek to improve ND users' experience, novel cybersecurity risks and immersive attacks become more prevalent.

5.2   Perception and Cognition

It is crucial to clarify the terms, relationships, and effects of perception, attention, and working memory on ADHD before examining the use of XR for the ADHD population.

The primary and defining characteristic of ADHD is thought to be inattentive conduct. Attention is a complex cognitive process that affects perception, memory, and decision-making to choose which pieces of information to engage with [76,77]. There are two definitions for attention; one defines attention as a finite resource for processing information [53,81] and another definition of attention is the mechanism by which information is selected to be processed with priority [16,21,53].

From young children to elderly individuals, it has frequently been linked to or associated with intelligence, information processing, executive function, comprehension, problem-solving, and learning [17]. According to research, the parts of attention and executive processes that are most frequently impacted by ADHD include working memory, response inhibition, sustained attention, divided attention, and selective attention [25,26,71].

Working memory (WM) is another term related to ADHD; it is the top-down, active manipulation of data stored in short-term memory [37]. WM is limited in both duration and capacity [82]. In contrast to long-term memory, which stores a large amount of knowledge over a lifetime, working memory is the little amount of information that may be kept in mind and used to carry out cognitive tasks.

WM deficits in ADHD are well established [37]. However, it is unclear which particular WM functions are impacted in this circumstance [53]. There is widespread consensus that WM and attention are related to ADHD. The predominant behavioral signs of hyperactivity and attention seem to be caused by working memory impairments [36].

The WebAIM website lists a number of cognitive impairments, including those involving memory, problem-solving, attention, reading, linguistics, and verbal and visual comprehension [62]. While some ND characteristics, such as difficulties with time management, concentration, organizational skills, teamwork, communication, and self-esteem, can be problematic in both traditional work environments and educational settings, ND individuals often possess unique talents that can boost productivity, quality, innovation, and engagement.

In addition, ND population reported multiple sensory challenges such as motion sickness, auditory stimuli, dizziness, nausea, exhaustion, headache, and spatial awareness [42]. The same study, explains these sensory barriers were primarily cited in relation to VR use.

According to the sensory integration theory [17], sensation has an impact on human growth, behavior, and function throughout the lifespan, but particularly in infancy. Having high or low thresholds for sensory stimuli and responding actively or passively to sensory input are two approaches by which individuals may struggle to integrate and interpret sensory information [17].

People with ND features feel sensory overload when using XR technologies; this is made worse by an excessive amount of multi-modal stimulation [42].

Sensory overload occurs when one or more of the senses are overstimulated. The processing power of human brains is constrained. Behavior, decision-making, and problem-solving skills can all be impacted by sensory overload. Mood, focus, and the capacity for clear communication can all shift as a result.

Auditory stimulants like loud music, many conversations going on at once, or irritating noises are extremely irritating to those with ADHD. Managing sensory overload in XR is one of the most challenges faced by both ND people and XR developers. It is believed that the most practical approach to prevent unpleasant experiences was to permit the customization of sensory settings. This reinforces the implementation of design approaches such as Human-Centered Design (HCD) and Community-based Participatory Research and Design (CBPRD) which are widely recognized designs or called people-centered approaches to address real-world problems [52]. Both approaches assist XR developers to involve ND people as partners in research and understand their unique and varying needs in order to design a safe immersive environment for this population.

The majority of XR studies had a correctional and therapeutic focus for ADHD population. For instance, Pollak et al. [61] reported that CPT embedded in VR (VRC-CPT) could have higher ecological validity and children with ADHD prefer VRC-CPT over classic CPT. XR could potentially provide a solution for inaccurate validity of existing ADHD assessment due to its ability to create standardized and extremely realistic virtual settings.

There are a few studies that provide some recommendations for designing attention-driven augmented reality (AR) interfaces [76]. Using layered interfaces created in accordance with the cueing and search concepts of attention theory, Bonanni et al. [11] decreased the users' cognitive load. In order to support visual search in AR situations, Lu et al. [47] evaluated an efficient subtle cueing technique that was less distracting. In order to direct the user's attention toward items outside the visual area, Biocca et al. [10] presented an attention funnel technique as a 3D cursor. Several studies examined the role on AR on student's performance. In [72] explains AR can improve academic outcomes by stimulating pupils' attention. The same study suggests the ADHD-augmented (AHA) pilot project with the goal of creating the AHA system as an educational tool that incorporates AR content into an already successful literacy program to address ADHD children's reading and spelling difficulties while fostering their engagement with the learning activities [72].

Another study [5] highlights the creation of an AR Serious Games (ARGS) to train focused and selective attention in kids with ADHD. ARGS seems to be a promising strategy that provides a welcoming setting for task enforcement, social support, and behavioral tactics. While these research concentrate on increasing the attention span in AR, another difficulty still exists: how to involve the user in an experience when certain distractions can be produced by the actual world as in AR, the user sees both virtual contents and the real world. Beside AR, several studies confirmed the advantages of virtual reality (VR) in cognitive performance, such as working memory, executive function, and attention.

Although everyone can experience sensory overload, it most frequently occurs in individuals with ADHD or other ND conditions. Numerous studies have shown that children with ADHD struggle to regulate their emotional responses to sensations and interpret sensory information [39]. Sensory overload in XR will affect their attention and sense of presence as there is a correlation between attention and user's performance in immersive VEs [78]. Attention plays an integral part in presence sensation in XR.

In addition, while there are many opportunities to offer useful supplementary information when actual and virtual objects are combined, there are also some negative impacts, such as split attention and increased visual complexity [76]. These cognitive difficulties could lead to increased distraction or cognitive overload [76]. As XR researchers seek to improve ND users' experience, novel cybersecurity risks and immersive attacks become more prevalent. (Sa/Se/Pr) challenges might have severe impacts on ADHD individuals compared to other people with ND features due to the correlation between attention and presence sensation in XR.

Social and emotional communication barriers, as well as repetitive and stereotypical conduct, are characteristics of ASD [79]. The hallmark of ASD is their complex sensory patterns that might affect social, cognitive, and communication abilities. One of the primary signs of ASD is thought to be difficulty interpreting the emotions and actions of other people. There have been multiple research focusing on the impact of XR on ASD population [79]. XR technology has been proven to be useful in boosting attention in ASD users due to its higher levels of motivation and engagement than other conventional mediums [77].

In study by [79], there is an indication of the implication of AR is being employed more and more in therapies for people with ASD in order to treat or lessen ASD symptomatology. Another study [24] claims that VR intervention can lead to hasten and improve the long-term acquisition of social skills. More specifically, VR assist people with ASD with recognizing others' emotions from their expressions and in social situations. [75] introduces a novel approach to quantify the security and privacy concerns raised by immersion attacks and other attacks and flaws that can negatively impact the user experience when using heads-up displays in social VRLEs by causing cybersickness.

According to British Dyslexia Association [13], difficulties with phonological awareness, verbal memory, and verbal processing speed are defining characteristics of dyslexia. Even though it is a lifelong condition, remedial and adaptive therapy can help control it [63]. In [38], there is an indication that dyslexia is correlated to a certain type of visual-spatial talent-an improved capacity to absorb spatial information globally (holistically) as opposed to locally (part by part). In another study, the main issues faced by dyslexic users are shared by the majority of Internet users are as follows; 1) confusing page layout; 2) unclear navigation; 3) poor color selections; 4) graphics and text too small; and 5) complicated language [45].

6 Conclusion and Future Works

ND individuals' XR accessibility demands and preferences have not received enough attention up to this point. We are all born and raised differently, therefore everyone is to some extent differently abled (a term that many ND people prefer). The theory of ND urges scientists to consider cognitive variations as natural expressions of human diversity, each with its own set of weaknesses and strengths. ND describes how diverse we are as human beings from a neurological perspective. We presented the spectrum of immersive attacks and vulnerable situations for the ND community, uncovered a critical evaluation of design guidelines, and highlighted the opportunities for quality user experience in XR.

The XR technologies have enormous potential benefits, but they also present new, significant hazards to computer security and privacy. Despite potential benefits of XR, the lack of user acceptance out of worries about privacy violations constitutes a barrier to diffusion in workplace environments. By design, most applications continuously receive and interpret sensor data remotely on a remote cloud somewhere placing users' and bystanders' privacy at risk.

There is a serious gap in contemporary XR technologies. To address such a gap, our future work will focus on providing a wide range of security and privacy-aware design aspects to address the requirements of the human condition. The plan is to combine XR and gamification into a simulation environment for various scenarios involving virtual people and objects. Such an environment will facilitate cyber attacks and reciprocal strategies focused simulations to promote trustworthiness (Sa/Se/Pr) in XR technologies.

References

1. Adams, R., Finn, P., Moes, E., Flannery, K., Rizzo, A.S.: Distractibility in attention deficit hyperactivity disorder ADHD: the virtual reality classroom. Child Neuropsychol. **15**(2), 120–135 (2009)
2. Aliman, N.M., Kester, L.: Malicious design in AIVR, falsehood and cybersecurity-oriented immersive defenses. In: Proceedings of the 2020 IEEE International Conference on Artificial Intelligence and Virtual Reality (AIVR), pp. 130–137 (2020)
3. Armstrong, T.: The myth of the normal brain: embracing neurodiversity. AMA J. Ethics **17**(4), 348–352 (2015)
4. Association, I.D.: Definition of dyslexia (2014). https://dyslexiaida.org/definition-of-dyslexia/. Accessed 10 Feb 2023
5. Avila-Pesantez, D., Rivera, L.A., Vaca-Cardenas, L., Aguayo, S., Zuñiga, L.: Towards the improvement of ADHD children through augmented reality serious games: preliminary results. In: Proceedings of the 2018 IEEE Global Engineering Education Conference (EDUCON), pp. 843–848 (2018)
6. Belsey, B.: Cyberbullying: an emerging threat to the "always on" generation. Recuperado el **5**, 2010 (2005)
7. Bernsland, M., et al.: CS:NO - an extended reality experience for cyber security education. In: Proceedings of the ACM International Conference on Interactive Media Experiences, pp. 287–292. ACM, Aveiro JB Portugal (2022)

8. Bertilsdotter Rosqvist, H., Chown, N., Stenning, A. (eds.): Neurodiversity Studies: A New Critical Paradigm. Routledge advances in sociology, Routledge, New York (2020)
9. Biederman, J., Faraone, S.V.: The effects of attention-deficit/hyperactivity disorder on employment and household income. Medscape Gen. Med. **8**(3), 12 (2006)
10. Biocca, F., Tang, A., Owen, C., Xiao, F.: Attention funnel: omnidirectional 3D cursor for mobile augmented reality platforms. In: Proceedings of the SIGCHI Conference on Human Factors in Computing Systems, pp. 1115–1122. ACM, Montréal Québec Canada (2006)
11. Bonanni, L., Lee, C.H., Selker, T.: Attention-based design of augmented reality interfaces. In: Proceedings of the CHI 2005 Extended Abstracts on Human Factors in Computing Systems, pp. 1228–1231. ACM, Portland (2005)
12. Brimo, K., Dinkler, L., Gillberg, C., Lichtenstein, P., Lundström, S., Åsberg Johnels, J.: The co-occurrence of neurodevelopmental problems in dyslexia. Dyslexia **27**(3), 277–293 (2021)
13. British Dyslexia Association: Definition of dyslexia. https://www.bdadyslexia.org.uk/news/definition-of-dyslexia. Accessed 10 Feb 2023
14. Canitano, R., Scandurra, V.: Psychopharmacology in autism: an update. Prog. Neuropsychopharmacol. Biol. Psychiatry **35**(1), 18–28 (2011)
15. Casey, P., Baggili, I., Yarramreddy, A.: Immersive virtual reality attacks and the human joystick. IEEE Trans. Dependable Secure Comput. **18**(2), 550–562 (2021)
16. Chun, M.M., Golomb, J.D., Turk-Browne, N.B.: A taxonomy of external and internal attention. Annu. Rev. Psychol. **62**(1), 73–101 (2011)
17. Cowan, N.: Working memory underpins cognitive development, learning, and education. Educ. Psychol. Rev. **26**(2), 197–223 (2014)
18. Cuervo, E., Chintalapudi, K., Kotaru, M.: Creating the perfect illusion: what will it take to create life-like virtual reality headsets? In: Proceedings of the 19th International Workshop on Mobile Computing Systems & Applications, pp. 7–12. ACM, Tempe Arizona USA (2018)
19. Dall'Acqua, L., Gironacci, I.: Using extended reality to support cyber security. In: Political Decision-Making and Security Intelligence: Recent Techniques and Technological Developments, chap. 8, pp. 146–166. IGI Global (2020)
20. Danielson, M.L., et al.: State-level estimates of the prevalence of parent-reported ADHD diagnosis and treatment among US. Children and Adoilescents, 2016 to 2019. J. Attention Disord. **26**(13), 1685–1697 (2022)
21. Desimone, R., Duncan, J.: Neural mechanisms of selective visual attention. Annu. Rev. Neurosci. **18**(1), 193–222 (1995)
22. Dewani, A., Memon, M.A., Bhatti, S.: Cyberbullying detection: advanced preprocessing techniques & deep learning architecture for roman Urdu data. J. Big Data **8**(1), 160 (2021)
23. Ellerweg, R.: Make frame rate studies useful for system designers. In: Proceedings of the 2018 International Conference on Graphics and Interaction (ICGI), pp. 1–8. IEEE, Lisbon (2018)
24. Frolli, A., et al.: Children on the autism spectrum and the use of virtual reality for supporting social skills. Children **9**(2), 181 (2022)
25. Fuermaier, A., et al.: Cognitive impairment in adult ADHD-perspective matters! Neuropsychology **29**(1), 45 (2015)
26. Fuermaier, A.B.M., et al.: Perception in attention deficit hyperactivity disorder. ADHD Attention Deficit Hyperactivity Disord. **10**(1), 21–47 (2018)
27. Geiger, G., et al.: Wide and diffuse perceptual modes characterize dyslexics in vision and audition. Perception **37**(11), 1745–1764 (2008)

28. Gugenheimer, J., et al.: Novel challenges of safety, security and privacy in extended reality. In: Extended Abstracts of the 2022 CHI Conference on Human Factors in Computing Systems. CHI EA 2022, ACM, New York (2022)

29. Halmøy, A., Fasmer, O.B., Gillberg, C., Haavik, J.: Occupational outcome in adult ADHD: impact of symptom profile, comorbid psychiatric problems, and treatment: a cross-sectional study of 414 clinically diagnosed adult ADHD patients. J. Atten. Disord. **13**(2), 175–187 (2009)

30. Hart, M.: Embracing dyslexia - crossing the chasm and saving lives (2020). https://mgiep.unesco.org/article/embracing-dyslexia-crossing-the-chasm-and-saving-lives. Accessed 10 Feb 2023

31. Heller, B.: Watching androids dream of electric sheep: immersive technology, biometric psychography, and the law. Vanderbilt J. Entertainment Technol. Law **23**(1), 1 (2020)

32. Jenaro, C., Flores, N., Frías, C.P.: Anxiety and depression in cyberbullied college students: a retrospective study. J. Interpers. Violence **36**(1-2), 579–602 (2021)

33. Jin, G., Tu, M., Kim, T.H., Heffron, J., White, J.: Evaluation of game-based learning in cybersecurity education for high school students. J. Educ. Learn. (EduLearn) **12**(1), 150–158 (2018)

34. Karantzas, G., Patsakis, C.: An empirical assessment of endpoint detection and response systems against advanced persistent threats attack vectors. J. Cybersec. Priv. **1**(3), 387–421 (2021)

35. Kennedy, R.S., Drexler, J., Kennedy, R.C.: Research in visually induced motion sickness. Appl. Ergon. **41**(4), 494–503 (2010)

36. Kofler, M.J., Rapport, M.D., Bolden, J., Sarver, D.E., Raiker, J.S.: ADHD and working memory: the impact of central executive deficits and exceeding storage/rehearsal capacity on observed inattentive behavior. J. Abnorm. Child Psychol. **38**(2), 149–161 (2010)

37. Kofler, M.J., Soto, E.F., Fosco, W.D., Irwin, L.N., Wells, E.L., Sarver, D.E.: Working memory and information processing in ADHD: evidence for directionality of effects. Neuropsychology **34**(2), 127–143 (2020)

38. von Károlyi, C., Winner, E., Gray, W., Sherman, G.F.: Dyslexia linked to talent: global visual-spatial ability. Brain Lang. **85**(3), 427–431 (2003)

39. Lane, S.J., Reynolds, S.: Sensory over-responsivity as an added dimension in ADHD. Front. Integr. Neurosci. **13**, 40 (2019)

40. Leitner, Y.: The co-occurrence of autism and attention deficit hyperactivity disorder in children - what do we know? Front. Hum. Neurosci. **8**, 268 (2014)

41. Lorenz, T., Reznik, N., Heinitz, K.: A different point of view: the neurodiversity approach to autism and work. In: Fitzgerald, M., Yip, J. (eds.) Autism - Paradigms, Recent Research and Clinical Applications. InTech (2017)

42. Lukava, T., Ramirez, D.Z.M., Barbareschi, G.: Two sides of the same coin: accessibility practices and neurodivergent users' experience of extended reality. J. Enabl. Technol. **16**, 75–90 (2022)

43. Maenner, M.J.: Prevalence and characteristics of autism spectrum disorder among children aged 8 years - Autism and developmental disabilities monitoring network, 11 Sites, United States, 2018. MMWR Surveill. Summ. **70**, 1 (2021)

44. Maskati, E., Alkeraiem, F., Khalil, N., Baik, R., Aljuhani, R., Alsobhi, A.: Using virtual reality (VR) in teaching students with dyslexia. Int. J. Emerg. Technol. Learn. (iJET) **16**(09), 291 (2021)

45. McCarthy, J.E., Swierenga, S.J.: What we know about dyslexia and web accessibility: a research review. Univ. Access Inf. Soc. **9**(2), 147–152 (2010)

46. Mcgee, M.: Neurodiversity. Contexts **11**(3), 12–13 (2012)
47. McNamara, A., Kabeerdoss, C.: Mobile augmented reality: placing labels based on gaze position. In: Proceedings of the 2016 IEEE International Symposium on Mixed and Augmented Reality (ISMAR-Adjunct), pp. 36–37. IEEE, Merida, Yucatan, Mexico (2016)
48. Merikangas, K.R., et al.: Lifetime prevalence of mental disorders in US. J. Am. Acad. Child Adoilescent Psychiatry **49**(10), 980–989 (2010)
49. Mhaldll, A.H., Schaub, F.: Identifying manipulative advertising techniques in XR through scenario construction. In: Proceedings of the 2021 CHI Conference on Human Factors in Computing Systems. CHI 2021, ACM, New York (2021)
50. Milosevic, T., Van Royen, K., Davis, B.: Artificial intelligence to address cyberbullying, harassment and abuse: new directions in the midst of complexity. Int. J. Bullying Prev. **4**(1), 1–5 (2022)
51. Mock, P., Tibus, M., Ehlis, A.C., Baayen, H., Gerjets, P.: Predicting ADHD risk from touch interaction data. In: Proceedings of the 20th ACM International Conference on Multimodal Interaction, pp. 446–454. ACM, Boulder (2018)
52. Morshedzadeh, E., Dunkenberger, M.B., Nagle, L., Ghasemi, S., York, L., Horn, K.: Tapping into community expertise: stakeholder engagement in the design process. Policy Des. Pract., 1–21 (2022)
53. Oberauer, K.: Working memory and attention - a conceptual analysis and review. J. Cogn. **2**(1), 36 (2019)
54. Ocay, A.B., Rustia, R.A., Palaoag, T.D.: Utilizing augmented reality in improving the frustration tolerance of ADHD learners: An experimental study. In: Proceedings of the 2nd International Conference on Digital Technology in Education (ICDTE 2018), pp. 58–63. ACM Press, Bangkok, Thailand (2018)
55. Odeleye, B., Loukas, G., Heartfield, R., Sakellari, G., Panaousis, E., Spyridonis, F.: Virtually secure: a taxonomic assessment of cybersecurity challenges in virtual reality environments. Comput. Sec. **124**, 102951 (2023)
56. Odeleye, B., Loukas, G., Heartfield, R., Spyridonis, F.: Detecting framerate-oriented cyber attacks on user experience in virtual reality. In: Proceedings of the USENIX Symposium on Usable Privacy and Security (SOUPS) (2021)
57. Ohl, A., Grice Sheff, M., Small, S., Nguyen, J., Paskor, K., Zanjirian, A.: Predictors of employment status among adults with autism spectrum disorder. Work **56**(2), 345–355 (2017)
58. Orji, J., Hernandez, A., Selema, B., Orji, R.: Virtual and augmented reality applications for promoting safety and security: a systematic review. In: Proceedings of the 2022 IEEE 10th International Conference on Serious Games and Applications for Health (SeGAH), pp. 1–7 (2022), ISSN: 2573–3060
59. Petracca, G., Sun, Y., Jaeger, T., Atamli, A.: AuDroid: Preventing attacks on audio channels in mobile devices. In: Proceedings of the 31st Annual Computer Security Applications Conference (ASAC 2015), pp. 181–190. ACSAC 2015, New York (2015)
60. Polanczyk, G., de Lima, M.S., Horta, B.L., Biederman, J., Rohde, L.A.: The worldwide prevalence of ADHD: a systematic review and metaregression analysis. Am. J. Psychiatry **164**(6), 942–948 (2007)
61. Pollak, Y., et al.: The utility of a continuous performance test embedded in virtual reality in measuring ADHD-related deficits. J. Develop. Behav. Pediatr. **30**(1), 2–6 (2009)
62. Renaud, K., Coles-Kemp, L.: Accessible and inclusive cyber security: a nuanced and complex challenge. SN Comput. Sci. **3**(5), 346 (2022)

63. Rodríguez-Cano, S., DelgAdoi-Benito, V., Ausín-Villaverde, V., Martín, L.M.: Design of a virtual reality software to promote the learning of students with dyslexia. Sustainability **13**(15), 8425 (2021)
64. Roesner, F., Kohno, T., Molnar, D.: Security and privacy for augmented reality systems. Commun. ACM **57**(4), 88–96 (2014)
65. Russell, G., Pavelka, Z.: Co-occurrence of developmental disorders: children who share symptoms of autism, dyslexia and attention deficit hyperactivity disorder. In: Fitzgerald, M. (ed.) Recent Advances in Autism Spectrum Disorders, chap. 17. IntechOpen, Rijeka (2013)
66. Rylaarsdam, L., Guemez-Gamboa, A.: Genetic causes and modifiers of autism spectrum disorder. Front. Cell. Neurosci. **13**, 385 (2019)
67. Schumacher, J., Hoffmann, P., Schmal, C., Schulte-Korne, G., Nothen, M.M.: Genetics of dyslexia: the evolving landscape. J. Med. Genet. **44**(5), 289–297 (2007)
68. Secnik, K., Swensen, A., Lage, M.J.: Comorbidities and costs of adult patients diagnosed with attention-deficit hyperactivity disorder. Pharmacoeconomics **23**(1), 93–102 (2005). https://doi.org/10.2165/00019053-200523010-00008
69. Shi, C., et al.: Face-mic: inferring live speech and speaker identity via subtle facial dynamics captured by AR/VR motion sensors. In: Proceedings of the 27th Annual International Conference on Mobile Computing and Networking, pp. 478–490. MobiCom 2021, ACM, New York (2021)
70. Spiel, K., Hornecker, E., Williams, R.M., Good, J.: ADHD and technology research - investigated by neurodivergent readers. In: Proceedings of the CHI Conference on Human Factors in Computing Systems, pp. 1–21. ACM, New Orleans (2022)
71. Thome, J., et al.: Biomarkers for attention-deficit/hyperactivity disorder ADHD. A consensus report of the WFSBP task force on biological markers and the World Federation of ADHD. World J. Biol. Psychiatry **13**(5), 379–400 (2012)
72. Tosto, C., et al.: Exploring the effect of an augmented reality literacy programme for reading and spelling difficulties for children diagnosed with ADHD. Virtual Reality **25**(3), 879–894 (2021)
73. Tseng, W.J., et al.: The dark side of perceptual manipulations in virtual reality. In: Proceedings of the 2022 CHI Conference on Human Factors in Computing Systems, pp. 1–15. CHI 2022, ACM, New York (2022)
74. University of Miami Miller School of Medicine: Cyberbullying linked to increased depression and PTSD, 22 January 2020. https://www.sciencedaily.com/releases/2020/01/200122080526.htm. Accessed 10 Feb 2023
75. Valluripally, S., Gulhane, A., Hoque, K.A., Calyam, P.: Modeling and defense of social virtual reality attacks inducing cybersickness. IEEE Trans. Dependable Secure Comput. **19**(6), 4127–4144 (2021)
76. Vortmann, L.M.: Attention-driven interaction systems for augmented reality. In: Proceedings of the 2019 International Conference on Multimodal Interaction, pp. 482–486. ICMI 2019, ACM, New York (2019)
77. Wang, K., Julier, S.J., Cho, Y.: Attention-based applications in extended reality to support autistic users: a systematic review. IEEE Access **10**, 15574–15593 (2022)
78. Wang, Y., Otitoju, K., Liu, T., Kim, S., Bowman, D.A.: Evaluating the effects of real world distraction on user performance in virtual environments. In: Proceedings of the ACM symposium on Virtual reality software and technology, pp. 19–26. ACM, Limassol Cyprus (2006)
79. Wedyan, M., et al.: Augmented reality for autistic children to enhance their understanding of facial expressions. Multimodal Technol. Interact. **5**(8), 48 (2021)

80. WHO: Definition of the concept of safety (1998). https://www.inspq.qc.ca/en/quebec-collaborating-centre-safety-promotion-and-injury-prevention/definition-concept-safety. Accessed 10 Feb. 2023

81. Wickens, C.D.: The structure of attentional resources. Attention Perform. VIII **8**, 239–257 (1980)

82. Wickens, C.D., Hollands, J.G., Banbury, S., Parasuraman, R.: Engineering Psychology and Human Performance. Psychology Press, London (2015)

83. Wiebe, A., Kannen, K., Li, M., Aslan, B., Andoro, D., Selaskowski, B., Ettinger, U., Lux, S., Philipsen, A., Braun, N.: Multimodal virtual reality -based assessment of adult ADHD: a feasibility study in healthy subjects. Assessment, 10731911221089193 (2022)

84. Williams, D.M., Nicholson, T., Grainger, C., Lind, S.E., Carruthers, P.: Can you spot a liar? Deception, mindreading, and the case of autism spectrum disorder. Autism Res. **11**(8), 1129–1137 (2018)

85. Zeidan, J.: Global prevalence of autism. Autism Res. **15**(5), 778–790 (2022)

86. Zhang, L., et al.: ADHDgene: a genetic database for attention deficit hyperactivity disorder. Nucleic Acids Res. **40**(D1), D1003–D1009 (2012)

87. Zulauf, C.A., Sprich, S.E., Safren, S.A., Wilens, T.E.: The complicated relationship between attention deficit hyperactivity disorder and substance use disorders. Curr. Psychiatry Rep. **16**(3), 436 (2014)

"Stay Out of My Way!": The Impact of Cookie Consent Notice Design on Young Users' Decision

Aysun Ogut$^{(\boxtimes)}$ (iD)

Sabanci University, 34956 Tuzla, Istanbul, Turkey
aysuno@sabanciuniv.edu

Abstract. Websites use *Cookies* to store the information and preferences of users and may collect this information for different purposes such as session continuity, customized experience for users, and a data source for the advertisement strategies of third parties. As the subject of data and user security becomes essential, the collection of these cookies without the consent of the users and the fact that they are not informed of the cookie collection has become a concern. Cookie consent notices have emerged to address this problem and to make users aware of the cookies. The main objective of this study is to understand how users respond to different cookie consent designs and whether the designs affect giving consent. Participants were asked to fulfill the tasks that include an item search from four different websites. However, while doing this, the main observation was how the participants reacted to the consent notice on these websites. The results of the study show that the acceptance rate of cookies is 100% for consent notices that occupy the middle of the page and prevent further action. In addition, the presence of a reject button or option for editing the preferences does not affect the consent rate considerably. Also, the detailedness or length of the text in the notice has no effect and all the participants declared that they did not read it. 90% of the participants said they accepted or closed it just to continue their task and remove the consent notice from the interface.

Keywords: Cookies · Consent Notices · Usability of Cookie Banners

1 Introduction

The number of websites displaying cookie consent notices has increased. One of the critical reasons for this is regulations that mandate users to be informed about the protection of their data. For instance, all websites belonging to the European Union and operating in these countries must comply with the GDPR, General Data Protection Regulation [1]. The regulation includes articles regarding how the cookie consent notices should be designed and failure to comply may result in penalties. However, these regulations are not global and there are many variations of cookie consent designs with different components. This diversity raises the question of which design provides better usability.

According to Habib et al. [2], for the cookie consent to be usable, the design should be descriptive and inclusive for the user's needs, the user should be able to undo the action they have taken, and attention should be paid to the points such as reducing the error rate in the selection. They suggested that the usability of the cookie consent that occupies a large portion of the page and contains all options is quite high.

In many cookie consent designs, texts insufficiently take place and there is a lack of buttons and options [3]. The fact that the text in the notice is not descriptive and complete may cause the user to not be informed enough, and also the absence of buttons may indicate that the user's behavior is interfered with.

The cookie consents and their proper design also have important effects in terms of user security. The existence of cookie consent helps users to be more aware of their security on websites [4]. So, the design not only affects the experience of the user but also enables them to manage their security and privacy.

Although the importance of cookie consent from the point of security and usability has been studied, how the design directs the user's decision has not been explored much. Do different cookie consent designs lead users to make different choices? This study tries to investigate how the location, reject and close options, and visibility of the cookie consent on the website interface affect the rate of consent to the collection of cookies.

Outcomes show that the consent notices in the middle of the page get the most interaction and consent for cookie collection. The reject button in the cookie consent does not make a big difference in user selection, while the addition of the close icon draws the interaction in this direction. The only purpose of interacting with the consent notice is to remove it from the interface for most of the users and they do not read the internal text at all. Also, the consent notice tends to be closed if it partially blocks the task element or switched to another page on the same website.

This paper first discusses the methodology of the testing, then analyzes the data from both testing and the questionnaire. After presenting the results, it makes an optimal design suggestion.

Ethics. This study involves human subjects. In this regard, the participants were informed about the study, and their consent was obtained at the beginning. Participants have been kept anonymous, and no identifying data was requested during the testing and questionnaire. Also, no additional information distinguishing the identities of these participants was recorded during the test observation.

2 Methodology

The main objective of this study is to understand the relationship between the rate of consent for cookie collection and the consent notice designs on the websites. Therefore, the following questions constitute the research questions:

- How does the *location* of the cookie consent notice on the website interface affect the rate of consent to the collection of cookies?
- How does the *presence of Close and Reject buttons* in the cookie consent notice affect the rate of consent to the collection of cookies?

– How does the *visibility* on the page (in terms of color and contrast) of the cookie consent notice affect the rate of consent to the collection of cookies?

Website designers and CMPs, consent management providers, take different tacks while deciding on the manner of how to represent preferences, such as demonstrating cookie notices to the users in a format of a pop-up that fills a major part of the screen or presenting them as a small banner at the bottom of the page that lets the users continue with limitations to choose some option for the cookies. In this study, different cookie banner designs were examined in terms of usability and effectiveness.

I worked with 10 participants and while choosing the participants, attention was paid to the equality of men and women. However, it is not intended to make any observations based on gender, ethnicity, or education level. The point considered was the previous knowledge of the user about the websites and cookie banners. For instance, if participants were chosen in a way that some had advanced knowledge about using a website while some had limited knowledge, the results could have been misleading. Thus, while deciding the participants, the internet users who have experience in navigating websites and have familiarity with website elements were selected. I assumed that people with longer browsing time would come across more cookie consent notices. The age range with the highest Internet use and familiarity with website elements is 12–24 [5] and considering the correct understanding of the study environment and the tasks, it was decided to work with participants between the ages of 15–24. Participants were randomly selected with their consent.

The testing was completed in a room by providing a computer to the participants. Throughout the study, all the sessions were recorded with their consent to ensure the reliability of the testing environment. The questionnaire was prepared via Google Forms, and they answered the questionnaire right after the testing, with the same computer that is provided to them.

As it is intended to monitor users' reactions to cookie consent during their daily website browsing, participants were not informed that their interaction with consent notices was being observed, to prevent extra attention from changing their decisions. On the contrary, participants were asked to complete small tasks on the websites. While they were performing the task, their behaviors toward the cookie banner, pop-up consent, and the buttons the notices have were recorded.

For the study, I determined four websites with four different cookie banner designs as experimental websites. Therefore, I selected Trendyol [6], Karnaval [7], Sahibinden [8], and Hurriyet [9]. These websites were not randomly selected, they have cookie banner designs with different aspects, only the value to be observed is different and other elements remain the same.

As seen in Fig. 1, the cookie banner appearing on Trendyol, an online shopping website, is placed at the bottom, in contrast to the color of the page. In other words, it can be easily noticed that there is a banner. There is no icon to close the banner or a reject button, only the accept button set as the primary action button. However, by looking carefully at the first line, there is an underlined link hidden in the text for the user to reject the cookie consent, but it is not in an easily noticeable position and a way for the user. It looks like a continuation of the existing information text.

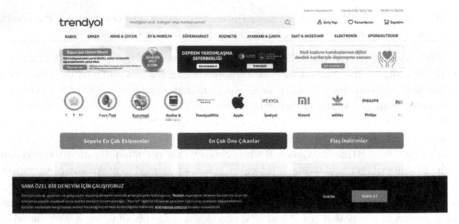

Fig. 1. Screenshot of Trendyol Main Page

Karnaval, a radio streaming website (Fig. 2), has a different design than Trendyol because the first thing to do is to handle it. Otherwise, it is not possible to operate on the website. It does not disappear when pressed anywhere other than this pop-up in the middle of the page. When the left button, Manage Options, is pressed, it is possible to choose whether to allow selected third parties. However, since there are many third parties, it may take a long time to perform this manually. This button is used in the primary action color as the Accept button and it may direct the user to press. The button that performs the same function has been placed as a link beside the accept button on Trendyol's website and has been implemented in a way that makes selection difficult.

Karnaval's cookie pop-up has the same functional buttons as the Trendyol cookie banner, so the main difference is the location. For the first research question (How does the *location* of the cookie consent notice on the website interface affect the rate of consent to the collection of cookies?), the comparison between Trendyol and Karnaval's cookie notices will reveal the reaction difference in terms of location. In this case, the independent variable is the location of the cookie banner.

The third website is Sahibinden, an online shopping website (Fig. 3). The reason to choose this website is when looking at the cookie banner, it has a similar location and color to Trendyol's, but the content of the buttons inside it differs. Unlike Trendyol, the Accept and Reject buttons are implemented with a clear explanation and designed with the same level of action, and there is also an icon to close the banner. The comparison between cookie banners implemented on Trendyol and Sahibinden websites addresses the second research question (How does the *presence of Close and Reject buttons* in the cookie consent notice affect the rate of consent to the collection of cookies?). The independent variable here is the reject and close buttons.

The last website is Hurriyet, a news website (Fig. 4). The cookie banner on this website is also located at the bottom of the website. The difference from other bottom-placed banners is that it almost becomes a whole with the page. While seeing the white background throughout the page, positioning the banner as white and indistinguishable from the other elements of the page may create confusion for the user. This banner also allows rejecting and closing the banner, just like in Sahibinden. Results for the third

Fig. 2. Screenshot of Karnaval Main Page

Fig. 3. Screenshot of Sahibinden Main Page

research question (How does the *visibility* on the page (in terms of color and contrast) of the cookie consent notice affect the rate of consent to the collection of cookies?) aimed to be observed by comparing Sahibinden and Hurriyet. While making this observation, the independent variable is the color of the cookie banner, that is, its distinguishability from the page.

Before starting the test on these four different websites, participants were informed about the experiment and stated that they were not tested and that the website was tested. Therefore, they could progress in the way and speed they wanted without pressure. Also, as an important remark, each website must be entered from an incognito tab during all tests because if the participant has visited this website before, there is a probability that the cookie banner will not appear. To eliminate the risk here, the participant was informed about opening an incognito tab at the beginning of each test case. The data collected in the test is what decision they made in the selection of cookie banners on websites: if cookie consent is being accepted, rejected, closed or preferences are being

Fig. 4. Screenshot of Hurriyet Main Page

set. The consent decision and reaction of the user through cookie banners were collected by monitoring these actions of the user during the test.

The participants were told that four different websites were tested for usability and that they would complete small tasks on them. I prepared a flow to ensure that all participants follow the same action sequence in the tasks. The steps are as follows:

1. Please open an incognito tab
2. Go to trendyol.com and wait for the page to load,
3. Type "White Backpack" in the search field and search for the product,
4. Click on the first result and add it to the cart,
5. The first task is done.
6. Open a new incognito tab,
7. Go to karnaval.com and wait for the page to load,
8. Press the search button in the top right corner,
9. Type and search for "Nilufer",
10. The second task is done.
11. Open a new incognito tab,
12. Go to sahibinden.com and wait for the page to load,
13. Type "Mercedes c180" in the search field and search,
14. Enter the first ad and click on the technical specifications button below,
15. The third task is done.
16. Open a new incognito tab,
17. Go to hurriyet.com.tr and wait for the page to load,
18. Click on the search icon in the top right corner,
19. Search for the word "School" in the new tab that opens,
20. Click on the third news,
21. The fourth task is done.

After the task was successfully completed, the main purpose of recording the decision regarding cookie consent was explained to the participant and the participant was asked about her/his intention. This intention and awareness were investigated with a questionnaire after the testing was over. While preparing questions, some of the questions from Habib et al. [2] were used since they constitute the questions with fundamental aspects of this topic.

In addition, before starting the actual experiment, I conducted a pilot study to make sure that the flow was working correctly and was applicable. The steps that needed to be changed were fixed before the actual experiment began. A minimum of confusion and error was aimed at the participant. For instance, it was checked if the banners were displayed correctly in each session.

3 Results and Analysis of Data

This study sought to understand the behavior of experienced internet users when cookie consent notices are displayed on various websites. Participants were all native Turkish speakers, and the questionnaire was conducted in Turkish to make sure that they create the browsing environment they are used to and that they are answered in the comfort of their native language. Half of the ten participants are female, and half are male, and the average age of these participants is 22. 90% of the participants are university students.

The data collected during the test was what action the participants took against the cookie banners, that is, how did they interact. There are five actions the user could take: Accept, Reject, Edit Preferences, Close, and No Choice. If they gave the cookie consent, *Accept,* if they refused, *Reject,* if they edited the selected cookies with their preferences, *Edit Preferences*, if they closed the banner from the close icon, *Close*, and if they continued their tasks without any reaction to the banner, *No Choice* data was collected. Details of all responses can be seen in Appendix.

3.1 Testing Outcomes

Trendyol. 70% of the participants doing the task on Trendyol's website, that is, the majority of them, continued their task while ignoring the banner, and the rest accepted. No user has rejected or edited their preferences from the settings. It can be said that since the reject action is included in the text, participants had difficulty finding it at first glance.

Karnaval. The results for Karnaval show that 90% of participants agreed to give consent for the cookie collection. The remaining 10% wanted to edit their preferences, but when they noticed that the process was taking a long time, they accepted all the cookies to return their task. It can be concluded that all users who entered Karnaval approved giving cookie consent since it was challenging to reject.

Sahibinden. The cookie banner on Sahibinden yielded various outcomes. 50% of the participants closed the banner without making a positive or negative choice, 20% consented to collect cookies, 20% did nothing, and the remaining 10% rejected. The variety of banner options, such as the "Reject All" and "Accept All" buttons with the same size and a visible close icon, may have contributed to this difference. When a close icon and a reject button are present at the same time, users seem to prefer closing rather than rejecting. In addition, at one time during this task, some of the participants stopped ignoring the banner and closed it, as it partially blocked the element to be clicked on.

Hurriyet. While approximately 70% of the participants who encountered Hurriyet's cookie banner did not engage in any interaction, the rest performed other actions equally. The banner was located at the bottom of the page and was smaller than the banners on other websites. In addition, because it was the same color as the background of the website and very complicated to notice, also it was not in a structure that drew the attention of the participants. However, although the variety of options remained, most of the participants preferred to ignore the banner.

3.2 Questionnaire Outcomes

To understand what their true intentions were and how much they noticed the cookie banners, a questionnaire was conducted right after the test. All participants stated that they completed the test without any problems. Then, they are asked if they remembered that they had made a privacy decision during the test. 40% of the participants remember that they took such an action, while the others do not remember or are not sure. Slightly more participants are not sure exactly whether they notice a cookie banner on all pages. Another question was why they reacted to the cookie banner. Categorization of the responses indicates that most users chose the action to access the web page interface to continue or because they made a random choice. No one here responded that they took this action because they want to protect their data or because this issue is important to them. 80% of the participants declared that the choice they made on the cookie banners was because they found it easiest to remove the banner from the interface. The remaining 20% stated they chose a random option. Most of the participants made a quick choice to continue with the tasks, they are aware of this and accept it. In addition, 70% of the participants declared they did not pay any attention to the options such as buttons, links, and icons on the cookie banner.

The texts on the banners were not read carefully by any participant. While 80% said that they had never read, 20% stated that they passed by skimming. This points to the question of how useful banner texts really are. No matter how short or how comprehensive the text is, the participant does not take the time to read it. For example, although there is more descriptive and visible text on the cookie pop-up of Karnaval, it was not read. Also, during the testing, it is seen that the participants did not read the text inside the consent notices.

Interestingly, although 60% of participants say that cookie banners and options were easy to understand, the same percentage say they felt like they have no control over cookies and their data. So, people are aware of the concept of a cookie banner, but they are not entirely sure about protecting their data with cookie consent.

To summarize, if the cookie consent is in a way that blocks access to the page, participants try to handle it somehow, they accept it to get rid of it or because they do not care. If the banner is located at the bottom, they usually do not take any action on it and the banner remains there. Apart from the acceptance rate, when looking at the total interaction rates with the banner (Accept, Reject, Closed, Edit Preferences), Karnaval has the most reacted cookie banner with 100%, Trendyol has the most ignored banner with 30% (Fig. 5).

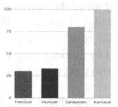

Fig. 5. Total Interaction in Cookie Banner on Each Website

Looking at the descriptive results of testing, the mode is *No Choice* for Trendyol, *No Choice* for Hurriyet, *Close* for Sahibinden, and *Accept* for Karnaval. When *how much control did you feel you had over the cookies used on the website?* asked the participants, between the range of 1–5 (1-none, 5-very), the mean is 2.3, the median is 1.5 and the mode is 1. The results for the question, *how easy was it for you to understand the cookie banner and the options on it?* show that between the range of (1-not easy at all, 5-very easy), the mean is 3.1, the median is 3.5 and the mode is 4. It can be commented that these results show most of the participants find the banner easy to understand, but they do not benefit from this convenience when it comes to real consideration.

4 Discussion

The first research question *How does the location of the cookie consent notice on the website interface affect the rate of consent to the collection of cookies?* was formed to explore the importance of the location of the banner for user selection. When comparing the results for Trendyol and Karnaval in which only the location is the independent variable and the other components are mostly identical, Karnaval has a higher consent acceptance rate than Trendyol. One of the most noticeable reasons for the greater interaction rate with the cookie consent of Karnaval is that it is in the middle of the page and does not allow further processing. The questionnaire results and testing results are also compatible. In the questionnaire, many of the participants stated that they interacted because they wanted the banner to be removed from the interface. Although the consent notice text on Trendyol is briefer than the text on Karnaval, neither one is read. The rate of consent to the collection of cookies is higher in cookie notice designs that appear in the middle and cover most of the page.

For the second research question, *How does the presence of Close and Reject buttons in the cookie consent notice affect the acceptance rate of the cookie collection consent?*, the results for Trendyol and Sahibinden were compared since they have similar cookie banner designs. For example, both have a black background color in the banner, and they have kind of similar text. The only difference is the presence of the Reject button and Close icon in Sahibinden (see Fig. 6 & Fig. 7). Although there is not much distinction in the design, the result differs. Comparing Sahibinden with the close icon and Trendyol without it, users seem to close the banner more than do nothing.

Although there are both reject and accept buttons on Sahibinden's banner, the interaction with either was not high as the close icon. It can be presumed that removing is coded in the mind more with a close icon than a reject button. Therefore, when removing the banner that appeared in front of the participant while performing the tasks, it caused the participants to use the close icon rather than the reject button. In response to the second research question, the reject button does not create much difference, but the close icon tends to be selected by participants. Also, almost no participant updated preferences and only one person who went into preferences gave up on editing them and accepted them all.

Lastly, the third research question analyzes *How does the visibility on the page (in terms of color and contrast) of the cookie consent notice affect the rate of consent to the collection of cookies?* by comparing the banners on Sahibinden and Hurriyet. Although the two banners included similar text and buttons, the cookie banner of Hurriyet was displayed in the same color as the background, in a smaller size, and looked like another component of the website (see Fig. 7 & Fig. 8).

Fig. 6. Cookie Banner on Trendyol

Fig. 7. Cookie Banner on Sahibinden

Fig. 8. Cookie Banner on Hurriyet

While half of the participants preferred to close Sahibinden's cookie banner from the closing icon, the same users continued their tasks without making any choices in Hurriyet. When looking at the rate of interaction with the cookie banner (Fig. 5), there is an interaction rate of 80% from Sahibinden, while this rate drops to 30% in Hurriyet. Participants' difficulties in seeing and distinguishing the banner in Hurriyet increase the ignore rate. In response to the third research question, it is difficult to conclude that the distinguishability of the banner on the page increases the rate of consent because only 10% of the participants on both websites accepted cookies.

Limitations. A limited number of participants were included in this study. The reason for utilizing this approach in this study is that the same results tend to be observed as the number of test users increases in finding usability problems [10]. However, if more banner designs and websites are aimed to check, the increase in the number of participants can contribute to obtaining further observations. In addition, since the participants cover a certain age range, another age group may yield different results. A small sample set of websites has been used throughout this study, but there are several websites with various cookie banner designs. Therefore, studies with a comparison of other designs may produce different outcomes. A short task flow was followed on the websites. If the duration of the tasks is longer, the reaction to the banner may change. For instance, participants may give a different reaction half an hour later to the banner that they did not make a choice at the first encounter. In this study, only the reaction given at the time of entering the website is discussed.

5 Conclusion

Multiple cookie consent designs were compared to comprehend the impacts of the design on usability. None of the participants who fulfilled the task on the websites focused entirely on cookie banner content and they affirmed that. Regardless of the design, it was not seen that the participants took the action to protect their data security and privacy. The most significant reason for interacting with the cookie banner is to remove it from the website interface to be able to continue the task. However, there have been different outcomes of separate designs.

The cookie consent located in the middle of the page increases the interaction rate and also increases the consent rate for acceptance of the cookies. Having a close icon on the banner increases the usability and interaction of the banner, while the reject button has no effect. However, from the user's point of view, it is the right of the users to have the opportunity to refuse cookies. Finally, the distinctive design of the banner such as color and contrast distinctions from the page also increases the interaction rate. No change is observed in the rejection or acceptance rate in the banners when all options are offered to the user, such as Accept, Reject, and Edit Preferences.

Considering all these data, a cookie consent positioned in the middle of the page and visibly separated from the original page, with a close icon, and accept/reject buttons forms an optimal design. The fact that the text in the banner is meaningful and consists of words that explain the concept can improve the perception. Instead of a sentence such as "We use cookies to improve your experience", sentences in which the keywords privacy, data, security, and third party are emphasized should be used. In this regard, my suggestion is to design a banner that is visually enriched and begins the text with a particularly emphasized keyword or sentence. With a 2-page cookie pop-up design with a well-emphasized consent text on the first page and accept, reject, or edit options on the second page, users' attention can be attracted. The important point in the implementation of this design is that the keywords in the text on the first page are highlighted. Although this study did not primarily focus on the text in the banner, further studies observing the effect of the banner text on the user's behavior will contribute to creating better-designed consent notices.

Cookie consent notices are one of the first elements that appear as soon as the page is loaded, and the user's first impression should be affected the fastest. Therefore, it has an important place to be designed remarkably. Developing a design that will not frighten or bore the user will also increase people's awareness of privacy-related issues. Raising awareness of the user with the correct design studies builds up trust in the interaction of the human with the computer.

Appendix

Testing results of participants.

Gender	Age	Trendyol	Karnaval	Sahibinden	Hurriyet
Female	21	No choice	Accept	Accept*	No choice
Female	24	No choice	Preferences	Close	No choice
Female	22	No choice	Accept	Reject	Reject
Female	22	No choice	Accept	No choice	No choice
Female	22	Accept	Accept	Close	Close
Male	22	Accept	Accept	Close*	No choice
Male	22	Accept	Accept	Accept	Accept
Male	23	No choice	Accept	Close*	No choice
Male	23	No choice	Accept	Close	No choice
Male	21	No choice	Accept	No choice	No choice
Total		**70% No choice** 30% Accept	**90% Accept** 10% Edit Preferences	**50% Close** 20% Accept 20% No choice 10% Reject	**70% No choice** 10% Reject 10% Accept 10% Close

*At first no choice, then changed

References

1. General Data Protection Regulation. https://gdpr-info.eu/. Accessed 21 Feb 2023
2. Habib, H., Li, M., Young, E., Cranor, L.: "Okay, whatever": an evaluation of cookie consent interfaces. In: CHI 2022: Proceedings of the 2022 CHI Conference on Human Factors in Computing Systems, pp. 1–27. ACM, New York (2022). https://doi.org/10.1145/3491102.3501985
3. Santos, C., Rossi, A., Chamorro, L., Bongard-Blanchy, K., Abu-Salma, R.: Cookie banners, what's the purpose?: analyzing cookie banner text through a legal lens. In: WPES 2021: Proceedings of the 20th Workshop on Workshop on Privacy in the Electronic Society, pp. 187–194. ACM, New York (2021). https://doi.org/10.1145/3463676.3485611
4. Degeling, M., Utz, C., Lentzch, C., Hosseini, H., Schaub, F., Holz, T.: We value your privacy… now take some cookies. Inform. Spekt. **42**, 345–346 (2019). https://doi.org/10.14722/ndss.2019.23378
5. Balčytienė, A., Vinciūnienė, A., Auskalniene, L. Mediatized participation and forms of media use and multiple meaning making: the Baltic perspective. In: Media Transformations, pp. 4–34. Vytautas Magnus University, Kaunas (2012). https://doi.org/10.7220/2029-865X.07.01
6. Trendyol. https://www.trendyol.com. Accessed 22 Feb 2023

7. Karnaval. https://karnaval.com. Accessed 22 Feb 2023
8. Sahibinden. https://www.sahibinden.com. Accessed 22 Feb 2023
9. Hurriyet. https://www.hurriyet.com.tr. Accessed 22 Feb 2023
10. Why You Only Need to Test with 5 Users. https://www.nngroup.com/articles/why-you-only-need-to-test-with-5-users. Accessed 22 Feb 2023

Evaluating Individuals' Cybersecurity Behavior in Mobile Payment Contactless Technologies: Extending TPB with Cybersecurity Awareness

Hana Yousuf[1], Mostafa Al Emran[1,2(✉)], and Khaled Shaalan[1]

[1] Faculty of Engineering & IT, The British University in Dubai, Dubai, UAE
mustafa.n.alemran@gmail.com
[2] Department of Computer Techniques Engineering, Dijlah University College, Baghdad, Iraq

Abstract. Mobile payment contactless technologies involve the transfer of sensitive financial information, making them a potential target for cyberattacks. Understanding cybersecurity behavior in these technologies helps to identify and address vulnerabilities that cybercriminals could exploit. Therefore, this research develops a theoretical model by extending the theory of planned behavior (TPB) with cybersecurity awareness to examine individuals' cybersecurity behavior in mobile payment contactless technologies. The developed model is evaluated based on data collected from 820 mobile payment contactless technology users using a hybrid structural equation modeling (SEM) and artificial neural network (ANN) approach. The results showed that the independent variables explained 52.9% of the variance in cybersecurity behavior. The PLS-SEM results supported all the suggested hypotheses in the developed model. Further, the ANN results indicated that cybersecurity awareness is the most important variable that affects cybersecurity behavior, with normalized importance of 100%. This is followed by perceived behavioral control (45%), subjective norm (38%), and attitude (33%). The results can inform the design and development of secure mobile payment systems and contribute to the broader field of cybersecurity research.

Keywords: cybersecurity behavior · mobile payment · contactless technologies · TPB · cybersecurity awareness · SEM-ANN

1 Introduction

The fourth industrial revolution introduced digital transformation using emerging technologies, such as artificial intelligence, the Internet of Things (IoT), and machine learning [1]. Moreover, the era of disruptive technologies has forced technology companies to transform their intention into enhancing and automating the services to become more accessible through customers' devices. An example of digital transformation is digital payment, where all transactions are made through a channel digitally using digital devices, such as computers, mobile phones, or points of sale [2]. Mobile payment is a transaction where the customers use their mobile devices to make transactions for buying goods through an ecosystem [3]. It is reported that the expected growth of mobile

© The Author(s), under exclusive license to Springer Nature Switzerland AG 2023
A. Moallem (Ed.): HCII 2023, LNCS 14045, pp. 542–554, 2023.
https://doi.org/10.1007/978-3-031-35822-7_35

payment technologies increases by 8.57% each year, indicating the willingness of customers worldwide to continue using these technologies [4]. Contactless mobile payment is a type of payment that uses mobile devices to handle the payment process through a digital platform using radio frequency identification and near-field communication [5].

In the era of COVID-19, contactless mobile payments have grown rapidly and increased opportunities for consumers and service providers [6]. It was the primary payment technology used during the pandemic to reduce human contact with common surfaces in processing payment transactions and reducing the spread of the virus. The benefits of these technologies also extended beyond the pandemic, where many scholars studied the adoption of mobile payments [7–10], with limited studies on mobile payment contactless technologies [6].

The importance of highlighting the cybersecurity behavior in mobile payment lies in the quick adoption of this technology without taking any precautions, especially cybersecurity behavior, to avoid any losses caused by performing improper behavior. In addition to different techniques used in mobile payment contactless technologies adoption, users' cybersecurity behavior toward mobile payment differs completely from users' cybersecurity behavior toward contactless technologies. Users' behavior towards mobile payments concerns all the technologies and regards the mobile as a means for payment, including credit cards, mobile wallets, and digital wallets. However, mobile payment contactless technologies are concerned only about the transactions made by the mobile wirelessly. As per the existing literature, the question of what impacts user cybersecurity behavior in mobile payment contactless technologies remains unexplored. Given that technologies are mainly concerned with user attitude, subjective norms, perceived behavioral control, and cybersecurity awareness (CSA), the effect of these factors on cybersecurity behavior in contactless technologies needs to be explored. To bridge this gap, the present study develops a theoretical model by extending the theory of planned behavior (TPB) with CSA. Understanding the determinants affecting user cybersecurity behavior in mobile payment contactless technologies can help identify areas of vulnerability and improve security. It also helps increase consumer trust in these technologies, which is crucial for widespread adoption and usage.

2   Research Gap

The research gap was identified by conducting a bibliometric analysis of the literature on mobile payment contactless technologies using the VOSviewer tool [11]. This approach is inspired by several earlier studies [12, 13]. The search was carried out on the published literature through the Scopus database in October 2022. The results of the bibliometric analysis are shown in Fig. 1. By critically analyzing the studies, it has been noticed that most literature is concerned with the technical challenges of using the technology. In addition, the analysis provided evidence that there is limited research on user cybersecurity behavior toward mobile payment contactless technologies.

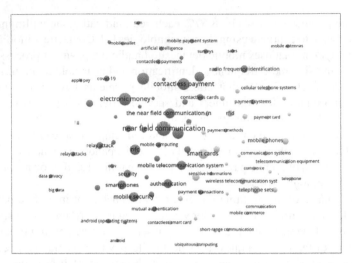

Fig. 1. The most frequent words in mobile payment contactless technologies studies.

3 Theoretical Framework and Research Hypotheses

We developed a theoretical model that extends TPB with CSA to investigate users' cybersecurity behavior toward mobile payment contactless technologies. TPB is selected in this study because it deals with the individual's psychological motivation to adopt new technologies. The lack of knowledge concerning what impacts cybersecurity behavior in mobile payment contactless technologies through the lens of the TPB factors also contributes to the selection of the theory. The TPB was developed to explain users' intention to adopt a behavior by measuring the user's attitude, subjective norm, and perceived behavioral control [14]. This theory is adopted in many studies, specifically in information technology, to predict users' behavior towards technology [15–17]. Previous research confirmed TPB factors' significance in information security awareness [18]. Another study measured the repurchasing intention of Chinese citizens by testing the effect of mediating TPB factors between customers' mobile usability and their satisfaction [19]. The present study assumes that cybersecurity behavior in mobile payment contactless technologies is influenced by individuals' attitudes, subjective norms, perceived behavioral control, and CSA. The developed model and its underlying constructs are shown in Fig. 2.

3.1 Attitude

Attitude, as per the TPB, is "the degree to which a person has a favorable or unfavorable evaluation of the behavior of interest" [14]. Attitude must be included as a factor to measure the level of engagement in security behavior. For example, a recent study showed a significant relationship between health practitioner attitude and engagement in cybersecurity behavior [20]. Another study concluded that attitude and threat awareness would enhance the user's security behavior [21]. Other research confirmed that the attitudes of healthcare practitioners could improve their security knowledge, which reflects

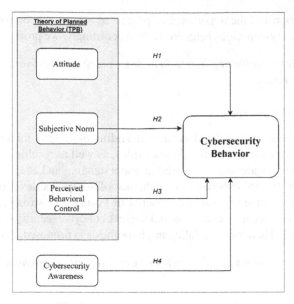

Fig. 2. The proposed research model.

in their behaviors [22]. From previous studies, attitude significantly impacts cybersecurity behavior towards mobile payment contactless technologies. Thus, the following is proposed:

H1: A positive relationship exists between attitudes and cybersecurity behavior.

3.2 Subjective Norm

Subjective norm refers to "perceived social pressure to perform or not to perform the behaviour" [14]. The effect of social and surrounding environments on the individual's behavior must be examined. Many studies have been conducted to confirm the relationship between subjective norms and cybersecurity behavior. For example, a study confirmed the impact of subjective norms on e-payment behavior in Cote d'Ivoire [23]. Moreover, subjective norms toward information security significantly impact an organization's behavior [24]. Given the significance of the subjective norms in the previous studies, we suggest the following hypothesis:

H2: A positive relationship exists between subjective norms and cybersecurity behavior.

3.3 Perceived Behavioral Control

Perceived behavioral control refers to "people's perception of the ease or difficulty of performing the behaviour of interest" [14]. A study examined the positive security behaviors towards using smart devices in Indonesia [25]. Their findings emphasized the significance of perceived behavioral control to engage in positive security behavior.

Another study approved the importance of perceived behavioral control in engaging in information security-conscious behavior [24]. Accordingly, we propose the following:

H3: A positive relationship exists between perceived behavioral control and cybersecurity behavior.

3.4 Cybersecurity Awareness

Cybersecurity awareness is defined as "understanding of security threats and their consequences, and information security policies rules, as well as resulting responsibilities" [26]. Cybersecurity awareness is essential in understanding and adapting proper cybersecurity behavior toward cyberattacks or threats [27–29]. The level of cybersecurity awareness was examined in a study conducted in Portugal. A strong relationship was found between cybersecurity awareness and the level of cybersecurity behavior of health professionals [20]. Therefore, the following hypothesis is proposed:

H4: A positive relationship exists between cybersecurity awareness and cybersecurity behavior.

4 Research Methodology

Over three months, a cross-sectional study was employed to examine the developed theoretical model. A web-based survey was conducted to collect data from users of mobile payment contactless technologies in the UAE. Non-probability convenience sampling techniques were used to collect the sample. The survey link and the purpose of the research were provided. A total of 1040 samples were collected. Data screening was conducted to cleanse the collected data, and 820 samples were used for further analysis.

The instrument is developed based on adapting items from the previous literature. The items of attitudes were adopted from [24]. The items for measuring subjective norms were adopted from [25, 30]. The items of perceived behavioral control were adopted from [25]. The items of cybersecurity awareness were adopted from several studies [31–35]. A five-point Likert scale was used to measure the items. The study followed a two-stage analytical technique to evaluate the proposed model. The first stage employs the PLS-SEM to test the hypotheses and identify the significance of the predictors of cybersecurity behavior. For the second stage, the artificial neural network (ANN) was used to rank the normalized importance of the significant determinants.

5 Results

5.1 Participants

The final sample size after data cleaning consists of 820 respondents. 52.8% of them were females, and 47.2% were males. For the participants' age, 12.7% is between 18 and 22, 19.8% is between 23 and 28, 31.5% is between 29 and 35, and 36% is above 35. Most participants are bachelor's degree holders (49%), followed by Master's/PhD degree holders (28.2%). Apple Pay is the most mobile payment contactless application used by UAE individuals (39.6%), followed by Samsung Pay (22.1%).

5.2 Measurement Model Assessment

The measurement model was assessed by testing the internal consistency reliability, convergent validity, and discriminant validity [36]. The reliability of the constructs was assessed by testing composite reliability (CR) and Cronbach's Alpha (CA). Table 1 shows that CA and CR values exceeded the threshold limit of 0.70 [37], which indicates robust reliability between the variables. Convergent validity was assessed based on average variance extracted (AVE) and factor loadings, as shown in Table 1. Convergent validity is accomplished as the loading of factors was >0.70, and the AVE values were >0.50 [37]. Discriminant validity was assessed by testing the Heterotrait-Monotrait ratio of correlations (HTMT) criterion at a threshold value of 0.85 [38]. As shown in Table 2, none of the values exceeded the threshold value of 0.85, which means the discriminant validity is confirmed.

Table 1. Reliability and convergent validity results.

Constructs	Items	Factor Loading	Cronbach's Alpha	Composite reliability	AVE
Attitude	ATT1	0.840	0.919	0.921	0.755
	ATT2	0.868			
	ATT3	0.889			
	ATT4	0.894			
	ATT5	0.854			
Cybersecurity behavior	CSB1	0.703	0.879	0.880	0.678
	CSB2	0.829			
	CSB3	0.876			
	CSB4	0.871			
	CSB5	0.826			
Cybersecurity awareness	CSA1	0.834	0.883	0.884	0.740
	CSA2	0.850			
	CSA3	0.888			
	CSA4	0.868			
Perceived behavioral control	PBC1	0.836	0.885	0.885	0.743
	PBC2	0.890			
	PBC3	0.856			
	PBC4	0.866			
Subjective norm	SN1	0.862	0.846	0.849	0.765
	SN2	0.874			
	SN3	0.887			

Table 2. HTMT results.

	Attitude	Cybersecurity behavior	Cybersecurity awareness	Perceived behavioral control	Subjective norm
Attitude					
Cybersecurity behavior	0.636				
Cybersecurity awareness	0.579	0.724			
Perceived behavioral control	0.691	0.697	0.666		
Subjective norm	0.807	0.639	0.579	0.705	

5.3 Structural Model Assessment

The evaluation of the structural model was performed using the coefficient of determination (R^2) and hypotheses testing. As shown in Table 3, the results provide strong support for all the proposed hypotheses. The R^2 refers to the structural model's predictive power. The literature suggested that R^2 values of 0.75, 0.50, and 0.25, respectively, describe substantial, moderate, or weak levels of predictive accuracy [39]. The results showed that the independent variables explained 52.9% of the variance in cybersecurity behavior, indicating satisfactory predictive accuracy.

Table 3. Structural path results.

Hypotheses	t-values	p-values	Decision
H1: Attitude → cybersecurity behavior	3.367	0.001	Supported
H2: Subjective norm → cybersecurity behavior	9.931	0.002	Supported
H3: Perceived behavioral control → cybersecurity behavior	5.505	0.000	Supported
H4: Cybersecurity awareness → cybersecurity behavior	3.040	0.000	Supported

5.4 Artificial Neural Network Results

ANN performs better prediction than conventional regression methods [40, 41]. The developed model in the present study has one endogenous construct (i.e., cybersecurity behavior). Thus, the research model has one ANN model only, as shown in Fig. 3. The model was examined using the ANN multilayer perceptron network in SPSS 23 software. The ANN structure has one hidden layer with several neurons [42]. For the model, the number of generated hidden neurons was three. The overfitting issues of the model were resolved by implementing a 10-fold cross-validation approach, where the data were segregated into the ratio of 90:10 for training and testing, respectively [43]. This approach is well-known in the research field for establishing the relative importance of the predictors [44]. The adopted activation function for the hidden and output layers of the model is a sigmoid function. Figure 3 shows that the model has four significant exogenous constructs: attitude, perceived behavioral control, subjective norm, and cybersecurity awareness. These exogenous constructs served as inputs for the model, whereas cybersecurity behavior (endogenous variable) was used as the output layer. The prediction accuracy for this model was assessed by the root mean square of error (RMSE) based on 10 generated networks [42]. The results reveal that the RMSE values for the model are in the range of 0.082–0.088 for training and 0.072–0.104 for testing. Therefore, the ANN model consistently created the predictor-output relationships and can fit the data effectively for better prediction.

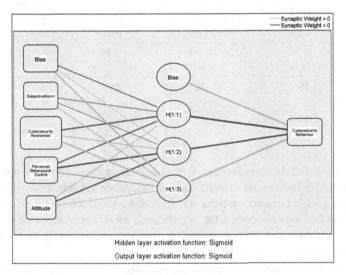

Fig. 3. ANN model.

5.5 Sensitivity Analysis

The contribution of each factor to cybersecurity behavior was assessed using sensitivity analysis. This analysis was conducted by calculating the normalized importance [45]. As shown in Table 4, cybersecurity awareness is the most important variable that affects cybersecurity behavior, with normalized importance of 100%. This is followed by perceived behavioral control (45%), subjective norm (38%), and attitude (33%).

6   Discussion

This study intended to examine the impact of psychological factors and cybersecurity awareness on users' cybersecurity behavior towards mobile payment contactless technologies. The proposed model was based on the TPB extended with the cybersecurity

Table 4. Sensitivity analysis results.

Neural Network	Subjective norm	Cybersecurity awareness	Perceived behavioral control	Attitude
Network 1	0.49	1.00	0.41	0.15
Network 2	0.27	1.00	0.58	0.33
Network 3	0.42	1.00	0.30	0.36
Network 4	0.31	1.00	0.42	0.27
Network 5	0.64	1.00	0.72	0.40
Network 6	0.38	1.00	0.33	0.23
Network 7	0.33	1.00	0.39	0.25
Network 8	0.25	1.00	0.38	0.34
Network 9	0.51	1.00	0.42	0.60
Network 10	0.24	1.00	0.40	0.32
Mean Importance	0.38	1.00	0.45	0.33
Normalized Importance %	38%	100%	45%	33%
Ranking	3	1	2	4

awareness factor. The data were collected from mobile payment contactless technologies users in the UAE. The results showed that the independent variables explained 52.9% of the variance in cybersecurity behavior, indicating satisfactory predictive accuracy. Moreover, the findings supported the significance of all the factors on cybersecurity behavior, which means that the proposed model is sound in predicting cybersecurity behavior through the lens of proposed external factors.

The results showed that users' attitudes toward mobile payment contactless technologies affect their cybersecurity behavior. As the user indicates a proper attitude to mobile payment contactless technologies, their appropriate cybersecurity behavior increases. This result is aligned with previous studies [20–22]. Moreover, the findings showed that perceived behavioral control was strongly correlated with cybersecurity behavior. This result means those who feel they have a high level of control over the technology are more likely to engage in safe and secure behavior when using it. This result comes in line with previous findings [24, 25].

Furthermore, the results showed that the subjective norm has a significant positive relationship with cybersecurity behavior, confirming previous studies' findings [23, 24]. This result means that the perceived social norms and expectations surrounding mobile payment contactless technologies strongly relate to how people behave concerning cybersecurity. The findings revealed that cybersecurity awareness strongly affects users' cybersecurity behavior, which aligns with the previous conclusions [20]. This result means that people with a higher awareness of the potential risks and dangers associated with mobile payment contactless technologies tend to exhibit better cybersecurity behaviors and practices. In other words, their cybersecurity awareness directly affects their actions and decisions in protecting themselves and their information when using these technologies.

7 Conclusion and Future Work

This research aimed to examine the factors affecting individuals' cybersecurity behavior in mobile payment contactless technologies. The hypotheses testing results supported all the relationships in the proposed model. The ANN results showed that cybersecurity awareness was the most important variable affecting cybersecurity behavior, with normalized importance of 100%. This is followed by perceived behavioral control (45%), subjective norm (38%), and attitude (33%). Theoretically, the study confirms the applicability of the TPB in a new application (i.e., mobile payment contactless technologies) with a new outcome rather than behavior (i.e., cybersecurity behavior). In addition, understanding the factors that impact mobile payment contactless technologies in collectivistic contexts such as the UAE has rarely been examined in the existing literature, which significantly contributes to the literature of these contexts.

Practically, the findings offer several managerial implications. Firstly, the results give software developers the knowledge to consider the critical factors in developing new payment applications. Secondly, policymakers are advised to encourage individuals to increase their cybersecurity awareness of cybercrimes and threats that may affect their payment transactions. Thirdly, by streamlining the application clearance procedure for these projects and encouraging the developers to develop a hybrid payment application considering the psychological and human components, decision-makers may assist in creating safe mobile payment technology projects. Fourthly, the functionality of mobile payment contactless applications should be improved by service providers to meet customer expectations and secure customers' payments in the event improper cybersecurity conduct occurs unintentionally. Additionally, banks should routinely hold an awareness session on appropriate cybersecurity behavior to use mobile payment contactless technologies efficiently.

The limitations of this study can be summarized as follows. First, the research did not examine the effect of moderating determinants in shaping cybersecurity behavior. Age, gender, and user experience must be examined in future studies as their role was neglected in the existing literature. Second, the present study did not include any qualitative methods in collecting data, such as conducting an interview or focus group. Thus, further research may assess the same population using mixed research methods to provide a deep understanding of cybersecurity behavior in mobile payment contactless technologies.

References

1. Al-Emran, M., Al-Sharafi, M.A.: Revolutionizing education with industry 5.0: challenges and future research agendas. Int. J. Inf. Technol. Lang. Stud. **6**, 1–5 (2022)
2. Rashid, H.: Prospects of digital financial services in Bangladesh in the context of fourth industrial revolution. Asian J. Soc. Sci. Leg. Stud. **2**, 88–95 (2020). https://doi.org/10.34104/ajssls.020.088095

3. Gong, X., Zhang, K.Z.K., Chen, C., Cheung, C.M.K., Lee, M.K.O.: What drives self-disclosure in mobile payment applications? The effect of privacy assurance approaches, network externality, and technology complementarity. Inf. Technol. People. **33**, 1174–1213 (2020). https://doi.org/10.1108/ITP-03-2018-0132

4. Statista: Mobile POS Payments - United Arab Emirates

5. Chabbi, S., Araar, C.: RFID and NFC authentication protocol for securing a payment transaction. In: 2022 4th International Conference on Pattern Analysis and Intelligent Systems (PAIS), pp. 1–8 (2022). https://doi.org/10.1109/PAIS56586.2022.9946661

6. Al-Sharafi, M.A., Al-Qaysi, N., Iahad, N.A., Al-Emran, M.: Evaluating the sustainable use of mobile payment contactless technologies within and beyond the COVID-19 pandemic using a hybrid SEM-ANN approach. Int. J. Bank Mark. **40**, 1071–1095 (2022). https://doi.org/10.1108/IJBM-07-2021-0291/FULL/PDF

7. Ariffin, N.H.M., Ahmad, F., Haneef, U.M.: Acceptance of mobile payments by retailers using UTAUT model. Indones. J. Electr. Eng. Comput. Sci. **19**, 149–155 (2020). https://doi.org/10.11591/IJEECS.V19.I1.PP149-155

8. Upadhyay, N., Upadhyay, S., Abed, S.S., Dwivedi, Y.K.: Consumer adoption of mobile payment services during COVID-19: extending meta-UTAUT with perceived severity and self-efficacy. Int. J. Bank Mark. **40**, 960–991 (2022). https://doi.org/10.1108/IJBM-06-2021-0262/FULL/PDF

9. Karjaluoto, H., Shaikh, A.A., Leppäniemi, M., Luomala, R.: Examining consumers' usage intention of contactless payment systems. Int. J. Bank Mark. **38**, 332–351 (2020). https://doi.org/10.1108/IJBM-04-2019-0155

10. Al-Saedi, K., Al-Emran, M.: A systematic review of mobile payment studies from the lens of the UTAUT model. In: Al-Emran, M., Shaalan, K. (eds.) Recent Advances in Technology Acceptance Models and Theories. SSDC, vol. 335, pp. 79–106. Springer, Cham (2021). https://doi.org/10.1007/978-3-030-64987-6_6

11. Van Eck, N.J., Waltman, L.: Software survey: VOSviewer, a computer program for bibliometric mapping. Scientometrics **84**, 523–538 (2010). https://doi.org/10.1007/s11192-009-0146-3

12. Al-Sharafi, M.A., Al-Emran, M., Iranmanesh, M., Al-Qaysi, N., Iahad, N.A., Arpaci, I.: Understanding the impact of knowledge management factors on the sustainable use of AI-based chatbots for educational purposes using a hybrid SEM-ANN approach. Interact. Learn. Environ. 1–20 (2022). https://doi.org/10.1080/10494820.2022.2075014

13. Al-Sharafi, M.A., Al-Emran, M., Arpaci, I., Marques, G., Namoun, A., Iahad, N.A.: Examining the impact of psychological, social, and quality factors on the continuous intention to use virtual meeting platforms during and beyond COVID-19 pandemic: a hybrid SEM-ANN approach. Int. J. Human–Computer Interact. (2022). https://doi.org/10.1080/10447318.2022.2084036

14. Ajzen, I.: The theory of planned behavior. Organ. Behav. Hum. Decis. Process. **50**, 179–211 (1991)

15. Josephng, P.S., Al-Rawahi, M.M.K., Eaw, H.C.: Provoking actual mobile payment use in the middle east. Appl. Syst. Innov. **5**, 37 (2022). https://doi.org/10.3390/asi5020037

16. Ogiemwonyi, O.: Factors influencing generation Y green behaviour on green products in Nigeria: an application of theory of planned behaviour. Environ. Sustain. Indic. **13**, 100164 (2022). https://doi.org/10.1016/j.indic.2021.100164

17. Al-Emran, M., Al-Nuaimi, M.N., Arpaci, I., Al-Sharafi, M.A., Anthony Jnr, B.: Towards a wearable education: understanding the determinants affecting students' adoption of wearable technologies using machine learning algorithms. Educ. Inf. Technol. **28**, 1–20 (2022). https://doi.org/10.1007/S10639-022-11294-Z/METRICS

18. Dinev, T., Hu, Q.: The centrality of awareness in the formation of user behavioral intention toward protective information technologies. J. Assoc. Inf. Syst. **8**, 386–408 (2007). https://doi.org/10.17705/1jais.00133

19. Sun, S., Law, R., Schuckert, M.: Mediating effects of attitude, subjective norms and perceived behavioural control for mobile payment-based hotel reservations. Int. J. Hosp. Manage. **84**, 102331 (2020). https://doi.org/10.1016/j.ijhm.2019.102331

20. Nunes, P., Antunes, M., Silva, C.: Evaluating cybersecurity attitudes and behaviors in Portuguese healthcare institutions. Procedia Comput. Sci. **181**, 173–181 (2021). https://doi.org/10.1016/j.procs.2021.01.118

21. Jansen, J., van Schaik, P.: The design and evaluation of a theory-based intervention to promote security behaviour against phishing. Int. J. Hum. Comput. Stud. **123**, 40–55 (2019). https://doi.org/10.1016/j.ijhcs.2018.10.004

22. Yeng, P.K., Fauzi, M.A., Yang, B.: A comprehensive assessment of human factors in cyber security compliance toward enhancing the security practice of healthcare staff in paperless hospitals. Information. **13**, 335 (2022). https://doi.org/10.3390/info13070335

23. Chen, A.N.: Subjective norms and demographic background on e-payment behavior in Cote d'Ivoire, pp. 150–162 (2018)

24. Safa, N.S., Sookhak, M., Von Solms, R., Furnell, S., Ghani, N.A., Herawan, T.: Information security conscious care behaviour formation in organizations. Comput. Secur. **53**, 65–78 (2015). https://doi.org/10.1016/j.cose.2015.05.012

25. Kautsarina, Hidayanto, A.N., Anggorojati, B., Abidin, Z., Phusavat, K.: Data modeling positive security behavior implementation among smart device users in Indonesia: a partial least squares structural equation modeling approach (PLS-SEM). Data Brief, **30**, 105588 (2020). https://doi.org/10.1016/j.dib.2020.105588

26. Tsohou, A., Holtkamp, P.: Are users competent to comply with information security policies? An analysis of professional competence models. Inf. Technol. People. **31**, 1047–1068 (2018). https://doi.org/10.1108/ITP-02-2017-0052

27. Rahim, N.H.A., Hamid, S., Kiah, L.M., Shamshirband, S., Furnell, S.: A systematic review of approaches to assessing cybersecurity awareness. Kybernetes **44**, 606–622 (2015). https://doi.org/10.1108/K-12-2014-0283

28. Razaque, A., et al.: Avoidance of cybersecurity threats with the deployment of a web-based blockchain-enabled cybersecurity awareness system. Appl. Sci. **11**, 1–21 (2021). https://doi.org/10.3390/app11177880

29. Nifakos, S., et al.: Influence of human factors on cyber security within healthcare organisations: a systematic review. Sensors **21**, 5119 (2021). https://doi.org/10.3390/s21155119

30. Yang, H., Yu, J., Zo, H., Choi, M.: User acceptance of wearable devices: an extended perspective of perceived value. Telematics Inform. **33**, 256–269 (2016). https://doi.org/10.1016/j.tele.2015.08.007

31. Ng, B.Y., Kankanhalli, A., Xu, Y.C.: Studying users' computer security behavior: a health belief perspective. Decis. Support Syst. **46**, 815–825 (2009). https://doi.org/10.1016/j.dss.2008.11.010

32. Blythe, J.M.: Information security in the workplace: a mixed-methods approach to understanding and improving security behaviours, p. 291 (2015)

33. Donalds, C., Osei-Bryson, K.M.: Cybersecurity compliance behavior: exploring the influences of individual decision style and other antecedents. Int. J. Inf. Manage. **51**, 102056 (2020). https://doi.org/10.1016/j.ijinfomgt.2019.102056

34. Hull, M., Zhang-Kennedy, L., Baig, K., Chiasson, S.: Understanding individual differences: factors affecting secure computer behaviour. Behav. Inf. Technol. **41**, 1–27 (2021). https://doi.org/10.1080/0144929x.2021.1977849

35. Li, L., Xu, L., He, W.: The effects of antecedents and mediating factors on cybersecurity protection behavior. Comput. Hum. Behav. Rep. **5**, 100165 (2022). https://doi.org/10.1016/j.chbr.2021.100165
36. Hair Jr, J.F., Hult, G.T.M., Ringle, C.M., Sarstedt, M., Danks, N.P., Ray, S.: Partial least squares structural equation modeling (PLS-SEM) using R: A workbook (2021)
37. Hair, J., Hollingsworth, C.L., Randolph, A.B., Chong, A.Y.L.: An updated and expanded assessment of PLS-SEM in information systems research. Ind. Manage. Data Syst. **117**, 442–458 (2017). https://doi.org/10.1108/IMDS-04-2016-0130
38. Henseler, J., Ringle, C.M., Sarstedt, M.: A new criterion for assessing discriminant validity in variance-based structural equation modeling. J. Acad. Mark. Sci. **43**(1), 115–135 (2014). https://doi.org/10.1007/s11747-014-0403-8
39. Hair, J.F., Hult, G.T.M., Ringle, C., Sarstedt, M.: A Primer on Partial Least Squares Structural Equation Modeling (PLS-SEM). Sage Publications, Thousand Oaks (2014)
40. Gbongli, K., Xu, Y., Amedjonekou, K.M.: Extended technology acceptance model to predict mobile-based money acceptance and sustainability: a multi-analytical structural equation modeling and neural network approach. Sustainability **11**, 1–33 (2019). https://doi.org/10.3390/su11133639
41. Jena, R.K.: Investigating and predicting intentions to continue using mobile payment platforms after the COVID-19 pandemic: an empirical study among retailers in India. J. Risk Financ. Manage. **15**, 314 (2022). https://doi.org/10.3390/jrfm15070314
42. Kalinić, Z., Marinković, V., Kalinić, L., Liébana-Cabanillas, F.: Neural network modeling of consumer satisfaction in mobile commerce: an empirical analysis. Expert Syst. Appl. **175**, 114803 (2021). https://doi.org/10.1016/j.eswa.2021.114803
43. Al-Emran, M., Abbasi, G.A., Mezhuyev, V.: Evaluating the impact of knowledge management factors on M-learning adoption: a deep learning-based hybrid SEM-ANN Approach. In: Al-Emran, M., Shaalan, K. (eds.) Recent Advances in Technology Acceptance Models and Theories. SSDC, vol. 335, pp. 159–172. Springer, Cham (2021). https://doi.org/10.1007/978-3-030-64987-6_10
44. Arpaci, I., Karatas, K., Kusci, I., Al-Emran, M.: Understanding the social sustainability of the Metaverse by integrating UTAUT2 and big five personality traits: a hybrid SEM-ANN approach. Technol. Soc. **71**, 102120 (2022). https://doi.org/10.1016/J.TECHSOC.2022.102120
45. Qasem, Y.A.M., et al.: A multi-analytical approach to predict the determinants of cloud computing adoption in higher education institutions. Appl. Sci. **10**, 4905 (2020). https://doi.org/10.3390/app10144905

Human-Centric Cybersecurity: From Intrabody Signals to Incident Management

Assessing User Understanding, Perception and Behaviour with Privacy and Permission Settings

Nourah Alshomrani[✉], Steven Furnell[✉], and Ying He[✉]

School of Computer Science, University of Nottingham, Nottingham, UK
{Nourah.Alshomrani,Steven.Furnell,Ying.He}@nottingham.ac.uk

Abstract. Nowadays, users face an increasing range of contexts in which they may wish to control access to and share their data. This includes mobile apps accessing sensitive data, cookies tracking user activity, and social media sites targeting users for advertisement. Existing studies have determined that many ordinary users are unable to make informed permissions-related decisions when giving permissions to apps due to a lack of understanding of permissions and interface issues. Today, primary web services, such as social networks, mobile phones, web browsers and the Internet of Things, provide a vast number of privacy settings to users, aiming to provide more control. Although privacy details and permission settings are often made available, they can fall short of capturing and communicating essential considerations which users care about or offering them a meaningful level of control. As a result, the situation for many users has become unmanageable, and they do not have sufficient and proper control of all permissions on different platforms. This paper presents initial findings from ongoing research that is aimed at investigating ways to improve communication with users and support their related decision-making. The analysis leads to the following conclusions: end-users do not read and misunderstand permission requirements, demonstrating a gap between knowledge, perception and behaviours about permissions and privacy settings. Therefore, it is reasonable to assist consumers by allowing them to manage and revisit their privacy settings easily. The number of privacy decisions is growing; therefore, it is unrealistic for ordinary users to manage all these privacy settings.

Keywords: Permissions · Privacy settings · User decisions

1 Introduction

Internet users face the need to control access to their data. Installing an application (app) requires a user to perform certain procedures to authorise access to their device's functions and sensitive resources such as the location, camera, internet connection, Wi-Fi, photos and storage. Individuals give these permissions via a consent form or privacy agreement. However, end users often neglect to read the terms of a permission request and, therefore, do not realise the disadvantages that could ensue.

© The Author(s), under exclusive license to Springer Nature Switzerland AG 2023
A. Moallem (Ed.): HCII 2023, LNCS 14045, pp. 557–575, 2023.
https://doi.org/10.1007/978-3-031-35822-7_36

Moreover, end users have vast amounts of choice when searching for a mobile app to install on their smartphones. Although privacy details and permission settings are often made available to improve users' privacy, this can fall short of identifying and communicating the essential considerations that users care about or offering them a meaningful level of control over web services or apps in expected ways. This indicates that regular users may not be able to make knowledgeable and informed decisions about what permissions to accept or disable while maintaining the usability of the online services or apps. Furthermore, consumers may face app usability issues while managing permissions using the current model, whereby individual permissions can be selectively disabled.

The increasing number of application programming interfaces (APIs) available to developers has fuelled the growth in smart apps accessing sensitive data such as a user's call logs, current location or camera. While the increase in the number of APIs leads to an increasing number of new apps, it also gives rise to new varieties of security and privacy risks, such as malware [1, 2]; another is that regular consumers may not be aware of how much sensitive data these online services access and for what purpose. Smart devices' access to sensitive information makes data privacy crucial.

Although privacy details and permission settings are often made available nowadays, they fall short in several areas. First, the number of privacy settings attached to every online service has its own permission settings, which makes it unmanageable for the user to go over each setting [3, 4]. Also, the available provided permission can fall short of providing the user control over what to choose to be private or not. This results in depriving the user of making knowledgeable and informed decisions about what permissions to accept or decline. In addition, usually, the device's permission settings are provided in a long, uneasy-to-read language that forces the user to accept whatever has been decided by the app provider. Several studies have shown that users are unable to make informed permissions-related decisions when giving permissions to apps due to a lack of understanding of permissions as well as interface issues [1, 5, 6].

The key challenges are how users can understand and control permissions for their devices while striking a balance between privacy and usability and how the permission and privacy settings model itself can be improved upon to help users reach this balance. Therefore, this study aims to use a survey to investigate users' understanding, perceptions and self-declared behaviours regarding their privacy and control permissions. Unfortunately, there is a lack of empirical research focusing specifically on online permissions and privacy settings for end-users with various online services of smart devices. Smart devices in this study include smartphones, tablets, laptops or other advanced technologies.

This paper analyses and evaluates users' understanding, perceptions and self-declared behaviours regarding their privacy and control permissions. Firstly, it discusses the literature review on three major topics: contextualisation of user privacy permission, privacy concern and usability of the privacy permission setting. This paper then presents the survey instrument as a methodology to study users' knowledge, perceptions and self-declared behaviours with permissions and privacy settings. The remainder of this paper presents the study's findings and conclusion.

2   Literature Review

This section focuses on three major topics: contextualisation of user privacy permission, privacy concern and usability of the privacy permission setting.

Permission serves the purpose of obtaining consent before accessing sensitive data. For example, an application offering a navigation function would request access to the consumer's location. However, many smartphone users are unable to arrive at an informed decision about permitting a mobile app to access sensitive data [7]. It is important to understand how users should be invited to respond to these permissions in a way that creates trust and positive behaviour regarding permissions-related decisions. Some studies also pointed out the need to provide more information to users on their mobile screens before requesting access to their private information [8, 9]. For instance, Fig. 1 provides two examples of messages that inform users about a permission request.

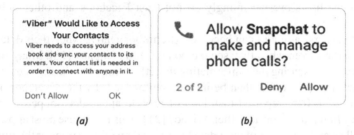

(a)   (b)

Fig. 1. Examples of permission request dialogue boxes on (a) iOS and (b) Android.

Looking at Fig. 1 the dialogue boxes may initially seem straightforward; however, there is some missing information. In Fig. 1a, the iOS application demands permission to access contact numbers, and the usage descriptions provided by the Viber app only give vague descriptions of how address book and contact data are used. App developers may not wholly and honestly inform the extent of their access to and usage of user data [10, 11]. In Fig. 1(b), the dialogue displays that Snapchat demands access to phone calls to make and manage them, yet, it does not inform the individual that it will also permit the app to access the phone status or ID (i.e. IMEI). End users could not be expected to have sufficient knowledge of the dangers of giving these permissions access from these brief descriptions.

Additionally, other relevant details are not provided, such as how the information will be used, and where it will be shared. Therefore, apps provide misinformation regarding privacy [12]. Such systems and platforms have various limitations that continually force consumers to overshare sensitive information due to the tension between usability and control [13]. Therefore, end users cannot make informed decisions about what permissions to disable or accept while still maintaining the usability of apps.

Ismail (2018) highlighted that there is a need to explore the understanding of users with respect to their exercising of their right to choose from the privacy settings offered to them. These often relate to the technical details of the device that an ordinary user may not be able to understand (e.g., broadcast WAP, Surface Finger, perform I/O over NFC, PUSH notifications) [14]. Current research has found that users typically make a decision on the basis of their intuition instead of knowledge because an ordinary user of a smartphone is unlikely to have a sound technical knowledge of smart devices and, as such, is unable to understand the risks of granting permission to apps [15, 16].

The Washington Post conducted a survey of over 1,000 internet users about how much they trusted social media companies such as Facebook, Youtube, Amazon, TikTok, Instagram, WhatsApp, Apple, Google and Microsoft responsibly handle users' browsing activities and sensitive data [17]. Consumers were asked whether they trusted the online services and platforms to 'a great deal', 'a good amount', 'not much' or 'not at all', or had no opinion about a certain company. Among the respondents, 18% stated they trusted Apple to 'a great deal', while only 14% stated as much of Amazon or Google. However, in the 'good amount' category, Amazon was the first ranked with 39%, then Google had 34%, and Apple had 26%. Finally, Apple's positive score was only 44%, then Google at 48% and Amazon at 53%. This indicates that users trust Amazon and Google to handle their personal data and internet browsing activities more than Apple, while the same users overwhelmingly do not trust Facebook and other online social networks.

Likewise, users' attitudes can become extremely negative when their data is shared with third parties, even when they see the benefit of a company [18]. Many individuals would rather allow sharing their information directly to improve the services that benefit them in exchange [19] rather than being commercialised (by the developer or service) [20]. Lim et al. (2015) reported that 17% of mobile app users stopped using an app because they found that it invaded their privacy [21]. This is because most app consumers are not at all aware of the risk of their data being used by other parties or the implications of data sharing. Accordingly, the growing surveillance of the invisibility of dataflows and passive digital footprints challenges the assumption that users control their privacy.

This recent stream of studies also focused on privacy issues in Android because Android devices have a huge market share and are also vulnerable to privacy-invading apps [22]. The literature review showed that there are usually three stages that an Android user goes through to make decisions related to using an app: download, install and runtime [22]. Herold & Hertzog (2015) found that users are unable to fully understand the purpose of permissions sought at the installation stage, therefore, hastily grant permission to just pass through the installation stage and operate the app [23].

Chen and Kim (2013) showed that on social media, high privacy concerns over unauthorized use and access impact users' behaviours. Individuals with high data privacy concerns tend to disclose less information on social media [24] or may stop using their social media accounts due to privacy concerns [25, 26]. Few studies looked into the willingness of users to allow mobile apps to share their location in order to be offered local services [27, 28]. It has been observed that Android devices, unlike iOS devices, are not pre-screened for potential security and privacy risks. Consequently, Android devices may be regarded as more prone to risks from privacy-invading apps than iOS devices. Therefore, it is imperative that the user is fully informed about the purpose for which permissions are sought, and this should be done at the downloading stage so that the user is able to evaluate the potential risk before an app is downloaded.

Several researchers have pointed out that most users are unable to comprehend the scope of access gained by mobile apps to their personal data [29]. Moreover, the researchers indicated the inadequacy and ineffectiveness of permission warnings to a user wishing to make sound decisions. It has also been observed that most users are unable to understand the nature, type and amount of data collected by the apps when they are granted permission [30]. Research in this area has also highlighted the semantic gap between the expectations of the users and the functionality of the app upon getting permission to access user data [34, 35]. Therefore, there is a great need to respond to permissions in a way that creates trust and positive behaviour regarding permissions-related decisions.

The privacy paradox refers to a phenomenon wherein individuals state they value privacy but act in ways that seem to show little concern for it [36, 37]. This "attitude-behaviour gap" [38] continues to complicate research and design-based attempts to assist users in the digital world in managing privacy. While people may want to protect their privacy in principle, they may need to see a realistic way to do so in practice. Therefore, individuals may have resigned to having their privacy routinely violated [39], thus negating any meaningful differentiation between what they say about their privacy and what to do to protect their information.

Overall, although there is available literature addressing users' knowledge, perception and self-declared behaviour, it has investigated each topic individually. The current research contributes to this body of knowledge by determining user perception, understanding and behaviour regarding permissions settings in general contexts such as website cookies, social media sites and mobile app permissions, and investigates them collectively in one survey.

3   Research Methodology

This research aims to study users' understanding, perceptions and self-declared behaviours regarding their privacy and control permissions. We chose survey as the research methodology as we aim to investigate users' knowledge, perceptions and behaviours on online permissions and privacy and gain a deep understanding of the literature and previous works on privacy and permissions in different contexts. There is a lack of empirical research focusing specifically on online permissions and privacy settings for end-users with various online services.

The survey was structured in four sections, as outlined below:

1. **Information about users' background and IT device usage:** Captures demographic information of our participants. They are asked to provide select their age, gender, education level, smart devices frequently used and their level of technology or digital knowledge.

2. **Users' knowledge about permissions and privacy:** Investigates users' understanding of permissions and privacy settings when using their smart devices. It presents questions to study their understanding and regularly read privacy policies for apps, websites and social media. It also covers the usability of the privacy information of online services such as mobile apps and the information for the permissions screens. Moreover, various questions are identified to evaluate their understanding of the permissions role on their devices.

3. **Users' perceptions about permissions and privacy:** Aims to identify users' feelings and perceptions of online activities and companies. It also discovers their feelings regarding their control over their sensitive data across different platforms and devices. Moreover, it investigates users' perceptions of managing their privacy settings with apps, social media and web browsing on their smart devices.
4. **Users' behaviour with permissions and privacy:** Asks participants about their privacy settings management while they use their online activities. In addition, it will uncover their behaviours regarding allowing or denying permission requests and online services using their sensitive data.

These sections were presented as a series of statements and respondents are asked to rate their level of agreement (total of 38 questions). Additional free-text comments boxes enable them to optionally expand upon their responses at the end of each section, bringing the overall total to 41 questions. Completing the full questionnaire was expected to take around 15–20 min and the survey required that participants should be 18 years or over and be regular users of IT devices or online services.

The survey was piloted with 35 people prior to the release of the full version, and modifications were made to the wording of some statements based upon their feedback. The study was approved via the School of Computer Science ethics committee [45]. The resulting survey was administrated using SurveyMonkey over a 2-month period in mid-2022. Participants were recruited via snowball sampling and via social media channels such as WhatsApp, targeting regular users with adequate technology/digital knowledge. A total of 494 valid responses were received. IBM SPSS Amos Version 28.0.1.1 (14) was used for most of the statistical analyses.

4   Survey Results and Findings

The majority (61.9%) of the participants were male (a total of 304, versus 187 females), and most were from Saudi Arabia. Additionally, most participants were from relatively young age groups, a pattern that showed that: (a) 18–34 years old grew up with the Internet and (b) 18–25 years old probably grew are in the era of smart phones. Furthermore, although the 35–44 age group might not have grown up with the Internet/web, they likely have had computers around them from an early age. Therefore, their interest and participation in technology-oriented research of these three younger age groups likely is high compared to those between 45 to 55 or above years of age. It also showed that participants from 18 to 44 years old are within the age of internet usage. Therefore, their native technology literacy interest is likely to be relatively high as borne out by the respondents' own self-assessments and they felt more interested in this study. It is evident that the young generation is relatively keener to take on new smart devices as compared to older populations. Therefore, the number of participants in this online survey mainly belongs to that age range (18 to 44 years). However, in self-reported data, it could not be ignored that participants may have a biased perception of their own technology skills and interests, which could impact the results of the study.

The country of origin of participants can play an important role in privacy and permission setting studies [31, 32]. Different countries have different laws and regulations regarding privacy, data protection, and personal information. Participants from different countries may have varying cultural attitudes and behaviours towards privacy, and this can affect their willingness to share personal information with apps and services. Additionally, certain countries may have a more advanced legal framework and enforcement mechanisms for data protection, which can influence the privacy practices of businesses operating in those countries [31, 33]. As a result, examining the country of origin of participants in privacy and permission setting studies can provide insights into regional differences in privacy behaviours and attitudes, and inform the development of privacy policies and regulations that are responsive to the needs of different regions. Although there were responses from 24 countries, 361 were from Saudi Arabia, and the only other considerable number of participants was from the UK (a total of 64). The remaining 54 responses came from the 22 other countries collectively.

Participants' education level can be an important factor to consider in privacy and permission setting related studies as it may affect their understanding and attitudes towards privacy. For example, some studies have shown that higher education level was associated with greater concern for privacy and more careful consideration of privacy settings. In this study, 82.8% of the respondents were educated earning a Bachelor's degree level or higher. Therefore, they are expected to be a more educated respondent group than the typical population.

4.1 User Knowledge About Permission and Privacy

This section explores users' knowledge and understanding of permissions and privacy when using their smart devices. It presents questions to study their understanding when reading privacy policies for apps, websites, and social media. It also covers the usability of the privacy information of online services such as mobile apps and the information for the permissions screens. Moreover, various questions are identified to evaluate their understanding of the permissions role on their devices.

Table 1 illustrates the descriptive statistics regarding the user knowledge about permission and privacy. In this and subsequent tables, the statements were rated on a 5-point scale Strongly Agree (SA) to Strongly Disagree (SD), with the respondents also having options for Agree (A), Neutral (N) and Disagree (D).

Over half of those surveyed reported that they do not have knowledge about when their personal data is being accessed by apps and other services on their devices. A possible explanation for this might be that participants do not read the privacy policies for apps and online services before giving permission to use their data. It is apparent from this Table 1 that very few of the participants can benefit from the privacy settings on their smart devices, such as managing who may access their data, read, delete or modify by the online web services. This could be the reason that they consider that privacy policies may protect their data from being shared or used, which shows a lower level of understanding of permissions and privacy.

All scale items were measured on a five-point Likert scale, with one more option, "Don't know", to give participants more flexibility and allow respondents to express their opinions sufficiently, ranging from Strongly Disagree (1) to Strongly Agree (5), with the numeric weights associated with each rating being used to calculate the Mean. The number of responses in this instance is 437 but reduces for some of the later questions as some respondents did not complete the questionnaire in full (the respondent total is therefore shown in each table caption).

Table 1. User knowledge about permission and privacy (n = 437)

Knowledge statements	%					
	SD	D	N	A	SA	Mean
I find privacy and permissions settings easy to understand	8.2	19.4	18.3	36.3	15.5	3.3
I read the privacy policies for apps and online services before giving permission to use my data	22.6	27.6	15.3	22	10.3	2.7
I understand the privacy policies for apps and services before giving permission to use my data	13.0	24.0	19.4	28.8	13.2	3.0
I think that accepting permissions may allow access to my personal information, even when I am not using the app or service	4.1	7.0	9.3	42.5	34.5	3.9
I think that a privacy policy protects my information from being shared	11.4	24.9	20.3	27.6	12.1	3.0
I think the privacy details in apps and other web services are understandable	10.7	27.4	26.3	25.4	8.4	2.9
I always know when my data is being accessed by apps and other services on my devices	20.1	31.1	16.0	21.9	6.4	2.6
I think that if I accept permissions, it may allow apps and services to read, modify, or delete my data on my devices anytime without notifying me	11.9	21.7	13.9	30.4	17.8	3.2
I usually understand what information those permissions are seeking to access to before giving my consent	8.9	19.9	20.3	40.7	7.5	3.1

The analysis showed that (36.4%) of participants agreed that privacy and permission settings are easy to understand. However, more than 50% of the participants disagree with reading the privacy policies before giving permission for online services to access their data. There are 42.6% of participants (the majority for that particular statement) who showed concern regarding their thinking that permission means to permit to access personal information even when they are not using apps/services. 40.7% of participants revealed that they understood and knew the purpose of the permission request before giving consent to the services provider.

Conversely, 38% (the majority of respondents for that particular statement) disagreed regarding the understandability of privacy details in apps and web services, which is alarming. Privacy information is presented in App stores, such as the Nutrition label for apps privacy information. One of the reasons for the lack of understandability is shared by a participant in another comment, such as the privacy statement are written by lawyers in small letters and very lengthy as well as hard to read and comprehend.

Therefore, accessible language, readable font, and font size are the primary elements that may motivate readers to read and understand the information.

Moreover, more than 50% of the participants may need help understanding which online services access their sensitive data on their smart devices. Around 33.6% of participants believe that their personal data cannot be read, modified or deleted from their smart devices after giving permission to access their sensitive data without notifying them. This indicates a lower level of understanding of permissions and privacy. Finally, more than a quarter of the participants do not have knowledge about what personal data those permissions are seeking to access before giving consent to access their data. In comparison, 20% of respondents to that statement did not give their opinion regarding the information those permissions would access before permitting access to their data.

Additionally, 38 people offered free text comments regarding their experiences with respect to the user knowledge towards permission and privacy. The thematic analysis of the comments showed several recurring themes, as listed below (with the number in parentheses indicating the number of comments linked to the theme):

- Lengthy and confusing terms of permission (5).
- Misleading privacy policies and disclaimers (5).
- Forced to agree to privacy policies to use apps (3).
- Personal information being shared without knowledge (2).
- Lack of privacy and the problem of using technology (2).
- Privacy policies protect the issuer not the user (2).
- Complexity and unclear nature of privacy measures (2).

Overall, the quotations highlight a common concern among users about the lack of transparency and accountability in privacy policies and the sharing of personal information. Respondents feel that privacy policies are often misleading and complex and do not adequately protect the user's privacy. It is evident that those users know the privacy and permission shared: "*it's all good, you cannot control what they do, it is deliberately too much to read or too hard to understand, you are forced to accept it or not be able to use things, I don't understand what it's about, I don't have the time to deal with it, and for their benefits or serving their interests*". Most of the time, respondents have believed that they are forced to do this, and they do not trust (e.g., misleading, deception, forced, lack of credibility, protecting the companies, violating policies for their benefits) in the issuer/companies who are collecting this data, for example, "*I think the privacy policy was created only for the legal protection of the trademark owner, there is no real benefit for us*". Other respondents have experienced having limited time to read lengthy information; the language of policy writing is complicated, and uncomfortable formatting used that created further difficulties for understanding and allowing, for example, "*need to be easy to get some understanding*". Most of the participants did not answer this question and selected to write none and leave the box.

4.2 User Perception About Permission and Privacy

This section investigates users' perceptions about permissions and privacy, including their feelings regarding their control over their sensitive data across different platforms and devices. Moreover, it discovers users' perceptions of managing their privacy settings with apps, social media, and web browsing on their smart devices. Table 2 shows the descriptive statistics about users' perceptions around permission and privacy.

Table 2. User perception about permission and privacy (n = 369)

Perception statements	%					
	SD	D	N	A	SA	Mean
I trust providers to protect my personal data	24.9	31.9	20.8	16.8	4.0	2.4
I am comfortable allowing other sites to access my accounts so that I can login to apps faster (e.g., "Login with Facebook/Google/etc.")	21.1	26.2	17.8	27.3	6.2	2.7
I am comfortable providing sensitive information to apps and services	37.9	33.6	14.3	10.8	2.1	2.0
I am comfortable with apps and services accessing data that I have created (e.g., pictures I have taken with my camera)	35.5	32.7	16.2	12.4	1.9	2.1
I am comfortable with apps and services collecting information about me	39.5	37.4	10.8	9.2	2.1	1.9
I am comfortable with my device camera and/or microphone to record me	43.0	24.3	10.3	15.4	4.3	2.1
I feel that I have sufficient control over how my personal information is collected and used	17.3	33.0	21.6	22.7	3.2	2.6
I am satisfied with the available explanations of how my apps and services will use my data	15.1	34.6	21.4	22.2	2.7	2.6
It is easy to identify the types or kinds of data I am sharing	14.9	29.2	24.6	23.3	4.6	2.7
It is easy for me to change the privacy settings in individual devices, apps and/or online services	10.0	21.4	17.0	37.6	10.0	3.1
I find it easy to manage permissions settings across the range of devices, apps and online services that I use	10.0	27.3	21.1	31.4	6.7	2.9
Privacy and permissions settings make it easy for me to understand how my data would be used	11.3	25.4	24.9	30.8	5.4	2.9

The analysis showed that (31.9%) of participants showed distrust on services provider to protect their personal data. On the other hand, 27.4% of participants felt comfort during allowing sites to access their social media account information for login in purpose that showed their trust in services provider to access and use their personal data. Majority of participants (37.7%, 31.4%, and 30.9%) are agreed that it is easy for them to change the privacy setting, manage the permission setting, and easy understanding how their data will be used by the services providers. Conversely, many participants (e.g., 37.9%, 35.5%, 39.6%, and 43.1%) did not feel comfortable to give access to their sensitive information, pictures, camera and microphone respectively which showed the negative perception of users.

Table 3 shows the percentages of the sensitive data that participants consider them as important to control and manage them regularly in the privacy settings. In the additional comments regarding the importance of personal data, one of the participants shared why personal information, such as names, emails and birth dates, is *"Extremely Important"* to consider whether to share or not because this vital information would lead to bad consequences. For example, *"personal data such as names and birth dates are vital information that would lead to very bad consequences once in the wrong hands as they may be used by scam groups who seek people of a particular age/background"*.

Table 3. The importance of user's personal information for sharing

Important of Personal Information statements	%					
	SD	D	N	A	SA	Mean
Your current location	7.0	9.2	9.4	25.7	44.9	3.9
Your name	11.9	17.0	14.9	24.3	29.0	3.4
Your date of birth	13.5	18.9	13.0	23.5	27.1	3.3
Your email address	9.7	8.6	10.5	31.9	37.4	3.8
Your social media identity	9.4	11.1	17.0	23.3	36.5	3.6
Your phone number	9.4	8.1	8.4	17.3	54.7	4.0
Your home address	13.0	8.1	9.4	10.3	56.6	3.9
Details about your device (e.g., type of device and network address)	14.0	14.9	16.5	21.6	28.7	3.3
Your photo and videos	19.2	6.2	5.9	7.3	58.5	3.8
Details of your calendar	20.0	13.2	12.4	19.7	31.7	3.3

Another comment regarding users' concern about forcing them to choose 'allow cookies', for example, *"I think we are forced to agree governments will have access to all the population data also I never understood the 'allow cookies'"*. The forced acceptance of cookers can raise serious concerns and distrust. One of the participants suggested that allowing permission requests should be associated with the nature of app use. For example, *"if we r using online supermarket for grocery shopping then obviously for that app, we need to provide our home address, phone number and email address for home delivery"*. Therefore, online services such as apps installed on smart devices raise privacy concerns since they may be used to profile user traits and preferences. Therefore, users should not be concerned regarding their personal information from the services provider regarding their sensitive data and privacy.

Ten participants shared thoughts on whether the user can control sharing different types of information about them. The key issues are listed below, along with the number of respondents raising related points in each case:

– Concerns about privacy and sharing personal information (7).

- Willingness to share information based on benefits and trustworthiness (3).
- The importance of personal information (2).
- Need for education about privacy and security (2).
- Accepting the need to share information for certain types of apps and services (1).

4.3   User Behaviour About Permission and Privacy

This section analyses users' behaviour with permissions and privacy and asks partici-pants about their privacy settings management while they use their online activities. In addition, it uncovers their behaviours regarding allowing or denying permission requests and online services using their sensitive data. Table 4 highlights the descriptive statistics regarding user behaviour regarding permission and privacy. Out of the 494 participants who took part in this study, only 38 participants shared their insights about users' behaviour regarding permission and privacy.

The analysis showed that the majority of participants, 50%, indicated that they do not take the time to read the privacy policies before using services and devices. One of the participants shared a subjective experience about this fact, such as the detail, understanding, reading and other problem with permission-related privacy info and privacy policies; for example, "*I think that the privacy measures that are always required are important, but because they are very many procedures, points and details and are not clear to the ordinary person who is not a specialist, they cause a complex, so to speak, not to read and agree without reading, and it is necessary to find a clearer and less complicated way and method*" and "Statement *is written by lawyers in small letter and very lengthy as well as hard to read and comprehend*". The other reason shared by the participants is that they are not giving permission requests because users may trust the service providers. For example, "*I find privacy policies quite misleading and/or indirect. That is usually -in my humble opinion- way for the app developers to make it easier to access data in order to sell it*". Conversely, 35.4% of participants revealed that they did not take the time to check the permission requested by the online service before giving consent. Conversely, 39.3% and 37.1% of participants (significant for this particular statement) agreed that they either think carefully about giving access to their information or prefer to decline the requests if the permission requests are regarding their sensitive data, respectively. Furthermore, 31.6% of participants showed their intention to identify the risks associated with the permission requests so that they can take optimal decisions based on the knowledge and facts. On the other hand, most participants (approximately 48% of responses fall between strongly disagree to disagree) said they usually did not turn off Wi-Fi when they were not using the device/app. For example, one participant said, "*I always turn off Wi-Fi but specifically for privacy-related reasons*".

After analyzing the quotes, some common themes emerged that could be linked to the statistical responses. The key themes and instances of occurrence are identified below:

- Carefully consider app permissions and privacy policies (4).
- Carelessness towards privacy (3).
- Difficulties understanding and reading privacy policies (2).
- Fear of identity theft (1).

Table 4. User behaviour about permission and privacy (n = 361)

Behaviour statements	%					
	SD	D	N	A	SA	Mean
I take the time to read privacy policies before using devices and services	22.4	31.8	19.6	16.6	6.3	2.5
I take the time to check the permissions requested that would access my data on my devices before giving my consent	13.3	22.1	14.4	34.0	13.3	3.1
I make a point of reviewing/regularly checking any privacy and permission settings on my devices	19.1	28.5	18.0	23.5	8.5	2.7
I decline permission requested that I perceive would collect sensitive information about me	4.9	5.5	16.9	37.1	33.2	3.9
I think carefully before allowing access to my information	4.9	8.3	16.9	39.3	29.3	3.8
I typically change my account privacy and permissions settings to limit the collection and use of my data	10.2	21.0	22.1	30.1	13.3	3.1
I take the time to identify the risks associated with the permissions requested	7.7	20.5	23.8	31.5	14.4	3.2
I usually deny requested for access to information I consider to be sensitive or personal	4.4	9.9	11.9	37.1	34.6	3.8

- Turning off Wi-Fi for privacy reasons (1).

   It was evident that the users were aware of the privacy and permission shared but felt that they were forced to do so as the service provider is not allowing them to use the app services before sharing their sensitive data, which is a genuine concern for them. For example, *"if you do not agree will be denied access to the site, or you cannot use the app"*. Similarly, *"I accept sharing my information because I am obligated to do so to work"*. They also found the policy writing language is too long and complicated to understand and agree to. For example, *"the privacy policy in most apps are very long, sometimes 5 or 6 pages, that is not easy to read & understand"*.

4.4 Summary Results

Table 5 uses the Likert scale that ranged from strongly disagree (1) to strongly agree (5) to determine mean and standard deviation of the responses observed across the different themes. The minimum and maximum values of responses also fall between the range of 1 to 5. The mean value is calculated from all the responses to statements within each of the three categories (i.e. knowledge, perception and behaviours), to give an overall value for each category. We screened out people who did not answer all questions in a given subset, and then ran reliability coefficients on the full data scores. The 'Don't Know' responses were excluded, so that the percentages are based on the total number of responses with Strongly Disagree to Strongly Agree answers.

Table 5. Summary results for the three dimensions

	Minimum	Maximum	Mean	Std. Dev	Median
User knowledge	1.1	5	3.09	.717	3.11
User perception	1.7	4.1	2.51	.739	2.42
User behaviour	1.2	4.9	3.19	.837	3.10

It has been found that all the values are average above three with regard to user knowledge and behaviours sections, which indicates that most of the participants agree with the given statements in the questionnaire Mean (3.09, 3.19) respectively. It was found (using composite indices that averaged their ratings on multiple items covering each topic) that survey respondents with a better understanding of permission and privacy settings significantly differed from those with negative. This was true when either: (a) discussing their use of privacy settings, (b) the time they take to manage their data, or (c) their considering privacy information as important. If users have negative perceptions, they may decline to provide access to service providers. This study showed that users are relatively uncomfortable and present a weak level of trust that can influence their actual behaviours towards privacy and permission settings with Mean (2.51).

Finally, the standard deviations for each category fall mostly under 1, which is a normal and acceptable range, and suggest a level of overall consistency in the respondents' views in each case.

Reliability was calculated using Cronbach's Alpha, which showed .76 for User knowledge, .87 for User perceptions, and .87 for User behaviours, for all proposed variables. A Cronbach's alpha value of .7 or higher is generally considered to indicate good reliability, meaning that the items on the scale or test are measuring the same underlying construct to a high degree. Therefore, the values of .76, .87, and .87 indicate that the questions or variables used to measure user knowledge, perception, and behavior about permission and privacy are measuring a consistent and reliable concept. As such, we concluded that our model variables were sufficiently valid to be constructed in the model as well as suitable for use in further analyses.

5   Discussion and Conclusions

As a result of our study that actual behaviours concern how much users are concerned about regularly checking and denying the service provider access to their personal information to keep their privacy and permission setting more secure. The relationship concerns technical and practical knowledge of smart devices and risks associated with giving specific access to a service provider. The complete knowledge about risks may prevent them from providing access to their personal data using privacy and permission settings. The user knowledge about permission and privacy includes questions about how many users have read, understand, and are ready to give access after knowledge about the risks associated with their data as it can influence their actual behaviours towards privacy and permission setting. The user perception includes trust, comfortable, feeling, and control when they are given access to the service provider for their sensitive data. If users have negative perceptions, they may decline to provide access to service providers. This study showed that users are relatively uncomfortable and present a weak level of trust that can influence their actual behaviours towards privacy and permission settings.

Previous studies of permissions and privacy issues have mainly focused on a specific context or domain, such as mobile app permissions, website cookies requests or social media permissions. According to [40], there are different scenarios when users deny permissions, such as denial rates varying from 10% to 23% according to permission type and from 5% to 19% across app categories of the Play Store. This supported our finding when more than 70% of our participants agreed with the statement to decline permission requested that would collect sensitive information about them. Around 33.6% of the participants believe that their personal data cannot be read, modified or deleted from their smart devices after giving permission without notifying them, indicating a lower level of understanding of permissions and privacy. A similar study showed that users commonly misunderstood the scope of permission requests and how online services could use their personal data [42]. Moreover, more than 68% think carefully before allowing access to their information. This finding provides insight into the burden on users to control and manage their data. Privacy and permission settings solution does not consider reducing users' cognitive burden (finding out about the risks of apps) or physical burden (navigating settings screens) when handling their settings.

It is found that regular consumers do not read and misunderstand permission requirements [44], which supports our finding. This demonstrates a gap between behaviours and knowledge about permissions and privacy settings. Thus, it is reasonable to assist consumers by allowing them to easily manage and revisit their privacy settings. The number of privacy decisions is growing; therefore, it is unrealistic for ordinary users to have the full benefits of all these privacy settings available on different platforms. In addition, the service providers even transfer some privacy protection responsibilities to the users [43].

End-users often lack motivation and time to manage the available settings when these mechanisms exist. According to Solove, internet users may not completely take advantage of all privacy controls available to them if they are designed to be self-managed [42]. Our findings clearly show that more than 47% did not make a point of reviewing /regularly checking any privacy and permission settings on their devices. Indeed, a recent PEW survey has found that 91% of users in the US feel they have less or no control over their data [41]. We found that more than 50% of our participants feel that they do not have sufficient control over how their personal information is collected and used. It has also been observed that most users are unable to understand the nature, type and amount of data collected by the apps when granted permission [30]. However, about 30% had the same result regarding privacy and permissions settings, that it easy for them to understand how their data would be used.

What is surprising is that more than 47% of our participants disagree with reviewing or regularly checking any privacy and permission settings on their devices. Where 18% of the participants did not provide their actual behaviours to this statement which is alarming fact. Although privacy details and permission settings are often made available, they can fall short of capturing and communicating the essential considerations that users care about or offering them a meaningful level of control. It is clear that, the number of privacy settings attached to every online service has its permission settings, making it unmanageable for the user to go over each setting. Moreover, the available permission can fall short of providing the user control over what to choose to be private. Thus, it deprives the user of making knowledgeable and informed decisions about what permissions to accept or decline. In addition, usually, the device's permission settings are provided in a long, difficult-to-read language that forces the user to accept whatever has been decided by the app provider. Consequently, users many not make informed permissions-related decisions when giving permissions to apps due to a lack of understanding of permissions and interface issues.

It is unclear whether brief privacy information may effectively make users aware of potentially risky practices. This paper addresses the question by studying the users' knowledge, perceptions and self-declared behaviours regarding privacy and permissions that users face on their devices. While generating insights on designing more usable privacy settings and options, these studies do not provide users with a privacy setting where they can set their preferences once and then link them to an individual app or service. These findings will help us toward developing a novel privacy and permissions framework for a new control privacy setting that enables consumers to express their privacy preferences once at the meta-level. Moreover, it can help consumers find and manage their sensitive resources in a more usable and accessible way. Therefore, the privacy setting assists users in configuring settings for specific permission across all apps and web services and individual apps via privacy settings. Finally, the privacy setting will show users the purpose information, assisting users in better understanding how an app might use sensitive information. The users will have the option to configure an app or online services privacy settings at the meta-level. The design interface for the privacy setting will depend on the survey results and looking towards the data collection to confirm the final design for users' privacy preferences. These findings draw our attention to the importance of considering points for the privacy setting interfaces to specifying the purposes of each permission access and checking the reason for each access to users' data (tracking, users' actions, functionality of the online service). Further work is required to assist users with a live privacy meter connected to the user's privacy preferences in the privacy setting to present the risk of the online service.

Acknowledgements. The authors would like to acknowledge the input from Julie Haney of the Visualisation and Usability Group at the National Institute of Standards and Technology (NIST) for her valuable input and comments into the design of the questionnaire instrument.

References

1. Felt, A.P., Ha, E., Egelman, S., Haney, A., Chin, E., Wagner, D.: Android permissions: user attention, comprehension, and behavior. In: Proceedings of the 8th Symposium on Usable Privacy and Security, SOUPS 2012, pp. 1–14 (2012). https://doi.org/10.1145/2335356.2335360
2. Zadeh, M.E., Kambar, N., Esmaeilzadeh, A., Kim, Y., Taghva, K.: A survey on mobile malware detection methods using machine learning (2022). https://doi.org/10.1109/CCWC54503.2022.9720753

3. Lin, J., Amini, S., Hong, J.I., Sadeh, N., Lindqvist, J., Zhang, J.: Expectation and purpose: understanding users' mental models of mobile app privacy through crowdsourcing. In: Proceedings of the 2012 ACM Conference on Ubiquitous Computing, pp. 501–510 (2012)
4. Smullen, D., Feng, Y., Zhang, S., Sadeh, N.M.: The best of both worlds: mitigating trade-offs between accuracy and user burden in capturing mobile app privacy preferences. Proc. Priv. Enhancing Technol. **2020**(1), 195–215 (2020)
5. Benton, K., Camp, L.J., Garg, V.: Studying the effectiveness of Android application permissions requests. In: IEEE International Conference on Pervasive Computing and Communications Workshops, PerCom Workshops, pp. 291–296 (2013)
6. Kelley, P.G., Consolvo, S., Cranor, L.F., Jung, J., Sadeh, N., Wetherall, D.: A conundrum of permissions: installing applications on an Android smartphone. In: Financial Cryptography and Data Security, FC 2012 Workshops, USEC and WECSR (2012)
7. Yus, F.: Smartphone Communication: Interactions in the App Ecosystem. Routledge (2021)
8. Betzing, J.H., Tietz, M., vom Brocke, J., Becker, J.: The impact of transparency on mobile privacy decision making. Electron. Mark. **30**(3), 607–625 (2019)
9. Kelley, P.G., Cranor, L.F., Sadeh, N.: Privacy as part of the app decision-making process. In: Proceedings of the SIGCHI Conference on Human Factors in Computing Systems, pp. 3393–3402 (2013)
10. Tan, J., et al.: The effect of developer-specified explanations for permission requests on smartphone user behavior. In: Proceedings of the SIGCHI Conference on Human Factors in Computing Systems, pp. 91–100 (2014). https://doi.org/10.1145/2556288.2557400
11. Liu, X., Leng, Y., Yang, W., Wang, W., Zhai, C., Xie, T.: A large-scale empirical study on Android runtime-permission rationale messages (2018). https://doi.org/10.1109/VLHCC.2018.8506574
12. Lin, J., Yu, W., Zhang, N., Yang, X., Zhang, H., Zhao, W.: A survey on Internet of Things: architecture, enabling technologies, security and privacy, and applications. IEEE Internet Things J. **4**(5), 1125 (2017). https://doi.org/10.1109/JIOT.2017.2683200
13. Olejnik, K., Dacosta, I., Soares Machado, J., Huguenin, K., Khan, M.E., Hubaux, J.-P.: SmarPer: context-aware and automatic runtime-permissions for mobile devices (2017)
14. Ismail, Q.: Crowdsourcing permission settings for mobile apps to help users balance privacy and usability. Doctoral dissertation, Indiana University (2018)
15. Alepis, E., Patsakis, C.: Monkey says, monkey does: security and privacy on voice assistants. IEEE Access **5**, 17841–17851 (2017)
16. Boroojeni, K.G., Amini, M.H., Iyengar, S.S.: Overview of the security and privacy issues in smart grids. In: Boroojeni, K.G., Amini, M.H., Iyengar, S.S. (eds.) Smart Grids: Security and Privacy Issues, pp. 1–16. Springer, Cham (2017). https://doi.org/10.1007/978-3-319-45050-6_1
17. Fathi, S.: More users trust Amazon and Google to handle their personal user data than Apple, survey suggests. MacRumors (2021). https://www.macrumors.com/2021/12/22/survey-amazon-and-google-user-data-more-than-apple/
18. Graeff, T.R., Harmon, S.: Collecting and using personal data: consumers' awareness and concerns. J. Consum. Mark. **19**(4) (2002)
19. Carrascal, J.P., Riederer, C., Erramilli, V., Cherubini, M.: Your browsing behavior for a big mac: economics of personal information online (2013). http://mozilla.org/firefox
20. Shih, F., Liccardi, I., Weitzner, D.J., Csail, M.: Privacy tipping points in smartphones privacy preferences (2015). https://doi.org/10.1145/2702123.2702404
21. Lim, S.L., Bentley, P.J., Kanakam, N., Ishikawa, F., Honiden, S.: Investigating country differences in mobile app user behavior and challenges for software engineering. IEEE Trans. Softw. Eng. **41**(01), 40–64 (2015)
22. Gu, J., Xu, Y.C., Xu, H., Zhang, C., Ling, H.: Privacy concerns for mobile app download: an elaboration likelihood model perspective. Decis. Support Syst. **94**, 19–28 (2017)

23. Herold, R., Hertzog, C.: Data Privacy for the Smart Grid. Taylor & Francis (2015)
24. Chen, H.T., Kim, Y.: Problematic use of social network sites: the interactive relationship between gratifications sought and privacy concerns. Cyberpsychol. Behav. Soc. Netw. **16**, 806–812 (2013)
25. McCay-Peet, L., Quan-Haase, A.: What is social media and what questions can social media research help us answer. In: The SAGE Handbook of Social Media Research Methods (2017)
26. Stieger, S., Burger, C., Bohn, M., Voracek, M.: Who commits virtual identity suicide? Differences in privacy concerns, Internet addiction, and personality between Facebook users and quitters. Cyberpsychol. Behav. Soc. Netw. **16**(9), 629–634 (2013). https://doi.org/10.1089/CYBER.2012.0323
27. Beierle, F., et al.: What data are smartphone users willing to share with researchers? J. Ambient. Intell. Humaniz. Comput. **11**(6), 2277–2289 (2019). https://doi.org/10.1007/s12652-019-01355-6
28. Schmidtke, H.R.: Location-aware systems or location-based services: a survey with applications to Covid-19 contact tracking. J. Reliab. Intell. Environ. **6**(4), 191–214 (2020)
29. Almuhimedi, H.: Helping Smartphone Users Manage their Privacy through Nudges (2017)
30. Shen, B., et al.: Can systems explain permissions better? Understanding users' misperceptions under smartphone runtime permission model. In: 30th USENIX Security Symposium (USENIX Security 2021), pp. 751–768 (2021)
31. Raab, C.: The role of national privacy law in shaping privacy attitudes and behaviors. Priv. Secur. Law Rep. **13**(7), 1–6 (2017)
32. Nguyen, L.T., Gligor, D.V.: Privacy attitudes and behaviors in the context of emerging technologies. J. Am. Soc. Inf. Sci. **66**(10), 2040–2049 (2015)
33. Pankowski, N., Kaminska, A.: The impact of national privacy laws on privacy behaviors in mobile applications. Priv. Secur. Law Rep. **16**(4), 1–6 (2020)
34. Wijesekera, P., et al.: The feasibility of dynamically granted permissions: aligning mobile privacy with user preferences (2017)
35. Mendes, R., Brandão, A., Vilela, J.P., Beresford, A.R.: Effect of user expectation on mobile app privacy: a field study. In: 2022 IEEE International Conference on Pervasive Computing and Communications (PerCom), pp. 207–214 (2022)
36. Kokolakis, S.: Privacy attitudes and privacy behaviour: a review of current research on the privacy paradox phenomenon. Comput. Secur. **64**, 122–134 (2017)
37. Barth, S., De Jong, M.D.: The privacy paradox–Investigating discrepancies between expressed privacy concerns and actual online behavior–a systematic literature review. Telemat. Inform. **34**, 1038–1058 (2017)
38. Woodruff, A., Pihur, V., Consolvo, S., Schmidt, L., Brandimarte, L., Acquisti, A.: Would a privacy fundamentalist sell their DNA for $1000... if nothing bad happened as a result? The Westin categories, behavioral intentions, and consequences. In: Symposium on Usable Privacy and Security (SOUPS), vol. 5, p. 1 (2014)
39. Woźniak, P.W., et al.: Creepy technology: what is it and how do you measure it? In: Proceedings of the 2021 CHI Conference on Human Factors in Computing Systems (2021)
40. Wijesekera, P., et al.: Android permissions remystified: a field study on contextual integrity. In: 24th USENIX Security Symposium (USENIX Security 2015) (2015)
41. Madden, M., Rainie, L.: Americans' attitudes about privacy, security and surveillance (2015)
42. Solove, D.J.: Introduction: privacy self-management and the consent dilemma. Harv. L. Rev. **126**, 1880 (2012)
43. Jesus, V., Pandit, H.J.: Consent receipts for a usable and auditable web of personal data. IEEE Access **10**, 28545–28563 (2022). https://doi.org/10.1109/ACCESS.2022.3157850

44. Linden, T., Khandelwal, R., Harkous, H., Fawaz, K.: The privacy policy landscape after the GDPR. In: Proceedings on Privacy Enhancing Technologies, pp. 47–64 (2020). https://doi.org/10.2478/popets-2020-0004
45. School of Computer Science Research Ethics Committee. Application for ethics approval - Online Privacy and Permissions Survey - Ref no. CS-2021-R49. Ethicsadmin@cs.nott.ac.uk (2022)

Capability Maturity Models for Targeted Cyber Security Training

Sabarathinam Chockalingam[1(✉)], Espen Nystad[2], and Coralie Esnoul[3]

[1] Department of Risk and Security, Institute for Energy Technology, 1777 Halden, Norway
Sabarathinam.Chockalingam@ife.no
[2] Department of Human-Centred Digitalization, Institute for Energy Technology, 1777 Halden, Norway
Espen.Nystad@ife.no
[3] Department of Risk and Safety, Institute for Energy Technology, 1777 Halden, Norway
Coralie.Esnoul@ife.no

Abstract. There will be more and more connected devices in use around the world with the evolution of technologies like Internet of Things. Furthermore, with the emergence of remote working, humans and critical systems in organizations are increasingly connected through the internet. At the same time, there is an increased rate of cyber-attacks. These are reasons why cyber security is critically important to contemporary society as these factors make most organizations even more susceptible to cyber-attacks. Such cyber-attacks are often initiated through the lack of awareness of humans in organizations. Therefore, humans are regarded as the weakest link in cyber security.

Effective and efficient cyber security training plays a crucial role to strengthen this weakest link. However, a factor that makes cyber security training not efficient in practice is the one-size-fits-all approach, instead of considering the current cyber security competence level of different personnel in the organization while choosing cyber security training. In this study, we mainly utilised Capability Maturity Models (CMMs) to tackle the above-mentioned challenge especially based on their applications in domains like e-learning. However, typical maturity levels used in such CMMs are not directly suitable for our application. Therefore, we relied on different levels of Bloom's taxonomy that are suitable for our application in determining the individual cyber security competence level. Finally, we illustrate the proposed framework using different examples involving specific group of personnel in an organization (i.e., Information and Communication Technology users). The main goal of this approach is to support the organization in strategically choosing targeted training activities for different personnel.

Keywords: Bloom's taxonomy · Capability maturity models · Cyber-attacks · Cyber security · Training

1 Introduction

Increasing digitalization and connectivity has been a trend over the years in different organizations across domains. It has improved efficiency, productivity, and decreased costs. Digitalization makes information easily accessible to those who need it, but it can also provide opportunity for adversaries who may want to steal, alter, or destroy it. Such adversaries may also look to gain access to critical systems and disrupt business operations. Therefore, it is important to safeguard sensitive information and critical systems against cyber-attacks using relevant security measures, such as access control, and encryption.

As technical security measures against cyber-attacks have improved and more widely used, adversaries have increasingly turned to social engineering techniques that can bypass technical security measures by targeting humans (i.e., system users) [1]. These techniques try to trick users into providing sensitive information such as passwords, clicking on phishing links that can result in installing malicious software (malware) in critical systems, which can then lead to data theft [2]. Social engineering attacks can be costly as they can shut down a business in some cases. On the other hand, it may require more time and resources to recover/restore normal operations after a successful social engineering-attack. An example is the ransomware attack on the energy and aluminum production company called *"Hydro"*. Ransomware attack is typically initiated via email. Ransomware is a type of malware, which locks the user out of their computer, encrypt their files, and demand a ransom to give back access [3]. The attack on Hydro spread across several parts of the organization in United States of America (USA) and Europe and estimated to cost 70 million USD [4]. In case users learn to recognise social engineering-attacks, they can to some extent identify and avoid falling for such attacks. In this way, users can also be seen as an important barrier for cyber-attacks. Therefore, an important way to keep systems safe is therefore to train/educate users to be able to recognise threats and perform correct preventive and mitigative actions.

Plant operators, safety engineers, and security professionals are among different groups of personnel who are responsible for the seamless functioning of Critical Infrastructures (CIs) [5]. On the other hand, in an organization, there are different groups of personnel like Information and Communication Technology (ICT), finance, and HR. As a part of their cyber security training, each group of personnel would have different learning objectives in addition to different topics of interest within cyber security. Furthermore, individuals within each group would have different competence level on each topic within cyber security. For instance, a person might be in an advanced level in the topic of phishing whereas another person might not have any idea about the topic of phishing. In this case, the former does not need to be trained again on the same topic of phishing, and rather needs to be trained on a different and/or advanced topic to make the training more efficient. On the other hand, the latter needs to be trained on the basics of phishing at first. However, the current one-size-fits-all approach in cyber security trainings are not optimally efficient in practice as they do not cater different individual needs [6]. More importantly, the management responsible for choosing trainings do not consider competence level of different individuals on the topics of interest within cyber security for their group. This is because there is a lack of methods that would help to determine individual cyber security competence levels in an organization.

Capability Maturity Models (CMMs) possess the potential to tackle this challenge especially based on their existing applications in cyber security [7], and e-learning [8] where CMMs were adapted and used to tackle similar challenges. CMMs provide a framework to assess the current maturity of an organization's process in a specific domain and support to gradually improve the maturity of it in the future [9]. CMMs are widely used in software development processes [10]. However, typical maturity levels in CMMs such as initial, managed are appropriate for assessing the maturity level of processes but not the competence level of people. Therefore, Bloom's taxonomy of educational objectives can be potentially integrated into CMMs to address this challenge. This research provides a framework to develop maturity models that helps to assess the competence level of different individuals on each topic within cyber security by addressing the research question (RQ): *"How could we integrate Capability Maturity Models (CMMs) and bloom's taxonomy of educational objectives to determine individual cyber security competence levels that support the planning of cyber security training in an organization?"*. The research objectives (ROs) are:

- **RO1.** To propose a CMM-based framework that would help to assess the individual cyber security competence level in an organization.
- **RO2.** To exemplify the proposed CMM-based framework through different examples.

The remainder of this paper is structured as follows: Sect. 2 provides an overview of CMMs in cyber security and e-learning in addition to the use of bloom's taxonomy as well as the different concepts of cyber security curricular framework. In Sect. 3, the proposed CMM framework is described with components from bloom's taxonomy and cyber security curricular framework. This framework is illustrated with different examples, using a group of ICT users in Sect. 4, followed by the conclusions and future work directions in Sect. 5.

2   Background: Methods Definition and Applications

2.1   Capability Maturity Models in Cyber Security and E-Learning

This section provides an overview of CMMs in cyber security [11–13] and e-learning [8, 14, 15] with a specific focus on the objective and components of each CMMs that would help to design our framework.

Barclay proposed a CMM to assess how an organization or a country is doing in terms of their preparedness to manage and respond to threats and vulnerabilities [11]. The proposed CMM has six different maturity levels: undefined (level 0), initial (level 1), basic (level 2), defined (level 3), dynamic (level 4), and optimizing (level 5). The underlying pillars which are used in this model to indicate the maturity level include: (i) attitude to threats and vulnerabilities, (ii) technological development, (iii) societal response, (iv) technical measures, (v) business measures, (vi) legal and regulatory measures, (vii) operational measures, and (viii) education/capability building measures. This would help organizations to determine their maturity level on different pillars/indicators considered. For instance, an organization might be in level 0 on the pillar *"attitude to threats and vulnerabilities"*, whereas they may be in level 2 on the pillar *"technological development"*. In this case, this would provide inputs to the management on which pillars need to be improved to reach an overall desired maturity level (example: level 1) in terms of their preparedness to manage and respond to threats and vulnerabilities in an organization. White developed a cyber security CMM which has five different maturity levels to determine the current level of preparedness in a specific community to prevent, detect, and respond to a cyber-attack [12]. The developed cyber security CMM has five different maturity levels: level 1 (security aware), level 2 (process development), level 3 (information enabled), level 4 (tactics development), and level 5 (full security operation capability). For instance, *"security aware"* implies that the community is aware of cyber security threats and issues, whereas *"process development"* means that the required security processes are established by the community to effectively deal with cyber security issues. The underlying pillars which are used in this model to indicate the maturity level includes: threats addressed, metrics, information sharing, technology, training, and testing. For instance, the goal of level 1 in this model on the underlying pillar *"information sharing"* is to establish information sharing committee. This would in turn help them to plan how to gradually advance on each pillar to the desired maturity level in terms of their preparedness to successfully prevent, detect, and respond to a cyber-attack.

Marshall et al. proposed a CMM for e-learning [8]. This CMM would help institutions to assess their current level in terms of their e-learning processes and develop a roadmap to reach the desired level in e-learning in the future. This CMM has five different maturity levels which include: (i) level 1 (initial) – focus on ad-hoc processes, (ii) level 2 (planned) – focus on establishing clear objectives for e-learning, (iii) level 3 (defined) – focus on establishing defined processes for development, (iv) level 4 (managed) – focus on ensuring the quality of both the e-learning resources and student learning outcomes, and (v) level 5 (optimizing) – focus on continual improvement. Each of these maturity levels rely on the four different underlying pillars which include: (i) student learning, (ii) resource creation, (iii) project management and support, and (iv) organizational management. Marshall et al. have also provided key requirements on each level for these four different pillars. Solar et al. proposed a CMM for Information and Communication Technology (ICT) in school education to assess the current level of an institution in terms of their ICT usage in school education and develop a roadmap to reach the desired level by gradually improving the ICT usage in school education in the future [14]. The major components of the proposed maturity model include: (i) leverage domains (educational management, infrastructure, administrators, teachers, and students), (ii) Key Domain Areas (KDAs – 25 in total) corresponding to each leverage domain, and (iii) measurable critical variables corresponding to KDA. The proposed maturity model has five different maturity levels (level 1 – level 5). In addition, this CMM introduces five different capability levels: (i) level 1 (initial), (ii) level 2 (developing), (iii) level 3 (defined), (iv) level 4 (managed) and (v) level 5 (optimized). These capability levels are determined for each critical variable in a KDA based on the responses from the institution. Furthermore, the capability level of a KDA is the weighted average of the determined capability levels of its critical variables.

The relevant components and structure from the above-mentioned CMMs are adapted to suit the purpose of this study which will be detailed in Sect. 3.

2.2 Cyber Security Curricular Framework

The *"Curriculum Guidelines for Post-Secondary Degree Programs in Cybersecurity"* is developed by a Joint Task Force on Cybersecurity Education [16]. This is based on a collaboration between international computing societies including ACM, IEEE-CS,

AIS SIGSEC, and IFIP WG 11.8. Experts were dedicated to creating thorough and adaptable curricular guidelines for cyber security education. This will then aid in the future establishment of programs and related cyber security educational initiatives. To support future program development, this report lists guidance to institutions seeking to structure their cyber security discipline by developing a thought model. This model defines the boundaries of the discipline and introduces cross-disciplinary views. The main concepts of this model and guidelines are introduced below to help to understand the framework, which will be detailed in Sect. 3.

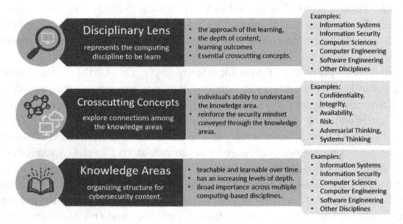

Fig. 1. Main Elements of Cyber Security Education Thought Model

The thought model shown in Fig. 1 illustrates three dimensions: knowledge areas, crosscutting concepts, and disciplinary lenses. These three dimensions are described as:

- **Knowledge Areas (KAs):** KAs are fundamental organizing framework for cyber security content. Each KA contains key knowledge that is widely applicable within and across different computing-based disciplines. KAs contain relevant Knowledge Units (KUs). KUs are thematic groups that include a wide range of linked topics and learning outcomes. Table 1 shows an example KA (i.e., Human security) including related KUs (i.e., social engineering, and awareness and understanding) and corresponding topics of each KU (i.e., The topics corresponding to social engineering KU include type of social engineering attacks, and detection and mitigation of social engineering attacks) [16]. Table 2 shows an example learning outcomes related to different topics contained in each KU [16].
- **Crosscutting Concepts:** This support students explore connections among the KAs and are critical to an individual's ability to comprehend the KA, independent of the disciplinary lens. The crosscutting concepts also reinforce the security mindset conveyed through each of the KAs. Confidentiality, Integrity, Availability, Risk, Adversarial Thinking, and Systems Thinking are the six concepts mentioned in this model to map and reinforce the security mindset when developing the cyber security discipline program.

- **Disciplinary Lens:** This represents the fundamental computing discipline upon which the cyber security program can be built. For the organization, this dimension represents the multi- and cross-disciplinary requirements to cover or begin learning and teaching cyber security.

Table 1. Knowledge Areas, Knowledge Units, and Topics - Example [16]

Knowledge Areas	Knowledge Units	Topics
Human Security	Social Engineering	Type of Social Engineering Attacks
		Detection and Mitigation of Social Engineering Attacks
	Awareness and understanding	Cyber Hygiene
		Cyber Vulnerabilities and Threat Awareness

Table 2. Knowledge Units, and Learning Outcomes – Example [16]

Knowledge Units	Learning Outcomes
Social Engineering	Demonstrate overall understanding of the types of social engineering attacks, psychology of social engineering attacks, and misleading users
	Demonstrate the ability to identify types of social engineering attacks
	Demonstrate the ability to implement approaches for detection and mitigation of social engineering attacks
Awareness and understanding	Discuss the importance of cyber hygiene, cyber security user education, as well as cyber vulnerabilities and threats awareness

2.3 Bloom's Taxonomy

A taxonomy that has been used in education to classify learning objectives is Bloom's taxonomy [17]. The original taxonomy categorized learning objectives into knowledge, comprehension, application, analysis, synthesis, and evaluation. An update of the taxonomy has been done to make it more appropriate for modern outcome-focused learning objectives [17]. In this update, the nouns have been replaced with verbs, while the category *"create"* has replaced *"synthesis"* and been placed as the last category. Table 3 shows the updated categories and their associated cognitive processes. These categories form a hierarchy, where the objectives on the right-hand side (Example: Create – Generate/Plan/Produce) are more complex than the ones on the left-hand side (Example:

Remember – Recognize/Recall) of the table. The objectives on the right-hand side in this way represents a deeper understanding of the topic. In the updated taxonomy, it is also recognized that there is some overlap within the categories and their underlying cognitive processes. The knowledge category from the original taxonomy has been incorporated as a second dimension that refers to the type of knowledge to be known: factual, conceptual, procedural, or metacognitive knowledge. Thus, each of the categories in Table 3 can be applied on any of the four knowledge types.

The taxonomy can be used to identify and plan instructional activities (e.g., [18]), which focused on the higher-level learning objectives, and to identify methods for assessing whether the learning objectives have been met (e.g., [19]). In assessment, the cognitive processes can be used as guide words for creating questions or tests for assessing students' competence level. For instance, students could be asked to recall definitions (remember); provide examples, classify, or summarize knowledge (to demonstrate understanding of the material); or use the knowledge in a new context by solving tasks (applying the material). In this way, individual learners can be tested to find their current competence level according to the learning objectives.

Table 3. Categories in Bloom's Taxonomy of Educational Objectives

Remember	Understand	Apply	Analyze	Evaluate	Create
1. Recognize 2. Recall	1. Interpret 2. Exemplify 3. Classify 4. Summarize 5. Infer 6. Compare 7. Explain	1. Execute 2. Implement	1. Differentiate 2. Organize 3. Attribute	1. Check 2. Critique	1. Generate 2. Plan 3. Produce

3   Proposed Framework

In this section, we describe our framework including main components, relationships between different components, and process corresponding to the use of the proposed framework.

As a part of the framework design, we elicited a set of requirements: (i) the framework needs to be adaptable for different type of personnel to be trained, (ii) the framework needs to be easily extendable in the future (for instance, including additional topics within cyber security), (iii) the framework needs to use common language (terminologies) as different organizations, and (iv) topics that need to be measured in each KU should be measurable through training assessments.

Firstly, in our CMM framework, we adapted leverage domains, KDAs, and measurable critical variables for our application from [14]. However, we adopted the notion of KAs, KUs, and topics from [16] and mapped it to leverage domains, KDAs, and measurable critical variables respectively, as they are relevant to our application. Figure 2 shows an example mapping in which we consider topics as measurable, like critical variables [14], in our framework especially in terms of individual competence level on each topic.

Fig. 2. Underlying Pillars Mapping – Example

Furthermore, in our framework, we adopted the list of KAs, KUs, and topics from the *Curriculum Guidelines for Post-Secondary Degree Programs in Cybersecurity* as it is comprehensive and flexible [16]. We can use the pre-defined list of KAs, KUs, and topics from the *Curriculum Guidelines for Post-Secondary Degree Programs in Cybersecurity* as the basis to discuss and shortlist topics that are relevant to the considered type of personnel to be trained involving relevant stakeholders in the organization. Depending on the needs of the organization especially considering the group of personnel to be trained, some KAs, KUs, and topics in the pre-defined list can be removed or changed in addition new KAs, KUs, and topics can be easily added depending on the evolution of the domain. For instance, in the *Curriculum Guidelines for Post-Secondary Degree Programs in Cybersecurity,* under the KU *social engineering,* there are four different topics including types of social engineering attacks, psychology of social engineering attacks, misleading users, and detection and mitigation of social engineering attacks. In case for a specific group of personnel to be trained, only two out of four topics are relevant (Example: types of social engineering attacks, and detection and mitigation of social engineering attacks), we can then easily remove the other two topics.

Moreover, in our framework, we used competence levels from bloom's taxonomy of educational objectives [17] instead of maturity and capability levels [14] as it is suitable in determining the individual competence level on different topics within cyber security. In addition, we introduced another level *"No Knowledge"* as it is relevant to our application. This is especially important when the trainee is not able to recall the training material (Example: Definition of phishing). In this case, the competence level of the trainee on phishing will be *"No Knowledge"*. We use the scale from 0 (*"No Knowledge"*) to 6 (*"Create"*) for competence levels from bloom's taxonomy of educational objectives. This can help to develop training material corresponding to each level in addition to prepare questions or tests on each level utilizing guide words for assessing individual cyber security competence level. For instance, if we want to test whether the competence level of the trainee is 1 or not (i.e., remember or no-knowledge) on the topic of phishing, we can ask the definition of phishing as a question. In case the trainee answers it, the trainee fulfills competence level 1. If not, the trainee fulfils competence level 0. However, the number of competence levels needed in a specific CMM can be adapted depending on the needs of the organization.

Finally, once we determine the individual competence level on each topic based on the test or assessment results, the competence level on corresponding KUs and KA can be determined using weighted average as it helps to reflect the relative importance on different topics.

The process involved in the use of the proposed framework includes: (i) group of personnel in an organization to be trained needs to be determined, (ii) appropriate KAs, KUs, and topics for the chosen group of personnel in an organization needs to be short-listed involving relevant stakeholders, (iii) number of competence level required needs to be decided based on the organization needs, (iv) training material and training assessment or tests for each competence level should be developed, (v) individual competence level of the trainee on each topic, corresponding KUs and KA needs to be determined, and (vi) based on the individual competence level and organization needs, appropriate cyber security trainings should be provided.

4   Illustration of the Proposed Framework – Examples

This section illustrates the process involved in the use of the proposed framework using different examples involving the group of ICT users in an organization.

Firstly, we defined the purpose and scope of our example CMM. This is illustrated through an example. We considered two different personnel in the organization: an ICT user (i.e., Alice), and the Chief Information Security Officer (CISO) (i.e., Tom), who is responsible for choosing cyber security trainings for ICT users. The current practice in choosing cyber security trainings for ICT users follows one-size-fits-all approach where all the ICT users receive the same cyber security trainings regardless of their existing competence. However, to provide appropriate and efficient cyber security trainings to the ICT user (Alice), the CISO (Tom) needs to know the current competence level of the ICT user (Alice) on relevant topics within cyber security (example: social engineering, privacy), otherwise the training may be inefficient or ineffective. The CMM which we develop will provide current competence level of an ICT user in an organization on relevant topics within cyber security.

Based on the inputs from the relevant stakeholders including the CISO (i.e., Tom), we shortlist appropriate KAs, KUs, and topics for the group of ICT users in which Alice belongs. The competence levels, in our example CMM, which we decide are as follows: level 0 – *"No Knowledge"*, level 1 – *"Remembering"* (i.e., the trainee remembers or recalls definition), level 2 – *"Understanding"* (i.e., the trainee is able to provide examples, classify, or summarize knowledge), and level 3 – *"Applying"* (i.e., the trainee is able to use the knowledge in a new context by solving tasks).

We chose the topics of information assets and phishing as examples for demonstrating the training material and training assessments in each competence level. Training on information assets is organized under the KA *"Organizational security"* as shown in Table 4. It covers knowledge about the types of data or information that is valuable for the organization and associated risks.

Table 4. Organization of the Curriculum Structure – Example

Knowledge Areas	Knowledge Units	Topics	Description for ICT User
Organizational Security	Risk Management	Information Assets	Know about information assets, their nature, different classifications and impact on confidentiality, integrity, availability
Human Security	Social Engineering	Types of Social Engineering Attacks	Know about phishing and spear-phishing attacks

Example training material and assessment questions for the topics of information assets, and types of social engineering attacks are presented in Table 5, and Table 6 respectively.

Table 5. Training Material and Assessment for Information Assets – Example

	Learning Objectives		
	Remember	Understand	Apply
Training Material	Definition of Information assets How are they stored? What are their classifications?	Description of examples of information assets, Examples: • Personally identifiable information • Research data • Confidential research results • Intellectual Property	Show some examples of information assets, their risks, and mitigations related to Confidentiality/Integrity/Availability, Examples: • Leaving printouts of confidential information in the printer room • Mitigations: locked printer room, identification required before printing • Having intellectual property on laptop. Mitigations: privacy screen protector, encrypted hard drive
Training Assessment	Multiple choice questions about the nature of information assets	Multiple choice task of things that can be information assets, Examples: • Operating procedures (correct) • Contracts (correct) • Information about how data is protected (e.g., network configuration) (correct) • Company funds/cash (wrong) • Expensive artworks (wrong)	Correctly identify mitigation measures for different information assets (could be assessed automatically) Describe your own information assets and their related risks (requires manual assessment)

In the example shown in Table 7, we considered human security as the KA, social engineering and awareness and understanding as the KUs in addition to four different topics. The example competence level is considered for the four different topics, to demonstrate how the overall competence level of corresponding KUs/KA can be determined. The individual competence level on each topic is usually based on training assessments. This individual competence level on each topic shows where an individual is lacking, and appropriate trainings can be planned.

Table 6. Training Material and Assessment for Phishing – Example

	Learning Objective		
	Remember	Understand	Apply
Training Material	As part of this training, videos highlighting the definition of phishing and spear phishing will be provided	As a part of this training, video listing ways to detect phishing emails such as mismatched URL, URLs with misleading domain name, Poor spellings, and grammar error	As a part of this training, we will video explaining ways to detect phishing emails through an example phishing email
Training Assessment	As part of this assessment, questions asking for the definition of phishing and spear phishing will be provided	As part of this assessment, questions will be provided to explain the ways to detect phishing emails	As part of this assessment, the trainee will apply the gained knowledge to classify phishing and legitimate email

Table 7. Competence Level on Different Topics – Example

KA	KU	Topics	Competence Level			
			0	1	2	3
Human Security	Social Engineering	Type of Social Engineering Attacks		X		
		Detection and Mitigation of Social Engineering Attacks				X
	Awareness and understanding	Cyber Hygiene			X	
		Cyber Vulnerabilities and Threat Awareness			X	

The competence level of a KU is the weighted average of the competence levels (CLs) of its variables $Topic_i$ (Eq. 1).

$$CL_{KU} = \text{Weighted average} [W_1 * CL(Topic_1), W_2 * CL(Topic_2), \ldots, W_n * CL(Topic_n)]/W_1 + \ldots + W_n \tag{1}$$

Weighted Average (KU)
Social Engineering = 2.5 (Weights Assumed: Type of Social Engineering Attacks = 1; Detection and Mitigation of Social Engineering Attacks = 3.)

Awareness and Understanding = 2 (Weights Assumed: Cyber Hygiene = 1; Cyber Vulnerabilities and Threat Awareness = 1.)

The competence level of a KA is the weighted average of the competence levels (CLs) of its variables KU_i (Eq. 2).

CL_{KA} = Weighted Average $[W_1 * CL(KU_1), W_2 * CL(KU_2), \ldots,$

$$W_n * CL(KU_n)]/W_1 + W_2 + \ldots + W_n \qquad (2)$$

Weighted Average (KA)

Human Security = 2 (Weights Assumed: Social Engineering = 2; Awareness and Understanding = 3.)

Data Security = (1 (3) + 2 (3))/3 = 9/3 = 3; This is a hypothetical example to show that the competence level of the user on data security is higher than human security. Therefore, it would allow the management responsible for choosing cyber security trainings to choose appropriately considering individual competence level on each topic in addition to weighted average on KU and KA.

5 Conclusions and Future Work Directions

Current one-size-fits-all approach in cyber security trainings does not cater varying needs of different groups of personnel within organizations. To address this issue, we proposed integrating CMMs and Bloom's Taxonomy of Educational Objectives to determine individual cyber security competence levels on different topics. This in turn would help management in choosing appropriate and efficient training for different groups of personnel. We illustrated the proposed framework using different examples.

This framework can contribute in several ways to increase the organization's capability in delivering cyber security training. The proposed framework can form the building blocks needed to establish clear objectives of cyber security training, establish defined processes, and ensure the quality of learning resources and learning outcomes. Describing a curricular framework and defining the required competence level for different employee groups will feed into the objectives of the cyber security training. Bloom's taxonomy is used in the framework as a basis for designing training and assessment material. This will provide a standardized way for producing training material that considers the desired competence level of the targeted employee groups in an organization. The establishment of required competence levels and defined curricula also provides the organization with an approach to ensure cyber security learning outcomes. The above-mentioned elements are only parts of the building blocks that are needed to enable the higher capability competence levels in the organization. Additional processes, competence building of the supporting staff as well as support tools are other elements that needs to be established.

A challenge corresponding to this framework can be that the assessment of employee competence levels and the resources required to do this. The lower-level learning objectives (Example: remember, understand) to a larger extent can be assessed by comparing the learner's responses to a correct answer, and can be done automatically. The higher-level objectives (Example: apply, analyze) involve more complex application of the knowledge learned and therefore is more difficult to perform automatically. Therefore, assessment at these levels likely to require more resources from the organization. In the future, the proposed framework needs to be evaluated in terms of effectiveness and feasibility in practice using a case-study based approach in an organization for a particular group of personnel.

Acknowledgments. This research is partially funded by the Research Council of Norway (RCN) in the INTPART program, under the project *"Reinforcing Competence in Cybersecurity of Critical Infrastructures: A Norway-US Partnership (RECYCIN)"*, with the project number #309911.

References

1. Breda, F., Barbosa, H., Morais, T.: Social engineering and cyber security. In: International Technology, Education and Development Conference, Valencia, Spain March (2017). https://doi.org/10.21125/inted.2017.1008
2. Salahdine, F., Kaabouch, N.: Social engineering attacks: a survey. Future Internet **11**, 89 (2019)
3. Richardson, R., North, M.M.: Ransomware: evolution, mitigation, and prevention. Int. Manag. Rev. **13**, 10 (2017)
4. Hydro: Cyber-attack on Hydro. https://www.hydro.com/en-NO/media/on-the-agenda/cyber-attack/
5. ICS-CERT: Recommended Practice: Developing an Industrial Control Systems Cybersecurity Incident Response Capability (2009)
6. Beyer, R.E., Brummel, B.: Implementing effective cyber security training for end users of computer networks. In: Society for Human Resource Management and Society for Industrial and Organizational Psychology (2015)
7. Rea-Guaman, A.M., San Feliu, T., Calvo-Manzano, J.A., Sanchez-Garcia, I.D.: Comparative study of cybersecurity capability maturity models. In: Mas, A., Mesquida, A., O'Connor, R.V., Rout, T., Dorling, A. (eds.) SPICE 2017. CCIS, vol. 770, pp. 100–113. Springer, Cham (2017). https://doi.org/10.1007/978-3-319-67383-7_8
8. Marshall, S., Mitchell, G.: An e-learning maturity model. In: Proceedings of the 19th Annual Conference of the Australian Society for Computers in Learning in Tertiary Education, Auckland, New Zealand (2002)
9. Paulk, M.C., Curtis, B., Chrissis, M.B.: Capability maturity model for software. Carnegie-Mellon University. Pittsburg, Software Engineering Institute (1991)
10. von Wangenheim, C.G., Hauck, J.C.R., Salviano, C.F., von Wangenheim, A.: Systematic literature review of software process capability/maturity models. In: Proceedings of International Conference on Software Process Improvement and Capability Determination (SPICE), Pisa, Italy (2010)
11. Barclay, C.: Sustainable security advantage in a changing environment: the cybersecurity capability maturity model (CM2). In: Proceedings of the 2014 ITU Kaleidoscope Academic Conference: Living in a Converged World-Impossible without Standards? (2014)
12. White, G.B.: The community cyber security maturity model. In: 2011 IEEE International Conference on Technologies for Homeland Security (HST) (2011)
13. Englbrecht, L., Meier, S., Pernul, G.: Towards a capability maturity model for digital forensic readiness. Wirel. Netw. **26**, 4895–4907 (2020)
14. Solar, M., Sabattin, J., Parada, V.: A maturity model for assessing the use of ICT in school education. J. Educ. Technol. Soc. **16**, 206–218 (2013)

15. Middleton, G.R.: A maturity model for intelligence training and education. Am. Intell. J. **25**, 33–45 (2007)
16. Burley, D., et al.: Curriculum Guidelines for Post-Secondary Degree Programs in Cybersecurity (2017)
17. Krathwohl, D.R.: A Revision of bloom's taxonomy: an overview. Theor. Pract. **41**, 212–218 (2002)
18. Athanassiou, N., McNett, J.M., Harvey, C.: Critical thinking in the management classroom: bloom's taxonomy as a learning tool. J. Manag. Educ. **27**, 533 555 (2003)
19. Sivaraman, S.I., Krishna, D.: Blooms taxonomy–application in exam papers assessment. Chem. Eng. (VITU) **12**, 32 (2015)

Designing and Evaluating a Resident-Centric Digital Wallet Experience

Sukhi Chuhan and Veronica Wojnas(✉)

Ontario Digital Service, Ontario Public Service, Toronto, Canada
{sukhi.chuhan,veronica.wojnas2}@ontario.ca

Abstract. This paper focuses on the results of usability testing of a self-sovereign digital identity (SSI) wallet prototype designed by the Ontario Digital Service User Experience team. The prototype was tested with 47 Ontario residents (with 29 participants cited in this research), and analyzed through moderated semi-structured interviews and short usability test tasks. The main themes from the sessions were related to security and recovery, scanning quick response (QR) codes, and connecting with service providers. Users had some preconceived notions about digital wallets, were apprehensive about the privacy and security of their personal information, and had a desire for a recovery protocol. The biometric authentication protocol raised concerns about inaccessibility to the wallet in case of device issues, and the QR code scanning process was not aligned with users' mental model and posed accessibility challenges. The concept of connections with service providers was also unclear. Based on these findings, we discuss recommendations around user-centric security and recovery framework and alternative accessible patterns for digital wallet experiences to support resident-level adoption.

Keywords: SSI · Digital Wallet · Usability

1 Introduction

82% of Canadians feel it is important that their provincial governments enable digital identity (ID) technology soon [1], and the security and privacy benefits of decentralized identity models in enabling access to online services are leading governments around the world to examine them as a viable approach. However, current digital wallets may pose usability issues that limit their ability to be a convenient tool for everyday use. As part of the Ontario Government's work on digital credentials and wallets, members of the Ontario Digital Service User Experience (UX) team designed a self-sovereign identity (SSI) digital wallet prototype (called 'Test Wallet' here) and tested it with Ontario residents ('users'). This paper will focus on the key themes discovered from residents' perceptions of a government-developed digital wallet and recommendations on how digital wallets can better meet their needs.

In this paper, we summarize the results of a usability test of a digital ID wallet based on existing SSI solutions and principles, conducted with a Figma prototype and live mobile application ('app') that are based on Aries framework specifications. We held 6 rounds of usability testing sessions with 47 participants, 29 of whom are cited in this research. Sessions were comprised of semi-structured interviews and collections of tasks simulating common contexts in which participants might be able to use their digital wallets and IDs (e.g. signing into a medical clinic, signing up for a gym membership).

We first provide background on SSI, government digital ID work, and wallet usability. We then move into a more detailed description of the above methodology, and our research objectives: (i) explore residents' impressions and sentiments towards the digital wallet, (ii) assess participant ability to complete key tasks with the digital wallet, and (iii) examine participant preferences for visual elements and navigation flows.

We then discuss our key findings. Participants' preconceived notions of digital wallets, based on their experiences with non-SSI wallets, provided them with a mental model of the concept that did not align with some of the aspects of our Test Wallet. In particular, users were caught off-guard by requirements to use biometrics, and suspected that the government might be collecting this information about them. They were also disappointed by a lack of recovery options, a concept that is basically a standard with online accounts. The concept of a connection with organizations that is central to SSI implementations, is unexpected and difficult to communicate in the wallet interface.

Based on our observations, we suggest enhancements to our design and areas for future exploration in digital wallet design.

2   Background and Related Work

2.1   Centralized Identity, Federated Identity Management (FIM), and Self-sovereign Identity (SSI)

Much of the internet operates on a centralized identity model, where users create a password-protected account unique to a given website, which is stored on a centralized database. Most users continue to experience at least some form of a centralized identity management system online: a 2020 survey by NordPass found that 7/10 of respondents claimed to have more than 10 password-protected online accounts, and 2/10 claimed more than 50 accounts [2]. Not only are multiple centralized identity accounts difficult for users to manage, but they can be risky – the Identity Theft Resource Center has recorded 422.1 million victims of identity breaches occurring in the United States over 2022 [3] resulting from attacks on centralized databases.

Federated identity management (FIM), also known as the user-centric identity model, arose in the early 2000s in response to pain points like those cited above, which were already beginning to become apparent. FIM's premise is to replace the separate account for each organization, with an identity account at a service provider called the identity provider (IDP). Any organization using that IDP would allow users to log in with their IDP identity account [4]. An implementation of FIM is web single sign-on. While FIM addresses the usability issue posed by centralized identity, the security issue remains present – possibly even more so, as IDP databases might become enticing targets for data breaches. Indeed, Twitter, one of the top 3 IDPs for web single sign-on in 2017 [5], was a victim of 2 of the largest data breaches in 2022 [3].

The decentralized identity model, also known as the self-sovereign identity (SSI) model, is a form of identity management that uses cryptographic techniques to enable users to share and verify their information directly in a privacy-protecting way. Distributed ledger technologies (such as, but not limited to, blockchain) are recently being used to accomplish this. SSI surfaced in 2015, as a response to existing centralized and federated identity models used by enterprise and government [4]. SSI differs from the preceding models in no longer relying on accounts. Instead, users and organizations use public/private cryptographic keys to create secure peer-to-peer connections and exchange information in digital identity credentials. These credentials are backed by public keys stored on blockchains or other trust registries that the party receiving the information can use to verify their authenticity [4].

SSI research until recently has prioritized architectural, privacy, and security considerations over usability [6]. Apart from the effects that poor usability could have on users' willingness to adopt a solution at all, Habib and Cranor point out that privacy choice interfaces used thus far have been limited in their effectiveness in part because of their poor usability [7], which makes this aspect of SSI worthwhile to explore.

2.2 Government and Digital Identity

Digital identity (ID) can be defined as "an individual's identity which is composed of information stored and transmitted in digital form" [8]. In practice, digital ID is an electronic version of government identification documents. Governments around the world have become interested in leveraging various identity models, including SSI, to enable digital IDs for various transactions. Sullivan traces digital ID's emergence as a distinct legal concept to 2006 in the United Kingdom, though she points out that earlier programs of capturing and using citizen information digitally had already existed in Europe prior to that time, such as in Belgium [8].

The implementation of government digital ID has generally happened at a federal level, though in some countries such as Australia, Canada, and the United States; subnational jurisdictions are involved in their own digital ID initiatives especially as it comes to specifically implementing digital driver's licences [9]. Digital ID is generally implemented as a collaboration between the government and private sector. The government may lead and fund the development and operation of digital ID infrastructure (though it may subcontract the actual development to a private company), such as with Belgium's initial eID [10]. Alternatively, it may collaborate with the private sector by developing the core digital ID infrastructure and providing access to select organizations to support and/or maintain it, such as Denmark's MitID [11] and Estonia's e-Identity [12]. Finally, it may tender the entire development and maintenance of digital ID to a private sector player or players who are given access to the tools to verify ID and issue credentials, such as Sweden's bank consortium-developed BankID [13].

In Canada, provinces and territories are responsible for developing their own digital ID programs, working towards a shared set of federal standards and establishing partnerships with one another using the non-profit Digital Identification and Authentication Council of Canada (DIACC) Pan-Canadian Trust Framework (PCTF) to promote interoperability [14]. The province of Ontario, where this research was conducted, is interested in a shared public-private collaboration approach along with sustained work with DIACC. Not all digital ID implementations leverage SSI, but the work in Canada is interested in this approach.

2.3 ARIES Identity Ecosystem

Bernal Bernabe, et al. discuss the ReliAble European Identity EcoSystem (ARIES) as an identity management framework that encompasses secure and trusted digital identity processes [15]. This framework includes feature specifications for products such as digital wallets including biometric requirements and decentralized storage, to promote an interoperable experience. The goal of ARIES is to reduce identity-related fraud which is an appealing prospect for government entities. According to its 2021 Annual Report, the Canadian Anti-Fraud Centre recorded a 114% surge in the occurrences of identity-related crimes since 2019 and anticipates this trend to persist and escalate [16]. The implementation of ARIES protocols can enhance practices of interoperability, security, and trust in the development of self-sovereign identity (SSI) digital wallets, particularly when dealing with government-issued identity documents.

2.4 Existing Research on SSI Digital Wallet Usability

Users interface with digital ID credentials and identity verification through software (usually mobile apps) known as "digital wallets." These are not to be confused with digital wallets (also known as mobile wallets) for financial or ticket transactions offered by banks, cryptocurrency exchanges, or mobile operating systems. Digital wallets abstract the complex, secure transactions taking place under the SSI model. Podgorelec, Alber, and Zefferer's literature review defines digital wallets as "software that operates in the remote or local environment and enables the storing, managing, and sharing of digital identity-related data. The digital identity wallet also provides secure storage for cryptographic material associated with digital identity-related data. With a digital identity wallet, the user controls and manages identity-related data" [17].

To enable users to truly make use of these features and exercise their full control over their personal data as the SSI model intends, digital wallets need to be usable. In recent years, there have been a few studies of commercial digital wallet usability, or usability of the concept of digital wallets. Sartor, Sedlmeier, Rieger and Roth evaluated users' perceptions of the usability of 4 commercial digital wallets, noting that even their generally technologically-experienced user group had trouble understanding SSI concepts despite finding the apps themselves easy to use [6]. Korir, Parkin, and Dunphy abstracted screens from 4 digital wallets to create a wallet prototype, finding issues with quick response (QR) code use and users' understanding of why errors might occur, as well as not understanding some of the technical specifics of the wallet (such as recoverability of credentials, or the issues with that under SSI) [18]. Owens, Anise, and Krause usability-tested a mobile authenticator that uncovered user concerns about smartphones and smartphone data or internet availability that could also apply to digital wallets [19].

Further back in the past, some research has been done about how the specific context of government ID interplays with users' perceptions of and willingness to engage with digital ID. Barzhananova and Smollander point out a number of non-technical assumptions in digital ID literature based on previous research, such as that users will actually use the service and know to take advantage of selective information disclosure [20].

Some possible causes might be found further back in time, when Halperin and Back-house surveyed participants in Europe about their perceptions of government digital ID specifically. Participants expressed some general concerns, but some government-specific concerns as well. For example, they specifically cited concerns with government information technology systems or overreach into their personal information [21]. Our research supplements some of these findings by testing a prototype that is inspired by commercial digital wallets, but customized to the context of government ID use cases. In this way, it seeks participants' impressions of digital wallets and their usability, within the particularly meaningful and plausible use case of government-developed wallets that store government-issued digital ID credentials.

3   Research Objectives

To gain insight into residents' experiences with an SSI digital wallet, we designed the Test Wallet and conducted usability testing sessions. This user study approach enabled the establishment of research objectives aimed at evaluating specific and future features of SSI digital wallets. These objectives included: (i) exploring residents' impressions and sentiments towards the digital wallet, (ii) assessing participant ability to complete key tasks with the digital wallet, and (iii) examining participant preferences for visual elements and navigation flows.

3.1   Prototype

The Test Wallet's design was conceptualized from existing Hyperledger ARIES agent patterns and W3C data format standards [22]. We analyzed interfaces from other digital wallets (e.g. eSatus, Lissi, and Trinsic) to inform feature prioritization and usability considerations. User flows followed common wallet design patterns while emphasizing the learnability of digital identity concepts as a means of improving user understanding [23].

The design decisions for the digital wallet were driven by the priority of accessible wallet interactions and the need for users to have flexible control over their credentials and wallet management. These considerations are reflected in the high-fidelity wire-frames that were developed as part of the design process. Using Figma as the primary design application, we were able to create an interactive prototype that demonstrated the main user tasks of onboarding, receiving a credential from an issuer and interacting with a verifier through a proof request. The prototype was developed as a React Native application to facilitate reliable testing with participants who were blind or had low vision.

The Ontario Design System was used in accordance with the government's specific visual identity policies and mobile components were styled using the Material Design System and Human Interface Guidelines [24]. However, the wireframes included in this paper are not specific to any particular implementation and can be interpreted more generally.

3.2 Method

The Test Wallet prototype was evaluated through six rounds of a semi-structured interview and usability testing. Five rounds utilized a Figma prototype, and the final round, which focused on accessibility, was shared through TestFlight, a platform for distributing and testing mobile applications. Sessions were live-moderated remotely and included a brief interview portion to understand participants' existing experiences with digital wallets and their perceptions of digital identity concepts. Participants were also asked to self-rank their comfort with technology using an adapted self-evaluation technology comfort scale. Following the interview questions, participants opened the prototype on their mobile devices and shared their screens so we could observe their behaviour and actions. Participants were asked to complete scenario tasks including the setup and onboarding of their wallet and receiving a foundational verifiable credential (VC) which had core identity attributes typically resembling an identity card (e.g. name, date of birth, address, photo). Users also interacted with verifiers through proof requests through contexts such as signing up for a gym membership and checking out from a library. Following the direct tasks, participants were asked about their overall experience and impression of a government-designed digital wallet as a resident.

We recorded and transcribed each interview, and following each round of usability testing, we conducted affinity mapping and open qualitative coding exercises on participants' impressions and contextual feedback to assess key themes and perceptions [25]. These open codes facilitated our documentation and prioritization of pain points, opportunities, and design update suggestions. After data was coded and synthesized, our design team worked on iterating the key digital wallet user flows necessary to increase residents' trust and comfort in using and understanding digital wallets and related identity products.

3.3 Limitations

To streamline the testing, several of our tasks omitted the biometric enrolment process for obtaining a foundational VC, instead starting with receiving the credential as an offer or having a few pre-existing credentials in the prototype wallet. This may have made certain tasks seem faster and more seamless than they would be in reality.

Due to time constraints and the priority we placed on testing visual interfaces, our test prototypes were not fully functional digital wallets and did not always behave exactly as they would in reality. For example, our Figma prototype's QR code camera view was a screenshot of a phone camera, rather than accessing the participant's device camera. In terms of accessibility testing, our scope was limited to blind and low-vision participants with Apple iOS devices, as we could only test with participants invited to our TestFlight account.

3.4 Participants

It was essential for this research to involve a diverse participant population with varying demographic characteristics, such as age, race and gender, and years in Canada, as well as different levels of comfort and experience with digital wallet technology. This approach, rooted in inclusive design principles, aimed to deliver a thorough qualitative evaluation that would take into account a diverse range of experiences [26]. This was critical in gauging the experiences of Ontario residents utilizing the Test Wallet. However, our participant pool consisted primarily of urban or suburban residents who were generally comfortable with their phones. Despite efforts to include diverse representation, our sample lacked Indigenous participants and perspectives on Indigenous data sovereignty and identity documents. Additionally, we had limited representation from rural and northern areas and from seniors (60+), which does not reflect the demographic distribution of Ontario's population [27].

All participants were Ontario residents and were recruited through the Code for Canada's Gathering Residents to Improve Technology (GRIT) participant pool [28]. Overall, our usability study involved 47 participants from Ontario, and post-study consent was obtained from 29 participants to allow their impressions to be reported in this paper.

4 Results

4.1 Initial Impressions

Jakob Nielsen posits that users form their expectations of a website based on experiences with similar sites [29]. To uncover the mental models that users have around how digital wallets should work from their related experiences, we spoke to participants about their experiences with digital wallet apps. We let participants define these terms as they saw fit, and heard about their impressions of similar products that were generally not SSI wallets (ranging from government-issued digital ID card apps, to mobile operating system wallets, to mobile cryptocurrency storage wallet apps).

About 33% of participants mentioned experiences with mobile operating system wallets, such as Apple Wallet or Google Pay, for either making payments or storing and showing tickets. Participants with such experiences tended to conflate SSI digital wallet apps with mobile wallets. Only 2 participants (7%), who both mentioned using cryptocurrency/decentralized finance wallets, anticipated some sort of SSI wallet patterns (such as selective disclosure) before using the Test Wallet.

Generally, participants were interested in the convenience promised by the Test Wallet and its potential to simplify interactions with government services. Among our participants, some 14% mentioned using (or having used) mobile operating system wallets to store payment methods. Government identity cards, such as driver's licences or health cards, were often the only thing standing between these participants and freedom from carrying a physical wallet at all. One remarked:

"It [mobile wallets] makes things easier. Sometimes I forget my wallet at home, or sometimes I deliberately leave it and am like 'I'll just pay with my phone'." - P5R6.

However, participants were also apprehensive with respect to both the privacy and security of the personal information stored in their wallet. This echoes Halperin and Backhouse's research [21] about perceptions of government digital ID in Europe, where participants expressed trust concerns with the concept based on risks to their information and privacy - due to unintentional actions by governments, intentional ones, or both. In our own study, participants expressed concerns about both of these types of risks:

"On one hand, we have to use identity in so many places that it helps to have it [available as a digital ID]. On the other hand - shades of Big Brother..." - P5R6.

This participant also exemplifies a concern of government overreach that affects user trust in digital ID and wallets. Another participant supplemented this thought with a contribution that might help increase trust in the product:

"Privacy laws are very important...the government should have lots of checks and balances in place." - P3R6.

Concerns about intentional misuse of personal data by government actors are not unfounded and might in some cases be inspired by reports from other countries. For example, in 2021 the Taliban took control over Afghanistan and gained access to databases collecting biometric data (including those for the country's e-tazkira digital ID) which allowed them to more easily seek out targets for reprisals [30].

"I think it might be easier to steal my identity if I have it on my phone." - P6R1.

This participant summarizes experiences with attempted and successful identity-based theft or fraud that others had also experienced. Participants noted that identity fraud is particularly difficult to recover from, and tended to initially associate the digital wallet with an increased risk of this type of fraud due to the potential for device hacks. Some participants were more vague about the security risks, drawing from experiences with centralized identity data breaches. The personal information for issuing physical ID cards is already stored in centralized government databases, but the modality of physical ID cards may hide this from users in a way that an app does not. Multiple participants mentioned reserving judgment or interest until the Test Wallet was widely used and they would have a chance to learn from others' experiences, or placing less-important credentials (such as loyalty cards) on it initially as a test before making the leap to government identity or bank cards.

Our participants generally rated themselves as comfortable with, and knowledgeable about, mobile devices. However, only one came into the study associating the wallet with decentralized identity storage. In many cases, participants instead extrapolated from their experiences with similar-seeming services (such as mobile wallets or payment systems, or digital IDs in other countries built on centralized models) to form their first impressions. Evaluating their knowledge and assumptions can be instructive in understanding how to describe concepts.

4.2 Usability Testing

The main themes that emerged from our usability sessions are categorized by the respective digital wallet user flows, which are as follows: wallet security and recovery (where participants stressed sentiments around biometrics), data storage and restoration. Secondly, participants' encounters with the connection-establishing method of scanning QR codes raised discrepancies between existing mental models and highlighted the importance of accessible design. Lastly, concepts such as connecting with service providers, which were simplified for the prototype wallet, still challenged participants in understanding and accepting the connection interactions. Despite efforts to ease the SSI wallet experience for participants, there were significant challenges and pain points from the resident perspective and each result category will outline the participant experiences with the wallet pattern.

4.3 Security and Recovery

As part of the app onboarding and setup process, the Test Wallet prototype initiated users with a welcome introduction screen which prompted them to assess their mobile device biometric settings. The wallet architecture relies on device-level biometrics to be enabled as a means of authentication to access the app. While usability constraints with using biometrics are recognized in existing research, namely the exclusion of mobile holders that lack the appropriate device hardware [31], the level of assurance required for the ARIES digital wallet necessitated the exclusion [15]. Participants who were familiar with biometric settings such as Touch/Face ID and Fingerprint Unlock when interacting with other high-security apps found the requirement to be standard practice, even citing ease and convenience, however, participants who did not use their device's biometric features, explained the following reasons:

"I never set up the face scanner… I never had the time…figured I'd set it up eventually but never got around to it." - P8R1.

"I have bank apps on my phone and I'm totally comfortable not using biometrics on it. (…) I understand it's advanced security, but this is just me not too comfortable with it." - P2R1.

One participant articulated the perception of government-related products requiring a biometric authentication, despite the wallet app relying on existing device system enrollment, as an unsettling concept and would instead advocate for other backup authentication options such as passcodes for broader resident-level comfort:

"I know certain people would be more comfortable using a passcode on their phone (…) I know why you would want to, but the general idea of the government requiring biometrics to access services, even if it's through a wallet app, seems a bit scary, somewhat." - P7R4.

Following the onboarding flow, participants began to question the premise of local digital credentials storage. In circumstances of system error in the biometric features or related device issues, participants highlighted their need to access their own data or be reassured of its impenetrability if the wallet app were to become inaccessible:

"What if you lose your phone? What if someone steals your phone?" - P4R2.

"I would like to have either the option to retrieve the information, like send me a message with a code and I can recover that information, or you to reassure me that it is deleted or encrypted and no one can use it. Help me feel more secure." - P2R1.

The Test Wallet currently lacks a recovery protocol due to storing credentials locally. However, our research indicates participants' strong desire for credential restoration, especially when locked out of the app, losing or obtaining a new device.

Inclusion Concerns with Biometric Requirements. Among some participants, concerns about the accessibility of biometric access were also raised. These were in response to the digital wallet only accepting a biometric entry and not permitting a passcode backup which perpetuated anxieties about being unable to access the Test Wallet. The singular user access via biometrics was considered especially problematic where multiple individuals required access to one device in scenarios such as dependent relationships and caretaking:

"I find it a little strange that you don't have the option to do one or the other [password versus biometrics]. What if you have arthritis and trouble using your phone [and need assistance]? I'm of a generation that is thinking about these problems." - P4R2.

As an acknowledgement of the multi-owner device circumstance, the Test Wallet prototype was iterated in later test rounds to account for additional biometrics potentially registered on a mobile phone. As part of the setup process, this feature required users to answer the question of whether additional biometric profiles were saved on the device. For an affirmative response, users were informed that all biometric profiles would have authentication access to the wallet. Following this step, the user would accept the system prompt to enroll their biometrics with the app. This updated decision point was met with varying degrees of success as most users explained that their device sharing happens on the basis of their passcode rather than enrolling biometrics as most mobile applications will still allow authentication through a system passcode.

4.4 Scanning QR Codes

The Test Wallet, like other SSI agent-based models, utilizes QR code scanning as a means of connecting to service providers [4]. Prior to performing any scenario-based usability tasks, participants anticipated using the digital wallet in some capacity to share information. These assumptions were backed by previous use of digital wallets and various methods of tap-to-pay/Near-field communication (NFC) mechanisms, completing app-to-app transactions or sharing QR codes through digital passes.

"I use my Apple Wallet, I've got my credit card loaded in there and all my rewards cards. I find it handy for events, having digital tickets instead of paper ones or screenshots." - P7R4.

"I would be ordering something on Skip [SkipTheDishes, a meal delivery platform and app] and I would choose 'Use mobile wallet' and then I could double-tap. I never really followed through with it and I don't know why but it was easy, understandable." - P7R6.

"Like what we have for the vaccine passport, I would think it should operate in the same manner [with businesses scanning the QR code]." - P2R3.

However, not all participants were familiar or comfortable with digital transactions and preferred analog approaches. These sentiments influenced outcomes once participants were exposed to scenarios where a QR code was presented for in-person services, for example interacting with an employee at a service desk. The consensus was split between assuming that further action involving the digital wallet was required, or whether they could show the device screen with the credential information itself.

"If they just need my name, I would [unhide] it [on the wallet app screen] and share that visually with the person at the counter." - P8R1.

Participants also wondered if they could scan a QR code with their regular mobile device's camera app and open the digital wallet and subsequent prompt in that manner:

"I would think...if I used my phone camera, it should open my Test Wallet to see what I need to share." - P6R4.

When prompted to interact with the QR code present in the scenarios, participants who were motivated to share identity attributes by showing their device screen still gravitated to selecting a particular credential depending on the scenario's context in hopes of selectively sending the information to the service provider. The Test Wallet included a "Scan QR code to share information" on the credential profile page in anticipation of this user behaviour, however, it inadvertently reinforced some participants' perception of selecting a particular credential source to share specific attributes rather than simply connecting with the service provider.

"I guess…because there's a button that says 'Scan code' and I saw the [QR] code I would instinctively scan code, but I might go to the wallet and see what I have and want to share. Or maybe when I scan the code, it will let me pick the cards I want to share." - P2R2.

Most participants had an existing mental model that QR codes contain sharcable data which they shared was formed from recent collective experience with the Proof of COVID-19 vaccination certificate. The service design involved showing the certificate's QR code for the verifier with the provincial COVID-19 Verify app to validate. Rather than interpreting QR codes as a means of connecting with service providers, participants questioned why the Test Wallet lacked a personal QR code containing attributes of their preference to share with others.

"I don't know if I can scan their QR and pass my information to them - this is new to me" - P5R2.

Overall, participants held a preconceived notion that QR codes were only for data sharing, not connecting with service providers. However, in the context of SSI digital wallets, users must scan QR codes to connect and respond to transaction prompts from service providers, which suggests alternative design considerations around connection methods.

Accessibility Issues with Scanning QR Codes. Participants with blindness or low vision tested the Test Wallet app via TestFlight, and faced difficulties in spatially locating QR codes without verbal guidance. Even with verbal guidance, the inaccessibility of QR codes to connect with service providers became apparent as screen reader technology lacked meaningful context explaining the QR code:

"As a blind person, it is frequently difficult to get my phone to line up with the QR code. Sometimes [VoiceOver reads] 'QR Code detected' and you go to tap your screen to access the information but by the time you do that, the camera's shifted slightly and you don't access the QR code…and so you have to line up your camera again." - P5R6.

Research recommendations from Korir, Parkin, and Dunphy also suggest a minimization of QR code reliance as it assumes users will be using both desktop and mobile devices simultaneously [18]. We observed that participants had different assistive technology set up on their mobile and desktop devices, and preferred using a particular device depending on their specific requirements and situational context.

4.5   Connecting with Service Providers

As seen in other SSI digital wallet connecting patterns, the holder first scans a service provider's QR code to receive an explicit connection request. Once approved, the user will receive the subsequent verification request and after the transaction is complete, the user remains connected with the service provider. This user flow (Fig. 1) presented some opportunities for improvement; first, users are withheld from the key interaction that they were expecting from the service provider, the verification request, by a connection request that does not bring users any upfront value. Secondly, the connection request adds a cognitive load by introducing a decision-making step and can increase friction in the transaction completion [32]. Lastly, the connection between the holder and service provider remaining after the transaction does not present the ability for users to revoke their consent after the transaction period. Users who may assume a fleeting connection with a service provider during the transaction period may not be aware of the persistent link established in their digital wallet.

In the Test Wallet, we tested connection prompts to service providers as occurring after the transaction to reduce the decision-making steps prior to the intended user goal of sharing credentials. Users were automatically connected to the service providers once they scanned the QR code and were empowered to maintain or sever the connection once the intended transaction was complete. The minimization of the connection concept was done intentionally to help users focus on the main transaction prompt; there was a callout box indicating that the organization had been temporarily 'Added to Wallet Contacts' on the verification request screen. The substitution of the term 'Contacts' for 'Connections' was done deliberately as a way to improve users' understanding of the connection model by leveraging the familiarity of the term 'Contacts' with the existing mental model of mobile phone contacts.

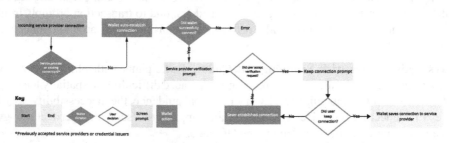

Fig. 1. The figure depicts the user flow for a holder making a decision on connecting to a service provider after a verification transaction. It shows the steps involved in evaluating and deciding on a connection, from reviewing the verification request to approving or declining the connection.

In observation of participants completing scenarios with the verification transactions, the majority of participants did not notice nor comment on the 'Added to Wallet Contacts' box (Fig. 2). When asked to interpret the content, participants reacted with questions and assumptions about the contact's role:

"I'm not too sure...'Contacts' is not a concept I'm familiar with in the context of wallets or digital information. I imagine it's a way to pre-approve giving information to certain places or destinations." - P7R4.

"If adding this person as a contact means they would be able to communicate with the app more frequently or bypass the request, I would want to know exactly what it does." - P2R2.

For a few participants, the word 'contact' introduced the idea that service providers were added to the mobile phone's directory, which indicates further content design iteration. The use of the word 'contacts' in some instances helped participants make a distinction that there was a communication channel established, evidence seen with participants referring to record management within the wallet:

"I'm assuming if I go into 'Contacts,' I can see where I've shown my information and what I've shared with them. It's a record." - P6R4.

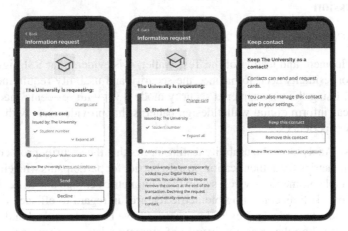

Fig. 2. These screens illustrate the steps for informing users about a new connection being added to their digital wallet contacts and allowing them to make a decision to keep or remove the contact. It shows visual screens of the process, including the initial notification of the new connection and the options to either keep or remove the contact once the user had successfully completed the verification request.

At the conclusion of the transaction, participants were presented with the option to maintain their connection with the service provider, leading to assessments of the connection's perceived value to the participant. The majority of participants would opt to sever or 'forget' the connection, however, the varied perception of a connection's role may have influenced this decision. Participants believed that maintaining a connection could fast-track proof requests and automatically send information to service providers with their next interaction. Some thought that it created a permanent data exchange between the user and service provider, which raised questions about trust:

"I don't want them to keep my connection...it's just me, I don't want to keep my information in too many places." - P2R1.

"It could be good or bad... (...) if I want to go back, I have their contact now. But it could be bad because do I trust this [Service Provider] with my ID? Do they have it?" - P8R2.

However, participants believed there to be value in keeping contact with organizations that they see themselves interacting with often:

"If it's the gym that I'm visiting often, I don't want them to keep asking me for the same [information]." - P7R2.

Our experiment with adding wallet connections automatically while presenting an ability for users to reflect on the connection's maintenance after the transaction completion indicates a desire for users to assess a connection value in their interactions with service providers. We found that participants' understanding and comfort with service provider connections were related to the type of organization and how often the participant anticipated interacting with them. Without repeated interactions with service providers, connectionless transactions may serve users' needs more appropriately.

5 Discussion

5.1 User-Centric Security

In the development and testing of the Test Wallet, it is evident that SSI digital wallets designed for residents need to balance the security and usability requirements of the experience. Using the user-centered security model [33] with residents' needs in consideration can inform digital wallet design patterns that provide users with secure and trustworthy experiences.

Biometrics. Analysis of the usability testing shows that the security protocol of solely requiring biometrics for authentication posed a barrier for participants who either did not have compatible biometric devices, set up their biometric settings due to device sharing or had personal beliefs contesting biometric features in regard to efficacy and privacy. User behaviours towards device-level biometrics have been researched and sentiments of concern regarding the transgressive use of biometric data have surfaced as a barrier to adoption [34]. This sentiment is compounded in products related to government, as it heightens suspicions related to surveillance state technology despite the architectural absence of these features within the application [35].

While biometric authentication was required as part of the ARIES high-level assurance of the wallet [15], one strategy employed to mitigate these misperceptions was through written content iterations. We explained that no biometrics were collected by the application or the government and that the digital wallet only relied on existing device features such as Touch/Face ID and Fingerprint unlock as a requirement for higher user security. These content updates were in an effort to align users' understanding of how the biometric authentication worked in the digital wallet application which was also necessary for users that had multiple biometric profiles stored on their devices. By simplifying technical information and presenting it in a way that was accessible to non-experts, users were made aware of the security measures in place for the digital wallet and the steps they needed to take to ensure their information remained protected [36] (Fig. 3).

It's important to note that these content changes cannot mitigate negative experiences for users where biometric authentication is not possible. During testing, participants expressed fear that biometric authentication may not always be reliable, a valid concern considering the documented discrimination in biometric systems [37]. The absence of biometric authentication use was also observed in participants that shared their devices with other individuals, typically in scenarios of caretaking or partnerships. One potential design alternative considered with ARIES-based digital wallets is allowing users to bypass biometric requirements for the wallet in exchange for limited capabilities. This may mean a lower level of assurance with stored credentials, however, this could be problematic for residents who expect to store their identity documents in a digital wallet designed to store government-issued credentials and are unable to do so. Further research

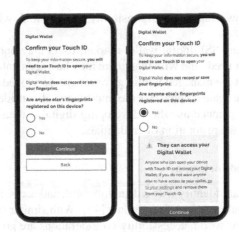

Fig. 3. A set of screens inquiring about multiple biometric profiles on the user's mobile device. If yes, the user is notified that these profiles can access the digital wallet, and the flow concludes with a prompt to confirm their biometric profile for the wallet.

and consideration should be given to the security requirements of digital wallets that can attain a high level of assurance and secure storage for stored credentials, and exploration around biometric authentication adoption.

Recovery. The usability testing results indicated a strong demand from participants for a recovery method for their digital wallet, especially in instances of authentication failure, or in situations of losing or obtaining a new device. Previous surveys have shown that more than 70% of Canadians expect their provincial governments to efficiently implement secure digital IDs [1]. These sentiments were also observed in testing with the expectation that government-issued digital credentials would be easily accessible, especially when stored within a digital wallet designed for that purpose.

Decentralized applications that have no solutions in place for backing up or recovering user data can be a hindrance to usability and adoption [38]. Our research showed that the tradeoff of higher security at the cost of storing VCs locally is not favoured at the cost of not being able to recover one's identity attributes. Methods such as biometrics have been offered as part of possible recovery protocols, however, there should be a thorough consideration of the users' expectations when determining an appropriate recovery mechanism. As seen in the research results, biometrics can pose unique barriers for residents and their interactions with digital wallets.

One potential opportunity for further exploration is secure cloud storage by key escrows [39]. Since residents likely understand the government's role in managing physical identity documents, this mental model could be extended with digital credentials. This method could be seen to improve users' experience if they were able to retrieve not only their previously issued digital credentials from government entities but the full backup of their digital wallet. However, this hypothesis requires further investigation to consider the policy implications of key escrow entities, such as the government, and to address questions of ownership and responsibility of credentials within a self-sovereign identity ecosystem.

With the developing SSI digital wallet market, users may opt to manage multiple wallets that serve their needs and with that, there may be a segmentation of government-issued credentials that are managed within government-developed digital wallets. With this possibility, it once again emphasizes the importance of considering residents' comfort levels and security concerns when developing digital wallets and the appropriate recovery protocol for the restoration of credentials.

5.2 Accessibility and Inclusion

Roughly 1 in 4 Ontarians identify with a disability [40], and accessibility for both public and private services online is enshrined in law [41]. With similar situations and laws in jurisdictions around the world, accessibility considerations are growing in importance. In addition, accessibility advocates point out that solving an accessibility issue for one population, often helps many others who may experience a similar need temporarily or in a certain situation [42]. There is significant room for digital wallets and VC interactions to become more inclusive, by at the least providing alternative options to users.

When VCs rely on QR codes to form secure connections and share information alone, they limit users in various situations from interacting with them securely. In our usability testing, we noticed some users with blindness or low vision finding it difficult to point their device at a QR code on their screen in order to obtain a VC or respond to a request. VCs themselves hold promise for accessibility to many of the same users: one participant with blindness remarked how having their card data read to them by a device's screen reader would have been much easier and provided more agency than their experiences feeling around in their wallet for an appropriate physical card, choosing the wrong card (between those of a similar shape), and relying on a sighted person nearby to help. Designers and developers of digital wallets should continue to explore alternatives to the QR code interaction, such as Bluetooth/Bluetooth Low Energy (BLE) or NFC-based interactions, to bring the accessibility benefits of wallets to all users.

This is not to mention additional issues for users who may have dexterity or mobility issues that limit how long or still they may be able to hold a mobile device in order for it to scan. In our study, such participants tended to use computers with alternative input devices to facilitate that process. Designers and developers of digital wallets should consider processes for obtaining and using credentials that could leverage non-mobile devices, or even possibly allow users to pre-select certain options on non-mobile devices to simplify interactions later on.

Another accessibility issue that came up during our studies involves the self-sovereign aspect of VCs. How can, or should, these models accommodate individuals who may need support to conduct digital transactions? VCs make an inherent assumption of binding between a device and the individual, and our own Test Wallet makes such assumptions and has security features to encourage them. However, users needing support will likely create workarounds for their support people or caregivers to help them manage their VCs. In such cases, designers need to consider balancing the ability to help users who wish to make such decisions, with the risk of misuse or abuse of these possibilities.

6 Conclusion

In this research, we designed and tested an SSI digital wallet prototype to assess provincial residents and their experience with government-issued identity products. We found that the Test Wallet made participants uneasy with its stringent biometric authentication protocol and lack of recovery process. There was also a misalignment of participants' mental models with the function of QR code scanning which raised key accessibility issues, particularly with blind and low-vision participants. Despite attempts to clarify the concept of connections, participants raised concerns about their purpose which prompted a re-examination of user learnability and connection-less verification methods. Our sessions also uncovered opportunities worth exploring further, such as the security framework surrounding biometrics and credential recovery, and accessible wallet patterns around multi-user devices and connection methods. Based on these findings, we find it important to continue exploring alternative design solutions for digital wallet experiences in order to support resident-level adoption.

References

1. Burak Jacobson Research Partners: Canadian Digital Identity Research 2020 (2021). https://diacc.ca/wp-content/uploads/2021/03/Canadian-Digital-Identity-Research-2020_Report_ENG_VF.pdf
2. Rawlings, R.: Password habits in the US and UK: this is what we found. https://nordpass.com/blog/password-habits-statistics/. Accessed 10 Feb 2023
3. Identity Theft Resource Center: 2022 Data Breach Report (2023). https://www.idtheftcenter.org/publication/2022-data-breach-report
4. Preukschat, A., Reed, D.: Self-sovereign identity: decentralized digital identity and verifiable credentials. Manning Publications (2021)
5. Corre, K., Barais, O., Sunyé, G., Frey, V. Crom, J.M.: Why can't users choose their identity providers on the web? Proc. Priv. Enhancing Technol. 75–89 (2017)
6. Sartor, S., Sedlmeir, J., Rieger, A., Roth, T.: Love at first sight? a user experience study of self-sovereign identity wallets. In: Proceedings of the 30th European Conference on Information Systems (ECIS 2022) (2022)
7. Habib, H., Cranor, L.F.: Evaluating the usability of privacy choice mechanisms. In: Eighteenth Symposium on Usable Privacy and Security (SOUPS 2022), pp. 273–289 (2022). https://www.usenix.org/conference/soups2022/presentation/habib
8. Sullivan, C.: Digital citizenship and the right to digital identity under international law. Comput. Law Secur. Rev. **32**(3), 474–481 (2016). https://doi.org/10.1016/j.clsr.2016.02.001
9. American Association of Motor Vehicle Administrators (AAMVA): Mobile Driver License Implementation Data Map. https://www.aamva.org/jurisdiction-data-maps#anchor formdlmap. Accessed 10 Feb 2023
10. De Cock, D., Wolf, C., Preneel, B.: The Belgian Electronic identity card (overview). In: 3rd Annual Conference of the Security Department of the Gesellschaft für Informatik (GI), pp. 20–22 (2006)
11. Agency for Digital Government: MitID – a unique public-private partnership. https://en.digst.dk/systems/mitid/mitid-a-unique-public-private-partnership/. Accessed 10 Feb 2023
12. Oyetunde, B.: The making of a giant: Estonia and its digital identity infrastructure. e-Estonia. https://e-estonia.com/the-making-of-a-giant-estonia-and-its-digital-identity-infrastructure/. Accessed 10 Feb 2023

13. BankID: Our History. https://www.bankid.com/en/om-oss/historia. Accessed 10 Feb 2023
14. Digital Identification and Authentication Council of Canada (DIACC): Frequently Asked Questions. https://diacc.ca/faq/. Accessed 10 Feb 2023
15. Bernabe, J.B, et al.: An Overview on ARIES: Reliable European Identity Ecosystem (2019). https://doi.org/10.1201/9781003337492-11
16. Canadian Anti-Fraud Centre: Canadian Anti-Fraud Centre 2021 Annual Report (2022). https://publications.gc.ca/collections/collection_2022/grc-rcmp/PS61-46-2021-eng.pdf
17. Podgorelec, B., Alber, L., Zefferer, T.: What Is a (digital) identity wallet? a systematic literature review. In: EEE 46th Annual Computers, Software, and Applications Conference (COMPSAC) (2022). https://doi.org/10.1109/COMPSAC54236.2022.00131
18. Korir, M., Parkin, S., Dunphy, P.: An empirical study of a decentralized identity wallet: usability, security, and perspectives on user control. In: Eighteenth Symposium on Usable Privacy and Security (SOUPS 2022), pp. 195–211 (2022). https://www.usenix.org/conference/soups2022/presentation/korir
19. Owens, K., Anise, O., Krauss, A., Ur, B.: User Perceptions of the Usability and Security of Smartphones as FIDO2 Roaming Authenticators. In: Eighteenth Symposium on Usable Privacy and Security (SOUPS 2022), pp. 57–76 (2022). https://www.usenix.org/conference/soups2021/presentation/owens
20. Bazarhanova, A., Smolander, K.: The review of non-technical assumptions in digital identity architectures. In: Hawaii International Conference on System Sciences (2020). https://doi.org/10.24251/HICSS.2020.785
21. Halperin, R., Backhouse, J.: Risk, trust and eID: exploring public perceptions of digital identity systems. First Monday (2012). https://doi.org/10.5210/fm.v17i4.3867
22. Sporny, M., Longley, D., Sabadello, M., Reed, D., Steele, O., Allen, C.: Decentralized Identifiers (DIDs) v1.0. W3C Technical report. https://www.w3.org/TR/did-core/. Accessed 10 Feb 2023
23. Nielsen Norman Group.: Measure Learnability. https://www.nngroup.com/articles/measure-learnability/. Accessed 10 Feb 2023
24. Ontario Design System. https://designsystem.ontario.ca/. Accessed 10 Feb 2023
25. Lucero, A.: Using affinity diagrams to evaluate interactive prototypes. In: Abascal, J., Barbosa, S., Fetter, M., Gross, T., Palanque, P., Winckler, M. (eds.) Human-Computer Interaction – INTERACT 2015. INTERACT 2015. Lecture Notes in Computer Science, vol. 9297, pp. 231–248 (2015). https://doi.org/10.1007/978-3-319-22668-2_19
26. Swan, H., Pouncey, I., Pickering, H., Watson, L.: Inclusive design principles. https://inclusivedesignprinciples.org/#principles. Accessed 10 Feb 2023
27. Government of Ontario: Ontario Demographic Quarterly Highlights Fourth Quarter (2023). https://www.ontario.ca/page/ontario-demographic-quarterly-highlights-fourth-quarter. Accessed 10 Feb 2023
28. Code for Canada: GRIT - Gathering Residents to Improve Technology. https://codefor.ca/grit/. 10 Feb 2023
29. Nielsen, J: Jakob's law of internet user experience. https://www.nngroup.com/videos/jakobs-law-internet-ux/. Accessed 10 Feb 2023
30. Guo, E., Noori, H.: This is the real story of the Afghan biometric databases abandoned to the Taliban. MIT Technology Review (2021). https://www.technologyreview.com/2021/08/30/1033941/afghanistan-biometric-databases-us-military-40-data-points/. Accessed 10 Feb 2023
31. Rountree, D.: What is federated identity? Federated Identity Primer, pp. 13–36. Syngress (2013). https://doi.org/10.1016/B978-0-12-407189-6.00002-9
32. Grant, W.: 101 UX principles: a definitive design guide. Packt Publishing Ltd. (2018)

33. Dodier-Lazaro, S., Abu-Salma, R., Becker, I., Sasse, M.A.: From paternalistic to user-centred security: putting users first with value-sensitive design. In: Proceedings of the CHI 2017 Workshop on Values in Computing (2017)

34. Bhagavatula, R., Ur, B., Iacovino, K., Kywe, S.M., Cranor, L.F., Savvides, M.: Biometric authentication on iPhone and Android: usability, perceptions, and influences on adoption. In: Proceedings of USEC 2015. Internet Society (2015). https://doi.org/10.14722/usec.2015. 23003

35. Franks, C., Smith, R.: AIC Research Report 20: Changing perceptions of biometric technologies. Australian Institute of Criminology (2021). https://apo.org.au/sites/default/files/res ource-files/2021-05/apo-nid312293.pdf. Accessed 10 Feb 2023

36. Office of the Privacy Commissioner of Canada: Data at Your Fingertips Biometrics and the Challenges to Privacy (2011). https://www.priv.gc.ca/en/privacy-topics/health-genetic-and-other-body-information/gd_bio_201102/. Accessed 10 Feb 2023

37. Castelvecchi, D.: Is facial recognition too biased to be let loose? Nature **587**, 347–350 (2020). https://doi.org/10.1038/d41586-020-03186-4

38. Liu, Y., Lu, Q., Paik, H.-Y., Xu, X.: Design patterns for blockchain-based self-sovereign identity. In: European Conference on Pattern Languages of Programs, pp. 1–14 (2020). https:// doi.org/10.48550/arXiv.2005.12112

39. Soltani, R., Nguyen, U., An, A.: Practical key recovery model for self-sovereign identity based digital wallets. In: IEEE 11th International Conference on Dependable Autonomic and Secure Computing, 11th IEEE International Conference on Pervasive Intelligence and Computing, 11th IEEE International Conference on Cyber Science and Technology, pp. 320–325. https:// doi.org/10.1109/DASC/PiCom/CBDCom/CyberSciTech.2019.00066

40. Government of Ontario: Accessibility for Ontarians with Disabilities Act annual report 2019 (2019). https://www.ontario.ca/page/accessibility-ontarians-disabilities-act-annual-rep ort-2019. Accessed 10 Feb 2023

41. Government of Ontario e-Laws: Accessibility for Ontarians with Disabilities Act, 2005, S.O. 2005, c. 11. https://www.ontario.ca/laws/statute/05a11. Accessed 10 Feb 2023

42. Holmes, K.: How inclusion shapes design (2019). https://www.youtube.com/watch?v=ZBj hniwwH8A&t=1250s. Accessed 10 Feb 2023

A Descriptive Enterprise System Model (DESM) Optimized for Cybersecurity Student and Practitioner Use

Ulku Clark[1,2], Jeff Greer[1,2(✉)], Rahmira Rufus[1,2], and Geoff Stoker[1,2]

[1] University of North Carolina, Wilmington, NC 28403, USA
greerj@uncw.edu

[2] Springer Heidelberg, Tiergartenstr. 17, 69121 Heidelberg, Germany

Abstract. This paper introduces the notion of a novel descriptive enterprise system model that is optimized for cybersecurity student and practitioner use, in a controlled classroom setting. Model-based system engineering theory provides guidance for the model design and use. The model is presented as a framework that needs to be detailed out for the enterprise being defended. There are two model benefits. First, is the analysis of how enterprise behavior impacts its attack surface structure and condition. Second is the ability to either abstract or decompose the enterprise attack surface structure at a level required for use case realization. The use case for this paper is the development of an enterprise risk treatment plan with a four-step work process. The four-step work process is shown to align with triple loop learning, a method recommended for improving cognitive skill levels and decision-making quality. Research shows enterprise cyber-defenders need high level cognitive skills.

Keywords: Digital Business · Model-Based Systems Engineering (MBSE) · Enterprise Cybersecurity · Cyber-Defender Cognitive Skill Development

1 Introduction

An objective of applied R&D at the University of North Carolina at Wilmington (UNCW) is the discovery of new means for improving enterprise cyber-defender performance capabilities. This includes both students interested in cybersecurity and adult learners who are employed as cybersecurity practitioners. One method of improvement is to develop skill sets amongst the student and adult learner population that foster proficiency in a particular sect of cybersecurity, which is within enterprise cybersecurity via model-based learning paradigms. The approach to minimize learning gaps via model-based learning motivated the preliminary development of the learning environment model described in this work.

1.1 Background and Motivation

Today every enterprise is a digital enterprise. It is only a question of what percentage of the enterprise has transitioned to a holistic digital process or simply specific capabilities that are subsets of the process. Additionally, there are digital titans, rising stars, and traditional enterprises undergoing varying levels of digital transformation (Rogers, 2016). The word enterprise is used because it universally encompasses for-profit businesses, non-profit organizations, and government entities. Within the cybersecurity knowledge domain, enterprise cybersecurity is unique and merits special consideration for two reasons. First, a modern digital enterprise is a large-scale, complex system of digital systems. Second, a modern digital enterprise coexists with and is dependent on its supply chain. Consequently, a modern digital enterprise and its supply chain presents the largest possible attack surface, with inherent risk, that needs to be treated for security objective achievement.

The emerging workforce required to develop, deploy, and securely operate the enterprise face challenges as the digital transformation is finalizing. Cybersecurity students and/or practitioners in training lacked a context for studying cybersecurity, primarily the lack of understanding about the overall operation, structure, and control of a modern digital enterprise.

One of the R&D team members was teaching a class in cyber-supply chain risk management. To help students better understand a cyber supply chain, its operation, structure, and control for security purposes, he used a modeling technique perfected over 15 years while working in the satellite communications industry. Students were taught how to create a supply chain map using applied graph theory in Google Earth, a geographic information system. Enterprises in the network were geocoded and assigned placemarks indicating their location on the surface of the earth. In applied graph theory these are known as vertices. Line strings were then defined to show the relationship between enterprises. In applied graph theory these are known as edges. Motivated threat actor information was then added into the model along with examples of direct and indirect supply chain attack vectors. Finally, other forms of relevant intelligence were embedded into the geographic information system model like a web link to MITRE's CAPEC (Common Attack Pattern Enumeration and Classification) website which cites 437 different types of supply chain attacks. The primary benefit of this type of teaching approach is that it enabled students to holistically view a cyber-supply chain as a system. The geographic information system model enabled a supply chain to be brought into the classroom for controlled learning purposes. Student feedback was favorable for this interactive virtual classroom experience.

This discovery provided insight on how to guide students through their learning curves such that they develop required knowledge, skills, and abilities (KSAs) required for professional success at an accelerated rate versus what is accomplished with experiential learning post-graduation. The R&D team then started to explore how this approach could be expanded upon for the purpose of teaching enterprise cybersecurity. A new modeling scheme needed to be developed or leveraged to encompass the entire scope of an enterprise's attack surface for cyber-defender proficiency building purposes.

1.2 Problem

There are several problems which need to be addressed when developing a modeling technique that will address student needs when studying enterprise cybersecurity.

First, is the need for a model to reflect a proper viewpoint for studying enterprise cybersecurity. Shown in Fig. 1 is NIST's view of Multi-Level Enterprise Risk Management. An enterprise cyber-defender's viewpoint needs to be at Level 1 when learning how to manage strategic risk. Consequently, the modeling technique needs to support the collection and presentation of relevant information needed for strategic risk management decision making.

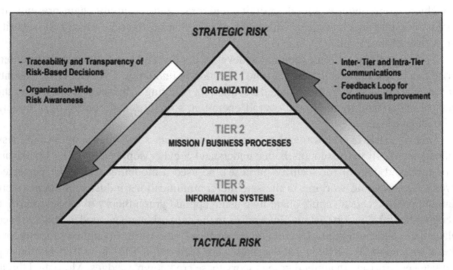

Fig. 1. Multilevel, Enterprise-Wide Risk Management, Reprinted from NIST SP800-53

Second, the scope and complexity of a system of digital systems is resident at Level 3.

Enterprise cyber-defenders are challenged at this level because they are a human entity with practical limitations in terms of how much information they can retain, process, and effectively act on over time. Enterprise cyber-defenders will benefit from a proven work process and decision-making support when working at scale with complexity. Consequently, the modeling technique needs to be capable of supporting both abstraction and decomposition of enterprise entity data based on cyber-defender need for the use-case they are working to resolve.

Third, cybersecurity students are taught today from the bottom up. They learn narrowly defined cybersecurity topics during their undergraduate education. Postgraduation, they learn how to apply their skills in the enterprise environment experientially. Consequently, the modeling technique needs to support the creation of an interactive virtual learning environment for a controlled classroom experience. Pilots learn to fly in a training simulator before walking onto the flight deck and taking control of a plane with passengers. Enterprise cyber-defenders will benefit from a training simulator to accelerate their learning curve and decision-making effectiveness.

2 Related Works

A directed literature search resulted in the discovery of similar work and useful ideas for creating a novel modeling approach. There were six findings of note. First, two researchers at the University of Bergan, in Norway, reported the best way to help people learn about the operation, structure, and control of a large-scale complex system is with a virtual learning environment and reality abstraction models (Skartveilt, 2014).

Second, the use of models in cybersecurity education is not a new concept. It has been used extensively in threat modeling (Schostack, 2014). One key concept from Schostack's work is the notion of enterprise attack surface (EAS) management. An enterprise's attack surface has inherent risk that needs to be treated. This is done with one of the standard ISO 31000 risk treatment options and deployment of security controls when appropriate. The process of treating attack surface risk converts it into a trust boundary at a level sufficient for achieving an enterprise's cybersecurity goals and objective.

Third, based on Skartveilt's work a search was conducted to discover the best method for developing reality abstraction models. There were several findings that highlighted the approach and benefits of model-based system engineering. In a book titled Effective Model Based System Engineering, the authors included chapters on its use in resolving several cybersecurity use cases (Borky, 2019).

Fourth, the National Institute for Standards and Technology (NIST) is actively promoting model-based system engineering (MBSE) to resolve cybersecurity problems. At the University of Bristol, in the UK, model-based cybersecurity engineering is being applied to autonomous vehicles as part of the Flourish Project (Robles-Ramirez, 2020). This provided further evidence to warrant the use of model-based systems engineering.

Fifth, the Department of Energy (DOE) just released its new Cyber-Informed Engineering Strategy (Kumar, 2022). They are promoting cyber-informed engineering as a best practice for assuring cybersecurity. They are building upon the original work of Nancy Mead's Security Quality Engineering Requirements (SQUARE) process (Meade, 2006). The unit of development work for the SQUARE process is a discrete IT project. It is interesting to think of how cyber-informed engineering practices can be extended to a modern digital enterprise which is a larger work unit.

Sixth, Kris Kobryn, principal owner of Pivot Point Technologies is reported to be one of the pioneers in model-based system engineering. He has developed and is promoting Cyber Modeling Language (CyberML) which is a proprietary ontology or modeling language that is optimized for cybersecurity use (Kobryn, 2013–2019). While not widely known or used it is a forward-thinking approach to evolving model-based system engineering for resolving cybersecurity use cases. Members of the Object Management (OMG) are currently working to optimize SysML, another modeling language, for cybersecurity purposes.

Upon reviewing related works it was interesting to note that while model-based system engineering theory is well known. What did not turn up in the search was specific guidance on its use in resolving enterprise cybersecurity use cases. A quick overview of model-based system engineering follows, then a more detailed presentation of its application for resolving an enterprise cybersecurity use case.

2.1 Model-Based System Engineering Tenets

There are five key model-based systems engineering tenets. First, is the recommendation to declare the System of Interest or SOI being studied. This is a scoping statement which brings focus to the work being performed within established boundaries. Second, is the recommendation to define a use case and problem that needs to be resolved. The use-case needs to identify the primary actors who are integral to the problem and their behaviors. Third, is the recommendation to use a four-step model-based system engineering work process to resolve the problem defined in the use case. The four steps are 1) model, 2) analyze, 3) design, and 4) implement. Fourth, is the recommendation to create and use a single parametrically defined data model. Functions then generate views from the data model for use-case realization. Fifth, is the recommendation to use a reference architecture when one is available. A reference architecture is a known proven approach for solving a problem. A reference architecture provides two benefits. First, it shortens the time for use-case resolution because it eliminates any discovery work regarding how to solve the problem. Second, it will result in a high-quality solution because it is a proven method that has delivered an acceptable result in the past. For UNCW's applied R&D initiative, the declared system of interest is a named modern digital enterprise. The use-case calls for a student to assume the role of a CISO tasked by the CEO to develop an effective enterprise risk treatment plan. A reference architecture is proposed for quickly developing a high-quality risk treatment plan.

3 Proposed Descriptive Enterprise System Model Framework

Shown in Fig. 2 is the proposed framework of a descriptive enterprise system model that is optimized for enterprise cybersecurity student and working practitioner use. The model is adapted from a model shown in the book Effective Model-Based System Engineering (Borky, 2019). The model shown in the book has three axes. There is a vertical axis of organization, a forward projecting axis of categories, and a horizontal axis of abstraction. It is titled, Architecture Taxonomy Defined by Three Fundamental Dimensions. To create a framework for a descriptive enterprise system model, the axes were renamed. The vertical axis is renamed the enterprise function axis, the forward projecting axis is now the enterprise attack surface structure, and the horizontal axis did not change. It is still the attack surface structure abstraction axis. What is significant about this framework is its ability to show how enterprise function or behavior impacts the structure and condition of its attack surface.

3.1 The Enterprise Function Axis

There is merit in decomposing the enterprise function axis into three time periods. The time periods are past, present, and future. Each period can be characterized by relevant management decisions and actions that impact the enterprise attack surface and its condition.

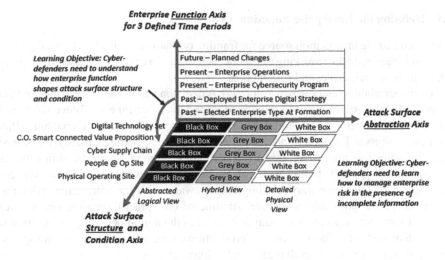

Fig. 2. A Descriptive Enterprise System Model Framework Adapted from a Model In <u>Effective Model-Based Systems Engineering</u> by Borky and Bradley, figure 1.2, page 13

3.2 The Enterprise Attack Surface (EAS) Axis

There is merit in decomposing the enterprise attack surface into five elements. They are 1) the digital technology set deployed for mission achievement, 2) depending on an enterprise's value proposition customer owned smart connected IoT products, 3) a cyber-supply chain purpose built for fulfilling enterprise digital needs, 4) people associated with the enterprise and 5) the physical operating site being defended. These five categories are a good start for further definition of the attack surface which follows.

3.3 The Enterprise Attack Surface Abstraction Axis

Abstraction is a useful and necessary approach for dealing with complexity. Entity items with similar characteristics can be referenced collectively versus individually. Attack surface categories are an abstraction of the underlying detail. Each category can be further decomposed into additional details when needed. Three different levels of abstraction are shown. They are black box, grey box, and white box. A black box is a logical entity, as seen by a cyber-attacker, with no supporting details. At the other extreme is a white box which is fully specified at the physical level. In between is a gray box for which some but not all information is known. Heavily abstracted information is useful when teaching. It helps prevent a student or cyber practitioner from being overwhelmed. Alternatively, fully detailed information is needed when managing operations.

4 Creating a Descriptive Enterprise System Model

The descriptive enterprise system model framework needs to be filled in or parametrically defined when creating a model. There are sources of information which can be used for this purpose. Recommendations are shown for each axis below.

4.1 Defining the Enterprise Function Axis

There is no single information source for framing out the enterprise function axis. Investigation is required when working to fill out each of the three recommended time-period when decisions are made, and action taken.

Consider when an enterprise was formed. A decision was made on what type of value proposition the enterprise would provide to an end-user. Joe Pine and Steve Gilmore in their book the Experience Economy, present the Economic Theory of Everything (Pine, Joe Pine Discusses The Experience Economy, 2016). They postulate there are five basic forms of value that are offered by enterprises. They are agrarian commodities that are life sustaining, products that provide functionality, services that provide convenience, experiences that are temporary psychographic rewards, and transformations which are beneficial permanent changes in state. At time of enterprise formation, one of these forms of value was selected and today it influences the digital operating technology set that is deployed for value proposition production. Selected operating technology is a subset of an enterprise's overall digital technology set.

Management decisions and actions taken in the past are also responsible for determining the currently deployed digital enterprise strategy. Decisions made include which digital technology to deploy. Who was it purchased from? Where is it physically located? What part of the enterprise mission does it support? Finally, which functional team/s maintains and uses it? The deployed digital strategy impacts every element of an enterprise's attack surface.

The current enterprise cybersecurity program determines the condition of the enterprise attack surface structure. Think of a state-machine. Condition 1, the attack surface is insecure if there is no risk treatment plan deployed. Condition 2, the attack surface is secure if a reasoned risk treatment plan is deployed. Condition 3, The attack surface is at risk if any of the assumptions or facts used in the risk treatment have changed. Cyber-defenders need to know how to assess and manage an enterprise's attack surface condition.

Current daily enterprise operations also impact the structure and condition of the attack surface. Enterprises experience employee turnover resulting in the need to onboard and offboard employees. There is also the periodic introduction of new digital technology or systems into operation.

Finally, the enterprise attack surface and structure can be impacted in the future. Merger and Acquisition activity is a known and reported period of vulnerability that needs to be managed from a cybersecurity perspective.

Enumeration and classification of enterprise decisions, actions, and their impact on the enterprise attack surface is a worthwhile exercise for cyber-defenders. An enterprise cyber-defender benefits from situational awareness and knowing which action to take at the right time. Literature searches revealed minimal information on this topic. Consequently, this is an area for further research in the future. Cybersecurity students and working professionals would benefit from an open source, information sharing website like other websites for threat intelligence. The proposed website would highlight behaviors known to impact enterprise cybersecurity. Noted behaviors would be an indicator of risk.

4.2 Defining the Enterprise Attack Surface Structure Axis

Shown in Fig. 3 below are five controlled information sources which can be used for framing out the enterprise attack surface structure axis. An enterprise's IT asset management system is a record of known digital assets. Product catalogs, sales, and distribution records are an indicator of any customer owned smart connected IoT products. Suppliers of digital goods and services should have a vendor master record in the enterprise's financial system of record. Alternatively, there is an accounting record of all financial payments too. A human resources or payroll system will have relevant information on people employed by the enterprise. Finally, the enterprise facility team will have information on the physical operating site and buildings being defended.

4.3 Defining the Enterprise Attack Surface Abstraction Axis

Defining the level of abstraction in the enterprise attack surface is dependent on the level of specificity required for use-case realization. It takes time to fully decompose an enterprise attack surface from a logical notion to a full physical description.

Cyber-defenders need to know the taxonomy of the digital infrastructure they are defending. For example, at level 0 there is the notion of an enterprise attack surface structure. At level 1, one of the attack surface categories is the digital technology set deployed for mission achievement. At level 2, it is possible to start decomposing the digital technology set into classifications of similar digital technology. This can include network enabling and network dependent technology. At level 3, network dependent digital technology can be decomposed further into classes of technology like IT, Endpoint Devices, OT, IoT, Communications, etc. This process of decomposition can be continued all the way down to a physical asset and its specification. What matters for the result is that the resultant information set meets requirements for use-case realization.

A literature search on enterprise digital infrastructure taxonomy was not all that productive which suggests this is another underdeveloped, yet important area for further exploration and development. Cybersecurity students and practitioners will benefit from being able to cite a digital infrastructure taxonomy like a doctor knows the bones in the human body.

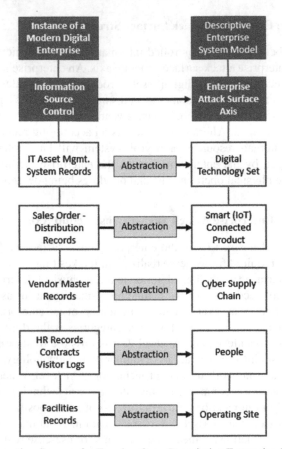

Fig. 3. Information Sources for Framing Out a Descriptive Enterprise System Model

5 Descriptive Enterprise System Model Application Domain

Once created, a descriptive enterprise system model is a useful artifact for teacher and student use in a controlled classroom setting. It is a representation of a modern digital enterprise. Shown is Fig. 4, is a proposed reference architecture (work process) for developing an enterprise risk treatment plan as called for in the use case. It is based on the model-based system engineering tenet of 1) model, 2) analyze, 3) design, and 4) implement. While the modeling technique creating a descriptive enterprise system model is novel, the process for creating a risk treatment plan is concurrent with conventional theory. Outputs from the work process are six analysis (2.1–2.6), a synthesized risk register which has been assessed (2.7), a risk treatment plan design using ISO 31000 risk treatment options and security controls as appropriate (3), and a plan of action with milestone (POAM) for risk treatment plan implementation (4).

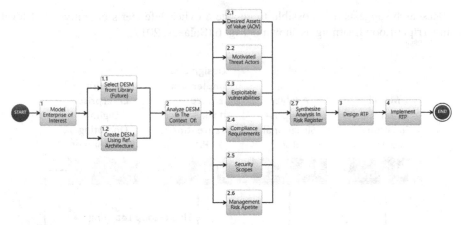

Fig. 4. Proposed Four-step Risk Treatment Work Process Using a Descriptive Enterprise System Model

6 Relevance

Researchers at Edith Cowan University in Australia have highlighted the need for enterprise cyber-defender to have high level cognitive skills (Ramsoonder N, 2020). They evaluated jobs in the NICE (National Initiative for Cybersecurity Education) framework in the context of Bloom's taxonomy which outlines six levels of cognitive skill as shown in Fig. 5. Enterprise cyber-defenders need to function at level 4 and above because they are dealing with uncertainty and need to design novel security strategies that are optimized for the enterprise they are being tasked to defend.

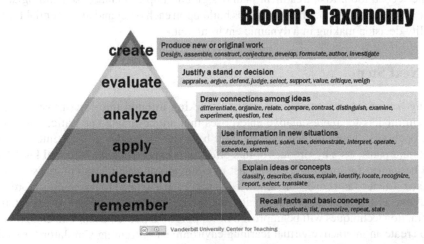

Fig. 5. Bloom's *Six Identified Levels of Cognitive Skill, Reprinted with Permission from* Vanderbilt University Center for Teaching

Research suggests it is possible to elevate a cyber-defender's cognitive skill level using Triple-Loop Learning as shown in Fig. 6 (Salakas, 2017).

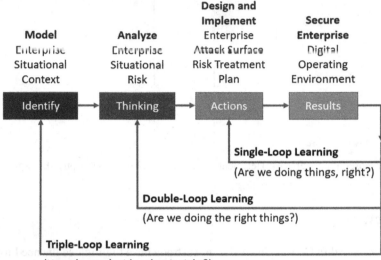

Fig. 6. Triple *Loop Learning for Effective Decision Making*

Note how the proposed reference architecture or four step risk treatment work process aligns with triple loop learning. The descriptive enterprise system model provides context for decision making in the third loop. Analysis provides assumptions for decision making in the second loop. Risk treatment plan design and implementation scheduling are the actions for the first loop. The three loops build upon each other and are essential for high quality decision making in a dynamic environment.

7 Next Steps

Going forward the research team will be working to build out descriptive enterprise system models for representative enterprises that are designated as critical infrastructure operators. These models will be used by students for developing enterprise risk treatment plans. As a by-product of this effort, it is expected that additional knowledge will be gained for creating a master list of behaviors impacting an enterprise's attack surface structure and condition. Knowledge will be also gained for creating a more complete master list of digital technologies and their taxonomy. Finally, it is expected the abstraction techniques will be improved in support of use case needs. The end objective is to create an interactive virtual learning environment or training simulator for student and working practitioner use while studying enterprise cybersecurity. It is hoped that the training simulator will help accelerate their learning curve and knowledge, skill, and ability development for greater effectiveness when defending a modern digital enterprise.

References

Borky, J.B.: Effective Model-Based Systems Engineering. Springer, Cham (2019). https://doi.org/10.1007/978-3-319-95669-5

Kobryn, C.: CyberML for Cybersecurity Architecture & Design. Pivot Point Technology Corporation, https://cyberml.com. Accessed 2013–2019

Kumar, P.: The U.S. Department of Energy's (DOE) National Cyber-Informed Engineering (CIE) Strategy Document. Office of Cybersecurity, Energy Security, and Incident Response. https://www.energy.gov/ceser/articles/us-department-energys-doe-national-cyber-informed-engineering-cie-strategy-document#:~:text=The%20U.S.%20Department%20of%20Energy%E2%80%99s%20%28DOE%29%20National%20Cyber-Informed,cycle%20of%20engineered%20systems%20t. Accessed 14 June 2022

Meade, N.: The square process. CISA-Department of Homeland Security, https://www.us-cert.gov/bsi/articles/best-practices/requirements-engineering/square-process. Accessed 30 Jan 2006

Pine, J.: Joe pine discusses the experience economy. YouTube. https://www.youtube.com/watch?v=M7rGBgn9jAI. Accessed 26 Aug 2016

Pine, J.: Theory of economic value (n.d.)

Ramsoonder, N.K.S.: Optimizing cyber security education: implementation of bloom's taxonomy for future cyber security workforce. American Council on Science and Education. https://american-cse.org/sites/csci2020proc/pdfs/CSCI2020-6SccvdzjqC7bKupZxFmCoA/762400a093/762400a093.pdf. Accessed 2020

Robles-Ramirez, E.: Model-based cybersecurity engineering for connected and automated vehicles: the flourish project. In: 11th Model Based Enterprise Summit, pp. 133–149. NIST, University of Bristol, Bristol. https://research-information.bris.ac.uk/ws/portalfiles/portal/237892738/Flourish_MBSE.pdf. Accessed 2020

Rogers, D.: On the digital transformation playbook. YouTube. https://www.youtube.com/watch?v=CPZvupB2W2A. Accessed 03 June 2016

Salakas, B.: Triple loop learning. Education Technology, https://educationtechnologysolutions.com/2017/03/triple-loop-learning/. Accessed 21 Mar 2017

Schostack, A.: Threat Modeling: Designing for Security. Wiley, Hoboken (2014)

Skartveilt, M.V.-L.: Visualization of complex systems-the two-shower mode. Psychol. J. http://psychnology.org/File/PSYCHNOLOGY_JOURNAL_2_2_VISTE.pdf. Accessed 2014

Human-Centric Machine Learning: The Role of Users in the Development of IoT Device Identification and Vulnerability Assessment

Priscilla Kyei Danso[1]([✉]), Heather Molyneaux[2], Alireza Zohourian[1],
Euclides Carlos Pinto Neto[1], Derrick Whalen[3], Sajjad Dadkhah[1],
and Ali A. Ghorbani[1]

[1] Faculty of Computer Science, University of New Brunswick,
Fredericton, NB, Canada
{priscilla.danso,alireza.zohourian,e.neto,sdadkhah,ghorbani}@unb.ca
[2] National Research Council (NRC), Fredericton, NB, Canada
heather.molyneaux@nrc-cnrc.gc.ca
[3] Information Technology Services, Port of Halifax, Halifax, NS, Canada
dwhalen@portofhalifax.ca

Abstract. Big data, Artificial Intelligence (AI), and Machine Learning (ML) have recently been posited as both a challenge and an opportunity for Human-Computer Interaction (HCI) research. Researchers and practitioners have also expressed concern about these systems' potential for favouritism, lack of transparency, and impartiality. We focus on the real-world utilization of various IoT devices and systems, communications technologies, and privacy and security considerations specific to the industry. We found that while the survey responses did validate some of our initial assumptions about privacy and security needs at Canadian ports, responses to the survey questions on IoT device and system usage and privacy and security needs were diverse, indicating an initial requirement for flexibility in UX design.

Keywords: Human-Computer Interaction · Machine Learning · Internet of Things · Security

1 Introduction

Recent literature on ethical issues surrounding AI systems shows a need for HCI research to bridge the gap between AI and HCI. Static recommendation models used by recommender systems are a quintessential example of a situation where the issue of "what precisely does a user like?" and "why does a user like this item?" are left unanswered [1]. These models are frequently employed to provide consumers with online services after being trained offline using data on past

---

A. A. Ghorbani—These authors contributed equally to this work.

A. Moallem (Ed.): HCII 2023, LNCS 14045, pp. 622–642, 2023.
https://doi.org/10.1007/978-3-031-35822-7_40

behaviour. Including societal norms and human values in AI systems could help address the biases in AI development and application [2].

Internet of Things (IoT) devices, can become entry points into critical infrastructure and be exploited to leak sensitive information [3]. In particular, ports are hubs for global supply chains connecting numerous operators, carriers and authorities and are particularly vulnerable to cyberattacks due to their reliance on information and communication technologies [4]. These interconnected systems operate with minimal consideration for cybersecurity risks [5]. The complexities of their ICT systems, with IoT devices, and their critical role as ports of entry into Canada make ports high risk for cybersecurity attacks, which could severely impact this country's economy and even National security [4]. The main goal of this research is to address this research challenge through device profiling, identification, intrusion detection and visualization while including end user feedback.

Our work involves training multiple Machine Learning (ML) algorithms to profile devices, identify vulnerabilities and communicate these issues with the end users. Our initial work is mainly focused on experiments with ML algorithms and standardizing data from reputable vulnerability databases tracking IoT vulnerabilities. In parallel with these activities, we have also been employing Human-Computer Interaction (HCI) methods in the system development and early stages of design using several methods. Firstly we recruited and are continuously working with an Expert by Experience (EBE) to discuss current issues in the field and validate our research directions. As a natural extension of this work, we collaborated with our EBE. We created a survey to elicit feedback from others within the industry to provide us with additional context to direct our research development.

HCI research is interested in how individuals interact with complicated systems, how to build tools and spaces for people to utilize, and how to create secure and comfortable systems and environments for the end user [6]. We employ ML techniques for IoT device profiling and identification. The development of ML systems that are dependable, credible, and realistic necessitates that pertinent interested parties, including developers, users, and subsequently the individuals who are directly impacted by these systems, get involved in the machine learning lifecycle [7]. Thus, to steer our research study in the right direction, the EBE is included to gather their perspectives on the various devices used in the ports, the technologies used at the ports, real-world experience, and other pertinent information.

This paper introduces and presents the findings of our survey. In particular, we focus on the real-world utilization of various IoT devices and systems, communications technologies, and privacy and security considerations specific to the industry. We found that while the survey responses did validate some of our initial assumptions about privacy and security needs at Canadian ports, answers to the survey questions on IoT device and system usage and privacy and security needs were diverse, indicating an initial condition for flexibility in UX design. These findings will be considered in the further refinement of our device profiling, identification, intrusion detection, and visualization research, and we also plan to test our proof of concept and initial UX design with the end users in our future work to elicit feedback further to incorporate into our development and design cycle.

2   Background

Internet of Things (IoT) is the new technological paradigm revolutionizing operations by improving efficiency, and automation [8]. IoT devices have been employed in different sectors and industries, including but not limited to retail, healthcare, industries, cities, ports, and buildings [9]. With the emergence of IoT, ports are gradually transitioning from more traditional approaches to operation [9]. With the concept of smart ports connected to smart cities, many ports are working towards enhancing performance and fostering entrepreneurial engagement between various relevant parties to accomplish horizontal and vertical supply chain convergence [10]. The fundamental idea behind the Internet of Things (IoT) is the interconnection of many "things" with the capacity to interchange and collect their data [11], as well as the simultaneous analysis of the acquired data to disclose insights and recommend actions that result in cost savings and increased efficiency [12]. The fundamental idea of the smart port is a seamless interconnection with its surroundings and industry stakeholders, in addition to other ports and logistics players worldwide, via a communications network [10]. These "things" in IoT are employed in smart ports and are comprised mostly of devices from different manufacturers with different communication, connection protocols, and applications [13]. Such heterogeneity presents security issues such as interoperability [13] and a need for unique device identification and profiling [14].

2.1   Current Security and Privacy Challenges in IoT

The proliferation of IoT devices and the potential permanence of their usage in every facet of our lives, coupled with their heterogeneity, makes them subject to different cyberattacks. IoT security solutions must defend against risks exclusive to traditional networking and enable safe and dependable communication for both kinds of human-device interactions [15]. Since IoT is a progression of the conventional, unencrypted Internet framework, where connectivity combining the digital and physical worlds converge, security is of utmost importance [16]. Below we highlight some critical privacy and security issues facing the Internet of Things.

2.1.1   Security Challenges
We outline the significant security challenges associated with implementing IoT in the port environments because it is the foundation for smart ports.

- **Object Identification and Locating in IoT:** Before other security concerns, identifying an object is the most crucial issue. The port's extensive array of tools and equipment require unique identification in case of an anomaly of the affected object. An effective item identification process highlights the object's characteristics while also identifying the object uniquely. A host can be uniquely identified on the Internet using a Domain Name System (DNS), a reliable identifying method. It is still susceptible to man-in-the-middle, and DNS cache poisoning attacks, among other types of attacks [17].
- **Continuous Availability:** It is risky for IoT platforms to continuously protect against constant and repetitive attacks like Denial of Service (DOS) attacks since they may influence the overall core ecosystem of reliant systems [18]. Making sure IoT services are available and ongoing while preventing any possible performance breakdowns and disruptions is the primary problem.
- **Authentication and Authorization:** Traditional authentication and authorization techniques such as public-key cryptosystems and id or password might not be appropriate for IoT devices, and networks due to their heterogeneity and complexity [17]. In the case of public-key cryptosystems, managing keys could become challenging due to the continually expanding number of devices. Hence, an attacker may use weak authentication techniques to append and impersonate rogue nodes or tamper with data integrity, invading IoT devices and network connections. In these situations, there is also a constant risk that the transferred and used authentication keys will be misplaced, destroyed, or tampered with.
- **Insufficient Physical Security:** Most IoT devices run on their own in unsupervised contexts [19]. With little effort, a malicious actor may easily gain physical access to such devices without authorization and then take over. As a result, the devices would then sustain physical damage from an attacker, who might also reveal the cryptographic techniques used, duplicate their firmware using a malicious node, or corrupt their control or data [20].

2.1.2 Privacy Challenges

IoT systems gather data that may be confidential to the ports, stakeholders or personal to a user. The following must be managed more effectively during implementation:

- **Transparency and the Ethics of Data Collection:** Due to the volume of information available in potentially complicated IoT ecosystems and the discreet techniques of data gathering, users are unaware of the data practices of IoT devices and their makers [21]. Personal information could be at risk due to the increased prevalence of linked devices. The widespread usage of equipment and networks with lax security postures contributes to some threats. The primary concern with the data collected is who will have access to it and how it will be used [22].
- **Massive Data Generation:** IoT devices are producing enormous data. While IoT tracking entails tracking a device, the goal is to comprehend the

behavioural patterns of the person using the device. The wealth of knowledge about the person, their actions, movements, and preferences give that information its value. Additionally, persistent patterns of location data associated with a certain device may provide insight into that device's position at specific times of day, ultimately revealing sensitive information such as the user's workplace or home [22].

- **Privacy Regulatory and Compliance Requirements:** The utilization of numerous networks, sensors, objects, and applications, along with the worldwide nature of IoT devices, have dramatically expanded this difficulty. As a result, data may be gathered, analyzed, evaluated, and utilized across numerous jurisdictions with various laws and regulations.

2.2   Current Solutions Proposed to Address the Security and Privacy Challenges in IoT

There are several security and privacy challenges in IoT. These include fixed access control, the challenge of building a standard system for various IoT devices, managing mass amounts of heterogeneous data, and the inherent resource limitations of IoT devices. Researchers are addressing these issues in multiple forms.

To address the fixed access control technique applied to privilege management and how interdependent actions affect IoT security [23], Jia et al. [24] proposed ContextIoT - a context-based authorization system for applied IoT systems that supports fine-grained contextual recognition for critical operations and runtime signals with rich content delivers contextual coherence.

It is challenging to build a standard defence system for heterogeneous devices because of the diversity of IoT devices, especially in industrial sectors [25] like smart ports. Therefore, it is vital to address how to find and solve the numerous security flaws present among the various IoT devices. Because each protocol differs from the others in terms of network security, researchers need to identify their most significant generic security flaws. Additionally, researchers should consider the security issues with a single protocol and any possible security threats linked to other protocols [23].

To address the issue of heterogeneity on the hardware level, Davidson et al. [26] designed and implemented an automated security analysis tool to provide an extensible platform for detecting bugs in firmware programs for some of the popular families of microcontrollers. The goal of the proposed solution by the authors is to verify the security properties of the simple firmware often found in practice.

Researchers are also addressing the issue of massive and heterogeneous data management. Li et al. proposed a storage management solution based on NoSQL called IOTMDS [27]. NoSQL systems provide high availability and performance. This study aims to delve into how to efficiently and intelligently store large amounts of IoT data while simultaneously looking out for data collaboration and exchange amongst various IoT apps. To enhance cluster performance and efficiently store data, two data preparation procedures were suggested in the design.

Most IoT devices do not deploy the essential defence mechanisms for the system and network because of the resource limitations of the IoT. Zhao et al. created and developed a lightweight solution that employs software fault isolation to redesign a compiled program and include a dynamic inspection before each risky action to improve system security for restricted IoT devices [28]. The intended outcome of the suggested approach is to offer an extreme case that its storage security and control flow trustworthiness standards are not broken and that devices may be trusted. Attacks on IoT devices are varied because of their heterogeneity and lack of appropriate security defences. Finding ways to recognize and defend against various attacks on IoT devices, such as a bonnet, Denial of Service (DoS), or Distributed Denial of Service (DDoS), is now a major challenge. Furthermore, how to detect these attacks is the difficult challenge at hand. However, McDermott et al. [29] offer a method for identifying botnet activity in IoT networks and consumer devices. A Deep, Bidirectional Long, Short Term, Memory based Recurrent Neural Network, was used to create a detection model (BLSTM-RNN). At the packet level, the detection was carried out with an emphasis on text recognition inside characteristics that conventional flow-based detection techniques would often overlook. The accuracy and loss are evaluated.

Device profiling and identification have emerged as a cutting-edge strategy that considerably reduces some, but not all, of the security concerns in IoT devices. The fingerprinting of a device is one of the well-known methods for device identification. The majority of the time, using device network traffic or physical properties, and behavioural patterns, there are numerous techniques to fingerprint the device. Similar to user authentication, device identification validates the legitimacy of the attached device to the network [30]. Due to the heterogeneity of the IoT ecosystem, accurate device identification is necessary but also challenging. Device identification describes a method that determines an IoT device based on its features. Cui et al. [31] described IoT device identification: *the input is various data collected from a device, e.g. sensors' data, network data, etc.; the output is a label for the IoT device indicating the type of the device.*

The five device identification techniques identified during our literature review are Fingerprinting, Machine Learning, Deep Learning, Manufacturer Usage Description (MUD), and Blockchain in Fig. 1. We review the works of different researchers for each identification technique.

Locality-sensitive IoT fingerprinting (LSIF), a unique method for identifying IoT devices, is presented by Charyyev et al. [32]. A locality-sensitive hash (LSH) function called Nilsimsa is used to construct the traffic profile of an IoT device from the flow of its network traffic. A signature database is then used to hold the relevant device target variable and produce a hash set. The highest average hash similarity score between each recorded device and the device being identified is

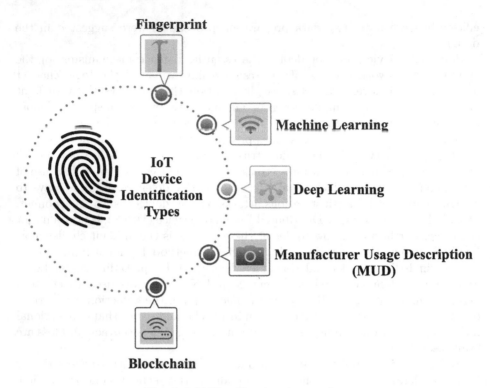

Fig. 1. IoT Identification Approaches.

computed. A comparison is made on the LSH of a new device joining the network and the hash values previously stored in the database.

To identify unauthorized IoT devices connected to a network, Yair et al. [33] used TCP/IP traffic network data for categorization by ML. The authors assume that the dataset adequately reflected each device type on the whitelist. To effectively identify IoT device types from the allowlist, features from network traffic data were extracted using supervised machine learning, especially Random Forest. Nine IoT device categories totaling 17 unique IoT devices were gathered and manually labeled to train and test multi-class classifiers. The trained classifiers obtained an average of 96% accuracy in detecting illegitimate IoT device types.

Jaidip et al. [34] detected IoT devices linked to a network using data from traffic data, precisely IoT devices not on the whitelist (unknown devices) using a deep learning approach. The method the authors suggested was based on representation learning and consisted of two experiments: one for detecting legitimate IoT devices in network traffic and the second for identifying illegitimate devices attached to a network. The proposed method identified known devices in a network with a maximum accuracy of 99.87% (Table 1).

Alam et al. [35] proposed a generalized fingerprinting approach based on blockchain technology to authenticate edge devices with distinctive PUF IDs (Physical Unclonable Function Identifications embedded in the device's memory

Table 1. Summary of device profiling and identification review. ML, F, DL, BC, and MUD each represent the different approaches used in the profiling and identification of a device Machine Learning, Fingerprinting, Deep Learning, Blockchain and Manufacturer Usage Description respectively.

No	Paper	Purpose	Algorithm/Tools	Type of Identification
1	[32]	IoT device identification using locality-sensitive hash (LSH) function	LSH function called Nilsimsa	F
2	[33]	Identify unauthorized IoT devices connected to a network	Random Forests (RF)	ML
3	[34]	Detect IoT devices in a network using data from traffic data	Neural Network	DL
4	[35]	Authenticate edge devices	Blockchain ledger BL	BC
5	[30]	IoT device profiling	Manufacturer Usage Description (MUD)	MUD

during production). They distinguish between a global and local component. While the global system verifies registered devices by anybody, anywhere, without being able to pinpoint the particular manufacturer, the local implementation allows defence-in-depth authenticity. The device identification is verified after a thorough approval process in which hashed values of both the blockchain ledger BL and gateway coincide.

Manufacturer Usage Description (MUD) [36] is a new standard created by the Internet Engineering Task Force (IETF). The MUD specification defines device profiles. An IoT device will submit a MUD URL along with its LLDP, DHCP, or X.509 request [30] when it initially joins an access control station. The MUD Manager converts this conceptual goal into a context-specific guideline and sent to the server. The server then enacts the policies on the network utilizing Access Control Lists (ACLs) for that IoT device's entry outlet. Then, depending on the maker's predetermined goal, accessibility to the device is granted.

3   Our Proposed System

The three primary components of the proposed framework are the device identification and profile, vulnerability analysis, and visualization or dashboard module. The primary motivation behind the proposed architecture is to have a compound system responsible for utilizing Machine Learning to detect the device type in a network while also evaluating and displaying their vulnerabilities. Although there are a number of processes that each component in the proposed system must go through, the work of Dadkhah et al. [14] provides a detailed explanation of these procedures. The surveys from the EBEs in our study were also used to evaluate our preliminary project findings and to highlight user interest areas that would be included in the final system design (Fig. 2).

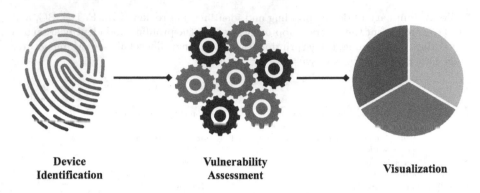

Device   **Vulnerability**   **Visualization**
Identification   **Assessment**

Fig. 2. System Flow.

4   Methodology

The first step to address this research challenge is to identify state-of-the-art IoT and logistics for the industry by investigating the most effective and commonly used devices, the resulting raw data, and possible attack threats. Initially, a literature review was undertaken, and findings were presented in an internal report; however, this search revealed little about the specific details of the devices used in the ports, technologies used at the ports, and the real-world experience. In order to understand the needs of operators at Port authorities as well as the devices commonly used within ports, we developed a survey whereby IT experts at the ports were asked to provide feedback on survey questions related to the current and future IoT needs, as well as devices used at the port. The survey was informed by our previous literature searches and was created with input and feedback from our EBE at the Port of Halifax. Participation was voluntary, and the survey was approved by NRC's Research Ethics Board (REB). In April, surveys were sent out via email to Port authorities with one reminder email. Eight port authorities were contacted by one researcher (including the five most important ports in Canada and three additional ports), and our EBE and four port authority representatives completed the survey. Data collection ended in August.

4.1   Demographics

From the survey responses, we can determine that most of the ports were medium-sized ports, employing 51–100 people. One larger-sized port, employing 201–300 people, filled out the survey (Fig. 3).

Responses to the question on how many IoT devices the ports currently have were varied, with two ports noting currently having between 0–500 IoT devices, one port having between 501–1000 devices and one port having more than 1000 (Fig. 4).

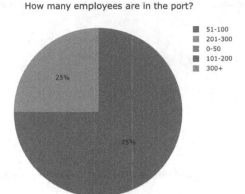

How many employees are in the port?

■	51-100
■	201-300
■	0-50
■	101-200
■	300+

Fig. 3. Number of employees.

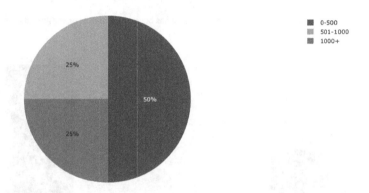

How many IoT devices do you currently have in the port?

■	0-500
■	501-1000
■	1000+

Fig. 4. Number of IoT devices.

Most of the ports reported high rates of implementing and considering privacy and security concerns in their current configurations (Fig. 5), with one exception discussed in more detail in the next section of this report.

Likewise, most of the ports also noted implementing and considering the use of monitoring, profiling, and tracking (Fig. 6), with one exception that is discussed in more detail in the next section of this report.

When asked which performance measures were significant, the accuracy of estimation and greenhouse gas emissions were the two most important performance measures to the ports (Fig. 7). In the written comments of the survey, two of the four ports noted that bandwidth for remote IoT and/or video devices could be a performance issue in their configuration. The largest port (P3) reported no problems with its configuration and rated all performance measures as 4 or 5.

All ports reported using cameras, sensors, and office accessories (Fig. 8). The port representatives were asked which devices they used in operations and given the ability to write in additional devices. A later question asked for more specific

To what extent privacy and secuirty concerns has been implemented or considered in your current configuration?

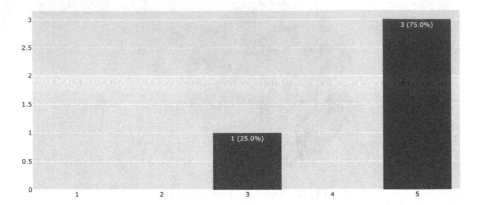

Fig. 5. Privacy and Security.

To what extent profiling/monitoring/tracking has been implemented or considered in your current configuration?

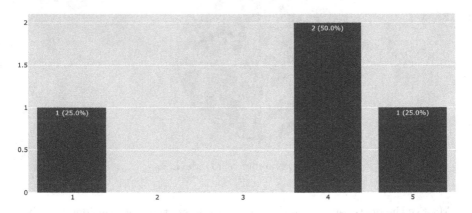

Fig. 6. Monitoring/Profiling/Tracking.

details about the types of sensors they employ at their port. One of the smaller ports noted having gates and access controls (a written response which they added).

All of the ports reported using Ethernet and 4G/5G, and most also use WiFi and RFID (Fig. 9). The largest port (P3) was the only one to report using LoRaWAN, and here they note that they do not use WiFi (which is contradictory to their response on a later question response); they also report not using GPS and Zigbee/Z-Wave.

Smart production management and smart parking lots were the two applications not employed by any of the ports surveyed (Fig. 10). Interestingly the

Which of the following performace measures are important to you?

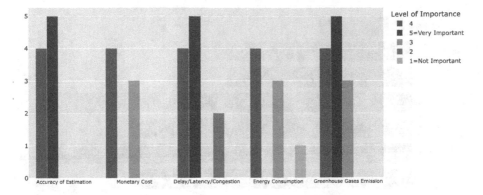

Fig. 7. Performance measures.

Which of the following devices do you use?

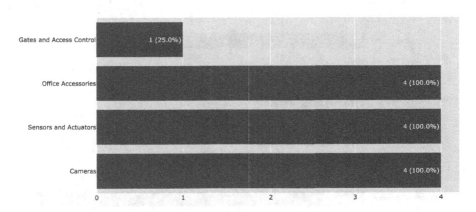

Fig. 8. Category of devices used.

largest port only reported currently operating smart operation management and Smart lighting, while one of the smaller ports reported using a greater variety of smart management systems (P1 noted using 5; P2 uses 3; P4 uses 2).

Many of the port authority representatives may know they need to expand their current usage of communication technologies. Not surprisingly, WiFi, Ethernet, RFID, and 4/5G were all required for all ports for land, and 4/5G and GPS for trucks in all four ports. Temperature, motion, image, dust, and wind sensors are currently employed in all ports (Fig. 11). There was a discrepancy between answers here with the use of LoRaWAN and an earlier question asking which communication technologies the ports currently employ (Fig. 9); however, the difference could be related to asking them which communication technologies they now use compared to which communication technologies they need.

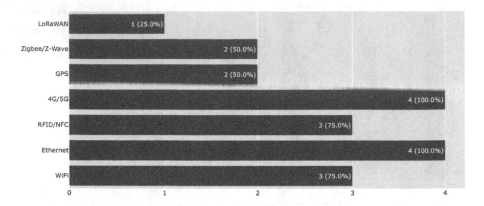

Fig. 9. Communication Technologies.

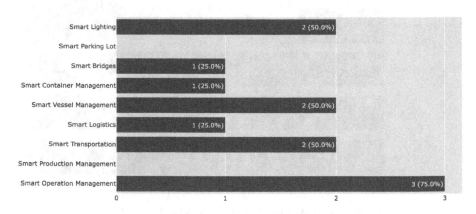

Fig. 10. Current application areas.

Temperature, motion, image, dust, and wind sensors are currently employed by all ports (Fig. 12). The largest port uses the most sensors (all but pressure, water, and gyroscopic sensors), but the smaller ports also employ many of the sensing systems; for example, P1 uses all sensing systems listed except water quality, chemical, acceleration, and gyroscopic sensors. P1 also wrote that they use water current sensors.

Not many ports currently use LoRaWAN, as we saw in Fig. 9; however, there is a need for it, especially for trucks and rail applications (Fig. 11), and here in Fig. 13 the majority of the respondents note an interest in employing and/or extending their use of the technology. Other technologies of note include WiFi, Ethernet, GPS, and, to a lesser extent, 4G/5G.

Which of the following communication technologies do you need to employ for which category?

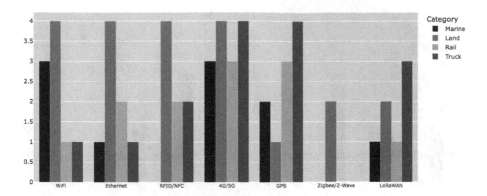

Fig. 11. Communication Technologies needed.

Which sensing system do you currently employ?

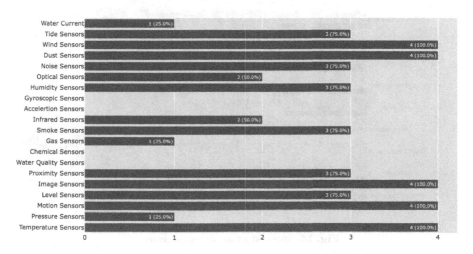

Fig. 12. Current sensing systems.

Smart transportation was noted as the number one application area of interest for employing or extending, followed by smart operation management (which three ports already use - Fig. 10), smart container management, and smart lighting (Fig. 14). While the most prominent port (P3) reported only using two application areas currently, they reported being very interested in all of the application areas listed, except for smart bridges and parking lots (marked "a little interested").

Most ports showed interest in employing and/or extending their image, dust, and wind sensor systems. All were interested in water quality sensors (Fig. 15). The ports had different responses to this question based on many factors, includ-

To what extent are you interested in employing or extending the following technologies?

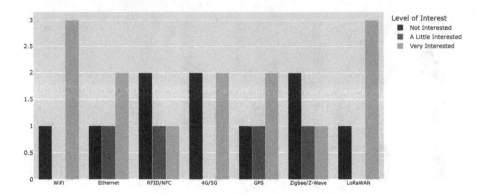

Fig. 13. Interest in communication technologies.

To what extent are you interested in employing or extending the following application areas?

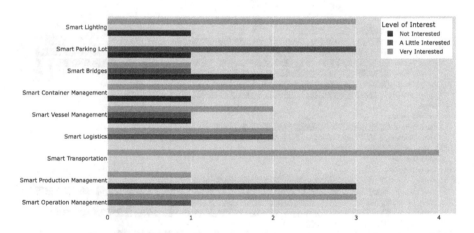

Fig. 14. Interest in application areas.

ing their current use of sensor systems, which will be detailed in the discussion section.

The port authorities were also asked which types of sensing systems were needed for which category: marine, land, rail, and trucks. All four ports reported needing temperature, motion, humidity, noise, dust, and wind sensors for land. Image sensors were reported as necessary for all aspects of operations within the port (marine, ground, rail, and truck); wind sensors were reported by 3 of the four ports as needed for marine operations; noise sensors were reported from 3 of the four ports as also required for marine, rail, and trucks. Three of the four ports reported needing tide sensors (which could indicate the difference between ocean ports and those located on lakes or rivers) (Fig. 16).

To what extent are you interested in employing or extending the following sensing systems?

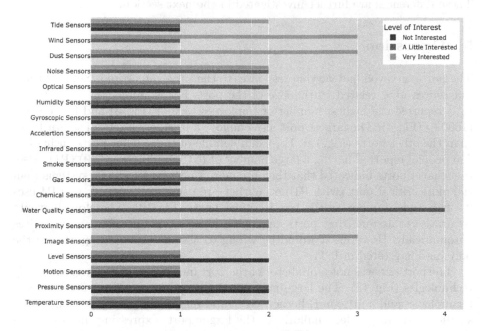

Fig. 15. Interest in employing/extending sensing systems.

Which of the following sensing systems do you need for which category?

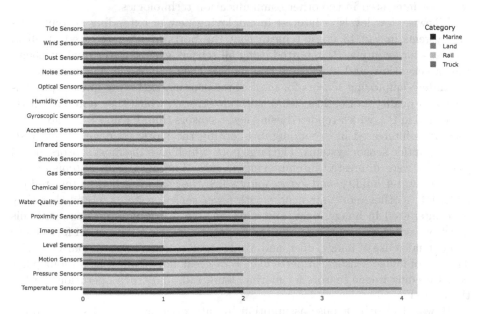

Fig. 16. Sensing systems for categories.

The responses from the ports to most of the survey questions were diverse. These differences are further investigated in the next section.

5 Discussion

The ports surveyed had varying responses to the survey questions. Some of these differences were related to the size of the port. For example, the largest port (P3) reported the highest number of employees (300+) (Fig. 3) and IoT devices (1000+) (Fig. 4). The largest port also employs a broader variety of sensor types than the other ports (Fig. 12). For example, one of the smaller ports (using 51–100 people) reported having a large number of IoT devices (over 500) (P1). Also, the smaller ports indicated that they use more smart management systems than the more critical port (with P1 noting they are using 5; P2 uses 3; and P4 uses 2 - the same number as the more critical port) (Fig. 10). Therefore it would be unwise to assume that ports employing fewer people use fewer IoT devices automatically. However, it would be wrong to assume that large ports are the only ones interested in IoT.

The port size was not a predictor of the port interest in employing/extending technologies (Fig. 13). The large port noted they were very interested in most technologies and a little in Ethernet, GPS, and Zigbee (P3). Likewise, one of the smaller ports responded similarly to the larger port, expressing interest in all the technologies aside from RFID (which they note they were a little interested in) (P2); however, P1 reported only being very interested in Zigbee, and P4 was only very interested in WiFi and Ethernet. Both P1 and P4 checked that they were not interested in the other communication technologies.

Likewise, low levels of interest in employing new or extending current sensing systems in Fig. 13 doesn't mean that the ports aren't interested at all in sensors - for example, P1 reported using all sensors except water quality, chemical, acceleration, and gyroscopic sensors - so they responded not interested in expanding/employing sensors for most of the sensors, excluding image, [proximity, water quality, noise, dust, wind, and tide sensors, which they noted is a little interested in P2, which reported using fewer sensors than P1 and P4, states that they were interested in expanding or adopting the motion, image, noise, dust, wind, and tide sensor systems. The large port, which uses the most sensors, noted that they were interested in employing or extending all sensor systems except pressure, water quality, and gyroscopic (which they said is a little interested in) (P3). P4, another more minor port with fewer sensor systems, noted that they were interested in image, dust, and wind sensors. All four ports answered this question very differently, but from the responses, we see a clear need for the use and extended use of image, dust, and wind sensor systems in particular (Fig. 15). The use of image sensors, in particular, is of great importance, as all four ports noted needing image sensors for marine, land, rail, and truck operations within the port (Fig. 16).

It would also be a false assumption to categorize larger and smaller ports as having different attitudes toward privacy and security. The largest port (P3) ranked privacy and security considerations and implementation as the highest consideration (5) and monitoring/profiling/tracking as the high consideration (4). Meanwhile, one more minor port noted privacy and security are of the highest consideration (5) and that they also highly implement/consider monitoring/profiling and tracking (5). This was the same port that reported having over 500 IoT devices (P1), which indicates they know they need to be aware and concerned about privacy and security within the port. They acknowledge the importance of monitoring, profiling, and tracking IoT devices. Similarly, another smaller port (P4) considered privacy and security highly assumed (5), and monitoring, profiling, and tacking were also considered (4).

However, not all of the responses about privacy and security from the ports were the same. One of the smaller ports (P2) noted that monitoring/tracking/profiling is not being considered (1); the same more minor port noted privacy and security concerns are not believed in the current configuration (answering "3" in the Likert scale).

The responses from P2 do not necessarily indicate that they are not interested in or aware of privacy and security concerns. Perhaps they suggest that they know that their port needs to do more. Their responses to the survey indicate they are interested in IoT solutions at their dock. The same port representative wrote in the study about having IoT for gates and access control, bandwidth challenges for video, smart operations management, smart transportation, and smart bridges. They also indicated that they are very interested in including or expanding upon in the future the port's smart operation management, smart transportation, smart vessel management, smart container management, smart bridges, and smart lighting (P2). Currently, P2 employs WiFi, Ethernet, 4G/5G, and Zigbee/Z-Wave. It is very interested in all technologies except RFID (which they indicated that they were a little interested in) P2 also currently employs various sensors such as temperature, motion, image, proximity, noise, dust, wind, and tide. They also indicated that in the future, they are interested in including and/or expanding upon motion, image, proximity, noise, dust, wind, and tide sensors. To further the conclusion that P2 is interested in growing their use of IoT, their final comment in the survey is that: "IoT solutions expected to grow in future" (P2).

6   Conclusions

Our study mixes training ML algorithms to profile devices and identify vulnerabilities with HCI approaches to direct and validate our research directions. Through our HCI work, we validated the importance of privacy and security at the ports and the priority, in particular, of image sensor systems. Several findings from the survey will inform our design outcomes, such as the importance of specific types of sensors and systems and the need for flexibility in UX design, as survey responses showed the diversity of the types of devices and systems used in the various ports. Questions related to the current and future IoT use in the ports support the idea of the growth in IoT at the ports and the need to support this growth with mindful privacy and security measures.

There are several limitations to our study. Our work was conducted during the Covid-19 pandemic, which limited our use of user studies. Meetings with the EBE were all conducted remotely, and the survey was administered online. Our survey contains a small sample size but within a relatively small population size, as there are only 17 Canadian Port Authorities recognized as such due to their strategic importance. Future work will involve engaging the EBE and other users for UX design and feedback through a cognitive walkthrough of the prototype.

Acknowledgments. The authors graciously acknowledge the support from the Canadian Institute for Cybersecurity (CIC), the funding support from the National Research Council of Canada (NRC) through the AI for Logistics collaborative program, the NSERC Discovery Grant (no. RGPIN 231074), and Tier 1 Canada Research Chair Dr. Ghorbani.

References

1. Gao, C., Lei, W., He, X., de Rijke, M., Chua, T.-S.: Advances and challenges in conversational recommender systems: a survey. AI Open **2**, 100–126 (2021). https://doi.org/10.1016/j.aiopen.2021.06.002
2. Lee, M.K., et al.: Human-centered approaches to fair and responsible AI. In: Extended Abstracts of the 2020 CHI Conference on Human Factors in Computing Systems (CHI EA 2020), pp. 1–8. Association for Computing Machinery, New York, NY, USA (2020). https://doi.org/10.1145/3334480.3375158
3. Rockefeller, S.: A kill chain analysis of the 2013 target data breach. Committee on Commerce, Science and Transportation, Tech. Rep. (2014)
4. Meyer-Larsen, N., Müller, R.: Enhancing the cybersecurity of port community systems. In: Freitag, M., Kotzab, H., Pannek, J. (eds.) LDIC 2018. LNL, pp. 318–323. Springer, Cham (2018). https://doi.org/10.1007/978-3-319-74225-0_43
5. Trimble, D., Monken, J., Sand, A.F.L.: A framework for cybersecurity assessments of critical port infrastructure. In: 2017 International Conference on Cyber Conflict (CyCon U.S.), pp. 1–7 (2017). https://doi.org/10.1109/CYCONUS.2017.8167506
6. Moustakis, V.S., Herrmann, J.: Where do machine learning and human-computer interaction meet? Appl. Artif. Intell. **11**(7–8), 595–609 (1997)
7. Vaughan, J.W., Wallach, H.: A human-centered agenda for intelligible machine learning. Machines We Trust: Getting Along with Artificial Intelligence (2020)
8. Jun, W.K., Lee, M.-K., Choi, J.Y.: Impact of the smart port industry on the Korean national economy using input-output analysis. Transp. Res. A Policy Pract. **118**, 480–493 (2018). https://doi.org/10.1016/j.tra.2018.10.004
9. Yang, Y., Zhong, M., Yao, H., Yu, F., Fu, X., Postolache, O.: Internet of things for smart ports: technologies and challenges. IEEE Instrum. Meas. Mag. **21**(1), 34–43 (2018). https://doi.org/10.1109/MIM.2018.8278808
10. Philipp, R.: Digital readiness index assessment towards smart port development. Sustain. Manag. Forum — NachhaltigkeitsManagementForum **28**(1), 49–60 (2020). https://doi.org/10.1007/s00550-020-00501-5
11. Minerva, R., Biru, A., Rotondi, D.: Towards a definition of the internet of things (IoT). IEEE Internet Initiative **1**(1), 1–86 (2015)
12. Davies, R.: The internet of things: opportunities and challenges (2015)

13. Noaman, M., Khan, M.S., Abrar, M.F., Ali, S., Alvi, A., Saleem, M.A.: Challenges in integration of heterogeneous internet of things. Sci. Program. **2022**, 8626882 (2022). https://doi.org/10.1155/2022/8626882

14. Dadkhah, S., Mahdikhani, H., Danso, P.K., Zohourian, A., Truong, K.A., Ghorbani, A.A.: Towards the development of a realistic multidimensional IoT profiling dataset. In: 2022 19th Annual International Conference on Privacy, Security and Trust (PST), pp. 1–11 (2022). https://doi.org/10.1109/PST55820.2022.9851966

15. Punla, C.S., Farro, R.C.: Are we there yet?: an analysis of the competencies of BEED graduates of BPSU-DC. Int. Multidiscip. Res. J. **4**(3), 50–59 (2022)

16. Hamad, S.A., Sheng, Q.Z., Zhang, W.E., Nepal, S.: Realizing an internet of secure things: a survey on issues and enabling technologies. IEEE Commun. Surv. Tutor. **22**(2), 1372–1391 (2020). https://doi.org/10.1109/COMST.2020.2976075

17. Zhang, Z.-K., Cho, M.C.Y., Wang, C.-W., Hsu, C.-W., Chen, C.-K., Shieh, S.: Iot security: ongoing challenges and research opportunities. In: 2014 IEEE 7th International Conference on Service-Oriented Computing and Applications, pp. 230–234 (2014). https://doi.org/10.1109/SOCA.2014.58

18. Kolias, C., Kambourakis, G., Stavrou, A., Voas, J.: DDoS in the IoT: Mirai and other botnets. Computer **50**(7), 80–84 (2017). https://doi.org/10.1109/MC.2017.201

19. Butun, I., Österberg, P., Song, H.: Security of the internet of things: vulnerabilities, attacks, and countermeasures. IEEE Commun. Surv. Tutor. **22**(1), 616–644 (2020). https://doi.org/10.1109/COMST.2019.2953364

20. Neshenko, N., Bou-Harb, E., Crichigno, J., Kaddoum, G., Ghani, N.: Demystifying IoT security: an exhaustive survey on IoT vulnerabilities and a first empirical look on internet-scale IoT exploitations. IEEE Commun. Surv. Tutor. **21**(3), 2702–2733 (2019). https://doi.org/10.1109/COMST.2019.2910750

21. Lipford, H.R., Tabassum, M., Bahirat, P., Yao, Y., Knijnenburg, B.P.: Privacy and the internet of things. In: Knijnenburg, B.P., Page, X., Wisniewski, P., Lipford, H.R., Proferes, N., Romano, J. (eds.) Modern Socio-Technical Perspectives on Privacy, pp, 233–264. Springer, Cham (2022). https://doi.org/10.1007/978-3-030-82786-1_11

22. Policy Group, R., et al.: The internet of things: an introduction to privacy issues with a focus on the retail and home environments. Office of the Privacy Commissioner of Canada (2016)

23. Zhou, W., Jia, Y., Peng, A., Zhang, Y., Liu, P.: The effect of IoT new features on security and privacy: new threats, existing solutions, and challenges yet to be solved. IEEE Internet Things J. **6**(2), 1606–1616 (2019). https://doi.org/10.1109/JIOT.2018.2847733

24. Jia, Y., et al.: ContextIoT: towards providing contextual integrity to appified IoT platforms. In: Network and Distributed System Security Symposium (2017)

25. Rubio-Hernan, J., Rodolfo-Mejias, J., Garcia-Alfaro, J.: Security of cyber-physical systems. In: Cuppens-Boulahia, N., Lambrinoudakis, C., Cuppens, F., Katsikas, S. (eds.) CyberICPS 2016. LNCS, vol. 10166, pp. 3–18. Springer, Cham (2017). https://doi.org/10.1007/978-3-319-61437-3_1

26. Davidson, D., Moench, B., Ristenpart, T., Jha, S.: Fie on firmware: finding vulnerabilities in embedded systems using symbolic execution. In: USENIX Security Symposium (2013)

27. Li, T., Liu, Y., Tian, Y., Shen, S., Mao, W.: A storage solution for massive IoT data based on NoSQL. In: 2012 IEEE International Conference on Green Computing and Communications, pp. 50–57 (2012). https://doi.org/10.1109/GreenCom.2012.18

28. Zhao, L., Li, G., De Sutter, B., Regehr, J.: ARMor: fully verified software fault isolation. In: 2011 Proceedings of the Ninth ACM International Conference on Embedded Software (EMSOFT), pp. 289–298 (2011)
29. McDermott, C.D., Majdani, F., Petrovski, A.V.: Botnet detection in the internet of things using deep learning approaches. In: 2018 International Joint Conference on Neural Networks (IJCNN), pp. 1–8 (2018). https://doi.org/10.1109/IJCNN.2018.8489489
30. Mazhar, N., Salleh, R., Zeeshan, M., Hameed, M.M.: Role of device identification and manufacturer usage description in IoT security: a survey. IEEE Access 9, 41757–41786 (2021). https://doi.org/10.1109/ACCESS.2021.3065123
31. Cui, L., Yang, S., Chen, F., Ming, Z., Lu, N., Qin, J.: A survey on application of machine learning for Internet of Things. Int. J. Mach. Learn. Cybern. 9(8), 1399–1417 (2018). https://doi.org/10.1007/s13042-018-0834-5
32. Charyyev, B., Gunes, M.H.: Locality-sensitive IoT network traffic fingerprinting for device identification. IEEE Internet Things J. 8(3), 1272–1281 (2021). https://doi.org/10.1109/JIOT.2020.3035087
33. Meidan, Y., et al.: Detection of unauthorized IoT devices using machine learning techniques. arXiv preprint arXiv:1709.04647 (2017)
34. Kotak, J., Elovici, Y.: IoT device identification using deep learning. In: Herrero, Á., Cambra, C., Urda, D., Sedano, J., Quintián, H., Corchado, E. (eds.) CISIS 2019. AISC, vol. 1267, pp. 76–86. Springer, Cham (2021). https://doi.org/10.1007/978-3-030-57805-3_8
35. Alam, S.R., Jain, S., Doriya, R.: Security threats and solutions to IoT using blockchain: a review. In: 2021 5th International Conference on Intelligent Computing and Control Systems (ICICCS), pp. 268–273 (2021). https://doi.org/10.1109/ICICCS51141.2021.9432325
36. Lear, E., Droms, R., Romascanu, D.: Manufacturer usage description specification. RFC Editor (2019). https://doi.org/10.17487/RFC8520. https://www.rfc-editor.org/info/rfc8520

Fail-Safe Automatic Timed Response Protocol for Cyber Incident and Fault Management

Zeth duBois[1]([⊠])[iD], Roger Lew[1], and Ronald L. Boring[2][iD]

[1] University of Idaho, Moscow, ID 83844, USA
dubois0720@vandals.uidaho.edu, rogerlew@uidaho.edu
[2] Idaho National Laboratory, Idaho Falls, ID 83415, USA
ronald.boring@inl.gov

Abstract. An operation modality sometimes referred to as Hybrid System Operation is increasingly prevalent as automated systems assume more control in industrial settings where regulatory guidelines continue to require the presence of human operators. This paradigm can lead to inefficient protocols due to process redundancy, sub-optimal incident response procedures, and encourage operator complacency with decreased situational awareness. This paper suggests a process framework that captures the adaptability of human oversight while retaining the fast low-error operations capable in computer logic. In our conception, the control system dedicates a response plan with sub-procedures of control setpoints with a total maximum safe time allowed to execute, and then present those summaries in a concise message to attending human operators. This we call Fail-safe Automated Timed Response (FATR). With a FATR safety assurance pre-plotted, the human operators may dedicate attention to diagnose system indicators to either confirm or deny system state, and either agree with the proposed plan or commit to alternate procedures.

It is our contention that a successful integration of this kind of HSO collaboration could lead to a) more efficient operations, b) increased safety, c) reduced operator stress, d) increased operator situational awareness, e) lead to improved industry standard guidelines, f) boost stakeholder confidence and relations.

Keywords: HSO · human reliability analysis · cybersecurity

1 Introduction

Nuclear Power in the United States produce around 20% of our low-carbon energy. Unlike renewables, nuclear power has high reliability. With a few exceptions the majority of US nuclear power plants were designed and commissioned in the 1970s and 1980s and the control technologies are representative of that era. In recent decades control systems have advanced with digitization of both backhaul and control systems. Simultaneously there is a global renaissance of nuclear

A. Moallem (Ed.): HCII 2023, LNCS 14045, pp. 643–655, 2023.
https://doi.org/10.1007/978-3-031-35822-7_41

power with new advanced reactors in various phases of conception, design, licensing, and commissioning. These new reactors can utilize new control system technologies to increase plant flexibility, reliability, and complement the capabilities of human operators [4].

New advanced reactors must fulfill stringent licensing requirements but advanced reactor vendors are also able to consider control room operations from a blank slate [4]. Optimizing total cost of ownership is critical to the adoption of advanced nuclear power plants. From talks with advanced reactor vendors it is clear that many of them have a "startup culture" mentality regarding new plant designs. Efforts are being made to reduce capital costs by manufacturing units in a factory setting and shipping them to their final locations. Vendors have the benefit of hindsight. They know that reactors will require support during their entire multi-decade life-cycle. Advanced reactor vendors are also treating subsystems as sub-assemblies that could be field swappable and reduce the bespoke engineering commonly associated with existing plants. New advanced reactors could potentially be fleet managed to reduce maintenance costs. Nuclear power is unique in that the fuel costs is low compared to the operational costs associated with staffing requirements. New plants are even considering remote operations and novel roles for control room operators [6].

Control room designs that utilize remote operations or centralized maintenance are vulnerable to cyber-security attack vectors that must be considered. Operating new plants may look and feel very different from current operations which rely on paper-based procedures and analog control rooms, much like driving Level 3 autonomous vehicles is very different from fully manual driving. An easily over-looked advantage in the antique model is a very low risk to cyber vulnerability by virtue of having analog systems or very early air-gapped digital systems with hardened physical security. Operators of new plants will likely need dedicated cyber-training and cyber-resources to navigate the new landscapes with cyber-risk components. Here we utilize the Rancor Nuclear Power Plant Microworld to prototype a novel framework for diagnosing and mitigating cyber threats.

Designing control systems and operational procedures for nuclear power stations requires compliance for the most stringent of regulatory oversight. Solutions which can achieve these high standards will surely meet the challenges set forth in industrial applications of equal or lower scale.

1.1   Background

Automated System Operations (ASO) for industrial scale operations are largely made possible by the advancements in Programmable Logic Controllers (PLC), remote sensors, miniaturization and ubiquitous electronics, and proliferation in digital communications. In practice, an ASO is a computer controlled system designed to follow optimal operational procedures. ASOs designed to monitor systems with physical sensors can analyze metered values to diagnose system state, and respond to impaired operations by executing scripted actions designed to restore optimal operating condition. Under equipment failure conditions, the ASO can engage emergency procedures to avoid or reduce further damage.

At its most fundamental, an *incident response* may be represented in three stages–those of awareness, decision, and reaction. In control environments with engineered procedures, we conceptualized these as *Attend, Commit, Act*. See Fig. 1.

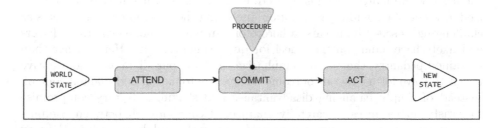

Fig. 1. Incident response diagram

A programmed incident response by computer will be faster and more reliable than a human response, which depends on organic perception, decision making, and motor response times. Additionally, humans may make errors in judgment and deviate from procedural guidelines, especially in complex or stressful situations.

However, ASOs may be unable to provide ideal response when presented with conditions that were not conceived of during program design. Automated controls are as effective and comprehensive as preconceived modeling allows. Accepting that automated control is imperfect, it is not only advisable to include human oversight, regulatory policies require licensed human operators to retain operational control in many domains, such as nuclear power and municipal water treatment.

It can appear that automated systems' instantiation in control operations is necessary to compensate for the failings of human operators, and that the human operators' attendance is required to ameliorate the failings of automation. It is the authors' opinion that a glass half-empty conception may foster a confusing landscape for the development of guidelines, control design, and the procedures that govern them. Instead, we seek a union with a sum greater than the parts.

1.2 Hybrid System Operations (HSO)

The growing prevalence of ASOs in industry present planners, regulators and engineers the challenge of integrating experienced human operators to provide efficient oversight. While the degree of operator oversight needed can vary depending on the application and context, it is generally recognized that human operators play an important role in ensuring safe and ethical moderation of machine automated control systems. Furthermore, humans can integrate contextual information that may not be readily available to an engineered controller, providing resiliency during unanticipated conditions. A control system that can offer autonomous operation modes while allowing human oversight is a Hybrid System Operation. These systems are designed to interact with human operators who retain ultimate override capability.

Any given HSO resides on a continuum between a fully automated and a fully manual system control. In contemporary industry settings it is increasingly unlikely to discover operations under control of exclusively manually or exclusively automated systems. Indeed, even as this century may be characterized as a one of expanding automation, including the development of systems as challenging as self-driving cars, a heretofore an unimaginable evolution, drivers will likely have hands on the wheel for quite some time [5]. Here, rather than sustained pedantry, the authors emphasize the HSO paradigm as an affirmative intent to solve for a superior outcome between automation and manual control. Instead of simply balancing disadvantages and striking arbitrary compromise to satisfy appearances, a carefully engineered collaboration between computers and humans can capture advantages from each modality, much in the way a well-managed professional kitchen expands multiple resources, offloading and distributing tasks as inputs, and then recombining outputs under the ultimate coordination of the head chef. See Fig. 2, depicting a typical HSO response workflow.

Conceived as a necessity to protect investment and public safety, hybrid systems are the executive positioned to minimize downtown due to performance degradation, and to avert or mitigate damage from catastrophic failures. Analogous to branches of government, engineers and the maintenance professionals are legislative architects, regulators and planners provide a judicial role, and the operators execute protocol under normal operation, prepared to respond to abnormal threat incidents. Training and experience must prepare operators to use best judgment in response to failures where no procedures are available. A well-executed HSO can mitigate threats to physical systems that go beyond component failure and procedural error, to include network breeches by malicious attackers meant to cause mischief or harm, i.e., cyber attacks.

1.3   Cyber Security

There is a growing desire and proliferation of remote operations enabled by network communications for cyber-physical systems, such as nuclear power. This presents the possibility for bad actors to use cyber-attacks to cause damage or loss. Because the limitations of skilled and well-funded attackers cannot be quantified before they are demonstrated, the vulnerability and consequences of cyber-attacks are difficult to quantify as traditional techniques like probabilistic safety analysis (PSA) cannot be used. Globally, several high-profile highly skilled cyber-attacks have occurred (Stuxnet, Ukraine power grid, Colonial pipeline) demonstrating that complacency is not a suitable alternative. A compromised system's final backstop may require human operator reasoning.

Cyber threats can range from simple denial of service attacks (DoS), ransomware hijacks, data theft, and targeted attacks on specific components utiliz-

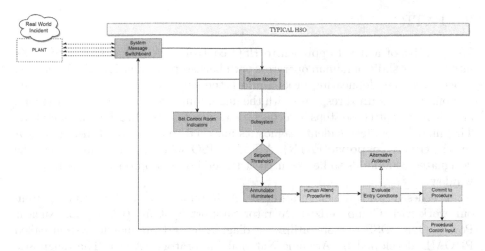

Fig. 2. Typical HSO showing computer activity blocks in purple, human in blue. (Color figure online)

ing zero-day vulnerabilities. Trends demonstrate that global cybercrime is projected to approach \$10T by 2025.

Inevitably, varying levels of hybridized system operations emerge under this threat. Operators need increased training and guidance to detect and respond to cyber-incidents. Of critical importance is the notion that the operator's primary responsibility is to the safety of the plant. Operator's actionable information during cyber-incidents may not trigger diagnostics systems to signal the presence or cause of a cyber-attack. Cyber intrusions would generally be undetectable from an operator's control room, especially if an attacker is only interested in information gathering. Cyber intrusions could also be disguised to look like sensor or component failures or may manifest as innocuous software glitches.

Our concept of HSO could be generalized broadly to cyber-physical system domains, but we are particularly interested in applications to nuclear power. Nuclear power is highly regulated, with well-defined requirements for operations, HMIs, operator training and licensing. As such, successful HSO concepts for nuclear power could be generalized to other less stringent domains.

Traditionally, nuclear power uses automated set-point controllers distributed throughout the plant, but the coordination of these controllers is entirely executed by human operators. Emerging advanced reactor designs have distributed control systems that can automate more control functions, like starting up the turbine. Microreactors are being conceived with nearly fully automated operations and remote monitoring.

HSO control environments can be a concern to stakeholders, as the domains of control can be ambiguous and complex, and the response to incidents are not entirely predictable. How often will a human operator override an otherwise ASO guided response with adverse outcomes? Under stress, could panic cause an operator to cause further system degradation?

2   FATR

We conceive of a novel approach to HSO control system that strives to safely integrate the skills of human operators with backstop automation. By developing procedures that delineating tasks a-priori, the control system dedicates chosen setpoints in a planned response with the maximum safe time allowed to execute, and then present those steps in a concise message to attending human operators. This model provides incident diagnostics matched to a scripted **fail-safe automatic timed response**(FATR). A FATR HSO will schedule and display the designated commands to be executed at the end of an appropriate safe response window.

The design and implementation of FATR builds on previous findings from our work with Computerized Operator Support Systems (COSS) for Nuclear Power. Our COSS concept utilized a diagnostic and prognostic system called PROAID developed by Argonne National Laboratory (ANL). The diagnostic and prognostic system was able to detect system small deviations from normal operations that could indicate leaks other system failures [3]. The COSS provided support to operators through an HSI similar to FATR and tailored computer-based procedures to mitigate fault states.

Our work demonstrated COSS was able to assist operators in mitigating faults that would normal lead to shutting down the plant. Over a series of operator workshops we refined the COSS concept and received positive feedback from operators regarding the concept. The primary distinction between COSS and FATR is that COSS utilized PROAID and tailored procedures for faulted components and did not consider cyber. FATR utilizes existing immediate action and emergency operating procedures. These procedures are amended with additional information to identify the possibility of cyber incidents. The design and operation of FATR has many similarities to COSS the usability is expected to generalize from our previous work.

The FATR delay time offers a safe window for human operators to conduct independent analysis. Human operators can dedicate attention to analysis according to current training procedures. For example, a main steam radiation alarm could indicate a steam generator tube rupture; or it could be a false flag caused by a component failure or a cyber-attack. The human must decide whether the indication is valid and may come to a different conclusion than would an ASO, which would not hesitate to follow rapid shutdown procedures, tripping the plant, disconnecting from the grid, potentially failing customer supply demands.

If the plant is under a cyber-attack or the radiation levels are normal and not caused by a ruptured steam generator, the human operator would have the opportunity to arrive at a different conclusion than the programmed ASO which can only follow preprogrammed logic. Provided the operator completes the analysis in the fail-safe time, she could override the ASO-scheduled response for a preferred outcome.

Current protocols for existing plants do not take into consideration the possibility of cyber scenarios as cyberattack vectors are limited due to the lack of digital infrastructure. The goal of our FATR HSO is to better prepare and assist operators in handling cyber events:

- a "cued" timed response that will execute in the time allowed, as proposed by Computerized Operator Support Systems (COSS),
- time for the operator to "take a deep breath" to consider the possibility of cyber-spoofing or instrumentation failures,
- delay time allows for parallel human analysis and override,
- serves to reduce procedure following complacency,
- cyber-specific training to suspect cyber events.

2.1 FATR Overview

The Fail-safe Automatic Timed Response (FATR) system is an assistive support system for hybrid operations. The FATR concept provides a Human System Interface (HSI) embedded in the plant's existing HSI. The goal is to maximize the speed and accuracy of automated control systems with the adaptability and resilience of human intervention, diagnostics, and decision making.

To capture the potential advantages present in HSO control environments, FATR delineates a workload division for the automated system and the human operators. On the machine side, a computerized process can sample sensor readings to diagnose a system state with sub-second processing time, and then execute prescribed actions dictated by expert policy without error or delay. However, the prescribed actions are only as good as the available data (system administrators and computer scientists will recognize GIGO–Garbage In, Garbage Out) and could easily misattribute states caused by component failures, misconfiguration, or instrumented masking cyber-attack to legit plant system failures. FATR allows for human operator parallax.

Nuclear power plants are complex systems of systems with usually slow temporal dynamics. As such the diagnostic window for minor and small faults can be on the order of minutes or even hours. A fully automated control system employed without integrated human troubleshooting would be **unable to take advantage of a safe response time**, simply operating prescribed procedure immediately with no broader considerations.

2.2 Projected Benefits of FATR

With the complexity of modern industrial plants, the task of operating and maintaining them can be overwhelming, leading to human error, reduced efficiency, and safety concerns. To address these challenges, FATR conceives of an efficient collaboration between scripted control logic and adaptable human oversight.

This technology is expected to provide numerous benefits, including more efficient operations, increased safety, reduced human operator stress, increased situational awareness, improved industry standard guidelines, and ultimately, boosted stakeholder confidence and relations.

The remainder of this section explores fundamental components that comprise FATR protocol.

2.3   FATR Protocol

The FATR protocol provides a decision tree encouraging on-site operators to select for optimal outcomes with minimal risk. Refer to Fig. 3.

Under normal operation, the COSS collects meter data from the remote plant sensors to monitor system state and provide a model for control room operators. The FATR HSI is a logic layer added in parallel with a dedicated display area and is granted episodic control permissions.

A FATR interdiction is triggered by subsystem trigger thresholds, which could be single meter out-of-tolerances or determined by more complex dependency functions. Set in-line with display annunciators that alert attending human controllers in traditional order, a minimal FATR HSI displays a synopsis, a counter, and two interactive buttons.

Commit Panel. The HSI for FATR requires minimal screen space. The *Commit Panel* should appear in a central control panel with easy visibility. It contains these features:

- countdown timer display window
- dynamic message window
- button a: Confirm
- button b: Oppose

If rendered in software, the interface for the commit panel could take many dimensions, but would likely be in a 4:1 to 5:1 ratio, width to height, and up to 800 pixels in width in typical screen pixel density monitors.

In plant mechanical, the panel group should be no less than 6 in. wide, with a minimum 3 in. wide timer window, and a minimum 5 in. digital readout window for messages. The two buttons could be rectangular at a minimum 2–3 in. with

Phases. The FATR protocol can be simplified to three blocks.

1. Ultimatum
2. Operator Assessment Procedure (OAP)
3. Commit

Ultimatum: When an incident is detected, the FATR logic plots response targets and the HSI directs operators to the procedure it will schedule for execution.

Operator Assessment Procedure (AOP): The HSI lists a documented procedure, in hard copy or digital page, depending on the institutional preferences, that provides criteria for the operator to determine whether FATR has identified a true event or false alarm potentially caused by faulty I&C or a cyber incident.

Commit: The operator chooses a course of action. Not all steps in a commitment are irreversible. Under FATR time limits, any queued automated responses can execute due to lack of timely action.

Process Flow. The HSI renders instructions to the interface varying by incident. A FATR interdiction has three possible flows:

1. Concur: presses "Concur: ..."
2. Oppose: presses "Oppose: ..."
3. Fail-safe: corrective action unsuccessful when timer runs to zero

Concur: Referencing the relevant procedure(s) for the present condition or incident, the operator has reviewed control room indicators and recommended guidance, and based on experience and judgment, CONCURS with the incident diagnosis presented in FATR HSI. If the operator signals "CONCUR" on the HSI, actions will proceed with **Scripted Incident Response** (SIR). The HSI will update according to script with next actions.

Oppose: Based on contextual information, the operators may also choose to OPPOSE FATR if they believe the plant is stable and requires additional troubleshooting beyond the control room. They will initiate an **Operator Incident Response** (OIR) by contacting the maintenance dispatch. Based on the information from OIR, dispatch will make contact with engineers and cyber analysts. If operators follow this path they would continue monitoring but would not take further actions until more information is collected.

Fail-Safe: The third possibility is that the fail-safe response timer expires during the operator assessment procedure and any corrective actions have not been successful. Effectively a default SIR, FATR will automatically initiate control commands determined by FATR's diagnosis and direct the operator to continue executing the appropriate procedure.

Fail-Safe Response Time Formula. The fail-safe response time (FRT) is the task timed granted to operators to conduct OAP. FRT is displayed at all times during a FATR interdiction in the commit panel as a total time counting backward to zero.

FRT is a visible countdown for human operators, but the computer has its own internal countdown summaries analogous to Card and Moran's GOMS [2] that it uses when it sets its operational plan. The internal timeline depends on control sequences in the given procedure that it may execute as required.

CFT is the product of **critical failure time** as derived by system engineers, and a safety factor multiplier less than 1. For example, a moderate SF could be set at 0.75, while a conservative SF might be as low as 0.5.

$$FRT = CFTxSF \qquad (1)$$

Scripted Incident Response (SIR). The FATR protocol is designed to be applied to incident response procedures as designated for the given industrial

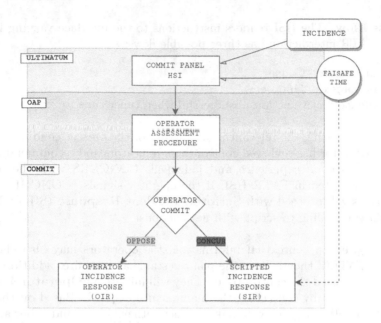

Fig. 3. FATR phases and flow logic

application. A SIR follows when the operator **CONCURS** with FATR's diagnostics, by matching entry conditions and secondary indicators. When the control system I&C is operating as expected, SIR is the most likely flow to follow.

Establishing a SIR requires a process analysis derived from written procedures. In nuclear plant operation, any given process flow moves through sequences typified by two classes of operations.

- Step, or sequence of steps, which can be automated
- Step, or sequence of steps, that the human is asked to do

The first class, automation-ready sequences, are control actions that the computer can execute rapidly with no danger of countermanding the operator's supervision. For example, in one variation of rapid shutdown procedure used in simulation, operators are instructed in three subsequent steps to manually trip the turbine, manually trip the reactor, and to activate safety injection. The order of these actions is of no literal consequence, but the expedience of execution may be. We believe nothing is gained by having the operators manually trigger these three actions individually, reading each instruction one block at a time.

However subsequent sequences in the same procedures request the operator to close multiple valves, stop pumps, and verify specified readings. Here diligence of the operator is of value, ensuring engagement, and maintained situational awareness. In short, ensuring human-(remains)-in-the-loop.

3   Implementation

To understand better the implications of a FATR HSO, a design exercise with quick prototype development and revisions is needed. We have designed human trial experiments to collect quantitative data, where adequate measures can be drawn, and survey data to assess situation awareness and stress. Naïve participants are sourced from university graduate and undergraduate students, and the opportunity to test experienced nuclear plant operators has also been confirmed. Pilot studies have begun.

3.1   Prototype

To successfully implement FATR, existing procedures must be reviewed and analyzed to discover how and where in a decision tree a FATR based COSS can improve performance. All solutions must be designed in a case by case basis, diagramming procedures using the FATR protocol.

Secondly, the HSI design requires a target platform, so that the controls contained by the commit panel may be custom fit with a suitable layout. Prototypes are conformed to dedicated real estate in the platform I&C.

Lastly, as the exploratory prototyping requires gathering data from participant trials, a simulation platform must offer scenario script control, and data capture capability. At a minimum, collecting control events, world script events, event times, and system status polling, are required. Some might make a case for eye and/or pointer tracking to provide further insight from attentional heatmaps.

3.2   Placement with Rancor

Rancor is a simplified Nuclear Power Plant Simulator developed by Idaho National Laboratory and the University of Idaho to support human factors research for Nuclear Power. Rancor contains the same systems and components as a pressurized water reactor but is simplified so that novice operators can control the plant. Rancor has a catalog of procedures for normal and abnormal operations and catalog of normal and abnormal scenarios that it supports.

Rancor is implemented in Windows Presentation Foundation allowing for modern HCI interactions to be quickly developed for prototyping and research purposes [1]. For this reason Rancor was selected as an environment to implement and examine FATR.

3.3   Procedures

FATR is designed to work with existing paper-procedures or computer-based procedure systems. FATR is linked to plant annunciator response procedures and is able to determine and direct operators to the correct procedure when a possible fault condition is detected. The procedures are modified so that they guide the operator though the necessary diagnostic steps to OPPOSE or CONCUR with FATR.

Procedures must be carefully considered to reveal the critical path. We consider the procedural logic for incident response by detailed block diagram analysis. Every block must be coded with consideration for its cognitive demand, urgency, and dependency graph. Numerical values such as delay time, n loops, and Boolean entry/exit conditions, will emerge to be coded in FATR procedure according to the protocol profile. As an example, refer to Fig. 4 for a block flow diagram for Loss of Feedwater scenario, with entry conditions noted at the head of each block, with a coded time variable.

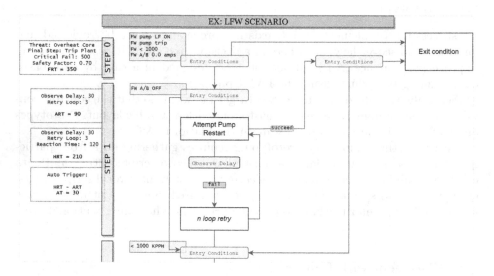

Fig. 4. Scenario diagramming with FATR protocol

3.4 Scenarios

Two general failures were considered during the prototyping process.

One failure considered, *loss of feedwater*, is caused by a single feedwater pump trip. When the pump trips the operator is directed to attempt to restart the pump. When the pump cannot be restarted FATR aids the operator in conducting a rapid shutdown of the plant. The operator then verifies the plant has been shutdown and completes some non-time critical activities to make sure the plant is in a safe shutdown state.

In the event the loss of feedwater is purely a cyber incident or a malfunction of I&C (the feedwater system is functioning normally and only the indications are faulty) the procedures assist the operator in diagnosing the condition and coordinating with maintenance.

The second failure we examined is steam generator tube rupture. If an actual SGTR is determined FATR assists in tripping the turbine and reactor. The operator can then isolate the steam generator and carry out the remaining mitigation procedures. Under conditions when there is no tube rupture, but instead faulty I&C misleading operators to think there is, a procedure without the cover of FATR might require the operator to trip the turbine and reactor unnecessarily.

4 Conclusions

The FATR protocol is a logical emergence of contemporary industrial control requirements. We observe a common fallacy in ad-hoc HSO that fail to capture the best features of human with computer system aids. We re-envision the collaborative framework for computer assisted human control environments by prioritizing a design protocol that allows for human ingenuity embedded with diligent automation.

References

1. Boring, R., Ulrich, T., Lew, R., Hall, A.: A microworld framework for advanced control room design. In: 12th International Topical Meeting on Nuclear Power Plant Instrumentation, Control, and Human-Machine Interface Technologies. NPIC & HMIT (2021)
2. Card, S.K.: The Psychology of Human-Computer Interaction. CRC Press, Boca Raton (2018)
3. Lew, R., Boring, R.L., Ulrich, T.A.: Computerized operator support system for nuclear power plant hybrid main control room. In: Proceedings of the Human Factors and Ergonomics Society Annual Meeting, vol. 63, no: 1, pp. 1814–1818. SAGE Publications, Los Angeles, CA (2019)
4. Nunes, I.L.: Human Factors and Systems Interaction, vol. 52. AHFE International (2022). Google-Books-ID: 4NyVEAAAQBAJ
5. Pearl, T.H.: Hands on the wheel: a call for greater regulation of semi-autonomous cars. Ind. LJ **93**, 713 (2018)
6. Poresky, C., et al.: Advanced reactor control and operations (ARCO): a university research facility for developing optimized digital control rooms. Nucl. Technol. **209**(3), 354–365 (2023)

Analysis of Country and Regional User Password Characteristics in Dictionary Attacks

Shodai Kurasaki and Akira Kanaoka[✉]

Toho University, Miyama 2-2-1, Funabashi, Chiba 274-8510, Japan
akira.kanaoka@is.sci.toho-u.ac.jp

Abstract. The degree to which passwords are robust to guessing has become one of the fundamental interests in password research. For example, a method has been proposed to calculate the robustness of password guessing as a password's strength and provide feedback. Measuring guessing robustness has been studied from several perspectives, but most studies are based on password datasets from US and European users. On the other hand, several studies have shown that the characteristics of passwords differ between countries and regions. However, there needs to be a more extensive analysis of guess-robustness due to differences in these data sets. In this study, a large password dataset was used to analyze the password characteristics of countries and regions from the perspective of guess-robustness. The results revealed differences in guess-robustness between countries and regions, as well as differences in guess-robustness given by the datasets used in the dictionary.

Keywords: Password Strength · Dictionary Attack

1 Introduction

Password strength is often improved by applying compositional policies and employing strength meters. Their strength has been defined heuristically, but recent research suggests that using robustness against guessing attempts as a strength metric is more suitable [1]. Efficient password-guessing methods include machine learning using dictionaries and guessing using dictionaries and modification rules (mangling rules). In both cases, the underlying dictionary data is essential.

On the other hand, several studies show that the characteristics of the passwords set by users vary significantly from country to country [2]. Since frequent passwords differ from country to country and region to region, it is necessary to prepare country-specific dictionaries to measure guess-robustness accurately. However, the differences in password-guessing success rates due to differences in dictionaries have yet to be discussed in detail. This study aims to comprehensively study the success rate of password guessing in different countries and

A. Moallem (Ed.): HCII 2023, LNCS 14045, pp. 656–671, 2023.
https://doi.org/10.1007/978-3-031-35822-7_42

regions using hashcat, a typical password guessing tool, and large-scale leaked password data and to clarify the differences in success rates and their characteristics.

The password dataset of over 1.4 billion passwords was split into country and region datasets, focusing on the TLDs in the email addresses. We then used these as dictionary files to perform password guessing. The dataset of the target to be guessed was also changed for each TLD, and a comprehensive, large-scale study was conducted to investigate how the success rate of guessing varied depending on the combination of the dataset of the TLD to be guessed and the TLD dataset of the dictionary to be used for guessing. The results showed that among the 4096 combinations, there were some combinations with very different guessing success rates and some dictionaries with average high guessing success rates. The study found that the differences were caused by the TLDs, i.e., by the characteristics of each country and region.

2   Related Works

The RockYou data breach in 2009 greatly influenced the large-scale analysis and application of passwords. In 2010, Weir et al. conducted a detailed analysis of the RockYou breach data, revealed statistical biases in the actual passwords created by users, and proposed using machine learning for guessing attacks [3]. Subsequent research has led to extensive research using large password datasets. In addition to investigating the characteristics of user-created passwords, the research expanded to include the effects of periodic expiry [4], password composition policies [5], the effects of password strength meters [6,7], and many others.

Methods for measuring password strength are another active topic in password research [8–12]. It has been applied in research to provide feedback to users on the measured strength, leading to the creation of stronger passwords. Tan et al. conducted an exhaustive evaluation combining methods such as composition policies and strength feedback when creating passwords. Their study recommended providing machine learning-based tolerance to guessing attacks as feedback and claimed that it is highly effective [1].

On the other hand, these studies are based on large leakage datasets, mainly in the US, including the RockYou dataset. There needs to be more discussion on whether the characteristics of passwords created by users in other countries and regions exhibit similar properties to those of US users. In 2014, Li et al. conducted a large-scale analysis similar to previous studies, focusing on Chinese users, showing significant differences [13]. In 2020, Mori et al. further expanded them to reveal differences with Japan, Taiwan, and India [2]. It has become generally recognized through these studies that the characteristics of passwords set by users differ between countries and regions.

The usefulness of using strength evaluation results for feedback, as shown by Tan et al. and the presence of national and regional password characteristic differences in these studies, suggests that strength evaluation may not be performed properly due to differences in the learning dataset during strength evaluation. This study aimed to investigate the extent to which differences in datasets ...

3   Dataset and Password Guessing Method

To analyze password characteristics, we used a dataset disseminated from the compromise of over 1.4 billion plaintext password/e-mail address pairs confirmed to exist in 2017 [14]. We call this dataset as "1.4B dataset."

While the ideal way to analyze password characteristics by country or region would be to split the 1.4B dataset by country or region, the 1.4B dataset used in this study does not contain clear labels such as "country" or "region." To the authors' knowledge, such a large dataset does not exist. Therefore, in this study, the top-level domains (TLDs) of e-mail addresses, which are assumed to be strongly influenced by countries and regions, were used as the basis for splitting the 1.4B dataset.

The TLDs used for the splitting were the seven "traditional gTLDs" and 254 "ccTLDs" listed on JPNIC's "Domain Name Types" web page [15], for a total of 261 TLDs. In order to create the dictionary datasets and the guess target datasets, we divided the 1.4B dataset by TLD and used 64 TLD (Fig. 1) datasets with more than 100,000 records out of the datasets for each TLD.

Appendix A lists the TLDs that were not used in this study.

Hashcat's rule-based attack mode was used as the password-guessing method. In rule-based attack mode, words in the dictionary are modified, cut off, or expanded based on rules to achieve comprehensive and efficient guessing. The dictionary used is the one described above and the best64.rules provided in hashcat are used as the conversion rules. The best64.rules contains 77 lines of rules, some of which are shown in Table 2.

Since hashcat displays the success rate, which indicates how many of the input passwords were successfully guessed, we use the success rate to analyze the characteristics of the passwords in this study.

The success rate of password-guessing was evaluated from two perspectives: guessing using the same TLD dataset as the dataset of the TLD to be guessed as the dictionary (we call this "self-TLD-guessing") and guessing using a different TLD dataset as the dictionary than the dataset of the TLD to be guessed (we call this "other-TLD-guessing").

The dictionary was higher than the 10001st most frequently occurring in the dataset for each TLD. For self-TLD-guessing, a 10-part cross-validation was performed, and dictionaries were created from the data excluding the data to be guessed.

4   Password-Guessing Results

4.1   Self-TLD-Guessing

Table 3 shows the top 10 success rates for password-guessing the TLDs of the 64 TLD datasets, and Table 4 shows the bottom 10. The dataset with the *cc*

Table 1. List of TLDs evaluated in this study

ar	at	au	be	bg	br	by	ca
cc	ch	cl	cm	cn	co	com	cz
de	dk	edu	ee	es	eu	fi	fm
fr	gov	gr	hk	hr	hu	id	ie
il	in	it	jp	kr	lt	lv	mil
mx	my	net	nl	no	nz	om	org
ph	pl	pt	ro	ru	se	sg	sk
th	tr	tw	ua	uk	us	vn	za

TLD had the highest success rate of 46.32%. On the other hand, the dataset with the lowest guess success rate was the dataset with the *th* TLD, with a guess success rate of 11.13%, showing a difference of about 35 points in success rate, indicating that there are differences in guess success rates among TLDs. The mean and median guess success rates were 21.88% and 20.88%, respectively.

4.2   Other-TLD-Guessing

Table 5 shows the top 10 success rates for guessing the other TLDs for the 4032 combinations of 64 TLD datasets, and Table 6 shows the bottom 10. The case with the highest success rate is the one in which the dataset with the *us* TLD was guessed using the *org* TLD as a dictionary, with a success rate of 27.95 On the other hand, the case with the lowest success rate was when a dataset with the *fi* TLD was inferred from a dataset with the *cn* TLD, with a success rate of 2.48 The difference in guess success rate was about 25.5% points, again showing a difference in guess success rate. The mean and median guess success rates were 11.29% and 10.72%, respectively.

4.3   Difference in Success Rate Between Self-TLD-Guessing and Other-TLD-Guessing

Figure 1 shows a box-and-whisker diagram of the success rate for self-TLD-guessing and the success rate for other-TLD-guessing. In addition to the mean and median, the quartiles show that self-TLD-guessing tends to have a high success rate. When looking at the TLD datasets for which the dictionary produced the highest guess success rate for the TLD dataset being guessed, the own TLD dictionary produced the highest guess success rate for 58 of the 64 TLD datasets.

Figure 2 shows a heatmap of the success rate for each TLD dataset to be guessed and for each TLD dataset used as a dictionary. The TLDs are listed from left to right in order of average success rate in password-guessing both for their own TLD dataset and for other TLD datasets, with higher success rates in red and lower success rates in blue. Columns with an average red color indicate TLDs with a high success rate as the TLD to be guessed. The further to the

Table 2. An excerpt of the rules contained in hashcat's conversion rules best64.rules and example of passwords converted by these rules

Rule	Password Example
Do nothing	password
Reverse the entire word	drowssap
Uppercase all letters	PASSWORD
Toggle the case of characters at position 0	Password
Append character "0" to end	password0
Append character "s" to end	passwords
Delete last character Delete last character Append character "e" to end Append character "s" to end	passwoes
Delete last character Delete last character Delete last character Append character "m" to end Append character "a" to end Append character "n" to end	passwman
Prepend character "e" to front Prepend character "h" to front Prepend character "t" to front	thepassword
Replace all instances of "o" with "0"	passw0rd
Delete character at position 2	pasword
Rotate the word right Rotate the word right Rotate the word right	ordpassw

left, the higher the average guess success rate. The diagonal component in red indicates that the self-TLD-guessing has a high success rate. Rows that are red, on average, indicate that the TLD has a high success rate as a dictionary TLD. The red lines in the lower part of the figure are TLD datasets that are highly resistant as guess targets but achieve a high success rate as a dictionary for guesses.

Apart from that, it can be visually seen that there are dictionaries with high and low success rates for guessing other TLDs as dictionaries, as well as TLDs with low success rates for various guesses.

4.4   Characteristics of the TLD Dataset Used for the Dictionary

The top 15 TLD datasets with the highest average guess success rate, when used as a dictionary, are shown in Table 7, and the bottom 15 in Table 8. The highest average success rate is 15.22% for *com*, and the lowest is 7.72% for *kr*. An

Table 3. Top 10 success rates of password-guessing in self-TLD-guessing based on 64 TLD datasets

TLD	(Country/Region)	Success Rate
cc	(Cocos Islands)	46.32%
vn	(Vietnam)	35.75%
lt	(Lithuania)	29.92%
us	(United States)	28.93%
bg	(Bulgaria)	28.55%
cn	(China)	28.18%
in	(India)	28.01%
au	(Australia)	27.96%
ro	(Romania)	27.94%
ca	(Canada)	26.13%

Table 4. Bottom 10 success rates of password-guessing in self-TLD-guessing based on 64 TLD datasets

TLD	(Country/Region)	Success Rate
th	(Thailand)	11.13%
fi	(Finland)	13.92%
be	(Belgium)	15.57%
ch	(Switzerland)	15.99%
tw	(Taiwan)	16.09%
eu		16.88%
tr	(Turkey)	16.94%
my	(Malaysia)	17.49%
kr	(Korea)	17.64%
jp	(Japan)	17.72%

overview of the ranking of the top 15 TLDs shows that the top TLDs are dominated by English-speaking countries and organizations (gTLDs). In contrast, Asian and European countries and regions dominate the bottom TLDs.

These show that using password datasets created by English-speaking users as dictionaries has, on average, a high success rate for guessing in other countries and regions, while using password datasets created by users in Asian and European countries as dictionaries does not have a higher success rate for other countries and regions.

In addition to the average success rate, the characteristics of each TLD are also evaluated from another perspective. The success rates for all 4,096 combinations of both self-TLD-guessing and other-TLD-guessing were then sorted in order of increasing success rate. We then looked at how many times each

Table 5. Top 10 success rates in password-guessing 4032 combinations of other-TLD-guessing by 64 TLD datasets

Dictionary TLD	(Country/Region)	Target TLD	(Country/Region)	Success Rate
org		us	(United States)	27.95%
net		us	(United States)	26.66%
edu		us	(United States)	26.24%
ca	(Canada)	us	(United States)	25.87%
com		us	(Unietd States)	25.16%
ca	(Canada)	au	(Australia)	25.14%
uk	(United Kingdom)	au	(Australia)	24.87%
gov		us	(United States)	24.86%
org		au	(Australia)	24.52%
net		au	(Australia)	24.39%

Table 6. Bottom 10 success rates in password-guessing 4032 combinations of other-TLD-guessing by 64 TLD datasets

Dictionary TLD	(Country/Region)	Target TLD	(Country/Region)	Success Rate
cn	(China)	fi	(Finland)	2.48%
kr	(Korea)	fi	(Finland)	2.69%
th	(Thailand)	fi	(Finland)	2.93%
vn	(Vietnam)	fi	(Finland)	3.02%
cn	(China)	nl	(Netherlands)	3.14%
cn	(China)	be	(Belgium)	3.21%
tr	(Turkey)	fi	(Finland)	3.28%
kr	(Korea)	nl	(Netherlands)	3.31%
tw	(Taiwan)	fi	(Finland)	3.35%
kr	(Korea)	be	(Belgium)	3.58%

TLD dataset appeared as a TLD dataset in the dictionary in the top 100 of the guess success rates. The results are shown in Table 9. Table 10 shows the results of the same study for the bottom 100. The number of occurrences of ca shows 9. It indicates that the ca TLD dataset was used as the dictionary in nine of the combinations with the highest guess success rate in the top 100. Again, the top TLDs include English-speaking TLDs, while the lower TLDs include a large number of Asian and European TLDs. Table 10 in particular, shows that Asian TLDs are more subordinate.

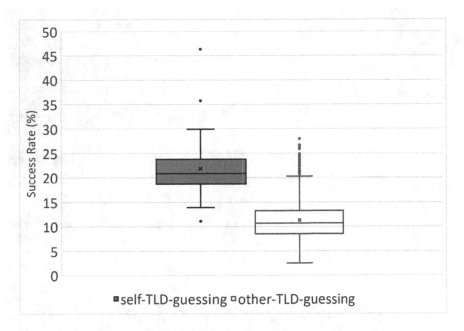

Fig. 1. Success Rate of self-TLD-guessing and other-TLD-guessing

Table 7. Top 15 TLD datasets with the highest average guess success rate when used as a dictionary

TLD	(Country/Region)	Avg. Success Rate
com		15.22%
de	(Germany)	15.08%
cz	(Czech)	14.83%
ca	(Canada)	14.66%
net		14.61%
org		14.14%
uk	(United Kingdom)	13.95%
fr	(France)	13.90%
au	(Australia)	13.57%
za	(South Africa)	13.34%
ru	(Russia)	13.31%
edu		13.25%
us	(United States)	13.17%
es	(Spain)	13.14%
pl	(Poland)	12.90%

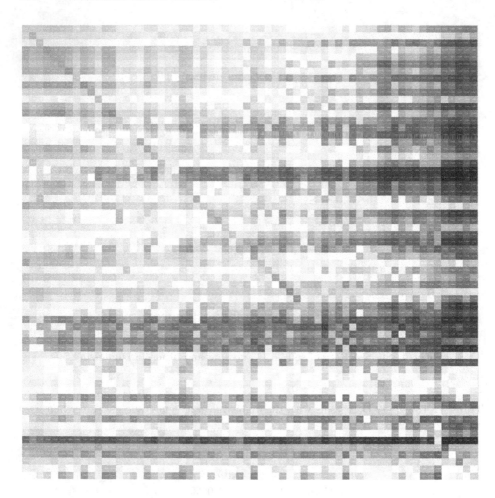

Fig. 2. Heatmap of the TLD dataset to be guessed and the success rate of password-guessing for each TLD dataset used as a dictionary

Table 8. Bottom 15 TLD datasets with the highest average guess success rate when used as a dictionary

TLD	(Country/Region)	Avg. Success Rate
kr	(Korea)	7.72%
tr	(Turkey)	7.85%
cn	(China)	7.88%
th	(Thailand)	7.90%
vn	(Vietnam)	8.33%
fi	(Finland)	8.49%
hr	(Croatia)	8.78%
ee	(Estonia)	8.97%
my	(Malaysia)	9.13%
il	(Israel)	9.34%
lt	(Lithuania)	9.37%
tw	(Taiwan)	9.38%
by	(Belarus)	9.65%
ua	(Ukraine)	9.97%
gr	(Greece)	10.10%

Table 9. Number of times each TLD dataset appears as a dictionary TLD dataset in the top 100 of password-guessing success rates

TLD	(Country/Region)	Num. of Appearance
ca	(Canada)	9
com		9
net		9
org		9
edu		6
uk	(United Kingdom)	6
au	(Australia)	5
us	(United States)	5
cz	(Czech)	4
de	(Germany)	3
gov	3	

Table 10. Number of times each TLD dataset appears as a dictionary TLD dataset in the bottom 100 of password-guessing success rates

TLD	(Country/Region)	Num. of Appearance
cn	(China)	15
kr	(Korea)	12
tr	(Turkey)	10
th	(Thailand)	9
vn	(Vietnam)	7
tw	(Taiwan)	5
lt	(Lithuania)	4
my	(Malaysia)	4
by	(Belarus)	3
hr	(Croatia)	3
il	(Israel)	3
ua	(Ukraine)	3

Table 11. Top 15 TLD Datasets with the Lowest Average Password-Guessing Success Rate when Used as Guess Targets

TLD	(Country/Region)	Avg. Success Rate
fi	(Finland)	5.41%
hu	(Hungary)	7.28%
be	(Belgium)	7.45%
nl	(Netherlands)	7.58%
eu		7.72%
jp	(Japan)	7.80%
cc	(Cocos Islands)	8.13%
lv	(Latvia)	8.25%
my	(Malaysia)	8.39%
th	(Thailand)	8.53%
tw	(Taiwan)	8.60%
pl	(Poland)	9.00%
se	(Sweden)	9.18%
ch	(Switzerland)	9.23%
fr	(France)	9.46%

Table 12. Bottom 15 TLD Datasets with the Lowest Average Password-Guessing Success Rate when Used as Guess Targets

TLD	(Country/Region)	Avg. Success Rate
vn	(Vietnam)	21.23%
bg	(Bulgaria)	17.19%
om	(Oman)	15.59%
us	(United States)	15.51%
cn	(China)	15.20%
ca	(Canada)	15.16%
au	(Australia)	15.14%
il	(Israel)	14.88%
cm	(Cameroon)	14.63%
uk	(United Kingdom)	14.38%
nz	(New Zealand)	14.10%
co	(Colombia)	14.06%
ie	(Ireland)	14.01%
net		13.95%
ph	(Philippines)	13.52%

Table 13. Number of times each TLD dataset appears as a target TLD dataset in the top 100 of password-guessing success rates

TLD	(Country/Region)	Num. of Appearance
fi	(Finland)	32
be	(Belgium)	14
nl	(Netherlands)	12
hu	(Hungary)	7
eu		6
ch	(Switzerland)	5
se	(Sweden)	4
cc	(Cocos Islands)	3
lv	(Latvia)	3
pl	(Poland)	3

Table 14. Number of times each TLD dataset appears as a target TLD dataset in the bottom 100 of password-guessing success rates

TLD	(Country/Region)	Num. of Appearance
au	(Australia)	13
us	(United States)	12
vn	(Vietnam)	12
ca	(Canada)	9
nz	(New Zealand)	7
gov		6
net		6
uk	(United Kingdom)	6
om	(Oman)	4
ie	(Ireland)	3

4.5   Tolerance to Password-Guessing Using Other TLD Datasets as Dictionaries

The top 15 TLD datasets with the lowest average success rate when targeted for guessing are shown in Table 11, and the bottom 15 in Table 12. The lowest average success rate is 5.41% for *fi*, and the highest average guess success rate is 21.23% for *vn*. An overview of the ranking of the top 15 TLDs shows that the top TLDs are dominated by European TLDs, while the bottom TLDs are dominated by English-speaking TLDs.

In addition to the average success rate, the characteristics of each TLD are also evaluated from another perspective. The success rates for all 4,096 combinations of both self-TLD-guessing and other-TLD-guessing were then sorted in order of decreasing success rate. We then looked at how many times each TLD dataset appeared as a target TLD in the top 100 of the guess success rates. The results are shown in Table 13. Table 14 shows the results of the same study for the bottom 100.

5   Discussion

5.1   Self-TLD-Guessing: Password Guessing by Own TLD Dictionary

Comparing self-TLD-guessing with other-TLD-guessing in Fig. 1, the overall success rate of self-TLD-guessing is higher.

Concerning the TLD datasets to be guessed, the highest success rate of guessing by the own TLD dictionary in 58 out of 64 TLD datasets suggests that self-TLD-guessing is more potent than other-TLD-guessing. This result may seem obvious, but it is supported by this evaluation experiment, as the details of such data have never been made clear before.

Related research has shown that the accuracy of password-guessing attacks varies depending on the dataset used for training, so it may be better to train each dataset separately to evaluate the tolerance to guessing attacks more accurately.

5.2   Versatile and Less Versatile Dictionaries

The TLD datasets used for the dictionaries with the highest password-guessing success rate were considered to be highly generic as dictionaries. The gTLD and English-speaking ccTLD datasets were the most common dictionaries with high versatility, possibly because there are more English-speaking TLD datasets than TLD datasets from other languages in the guess target.

The TLD datasets used for the dictionaries at the lower end of the guess success rate are considered to be less generic as dictionaries. The high number of Asian and European country and region TLD datasets as less generic dictionaries can be attributed to the low usage of their ccTLDs by users from non-English speaking countries and other regions.

5.3   Guess-Tolerant and Weak Guess-Tolerant TLDs

The TLD datasets analyzed with low guessing success rates were highly resistant to guessing. European TLDs were the most common targets with high guess resistance, possibly due to the low usage of their ccTLDs by users in non-English-speaking and other regions.

On the other hand, the TLD datasets analyzed with a high success rate are also considered to have weak guess tolerance. The analysis targets with weak guess-tolerance include many TLD datasets from English-speaking countries, which may be because there are more TLD datasets from English-speaking countries in the dictionary than from other language-speaking countries.

5.4   Appropriateness Between Dictionary-Listed Words and Change Rules

The rules in best64.rules, the set of rules for changing words in the dictionary used in this study, show that the rule is to add "the" at the beginning. However, taking "sakura" as an example, which is one of the top passwords that Japanese users are likely to use, it is unlikely that "the" is added to the beginning of the string to make it "thesakura." In addition, the large number of English-speaking TLD datasets found as highly generic dictionaries and weakly guessable targets suggest that some of the best64.rules were created by English-speaking users or with English-speaking users in mind. There may be rules in each language that are not universal but are due to specific language characteristics.

From the above, the versatility of each TLD dataset as a dictionary and the tolerance to guesses as a target is also influenced by the rules for changing the words in the dictionary. It would be better to create and use a set of rules for changing words in the dictionary that includes rules suitable for each language, in addition to rules that are likely to be universally applicable, such as "invert strings."

6   Conclusion

This study aimed to investigate the differences in the success rate of password-guessing attacks by country and region and to identify their characteristics. To investigate password characteristics, instead of dividing the compromised dataset of plaintext password/e-mail address pairs by country and region, we divided it by TLD of the e-mail address and created dictionaries and guessing targets from each TLD dataset, which were then evaluated using password guessing attacks.

As a result, it was found that the success rate of password-guessing attacks differs significantly depending on the dictionary and the dataset used for the guessing target. Furthermore, the results showed that the differences were related to language and region and that, in addition to the characteristics of the language itself, the tendency to change passwords at the time of setting may also differ between languages and regions. These results indicate that the password strength evaluation to date may not correctly indicate the strength of passwords.

Acknowledgements. This work was supported by JST, CREST Grant Number JPMJCR22M4, Japan.

Appendix

A   List of TLDs Excluded from Evaluation in this Study

Table 15. List of TLDs excluded from evaluation in this study

ac	ad	ae	af	ag	ai	al	am
an	ao	aq	as	aw	ax	az	ba
bb	bd	bf	bh	bi	bj	bl	bm
bn	bo	bq	bs	bt	bv	bw	bz
cd	cf	cg	ci	ck	cr	cu	cv
cw	cx	cy	dj	dm	do	dz	ec
eg	eh	er	et	fj	fk	fo	ga
gb	gd	ge	gf	gg	gh	gi	gl
gm	gn	gp	gq	gs	gt	gu	gw
gy	hm	hn	ht	im	int	io	iq
ir	is	je	jm	jo	ke	kg	kh
ki	km	kn	kp	kw	ky	kz	la
lb	lc	li	lk	lr	ls	lu	ly
ma	mc	md	me	mf	mg	mh	mk
ml	mm	mn	mo	mp	mq	mr	ms
mt	mu	mv	mw	mz	na	nc	ne
nf	ng	ni	np	nr	nu	pa	pe
pf	pg	pk	pm	pn	pr	ps	pw
py	qa	re	rs	rw	sa	sb	sc
sd	sh	si	sj	sl	sm	sn	so
sr	ss	st	sv	sx	sy	sz	tc
td	tf	tg	tj	tk	tl	tm	tn
to	tp	tt	tv	tz	ug	um	uy
uz	va	vc	ve	vg	vi	vu	wf
ws	ye	yt	zm	zw			

References

1. Tan, J., et al.: Practical recommendations for stronger, more usable passwords combining minimum-strength, minimum-length, and blocklist requirements. ACM (CCS 2020) (2020)

2. Mori, K., et al.: Comparative analysis of three language spheres: are linguistic and cultural differences reflected in password selection habits? IEICE Trans. Inf. Sys. (2020)
3. Weir, M., et al.: Testing metrics for password creation policies by attacking large sets of revealed passwords. In: Proceedings of the 17th ACM Conference on Computer and Communications Security (2010)
4. Zhang, Y., Monrose, F., Reiter, M.K.: The security of modern password expiration: an algorithmic framework and empirical analysis. In: Proceedings of the 17th ACM Conference on Computer and Communications Security (2010)
5. Kelley, P.G., et al.: Guess again (and again and again): measuring password strength by simulating password-cracking algorithms. In: 2012 IEEE Symposium on Security and Privacy. IEEE (2012)
6. Ur, B., et al.: How does your password measure up? The effect of strength meters on password creation. In: 21st USENIX Security Symposium (USENIX Security 2012) (2012)
7. Wheeler, D.L.: zxcvbn: low-budget password strength estimation. In: 25th USENIX Security Symposium (USENIX Security 2016) (2016)
8. Dell'Amico, M., Michiardi, P., Roudier, Y.: Password strength: an empirical analysis. In: 2010 Proceedings IEEE INFOCOM. IEEE (2010)
9. Castelluccia, C., Dürmuth, M., Perito, D.: Adaptive password-strength meters from Markov models. In: NDSS (2012)
10. Ur, B., et al.: Measuring real-world accuracies and biases in modeling password guessability. In: 24th USENIX Security Symposium (USENIX Security 2015) (2015)
11. Golla, M., Dürmuth, M.: On the accuracy of password strength meters. In: Proceedings of the 2018 ACM SIGSAC Conference on Computer and Communications Security (2018)
12. Pasquini, D., et al.: Reducing bias in modeling real-world password strength via deep learning and dynamic dictionaries. In: 30th USENIX Security Symposium (USENIX Security 2021) (2021)
13. Li, Z., Han, W., Xu, W.: A large-scale empirical analysis of Chinese web passwords. In: Proc. 23rd USENIX Security Symposium, pp. 559–574 (2014)
14. Luku, I.: 1.4 billion user credentials found on the dark web. IT governance. https://www.itgovernanceusa.com/blog/1-4-billion-user-credentials-list-found-in-the-dark-web. Accessed 23 May 2022
15. JPNIC: Domain name type. https://www.nic.ad.jp/ja/dom/types.html. Accessed 09 Feb 2023

Cyber Technologies, Machine Learning, Additive Manufacturing, and Cloud in the Box to Enable Optimized Maintenance Processes in Extreme Conditions

Kasey Miller[✉] and Johnathan Mun

Information Sciences Department, Naval Postgraduate School (NPS), Monterey, CA, USA
{kcmiller1,jcmun}@nps.edu

Abstract. Routine maintenance processes (e.g., peacetime conditions) are not optimized for extreme maintenance conditions (e.g., aircraft or ship battle damage repair, extreme cold Alaska pipeline repair, and COVID-19 depot repair processes). In extreme contexts, modern information technology (e.g., machine learning [ML], additive manufacturing [AM], and Cloud in the Box [CIB]) is typically not being leveraged to optimize productivity and cycle time in these maintenance processes. Literature on process optimization does not address the use of modern technology for optimization in extreme maintenance conditions. This research aims to test the value added to information technology to optimize process productivity and cycle time for extreme maintenance conditions. It will extend the use of process optimization theory to include the effect of modern information technology as well as extreme maintenance contexts. This research is critical because failure to make correct repairs can affect the organization at its most vulnerable cyber infrastructure.

Keywords: Economics of IT · Extreme Maintenance · Cyber Security · Process Optimization Theory · Real Options · Machine Learning · Cloud in the Box · And Additive Manufacturing

1 Introduction

The current extreme maintenance conditions present many repair, cyber, and maintenance challenges. These challenges include the availability of technical data or specifications to make the repairs, the lack of parts, and insufficient decision support aids to assist with transforming data into information and knowledge to make timely decisions. The lack of timely information increases the risk to the repair and the employee and leads to uninformed and suboptimal decisions, especially in edge networks. For example, the naval enterprise system architecture (ground and aviation) has limited technical data in these edge networks. The communication limitations of the edge networks have exposed interaction-based failures as a driver of how inefficient systems currently exchange information. This problem requires us to be smarter with naval maintenance

A. Moallem (Ed.): HCII 2023, LNCS 14045, pp. 672–684, 2023.
https://doi.org/10.1007/978-3-031-35822-7_43

resources. According to Arthur (2009), "innovation" combines what is new with what is useful and may be what is required to overcome the limitations in extreme maintenance conditions. In modern organizations, innovation focuses on information technology (IT) and knowledge management (KM) professionals at the enterprise level. Information systems should provide mechanisms to enable leadership to make data-driven decisions at all levels with data available to leverage new IT technology (i.e., machine learning [ML], additive manufacturing [AM], and Cloud in the Box [CIB]). When deploying new IT solutions in organizations, it is hard for data scientists to gather the required data on decisions that impact the employees (Leonard-Barton & Kraus, 2014). If the local maintenance personnel deliver innovative repair decisions aided by IT to solve challenges, their processes can be optimized, and the data can provide value to the organization. Currently, limited common aviation maintenance knowledge and process optimization are available for extreme maintenance conditions, and that knowledge is not passed from one generation of maintainers to the next.

2 Purpose Statement

The purpose of this research is to test the value added to information technology (i.e., AM, ML resource requirement prediction, and CIB) to optimize process productivity and cycle time for extreme maintenance conditions. The research will extend the use of process optimization theory (Castillo, 2011) to include the effect of modern information technology in extreme maintenance contexts. This research is essential because there is a gap in the process optimization literature with regard to extreme maintenance conditions and the use of modern technology for optimization. It is critical because failure to make correct repairs can affect the organization at its most vulnerable cyber infrastructure. Cyber risk can be reduced by leaders being actively involved and utilizing emerging technology when available (Vanajakumari et al., 2021).

2.1 Research Goals

The goal of the research is to make a theoretical contribution to the domain of Economics of Information Technology (EOIT) with new IT technology to provide process optimization for decision-makers in terms of productivity and cycle time for extreme maintenance conditions. The research will provide confidence in the decision-makers' predictions based on information realized in actual outcomes (productivity/cycle time). The organization will need to adjust its maintenance methods through Business Process Reengineering and revolutionize its IT architecture with AM, ML, and CIB. The ML analytic data problems involve three dimensions to meet the challenges—algorithms, machines, and people (Stoica et al., 2017). Decision-makers can address overall risk management values and adjust the individual data within the CIB. The ML provides human agents with information to adapt, improve repair decisions, and reduce risk. As expeditionary and maintenance information flows throughout the CIB, the technical data for repair is constantly reviewed and updated based on the repairs required. The ML engine should provide the automation required to provide technical data to the maintenance personnel in real time. Machine learning, in this context, focuses on accessing technical data, and the algorithm learns with feedback from the maintenance experts and acceptable risk thresholds. Thus, we propose an Information Science–based investigation of the robustness of extreme maintenance methods.

3 Research Hypotheses

Research opportunities for naval maintenance for decision-makers, maintenance person nel, and data scientists can determine how to fuse new IT technology to enable process optimization in decision-making. The hypotheses below will be assessed with statistical methods discussed later in the methods section:

- Hypothesis 1: ML improves cycle time compared to traditional prediction methods.
- Hypothesis 2: ML causes process productivity to improve.
- Hypothesis 3: AM decreases cycle time compared to traditional supply chain parts acquisition methods.
- Hypothesis 4: AM increases productivity compared to traditional supply chain parts acquisition methods.
- Hypothesis 5: Cloud-in-the-Box (CIB) technology improves cycle time compared to traditional reach-back methods.
- Hypothesis 6: CIB improves productivity compared to traditional reach-back methods.

4 Contribution to Knowledge

This research will make theoretical contributions to Information Sciences through EOIT by gauging the ability of new IT technology to impact productivity and cycle time in extreme maintenance conditions. Theories in the EOIT are economic theories that consider the effects of introducing Information Technology (Shapiro & Varian, 1999; Goldfarb & Tucker, 2019). Based on EOIT theory, researchers may hypothesize the effects of these inputs on the firm's output and then test them empirically against organizational accounting data. Hitt et al.'s (1994) use of the theory led them to conclude that information technology affects an organization's output and productivity.

This research seeks to extend process optimization theory to extreme maintenance conditions. Process optimization theory is focused on the variables that predict productivity improvements (Castillo, 2011). In process optimization, value added can be calculated at the component process level (Housel & Kanevsky, 1995). In extreme maintenance, the overall process can be broken down into subprocesses. Even if the outputs of the subprocesses are different, they can be compared by using common units (e.g., Knowledge Value Added units [KVA]).

The research will generate new artifacts relying on KVA to optimize maintenance conditions that integrate with ML, AM, and CIB technology to increase productivity and decrease cycle time. These new artifacts will model and leverage new cyber technology, as seen in bioinformatics, into decision support systems. These new approaches can potentially assist decision-makers by speeding up the data-to-decision (D2D) times and reducing risk. This research's end state and contribution are to extend EOIT and speed up the D2D times by addressing theoretical gaps in extreme maintenance conditions with process optimization through the use of a simulation.

When applied early in the design cycle and experimentation process, the methods presented in this research increase IT portfolio management and decision-making in an operational context in hypothesis-generation efforts (Albert & Hayes, 2002). The research will use Monte Carlo simulation with real options to assess the value of these new IT technologies. For example, the testing methods would look at the current as-is extreme maintenance process and assess the to-be process with quantitative methods through the simulation process, which is an excellent place for IT to add value to current extreme maintenance.

5 Review of Literature

This literature review explores theories of EOIT, including Business Process Reengineering (BPR) and process optimization. The study will analyze theories in decision-making with a deeper dive into emerging technologies that can assist in extreme maintenance. These theories of EOIT and decision-making are well-grounded in the field of information sciences. We see the work of Herb Simon in decision-making and complexity theory used as a foundation for KVA measurement. While the emerging technologies discussed are also used in other contexts in the domains of science, they provide significate process optimization possibilities. We see ML used in the medical field to review massive amounts of data and predict medical treatments (i.e., bioinformatics). For EOIT, AM has offered parts being made on-site reducing the time required for inventory reduction in the supply chain. Additionally, CIB technology extends network theory offering high-speed computing at the edge where it is needed to make a data-driven decision.

5.1 The EOIT, BPR, and Process Optimization

The economics of IT is often used to evaluate the functioning of an organization with the introduction of technology (Shapiro & Varian, 1999). EOIT is based on accounting principles accepted as the economic and international standard for over 500 years. These accounting principles are historical in nature and deterministic. When forecasting, the models look to the future and are probabilistic. EOIT is a large theory that includes sub-theories within it. A few EOIT sub-theories explored in the research are productivity theory, Business Process Reengineering (BPR), and process optimization theory. Hitt et al. (1994) introduce the productivity theory by utilizing the productivity construct to measure whether the emerging technology is effective. In accounting, productivity is calculated in terms of process output divided by input at the corporate level. The organization uses output as the item of interest being produced (e.g., widget, repaired aircraft), and the input construct consists of items required to produce the output (e.g., labor and materials); these inputs are factored in as a cost. Value caused by IT is another essential construct and is an enduring concern in EOIT; it is one without a definitive resolution (Housel & Bell, 2001; Mirowski, 2009). One popular research method to measure the "value" that this research will leverage is KVA, which reduces the subprocess outputs to standard units (e.g., value) that can be measured across subprocesses to evaluate and optimize the performance of the overall process (Housel & Kanevsky, 1995). An organization can convert inputs to outputs in differing combinations to create any specific level of output. This is possible through a production function that can attribute each input's contribution to the output measured by gross marginal benefit. Finally, the market is measured in equilibrium, with no excess demand.

The process optimization theory is focused on productivity improvement (e.g., information technology and process flow). It also provides a conceptual framework for process optimization as well the key optimization parameter productivity (i.e., output/input). This line of research typically uses modeling and simulation to estimate productivity improvements using various optimization options (e.g., using information technology). The Business Process Reengineering (BPR) approach is used to radically optimize processes, typically through the use of modern technology (Hammer, 1990). Process optimization theory typically focuses on incremental improvements in process productivity. The BPR approach focuses on radical process productivity improvement, most often using cyber technology (e.g., AM, ML, and CIB).

Process optimization theory predicts productivity improvements with statistical methods to maximize award functions through subprocess refinement (Castillo, 2011). It conceptionally and operationally defines process optimization in terms of productivity. This leads to the modeling and simulation of process optimization through real options and portfolio opportunities (Mun, 2015). The success of organizations is tied to the efficiency and effectiveness of their core processes (Niedermann & Schwarz, 2011). Process optimization usually involves BPR to refine the processes and focus on greater gains in productivity. The gap in the theory is that it does not provide artifacts or models that include the extreme maintenance case, nor does the theory account for the potential use of modern information technology.

5.2 Decision-Making with ML

Decision-making research has been explored heavily with ML in bioinformatics. According to Adams (2022), bioinformatics is a scientific discipline using certain ML technology to collect, store, analyze, and disseminate biological data and provide information for medical-based decisions. In health care fields, bioinformatics is utilized to make cancer predictions, such as mortality rates and when future treatment is required, and treatment decisions. These predictions and treatment decisions are analogous to repairs on human-made systems (e.g., aircraft). It is reasonable, then, that bioinformatics ML technology should be able to assess risk and assist in supply chain maintenance decisions.

In edge decision support systems, decision-making and problem-solving should be partnered with intelligent machines to achieve productivity and suitable courses of action (Simon et al., 1987). John Boyd's Observe Orient, Decide, and Act (OODA) Loop describes the decision-making cycle and can be combined with transformative technology to speed up the decision-making cycle (Phillips, 2021). ML partners with human agents in a highly proficient and complex way and provides optimization opportunities (Glikson & Woolley, 2020). ML–assisted decision-making solves complex logistics and manufacturing problems where the solution maximizes the sum of the award over time (i.e., inventory management). Complex decision-making in an extreme maintenance context can predict courses of action when aided by ML technologies (Zhao et al.,

2016). Therefore, it is logical to combine the benefits of ML to address problems through multiple systems and their data sources (Russell, 2020).

The stakeholders in this research are a subset of decision-makers, maintenance professionals, and data scientists.

Overcoming the technology challenges while maintaining data availability is critical cyber work. Even with the diversity of the systems within the organization, there is a demand for time-sensitive information (Miller et al., 2021). To merge ML engines, the organization will have to implement data governance at the enterprise level. The overall reliability and availability of the ML will be gauged by the ability to access individual systems when required to migrate authoritative data into one location or a few corresponding locations where ML can act on the data like a CIB. Predictability means that models are reliable and the data are representatively complete. The "gauge" is assisted by data standards, network science, and sharing problems. The process and design have more potential than the described application (e.g., cybersecurity and IoT modernization decisions). The end state is merging ML technology to take full advantage of decision support with increased system reliability and data availability. This knowledge architecture can offer a diffusion of ideas in an adaptive learning environment (Schön, 1971).

5.3 AM

Additive manufacturing requires reliable complex systems that take in technical data to create the parts with the proper materials (e.g., parts that machines require to handle the stress of aviation fatigue). Huang et al. (2015) explained that in complex systems, manual methods exist for calculating reliability, and a new process could automate this approach within an extreme maintenance AM context with limited bandwidth. The technical data AM machines use are often 3D high-fidelity drawings specific to certain devices. Aerospace and defense manufacturers typically require software modules with unique data that require additional functionality when considering the risk requirements. Risk calculation tools could explore where these AM machines and data make the most sense to utilize. Mun and Housel (2010) explain how using real options for risk evaluation with simulation can allow for a dynamic assessment to rapidly optimize processes in civilian and DoD settings with additive manufacturing.

When applied early in the additive design cycle and experimentation process, the methods presented in this research can increase productivity in an operational context in hypothesis generation efforts (Albert & Hayes, 2002). The productivity of these maintenance processes through various technologies, such as AM, should be explored (Housel, Ford, Mun, & Hom, 2015). New technological innovations, such as AM, pave the way for less expensive products and services (Wooten, 2021). The technical 3D data can be significant in size for these AM machines, so locally storing the data in CIB would be ideal in a bandwidth-restrained environment.

5.4 CIB

Cloud-in-the-box technology is based on network theory. A supply chain is a network. These networks are made up of organizations and resources (e.g., labor and materials) that lead to creating and maintaining a product or system (Lutkevich, 2021). A supply chain consists of manufacturers, material delivery, and assistance in repair and delivery to a customer. A risk to the supply chain can impact maintenance risk. In aviation, maintenance and mission risk can be quantified. Risk determination is conducted manually; however, it is not a stretch for machines to find correlations and structural relationships that are not readily apparent to humans. Furthermore, all risks have time horizons, and risk mitigation occurs as the remaining time and uncertainty are reduced (Mun, 2015). Additionally, Huang et al. (2015) address a manual method of calculating reliability in complex systems, and a new ML process could augment this approach within a tactical edge CIB context. This would allow for a dynamic enough process to adapt to rapidly changing missions and tactical edge settings. Positive feedback can provide the dynamic state changes required to measure mission-based risk. When applied early in the CIB design cycle and experimentation process, the methods presented in this research increase CIB reliability in an operational context in hypothesis generation efforts (Albert & Hayes, 2002).

Aviation data sources and availability in the DoD should continue to adopt a Net-centric Data and Service Strategy (NCSS). According to Grimes (2006), NCSS makes "data assets visible, accessible, and understandable. This strategy also establishes services as preferred means by which data producers and capability providers can make their data assets and capabilities available" (p. i). When components fail, humans can discover correlations through manual analysis; however, this analysis is time-intensive and often incomplete (O'Connor & Kleyner, 2012). Furthermore, inadequate static CIB models, not understanding extreme maintenance environments, and system integration significantly overburden leadership (Nielsen et al., 2012). According to Jamshidi (2009), using Extensible Markup Language (XML) technology is a preferred way to exchange data between disparate systems. Cloud technology leverages big data and dockers with data pipelines of various sizes and scales (Stoica et al., 2017). Once the data pipelines exist, the simulations provide a means to model the complexity of those data connections.

Implementing ML across the organization is a costly but urgent necessity. Many of our cyber and defensive adversaries are years ahead of the United States in making this transition and, therefore, are deploying much more sophisticated analytical capabilities. Often it is challenging to recognize that ML is being used, making analysis efforts difficult (Hoadley & Lucas, 2018). The DoD has invested billions of dollars in adopting rapidly evolving IoT or intelligent devices, exponentially increasing the volume of data points collected globally. Without adopting ML engines, the significance of these data points can be lost along with any competitive edge we may have gained within global cyber and military operations. To ensure mission success, the DoN should leverage new reliability architecture and availability models, including Future Knowledgebase Systems of Systems (FKSS) with technology like commercial off-the-shelf (COTS) products, machine learning, and cloud computing with big data (Miller et al., 2019).

5.5 Review of Relevant Theories and Definitions

Existing models and theories used to assist the researchers in answering the questions and expanding the field of data science and information science include the following:

- Economics of Information Technology (Jowett & Rothwell, 1986)
- Process Productivity Measurement
- Measuring and managing knowledge (Housel & Bell, 2001).
- Decision-Making Theory (Edwards, 1954; Simon et al., 1987)
- Sustainable Value Creation (Housel & Shives, 2022)
- ML for Predictive Maintenance (Susto et al., 2015)
- Research on Decision Support Systems for Maintenance (Liu et al., 2006)

If these theories and models are expanded and utilized correctly, systems and applications would freely and securely exchange data and information in the CIB and provide insights to the knowledge workers and commanders. The context diagram in Fig. 1 compares the current process of multiple independent systems to some interconnections, e.g., Service Oriented Architecture (SOA) to a flat consolidated architecture for a CIB.

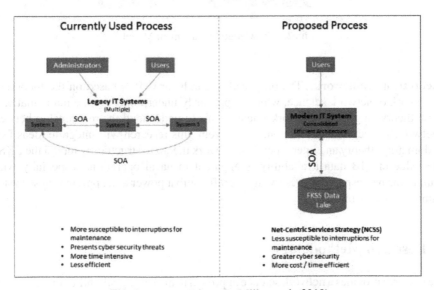

Fig. 1. Context Diagram (Miller et al., 2019)

The proposed strategy on the right offers an NCSS model with gains in efficiency and security at a reduced cost. As discussed in the system architecture and CIB connections, "expeditionary and interoperable exercises become increasingly reliant on technology, issues stemming from inabilities to synchronize and collaborate between garrison and deployed forces have necessitated more integrated and modernized networking tools. These critical issues can only be rectified if the DoD recognizes and embraces the value of technological innovations to improve the dynamic capabilities of IT platforms" (Miller et al., 2019, p. 78). These modern capabilities can provide CIB efficiency and leverage

ML and AM. The knowledge management architecture in Fig. 2 will be a starting point for our inquiry and will build on knowledge flow theory (Nissen, 2006).

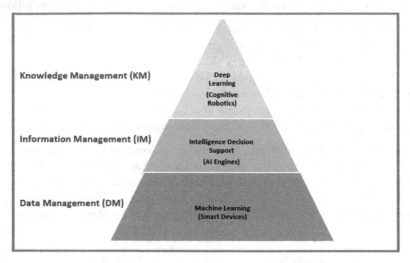

Fig. 2. Knowledge Management Model

Theoretical Framework. The proposed research for CIB is based on the theoretical framework of network science, which is primarily underpinned by the mathematics of graph theory. In general, network science aims to understand the relationship between a network's structure and function. In that vein, this research will integrate ideas from random graph theory and interdependent network theory to structurally model the FKSS. The value of CIB data availability is apparent in naval operations, especially when shaping the battlespace by preserving aircraft combat power and applying these system maintenance capabilities.

6 Research Methodology

The research provides a network science approach to measuring reliability in a CIB while considering the operational risk to systems availability and the warfighter. Although military network environments may be dynamic, patterns even within tactical meshed networks may utilize ML (Bordetsky et al., 2019). This research presents a design experiment as a possible CIB reliability and AM data availability model using ML. The design will work to expand on SoS availability and reliability models. CIB reliability can be measured and adjusted to offer greater data availability. The research methodology addresses specific challenges to SoS reliability by offering a network science approach focusing on a scale-free network's hubs. In doing so, we present a new process to measure the SoS reliability and availability to enable the decision-maker to make informed adjustments to the SoS at the hubs. New processes, logic, and a use case will be analyzed.

This theoretical, quantitative study will be conducted in two phases: analytical and simulation. Existing ML predictive maintenance research can be expanded to aviation maintenance (Susto et al., 2015). The focus of this research is the aviation maintenance domain. Multiple simulations, including model-based system engineering (MBSE) simulation, will be applied to evaluate new approaches to tactical edge networks expanding on current methods.

6.1 Design of Experiment (DOE)

Some data will be augmented with ML used in bioinformatics and compared with current methods as a benchmark. The simulation will evaluate whether the models will work, and this research will be a template for further field experiments and other endeavors. A full-fledged proof of concept to predict aircraft readiness, given a limited amount of data, will be a goal. Types of simulations that will be utilized in the research include existing Real Options Process Optimization models with Monte Carlo Simulation (Mun & Housel, 2010).

As discussed earlier, extreme maintenance in an edge network context will provide the data for the baseline and to-be model. The metrics determine the value of our model to measure its accuracy and precision. The research ML, AM, and CIB design framework can be displayed with a $2 \times 2 \times 2$ factorial where the research constructs' theoretical relationships fit well.

The experimental design considers the effects of various conditions of data independent variables (IV) with dependent variables (DV) with a series of data analyses to test our model. Quantitative models, such as regression analysis, can be performed on the data. The data analysis can consist of ANOVA, MANOVA, Nonlinear Regression, Parametric vs. Nonparametric tests, Monte Carlo methods, and distributional curve fitting based on the Bayesian probability formula. The DV, productivity and cycle times are affected by the relationship between IV, AM, and decision-making, with ML and CIB as shown in the $2 \times 2 \times 2$ factorial. The research design framework can be displayed with a $2 \times 2 \times 2$ factorial matrix to show the DVs' and IVs' relationships, as illustrated in Fig. 3.

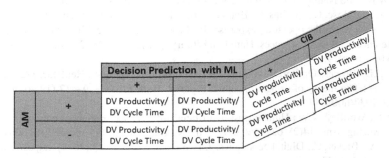

Fig. 3. Research Design Testable Framework

7 Analysis of the Research

Much of the analysis of the research will be conducted by real option simulations. Some of the assumptions and limitations are included to set the boundary conditions for the research analysis. This research will be conducted from the perspective of a Leibnizian (Analytical-Deductive) inquiring system in which the guarantor of the knowledge claims is the self-evidence of the inputs and the deductive soundness of the operations. The validity of this research will be established through a clear explanation of the input selection reasoning, a detailed explication of all derived analytical expressions, and a comparison between simulation results and the theoretical predictions of the derived analytical expressions. The complex system data analytics for cyber reliability and availability can be processed and automated with ML (Maule, 2020).

8 Conclusion

This research is significant, particularly given the complexity of process optimization theory with extreme maintenance conditions with an artifact that integrates edge networks with data science to increase information cyber availability. This research should speed up the data-to-decision (D2D) times and productivity to reduce risk (e.g., aircraft downtime) and may apply beyond extreme maintenance conditions.

Author Statement. The views expressed in this paper are those of the authors and do not reflect the official Navy policy or position of the NAVAIR, Department of Defense, or the U.S. Government. This paper is not a product of NAVAIR.

References

Adams, D.: Bioinformatics. Genome.gov. (2022). https://www.genome.gov/genetics-glossary/Bio informatics. Accessed 11 Nov 2022

Albert, D.S., Hayes, R.: Code of best practice: experimentation. Office of the Assistant Secretary of Defense, Washington, DC, Command and Control Research Program (CCRP) (2002)

Arthur, W.B.: The Nature of Technology: What it is and How It Evolves. Penguin Group (2009)

Bordetsky, A., Glose, C., Mullins, S., Bourakov, E.: Machine learning of semi-autonomous intelligent mesh networks operation expertise. In: Proceedings of the 52nd Hawaii International Conference on System Sciences. Hamilton Library, pp. 1221–1228 (2019). https://doi.org/10.24251/hicss.2019.149

Castillo, E.D.: Process Optimization: A Statistical Approach. Springer, Heidelberg (2011)

Edwards, W.: The theory of decision making. Psychol. Bull. 51(4), 380–417 (1954). https://doi.org/10.1037/h0053870

Glikson, E., Woolley, A.W.: Human trust in artificial intelligence: review of empirical research. Acad. Manag. Ann. 14(2), 627–660 (2020). https://doi.org/10.5465/annals.2018.0057

Goldfarb, A., Tucker, C.: Digital economics. J. Econ. Lit. 57(1), 3–43 (2019). https://doi.org/10.1257/jel.20171452

Grimes, J.G.: Department of defense net-centric spectrum management strategy (2006). https://doi.org/10.21236/ada454462

Hammer, M.: Reengineering work: don't automate, obliterate. Harv. Bus. Rev. 1–8 (1990)

Hitt, L., Brynjolfsson, E., Walsham, G.: The three faces of it value: theory and evidence. In: ICIS 1994 Proceedings (1994). https://aisel.aisnet.org/icis1994/69

Hoadley, D.S., Lucas, N.J.: Artificial intelligence and national security. Report, Congressional Research Service, Washington DC (2018). https://digital.library.unt.edu/ark:/67531/metadc1157028/

Housel, T.J., Bell, A.H.: Measuring and Managing Knowledge. McGraw-Hill/Irwin (2001)

Housel, T., Ford, D., Mun, J., Hom, S.: Benchmarking naval shipbuilding with 3D laser scanning, additive manufacturing, and collaborative product lifecycle management. Acquisition Research Program Report No. NPS-AM-15-126. Naval Postgraduate School, Monterey (2015). https://dair.nps.edu/handle/123456789/2650

Housel, T., Shives, T.: In a conceptual model to account for the contribution of sustainable value creation in the public sector. In: 17TH EIASM Interdisciplinary Conference on Intangibles and Intellectual Capital - Non-Financial and Integrated Reporting, Governance and Value Creation Special Track On, Intellectual Capital and Public Sector (2022)

Housel, T., Kanevsky, V.A.: Reengineering business processes: a complexity theory approach to value added. INFOR: Inf. Syst. Oper. Res. 33(4), 248–262 (1995). https://doi.org/10.1080/03155986.1995.11732285

Huang, Y., Pan, X., Hu, L.: Rapid assessment of system-of-systems (SoS) mission reliability based on Markov chains. In: 2015 First International Conference on Reliability Systems Engineering (ICRSE). IEEE (2015)

Jamshidi, M.: System of Systems Engineering Innovation for the 21st Century. Wiley, Hoboken (2009)

Jowett, P., Rothwell, M.: The Economics of Information Technology. Macmillan, New York (1986)

Leonard-Barton, D., Kraus, W.: Implementing New Technology (2014). https://hbr.org/1985/11/implementing-new-technology. Accessed 27 Oct 2020

Liu, M., Zuo, H.F., Ni, X.C., Cai, J.: Research on a case-based decision support system for aircraft maintenance review board report. In: Huang, D.-S., Li, K., Irwin, G.W. (eds.) ICIC 2006. LNCS, vol. 4113, pp. 1030–1039. Springer, Heidelberg (2006). https://doi.org/10.1007/11816157_125

Lutkevich, B.: What is a supply chain? - Definition, models and best practices. WhatIs.com (2021). https://www.techtarget.com/whatis/definition/supply-chain. Accessed 11 Nov 2022

Maule, R.: Acquisition data analytics for supply chain cybersecurity. In: Proceedings of the Seventeenth Annual Acquisition Research Symposium, pp. 1–11. Naval Postgraduate School (2020)

Miller, K., O'Halloran, B., Pollman, A., Feeley, M.: Securing the internet of battlefield things while maintaining value to the warfighter. Inf. Warfare J. 18(2), 74–84 (2019)

Miller, K., Bordetsky, A., Mun, J., Maule, R., Pollman, A.: Merging future knowledgebase system of systems with artificial intelligence/machine learning engines to maximize reliability and availability for decision support. Milit. Oper. Res. J. 26(4), 77–96 (2021). https://doi.org/10.5711/1082598326477

Mirowski, P.: Why there's (as yet) no such thing as an economics of knowledge. In: Kincaid, E.H., Ross, D. (eds.) The Oxford Handbook of Philosophy of Economics. Oxford University Press (2009)

Mun, J.: Readings in certified quantitative risk management (CQRM): applying Monte Carlo risk simulation, strategic real options, stochastic forecasting, portfolio optimization, data analytics, business intelligence, and decision modeling. IIPER (2015)

Mun, J., Housel, T.: A primer on applying monte carlo simulation, real options analysis, knowledge value added, forecasting, and portfolio optimization. NPS Acquisitions White Paper (2010). https://doi.org/10.21236/ada518628

Niedermann, F., Schwarz, H.: Deep business optimization: making business process optimization theory work in practice. In: Halpin, T., et al. (eds.) BPMDS/EMMSAD -2011. LNBIP, vol. 81, pp. 88–102. Springer, Heidelberg (2011). https://doi.org/10.1007/978-3-642-21759-3_7

Nielsen, M.: Reinventing Discovery: The New Era of Networked Science. Princeton University Press (2012)

Nissen, M.E.: Harnessing Knowledge Dynamics. IRM Press (2006)

O'Connor, P.D.T., Kleyner, A.: Practical Reliability Engineering, 5th edn. Wiley, Hoboken (2012)

Phillips, M.S.: Revisiting John Boyd and the OODA loop in our time of transformation. Defense Acquisit. J. L(5), 8–11 (2021). https://www.dau.edu

Russell, S.J.: Human Compatible: Artificial Intelligence and the Problem of Control. Penguin Books (2020)

Shapiro, C., Varian, H.:Information Rules: A Strategic Guide to the Network Economy. Harvard Business School Press (1999). https://doi.org/10.2307/1183273

Simon, H.A., et al.: Decision making and problem solving. Interfaces 17(5), 11–31 (1987). http://www.jstor.org/stable/25061004

Stoica, I., et al.: The Berkeley data analysis system (BDAS): an open-source platform for big data analytics. Technical report AFRL-RI-RS-TR-2017-173. University of California, Berkeley (2017)

Susto, G.A., Schirru, A., Pampuri, S., McLoone, S., Beghi, A.: Machine learning for predictive maintenance: a multiple classifier approach.IEEE Trans. Industr. Inform. 11(3), 812–820 (2015)

Vanajakumari, M., Mittal, S., Stoker, G., Clark, U., Miller, K.: Towards a leader-driven supply chain cybersecurity framework analysis of security features and vulnerabilities in public/open Wi-FI. J. Inf. Syst. Appl. Res. 14(2), 42–52 (2021)

Wooten, J.: Failure is not fatal, but failure to change might be. Defense Acquisit. J. L(5), 31–36 (2021). https://www.dau.edu

Zhao, Y., Kendall, T., Johnson, B.: Big data and deep analytics applied to the common tactical air picture (CTAP) and combat identification (CID). In: Proceedings of the 8th International Joint Conference on Knowledge Discovery, Knowledge Engineering and Knowledge Management (2016). https://doi.org/10.5220/0006086904430449

Person Verification Based on Multipoint Measurement of Intrabody Propagation Signals

Isao Nakanishi$^{(\boxtimes)}$ (ID), Tomoaki Oku, and Souta Okasaka

Tottori University, Tottori 680-8550, Japan
nakanishi@tottori-u.ac.jp

Abstract. Previous studies have investigated the potential of intrabody propagation signals for use in biometrics. However, the verification performance of this approach is not yet sufficient and must be improved. In this study, we performed multipoint measurements on the human palm and other points on the body and examined the verification performance when fusing individual features or verification results obtained by multipoint measurements. The effect of multipoint authentication was confirmed but was found to be not very strong.

Keywords: Biometrics · Intrabody propagation signal · Multipoint measurement · Feature level fusion · Decision level fusion

1   Introduction

Recently, fingerprints and face images have been employed for user authentication in smartphones. Unlike conventional passwords and pattern locks, these bodily features are convenient since they do not require users to remember anything. However, because they are located on the body surface, they are vulnerable to capture by others and can be abused for spoofing. The "gummy finger" is a famous example [1].

We have studied the use of an intrabody propagation signal as a biometric that is not exposed on the body surface. The intrabody propagation signal is particularly suitable for systems requiring continuous authentication during use. In previous studies, we examined verification performance on forearms [2], palms [3], and several other parts of the body [4]. However, we found no large differences in verification performance among these body parts.

In this study, we aim to improve verification performance by fusing individual extracted features or verification results from multipoint measurements of intrabody propagation signals as an alternative to conventional single-point measurement. First, we examine verification performance by multipoint measurements on the palm using newly produced dedicated measuring devices. Next, we evaluate the verification performance by multipoint measurements on the body using intrabody propagation signals measured in our previous study [4].

A. Moallem (Ed.): HCII 2023, LNCS 14045, pp. 685–700, 2023.
https://doi.org/10.1007/978-3-031-35822-7_44

2 Person Verification Using Intrabody Propagation Signals

The intrabody propagation signal is obtained by using intrabody communication technology [5,6], which utilizes the human body as a transmission path. According to the transmission mechanism, intrabody communication technology is roughly divided into the current method and the electric field method. In our research, we adopt the electric field method, which exploits the fact that the dielectric constant of the human body is greater than that of air. When a high-frequency signal is passed between electrodes at the transmission side, a leakage electric field is generated around them, propagates on the body, and is detected as a voltage change at electrodes at the receiver side. We call this voltage change an intrabody propagation signal. The generated electric field varies depending on the body composition (muscle, fat, epidermis, etc.), giving each individual a set of unique propagation signal characteristics that can be used to verify their identify. The intrabody propagation signal is not exposed on the body surface; therefore, it has less risk of being stolen and is resistant to spoofing. In addition, the intrabody propagation signal can be used for liveness detection, which prevents the use of artificial body parts in authentication.

Initially we started with evaluation of the intrabody propagation signal on the forearm [2], but in recent years we have been evaluating it on the palm assuming its practical use [3]. In daily lives, humans use their palms to touch or grip various things, such as smartphones, pointing devices on computers, and steering wheels on cars. If an authentication system using the intrabody propagation signal could be incorporated into the object the user touches or holds while using a system, biometric information about the user could be extracted without the user's awareness, allowing continuous authentication. In our previous study [4], we evaluated the verification performance of several parts of the body other than the palm.

2.1 Propagation Signal

Assuming use of the palm as the verification point, the schematic diagram of the intrabody propagation signal is illustrated in Fig. 1. The signal to be propagated is circulated through electrodes at the transmitting side, and then the propagated signal is extracted between electrodes at the receiving side, where the electrical ground (GND) is in common with the transmitter side. The current is 20 mA since the guideline of the ICNIRP (International Commission on Non-Ionizing Radiation Protection) stipulates that the permissible current that can flow through the human body is under 20 mA in a 100 kHz–110 MHz waveband [7].

In this study, a signal is composed of sine waves with different frequencies, the same amplitude, and zero phase. Figure 2 shows the signal used in this experiment; its frequencies are integers from 1 MHz to 50 MHz.

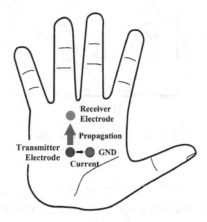

Fig. 1. Schematic diagram of intrabody propagation signal.

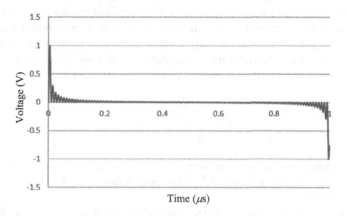

Fig. 2. A representative signal to be propagated [8]. ©2022 IEICE

2.2   Feature Extraction

As an individual feature, an amplitude spectrum is extracted from a propagated signal using FFT (fast Fourier transform). However, the intrabody propagation signal varies among individuals and also with each measurement in a given individual. Thus, a detected propagation signal is divided into several regions, a period of which corresponds to the fundamental period of the signal to be propagated, and then an amplitude spectrum is extracted from each region, and ensemble averaging is performed using the amplitude spectra of all regions. As a result, an averaged amplitude spectrum is obtained. The fundamental period of a propagated signal is known since frequencies are never changed through propagation.

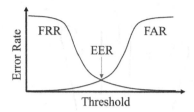

Fig. 3. Definition of EER.

2.3   Verification

The averaged amplitude spectrum can be used to verify whether a user is authorized or not. In the enrollment stage, intrabody propagation signals of all users are measured several times. By ensemble-averaging some spectra of each user, a template, which is used for comparison in the verification stage, is obtained and stored in an authentication system. In the verification stage, an intrabody propagation signal is measured from an applicant who claims to be a user, and his/her amplitude spectrum is tested with a template of the user. The test (verification) is performed using Euclidian distance matching[1], defined as

$$d = \sqrt{\sum_{i=1}^{N}(a_\mathrm{i} - b_\mathrm{i})^2}, \tag{1}$$

where a_i are template data, b_i are test data, and N is the number of data. If the distance d is shorter than that set by the verification threshold, the applicant is verified as the user.

Here, the larger the threshold, the higher the level of security of the authentication system. Even regular users may be rejected when the threshold is set high, and thus the authentication system is degraded. Inversely, a lower threshold improves usability, but nonregular users may be accepted, thereby degrading security. That is, a trade-off between security and usability exists when setting a threshold in an authentication system. The rate of rejected data of regular users to all regular users' data is called the false rejection rate (FRR), and that of accepted data of nonregular users to all nonregular users' data is called the false acceptance rate (FAR). When these rates are graphically represented in a vertical axis with a threshold in a horizontal axis, the FRR and FAR curves intersect at one point, as illustrated in Fig. 3; this point is called the equal error rate (EER) and is used as a verification performance index. A smaller EER indicates better performance.

---

[1] In our previous research we used a support vector machine (SVM), which is a machine learning method [4]; however, Euclidian distance matching is used in this study.

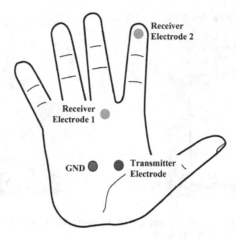

Fig. 4. Measurement at the index fingertip and the base of a middle finger.

3 Multipoint Verification in the Palm

In our previous studies [2–4], an intrabody propagation signal was measured at a single point and verification performance was evaluated using a single point-measured signal. If the intrabody propagation signals are measured at multiple points on the body, individual extracted features or verification results from the multiple points can be fused. This may improve verification performance.

In this section, we examine the methods for multipoint measurement of intrabody propagation signals in the palm and evaluate verification performance when fusing individual extracted features (feature-level fusion) or verification results (decision-level fusion) from the measured signals.

3.1 Measurements and Verification at the Fingertip and Finger Base

First, we compared the amplitude spectra by making a measuring device where a transmitting electrode was set on the palm, similar to the conventional manner, and receiving electrodes were placed on the tips of the index and ring fingers. However, there was no difference between those spectra. Even if the number of individual features is doubled by fusing two spectra, if they are the same, the verification performance is not improved and the effect of multipoint measurement is not achieved. The reason why there was no difference in two amplitude spectra is thought to be that their propagation distances were about the same.

Thus, we considered that different propagation characteristics could be obtained by measuring at the index fingertip and the base of a middle finger. The electrode positions are illustrated in Fig. 4. The measuring device and an image of measurement are presented in Fig. 5. The part that the palm touches was molded with silicone, and guide bars (acrylic rods) were attached to fix the position of the hand.

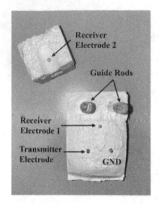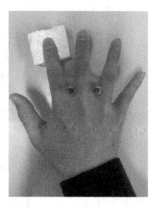

Fig. 5. Measuring device and an image of measurement at the index fingertip and middle finger base [8]. ©2022 IEICE

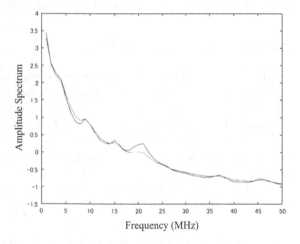

Fig. 6. Comparison of amplitude spectra at the fingertip and finger base of a subject [8]. ©2022 IEICE

In the measurement, the subject sits in a chair, wipes his/her palm with an alcohol sheet, dries the palm with a hair dryer, and places the palm on the measuring device along the guide bars. Propagated signals are then measured while the subject sits at rest.

Amplitude spectra at the fingertip and finger base are compared in Fig. 6. Each spectrum was obtained by averaging 10 amplitude spectra at each measurement point per subject. In the range of 5 MHz–25 MHz, there were differences between spectra; thus, we confirmed that different features could be obtained from measuring multiple points having different propagation distances.

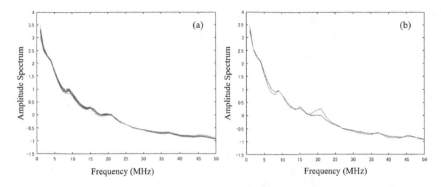

Fig. 7. Intraindividual variation in amplitude spectra at fingertip (a) and finger base (b).

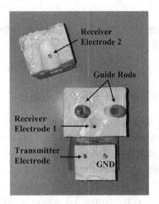

Fig. 8. Measuring Device B [8]. ©2022 IEICE

On the other hand, intraindividual variation in amplitude spectra extracted from the finger base was larger than that in amplitude spectra from the fingertip. Figure 7 shows the intraindividual variation in amplitude spectra at the fingertip and finger base. The difference in variation between receiving electrode locations is attributed to a leaked electric field propagated on not only the palm but also the silicone base. As indicated in Fig. 5, the receiving electrode at the fingertip and the transmitting electrode on the palm were placed on different silicone bases while the receiving electrode at the finger base was placed on the same silicone base as the transmitting electrode. This difference might result in differences in intraindividual variation.

Thus, as shown in Fig. 8, we made a new measuring device, in which the receiving electrode at the finger base is placed on a different silicone base than that for the transmitting electrode. For convenience, this measuring device is called B, and for comparison, the measuring device in Fig. 5 is called A.

Figure 9 shows the intraindividual variation in amplitude spectra at the fingertip and finger base using B. It is clear that the intraindividual variation

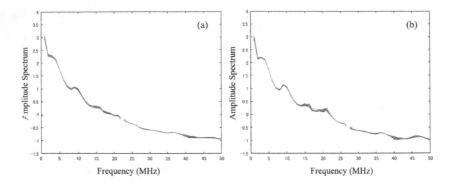

Fig. 9. Intraindividual variation in amplitude spectra at fingertip (a) and finger base (b) using measuring device B.

observed when using A was reduced by using B. Separating the receiving electrode from the transmitting one is effective for reducing intraindividual variation; however, it may be difficult in practical situations.

3.2   Evaluation of Verification Performance

We evaluated the verification performance in the multipoint measurement of the intrabody (palm) propagation signal. Twenty subjects participated. All were male students at our university between the ages of 22 and 24. Measurements were performed once or twice a day, at intervals of at least 4 h, for approximately 20 days. There were 20 sets of data for each subject; 10 sets of data were used to make a template and the remaining 10 were used for the test (verification). The number of dimensions in an individual feature was 50, which corresponds to the number of integral frequencies between 1 MHz and 50 MHz.

Verification Performance at a Single Point. Verification performance at fingertip (FT) and finger base (FB) points is shown in Table 1, which presents EERs only when there were 30 or fewer dimensions. Colored columns indicate the smallest EER in each device and position. The best EER at a single point is approximately 32%.

Here, the number of dimensions in the table does not correspond to the number of dimensions in a feature. Using 10 amplitude spectra for making a template of each subject, the ensemble-averaged spectrum was obtained and then intraindividual variation at each frequency bin were calculated. In addition, using the 20 averaged spectra from 20 subjects, the interindividual variation was determined. A smaller ratio of intraindividual variation to interindividual variation at a frequency suggests that the frequency is more effective for verifying individuals. Thus, the frequencies were rearranged in ascending order of their ratio and the order corresponded to the number of dimensions. Even though A and B had the same number of dimensions (order), the frequencies involved may have been different.

Table 1. EERs (%) at the fingertip and finger base and those when the two features were fused with the same number of features.

Num. of Dimen.	Device A			Device B		
	FT	FB	Fused	FT	FB	Fused
1	36.1	34.8	33.7	35.7	32.0	36.3
2	35.8	34.8	34.0	33.0	32.1	33.0
3	35.2	35.5	33.7	33.4	33.6	33.4
4	35.4	37.0	33.7	34.0	32.0	34.8
5	35.0	36.5	35.0	33.0	31.1	36.0
6	34.6	37.2	32.9	33.0	31.5	35.8
7	34.0	35.5	31.7	32.9	32.0	36.0
8	34.5	34.3	32.2	33.0	31.9	36.0
9	32.9	33.9	34.0	32.5	33.0	36.0
10	34.0	35.3	34.0	33.1	33.5	37.0
11	33.6	35.0	34.8	32.8	32.5	36.1
12	34.3	34.7	34.4	33.8	32.8	37.0
13	33.5	35.5	35.0	33.3	32.5	36.7
14	36.0	35.0	36.7	34.0	32.0	36.8
15	35.9	34.0	36.7	34.0	32.7	36.5
16	35.5	33.6	36.2	34.5	32.5	36.0
17	35.7	33.6	37.0	35.0	32.4	37.5
18	35.8	34.1	37.0	37.0	32.5	39.0
19	35.8	34.0	37.0	37.5	32.0	39.0
20	36.4	34.4	37.5	37.4	32.0	38.9
21	36.5	34.0	37.0	37.5	32.1	38.8
22	36.5	34.1	38.0	37.5	31.9	38.7
23	36.6	34.5	38.0	37.0	31.4	38.0
24	36.5	34.5	39.0	37.2	31.6	38.2
25	36.5	34.0	39.0	37.0	32.0	38.3
26	36.5	32.9	38.1	37.2	31.6	37.9
27	36.5	32.5	38.9	37.1	31.7	37.3
28	36.5	32.5	39.0	38.0	32.6	38.0
29	36.7	32.0	38.9	37.5	33.4	38.3
30	37.0	32.1	39.3	38.0	32.8	39.0

Feature-Level Fusion. Verification performance was assessed when the individual features obtained at the fingertip and finger base were fused. The spectral elements at the same dimension (order) in the two features are directly concatenated as a fused new feature with double the number of dimensions.

EERs using the new, fused feature are indicated as "Fused" in the table. For A, the smallest EER was obtained when there were 7 dimensions, and this EER value was smaller than those obtained by single-point measurement; therefore, the effect of fusing features by multipoint measurement was confirmed. On the other hand, for B, the smallest EER was obtained when there were 2 dimensions; however, this EER value was not smaller than the EERs obtained by single-point measurement, and therefore the effect of fusing features was not confirmed.

Thus, we examined all combinations (50 × 50 = 2500). Although we do not show all the results, the best EERs are presented in Table 2. In both devices, EERs were reduced in comparison with those when the same number of features were fused. In addition, these EERs were smaller than those obtained by single-point measurement; therefore, the effect of multipoint measurement (authentication) was confirmed.

Table 2. The best EERs (%) in all combinations when fusing features at the fingertip and finger base.

Device	Num. of Dimen.		EER (%)		
	FT	FB	FT	FB	Concatenated
A	5	26	35.0	32.9	31.5
B	3	1	33.4	32.0	28.5

Decision-Level Fusion. Next, we evaluated verification performance by fusing the verification results (decisions) from the fingertip and finger base. In decision-level fusion, the logical product (AND) and sum (OR) were performed. For AND, an applicant is regarded as genuine only when both results claim that the applicant is genuine. For OR, when at least one of the two results claims that an applicant is genuine, the applicant is regarded as genuine.

Tables 3 and 4 show the best EERs when performing AND and OR, respectively. For AND, EER was improved in B; however, EER was not improved even when fusing A. For OR, EERs were improved in both devices; therefore, OR was superior to AND. The smallest EER value was the same as the smallest one obtained in the feature-level fusion.

Considerations. The above results confirmed that multipoint authentication improved verification performance. However, the effect of the improvement was limited.

When features with the same number of dimensions are fused, the number of fused features is doubled; therefore, the verification performance was expected to be improved. However, such improvement was not achieved except for the small number of dimensions A. If the characteristics of a feature are stable, increasing the number of feature dimensions expands the feature space and makes it easier

Table 3. The best EER (%) when fusing by AND.

Device	Num. of Dimen.		EER (%)		
	FT	FB	FT	FB	AND
A	9	25	32.9	34.0	32.9
B	8	2	33.0	32.1	30.2

Table 4. The best EER (%) when fusing by OR.

Device	Num. of Dimen.		EER (%)		
	FT	FB	FT	FB	OR
A	2	1	35.8	34.8	31.8
B	10	5	33.1	31.1	28.5

to verify individuals. However, intrabody propagation signals as dynamic biometrics have large intraindividual variation, so increasing the number of feature dimensions increases the variation and does not make verification easier.

On the other hand, in the investigation using all combinations of two features, EERs were decreased by fusing features. This confirmed the effect of fusing features. However, features with few dimensions were fused in that investigation. For instance, in the case of B, there were 3 dimensions at the fingertip and 1 at the finger base. Together they were four-dimensional. The decrease in EERs might be due not to the increased dimensionality by fusion but rather to robustness. Even if the verification result by one feature is incorrect, that by another feature prevents the error. Furthermore, in single-point verification, 9 dimensions at the fingertip and 5 at the finger base achieved the highest verification performance. Therefore, fusing the best-performing features does not achieve the best performance. The present study yielded no insights into the feature combination that achieves the best verification performance.

4   Multipoint Verification in the Body

We also evaluated verification performance when fusing features or results at multiple points in the body. Strictly speaking, we should simultaneously measure intrabody propagation signals at multiple points. In this study, however, we used the database of intrabody propagation signals, which in our previous study [4] we had measured successively at multiple points on the body, assuming that those measurements were performed simultaneously. The transmitting electrode was placed on the right palm and the receiving electrodes were placed on the right wrist, left palm, right ear, and left ankle as illustrated in Fig. 10(a). These positions are not covered by clothing and placing electrodes there causes no inconvenience. The devices for measuring them and the images of measurement are pictured in Fig. 10(b).

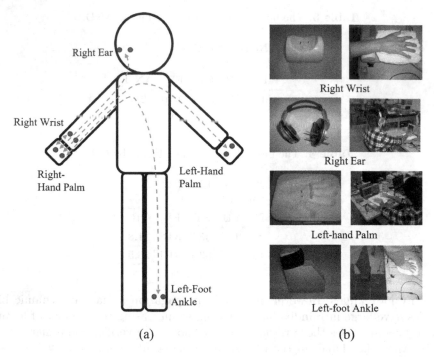

Fig. 10. Multipoint measuring. (a): Electrode positions; (b): measuring devices and images of measurement.

There were 15 experimental subjects, all of whom were male university students. For measurements other than the ankle, the subject sat in a chair; the ankle was measured while the subject was standing. The measurements were performed twice a day at intervals of at least 4 h. In total, there were 20 sets of data at each measuring position for each subject. From those 20 measured sets of data, 10 were used to make a template for verification, and the remaining 10 were used for evaluating verification performance.

Table 5 describes the verification performance at each measurement point obtained in Ref. [4]. As a reference, the verification performance at the palm is also presented. Their averaged EER was 41.5%. Euclidian distance matching,

Table 5. Verification performance at each measurement point [4].

Position	EER (%)
Right palm	40.1
Right wrist	40.7
Right ear	44.0
Left palm	41.3
Left ankle	41.3

which is the simplest verification method, was applied; therefore, the verification performance was generally low. As we demonstrated previously [4], verification performance can be improved by introducing machine learning such as that by a support vector machine (SVM).

4.1 Multipoint Verification Performance

As in the case of multipoint measurement on the palm, we examined feature- and decision-level fusions using intrabody propagation signals measured at the five points.

Feature-Level Fusion. First, feature-level fusion was performed by simply concatenating the features, which are amplitude spectral elements extracted from intrabody propagation signals measured at multiple points. Verification performance by feature-level fusion is presented in Table 6. For cases with 4 or fewer points, various combinations were used to select measurement points at each case and their EERs were different; thus, their averaged value is indicated. While EERs were more than 40% at a single point, they were reduced to 30%. In addition, since the EERs decreased as the number of points increased, the effect of multipoint verification was also confirmed in the body.

Table 6. Verification performance by feature-level fusion in the body.

Num. of Points	EER (%)
2	38.2
3	35.8
4	33.9
5	33.2

AND and or Fusion. Next, verification performance by decision-level fusion, AND, and OR is shown in Table 7. As with the previous results, these are averaged values of all combinations for each case. As with the feature-level fusion, EERs were reduced in comparison with those obtained at a single point, and EERs decreased as the number of points increased. In particular, the OR fusion at 5 points achieved the best performance in decision-level fusion.

Table 7. EERs (%) by AND and OR fusion in the body.

Num. of Points	OR	AND
2	39.1	39.7
3	37.1	39.5
4	35.5	39.0
5	34.0	38.2

Fusion Based on Majority Voting. We examined fusion based on majority voting as decision-level fusion. The results are presented in Table 8. In the case of 2 points, it was impossible to take majority voting, so we examined the majority voting of 3 points or more by changing the number of points (threshold) considered to be the majority. In agreement with our previous results, when fusing 3 and 4 points, the EERs were the averaged values of all combinations. The majority vote of 5 points with a threshold of 2 achieved the second-best verification performance in this study.

Table 8. Verification performance based on majority voting.

Num. of Points (Threshold)	EER (%)
3 (2)	38.2
4 (2)	36.9
4 (3)	37.6
5 (2)	34.7
5 (3)	36.6
5 (4)	37.3

Figure 11 summarizes all of the results obtained in this evaluation. In general, verification performance depends on the number of features, dimensions, or points; therefore, comparisons with the same number of features, dimensions, or points enables us to fairly compare the verification performance of fusion methods. The EER when there is 1 point is the average of EERs of 5 measurement points obtained at the single point evaluation.

From these comparisons, we see that the verification performance is higher in the order of simple concatenation (SC), OR, 2-point majority vote (MJ2), 3-point majority vote (MJ3), 4-point majority vote (MJ4), and AND. The AND fusion accepts applicants only when they are regarded as genuine at all measurement points; this increases the false rejection rate, thus degrading verification performance. This phenomenon is also found in the majority voting. As the number of points considered to be the majority increased, the verification performance deteriorated. In the OR fusion, applicants are accepted if they are regarded as genuine at least 1 point, so verification performance is not degraded. In the decision-level fusion, such as majority vote, OR, and AND, the robustness, defined as the covering of false decisions at measurement points by correct decisions at other measurement points, improves the verification performance as the number of fusing points increases; however, the final verification performance basically depends on the verification performance at each measurement point. On the other hand, the feature-level fusion, such as the simple concatenation of features, increased the number of feature dimensions (measurement points); therefore, it expanded the feature space and resulted in improved final verification performance.

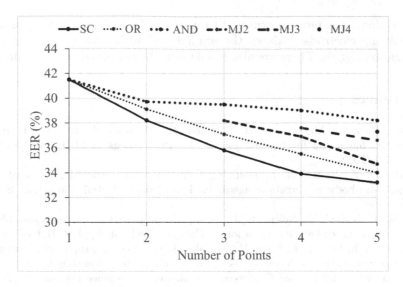

Fig. 11. Relation between number of points and verification performance.

5   Conclusions

In this study, we examined the verification performance of multipoint authentication using intrabody propagation signals. In the palm, intrapalm propagation signals detected at the fingertip and finger base were fused at the feature and decision levels, and their verification performance was evaluated. The effect of fusing was confirmed but was not outstanding. On the other hand, we evaluated verification performance by fusing intrabody propagated signals measured at several body-surface points. The effect of fusing was also confirmed. In particular, as the number of points increased, verification performance improved. However, the effect of fusing was not outstanding here either. The effect of improving verification performance by multipoint authentication using intrabody propagation signals may be limited.

In the case of multipoint measurement on the body, unlike in the case of measurement on the palm alone, we did not examine the fusing of effective spectral elements for verification or the selection of the best combination of features or results from all combinations. This should be studied in the future.

As shown in Figs. 7 and 9, the amplitude spectral elements of intrabody propagation signals decrease as the frequency increases. In this study, those spectra were directly used as feature values. However, if there are large differences between feature values, verification performance depends on only the features that have large values, and the effectiveness of fusing multiple features is lost. It may be effective to introduce normalization in spectral elements.

To realize multipoint authentication, multiple transmitting/receiving systems of intrabody propagation signals are required. Therefore, the cost and computational amount are expected to increase. In addition, wearing multiple transmitting electrodes reduces the usability of authentication via intrabody propagation signals. These are also problems to be discussed in the future.

References

1. Matsumoto, T., Matsumoto, H., Yamada, K., Hoshino, S.: Impact of artificial 'gummy' fingers on fingerprint systems. In: Proceedings of SPIE. vol. 4677, pp. 275–289 (2002)
2. Yorikane, Y., Nakanishi, I., Itoh, Y., Fukui, Y.: Biometric identity verification using intra-body propagation signal. In: Proceedings of 2007 Biometrics Symposium (2007)
3. Inada, T., Sodani, Y., Nakanishi, I.: Intra-palm propagation signals as suitable biometrics for successive authentication. J. Comput. Technol. Appl. 7(2), 65–72 (2016)
4. Nakanishi, I., Ogushi, I., Nishi, R., Murakami, T.: Effect of propagation signal and path on verification performance using intra-body propagation signals. In: Proceedings of 2017 International Conference on Biometrics Engineering and Application (ICBEA2017), pp. 80–84 (2017)
5. Zimmerman, T.G.: Personal area networks: near-field intrabody communication. IBM Syst. J. 35(3–4), 609–617 (1996)
6. Hachisuka, K., Takeda, T., Terauchi, Y., Sasaki, K., Hosaka, H., Itao, K.: Intra-body data transmission for the personal area network. Microsyst. Technol. 11, 1020–1027 (2005)
7. International Commission on Non-Ionizing Radiation Protection(ICNIRP), "Guidelines for limiting exposure to time-varying electric, magnetic, and electromagnetic fields (up to 300 GHz)," Health physics, vol. 74, no. 4, pp. 494–522 (1998)
8. Nakanishi, I., Oku, T., Okasaka, S.: Person verification using intra-body propagation signal verification performance by multipoint measurements (in Japanese), IEICE Technical Report, vol. 122, no. 197, BioX2022-61, pp. 32–37 (2022)

Correction to: A Privacy-Orientated Distributed Data Storage Model for Smart Homes

Khutso Lebea(iD) and Wai Sze Leung(iD)

Correction to:
Chapter 13 in: A. Moallem (Ed.): *HCI for Cybersecurity,*
Privacy and Trust, **LNCS 14045,**
https://doi.org/10.1007/978-3-031-35822-7_13

In an older version of this paper, incorrect affiliation, "Springer Heidelberg, Tiergartenstr. 17, 69121 Heidelberg, Germany" was found. This has been removed.

The updated version of this chapter can be found at
https://doi.org/10.1007/978-3-031-35822-7_13

Author Index

A. Moallem (Ed.): HCII 2023, LNCS 14045, pp. 701–702, 2023.
https://doi.org/10.1007/978-3-031-35822-7

Printed in the United States
by Baker & Taylor Publisher Services